Copyright © 2018 Read Books Ltd.
This book is copyright and may not be
reproduced or copied in any way without
the express permission of the publisher in writing

British Library Cataloguing-in-Publication Data
A catalogue record for this book is available from
the British Library

Eng^d by W.Holl from the original by Nasmyth.

CHAPTER I.

BURNS THE BOY.

THE title here proposed, while in one sense ideally appropriate, is in another as certainly a misnomer—the Life of Robert Burns. In one sense, Burns was the most intensely living man modern times have produced—had a perpetually active and seething brain; a heart beating in big and almost audible throbs; a "pulse's maddening play;" the most living and eloquent lips that ever spoke in Scotland; a hand that if you touched it threatened to *burn* your's : from the sole of the foot to the crown of the head he was a Man, and forms, thus, one of the best themes for biography. But, in another view, his life was so short, so fragmentary, so contradictory to itself, that the words, the Life of Robert Burns, sound like cruel irony—sad, shadowed, and incoherent as it was; and the feeling is not lessened, but increased, and the disturbance of the whole rendered more painful and mysterious, by the Arabesque border of wild happiness and lofty inspiration, too, by which it was begirt, but never either penetrated or pervaded. Besides the difficulties connected with such a strange, exceptional existence as was his, there meets us also on the threshold of our enterprise the fact that the tale of his life, with its union or disunion of elements, has been so often told, that it seems hopeless to seek to give it any new interest, or to draw from it any stronger moral than has been drawn. Nevertheless, we have decided to attempt it, and to do our best. Burns' life, said an accomplished gentleman to us the other day, must be written with the heart, and this qualification for writing it we unhesitatingly claim. We add, it should be written with determined honesty, and to that too we lay fearless claim.

Robert Burns was born on the 25th of January, 1759. His father was William Burns or Burness, a native of Kincardineshire, usually called the Mearns, westward from Glenbervie, which was the cradle of the Burness family. The country is called the *Howe* or Hollow of the Mearns, a fertile region lying low between two ridges of hills—the ridge of Garvock on the south side, and those of Strathfenella or Strath-findlay and Auchcairnie on the north. Laurencekirk, the birthplace of James Beattie, and connected with the memory of Lord Gardenstone and the still more famous Lord Monboddo, stands the centre or capital of this beautiful district. Eastward the ground rises, while it gets more bleak, and swells gradually into heights, partly arable and partly moorish; and among these heights is Glenbervie, from which farther on there is a deep and rapid descent toward Stonehaven and the sea. Burness, Burnes, and Burns, as the name is variously spelled, is derived from the Anglo Saxon Beorn, "a chief," with the affix *nes* for possession. The name De Burnes is found early in English records. The name of Brunhouse of Kair, in the county of Kincardine, appears as early as the reign of Robert the Bruce. In 1547 we find persons named Burnes renting the lands of Inchbreck, in the parish of Glenbervie. One of these, named William, took in Glenbervie a farm called Bogjorgan, where he died in 1715. Before his death he gave up the farm to his sons, William and James. After holding it some time at a joint lease James removed to Inches, a farm in the same county, while William remained in Bogjorgan. Robert Chambers gives a copy of the inventory of the homesteading at Bogjorgan at the time of the separation—a document remarkable among other things for spelling the name *Burnasse*. William Burness had a son (or, Dr. Rogers says, a brother), who settled in the farm of Brawlinmuir, Glenbervie. On one occasion he outwitted some caterans who were hovering in the neighbourhood, and who ultimately entered his house to rob it, by concealing his money in the nave of an old wheel, which lay in the jaw-hole before the door as a kind of stepping-stone. One of his sons, Robert Burnes, rented the lands of Clochanhill, six miles west from Stonehaven, on the estate of Dunottar, which belonged to the Earl of Marischal. He had three sons, James, Robert, and William—1st, James, who went to Montrose, and became the father of the Writer there, who corresponded with the poet, and the great-grandfather of the famous Sir Alexander Burness of Bokhara and Cabul memory; 2nd, Robert, who left his father's house, as we will see immediately, at the same time with his brother, William, for England, remained there for a number of years, and died at Ellisland in 1789; and 3rd, William, the father of the Scottish Bard.*

Robert Burns himself fostered the belief (in which there is also some traditionary credence)—the wish being with him father to the thought—that some of his ancestors were "out" in the Rebellion. The author of the "Chevalier's Lament" and "Drummossie Muir" had a strong Jacobitical prejudice, mingling in his bosom with that patriot passion of which he speaks to Dr. Moore, and "which was to boil on in his bosom till the flood-gates of life were to shut in eternal rest;" and we might wish that it had been yet stronger, since in this case it might have inspired a hundred Jacobite melodies as good as those we now possess—better they could hardly be. Some of his remoter relations may have shared in the Rebellion of 1715-16; but his father was not born then, and procured ere he left his home a certificate that he had no part in the late "wicked rebellion."

William Burness and his elder brother, Robert, left Clochanhill together — driven southward by the same stress of poverty. Gilbert Burns tells us that they parted on the summit of a hill on the confines of their native place—very probably on the top of Garvock, with its wide view northward of the Howe of the Mearns, its fields of billowy grain, edged by a margin of blue hills soaring upwards to the loftier heights of Wirren, Caterthun, and Clochnaben; and southward of the ocean, with "ships dim-discovered dropping from the clouds" in the distance, and the coast from Bervie to Montrose and the Red Head stretching below. From this the coast road strikes away to Montrose, and thence to Edinburgh, *via* Dundee; while, on the other side, a road goes right through the Howe of the Mearns, by Brechin, to Perth, and thence to England. At this point the brothers had to part—the one going to Edinburgh, the other to England. And there would be here the elements of a tragedy, for both the men were of the blood of Burns; and with tears in their eyes, and anguish like despair in their hearts,

* See Dr. Rogers' excellent and most researching book on the "Genealogy of Burns," 1877.

they would tear themselves asunder—Robert, we suppose remaining last on the hill, and watching his brother William slowly descending toward Den Fenella and St Cyrus, and often turning back to the summit to take a last look—it is the last—of his younger brother. They never met again. William hied him to Edinburgh, and there, or in its immediate neighbourhood, procured some employment as a gardener, working and faring hard, and always contriving to save and send a little money home to Clochanhill to gladden the hearts of his aged parents. Once a bank note of some value arrived. They stared at it with astonishment. They had perhaps seen such a thing before only in the hands of haughty lairds or cruel factors, at an unapproachable distance. But now that it was theirs, as the schoolboy feels to his first shilling, they hardly know how to use it. Had the poet been there, he who wrote verses about a bank note and often on bank notes, might have inscribed a sonnet or a song on the "First Bank Note (and the Last) in Clochanhill."

From Edinburgh William Burness found his way to the West; but found it not, alas! more genial or hospitable than the East had been. He got a situation first under the laird of Fairlie, and then under Crawford of Doonside. He afterwards leased seven acres near the Bridge of Doon as nursery ground. Here he built the "auld clay biggin'" with his own hands, and on 15th December 1757, brought home to it Agnes Brown, his young bride. The poet's mother was a comely person, with red hair bordering on yellow, and with fine dark eyes, which she left, along with a poetic temperament, as a legacy to her son. She had been taught to read, but not to write. Her memory was stored with old ballads and songs, which she sang uncommonly well. She was of exceedingly active habits, of a cheerful disposition—a helpmeet to her husband and a kind mother to her children. Having been early left "a mitherless bairn"—sent out from her home to the care of a maternal grandmother, and afterwards mistrysted, as they say in Scotland, with a love affair— her career was to some extent prophetic of her son's. The low deal chair in which she nursed all her children is still preserved in Closeburn Hall, in Dumfriesshire, the seat of Sir James Menteith. William Burness was thirty-one years of age, and Agnes Brown twenty-six, when they were married. No epithalamium was sung at their nuptials, no marriage presents of value given to the young couple, although there would be the usual reels and rejoicings of a Scottish wedding; but here was a more memorable conjunction than Astronomy has ever recorded—rustic loveliness, sense, and sensibility in Agnes Brown, united to strong intellect, high moral principle, and indomitable perseverance in William Burness, recalling the fine words of Gerald Massey—

> "See Strength and Beauty, hand in hand,
> Step forth into the golden land."

Alas! in this case, however, it was no golden land, only a humble house with a *but* and a *ben*, a hut, in which the boy Burns was to appear thirteen months afterwards; and beyond a piece of garden ground bordering on the sea, with the old road from Ayr to the south on its edge, a spot altogether consecrated to the genius of poverty and toil. But the "golden land" lay in their mutual love, and that was soon to be sealed by the birth of the most extraordinary man in native power and genius Scotland ever produced.

Thirteen months passed away in love and labour, the love sweetening the labour, the labour strengthening the love, till at last the consummation arrived. But Burns, who was not in the roll of common men, could not be like common men in the circumstances of his birth. No Owen Glendower prodigies, indeed, were to attend his arrival amongst us. It was fit that the handsel of Nature's great Scottish poet should be given by one of the genuine blasts of his own stormy sky. Not, indeed, on the 25th January, 1759, but some days afterwards (Gilbert Burns says, on the 3rd or 4th of February) came a loud tempest with lashing rains—

> "That *day*, a child might understand,
> The Deil had business on his hand."

But if his purpose was to destroy or drown his future bard and murderer (who, as Dr. Waddell intimates, scoffed him out of belief, if not of being), his purpose was foiled. True, the two jambs of the "auld clay biggin'" threw the gable off its centre, and it falling down got so shattered that it was thought necessary to carry the squalling poet through the storm to a neighbour's house, where he remained a week. The horoscope of the hapless Duke of Buckingham was thus read by Davy Ramsay ("Fortunes of Nigel")—

> "Full moon and high sea,
> Great man shalt thou be;
> Red dawning, stormy sky,
> Bloody death shalt thou die."

That of Burns, to a poetic augur vaticinating on the ground of this storm, might seem to portend wild tumult and skiey wrath, ending in safety, the poet triumphing over the tempest which sought his life, the storm of calumny, opposition, and passion subdued into peace. But, alas, No!*

Many years ago (in June, 1846) we visited the "auld clay biggin'," at that time (and we believe still) a hostelrie for dispensing Burns' beloved beverage, and other good things of this life. We remember one rather odd circumstance: when looking at the concealed bed in which the poet was born, our companion (the gifted Rev. Dr. W. B. Robertson of Irvine, the orator and poet of the West) exclaimed, "Here's a laddie, here's wee Bobbie Burns!" A cry from the bed confirmed the words, and drawing near we tried to complete the *glamourie* of the scene by imagining that this boy who lifted up his arms and smiled was the inspired child to whose birthplace, in that humble cottage, the civilized world has flocked for wellnigh one hundred years. From the cottage we pursued the road along which Tam O' Shanter led his weird and tipsy gallop to Alloway Kirk (which seemed too small a stage for such a phantasmagoria as was transacted there, as though "Macbeth" were enacted in a barn-loft), but found metal more attractive in the grave-stone† erected by the poet to the memory of his parents, which, although not to weeping given, touched us to tears by the simple pathos of the story it tells of them, and the feeling it discovered in him. After this the elaborate monument on the Doon seemed an impertinence; but the haunted bridge restored and intensified the spirit of the spot, receiving and shedding down the magic light of the Past upon the stream, which combined music and legendary mystery in the murmur of its immemorial waters. How thankful we were from all we had heard of it, that we had not been present, as we once intended to have been, at the Burns' Festival in 1844. To-day there had been a partial disenchantment, then it had been total; and how terrible always is the fall of a long-cherished ideal to a young enthusiast!

Of the infant years of the poet we know little. The first glimpse we get of him is sitting at his father's fireside, listening to the ballads and stories of an old woman, one Betty Davidson, a relation of the family; and, as Wandering Willy says in "Redgauntlet," she had "some fearsome anes, that mak the auld carlines shake in the settle, and the bits o' weans skirl on their minnies out frae their beds." Her stories roused in Burns the sleeping elements of wonder and poetry, and probably fascination would sometimes overpower fear, and he would cry out in spirit with Outis in the "Odyssey," "More, give me more, it is divine!" He owns to the feeling continuing in after life; and if so, how strong it would be in early days! William Burness sent Robert in his sixth year to a little school at Alloway Mill, taught by one Campbell, who, however, soon migrated to a better place in Ayr, and William Burness united with some neighbours in employing a young man, named John Murdoch, as teacher to the children of several families. This worthy man taught Robert and his younger brother, Gilbert, English and English grammar, besides writing, and was much gratified by their proficiency. Murdoch lent him the "Life of

---

* See, in reference to Burns' Cottage, Appendix, No. I.

† "Grave-stone," see Appendix, No. II.

Hannibal," and two years after he got from a blacksmith who shod their horses the "Life of Sir William Wallace," which he read with the utmost avidity and with important results, for it poured into his veins that tide of Scottish prejudice of which he predicates, as we have seen, the life-long endurance.

In 1766 his father left his cottage at Alloway, and took the small farm of Mount Oliphant, two miles off. Robert, however, and Gilbert continued to attend Murdoch's school, till at the end of two years he removed to Carrick. It was on a parting visit of the excellent Dominie to the cottage that there occurred the famous scene at the reading of "Titus Andronicus," where the whole party were so much moved at some of the melodramatic horrors of the play that they were all dissolved in tears, and Robert threatened, if it were left in the house, to burn it. Dr. Currie it is, we think, who asks why this silly play is still bound up with the writings of Shakspeare? But although it is certainly far inferior to his usual mark, there are passages in it (witness Aaron's address to his black illegitimate child by the queen) which bear the stamp of Shakspeare. Schlegel remarks that Shakspeare alone was capable of producing either its beauties or faults, although Hazlitt thinks Marlowe, who was only a little lower than the Myriad-minded, might have written it. Perhaps Shakspeare added the better passages to the play, just as Burns himself often made an old, stupid, and scandalous ballad his own by inserting some stroke of consummate wit or genius. It is curious that Murdoch preferred Gilbert to Robert, and thought, because the former was the merrier of the two, that he was more likely to turn out a poet. Little did he see what a deep current of enthusiasm was running below, or knew what dark stern cogitations were saddening the brow of the wondrous boy, who already knew that he was a "poor man's son," and was already noted for a sturdy stubborn something in his disposition, for an "enthusiastic idiot piety," and whose mirth at all seasons of his life was only the silver lining on the cloud of the thickest melancholy!

From the date of Murdoch's departure William Burness undertook himself the charge of his children's education, and whiled away the heavy labours of the farm by conversing familiarly with them on useful subjects. He borrowed Salmon's Dictionary for them—made it their text-book in Geography; and instructed them in Natural History and Astronomy out of Derham's "Physico and Astro Theology" and Ray's "Wisdom of God in the Creation," a book once very popular, till supplanted by Paley's works, as these in their turn have been supplanted by the "Bridgewater Treatises"—very different fare from Thomas Boston's "Fourfold State," so strongly recommended (see the "Life of Thomas Davidson, the Scottish Probationer"), and with what slender results and left-handed gratitude to the gifted author of "Ariadne in Naxos." Burns, however, had read, and refers more than once to, honest Thomas' book; and whatever he might think of its religious theories, he no doubt did ample justice (as Carlyle also does) to Boston's excellent motives and thorough simplicity of character. Burns became acquainted, too, with Stackhouse's "History of the Bible" (afterwards edited by the venerable Bishop Gleig, of Stirling, father to the author of the "Subaltern" and the "Life of Warren Hastings"), and with a collection of letters by eminent writers, which became his standard and model for epistolary composition. When about thirteen or fourteen years of age, he and Gilbert were sent to the parish school of Dalrymple, three miles from their home, for a summer quarter, to improve their handwriting; and about this time Robert got hold of some of Richardson's, Fielding's, Smollett's, Hume's, and Robertson's works. Shortly after, his old master, Murdoch, was appointed English teacher in Ayr; and resuming his acquaintance with the Mount Oliphant family, he lent Robert Pope's works, and took him, at his father's desire, to Ayr to assist him in revising his grammar and learning a little French. Burns was advised to begin Latin, too; but proceeded only a short way in that study—not farther, he used to say waggishly, than to understand the words, *Amor vincit omnia*, although he resumed it occasionally afterwards; and whenever any reverse of fortune or disappointment befell him, he was wont to hum, "But I'll to my Latin again," as he snatched up Ruddiman. Some of his biographers have regretted that, along with the Bible and the ballads of Scotland, Burns had so much intercourse at this time with "shallow, sharp, and polished writers, like Pope, Addison, Swift, and Steele, with their stilted stops and methodical periods." In this slump judgment we do not agree. These writers alone might have been bad models; but united to others of a loftier mood, they materially assisted the education of his taste, and aided him in acquiring such a comparatively correct prose style as his letters exemplify. They gave him the *form;* his own genius supplied the *fire.* They helped him, as ruled paper helps a beginner in the art of writing. Nor can we coincide with this estimate of the authors referred to. Surely Addison is one of the sweetest and most natural writers in the language. We knew a very clever and scholarly man who used to say that he would rather have written the "Vision of Mirza" than all Byron's poetry; and Burns himself speaks of his early delight in perusing that exquisite allegory. Pope, according to Sir Walter Scott, was a "Deacon in his trade"—the finest of artists, and not the least gifted of poets, although too often, as his defender Lewes has it*—

* "Lewes" (see Boswell's "Johnson"), author of some noble stanzas about Pope, much prized by Dr. Johnson.

> "Malice, Pope, denies thy page
>   *Its own* celestial fire;
> While critics and while bards in rage,
>   *Admiring, won't admire.*"

And to call Swift—the masculine, the ingenious, the sensible, the master of strong, simple, sinewy English, the greatest satirist of his age, the wittiest man in the wittiest nation of the world, and if you will, the ablest libeller of human nature that ever lived—"shallow," is to betray a narrowness of judgment and a want of appreciation of one of the giants of British literature as strong and as unique, in his *own style*, as Shakspeare or Milton. Apart from what Burns derived from the wits of Queen Anne (we will show by and by it was not unmixed good) and the poets of the Elizabethan period (the latter very imperfectly known to him), he must have reaped a great deal of advantage from such master novelists as Richardson, Fielding and Smollett; and such historians as Hume and Robertson. The one class tended to educate his feelings and develop his dramatic power, a power he possessed in a great measure, and often used, though he never wrote a play; and the second, to enlarge his views and to strengthen his understanding. Burns read, Gilbert tells us, two volumes of "Pamela," a novel which, from its subject and its heart-rending pathos, must have been peculiarly suggestive to him at this period of his life.

At Ayr Burns continued three weeks in Murdoch's house, diligently employed in learning French. Murdoch in a long letter gives an interesting account of this visit, which was terminated by the coming on of harvest, at which Burns, who at fifteen did the full work of a man, could not be spared. The most notable thing in this letter is its panegyric on William Burness, who seems to have been one of Nature's uncrowned nobility—a man almost perfect —not of that kind of virtue either which must be taken for granted, but which was tested by every kind of severe suffering, except that of remorse for gifts misused, opportunities neglected, and errors committed. That was the lot of his son; but ere we place him hopelessly beneath his father, let us remember that no meteor rays streamed before the parent's eyes, no passions hot as those of a hundred hearts beat in his bosom. Robert Burns did, at all events, to his father what no Murdoch or Gilbert Burns could have done for him, he repaid the gift of life with immortality. It was of his father he said—

> "Then kneeling down to Heaven's Eternal King,
>   The priest, the father, and the husband prays."

Before closing this chapter we may merely pursue for a moment the fate of John Murdoch, the excellent preceptor of the poet. After Burns left for the harvest rigg Murdoch often visited him at his father's house, and helped him with his learning. He continued for some years a respected citizen and teacher in Ayr, till a quarrel in his cups with Dr. Dalrymple, the all-powerful parish minister there, forced him to migrate to London, where he became a private teacher of French, and wrote some books on the French language—such as, "A Radical Vocabulary of the French Language," "On the Pronunciation and Orthography of the French Language," a "Dictionary of Distinctions." He also rendered valuable assistance to Walker when preparing his excellent "English Dictionary." He heard in the midst of the mighty London of the fame of his pupil, and could scarcely for a while believe that this prodigy of genius had ever walked by his side along the whitening ridges of Mount Oliphant, or lain in bed with him conjugating French verbs! He soon warmly welcomed his rise, but never seems to have thought of comparing him for a moment with his father. Murdoch's connection, however, with Burns was of service to him in his declining years. Although he had taught English to many distinguished persons in London, such as Talleyrand, he fell into poverty and ill-health. An appeal was made on his behalf to the friends and admirers of Burns, who raised some money to relieve his wants. He died in 1824, aged seventy-seven, having survived for twenty-eight years his excitable and ill-starred scholar.

CHAPTER II.

BURNS THE YOUTH.

THUS for eighteen years had the life of the boy Burns sped away. Working in the harvest field like a Titanic slave, and spending his evenings after his own heart; his summer nights in wandering through the country by haunted stream or sounding ocean, a book often in his hand; his winter nights in devouring Stackhouse, Smollett, and Robertson; his Sabbaths in listening to Dr. Dalrymple, or some nearer Presbyterian oracle; and his private hours, by night or day, in thoughts too deep for tears, in communings with his own hungry heart, in conjectures on his future destiny, as yet unblest by any delightful "Vision," and in melancholy reflections on man and the world. He was little regarded by anybody, unless indeed by his father, who always saw in Robert the promise of an extraordinary man. He speaks of the cheerless gloom of a hermit, and the unceasing toil of a galley slave, as comprising his whole existence up to his sixteenth year. Yet, we doubt not, he was then often happy, happier than in after days, and that for two good reasons—first, he was young, and the basis of youth is Hope; and, secondly, he was virtuous, and the usual attendant of virtue is Peace.

One cause of his sufferings was their poor farm. Mount Oliphant resembled Rip Van Winkle's farm; it was "the most pestilent piece of ground in the whole country," and Gilbert Burns tells us it continued unimproved and unimprovable, and notwithstanding the extraordinary rise in the value of land in Scotland about the time he wrote, let at £5 lower than the rent paid for it by his father thirty years before! The family laboured very hard, and fared very poorly—never for years tasting butcher's meat, and working themselves without any servant. Robert began to feel those fits of deep depression which never altogether left him, and in the evenings was often afflicted with a dull headache, exchanged afterwards for a palpitation of the heart, and a threatening of fainting and suffocation in his bed in the nighttime, which made him sometimes arise and plunge himself into a tub of water which stood in the room.

At Whitsunday, 1777, the family left Mount Oliphant for Lochlea (pronounced *Lochly*), in the parish of Tarbolton. This farm lay on a rising ground to the north of the Ayr, was bleak and uninteresting in aspect, but from some of its braes commanded a fine view of the Carrick hills on the left, and of Arran and the other islands of the Frith of Clyde on the right; of Ailsa Craig too, that "craggy ocean pyramid" which Keats has sung. Burns must, from this and many other points, have often seen these striking objects; but it is curious how seldom he alludes to them in his poems, only once, we think, to Ailsa—

"Meg was deaf as Ailsa Craig"—

and never, so far as we remember, to the dark mass of mountains rising to the west, and known now to travellers from every part of the globe as the hills of Arran.* How often must he have seen the sun going down in gold or blood behind these black battlements; Jove pausing ere he dipped his orb, so beautiful and large, in the sea beyond them, and his own beloved Venus trembling as it shone a bulb of light in the orange sky of evening above them! But of all this his poetry, so full of allusions to the simpler features of Ayrshire scenery—her "burn stealing under the lang yellow broom," her "milk-white thorn that scents the evening gale," her Doon with her "far-fetch'd floods," and her moors "red-brown wi' heather bells"—is entirely silent. Nor do twenty lines in all his works attest any interest in or admiration of mountain scenery, and his verses on the "Fall of Foyers" and "Taymouth" are miserably poor, and like his Doon floods, "far-fetch'd." His contemporary, Cowper, yearned for mountains, but never expected to see them, unless he saw them in Heaven, and that to him, poor fellow, seemed a doubtful prospect; but Burns saw them every day from his plough, gave them his admiration doubtless, for he had a strong sense of the picturesque and sublime, but preferred to sing the "Braes of Ballochmyle" and the "Castle of Montgomery," nay, the "Mouse" running away from his ploughshare, and the "Daisy" crushed below it.

William Burness took his farm at Lochlea, of one hundred and twenty acres, at twenty shillings an acre, which Robert Chambers thinks a high rent for these days.

* Alexander Smith, whose "Life of Burns" we did not read till after writing this portion of our own, alludes, we observe, to this.

LIFE OF BURNS.

Nevertheless, matters at first rather prospered here with the Burns family. They stood, as the Highlanders phrase it, "shouther to shouther," and worked efficiently and well together — a family of poverty and "industrious peace." At this time a rather important event took place in the poet's history. His mother, originally from Craigeston, in the parish of Kirkoswald, had a brother living at the farm of Ballochneil, about a mile from the village of Kirkoswald—Samuel Brown by name, at once a farm labourer, fisherman, and dealer in wool. Burns resided with his uncle in a farm house which he occupied along with his brother-in-law, Niven, the farmer, his own wife being dead; and walked every morning to the village school at Kirkoswald. The coast of Carrick, near this, is the commencement of a long line of sea margin, extending by various reaches and windings from Ayr to Girvan, and thence to Stranraer, and thence to Wigton, and thence to that romantic region below Creetown, called usually Guy Mannering's country. Carrick, though far away from this, may be said to begin the waving line which, after many bendings, culminates in one of the most interesting spots in all the south of Scotland, both in itself and its associations. One rugged band then united all this tract of sea coast. It was, from Kirkoswald to Kirkcudbright, the haunt of a smuggling population; the Isle of Man forming a midway station between it and France, Ostend, and Gottenburg. We must not judge, however, of the Kirkoswald smuggler by Vanbeest Brown, *senior*, or Dirk Hatteraick. He was half smuggler, half farmer, jolly, kindly, though somewhat rude and riotous. Burns' uncle, Brown, belonged apparently to this type. The coast extends for many miles, and is backed by bare though green hills or uplands, surmounted at one place by the point on which formerly stood the Castle of Turnberry, famous in the history of Robert the Bruce, where the hero of Bannockburn "shook his Carrick spear." The village of Kirkoswald stands a mile or two inwards, in a sequestered nook. It was altogether a spot admirably adapted for the training of a young poet, and the four months spent by Burns here form one of the most pleasing and pregnant episodes in his early history. It is true, he tells us, that he learned "now to fill his glass and to mix without fear in a drunken squabble," which, by the way, shows that he had been habitually temperate before. But he here got acquainted with wild men and wild usages, saw wild scenery, bathed his young system and his soul, too, in the salt breath of the ocean, and met the first rough model of his inimitable "Tam o' Shanter." This was one (of whom more afterwards) Douglas Graham, whose farm of Shanter (its steading is now down, and its identity is somewhat indistinct, the farm having been divided into two) lay on a slope near the site of Turnberry Castle, and who was a good decent man to be a habitual smuggler and occasionally a hard drinker, and whose wife, Helen MacTaggart, was as fearful and superstitious as the Kate of the poem.

Hugh Rogers, who taught Burns mensuration and geometry, was an eminent teacher, and distinguished also as a land-surveyor—narrow, however, in his views; and this led him into certain disputes with his distinguished pupil, in which, as might have been expected, the Dominie came off second best. Unluckily, on one occasion, Rogers committed himself to a public discussion before his school, about the comparative value to society of a general and a merchant, with Burns, and was completely discomfited, to his own confusion, the satisfaction of his opponent, and the uproarious delight of the scholars. Burns' great associate at the time was John Niven, afterwards of Kilbride, a very successful man in business, and ultimately a land proprietor. On one occasion they treated their teacher to a jug of ale in an inn kept by two gentlewomen, Jean and Ann Kennedy, the former of whom figures in "Tam o' Shanter" as Kirkton Jean—

"Thou drank wi' Kirkton Jean till Monday."

Their house was a respectable one of its sort, and called usually "The Ladies' or Leddies' House."* Niven hailed from Maybole, and when he returned there from school on the Saturdays, these precious breathing times to scholars, Burns accompanied him, and their talk to and fro was of an elevating and inspiring character. First in his studies, first in debate with his teacher, first in his talk with his school companions, Burns was not first in manly exercises, such as putting the stone, wrestling, and leaping, although in these, too, he excelled. But here Niven was his Evil Genius, and always triumphed. Burns found his revenge, however, in drawing his successful rival into an argument about some speculative point, in which he generally regained his laurels.

And now he fell in love in a characteristic fashion. The original school at Kirkoswald was destroyed, and for it was substituted a room opposite the churchyard. Behind this room, on a high slope, was a succession of "kail-yards" attached to various cottages. Across this unromantic locality there shot a vision of female beauty, which quite dazzled the eye of Burns. He had gone out to take the altitude of the sun—fit employment for a young poet! But a star came between him and old Sol. Sines and cosines, quadrants and parallaxes, were alike confounded and put to flight when Peggy Thomson, daughter of a neighbouring cottager, came out to the garden, according to one of his biographers, not to gather flowers, but to cut down a cabbage for the family dinner! This, he says, completely overset his trigonometry. *Amor vincit omnia* became his motto. To see Peggy, to steal out and court

* See Note on "Tam o' Shanter" in Poems.

Peggy, and ultimately to vent his feelings on Peggy in song, was henceforth his care till he left Kirkoswald. He renewed his acquaintance with her temporarily afterwards; but her image left little permanent effect on his mind.

Chambers tells the following anecdote about Burns when he resided at Kirkoswald:—One day, as he was walking slowly along the street of the village in a manner customary to him, with his eyes bent upon the ground, he was met by the Misses Biggar, the daughters of the pastor of the parish. He would have passed without noticing them, if one of the young ladies had not called him by name. She then rallied him on his inattention to the fair sex, in preferring to look to the inanimate ground, instead of seizing the opportunity afforded him of indulging in the most invaluable privilege of man—that of beholding and conversing with the ladies. "Madam," said he, "it is a natural and right thing for man to contemplate the ground from which *he* was taken, and for woman to look upon and observe man from whom *she* was taken." This, adds Chambers, was a conceit; but it was the conceit of no "vulgar boy." It was not, however, original with Burns. A respected correspondent, John Cuthbertson, Esq., formerly the able English master of the High School, Dundee, now residing near Troon, Ayrshire, writes us as follows:—"There was an edition of L'Estrange's 'Ruins of Quevedo' published in Glasgow in 1753. It is coarsely printed on coarse paper, and must have been sold for a price not exceeding sixpence. At page 24 a young woman is represented as saying to a duenna who had admonished her, 'Let the men look downwards toward the clay of which they are made; but man was our original, and it well becomes us to keep our eyes upon the matter from which we came.'" He adds, "If Burns had got the idea from Quevedo, he must have read at least one book more than the list given by Chambers contains, and I believe he had perused dozens more. Burns, if he ever used the words, which I doubt, might have got them from this Glasgow translation."

He returned home from this visit, he tells us, very considerably improved. Some think that it was at this period that he composed his song, "I Dreamed I Lay where Flowers were Springing," some of the lines in which bear a resemblance to Mrs. Cockburn's "Flowers of the Forest." Chambers says that his lines on "Peggy Thomson" were not written till he renewed his acquaintance with her, years after he had seen her at Kirkoswald. Burns tells us that, while in Carrick, he read Thomson's and Shenstone's works for the first time. Even the languid sentimentalism of Shenstone found some reflection in his inflammable bosom, as his "Vision" proves; but how much more must he have sympathized with the solemn grandeur, the difficult swell, like that of a labouring sea, the natural piety, the genuine enthusiasm, the sudden and savage dash of some of the pictorial touches, like the style of Salvator Rosa, and what he calls the "landscape glow" of the great author of the "Seasons," on the crowning of whose bust he was afterwards to indite a poem! He commenced, immediately after leaving Carrick, a habit of letter-writing, which led by and by, through much practice, to excellence; his correspondence being, if not his highest, yet one of his distinct and undeniable claims to enduring fame. He began by studying and imitating the letters of the "Wits of Queen Anne," a collection of which he had procured; but soon (as Wordsworth says of the Sonnet) in his hands "the thing became a trumpet," and some of Burns' letters are among the most eloquent ever penned. Once engaged in letter-writing, he found it a fascination. "Though he had not three farthings' worth of business in the world, every post brought him as many letters as if he had been a broad plodding son of daybook and ledger." He read also at this time "Tristram Shandy" and the "Man of Feeling" with special delight—the one for its riotous oddity, wild humour, and touches of Shakspearean tenderness; the other for its delicate vein of pathos and charming style. Often, too, he took up the lyre, and swept the chords with energy; but his full mastery over it was not yet attained.

His career at Lochlea was for some years uneventful. The Burns family was all that time a virtuous household, though exceeding poor; hard-wrought, but contented; singularly self-contained, and mingling little with their neighbours; distinguished by a certain superiority of manners and refinement of taste, and sure to be found, all of them, at meal times reading while consuming their victuals. Such families were once not uncommon in Scotland, and even still, in hamlets among the hills or in lonely country-sides, a few may be found. We fancy a kind of *hauteur* and reserve in their manners, as of a family dwelling alone, and not reckoned among the common herd; and this certainly characterized Robert Burns himself. He was as proud as Lucifer, or rather (to imitate a witticism of De Quincey) Lucifer was as proud as Burns.

Up to his visit to Irvine in his twenty-third year, Burns seems to have been one of the brightest, funniest, happiest, and most virtuous of young men. Gilbert went with him to the peat-moss, and he seemed to set it on fire by the quick, lightning-like play of his raillery and thick-coming fancies. His audience then was rather few than fit, consisting of some farm servants engaged at their laborious employment of delving, wheeling, and stacking peats under a burning summer sun; but soon their sides were sorer than their limbs, and more wearied, while the peasant youth was darting up from among the hags the flashes of his eye and the coruscations of his wit and genius. An old man near Catrine used often to tell our excellent friend, Dr. Hamilton MacGill, foreign secretary to the United Presbyterian Church, that he remembered a string of carts going to a quarry for lime, all of them abandoned by their drivers, who had gathered round the cart of Burns, who, by shooting round shafts of fun, was exciting screams and shouts of laughter, while some of the weaker recipients, we venture to say, were rolling helpless on the ground. It was, we think, the same man who, when a boy, saw Robert and Gilbert digging a lint hole. "What are you doing there?" said he. "Making a grave for the *Deil*," replied Robert. "*Catch him first*," cried the boy, on which the poet exploded in convulsions of laughter. The mention of the Deil always tickled rather than terrified the author of the "Address."

The other members of the family of Lochlea were not destitute of literary aspirations. Agnes, while milking the cows with her two sisters, would repeat the old Scottish songs she had picked up—the "Flowers of the Forest" (in the first form of that plaintive ditty), "Sir James the Rose," and some of the versions of the Psalms, specially the 145th in our Scottish collection. Gilbert Burns was a man of reading, and, for the time, of cultivated understanding, although that exuberance of spirits attributed to him in early days by Murdoch seems to have departed and gone over to his elder brother, who at this time of his life was of a most joyous and indulgent temper. Gilbert was in the harvest field a sullen, stern task-master; but when he spoke harshly to any of his young labourers, Robert would take their part, and cry, "Oh, man, ye're no for young folk." Nor can we wonder though the author of "The Winter Night" should think with pity on those "poor dumb mouths," the "owrie cattle," the robin red-breast, friend and bewildered guest of man, the "silly sheep" and "ilk happing bird, wee helpless thing;" and never did poet, unless we except William Cowper or Professor Wilson, exhibit more sympathy, whether in his song or in himself, with "the creation made subject to vanity, and groaning and travailing in pain together until now." And it is hinted that the crushed and trampled ones knew their benefactor—knew the man who, in the "Twa Dogs," had sounded their very souls (if souls they have), had gauged their sufferings, and had shared in their gladness, when, at the sight of "the innocent wee things" in the cottage at play—

"They for joy had barkit wi' them."

It was altogether a happy home that of Lochlea. Poverty might be looking in at the window, but had not yet entered the house. The excellent father was yet strong to labour, as well as wise to advise. And the hot passions of the eldest son, which were to form such an element of disturbance to himself and his friends, still slumbered like morning clouds, which look calm and bright till—

"Slowly charged with thunder they convey
Terror to earth and tempest to the air."

And it is to the period of his life now at hand that we would specially apply the lines of Wordsworth—

"Of him that walked in glory and in joy,
Behind his plough upon the mountain side."

In our next Chapter we will look at him as developed into the Ploughman Poet. But although advancing to this stage he got more fame, we suspect his pleasures were hardly so pure and simple as they had been in Lochlea. The cause of this will presently appear.

CHAPTER III.

BURNS THE PLOUGHMAN-POET.

BEFORE settling down as a farmer, Burns' fancy was crossed by a new ambition, which promised to alter his entire scheme of life, and which might have led him to fortune and forgetfulness! Feeling that the outlook of a poor plough-boy was but a gloomy one; aware that, as he tells Dr. Moore, the only two openings by which he could enter the Temple of Fortune were the gate of niggardly economy, and the path of little chicaning bargain-making, both of which he detested—the one as narrow, the other as contaminated; and having a desire, besides, to marry (Ellison Begbie is supposed at that time to have been his flame, who afterwards jilted him)—he turned his attention to flax-dressing, in which he had tried some experiments along with Gilbert at Lochlea, and removed to Irvine to set up his trade. Irvine, now a thriving seaport, was then the emporium of the flax-dressing trade, generally in connection with farms on which the material was raised. Here Burns became connected with a man named Peacock, whom the poet, in a passage of his letters which has not been printed, has strongly denounced. He possibly had cheated Burns while teaching him his calling. The cottage where he plied his trade stood on the Smiddy Green, one end being devoted to the work, the other employed by an individual in keeping workhorses. Flax-dressers, or hecklers, as they were often called, have been in Scotland a superior, though peculiar class of men. In the town where we now write (Dundee), they were, we have heard, in the first half of the century, noted for their knowledge, irregular diligence, occasional *bouts* of dissipation, great interest in politics, and expertness in political discussion. The most powerful speakers who, at the time of George Kinloch's banishment, stirred the fierce democracy of Dundee, were hecklers. Their manners, however, and their habits, were often coarse. We suspect that Burns in Irvine was thrown among a similar class, and his very superiority led him into snares. He was noted for his powers of conversation. But the inspired heckler found rough and ready logic more popular than poetical talk. Little else, we believe, is remembered of him in Irvine than his melancholy. The uncongenial and unsuccessful trade, the rude society the scoundrel partner, his distance from home, and, it may be, a certain looseness of habits here acquired, reacted violently on his spirits, and made the brightest man in the west of Scotland for a year a gloomy hypochondriac. Yet one precious fruit grew on, and has fallen to us from the baleful tree—we refer to the beautiful letter to his father, dated December 27, 1781. This itself seems to cast doubt on the insinuation Professor Walker throws out on the authority of somebody, who boasted that he had taught Burns looser ideas of religion in Irvine. The expression is of course very vague; but if the opinions taught him were really loose, and not simply somewhat bolder than his former sentiments, they do not seem to have rooted themselves very deeply. The heart, at least, of the author of that noble letter was right, and—

> " The heart aye's the part, aye,
> That keeps us richt or wrang.'

Yet temptation seems to have attacked him in Irvine from another direction. Here he met with one Richard Brown (afterwards, we have been assured by persons who knew him, a very respectable man and citizen), who had been at sea, and talked of illicit love with the levity of a sailor, although Brown was wont to say that Burns had nothing to learn on that subject when they got acquainted. This must refer to his Irvine experience, since we have Gilbert Burns' testimony and his own that his life in Lochlea was pure. An account of Brown's romantic history and his influence on Burns' mind may be read in the poet's famous letter to Dr. Moore. We find him writing to Brown afterwards with great affection. Burns seems seldom, if ever, to have lost a friend. He "grappled them to his heart with hooks of steel." He had a high theoretical idea of the value of friendship; and practically his friendships were about as strong as his loves, and considerably less fickle. " The lover and the friend " he invariably classes together. Brown had a taste in other directions than the fair sex. He liked poetry, and Burns alludes in one of his letters to a Sabbath day they passed in Eglinton woods, then, as now, very beautiful and umbrageous, when Brown urged Burns to send some verses he repeated to a magazine—a hint which flattered Burns' vanity, although he did not act on it.

Burns, we saw, had written the plaintive letter to his father on the 27th December, 1781. We find him with characteristic volatility welcoming in the New Year on the 1st of January, 1782, in a carousal so prolonged and excessive, that during it his flax shop took fire, was burned to ashes, and himself left, "like a true poet, without a farthing." He did not, however, return to Lochlea till March, as is proved by his sister's statement and by his initials inscribed by himself, with the date (1782), on the chimney-piece of the little garret where he slept.

The gloom which had cast its shadow over Burns' later days at Irvine came home with him, although it seems gradually to have yielded to various influences—to the summer weather which began, to his resumption with redoubled energy of his labours in the field, to the counsel and company of his father, and to the happy fraternal influence of Gilbert. Whatever might have been his habits in Irvine, and although changed perhaps in tastes, he resumed in Lochlea the same hard-faring and temperate life as before. He engaged, however, as we shall see, in some love affairs, although none of much consequence. He attended, as he had done once before, a dancing school. He began in rivalship with David Sillar (his "Davie"), who was a very respectable poetaster and a "prime fiddler," to practise the violin—sometimes on a bad day, when he was unable to work in the fields, and sometimes early in the morning, when he would break up the kitchen *gathering coal*, and alarm the family by his untimely scrapings. Fiddling is not a very common accomplishment, we think, of poets. Dr. Croly, indeed, according to Barry Cornwall, was a good violinist, although in his later days, when we knew him, he had resigned the practice as unsuitable to his years, if not to his profession. Burns never succeeded in it, nor in the German flute, and his voice was tuneless and rough as a boar's; yet he could read music, and was keenly susceptible, need we say? to the charms of song. But his chief employment now was the plough, and his chief relaxation and solace was poetry —and lo! the Ploughman Poet! He restrung, he tells us, his lyre with renewed vigour.

Six or seven years before this he had written, as we have seen, his pretty "I dreamed I lay where flowers were springing." He tells us he had even sketched the plan of a Tragedy, and has retained one speech from it; supposed to have been spoken by a great oppressor, by whom he meant the factor who had ground down his father for his arrears at Mount Oliphant. It reads rather like a bit of Young's "Revenge" than of Shakspeare. Afterwards he is said to have composed a song on every tolerably looking girl in the parish, and finally, one in which they were all included. Such ditties he usually destroyed. A beautiful one has survived—"My Nannie, O," and it is certainly one of the sweetest and tenderest of all his strains. The river of the song, beyond which were the Carrick hills, visible from Lochlea, was the Stinchar or Stinsiar, for which he afterwards substituted, as a more euphonious title, the Lugar, a stream which belonged to a different district. At this our friend, the late excellent David Jamieson, U.P. minister in Kilmarnock, was very angry, and has justly abused Burns and Burns' editors for it in his volume of poems, "Scenes of Youth." Nannie was one Agnes Fleming, in Tarbolton parish, a farmer's daughter and a servant, of no special attractions, and who knew Burns very slightly—only, indeed, so far that he once told her he had written a "sang" on her. It is interesting to know that his father lived to see and to be much gratified by this song, which is indeed pure as the "opening gowan wat wi' dew." It was followed by his scornful ditty, "O Tibby, I hae seen the day," inscribed to a proud minx named Isabella Steven or Stein. There were some other love strains, which may be more appropriately treated when we come to the list of his early loves in the next chapter. His gloomy state of mind at Irvine inspired the copy of verses called "Winter," with the two lines so affecting in their simplicity of bitterness—

"The leafless trees my fancy please,
  Their fate resembles mine."

also his "Prayer Written under the pressure of Violent Anguish." He had flung off this untimely load ere he struck up the cheerful strain—

"My father was a farmer upon the Carrick border,"

which, though written in a ranting style, is a piece of real genius. Many of his poems were composed at the plough—notably, "Poor Mailie." Burns had bought a ewe and two lambs, and the ewe was tethered in a field adjoining the house of Lochlea. He and Gilbert were going out with their team, when Hugh Wilson, a curious, awkward-looking boy, clad in plaiding, came, with much anxiety in his face, to tell that the ewe had entangled herself in the tether, and was lying in the ditch. Robert caught up the humour in Hughoc's look and the pathos in Mailie's position at once; and after relieving the ewe, went, with eyes sparkling, to the plough, composed the poem there, and repeated it to his brother in the evening. To those who remember their own boyhood, and what a Scotch boy especially is, the best touch in all this simple and quaint effusion lies in the words—

"Now, honest Hughoc, dinna fail
  To tell my master a' my tale;
And bid him burn his cursed tether,
  And for my sake thou's get my blether."

To the same period (founded partly on a black-letter English ballad) belongs "John Barleycorn," as spirited an

Anacreontic as ever flowed from the lyre of the Teian Bard, of Herrick, Tom Moore, Byron, or Lytton Bulwer, whose exquisite song in the "Last Days of Pompeii" has seldom been equalled; * and the rest of the Bacchanalian brotherhood. Yet Burns, when he wrote it, was habitually a water drinker; when he did drink, it was in great moderation, and his whole expenditure on himself was £7 per annum.

"Ye generous Britons, venerate the plough," cries Thomson; and Burns, since Thomson's day, has supplied a new reason for obeying the command. Since the plough of Cincinnatus, no plough that ever cut the furrow can be named for interest with the plough of Burns. And what was a Roman patriot, however august and disinterested, to our large-hearted poet, whose bright-blazing meteoric eyes seemed to be piercing into the deep of thought and feeling, while his ploughshare was cutting through the clods a way for the seed, the blade, and the full corn in the ear—the divinity of whose daily toil was proved and complemented in his experience by the inspiration which descended from above, and seemed the witness of the gods to his humble, honourable calling here, and their prophecy of his eternal fame hereafter. To refer to an image Burns used himself afterwards, Elisha was not a prophet till he left the plough; but to Burns the shaft of the plough was his rod of inspiration and command, as his mind moved in the wind of the spring day, and his genius expanded and caught the colours of the April sun. Never was our poet more manly, more simple, often so bald, but always so beautiful, as in those poems and songs which, composed at the plough, he was to commit to his immortal page, leaning over his table or chest in his little Lochlea garret ere he went to rest!

His labours at the plough were diversified by various excursions on Sabbaths, and walks in the evenings on other days. The story of Wallace, as recounted by Blind Harry (abridged by Hamilton of Gilbertfield), had made a very deep impression on Burns' mind, especially the words—

"Syne to the Leglen wood, when it was late,
He made a silent and a safe retreat."

This wood was in his own locality, and he chose, he tells us, a fine summer day to visit it and explore every den and dingle where he supposed his heroic countryman to have been. No wonder though his heart glowed with a wish to make a song on him in some measure equal to his merits. But two things were yet wanting to the birth of—

"Scots, wha hae wi' Wallace bled"

—the wild moors of Galloway, and a mood caught from the thunder-cloud and the tempest which was beating on the brow of the poet, careering through it—the Spirit of the Storm! A poem on Wallace, written in the Leglen wood at this time of his life, would have been, we fear, a tamer affair. Surely the sternest Sabbatarian would hesitate ere he condemned in a poor man's life such precious breathing times (to quote again the words of Gilbert Burns) as this. It did not imply the forsaking of the assembling of himself entirely, or habitual religious disloyalty. Burns was generally found by his father's side in the house of God on the first day of the week. But sometimes his spirit moved him to spend the Sabbath in his own way—in shall we say for him a higher, holier fashion? to worship God in the solitary woods, or by the murmuring shores of the sea; there often, too, to seek after, if he might peradventure find, the Ideal of his Art, which appeared glimpsing away, yet beckoning him to follow, like a coy maiden, into the depths of the forest; and there sometimes, as he did to his silent, entranced brother, Gilbert, to repeat the newly composed effusions of his mind; and might not Nature be figured as becoming more deeply still to listen to the inspired numbers of the "Cottar's Saturday Night," and to scan the glowing features of a poet as he passed "sounding" on his way? There are no such Sabbath-breakers now!

Robert Chambers describes Burns ascending an eminence during the agitations of Nature, striding along a summit while the lightning flashed around him, and amidst the howling of the tempest apostrophizing the Spirit of the Storm. We remember no authentic record elsewhere of any such high-wrought and affected raptures. Here is his own well-known, simple, and truly sublime picture of his actual experience. "There is scarcely any earthly object gives me more (I do not know if I should call it pleasure, but something which exalts me, something which enraptures me), than a walk on the sheltered side of a wood or high plantation on a cloudy winter day, and hear the stormy wind howling among the trees and raving over the plain. It is my best season for devotion; my mind is rapt up in a kind of enthusiasm to Him who,

---

* "In the veins of the calyx foams and flows
    The blood of the Samian vine;
But, oh! in the goblet of youth there glows
    A Lesbium more divine.
Bright, bright, as the liquid light,
    Its waves through thine eyelids shine.

"Fill up, fill up, to the sparkling brim,
    With the juice of the young Lyæus;
The grape is the key that we owe to him,
    From the jail of the world to free us.
Drink, drink, what need to shrink,
    When the lamps alone can see us?

"Fill up, fill up, while I quaff from thine eyes
    The wine of a softer tree;
Give thy smiles to the god of the grape, thy sighs,
    Beloved one, give to me.
Turn, turn, my glances burn,
    And thirst for a look from thee."

LIFE OF BURNS.

in the language of the Hebrew bard, 'walketh on the wings of the wind.'"

This is an extract from a Common-place Book Burns began to keep in April, 1789, and which will be found elsewhere. It contains many pithy and many poetical remarks; and coming from so young and inexperienced a man as Burns was then, is more wonderful than even his songs or poems, and ranks, though on a smaller scale, with the Journals kept by Byron, Foster, and Sir Walter Scott, as probably the very best in the literature of our country. We might have mentioned that Burns had, some time previously, established at Tarbolton a debating club, called "The Bachelors," a long history of which, written by the poet, has been preserved.

Thus ran on the life of the bard for two or three years, peacefully, honourably, and on the whole happily, although not without some aberrations unknown to his career ere he saw Irvine, with its bay, and links, and steeple. In those years, as with Rousseau, "Early love his Psyche's zone unbound," but it could be hardly said that she hallowed it with loveliness. If there was delight there was disenchantment, too, and perhaps he might have exclaimed with his brother Byron—

"The tree of knowledge has been plucked – all 's known."

We gather this from expressions in his "Journal," and from the guarded evidence of his friends, as well as from the dying words of his father immediately to be quoted. Meanwhile, that excellent man was fast sinking to the grave. He was not old, only sixty-three; but he was quite broken down by severe labour, anxiety, and misfortune. Burns, in a letter dated 21st June, 1783, gives a very distressing account of the general condition of the small farmers of the period—a state of things which, along with a dispute about his lease, preyed terribly on his father's constitution, and bowed him to the dust. Indeed, he was only saved from the horrors of a jail by a consumption; and in fine, on the 13th of February, 1784, he breathed his last. There were present only Mrs. Begg and Robert. She was crying bitterly, and her father tried to comfort her, although only able to murmur out a few words, closing with an injunction to walk in virtue's paths and to shun every sin. He paused, and then said there was one of his family for whose future conduct he felt some anxiety, and repeated the expression; when Robert stepped up to the bedside and said, "Oh, father, do you mean me?" The old man replied, "Yes;" and the poet turned round to the window, his eyes shining through tears, and his heart heaving with sobs. What a scene for a painter—a Wilkie, Harvey, or Paton! The good old man on his dying bed; the February sun shining dim and "mottie through the reek," and showing his "lyart haffets" waxing thin and bare; his pale, stern, and composed features, and his frame and aspect—purged, earnest, resolute, and stripped, as of one who was immediately to join a spiritual company; his eye fixed on his erring but beloved son; the daughter dissolved in infantile sorrow; and Robert, with his face, and its expression of anguish, and its large eloquent tears, hid as in that picture of ancient Greece, where the painter employed to paint Agamemnon's grief at the sacrifice of Iphigenia made himself immortal by not painting it at all, but drew a curtain over the unutterable tragedy; and assuredly Burns' countenance, with that blended look of sorrow, remorse, and shame, no pencil could adequately depict. Old William Burns was carried to the banks of the Doon, where he had begun his married life. The coffin was placed between two horses ranked before each other in tandem-fashion, and followed by his neighbours and family also, all on horseback, to Alloway kirkyard. There, in that spot, which of all spots bears most emphatic witness to the triumphs of his son's creative genius—near the "winnock bunker in the east"—lies William Burns. Robert erected a simple tombstone over his remains, having the following stanzas from his own pen:—

"Oh ye whose cheek the tear of pity stains,
 Draw near with pious reverence and attend!
Here lies the loving husband's dear remains,
 The tender father, and the gen'rous friend;
The pitying heart that felt for human woe;
 The dauntless heart that feared no human pride;
The friend of man, to vice alone a foe,
 'For even his failings leaned to virtue's side.'" *

Seldom, as said before, have we felt more than when contemplating this simple stone and inscription. While recording on a page, as immortal as is the "Cottar's Saturday Night," the virtues of the father, it seemed an unanswerable certification also of the heart, the filial piety, the nobility, and the essential Christianity of the son. It completed in thought, and rendered eternal, the link of reconciliation which seemed broken at the deathbed of the former, and you longed for some vacant space on which to inscribe the words, "They met in Heaven!"

Mrs. Begg has told us much of the excellence of the father. Twice only had she seen him angry—once when returning exhausted and irritated from some interview with factors and writers anent the unfortunate lawsuit, he found a young man, one of his servants, wasting hay; and another time when an old man, to whom he had been very kind, had told a falsehood about him. As he rebuked the foul-mouthed railer Mrs. Burns gave him a reproachful look, on which he sternly cried, "There must be no gloomy looks here." This was, so far as she could say, the first and the last time on which he ever said a harsh thing to his wife. When Mrs. Begg was employed in herding the kye her

* See Appendix, No. I.

father would approach and tell her about the grasses and wild flowers, to beguile the tedium of her solitary calling; and as she was afraid of thunder, he, whenever it threatened a storm, would come to her to soothe her terrors. We may as well add here, that Mrs. Begg used to say to an esteemed friend of ours, "Oh! Mr. S.,* my brother Robert was not the vile man they make him out to have been, he was a good, pious, God-fearing man, like his father!" *Valeat quantum valere potest.* It was certainly truer than the other version of his character.

CHAPTER IV.

BURNS THE YOUNG LOVER.

ERE we must retrace our steps a little, and tell the story of what are called Burns' "Calf Loves;" and this chapter, while it may be sweet, must be short, his grander *belles passions* being a good way forward in his life.

All who have read his magnificent letter to Dr. Moore (one of the finest of autobiographical sketches ever penned —how incomparably superior to those of Hume, Sir Walter Scott, or even that admirable one of Gibbon) remember his description of his first love, his partner in the harvest-field—"the bonnie, sweet, sonsy lass." Shakspeare in none of his love plays, the purest as well as most beautiful in the language, has surpassed in delicacy the following words:—"How my pulse beat such a furious ratan when I looked and fingered over her little hand to pick out the cruel nettle stings and thistles." To her singing power, too, he attributed his first initiation into poetry. Best of all in this little Idyl is Burns' brave panegyric on love, "that delicious passion" which had led him into so many scrapes, but which he was still determined to hold the first of human joys, our dearest blessing here below. We are reminded of Wordsworth's Ruth, who had been ruined greatly through the freedom of her rural life and the influences of scenery on her solitude; but the poet says—

"The engines of her pain—the tools
    That shaped her sorrow—rocks and pools,
        And airs that gently stir
    The vernal leaves, she loved them still,
    Nor ever taxed them with the ill
        That had been done to her."

So Burns loved and lived to love, notwithstanding all the evil and misery it had caused him, and might with Byron sing that he was,

"In spite of tortures ne'er to be forgot,
    The slave again of love."

With the harvest this early passion seems to have passed. Nelly Kirkpatrick was his inamorata's name, the daughter of the blacksmith who lent him the "Life of Wallace," and he wrote on her his copy of verses, "Handsome Nell." The next of his flames was Peggy Thomson, whom he saw and fancied in the garden of Kirkoswald. He met her again in the summer and autumn of 1784, and composed on her then the fine simple song—

"Now westlin winds and slaughtering guns
    Bring autumn's pleasant weather."

Judging from a brief letter written by him in the November of that year to Thomas Orr of Park, he had by that time got off with the old love, and was trying to be on with a new. At all events, Peggy vanished from his view for ever and a day.†

The love customs and courtships of these days, and long after in Scotland, were very peculiar. When twilight fell fairly over the landscape, the young farmer or ploughman or weaver, it mattered not how hard had been his work during the day, or how early he must rise next morning, determined to have a "canny hour at e'en" amang the lasses. Often he would go *impransus,* and it was thought mean, we remember, in one villager that he would never go out a courting till he got his supper! Frequently he went alone and stealthily, like the hero of "My Nannie O;" and sometimes he would go along with a companion or two, with one either on his "ain hand" or acting as a "blackfoot." Not unfrequently they were in

---

* William Smith, formerly editor of the *Whitehaven Herald,* and nephew of Thomas Aird.

† No! for we find him in the Glenriddell MS. speaking thus of her:—"Poor Peggy, her husband is my old acquaintance, and a most worthy fellow. When I was taking leave of my Carrick relations, intending to go to the West Indies, when I took farewell of her, neither she nor I could speak a syllable. Her husband escorted me three miles on my road, and we parted with tears."

these evening walks watched by rivals, who followed their footsteps till they saw them fairly housed, and then either boldly entered themselves or knocked at the window to interrupt the fair fellowship. Occasionally battles between the different opposing lovers, fierce and bloody as bull-fights, took place. Sometimes the swain himself knocked or threw gravel on the window-pane as a signal for her to come out. Sometimes, as with Jenny's sweetheart in the "Cottar's Saturday Night," a modest tap proclaimed his presence, and then he entered and became one of the family for the evening. Sometimes the lads and lasses would adjourn to the barn yard and have a glorious game at *barley brax* (a sort of "hide-and-seek") among the stacks. Often there would be lonely walks—and then

"What sighs and vows
Amang the knowes!"

Sometimes the maiden would accompany the lover halfway home again, and sometimes the swain would do this instead of the maiden. Jenny Rintherout in the "Antiquary," it will be remembered, after flirting all night in the fisherman's cottage, was accompanied homewards by poor Steenie (drowned the next morning); and Scott adds, "at what hour he returned the deponent sayeth not." Distance and time on these occasions were entirely forgotten, and the lover cared not "though the night were e'er so dark and he were e'er so weary," and the nearer the morning the sweeter the enjoyment. Sometimes the lover was privileged to enter the chamber of his "Sleeping Maggie" and spend the night there. Sometimes, no doubt, scandal and shame were the results, but usually the intercourse was innocent, and if there were "mistaks" at times they were almost always "southered" afterwards by matrimony; and perhaps, on the whole, these customs were fraught with as little mischief as the more refined but equally seductive love affairs of capitals. In this Robert Burns mingled with his characteristic ardour as a man and a poet. Gilbert Burns tells us he was not aspiring in his loves, and was as ready to court the servants as the daughters of the farmer, who, indeed, at that day could hardly be distinguished from each other in dress or language or manners. David Sillar was struck at the poet's facility in addressing the fair sex, and at the freedom and ease with which he entered into conversation with them. They seemed his natural game. They were from first to last the stars of his destiny. In one point he differed from his kindred spirit, Lord Byron, all whose loves—Mary Duff, Miss Chaworth, Miss Millbank, Lady Caroline Lamb, the Countess Guiccioli, and many others—were more or less beautiful; while according to the Ettrick Shepherd, who had seen a number of Burns' flames, they were for the most part very plain-looking, if not repulsive. Yet Burns told some one, that when he first met a highly refined and cultivated woman, she seemed in contrast with those in humble life, something quite new and dazzling—almost taking away his senses and breath; while *men*, on the other hand, of intellect and worth, were much the same in all ranks. It was not his want of discrimination, nor latterly of a high standard; it was his overpowering imagination, and his blinding passions, which made his dowdies divine, and "gave Helen's beauty to a brow of Egypt." And his feeling to some of his sweethearts could hardly be called love; it was rather a half-drunken dream, from which he was continually awaking.

Surely there was something far higher and holier in his heart when he wrote that sweetest of love songs, trembling with tenderness, radiant with sentiment, full of that love which is "indestructible"—"Mary Morison." Who that maiden was is for ever a mystery. There was one Morisson, a cabinetmaker in Mauchline, who might have had a daughter called Mary, and she might have been an early love of Burns; that is all we can say. Dr. Waddell errs, we think, in calling her an indifferent or unconscious maiden, for how then could the poet speak of—

"The wished, the trysted hour?"

It is evident he is jealous of her, afraid she should "wreck his peace;" but while he loves her to distraction, he struggles hard to believe it impossible that she can or will act thus—

"A thought ungentle canna be,
The thought o' Mary Morison!"

And was there ever such wooing, so instinct with the very soul of love and poetry, as in the lines ending—

"Ye are na Mary Morison!"

Along with "Mary in Heaven," "Mary Morison" is Burns' finest love song—so thought William Hazlitt. Indeed, we rather prefer Mary on earth, Mary at the window, to Mary in the skies! The "Riggs of Barley" has less ideal love, but has much human interest. It is a pre-Raphaelite sketch of a genuine Scotch courtship. We remember overhearing, many years ago, two young men discussing its purity—one maintaining that it excited luscious ideas, the other that it might do so in him, but not necessarily in others; taking, in short, the *honi soit qui mal y pense* ground, and we rather inclined to this view. The sweet name Annie (Ann is not such a favourite name) might suggest that the heroine was worthy of her name, and of Burns' muse. But it seems she was one Anne Merry (daughter of John Rankine, according to some), a tall and masculine-looking dame, who ultimately kept a house of public entertainment in Cumnock, who had had an early nocturnal adventure with the poet, but all whose beauty was lent her by the moon shining on the corn riggs.

She even expressed surprise to Burns that he had written a song about her, and he replied, "Oh, I was just wanting to gie you a cast amang the lave." But she, according to Robert Chambers, would all her life-long sing the song, "the Riggs of Barley," and speak tenderly of the memory of the poet.

Another of his songs had a more complex history. This was that entitled "Montgomery's Peggy." This was a kind of superior servant, who lived in the house of Mr. Montgomery of Coilsfield. Burns happened to sit in the same seat with her in church; and Robert Chambers hints that this might have put it into his head, like Dumbiedykes, who says of his intended bride, "It's the Laird of Lickpelf's youngest daughter, she sits next us in the kirk, and that's the way I cam' to think o't;" but Burns was not a Dumbiedykes, and perhaps to render a more poetic reason for it, she sang divinely; and then his experience might be that of one poet thus described by another—

"When one summer's Sabbath eve a voice
Rose in the church, like some intense perfume,
The very strength of softness, balm of power,
His heart went up upon it as on wind,
And on its cadences came down again,
His own no more!"

He entered on a brisk fire of *billets-doux* immediately, then wrote his song in her praise, and finally found, when he meant ulterior measures and began to think of matrimony, that Peggy's heart was already pledged to another!

But we have shot too far ahead, and must beg a thousand pardons of Ellison Begbie, the passion of Burns for whom once threatened to be rather a serious affair. She was the daughter of a small farmer in Galston, but was servant with a family on the banks of the Cessnock, two miles from Lochlea, and here Burns first knew her. She was hardly beautiful, but had a good mind, a graceful carriage, a fine figure, a fascinating manner, "twa sparkling, roguish een," and a fair education. This made her a general favourite; and Burns is reported, even after meeting Miss Burnet, Margaret Chalmers, Charlotte Hamilton, &c., to have said that Ellison Begbie could bear comparison with any of them in mind, and was, of all the women he ever seriously addressed, best fitted to have been his life-companion. At all events, he was violently enamoured, addressed to her some very carefully, if somewhat formally composed letters, and wrote a song called "Cessnock Banks," in which the poet actually pelts her with similes, like sugar-plums on a carnival night. Cromek preserved this poem in his "Reliques," and tells us he got it from the oral communication of a lady residing in Glasgow, whom the poet in early life affectionately admired. It is not likely this lady would have cared to retain a long copy of verses about a rival, and we agree with Chambers in thinking that she was the veritable Ellison herself, who, perhaps, lived to regret that she had not tried her hand in reclaiming the irreclaimable poet. Certain only it is, that she refused his offer of marriage—and it might be better for both.

His sister used to tell a curious anecdote connected with this amour. Burns sometimes was very late in returning from Cessnock banks, and one night his worthy father sate up to let him in and administer him a rebuke for his irregular hours. He asked his son where he had been, and Burns, by way of making an apology, told him that he had met the Deil in coming home, and described the meeting much as he did afterwards in his famous "Address":—

"Ae dreary, windy, winter nicht,
Wi' you mysel' I got a fricht."

William Burns was so electrified by his son's description that he quite forgot the reproof, and perhaps (like David Deans with Reuben Butler at his offer of marriage to Jeanie, who produced one, nay two, aged bottles of strong ale, in contrast with his usual habits), he would treat his son to the best in his humble house, and sit up long listening entranced to Robert, who that night, what with love and starlight and the fright he had got with the Deil, was inspired, and talked far above singing till "the wee short hour ayont the twal!"

Burns had great delight in linking his loves with the streams near which his favourites dwelt. Ellison Begbie was the "Lass of Cessnock Banks;" Mary Campbell is for ever associated with—

"Ye banks and braes and streams around
The castle o' Montgomery.

Jean Armour's image is reflected, now in the Ayr and now in the Nith; and Charlotte Hamilton, his ideal love, wandered to his eye for ever along the banks of the "Clear Winding Devon," and he still saw her there as he indited his last song—

"Fairest maid on Devon banks,
Winding Devon, crystal Devon."

One is reminded of Byron's verses to the river Po, which he too connected with the form of Madame Guiccioli :—

"River that rollest by the ancient walls,
Where dwells the lady of my love, if she
Walks by thy brink, and still perchance recalls
One faint and fleeting memory of me."

Such is a list of Burns' early loves—all of them interesting, all of them connected with fine effusions from his young genius, and all of them, we believe, innocent. But he had not yet met with his "Ain." Still the two destined to exert such influence on each other, and to be identified so closely and for ever, were now drawing near, were almost now arrived at their trysting tree.

CHAPTER V.

BURNS AT MOSSGIEL.

E might perhaps rather have entitled this chapter, "Burns, Farmer and Poet;" for now for the first time he possessed, out of Parnassus, acres which he could call his own. At Martinmas, 1783, Robert and Gilbert Burns took the farm of Mossgiel, a few miles from Lochlea, but situated in the parish of Mauchline, and within one mile of the village of that name. We visited some years ago the snug steading which still bears the name of Mossgiel, saw near it the field where Burns, as Wordsworth has it, "ploughed up the daisy," and enjoyed a glimpse of the fine undulating country beyond Mauchline and toward Kilmarnock in all the green glory of June. It was pleasing while walking along the road, which slopes gently from Mauchline to Mossgiel, and is begirt by trees, to remember that it was by this the poet must often have returned homewards from his engagements at the village —from kirk, market, Poosie Nancy's, and visits to some of his famous Mauchline belles. Mossgiel consisted of one hundred and eighteen acres of cold, clayey soil, on a bare upland to the east of Mauchline.

The Burns family, by ranking themselves creditors to their father for arrears of wages due them for their labours on his estate, had rescued from his creditors and the lawyers some portion of the stock of the farm to enable them to begin on their own account. Gilbert says, "Robert and I took the farm of Mossgiel, consisting of one hundred and eighteen acres, at the rent of £9, from Mr. Gavin Hamilton, as an asylum for the family in case of the worst. It was stocked by the property and individual savings of the whole family, and was a joint concern between us. Every member of the family was allowed ordinary wages for the labour he performed at the farm. My brother's allowance and mine was £7 per annum cash; and during the whole time this family concern lasted, which was four years, as well as during the previous period at Lochlea, his expenses never in any one year exceeded his slender income. His temperance and frugality were everything that could be wished."

Dr. Currie and Gilbert Burns both coincide in denying Robert much skill as a farmer. Nobody held the plough better; nobody had a more elegant cast of the hand while sowing than he; but his knowledge of markets, rotation of crops, and other mysteries of husbandry, was slender; and he would often, in following his whim or indulging his social propensities, neglect his farming duties. It would be much with him as it was with James Hogg at Altrive, of whom his successor on the farm, "Old Scottie," a venerable worthy of ninety-four, recounted to us in 1859 the following anecdote:—His wife came once to Hogg and told him that a fine and favourite mare was dangerously ill, and a farrier should be sent for. The reply was—"I canna attend to her joost now, for I'm going up the hill to shoot a 'mawkin' for oor dinner." He went up the hill accordingly, shot the "mawkin," and when he came down found the mare dead. Burns always referred those who came to him on business matters to his brother—"Oh, talk to my brother about that." Yet it has been said by good authorities that Gilbert, too, knew more about the theory of farming than its practice. Both, however, brought industry, good intentions, and honesty, if little capital and experience, to the firm. Robert in the summer of 1784 was far from well. His disease seems to have been irregular action of the heart—a distemper which, in another form, perplexed and annoyed him all his life. At this time, as well as before, he kept a tub of water by his bedside, and by plunging in got temporary relief. Some may say that the wet-sheet or water-cure, applied internally as well as externally, would have saved him from the ruin that followed. Much good they might have done him; but, alas! he had passions raging within him with which water or whisky either had at that time little to do.

Along with this irregular action a worse calamity befell him;[*] a serving girl, Elizabeth Paton by name, in his family bore him a child, and this, although he tried to set it at defiance, and laugh it over, glorying in his shame, undoubtedly gave him the keenest anguish; and, perhaps, his chief consolation under it was the fact that his father was now "where the wicked cease from troubling," and where the thought of human aberrations, even those of a dear son, cannot disturb eternal peace. In this dark

[*] See Appendix, No. III.

season he applied at moments, too, to celestial aid, sought comfort in God, although it may be (as Pollok has it), "he sought reluctantly and therefore was not heard." His prayer, or rather prayers, for there are two of them—"A Prayer in the Prospect of Death," and stanzas on the same occasion—have been preserved, and are on the whole noble strains of devotion and contrition. Perhaps it is rather daring in him to point to the passions of his nature, and to trace them upwards to God as their author—

" Thou know'st that thou hast formed me
With passions wild and strong,
And list'ning to their witching voice,
Has often led me wrong."

But it is the daring of high reverence, and of one who cannot even in penitence be unjust to himself, or, like David, take what may seem to some the one-sided view—

" Gainst Thee, Thee only, have I sinned.'

Robert Chambers says, with great truth and good feeling, "It is strange that we so often hear of the faults of Burns, and of the defences advanced by his friends, and that so little notice has been taken of what at once attests the reality of these faults, and most powerfully pleads their pardon—the deep unostentatious penitence of the Bard himself."

It is somewhat difficult to reconcile the sincere contrition of these verses, and the spirit in which he describes the same incident in his history in his epistle to that facetious gentleman, John Rankine. Burns "before and after dinner" will not solve the mystery, for the poet at that time was a very sober man, as a rule, and his after-dinner hours were spent at the plough. Two considerations will in part explain it: first, the great exuberance of his animal spirits, which after deep depression rose to a higher pitch, for as he says himself, he had "aye a heart aboon a'" his calamities; and, secondly, there was a great deal of the chameleon about him; he took his colour from his acquaintances, even when far inferior to himself, and was equally at home with John Rankine and Dugald Stewart, with "Racer Jess" and Charlotte Hamilton, with Dr. William Robertson and Willy Nichol. And this, if it was his weakness as a man, was his power as a poet and essential dramatist, the Shakspeare of Scotland. He became all things by turns, and was seldom himself, because he was everybody else. The grand blunder of many in reference to Burns is first admitting his exceptional character, and then expecting him to be altogether unexceptionable. First, they take him at his own word, "I am Spunkie;" and then they look in a "Will o' the Wisp" for the regularity of a planet and the fixity of a star.

Rankine was hardly worthy to be a confidant or companion to Robert Burns. He was famous for his practical jokes; he had on one occasion, by putting in whisky instead of hot water in a kettle, overcome the sobriety of an "auld-licht" elder, and had extemporized a dream which made all the countryside ring with laughter. It is thus recounted by Allan Cunningham :—" Lord K——, it is said, was in the habit of calling his familiar acquaintances *brutes*— ' Well, ye brute, how are you the day?' was his usual mode of salutation. Once, in company, his lordship having indulged in this rudeness more than usual, turned to Rankine and said, ' Brute, are ye dumb? hae ye nae queer story to tell us?' ' I hae nae story,' quoth Rankine; 'but yestreen I had an odd dream.' ' Out with it by all means,' said another. 'Well,' said Rankine, 'I dreamed I was dead, and that for keeping other than good company on earth, I was sent down stairs. When I knocked at the low door, who should open it but the Deil. He was in a rough humour; and he said, ' Who may ye be, and what's your name?' ' My name,' quoth I, ' is Rankine, and my dwelling-place was Adamhill.' ' Gae wa' wi' ye,' quoth Satan, ' ye canna be here; you're ane o' Lord K.'s *brutes*; hell's fu' o' them already.' This sharp rebuke, it is said, polished for the future Lord K.'s speech."

Burns had been in Lochlea a freemason, and soon rose to be depute-master to the Fraternity. It is hard to say what effect this had upon his morals. Chambers represents him as entirely indifferent to the indulgences connected then with Freemason Lodges; but this is surely refining ridiculously. Burns enjoyed these from his first to his last, from Irvine to Dumfries, as the whole tenor of his life and writings shows; but it was long ere they to any degree overpowered his will, and probably of all Mason Masters he was at first the most exemplary, just as the Excise Books (see *Chambers' Journal* and our Appendix) have recently proved that he, of all the gaugers of Scotland, was among the most regular in his habits, although a little allowance was made for him as a "Poet." ("He is a poet, and does pretty well," are, we think, the words). He continued his "Commonplace Book," and inserted in it from time to time scraps of prose and short poems, such as "No Churchman am I for to rail or to write;" and one of his most characteristic copies of verses, entitled "Rantin' Rovin' Robin,"

" There was a lad was born in Kyle."

In one of the letters of this date he gives rather a plain than pleasant account of the famous Lucky Buchan, the Joanna Southcote of Scotland—an account containing a hit here and there worthy of the author of the "Holy Fair." Burns was always, in reference to every form of fanaticism, a clear seer and a bold speaker, denouncing it as an offence to the intellect, an outrage to common sense, and a scandal to religion. One of his verses of this time seems to point to the Coming Woman, to Jean, whose acquaintance he was making—

> "Though cruel fate should bid us part
>   As far 's the Pole and Line,
> Her dear idea round my heart
>   Should tenderly entwine.
> Though mountains frown and deserts howl,
>   And oceans roar between,
> Yet dearer than my deathless soul
>   I still would love my Jean."

He had not been long in Mossgiel till he met with Jean. She was the daughter of a master mason, named James Armour, in Mauchline village. He met her first, it is said, at a penny ball which took place at the close of a race in the village, which usually occurred in the end of April. The poet and Jean were in the same dance, but not as partners. Burns had a dog, which followed him into the room, and created some confusion and fun by tracking his master wherever he went; and he laughingly said to his partner (whoever she was) that he wished he could get any of the lasses to love him as well as his dog did. One day after, he was passing through Mauchline Green where Jean was bleaching clothes; she cried on Burns, whose dog was running among them, to call him off. This led to a conversation, in which Jean, who had overheard his remark at the ball, asked him playfully if he had got any of the lasses yet to love him as well as his dog.* This was the prelude of an intimacy, and Jean speedily became the Ruling Star of his heart—we might rather say, the Moon in his sky, not altogether unattended by sister planets—peerless, but seldom quite alone.

Our readers will at this point do well to turn up Burns' famous lines on the Mauchline belles. None of them, however, seemed ever to have any chance with Jean, attractive as they appeared to others. There might have been betwixt Burns and Jean a mutual fascination—that meeting of eyes and souls at once and for ever, that love at first sight, in one or both, which is said frequently to precede and prophesy marriage. And although there were, as we have hinted and will afterwards see, others for whom Burns felt a strong and pure tenderness amounting to love, he never ceased to regard Jean (except perhaps for a short period after her burning the marriage lines) with a degree of respect as well as affection. To reconcile these apparently jarring facts we do not attempt, and know not how it can be done, nor do we mean to assoilzie Burns from blame in the matter; but he was, as we have said, an altogether exceptional being—a burning man—susceptible, passionate, and imaginative beyond the measure of a score of ordinary men; and we must just judge of him as he was and take him as he is, for better for worse, and on the whole be thankful for him. His own words were true—

> "He 'll be a credit to us a',
>   We 'll a' be proud o' Robin."

* See this scene well rendered in Stirling's "Burns in Drama."

And now from the root of a fixed love there burst out a most extraordinary efflorescence of poetry. Robert Chambers remarks that "the mass of poetry which gave Burns his principal fame came from him in a period not exceeding fifteen months. After that it became, comparatively speaking, exhausted." No doubt his poetry seemed exhausted by or shortly after that time; but it was the marvel of this most marvellous man that after one vein shut, another and a more copious and a sweeter one opened, and the cessation of his Poems was only the commencement of his Songs—songs written, like the last novels of Scott, amidst misery, bodily disease, and ruin. We add an element which did not belong to Scott, which did belong to Burns, and which adds mightily to the wonder—Remorse. We know only one parallel to this, and it is obviously not complete—the case of Byron's later works, which, considering the circumstances in which they were written—expatriation, contumely, dissipation, a broken heart and constitution, and a fevered brain—are now generally judged superior to his earlier ones. How different from some other poets of the period, who have outlived their genius and its true works for a quarter of a century, and who, if they still continue to write, it is in a style of helpless self-imitation or stilted exaggeration, which is more lamentable than would be utter silence! "Superfluous lags the veteran on the stage" is bad enough, but "Superfluous struts the veteran on the stage" were far worse!

Thus Burns sings shortly after seeing Jean Armour:—

> "When first I came to Stuart Kyle,
>   My mind it was na steady;
> Where'er I gaed, where'er I rade,
>   A mistress still I had aye;
> But when I cam' roun by Mauchline toun,
>   Not dreading any body;
> My heart was caught before I thought,
>   And by a Mauchline lady."

And this fixity in his affections seems to have had a centralizing influence on his genius. Previous to this he had a vague ambition, he tells us—

> "For poor auld Scotland's sake,
>   Some usefu' plan or book to make,
>   Or sing a sang at least."

Now his "Commonplace Book," dated August, 1784, shows that this wish, after beating wildly about, had found an opening, since in it he expresses a desire to be the Ayrshire bard, and to make "the fertile banks of Irvine, the romantic woodlands and sequestered scenes in Ayr, and the heathy mountainous source and winding sweep of Doon emulate Tay, Ettrick, Tweed." Few young poets but have felt a similar ambition in reference to their natal streams and valleys. But Burns got his wish and more, and became not only Ayrshire's, but Scotland's bard. All these extracts from the "Commonplace Book" of this year are peculiarly interesting; they are the flutterings of the wings of the caged bird against his bars, and portend the long, strong, exulting flight that was before him.

One thing remarkable about this wonderful series of verses is their occasional character. Young poets, like Kirke White, Shelley, Keats, and Pollok, seize eagerly on some big sounding theme, such as "Time," "The Cloud," "Hyperion," "The Course of Time;" Burns takes up familiar matter of to-day—

"Some natural sorrow, grief, or pain,
Which has been and may be again."

And hence almost every one of his Mossgiel poems bears specially on his own history, and they become as a whole an unintentional autobiography. One of his first is his "Epistle to Davy, a Brother Poet, Lover, Ploughman, and Fiddler." In it he produced a thought he had long rolled in his mind, like a "pebble in the ocean," that in the last extremity of his fortunes to beg was still a *dernier ressort*—

"The last o't, the warst o't,
Is only but to beg!"

He introduces, too, a panegyric, too flowing and eloquent to be insincere, on his Jean, coupling it with a word for Margaret, David Sillar's beloved, who was not fated to become his wife. Margaret Orr, by the way, was servant to Mrs. Stewart of Stair. Burns had lent Margaret some of his songs, which she showed her mistress, who, being a woman of taste and sensibility, was very much delighted with them, and requested the author to come up to the drawing-room; and for the first time his clouted shoon and (in his own words) "clouterly carcase" came in contact with a Turkey carpet, and he, no doubt with a little trepidation, found himself in the presence of a fashionable lady. He never feared the face of man, but he did fear the terrors of a beautiful and accomplished woman. Mrs. Stewart, however, seems to have become his warm friend.

In a different vein he wrote "Death and Dr. Hornbook." One John Wilson, the well-known story assures us, a schoolmaster in Tarbolton, added to his ill-paid occupation that of a grocer, and ultimately a druggist—was, in plain English, a quack. In this complexity of calling he rather prospered; and Burns would not have disturbed him in any of them had he not encountered Wilson at a Mason-lodge meeting, where, we presume, the "clachan yill" had made both a little "canty," and where the apothecary made a needless display of his medical knowledge. Burns contradicted him; and still fired with the dispute that followed, composed on his way home this admirable satire, and repeated it to Gilbert the next morning as he was holding the plough, and Robert was letting water off the field beside it. It, along with a dispute with the heritors, had the effect of blowing the unlucky Dominie out of Tarbolton. Yet after some years in the Gorbals, Glasgow, settled as a teacher and session clerk, Wilson became a much respected though pedantic little man; and used, it is said, in his cups (for, like Bailie Jarvie's "feyther afore him," "he took a glass at an *orra* time") he used to drink the memory of Burns, and thank him for the good office he had done him in cutting short his Æsculapian career. He died at a great age in 1839.

"Death and Dr. Hornbook" shows a daring genius, apart from its satirical vein; and his description of the grim skeleton has never, we think, been equalled in poetry, unless by the late Thomas Davidson ("Scottish Probationer") in one of his poems—the "Hobgobliniad"—and which pushes the grotesque still further, and abates not an atom of the grisly grandeur.

There was on Fastern's E'en (Shrovetide) a "rocking" at Mossgiel—a social meeting, borrowing its name from the old custom of country women spinning on a rock or distaff. At this meeting, among other songs, one was sung purporting to be by an elderly man residing in Muirkirk called John Lapraik (a name presumed to be a contraction of Leprevick, the name of a distinguished early printer in Scotland). The song is supposed to be addressed by a fond husband to his wife, and is very tender and simple, although we believe it is not by Lapraik at all, but borrowed from an older source. To Burns it was quite new; and with all the frank enthusiasm of his nature, he determined instantly to write to the old poet. The result was the excellent poetical epistles to John Lapraik. Lapraik sent a poetical reply to Burns' first letter by the hand of his son, who found the poet in the field sowing. When he gave him the letter, Burns said, "I am not sure if I know the hand;" but when he opened it, he became so engrossed that he let go the sheet holding the grain, and it was half emptied ere he perceived his loss. Lapraik was encouraged by Burns' approbation to publish a volume of verses; but like David Sillar's, and those of a hundred other imitators of Burns in that period, it had no success. We have seen, however, the verses Burns admired so much quoted in collections of poetry of this century.

We will speak afterwards of Burns' religion. He was about this time plunged into the thickest polemical strife. Two theological parties were then engaged in war to the knife in the west of Scotland. One consisted of the Old Whigs, who held to the unmitigated Calvinism of the Confession of Faith; the other of a Broad Church School, come prematurely on the stage, who professed a more latitudinarian creed, bordering with some on Arianism, with others of a decidedly Arminian type, and with Burns verging at one time, he tells us, on "the daring path Spinoza trode," although this apparently he had forsaken

LIFE OF BURNS.

some time before. Whatever might be his settled speculative opinions, his heart sympathies and his floating talk were all with the "New Light." In this he followed the example of his father, who had written a little manual of belief for the use of his children, in which semi-Arminian views were very sedulously inculcated.* In this, too, he obeyed the impulses of his own bold and unfettered intellect, and gratified his love of wild and witty talk. He tells us he used on Sabbath intervals to puzzle Calvinism with great heat and indiscretion. Nor did he confine himself to conversation, but lifted up his mighty pen on the liberal side. First came his poetical epistle to John Gowdie of Kilmarnock, a well-known eccentric of the day —a worthy man, but a sad heretic—who had published a volume of essays, containing what were thought very heterodox sentiments, and called in irony, "Gowdie's Bible." This, along with John Taylor of Norwich's "Scripture Doctrine of Original Sin," was the *Vade mecum* of the "New Lights." Then followed his more celebrated "Twa Herds, or the Holy Tuilzie." One of these was the Rev. John Russell, then of Kilmarnock, subsequently of Stirling. In Professor Wilson's essay, prefixed to Blackie's edition of Burns, will be found a picturesque description of this gentleman's preaching, which seems to have frightened even Christopher North. He was called Black Russell from his dark complexion— was a big, brawny man, had a stern look, a voice like a bull's, and tremendous energy of address. We remember his son, who was minister of Muthil, Perthshire, and was a smaller edition of his father—a vehement, earnest, excellent man, of the highest Calvinistic views, whose preaching was so popular that little parties often used to walk from parishes seven or nine miles off every Sabbath to hear him. They were called "Muthilites;" and we were wont to watch them returning on the Sabbath evenings of summer from a journey of at least sixteen miles, back and forward, to their homes in Comrie, Perthshire. We heard Mr. Russell preaching once at the Old Church tent of Crieff on a Sacramental Sabbath evening, and the echoes of his very powerful voice linger in our ears still. Burns would have called it, not speaking, but "rowting." He had not his father's full physical energy; after his usual Sunday's work, would lie vomiting bile all the evening; and died in middle life. A volume of his sermons was published, to which Dr. Chalmers supplied a preface.

Black Jock had had a quarrel with Alexander Moodie of Riccarton, another zealous advocate of the Auld Licht. Some say, according to Chambers, that they were riding home one evening when Moodie, in a sportive frame, tickled the rear of his neighbour's horse. The animal performed certain antics along the road, much to the amusement of the passers-by, but greatly to the discomfiture of Black Jock, who afterwards learning the author of the trick, never forgave Moodie for it. There were other grounds of quarrel; and in a dispute about parochial boundaries, which came to the Presbytery, "The Twa Herds" lost their temper, and abused each other at a terrible rate, to the great scandal of their party, and the intense amusement of Burns, who was present, and soon after recorded their unseemly dispute in lines of imperishable fun. "The Twa Herds" was the first of Burns' poems to see the light, and became very popular. Many of the clergy, as well as laity, received it "with a roar of applause." A copy found its way to Ochiltree, where one William Simpson, himself a rhymer and a choice spirit, was parish schoolmaster. He addressed a rhyming epistle to Burns, warmly commending his poem and his genius generally. Burns replied in one of the noblest of his poetical effusions, the "Epistle to William Simpson," adding as a postscript an allegorical account of the New Light controversy, which, though clever, is certainly a falling off from the previous letter. Burns did not always, like ladies, put the pith into the postscript. We notice here how a little genuine praise never failed to rouse our poet to his full mettle—acting like that barley of the gods of which Homer speaks, on the coursers of Achilles. Usually the strong man is excited, the weak man enervated, by the "voice of praise." Dr. Johnson, indeed, was thankful for the praise of every human being; but Burns weighed and analyzed before he swallowed what came to his share. Two stanzas in this epistle to Simpson should be written in gold—one is that on Wallace—

"At Wallace' name what Scottish blood," &c.

What a raw and bloody glory shines out of the line—

"Still pressing onwards, *red wat-shod!*"

It is, indeed, as Carlyle says, too "frightfully accurate for Art." The second was a great favourite with Coleridge—

"The Muse, nae poet ever fand her,
Till by himsel' he learned to wander
Adoun some trottin' burn's meander,
An' no think lang,
While he can stray and pensive ponder
His heartfelt sang."

Thus it often was with Burns himself; his genius supplied the matter, the river the melody of the strain.

The success of the "Twa Herds" brought to Burns a new lot of acquaintances, chiefly among the New-light clergy, who, in a church so Calvinistic as the Scotch, were so far in a false position (and this always reacts in some way, either on comfort or character), but had nevertheless many virtues, and a liberality of spirit quite after Burns'

* See Appendix, No. IV.

own heart. Such were the Shaws, MacGill, and young MacMath of Tarbolton, afterwards a victim. Burns had long known Gavin Hamilton, writer in Mauchline; indeed, he was his landlord as well as his boon companion. Hamilton was a careless clever fellow, generous and good-hearted, but by no means rigidly righteous; given to lift his potatoes on Sabbath days, and to other peccadilloes. This brought him in contact with the kirk session. These courts were once all-powerful in Scotland. Infinitesimally small were the cases and crimes which they intermeddled with. How their members spent their Sabbath evenings, how they feed or fed their servants, how they paid their butter accounts—such were some of the thousand and one questions on which these inquisitors insisted, and for defalcation or omission in which they summoned high and low to their tribunals. After the Secession began new subjects of investigation were started, as to what was called occasional hearing; and those who attended any church but their own, even when there was no preaching there, were sisted and severely dealt with. We have heard of a waggish elderly man who was summoned to appear at a Seceder session to answer for going one day to attend service in the Established Church, when there was none in his own. He said in defence, "Maister Moderautor, I aye thocht Heeven was a great muckle place; I never kent till noo that it was built to haud only a wheen (few) Seceders!" The naïvete of the reply saved him from censure. Gavin Hamilton was not of the submissive kind, any more than honest old Tam Brough; he wrote the session a plain-spoken letter; he set Daddy Auld, the minister, a very good but narrow man, and his ruling elder, William Fisher (Holy Willie), at defiance, and carried the case from session to Presbytery, and Presbytery to Synod; got, in fine, a certificate of being free from all church censure, and thus gained the victory. He was greatly aided in this by Robert Aiken, writer in Ayr, who was a natural orator, to whom Burns afterwards inscribed his "Cottar's Saturday Night," and who pled his cause with great ability. And to gratify him Burns "loused his tinkler jaw" on his enemies, in the most freespoken and fearless of all his satires, "Holy Willie's Prayer." Holy Willie—

"That leein', cheatin', prayin' billie,"

was found guilty afterwards of embezzling the church funds, and ultimately died in a ditch. Altogether, including Burns' blasting touch, Willie's punishment was greater than he could bear. He was hardly worth such fiery powder and shot from such a marksman.

Meanwhile Mossgiel was not thriving as a farm; and what with bad seed one year, and a wet season another (1785), had become a losing concern. This no doubt threw Burns back more determinedly on his intellectual resources and poetical pursuits. Hitherto he had only been a local celebrity, and had he died at this time, would have scarcely been remembered out of Ayrshire. But he now took a flight which must, in any circumstances, sooner or later have brought him into the sight of all Scotland, and of the world—he wrote the "Cottar's Saturday Night." Everybody remembers the feelings of his brother Gilbert, when he heard Robert repeating it to him on a Sabbath day. To Gilbert it must have come more refreshingly, as he and their family had been annoyed at the recent desecration, as they thought, of his genius, in inditing "Holy Willie's Prayer" and so forth. What a bound up from this "Devil's kitchen work," as the Germans talk of, to such a divine close as that of the "Cottar's Saturday Night," which approximates, in simple yet rounded majesty, the climaxes of Isaiah or the glowing perorations of Paul. Some suppose that the approbation which his brother, known by Robert to be an excellent judge of literary matters, gave this masterpiece, as much by the tremulous and tearful enthusiasm of his face and bearing as by his words, encouraged him to think of publishing a volume of poems, and that this accounts for the extreme rapidity with which poetry flowed from him all this winter and spring. It is, indeed, certain that he composed in this short period such poems as the "Mouse," "Hallowe'en," "Man was Made to Mourn," "Address to the Deil," "The Jolly Beggars," the "Vision," the "Epistle to James Smith," the "Author's Earnest Cry and Prayer," the "Twa Dogs," the "Ordination," and "Scotch Drink." But some of these pieces were surely prompted by a higher motive than the mere prospect of seeing them in print. They are pure, gushing inspiration. Was he thinking of "gude black prent" when he sent his poetical "Hail, fellow, well met," after the mousie scampering from his plough? Was he thinking of Johnnie Wilson and his Kilmarnock press when, in the "auld clay biggin',"

"Ben in the spence, right pensively,
He gaed to rest,"

and was kept sleepless by the most glorious "Vision" that ever visited poet in his youth, since Shakspeare dreamed the "Midsummer Night's Dream?" Was there any anticipation of coming fame, or of the title of Satan's laureate, in the tumultuous glee which flashed in his eye when he indited the words—

"O Thou! whatever title suit thee,
Auld Hornie, Satan, Nick, or Clootie?"

Was aught in his veins but the most Shakspearean riot that ever revelled therein, when he peeped through the bole of Poosie Nancy's, and saw the devilry of dissipation, the Bacchanalian abandonment, the wild orgies, as of a Scotch Walpurgis Night, which were being celebrated in it? No doubt, when he wrote "The Twa Dogs" he was thinking of publication; but it, with all its admirable sense and satire, and one or two inimitable touches of nature, is of a much less inspired mood than the others, and has more method than magic in its web.

Some of these pieces were composed at the plough, when neither had his eye waxed dim nor had his natural strength abated. There, of course, he sang the "Mouse." And there, turning his sad eye across the melancholy November landscape, over which the weary winter sun was going down, he breathed out the monody—matching with that "Prayer of Moses, the man of God," the Ninetieth Psalm—one thought in which De Quincey, slow to praise the Scottish poet, recognizes the hand of a master—

> "See yonder poor o'erlaboured wight,
> So abject, mean, and vile,
> Who begs a brother of the earth
> To give him leave to toil."

Often he composed, and still oftener he transcribed, in the little garret above the *but* and the *ben* of the farmhouse of Mossgiel. In this garret there was a little window in the roof, through which he might see the stars. A small curtainless bed stood in the room where the two brothers slept. Under the window was a little deal table with a drawer; on the table the poet wrote, stooping as he did so, and in the drawer he deposited his verses. Scarcely has he left for the fields again, to his afternoon labour, till we see his young sister, afterwards Mrs. Begg, silently stealing up stairs into the Sanctum to peruse the poems her brother had left there. Conceive her, as she reads the "Mouse" or the "Vision," enjoying one of the purest pleasures possible on earth—a relative and young enthusiast reading the finest poetry of the age, and whispering every now and then to herself, Can these actually be the compositions of my brother? Let us trust that she sometimes stole them from the desk for an hour or twain, and showed the better of them to his and her mother.

Burns when he composed the "Mousie" was not alone. A youth, called John Blane, who was guiding the four horses which were then required for the plough, remembered the incident, and his running after the "wee beastie" to destroy it, but was checked by Burns, who immediately after became abstracted and thoughtful. Blane, who became a stage-coachman, told afterwards a stranger he met on the coach that Burns came into the stable in the evening and read him the poem, and asked, "What he thought of the Mousie now?" He added that the poet, while he was with him, though he did sometimes indulge too freely, was a kind master, and regularly made family worship night and morning.

Even before his father's death Robert had taken a part in this exercise, reading the chapter, and giving out the psalm. Afterwards, as the head of the house, he took on himself the whole of the service. Some of his family remembered distinctly Robert's practice, and Mrs. Begg used to say that she never in her life heard such prayers as her brother's; and we can easily conceive from specimens of his prayers which have been preserved in rhyme, that his family devotions would be distinguished by great fervour, eloquence, and pathos, and not less by simplicity and sincerity—the two main elements of true prayer.

The Mauchline of this period must have been quite a caravansera of queer characters. Besides its famous belles, were several females of more questionable notoriety: Nanse Tinnoch, with her hostelry, where Burns pretended to be a nightly visitor, although the "Lucky" herself said that she scarce knew the colour of his coin, and that his half mutchkins were mostly myths—"Poosie Nancy," with her rough, roaring public, crowded with strollers of every kind, and floating with "Kilbagie," the "blue ruin" of Ayrshire (although distilled at Clackmannan), where Disrespectability lifted up her unabashed head and held "leets and lawdays" under the astonished midnight; and "Racer Jess," her daughter, a sort of unbreeched Goose Gibbie (see "Old Mortality"), who ran races for wagers, and unmatched for swiftness of foot, carried messages through the country — an Iris unballasted either by chastity or laziness. Then there were sundry male curiosities: wee James Smith, the "sleest, pawkiest thief" in all Burns' acquaintance—a dark-complexioned, clever, little man, who talked wondrously well, and yet had the sense to yield the *pas* to the Mossgiel ploughman; some noble specimens of the old Covenanting character—stern livers, high thinkers—men who read Calvin in translations and Dr. Owen in English, and criticized sermons severely, and prayed long, and mourned over modern degeneracy, and were themselves entitled to do so, being firm to their principles as Arran or Ailsa Craig (James Humphrey was a very fair specimen of this class)—not to be confounded with a class, who were also there, of "yill-caup commentators," who discussed religion in change-houses, and hiccupped most undeniable orthodoxy as the wee short hour was about to strike on the dull, cold ear of Night; of this latter class "Holy Willie" being the *facile princeps*.

Such a fertile field even Mauchline opened to Burns' genius; and he made the most of it, especially in his "Holy Fair" and "Jolly Beggars." Dr. Walter Smith said not long ago, with more point than felicity, that "the reading of this latter *brochure* leaves a bad taste in the mouth." This perhaps depends a little on the state of the mouth that tastes it. At all events, it is not what James Hogg would have called a "wersh" taste which it leaves, but one of tingling gusto; and no one but must admire the marvellous variety of badness in its characters —all bad, none odious; the excessive spirit of its writing, especially its songs, and the wild harmony produced from the heterogeneous materials, so that a naked dance of Satyrs assumes almost an ideal aspect; and the movement is graceful, as if it took place to some such music as Ariel played to Stephano, Trinculo, and the other bewildered and tipsy ones of the "Tempest"—ending in a storm chorus which gives an apotheosis to Blackguardism. Burns drew it from the life; but while John Richmond and James Smith, who had accompanied him to the sight, applauded it to the echo, his brother and mother deplored it, and at her request the good-natured bard laid the poem aside, and for years forgot its existence.

The "Holy Fair" seems to have been a rather late production, but one that breathes the same spirit which was indeed the spirit of a year or two of his life—the spirit of reckless satire and of dare-devil revelry—a spirit which was to appear afterwards in short and desperate snatches toward the close of his career. There is a freedom of touch and of motion in this poem which he never surpassed. The whole (as is true also of "Tam o' Shanter") runs out as from a mould, and reads like a single sentence. There is all the French elasticity without the French *persiflage* or heartlessness, although there may be a smack of the pleasure of the stolen waters and the bread eaten in secret. A man eating pork with great relish once paused and said, "I wish I were a Jew." "Why?" was the answer; "for in that case you would not enjoy your favourite food." "Yes; I would then have the pleasure of eating it, along with the *gust of sinning*." Burns must have felt this gust while composing the semi-scandalous but excessively clever poem, "The Holy Fair." It is entirely original, with the exception of its best and worst word, *damnation*. Tidings of *salvation* it had been; but at Dr. Blair's suggestion was changed to what it is, and Burns was but too ready to acknowledge the obligation.

About the same time Burns came forward as the Laureate of Scotch whisky, of which, says one of his biographers, he was no lover, and yet speaks very like one. That article was then severely taxed, not so much for moral motives as because the English distillers had a jealousy of the Scotch. When the obnoxious impost was taken off, Burns expressed his gratitude in some well-known verses. He had previously commended the spirit with a gusto and an eloquence which showed more than a theoretical appreciation thereof. Perhaps further on in his history he might, like Esop with his dish of tongues, have given the *per contra* of his warm and rather one-sided panegyric. Yet there is one stanza of genuine poetry—

"Nae cauld, faint-hearted doubtings teaze him;
Death comes, with fearless eye he sees him,
Wi' bluidy hand a welcome gi'es him;
And when he fa's,
His latest draught of breathing lea'es him
In faint huzzas."

This, with all deference to poor Burns, is rather the spirit of the bard than of the barley. Unquestionably Burns wrote many of his poems and songs in an overexcited state, but as certainly the very best of them flowed from him when he was in his normal condition; although even in that normal state, when in the eye of Nature, he might say with Coleridge that he was—

"Inspired beyond the guess of folly,
By each rude shape and wild unconquerable sound!"

His fault was that in later life, as his spirits fell low and his hypochondria deepened, his genius sometimes condescended, like the Britons with the Saxons, to call in auxiliaries, which ultimately led that haughty power in chains. John Gowdie, author of "Gowdie's Bible," is said to have visited Burns, who behind a stook read him some verses which greatly pleased him, and he invited him to visit Kilmarnock, where at Gowdie's table he met such local notorieties as Major Parker Paterson, town clerk, Dr. William More, and Mr. Robert Muir, merchant, afterwards a great friend and correspondent of the poet.

Kilmarnock has produced or harboured men of no little eminence, such as an eccentric but very clever United Secession clergyman, Robertson by name; his successor in ability and eccentricity, Dr. John Ritchie, afterwards "Voluntary John of Potterrow," Edinburgh; Dr. James Morison, the learned and able founder of the Morisonian sect in Scotland; and, besides many others, our recent friend Alexander Smith of the "Life Drama." Burns might have known the first mentioned of these, Robertson, although we have no evidence that he did. When he first visited "Auld Killie" he found it in a state of great excitement about a minister. For forty years Moderatism —under, first, one Lindsay, who was shrewdly suspected to have owed his appointment to his wife, Margaret Lauder, who had been housekeeper to the Earl of Eglinton (*verb. sat sap.*), and hence Burns' lines—

"Curst common-sense, that imp o' Hell,
Cam in wi' Maggie Lauder;"

and, secondly, under a Mr. Mutrie—had walked the course. But now both ministers were dead, and a young and zealous highflier, James Mackinlay by name, was appointed, and the Moderates in wrath prevailed on Burns, their willing organ, to vent their chagrin and his own in rhyme. Hence the "Ordination," written in a style of fierce, personal, and polemical satire, which Burns practised rather often at this time, and which, although excessively poignant and clever, never even approached the higher reaches either of his wit or his genius. It, however, like the rest of such pieces, created a roar of applause—a roar which has got fainter and fainter as time has elapsed, and as the event and the characters which suggested it have sunk into oblivion. We think that Mackinlay, the hero of the poem, became less popular afterwards with his partizans, owing to a marriage with his servant. He was a man of good elocutionary gift, but of ordinary intellect.

Burns takes more general ground in his next poem. This, which forms a kind of spur upon a chain of vigorous pasquinades, is his "Address to the Unco Guid," and the last verses, so well known—

> "Then gently scan your fellow-man,
> Still gentler, sister woman,"

constitute a living moral and truly Christian inference from such miserable hurley-burleys as "Holy Fairs" and "Ordinations." They stamp Burns a great moralist—a title he deserves none the less but all the more from his occasional aberrations, and corroborate Curran's statement about the "sweet morality of a Burns," which some have thought paradoxical. He could—

> "Others teach their course to steer,
> But run himself life's mad career;
> Wild as the wave."

Besides other productions of a wildish tone and temper, such as the "Louse" and "The Inventory," belonging to this prolific period of his history, we may close by mentioning his deliciously natural and pathetic poem, "The Auld Farmer's New Year's Salutation to his Auld Mare Maggie." On animals of every variety, and especially on those within the reach of the cruelty or caprice of man, Burns always shone, because he always sincerely sympathized with them. And if some hypercritics call him, therefore, the "Bard of the Brutes," nay, a sublimer brute himself, we care not. It was as a friend, an advocate, a mediator between them and man, that he spake; and that mission was not only a high one in itself, but qualified him to discharge his loftier and later one, the proclamation of universal charity and brotherhood—the publication of peace on earth and good will to men, in the immortal words—

> "When man to man the world o'er
> Shall brithers be and a' that."

CHAPTER VI

BURNS IN THE NADIR.

ADIR, most people know, is the point diametrically opposite to the zenith, the lowest pole in the horizon. Burns uses the word with a different bearing when he says, in his letter to Dr. Moore, "The baleful star which had so long shed its blasting influence on my zenith for once made a revolution to the *Nadir*." The darkest hour usually precedes the dawning. And assuredly this was the case with Burns. The presentiment or prophecy which crossed his soul at the sight of the "Mouse"—

> " I backward cast my e'e
> On prospects drear;
> And forward, though I canna see,
> I guess and fear!"

was now about to be fulfilled. Evil deeds are often punished long ere they occur by misery which appears causeless in the offender at the time, who is in this way "paid in advance" after a terrible fashion. Burns might have read a rehearsal of his own fate in that of Peggy K——, the daughter of a landed proprietor in Carrick, whom he met, admired as one of the first accomplished young ladies of the upper classes he had ever seen, and on whom he wrote the song "Young Peggy." Her fate was wretched, although it is only indicated, not fully stated in any biography we have read. At seventeen, engaged to an eligible lover in her own rank of life, she was hanging already over the precipice, and doomed to lose first her good name, and afterwards her young life. We might conceive her referred to in the lines on the "Daisy"—

> "Such is the fate of artless maid,
> By love's simplicity betrayed,
> And guileless trust."

And if so, this is but a pendant to the stanza which follows :—

> "Such is the fate of simple bard,
> On Life's rough ocean luckless starred,
> Till billows rage and gales blow hard,
> And whelm him o'er."

Charles I. had, it is said, a look of dim, settled sadness on his face, which was thought to prognosticate a violent death. And amid all the fun and riot of Burns' poetry, there peers out ever and anon a look in which one may read strange matters and woeful prophecies, even as on his face, above the blaze of his bright black eye and the mirth that lurked about his mouth and chin, there lay a dark, unmoved cloud of profound and melancholy feeling—not merely of reflection, not at all of fear : it was a face confronting and defying the scowl of Destiny !

We linger as long as we can ere we venture to narrate the lamentable events which now occurred in the poet's history, and may first record for praise one man in Ayr who was of material service to Burns' success as a poet. This was Robert Aiken, to whom, as we saw, his "Cottar's Saturday Night" was inscribed as—

> "My loved, my honoured, much respected friend."

Aiken was a writer and tax collector. He was a man of great natural eloquence, as we have seen from his successful defence of Gavin Hamilton ; and above all, he was a warm admirer and powerful reader of poetry. He was said by Burns to have read him into fame. Wherever two or three were gathered together, the enthusiastic Aiken was sure to introduce the name and read the poetry of Burns. He had two criteria of good poetry : it was good if, first, it brought tears to his eyes ; and secondly, if it made the buttons of his waistcoat "skelp." Once, when reading a poem on the death of Burns by some admirer or other, the latter catastrophe was produced : his vest had burst open, while his eyes were streaming. It reminds us of a late eccentric, clever, but very nervous clergyman in Newcastle, who was always imagining himself at the point of death with one imaginary disease or other. One day, walking in the country with a friend, he suddenly got pale as a corpse, and exclaimed, "It's all over now ; did you not hear that dreadful sound ? Some vital part of my interior has burst, and I have only a few minutes to live." On investigation it was found that he had broken his waistband ! This, the crack of doom to him, was the signal of loud and inextinguishable laughter to his companion and to everybody else. On one occasion Aiken, who was a nephew of Dr. Dalrymple, Ayr, made a speech at a private party about his venerable uncle, which melted the whole assembly into tears. An Irish officer, blubbering like a child, looked round on the company, and exclaimed, "Can you tell me the *maning* of this?" One is reminded of Dandie Dinmont—"Deil 's in the man; he has made me do that I have not done since my auld mither dee'd!" To use a vulgar expression, Burns and Aiken "jumped at each other," and became fast friends. Nor did the relation of patron and patronized produce its usual unhealthy effects. The choice of Aiken to head the "Cottar's Saturday Night" was enough to stamp him as a worthy and noble man, whatever might be his faults and failings; and Aiken reciprocated and in some measure repaid the honour.

It was in the spring of 1786 that Burns' sorrows came upon him, as usual in a complex form. His farm was becoming every year a more ruinous concern. How much this was the effect of misfortune, and how much of Burns' engrossment with society and literary matters, cannot now be ascertained. Both probably contributed. Burns often acknowledges that he was not a good man of business or farmer, and few of his kindred are—

"The enthusiast Fancy was a truant ever."

But let us remember that the very greatest of England's tuneful tribe have been regular and laborious men—Shakspeare, Milton, and Wordsworth. But Burns, with perhaps as bold and broad a sail as these men, wanted their ballast; and ere he had time to take it in, he died. But while his farm was going wrong, other circumstances were clouding his horizon. He had now for nearly a year known and loved Jean Armour. She was rather more than an average specimen of a Scottish maiden of the middle rank of life, although, we have heard, counted a little "glaikit" by the matronage and female critics of her neighbourhood. She was tall and well built, rather than particularly good-looking. But she had fine dark eyes, a complexion slightly olive, and a bewitching smile. She sung and danced well. In her latter years, and after the poet's death, she seems to have been all that was sensible, respectable, and motherly. Burns' love for her was not romantic, like that he felt for Mary Morrison and Mary Campbell; nor ideal, like that he felt for Charlotte Hamilton; nor a compound of desire, vanity, and literary sympathy, like that he felt for Clarinda: it was a fresh, warm, and hearty outcome of his physical and passionate nature—a young man's love for one he did not look at from afar with chivalric and awestruck affection, but whom he knew familiarly, met often, and clasped to his bosom when he did so, sans phrase or form. It may be that the prejudice felt by the Armours at "Rab Mossgiel" kept him out of the house, and led to private assignations and the train of dangerous consequences flowing therefrom. Jean, at all events, became as "ladies' love to be," &c., and the effect of the *eclaircissement* was disastrous to our poet. Jean urged Burns to give her a written acknowledgment of her as his wife, an act equivalent in Scottish law to a marriage. At first Burns refused to consent to this arrangement; but an interview with her melted his resolution, and he gave her what she desired. Jean's object was to conciliate her parents, but in this she failed. Old Armour, who had no great idea of Burns from the beginning, and who overrated the value of his daughter, knew well, too, that Mossgiel was not thriving. Had this event occurred a year afterwards, it had been different; but the daughter of a stone-mason was thought too good a match for the bankrupt and unfortunate poet. Armour sought to annul the marriage, and prevailed on Jean to surrender to him the paper, which he put into the hands of Mr. Aiken, Ayr. In vain did Burns offer to go to Jamaica to better his condition, promising to come back in some years and claim Jean as his wife; in vain did he offer, if this plan failed, to become a common labourer, to support his wife and her expected family. Armour was inexorable, and Jean, too, at last yielded to the strength of his persuasions and threats; and as she had previously given up the paper, she now surrendered the poet. We neither deeply blame nor greatly wonder at her conduct. Like Lucy Ashton, she was sore beset by the influence of father, mother, family, public opinion, and had nothing to support her but her love to a man who was standing at the lowest point of depression, with no fortune, little fame, and a damaged moral reputation. She was too melancholy and utterly depressed to sing, as Burns represented his former sweetheart singing—

"The rantin' dog the daddie o't."

She became the most miserable of women, and her misery only wanted one element to make it despair, and that, too, seemed at this time very near—the madness or suicide of her poet-lover. And now came the darkest point in Burns' history, unless his rejection at Dumfries at a later date was a yet deeper deep, because succeeding a great triumph. Hugely indignant at Jean, yet loving her still, he ran, he tells us, into dissipation of every kind, attending mason-lodges and other merry meetings, vainly seeking "to drown in rant the heartache of the night." He wrote "Laments," odes to "Ruin," and so forth, forcing out thus a brief and imperfect solace to his woes. All, all were found miserable comforters—

"'Hungry Ruin' had him in the wind."

A hundred plans of extrication from his difficulties floated through his mind. At last one of some feasibility presented itself; he would go to the West Indies, and to purchase a passage would publish a volume of poems. Gavin Hamilton advised him to do so, and Burns eagerly consented. Proposals of publication and subscription papers were instantly thrown off.

While pressed down by these woes, and with the cares of publication coming upon him, this extraordinary being was engaged in an under-plot of passion and sorrow, enough itself to have crushed many ordinary men to the dust; we refer, of course, to the history of Mary Campbell, or "Highland Mary." She was of Highland extraction, from Dunoon, and daughter of a sailor in a revenue cutter, whose family resided in Cantyre. She had spent some of her earlier years in the family of the Rev. David Campbell of Loch Ranza, in Arran, a relation of her mother's. She became a servant in the family of Gavin Hamilton in 1785, acting as nurse-maid to one of his sons. She is said not to have been peculiarly graceful or feminine, but very sweet and artless. The tradition of the village generally attests her purity, although calumny has not spared her connection with Burns. She was sprightly and blue-eyed. She knew Burns some time before their final courtship, although Mrs. Begg remembers no reference to her from her brother's lips except once, when he told John Blane that Mary had refused to meet him at the Old Castle—a ruined priory near Gavin Hamilton's house.

Spurned by the Armours, and given up by Jean, Burns reverted to Mary, who was residing as a dairy-maid in Coilsfield House; resumed his acquaintance with her; and, in fine, determined to affiance her to himself for ever. They met, as everybody knows, for this purpose on the banks of the Ayr, diverging probably to the woods of the Fail—a tributary stream which washes the domain of Coilsfield—on the 14th of May, 1786, a Sabbath day. They stood on opposite sides of a small brook, laved their hands in the stream, and exchanged Bibles—Mary giving her lover a plain Bible in one volume, Burns presenting her with a handsome one in two. On a blank leaf of one of the volumes was inscribed in Burns' hand the words, "And ye shall not swear by my name falsely, saith the Lord (Levit. xix. 12); and on the second, "Thou shalt not forswear thyself, but shalt perform unto the Lord thine oaths" (Matt. v. 33). On the blank leaf of each was Burns' name inscribed, along with his mason-mark. We see it reported in a recent number of the *Scottish American Journal* that Mary's mother after her death gave the two-volumed Bible to her other daughter, Annie Campbell, along with a lock of Mary's hair, who in her turn gave each of her two daughters one of the volumes. But they became, it seems, the cause of discord in the two families; and to remove this one William Anderson, a mason, son of one of the families, bought from the two sisters each her copy, carried them out to America when he emigrated there in 1834, and thence they were sent home to Ayr to the trustees of the Burns monument, and are deposited there.

Mary, who seems now to have fixed to be Burns' wife, and to go with or after him to the West Indies, returned and spent the summer with her parents. She crossed the Clyde to Greenock to visit some relatives, and to have a parting interview, some say, with Burns before he went abroad; but in the house of a relative, Peter MacPherson, a ship-carpenter, she fell ill of a fever, caught while waiting on a sick boy, her brother, Robert Campbell. And in spite of an amulet prepared by her superstitious friends in the Highlands—consisting of seven smooth stones, picked up at a cross burn and boiled with new milk—which she had to swallow, Mary died, it is supposed in October, 1786, and lies now in the West Churchyard, Greenock, in a mean part of the town, but with a tall elegant monument over her. Fortunate, may we not say, she! to have departed so early to the "Land o' the Leal!" With Burns probably she would not have been happy; and have not his two immortal songs reared such a mausoleum over her dust,

"That kings for such a tomb might wish to die!"

He addressed several songs to her while she lived, such as "My Highland Lassie," "Will ye go to the Indies, my Mary?" but he never mentioned either his engagement or her death to any of his relatives. We will see what Mrs. Begg tells about this by-and-by. In the Scottish journal referred to it is said, that after Mary's death Burns went to her abode and asked some token of her; but her mother, who disliked him, sternly refused. Others, however, maintain that the mother was more friendly to the poet than was the father, and spoke well of him as a "real warm-hearted chiel, though she did not think her sweet lassie would have been happy with such a wild and profane genius," and probably she was right.

During the troubled time extending from his disgrace with the Armours, and his appearance on three successive Sabbaths to be rebuked in the church for his incontinence, down to the publication of his poems, Burns' life was by no means uneventful. There was a certain Elizabeth Black— who ultimately ended as a very respectable hostler wife in Alva, and who was probably known to our late friend, Dr. Eadie, of Glasgow, a native of Alva, and who must have been a youth of eighteen when Mrs. Black died—who boasted that she knew Burns in his early days, and that he wrote on her the song, "From thee, Eliza, I must go." About this time, too, he saw the "Bonnie Lass o' Ballochmyle," Miss Wilhelmina Alexander, sister of Claud Alexander, Esq., a gentleman who had enriched himself in India and bought Ballochmyle. We visited the place some years ago, and admired exceedingly its rich-wooded braes and distant prospect of the Ayr and the village of

Catrine, and fancied below the trees the vision of beauty still passing, and the musing poet still standing with folded arms and looks of insatiate admiration, like one transfixed by Love's lightning and rooted to the spot. It was some months afterwards that he sent her the exquisite song, of which Miss Alexander (prepossessed against Burns by some village gossip) took no notice, but which she lived to value very highly, and to say of the original copy, that she would never part with it. Her nephew, Mr. Alexander, erected a bower at the spot, and there a facsimile of the song and the accompanying letter was framed.

Burns' pen did not lie idle during these anxious and miserable months. He wrote songs, dedications (to Gavin Hamilton), *jeux d'esprit*, such as "The Calf," composed on the Rev. James Steven, of London and Kilwinning, his famous "Tam Samson," &c. We saw that subscription lists had been thrown off, and the announcement of his volume as advenient had created a buzz through Kyle, Carrick, and Cunningham, if not through Renfrewshire and Lanarkshire; for in these shires, and beyond them, many had begun to hear of the fact that there was a great poet rising among them—

> " At times a warning trumpet blown,
>   At times a stifled hum,
>   Told Scotland from his mountain throne
>   Her KING did rushing come."

He had nearly, like Joseph, come out of prison to reign.

He was now called upon to give security for the maintenance of Jean's expected offspring. This from sheer poverty he was unable to do, and was obliged in consequence to skulk in a farm-house belonging to a relative of his (an aunt), named Allan, in Old Rome Forest, near Kilmarnock, lest he should be clapt into jail. His *Nadir* was now at its deepest, when there arose in the July sky of 1786 the first streak of his undying fame.

CHAPTER VII.

BURNS IN ASCENSION.

HIS volume was published by John Wilson, Kilmarnock, and went immediately to the heart of that country-side; old and young read it with equal avidity and unmingled delight. Plough-boys and maid-servants gladly gave their "sair-won penny fee" to get possession of the poems of Burns. Many wept blessed tears over the "Cottar's Saturday Night;" many laughed day and night over the "Address to the Deil" and the "Holy Fair:" all were enchanted with the ease, the power, the nature, and the truthfulness of the pictures of Scotland—its life, scenery, and manners. His early friends and patrons felt pride as well as pleasure in their hearts. Some, indeed, might not be able to believe for very gladness that these "old familiar faces" were so beautiful and so striking after all: was this really the "Vision" they had heard Bob Aiken read? Others took the credit, perhaps, of predictions they never made, and criticisms in his favour they never uttered. The inhabitants of Mossgiel alone, we are told, no copy of their friend's immortalities reached, although there, too. the echo of his fame was heard with surprise, pride, and pleasure. "Had our father only been living to see this day!" some of them would exclaim. The edition of six hundred speedily disappeared; another of one thousand was projected, and Burns became for the first time in his life the master of £20! The success of a first work is felt by all authors to be exhilarating. But never perhaps in the history of literature was there such a sudden bound as in the case of Burns from misery, contempt, poverty, and semi-madness, to present popularity and the prospect of future fame and competence. Were, not a reprieve, but a royal crown given to a criminal at the gallows, it would be only a type of the suddenness of the transition and the thoroughness of the triumph!

John Wilson was a bookseller in Kilmarnock, who afterwards throve in the world; and removing to Ayr, started the first Ayrshire newspaper — the *Ayrshire Advertiser* — which became a good property. Burns, while watching the publication and correcting the proofs, was a great deal in Kilmarnock. The first edition did not contain some of the best pieces—"Death and Dr. Hornbook," "A Prayer in prospect of Death," &c.—which were all then composed, and a number of others which he wrote afterwards—such as his "Address to Edinburgh," the "Brigs of Ayr," and the "Address to a Haggis." Jamaica was still in his view. He had made an engagement with Charles Douglas, of Port Antonio, to act as book-keeper on his estate for three years, at £30 a year. He had even been afraid he would have to indent himself —*i.e.*, become a bound apprentice—that Mr. Douglas might pay his passage. And as soon as he possessed nine guineas, he took a steerage passage in a vessel which was to sail from Greenock in September.

Burns' spirits seem to have, as might have been expected, continued good for a time after the success of his book. He went from town to town collecting his moneys, and meeting with old and new friends, cracking jokes, attending social meetings, and making such rhymes as these (he was mounted on a sorry hack, like that of Andrew Fairservice, ycleped "Souple Sam," *lucus a non lucendo*):--

> " Here comes Burns
>   On Rosinante;
> She 's d—— poor
>   But he 's d —— canty."

He had returned to Mossgiel, and was living quietly there, when one evening (September 3) a brother of Jean's came in to tell him that she had born him twins—a boy and a girl. The Mossgiel family took the boy and the Armours the girl, who soon, however, died. Jean had visited Paisley in March, had lived with her uncle, Andrew Purdie; and reports of her borrowing money and flirting with a young weaver there, called Robert Wilson, originally from Mauchline, had reached Burns, and made him very miserable. He had a lurking liking for her still, and perhaps she became yet dearer to him after her *accouchement*. He says, "A very fine boy and girl have awakened thoughts and feelings that thrill now with tender pressure, and now with foreboding anguish, through my soul." A number of the gentry of the county began to show Burns flattering attention; and perhaps if he had remained and taken root in Ayrshire, it had in the long-run been better for him, alike commercially and morally. One was MacAdam of Craigengillan, to whom he addressed

BURNS STATUE, KILMARNOCK.

ENGRAVED BY W. ROFFE, FROM THE STATUE BY W. G. STEVENSON.

WILLIAM MACKENZIE, LONDON, EDINBURGH & GLASGOW.

a copy of verses; another was Sir William Cunningham of Robertland; a third was Mrs. Stewart of Stair, of whom we heard farther back. He sent her a collection of his own published songs, including the "Lass of Ballochmyle," in a highly complimentary but sincere-seeming letter. There was another and, in a social position, a humbler friend, who turned out of greater service to the poet. This was the Rev. George Lawrie of Loudon, a parish in the neighbourhood of Mossgiel. Lawrie was an accomplished man himself, and the friend of men that were more so still. He had been the means of introducing MacPherson's Ossianic fragments to Dr. Blair, and was intimate with him, with Blacklock, Robertson, and others. He had read Burns' poems, and had sent a copy to good Dr. Blacklock for his opinion. Burns spent a night in his house, which was the abode of refined yet hearty hospitality—the ideal of a Moderate minister's dwelling. There were his host, his pleasant lady, a young son, a daughter, beautiful and accomplished, who could play on the spinet—an instrument new to Burns—another daughter in her teens, and some children. There was in the manse (tell it not to "Daddie Auld;" whisper it not to "Holy Willie!") after supper a dance, in which the poet ploughman danced with Miss Lawrie—keeping time admirably, as she afterwards said. How commonplace all this looks to us now, but what a rare treat to him. Heart full, he retired to bed; but being somewhat late in rising the next morning, the son went to inquire for him; and meeting him on the stairs, asked him how he had slept. "Not well," replied Burns; "I have been praying all night. If you go up to my room, you will find my prayers on the table." These were his "Lines Written at a Friend's House." Miss Lawrie had also a scrap of verse from Burns' pen, beginning—

"The night was still, and o'er the hill.' *

He seems to have remained with this delightful family till the afternoon, and left them, carrying away and leaving regret. Mr. Lawrie, no doubt, would lament that such a noble being was quitting his native land so soon, and for ever. As usually happens, in proportion to the exquisite delight of the previous day, in such contrast to Burns' ruder revelries and coarse society, was the deep rut of the reaction. He became very, very sad. It was a lowering evening in autumn, with the clouds driving over the sky, the wind whistling through the rushes and long spear grass, and cold pelting showers striking ever and anon upon the face of the solitary traveller. It was altogether such another night, *mutatis mutandis*, as fell dark over poor Shelley, our truest poet and sincerest man since Burns, in Italy when he sung—

* See Poem.

"O wild west wind, thou breath of autumn's being."

He found a solace in his noble ode to the "West Wind," which he wishes to become the trumpet of a prophecy, and to—

"Drive his dead thoughts over the universe,"

and asks the question"—

"If Winter comes, can Spring be far behind?"

Burns' mood, if more hopeless, was more subdued, as he composed, striding along, "the last song he was ever to measure in Caledonia"—

"The gloomy night is gathering fast,
Loud roars the wild inconstant blast;
Yon murky cloud is foul with rain,
I see it driving o'er the plain.

Farewell, old Coila's hills and dales,
Her heathy moors and winding vales;
The scenes where wretched fancy roves,
Pursuing past, unhappy loves.

Farewell, my friends, farewell, my foes!
My peace with these, my love with those.
The bursting tears my heart declare—
Farewell the bonnie banks of Ayr!"

We cannot exactly fix the date of the evening Burns composed this song; it was in autumn, 1786, probably in the close of August. On the 3rd September he heard, we saw, of the birth of his twins; and a day or two after came tidings to Mossgiel which entirely altered the course of his destiny. The history of Thomas Blacklock is well known. He was born in Annan; when six months old he became blind through small-pox, but was carefully tended and taught by his father, and afterwards, being a great favourite from his gentle temper, he was never without some companion to help him in his studies. At the age of twelve he wrote verses. At twenty he came to Edinburgh, where he was instructed in Latin, French, and other languages, acquiring French chiefly in conversation with a French lady, the wife of Provost Alexander. He published in 1754 an edition of his poems, and soon after a quarto edition by subscription, which brought in a considerable sum of money. He now devoted himself to the study of theology, and was presented to the parish of Kirkcudbright; but being opposed by the parishioners on account of his blindness, ultimately withdrew on a moderate annuity. He married the daughter of a Dumfries surgeon, named Johnstone, who was a great blessing to him. He resided finally in Edinburgh, and supported himself by keeping boarders. He was a most amiable and excellent man, and after attaining a respectable place among the literati of Scotland, and issuing a number of books, he at last died in 1791, aged seventy. He was the means of drawing out of obscurity a number of young men, and helping them forward in life. And now he performed the best deed of all in befriending Burns. We can conceive the joy wherewith Burns, heavy laden under the burden of many cares, read the letter which Mr. Lawrie kindly forwarded him from Dr. Blacklock, praising his poetry, and urging him to issue a second edition. Assuredly, if this letter found the poet in the harvest field, he would work no more that day! He did not, however, (though he seems to say so himself in his letter to Dr. Moore), hurry instantly to Edinburgh, but remained at Mossgiel for two months. During this period he wrote the "Brigs of Ayr," inscribing it to the architect of the new brig, Mr. Ballantyne, a special friend. He began to cherish the idea of becoming an exciseman. One day as Mrs. Begg was working at her big wheel, the harvest being over, and Robert and Gilbert being in the apartment, a letter was handed in to the former. He snatched it eagerly, went to the window, opened, read it, and she saw a look of the intensest anguish crossing his face as he went out without uttering a word. It was the news of Mary Campbell's death! Dugald Stewart, who resided at Catrine, a few miles off, had heard of Burns and his wonderful poems from Mr. Mackenzie, a clever surgeon in Mauchline. He invited him, along with Mr. Mackenzie, to dine at his house, and there happened to have called there by accident Lord Daer, the son of the Earl of Selkirk, who had been one of Dugald Stewart's pupils. Burns has recorded his impressions of the young lord in his well-known verses, and Stewart in his equally well-known letter. He wrote about this time a "canty" rhyming letter to one William Logan, a retired major, who lived at Park, near Ayr. He now, too, began his intimacy with Mrs. Dunlop of Dunlop. This lady, a daughter of Thomas Wallace of Craigie, and reputed a descendant of the great Sir William, had been afflicted by a long severe illness, preying with peculiar heaviness upon her spirits, when a copy of Burns' poems was laid by a friend on her table. She opened it at the "Cottar's Saturday Night," and like Gilbert when he heard it recited, was absolutely electrified. It acted like a charm; and she instantly sent off a messenger sixteen miles to Mossgiel, with a letter to Burns, desiring half a dozen copies of his poems, and requesting him to call at Dunlop House. This was the beginning of a correspondence which continued during the poet's life. He again visited Mr. Lawrie's manse, and had a kind of tift with Mrs. Lawrie about the case of Peggy K——, mentioned before; Mrs. Lawrie blaming him for undue severity on "sister woman," not a common fault with him, and he replying in lines which may be found among his poems. The *Edinburgh Magazine* for October, edited by James Sibbalds, a literary bookseller, published a most favourable criticism on his volume. He now definitely abandoned all intentions of going to Jamaica, and fixed to start for Edinburgh on the 27th or 28th of November. Mr. Ballantyne, of Ayr, hearing that Burns was prevented from printing another edition of his poems by want of money to pay the printer, generously offered him £27 for the purpose; but advised him to go to Edinburgh as the best place for publishing. Not long before he started there was a *Gaudeamus*, probably on the 10th of November, in the St. James Lodge of Masons, of which Burns was a depute-master, and which met in a small inn kept by one Manson. John Lees, who survived "Brother Burns," spoke of it as an "awfu' nicht." Burns came to it in a pair of buckskins, out of which he would pull the other shilling for the other bowl till it was five in the morning!

At last, on the 27th of November, 1786, he set off for Edinburgh, a distance of sixty miles. It used to be currently said that he walked on foot, although, as we shall immediately see, Gilbert Burns asserts that he rode upon a borrowed pony. But, at all events, whether on foot or horseback, he travelled "crooning" to himself his favourite lines—

> "As I cam o'er by Glenap,*
> I met an aged woman,
> Who bade me keep up my heart,
> For the best o' my days were coming."

* Glenap, a romantic glen in the south of Ayrshire, near Ballantrae.

CHAPTER VIII.

BURNS AT THE ZENITH.

BURNS' Glenap soothsayer was, like her of Endor, so far right and so far wrong in her vaticination. The morning was coming, and also the night. The best and the worst days of Burns were now before him. Edinburgh was to raise and to ruin him.

Gilbert Burns says that he rode on a pony, borrowed from a friend; and Robert Chambers corroborates the statement, with the additional evidence of Mr. Archibald Prentice of the *Manchester Times*, a relative of the late Mr. Prentice of the *Glasgow Chronicle*, and a most worthy man, with whom we, too, had some literary correspondence. Mr. Prentice writes a letter to Professor Wilson, published in the *Edinburgh Intelligencer* for March 8, 1841. In it he states that through an Ayrshire friend—George Reid of Barquharry—Burns had become acquainted with Mr. Prentice's father, the farmer of Covington Mains, who testified his admiration for his poetry by subscribing for twenty copies of the second edition. (It should be twelve only, as we see in the list of the subscribers' names). It was arranged by Mr. Reid that Burns should, on his journey to Edinburgh, make the farm-house at Covington Mains his resting-place on the first night. All the farmers in the parish had read with delight the poet's then published works, and were anxious to see him. They were all asked to meet him at a late hour; and the signal of his arrival was to be a white sheet attached to a pitchfork, and set on the top of a corn-stack. "The parish is a beautiful amphitheatre, with the Clyde winding through it; and my father's stack-yard, lying in the centre, could be seen from every house in the parish. At length Burns arrived, mounted on a pony borrowed from Mr. Dalrymple, near Ayr. Instantly was the white flag hoisted, and as instantly were the farmers seen issuing from their houses, and converging to the point of meeting. A glorious evening, night, morning, followed, and the conversation of the poet confirmed and increased the admiration created by his writings. Next morning he breakfasted with a large party at the next farm-house, tenanted by James Stoddart; took lunch, also with a large party, at the Bank with John Stoddart, my mother's father; and rode into Edinburgh in the evening on the 'pownie,' which he returned to the owner a few days afterwards by John Samson, the brother of the immortal Tam." This is Mr. Prentice's statement. We got a letter some years ago, when editing Nichol's Edition of the Poets, from a gentleman in Carnwath, giving us a few particulars of Burns' visit, a little different from this. He says that the sheet was hoisted from Covington Hill, being a spot visible from a considerable distance. Burns did call in passing at John Stoddart's, but he did not alight. Stoddart remarked that they were in great confusion, as they had a bride in the house. "Weel, weel," said Burns, laughing; "Heaven send the lassie good luck." Good luck accordingly followed the blessing of the bard. The lassie became the mother of a numerous family, who all did well in the world. One daughter settled in Moscow, became milliner and dressmaker to the Empress of Russia, acquired a large fortune, and returned to her native country.

We have strong doubts if this event, of the occurrence of which there can be no doubt, took place on Burns' first visit to Edinburgh. He is generally said to have performed that journey on foot, and to have been so fatigued with the walk that he was indisposed for some days—an indisposition to which he alludes in his letters, and which is more likely to have been produced by a long walk than by a ride, unless, indeed, the hospitalities of the Mains had been excessive; and certainly three meals in so short a compass of time, at the then rate of convivial living, was hard work. It is scarcely, however, likely that the farmers would have gathered to meet him unless they had been previously acquainted with his poems. But the circulation of his first edition had been limited, and was almost entirely confined to Ayrshire. The enthusiasm in Carnwath was more probably produced by Mr. Prentice's extra copies of the second edition (see Chambers', vol. i., Appendix), circulated by him among his neighbours, and Burns had afterwards occasion more than once to pass that way.

The same Carnwath gentleman (it is twenty years since he wrote us, and we regret exceedingly we have neglected to preserve his name) told us in his letter another story connected with Burns. In the spring after he died Thomas Nimmo, a native of Carnwath, having received his discharge from the army in England, was travelling home with his comrade. Passing through Dumfries, they inquired the way to St. Michael's Churchyard, to visit the poet's grave. Following a footpath through the wilderness of ornamental structures which deck that famous burying-ground, they looked round for a stone to tell them where he slept. Not finding anything of the sort, they made up to a female in deep mourning who was sitting on the ground a little farther on. Nimmo thus addressed her—"Mistress, we are strangers, and would feel obliged if you would show us the grave of Burns." Pointing to the narrow mound at her feet, and bursting into tears, she said—"That, soldiers, is his grave, and I am his widow." The poor fellows apologized for disturbing her sorrows, and went on their way. It were a good subject for a painter—Jean Armour at the grave of Burns while no monument marked the spot.

No word or prospect of the grave on the 28th November, when the eye of Robert Burns first rested on the towers and temples, the Castle and Calton Hill, of Auld Reekie. Worn out and wearied a little by long walking he might be, but his spirits were high. "Hope rose before him like a fiery column, the dark side not yet turned," and the Sybil's song was yet sounding in his ear. Did a sunbeam from the Day-star, setting over his beloved West, strike upon the Castle-rock as he entered, preceding and announcing the arrival of the brightest of Scotland's sons? or did dark and ominous clouds, black with more than the gloom of November, gather on the brow of Arthur's Seat, as the man doomed to be first the enslaver and then the victim of the proud city was slowly approaching the scene of his glory and his shame? Certain it is that he entered Edinburgh entirely unknown, and perhaps unnoticed, unless a curious townsman might ask what travel-soiled, slouching peasant, with those marvellously bright eyes, is that, and had ere he passed ceased even to wish for a reply. The feeling of one for the first time entering London is usually that of intense insignificance, produced by the enormous crowd of human beings. The feeling of one entering Edinburgh is wonder at the grand objects and grander associations of the place: the shadow of the Castle falls on him like a thunder cloud, and he dares hardly breathe as Holyrood, with all its memories of kings and crimes which had so long dwelt in his imagination, starts up to his eye, like a bloody spectre from his low lair in the valley. Burns, it is likely, after some such solemn thoughts in his mind at the first sight of Edinburgh, had to consider the practical question, where was he to sleep, and could think of no "howff" whatever save the lodging of honest John Richmond, once a clerk with Gavin Hamilton, and a jolly companion of the poet's, now residing in a single room in Baxter's Close, Lawnmarket, for which he paid three shillings a week. Joyfully does the humble clerk rise from his chair to welcome Burns, and a long night might they spend, conversing on the news of the West, ere the wearied poet retires to his bed. The next day he is unwell, and keeps it, and has no doubt many a sad and sombre thought as he now more fully realizes his solitude in the great city. It is said of Carlyle that when he first transferred himself to London, and commenced his then thankless and unappreciated literary work, he sat down with the *sternest determination*. And no doubt Burns would summon up his most iron resolution, too. After his brief indisposition was gone he began, as Nanty Ewart has it, a "cruise about Auld Reekie." He would visit the Castle and gaze delighted on the distant shores of Fife; the rising palatial streets of the New Town; the huge dusky masses of the Old, surmounted by the Lion of Arthur's Seat, never looking more leonine than from this point; to the west the Highland mountains, scarce visible through the dim light of November; and "the moors and mosses many" of his own Ayrshire he would try, like poor Harley in the "Man of Feeling," to shape to himself in the clouds, and resign the task with a sigh. On his way from Holyrood, with its teeming and tragic stories, he found out the grave of Fergusson, and kneeling down, kissed the sod. According to Allan Cunningham, he visited the shop which had been once that of Allan Ramsay, taking off his hat as he entered; and when afterwards introduced to Creech the bookseller, that knowing worthy remembered he had been in his shop before, inquiring if *that* had been the shop of the author of the "Gentle Shepherd." Still was he almost entirely unknown, and had to retire, grumbling a little and dissatisfied, to his humble bed and companion in the Lawnmarket. No doubt he felt dull enough at times, and as Crabbe, when struggling for subsistence in London, sometimes exclaims, "O, Sally (afterwards Mrs. Crabbe), for you!" so Burns may have often sighed for his Jean, to whom, if she could not soothe, he might at least whisper his sorrows.

Help, however, was near him, and it was to come, after all, from the banks of the Ayr. Worthy Provost Ballantyne was to be the *Deus ex machina*. He had introduced Burns to Dalrymple of Orangefield. Now, the said Dalrymple was one of three gentlemen who had married sisters, all very rich, although all sprung from a poor violer in Ayr called Hugh M'Guire, who had been kind to one MacRae, afterwards Governor MacRae of Madras. He, having no children of his own, adopted those of the humble M'Guire. Lord Glencairn married M'Guire's eldest daughter; Lord Alva, a Lord of Session, married the second; and Dalrymple of Orangefield the third. Thus a chain of patronage was woven for our poet. Dalrymple introduced him to the Dowager Lady Glencairn, and to her amiable son, Lord Glencairn; and through a younger brother of his, who married the sister of the Earl of Buchan and the famous Henry Erskine, Burns also got into that circle, the most brilliant then in Edinburgh. Mr. Dalziel, Lord Glencairn's factor, had spoken of Burns as the author of the Kilmarnock volume to his lordship. And also, most fortunately, Creech, the sagacious bibliopole, had been the tutor of Glencairn, and the earl introduced our poet to his notice, although, like most booksellers, he was in no hurry to close with him, saying, as an eminent and really excellent bookseller said once, "As to the merit of the book and its interest there can be no doubt; the question of sale is what I have to consider." Within a few days of Burns' arrival in Edinburgh he seems to have met Glencairn and Dalrymple, although where and how is somewhat uncertain. His first interview with Henry Erskine is characteristic. It was at the Canongate Kilwinning Lodge of Freemasons, where Henry Erskine was Past Master. They became intimate in an instant, and although they do not seem to have met very often, their friendship never cooled. It was a singular family that of the Erskines. Lord Buchan was a fool (of some talent); Thomas (Lord) Erskine, was a fool of transcendent forensical genius, whose flights of fancy and eloquence seem absolute inspiration, rivalling those of Curran, and little inferior to Burke's, but who, in private and domestic life, displayed the most reckless imprudence; and Henry was a man of sense, wit, learning, patriotism, and piety. Lord Buchan afterwards, when Burns had gained the shore, encumbered him with some bungling help; but Henry and Glencairn were the real architects of his fortune. Henry Erskine trumpeted his fame in every direction to which his influence as the first lawyer at the bar extended, and Lord Glencairn pledged the Caledonian Hunt, one and all, to subscribe for the second edition; so that, by the 7th December (nine days after his arrival) Burns was able to write to Gavin Hamilton in the following style:—"I am in a fair way of becoming as eminent as Thomas à Kempis or John Bunyan. And you may expect henceforth to see my birthday inserted among the wonderful events in the "Poor Robins" and "Aberdeen Almanacs," along with the "Black Monday" and the "Battle of Bothwell Bridge." And his soul has prophesied truly!

Dugald Stewart, too, was working for him. He had brought his Kilmarnock copy of the poems to Edinburgh and showed it to Henry Mackenzie the "Man of Feeling," (the neglect of whose pathetic and classical works is a disgrace to our age), who from the sofa of the "Lounger," which he then occupied, flung a smile upon it, which was at that time fame. Lord Craig had previously spoken of Michael Bruce's poems in the "Mirror" in a kindly fashion; but Mackenzie, far more eulogistic, dared to mention Burns in the same sentence with Shakspeare, and to call him by a name he has never yet lost, "the heaven-taught ploughman." We question if any Edinburgh critic before or since (always excepting Christopher North) would ever have ventured on such generous audacity. Assuredly Lord Jeffrey never would.

And now the folding-doors of Edinburgh fashionable society were thrown wide open to our Ayrshire Bard, more widely than they were to Dr. Johnson thirteen years before, more widely than (so far as we know) they were to Edmund Burke two years before. Edinburgh had then a grand cluster of literary and other celebrities within its walls. David Hume, indeed, the greatest of them, had been ten years dead; but there were still Hugh Blair, the pleasing critic and smooth sermon-writer; William Robertson, the world-famous historian and powerful Churchleader; Adam Smith; John Home, the popular dramatist; John Erskine, the manly and outspoken Calvinistic divine; John Logan, the poet and popular sermon-writer; Dr. A. Webster, the clerical humorist and founder of the Scottish Clergy's Widows' Fund; Dugald Stewart, the eloquent and accomplished philosopher; Henry Mackenzie, the Addison of Scotland. Among the Lords of Session were Lord Kames, the astute critic; Lord Hailes, the learned annalist; Lord Craig, the refined essayist; Lord Auchinleck, best known as having given life to Bozzy, even as Bozzy is best known for having confirmed the immortality of Johnson; and still keeping to a lofty platform, Adam Ferguson, the Roman historian, and Lord Monboddo— whose strange theories, after a century's sterility, seem of late showing symptoms of vitality—dear to Burns, however, not for his original and daring speculations, but as the parent of Miss Burnet, the loveliest vision in female form and actual life which ever flashed on his enraptured eye! In lower regions there were Gilbert Stuart and William Smellie, of the latter of whom we shall hear more hereafter. There were then three ladies of some literary note— Lady Ann Barnard, author of "Auld Robin Gray," Jane Elliot, author of the first, and Mrs. Cockburn, the accomplished author of the second version of the "Flowers of the Forest." These and the others we have already mentioned, Lord Glencairn, Henry Erskine, and the members of the Caledonian Hunt, were among the leading luminaries of Edinburgh society when Burns burst amongst it like a meteor, and continued there till it was discovered that a meteor, when it shines too long, is less useful in a drawing-room than an Argand lamp, and being somewhat wild and lurid withal, had better vanish.

The first impression he made was unprecedented. Within a month of his arrival in Edinburgh he had been at the *routs* of Jane, Duchess of Gordon, who was then the queen of fashionable society, and who said that no conversation had ever so completely carried her away as that of Burns; had attended meetings of the Caledonian Hunt, where Lord Glencairn took him by the hand with an air so affable, and a smile so kind, that he seemed "to be a stronger proof of the immortality of the soul than any philosopher can furnish—a mind like his can never die" (like Fuseli, who said once to a coxcomb who was denying human immortality, "I don't know if *you* have an immortal soul, but by ——, *I know I have*"); had met with Lord and Lady Betty Cunningham; had got ten guineas anonymously from a gentleman he discovered to be Patrick Miller of Dalswinton, afterwards his landlord; had mingled familiarly with Dr. Robertson, Dr. Blair, Dr. Gregory, Mr. Frazer Tytler, Mr. Mackenzie, and Dr. Adam Ferguson, and had been once or twice at the elegant suppers of Lord Monboddo; and while his lordship was classifying his guest as a very superior offshoot from the ape, Burns was regarding his host's daughter as only a little lower than the angels. Returning from his first visit from Lord Monboddo's house, he was asked, "Did you admire the young lady?" he replied, "I admired God Almighty more than ever; Miss Burnet is the loveliest of all His works!" It was at this time, when the city was all bright and joyful, and full of hope to him, that he wrote his beautiful address to Edinburgh. His honeymoon with her had not yet, but was soon to, come to a close.

There are a hundred testimonies to the power of Burns' talk, to the modesty of his demeanour, and the regularity of his habits at this trying period. His conduct and conversation were equally admired. His manner was modest, yet thoroughly self-possessed; his talk rich, yet well regulated; and whatever he might think in his heart, he seemed always to be rather borrowing light from, than reflecting it on, the luminaries of the metropolis. This was the more edifying as, in reality, he possessed as much talent as any ten of these *litterateurs*, and more genius than all of them put together. Dr. Johnson, in 1774, had frightened and fluttered these Volscians in Corioli, and Burns might have done the same had he not come straight from the plough, and felt the cold shadow of the patronizer over him. And we doubt not that a certain relief from restraint, along with the sense of conscious though curbed superiority, mingled with his feelings as he returned from these splendid suppers to his humble bed in the Lawnmarket* with John Richmond.

Burns' appearance and dress at this time neither added to nor detracted much from the impression he produced. When Scott met him he was dressed like a farmer, who had put on his best to dine with his laird. And, according to other authorities, his best was a suit of blue and buff—the colours of the Whig party, afterwards transferred to the cover of the *Edinburgh Review*—with buckskin breeches and top boots. His hair was tied behind and spread out over the forehead; but he wore no powder,

* Richmond's landlady's name was Carfrae, and he occupied a rather spacious apartment.

though that was the fashion of the time. We once saw on the street of Dumfries a descendant of his who was said to be a fac-simile of the poet—liker than all the portraits; and he helped us to our idea of Burns as a man of middle stature, seeming so, at least, from a stoop contracted at the plough; with broad brow, rather low and palpitating with thought and suffering; dark eyes, shivering in their great round orbs like the star Venus in the evening, west; with nostril slightly curved upwards, dusky skin (recalling Carlyle's description of Camille Desmoulin's face of "dingy blackguardism, wonderfully irradiated with genius, as though a naphtha lamp burned within it"), thick black hair, and rather indecisive chin and cheek. Burns' conversation will occupy our critical attention afterwards. In Edinburgh he would probably somewhat mitigate the dictatorial tone which Dugald Stewart calls its only fault, and altogether restrain its excesses of humour bordering on riot, and of daring verging on profanity. His address to females—not to ladies merely, but to the sex—was extremely deferential and winning. Probably Dr. Robertson somewhat exaggerates when he says that his conversation was a fuller outcome of his mind than his poetry, which he rated high, and than his letters, which he rated higher. Few will grant this latter statement, and we have our doubts as to the accuracy of the other. The marvel of those literary men could not be altogether explained on the principle implied in Balaam's supposed line addressed to his loquacious ass—

"Mon ane parle, et même il parle bien!
"My ass speaks, and speaks well, too!"

Yet something of this feeling mingled with their appreciation of Burns' talk. Wonderful in itself, it was far more so as coming from a rustic. Perhaps, too, they never thought of measuring themselves with him, or of talking their best before him. They looked on him as a performer on the stage, to whom it was enough that they furnished a cue now and then. Dr. Robertson would as soon have thought of encountering with his eyes those of David Garrick when his transport of divine fury in "Lear" was at the highest, as those of Burns as he was reciting his "Vision" or the "Gloomy night is gathering fast." They admitted, and never thought of contesting, his superiority, just as they would have bowed before some superb specimen of an African lion or Bengalian tiger. Even Burke, the only man then living entitled to take the *pas* of Burns, would have paused before he sought to have a passage of arms with such a prodigy. In one point none of the Edinburgh conversers would have the slightest chance with the Ayrshire Ploughman, and would be always willing to give him his own way; and that was in *feeling*. Henry Mackenzie had put all his pathos in his novels; there was little in his talk, and the others had none. Here Burns was unaffectedly and habitually strong. He shed tears when he saw Bunbury's print and read Langhorne's lines, so near was his heart to his eyes; and he had the power of producing tears as easily. Tears are seldom seen in drawing-rooms, and when they do arise, it is usually to the magic of music or song. But Burns' talk was often a sad, sweet melody, and as fraught with genius as with sorrow. It was this which carried the Duchess of Gordon off her feet, and perhaps made other ladies of susceptibility disposed to exclaim as they felt his fascination, like Ada to Cain, when Lucifer was drawing her into his weird suction—

" Save me, save me from him! "

Lockhart's powerful description of Burns' *debut* will occur to our readers. But we do not think it quite so just as it is powerful. It attributes to the Edinburgh magnates a spirit of emulation, if not of envy to Burns, which we believe the abler and better of them never felt, either then or afterwards. John Hume, alone, in one of his letters we remember, speaks of the Ayrshire Ploughman as a popular delusion or *humbug*, from which assuredly the public would one day awaken. In this, however, he was singular and wrong. If the public, and the Edinburgh literati, too, did turn away from Burns for a season, it was owing to other causes than change of mind as to the merits of his poetry, although in this they acted, we think, coldly and unwisely, pushing the ostracism too far. But the former fact has not, we think, been sufficiently noticed by his biographers.

It was not even yet, however, all plain sailing with Burns. He had difficulties about the printing and getting out of his second edition. There is a story told of him calling one day on a printer in Edinburgh, to inquire about the printing of a volume of poems. The printer was not at all prepossessed by his appearance and manner, which were at once plain and a little pretentious, and thought him a cracked poetaster. So he regarded him superciliously, and spoke of receiving guarantees of payment for any such undertaking. Burns went away in high dudgeon; but not till he had taken out of his pocket and poked in the man's nose sundry coins of the realm, to show of course that he was no beggar. Soon after the typographer discovered who his visitor was; and to complete his mortification, when some rural bard from Aberdeenshire called and offered him a volume of poems, he accepted it, and it turned out a total loss.

Burns went, on December 21, to attend a meeting held to celebrate the birthday of Charles Edward. The Jacobite feeling in Scotland had in forty years nearly expired, and so it had in Burns' bosom. He carried only embers to embers, and yet he produced an ode upon the occasion, of which Dr. Currie has preserved a few stanzas. In this incident we see a proof that Burns was already becoming known beyond the fashionable and literary circles of Edinburgh; although it is doubtful if this were altogether an enviable position. It led to encroachments on his time, probably to temptations, and certainly brought him into company not quite worthy of him. On the 13th of January, 1787, we find him at a great Mason-lodge meeting, where the Grand Master proposed his health as Caledonia's Bard, Brother Burns; and he, trembling in every nerve, made the best return in his power, and was consoled, while sitting down amidst the vehement applause of the audience, by overhearing the loud whisper of the Grand Master, " Very well indeed! " How we wish that Wilkie or some other genuine Scottish painter had given us this scene in colours—" Burns at a Grand Mason-lodge Meeting! " Alas! that of this splendid meeting, with all its grand worshipfuls and grand officers, nobles, lawyers, squires, and merchants, that one trembling figure, Brother Burns, sitting down bashful and blushing to the toe-points, and comforted by a friendly compliment accented aloud for his ear, is the only figure that would now be recognized!

In this transition time, between his first arrival in Edinburgh and the publication of his second edition, we notice some pleasing incidents in his history and traits in his character. Still he had not forgotten his true-hearted Ayrshire friends, and might have sung, had he then produced, the beautiful and melting strain—

" Of a' the airts the win' can blaw,
I dearly lo'e the West."

He kept up correspondence with John Ballantyne, Gavin Hamilton, Dr. Mackenzie, and others of his bosom cronies. He wrote also to Mrs. Dunlop, who introduced him, through his writings, to Dr. Moore, famous in his day for his two novels, both of which we happen to have read (few, we suspect, can say so now-a-days)—" Zeluco " and " Edward "—the one a kind of sulphureous Byronic tale, the other a much more pleasing and unpretending production; also, for his " Views of Society and Manners on the Continent," popular, too, once, and legible still, but who is remembered by people now chiefly as the father of Sir John Moore, and the friend of Robert Burns.

Burns gradually surrounded himself, or was surrounded, by a somewhat lower set of associates than the Caledonian Hunt or the Monboddo circle. Perhaps he did this from taste, as Dandie Dinmont preferred the society and viands of Mrs. Allan, Guy Mannering's housekeeper, to those of the Colonel's dining-room; or perhaps he did so to secure greater freedom in his talk and deportment. Among them were men of great ability, such as Willie Nicol of the High School, Nasmyth the painter, and Smellie the printer. Smellie was a very remarkable man, full of various knowledge, particularly in natural history, of rough humour and sagacity—the only man of the circle quite a match for Burns in conversation and repartee.

Burns used a claymore, sometimes a dirk; Smellie wielded a sledge hammer, more formidable and resistless still. In Smellie's forgotten memoirs we find a strange story, which we may quote, as we think it is very little known. Smellie and his friend Greenlaw entered into an agreement, which was reduced to writing, signed with their blood, and formally sealed by both parties, in which they mutually engaged that whoever should die first should return, if possible, and give an account of the world of spirits, under the proviso that if the deceased did not return by the expiration of twelve months, it was to be concluded that he was not permitted to come back. Greenlaw died on the 26th June, 1744. When the year subsequent to his death had nearly expired, Mr. Smellie became exceedingly anxious about the expected visit. After losing several nights' sleep successively in watching for the reappearance of his deceased friend, he fell fast asleep one evening in his elbow chair, when, in a dream, he saw a vision of Greenlaw attired in the usual costume of a ghost. This phantom, addressing him with an impressive solemnity of tone, informed him that he had experienced great difficulty in procuring permission to return to the earth according to their agreement; that he was now in a much better world than the one he had left; and yet that the hopes and wishes of its inhabitants were by no means satisfied, as, like those of the lower world, they still looked forward to the hope of reaching a higher state of existence. Both Smellie and Lord Monboddo, two of the ablest men of the time, were convinced of the supernatural character of this dream. We rather like the theory it implies, of future existence rising in an everlasting series of progression and improvement toward a roofless heaven.

In Smellie's office Burns was a frequent visitor, appeared in his buckskins and buff, cracking his whip and his jests, and had one stool appropriated to him, which, as far down as 1844, was extant, and known as Burns' stool. Sir John Dalrymple (a well-known humorist of that age, author of a very clever *jeu d'esprit* on a "Country House") had one day unwittingly occupied it, and was requested to surrender it to Burns, who stood by unknown to the baronet. "I won't surrender my seat to that impudent, staring fellow." "That's Burns the Poet." "Good gracious!" said Dalrymple, "give him all the seats in the house!" Smellie introduced Burns to a club called the "Crochallan Fencibles" (Crochallan, from the title of a Gaelic song sung by Douglas the landlord, *Chro Chalein*, "Colin's Cattle" and "Fencibles," from certain regiments bearing his name for fighting in the American war), including Smellie, William Dunbar, W.S., Willie Nicol, and others. Dunbar gave Burns a copy of Spenser's "Faëry Queen," and he undoubtedly would lose no time in plunging amidst the beautiful and mystic mazes of that poem, although we think he would value it less than Shakspeare or Milton, would feel more faith in than love for it, while hope especially would be required to sustain him to the close. He had been rather long in seeking out Blacklock, his generous friend; but found him at last, and greatly enjoyed the warm grasp of his hand (there is none so warm as that of a fine-hearted blind man) and the glimmer of his eyes, which never rolled so much to see the day and the poet's face with it, as now. To Nasmyth he sat for his portrait, which Beugo engraved, and which has been so often reproduced — unquestionably a good likeness, although Scott thinks it less massive than the original. Nasmyth once had dined with Burns; and having both exceeded the bounds of moderation, they agreed not to go to bed, but to make an expedition to the Pentland Hills. On their way, hearing a loud noise in a cottage, and entering in, they found a man who had suddenly been bereft of his reason. The effect of the cries and gestures of the lunatic upon Burns' nerves, somewhat shattered by the revel of the previous night, was appalling. After rambling all night they returned to Roslin to breakfast, which the hostess (a Mrs. David Wilson) supplied in the old Scotch style; and Burns, in his gratitude, scrawled on the reverse side of a wooden platter the verses—

"My blessings on you, honest wife,
 I ne'er was here before,
You've walth o' gear for spoon and knife;
 Heart could not wish for more.

Heaven keep you clear of sturt and strife,
 Till far ayont four score;
And by the Lord o' death and life,
 I'll ne'er gae by your door."

The Second Edition at last appeared in 1787. It was prefaced by a dedication to the Caledonian Hunt, and followed by a list of subscribers amounting to 1500 names, and accounting for 2800 copies. It was the first copy of Burns we ever read, when eight or nine years old, is a large thick octavo, and is for the age beautifully got up and printed. We met it again lately, and find among the list of subscribers (besides those enumerated by Chambers, which are chiefly nobility and gentry) the following distinguished names:—Miss Burnet, Dr. Blair, Dr. Blacklock, Dr. Black, Mr. Brougham of Brougham Hall (Lord Brougham's father), Rev. George Baird (afterwards Principal Baird), David Bridges,* John Clerk (Lord Eldin), Dr. Carlyle, (Jupiter Carlyle of Inveresk), Dr. Cullen, Alexander Wood, Professor Dalziel, Henry Erskine, Dr. Gregory, Lord Hailes, Malcolm Laing, Adam of the High

---

* Father of old David Bridges, "Director-General of the Fine Arts," as the Blackwood wags christened him, a singularly smart and sagacious man, famous for his pun at a masquerade. To one who asked him, "Mr. Bridges, on which of the bridges do you collect the pontage?" "On the *Pons Asinorum*, sir; fools and asses pass free; you may go on, sir."

School, Dr. Adam Ferguson, historian of Rome, Dr. Robertson, historian of Scotland, Dr. Henry, historian of England, Rev. Henry Hunter, afterwards of London Wall (translator of "Paul and Virginia," author of "Sermons"), Rev. Mr. Greenfield (father of Lord Rutherford, who had to flee from Edinburgh owing to a frightful scandal, and was thought long by some the author of the Waverley Novels), Dugald Stewart, Henry Mackenzie, Adam Smith, Gilbert Burns, besides other names, some from the Colonies, the Continent, and America, a good many from England, the most from Glasgow and the west of Scotland. In this new edition Burns inserted a number of pieces, some old, but which he had not previously ventured to print; such as "Death and Dr. Hornbook," "The Ordination," "The Unco Guid," "John Barleycorn," and a few other small poems and songs. The "Brigs of Ayr," "Tam Samson's Elegy," "A Fragment," and an "Address to Edinburgh," had been composed since his first volume appeared, but were now published for the first time in the second. It was received with enthusiasm, and perhaps more warmly welcomed in the Modern Athens than any volume of poems had hitherto been, or was to be, till "The Lay of the Last Minstrel," eighteen years after. Burns had written some lines intended to be inserted under the Earl of Glencairn's picture, and requested permission to print them in the new volume; but for whatever reason the lines do not appear. The price was five shillings. The Caledonian Hunt took one hundred copies at a guinea the copy ; Creech took five hundred copies (for sale, of course); the Earl of Eglinton took forty-two copies ; the Duchess of Gordon, twenty-one ; Robert Muir of Kilmarnock, forty. Some Scottish Colleges abroad also subscribed.

Accounts of Burns' private bearing at this time abound from various writers, ranging from Professor Walker to Sir Walter Scott. We knew Professor Walker in our boyhood, attended his Humanity or Latin class in Glasgow, and received kindness from him. He was a man of very considerable learning, classical taste, and a warm heart. He had, however, a certain degree of pedantry and *petit maitreship* about him, and had been rather spoiled by acting as a tutor in some noble families. To tutors, as a rule then, the frivolities and conventionalisms of the great were sure to adhere, along with a portion of the polish. His measurement of Burns at this period is more that of a martinet than of a manly critic. Hear this, for instance. " His eye was full of mind, and would have been singularly expressive under the *management* of one who could employ it with more art for the purpose of expression." Think of managing by art the expression of two eyes which were compared to two chariot lamps flaming on through a dark night! Manage the eye of Mars as we have seen him this year (1877), glaring fiery red and large as Jove, across a narrow gulf, at Saturn! Professor Wilson has dwelt with merciless force on some similar platitudes in Walker's description of his interview with Burns at Dumfries. Still Walker loved Burns, and speaks of him always with respect as well as affection. He saw his faults; but he evidently regarded him as a man of sterling worth, as well as of transcendent genius, although he had not cultivated the graces under the Duchess of Athole, nor studied the humanities under the amiable and learned Josiah Walker, author of the " Defence of Order" (mercilessly mangled and reduced to chaos by Lord Brougham in the *Edinburgh Review*), and who was better at defending the order of his country than maintaining that of his class. Peace to his memory! We see still his big burly brow, his tall erect figure, his solemn spectacles, his formal manners, disguising an excellent disposition and a very upright character; and hear him still reading to his class (which was that morning supplemented by the presence of Thomas Campbell, then Lord Rector of Glasgow University) a lecture on "Poetry," of great polish and erudition. He wrote "The Defence of Order," a "Life of Burns," and "The Vision of Liberty." He was the Professor, Burns was the Poet, of Humanity.

Walker touches tenderly here on Burns' frailties, although he memorizes the fact that when Burns, at Dr. Blair's table, was asked to name the public place where he had got the most gratification, he named the High Church, and Mr. Walker, the colleague of his entertainer—an excellent preacher doubtless, but whom Dr. Blair naturally rated less highly than himself. Burns probably perceived his mistake in a moment in the astonishment of the company and the silence of his host, but with admirable prudence never alluded to it till years had elapsed, when he expressed to the worthy tutor of Athole his poignant regret. On another occasion he called a clergyman a —— blockhead for first abusing and then misquoting Gray's " Elegy" —" a piece of insolence unpardonable," quoth Christopher North, "at such an early meal as breakfast." These were *lapsus linguæ*. But Dugald Stewart, a higher authority than Josiah Walker, assures us that Burns' conduct and conversation were all that could be wished, that his sense of religion was then very strong; and though he did hear rumours of indulgence and low society, he saw nothing in his own experience but temperance and decorum. Indeed, Burns told him that the weakness of his stomach was such as to deprive him of all merit in his sobriety. It is curious, however, that we never hear of this weakness again till near his end, nor had heard of it before. It was probably brought on by his change of diet in Edinburgh.

Scott's description is too well known to need quotation. Langhorne, the author of the lines which made Burns weep, and which Scott recognized as his, preached in Lincoln's inn Chapel, and besides being popular with the intellectual class among whom he laboured, wrote some well-known works, such as a translation of "Plutarch's Lives" and "The Country Justice," containing the lines referred to. All that Burns said to Scott, after his modest interference, was, "Ye'll be *a man yet*," but it fell like a drop of poetic baptism on his brow.

Robert Chambers thinks that Edinburgh did as much for Burns as might have been expected; and yet it amounted only to the paltry sum of £500. He said they did not appreciate Burns so highly as we do, and that the sum raised was very respectable from their point of view. We are forcibly reminded of Burns' own words anent Fergusson—

"A curse upon your whunstane hearts,
 Ye Embrugh gentry;
A tithe of what ye waste on cartes (*cards*),
 Wad stowed his pantry."

The Edinburgh people appreciated Burns intellectually well enough. They gave him plenty of claret and praise; but he could well have wanted a moiety of the first, and the second, even when it was not sheer flummery, did him more harm than good. But they gave him little solid cash, found for him no congenial position, and what was worse, he got accustomed while amongst them to habits and society which unfitted him for the drudgeries and companionships of a country life. To return from venison and champagne to "haggis" and "tippenny;" from the society of Dugald Stewart, Archibald Alison, and Lord Glencairn, to "slee Jamie Smith" and rattling John Rankin; and from Eliza Burnet and the Duchess of Gordon to Jean Armour and Elizabeth Black—was a downcome. To alter what Carlyle says of Edward Irving—"Edinburgh forgot this man, who, alas! could not in his turn forget." We may apply to poor Burns the words of Cowper to the gentle savage, "Omai," who after visiting London, and being admitted to its best society, had to return to his native isles:—

' The dream is past, and thou hast found again
  Thy cocoas and bananas, palms and yams,
 And homestead thatched with leaves; but hast thou found
  Their former charms? and having seen our state,
 Our palaces, our ladies, and our pomp
 Of equipage, our gardens and our sports,
 And heard our music, are thy simple friends,
 Thy simple fare, and all thy plain delights
 As dear to thee as once?"

There was this difference: "Omai" probably wondered that he, a simple savage, should ever have been admitted among society so superior. But Burns had learned in Edinburgh, if he had not learned before, that he was one of Nature's nobility—equal, and more than equal, to the men he met there; and knew that they were to continue to fatten on a birthright he had lost by no fault of his as yet, while he was to be driven away to herd with an inferior grade the rest of his life. If he was too proud for a pension, was there no post they could have found for him of a semi-literary cast? no secretaryship in the then University, like that which broke the fall and made the little fortune of Alexander Smith? no teaching situation in one of their academies or schools? no position in which he might have prosecuted his studies, and obtained a competence, with the hope, too, of rising to a situation better adapted for his extraordinary powers? Perhaps it is too extravagant to think of a plan being started and funds being raised for sending Robert Burns to College. Yet men long after his time of life (twenty-nine) have been sent there, and have profited mightily by their mature studies. Scott, who knew Edinburgh well, speaks of the efforts made to help Burns as extremely trifling. Alas! we fear that the Coleridgean chaplet of henbane, nettles, night-shade, and other dung-hill weeds and flowers of darkness, must continue to adorn

"The illustrious brow of Scotch nobility."

If this be called inconsistent with what we previously said about his Edinburgh patrons being induced to withdraw from Burns by rumours affecting his morals, it will be noticed that we stated, without wholly defending, their conduct in this matter. Besides, his behaviour at first in Edinburgh was irreproachable, and it was then especially that they were called upon to do something effectual in his behalf.

Many of the friendships Burns formed in Edinburgh he believed to be very fragile, and they proved so. There was one valuable one, however — his connection with Robert Ainslie. This gentleman survived Burns long, and became a worthy Writer to the Signet in Edinburgh, an elder in the Church of Scotland, and, we think, the author of a little religious *brochure* once very popular in Scotland—"A Father's Gift to his Children." In his youthful days he was gay and gamesome as a young buck, acting as an apprentice to a Mr. Samuel Mitchelson, a writer in Carrubbers Close, an acquaintance of Smollett's —about twenty years of age when Burns first knew him, and distinguished by his bonhomie and kind-heartedness, as well as by his young literary enthusiasm. Burns and he became very intimate. Probably they often heard together the chimes of midnight, but one anecdote is very creditable to the temperance of both. Burns called on Ainslie one spring afternoon. Ainslie produced a bottle of excellent wine. Burns exclaimed, "We don't require any artificial stimulus to sharpen our wits," and proposed a walk to Arthur's Seat; and Ainslie used to declare that he never found the poet more delightful than during that walk and the sober tea-drinking which followed. Burns was now revolving a visit to the South, and Robert Ainslie, a native of Berwickshire, agreed to go along with him.

CHAPTER IX.

BURNS IN THE SOUTH, WEST, AND NORTH.

BURNS, ere leaving Edinburgh, had got acquainted with James Johnson, an engraver, who was already projecting his "Museum of Scottish Songs," with their appropriate tunes, to which the Poet became a contributor, sending him "Green Grows the Rashes" and "Young Peggy blooms the fairest Lass."

He left Edinburgh 5th May, 1787, along with Ainslie, for Berrywell, near Dunse, where the father of the latter, land-steward to Lord Douglas, resided. He travelled on horseback, and had just mounted when a letter was shot into his hand from Dr. Blair (which will be found in the Correspondence). It is kind, but formal and stilted. It recommends Burns to take time and leisure to mature and improve his talents, "for on any second production you give to the world your fate as a poet will very much depend." Burns laughed, thrust the letter into his pocket, and exclaimed, "Thank you, doctor; but whiles a man's first book, like his first bairn, is his best." It was, in fact, Burns' first and last book. He was constantly adding to it, and new editions of it were issued, but no supplementary volume ever appeared in his lifetime.

Perhaps the moment when Burns mounted his horse for the South may be called his completed culmination. He was leaving Edinburgh triumphant in literary success, and outwardly unstained, respected, and beloved by several circles—leaving it a free, unfettered man, with a little money in his pocket, a kindred spirit by his side, the lands of Scottish romance and poetry before him, and the blue sky of early summer above him, reflecting the joy of his bosom; and he felt with George Herbert as if

"There was no month but May."

Ayrshire, with all its sorrows and humiliations, was far distant. And yet now and then as he rode gaily along, and, like the Canterbury Pilgrims, carolled as he pursued his way, his prophetic soul might whisper to him that, though the main wing of the storm was scattered—

"The sullen rear
Was, with its stored thunder, labouring up."

He was carrying his temperament, his pride, his passions, as well as his genius and his prestige, with him to the South; and if with the latter there was great glory, with the former there was danger equally great. He was ostensibly in this journey a farmer in search of a farm; less ostensibly, he was a "Cœlebs in search of a wife," and we find him more than once on the point of finding, or rather being found of, one. But his matrimonial destiny did not lie—perhaps it had been better had it lain—in the South.

We quote here the "Journal" as far as Carlisle, and append a few remarks :—

"Left Edinburgh (*May* 5, 1787)—Lammermuir hills miserably dreary, but at times very picturesque. Langtonedge, a glorious view of the Merse; reach Berrywell. Old Mr. Ainslie an uncommon character—his hobbies, agriculture, natural philosophy, and politics. In the first he is unexceptionably the clearest-headed, best-informed man I ever met with; in the other two, very intelligent. As a man of business he has uncommon merit, and by fairly deserving it has made a very decent independence. Mrs. Ainslie, an excellent, sensible, cheerful, amiable old woman.* Miss Ainslie—her person a little *embonpoint*, but handsome; her face, particularly her eyes, full of sweetness and good-humour; she unites three qualities rarely to be found together—keen, solid observation; sly witty observation and remark; and the gentlest, most unaffected female modesty. Douglas, a clever, fine, promising young fellow. The family-meeting with their brother, my *compagnon de voyage*, very charming—particularly the sister. The whole family remarkably attached to their menials: Mrs. A. full of stories of the sagacity and sense of the little girl in the kitchen. Mr.

---

* The account of the Ainslie family is not more flattering than we believe true. Of Rachel's fate we know nothing, but that she died in single blessedness. Her brother Robert had several daughters and a son. His eldest daughter was very beautiful, and married, we believe, a Dr. Farquharson of Edinburgh. His younger, Esther, married the Rev. John Robertson, Secession minister of Dunse. She had been originally engaged to Swinton of Swinton, Berwickshire, who died before marriage. Before marriage she kept the house of Douglas Ainslie of Cairnbank, near Dunse, who was a writer, and factor for many estates in the county, made a great deal of money, and left it partly to Esther and partly to a nephew, Sir Douglas Ainslie, whose only child is now Mrs. Grant Duff. Chambers says that Robert Ainslie, whom he met often, always spoke of Burns with the greatest affection, as the finest fellow as well as the greatest genius he ever knew.

A. high in the praises of an African, his house-servant; all his people old in his service. Douglas's old nurse came to Berrywell yesterday to remind them of its being his birthday.

"A Mr. Dudgeon,* a poet at times, a worthy, remarkable character—natural penetration, a great deal of information, some genius, and extreme modesty.

"*Sunday (May 6)*—Went to church at Dunse—Dr. Bowmaker, a man of strong lungs and pretty judicious remark; but ill-skilled in propriety, and altogether unconscious of his want of it.

"*Monday (May 7)*—Coldstream—went over to England—Cornhill—glorious river Tweed—clear and majestic —fine bridge.

"Dine at Coldstream† with Mr. Ainslie and Mr. Foreman; beat Mr. F. in a dispute about Voltaire. Tea at Lennel House with Mr. Brydone. ‡ Mr. Brydone a most excellent heart, kind, joyous, and benevolent, but a good deal of the French indiscriminate complaisance—from his situation, past and present, an admirer of everything that bears a splendid title or that possesses a large estate. Mrs. Brydone § a most elegant woman in her person and manners, the tones of her voice remarkably sweet; my reception extremely flattering. Sleep at Coldstream.

"*Tuesday (May 8)*—Breakfast at Kelso—charming situation of Kelso—fine bridge over the Tweed—enchanting views and prospects on both sides of the river, particularly the Scotch side; introduced to Mr. Scott of the Royal Bank, an excellent, modest fellow—fine situation of it—ruins of Roxburgh Castle—a holly-bush growing where James II. of Scotland was accidentally killed by the bursting of a cannon. A small old religious ruin and a fine old garden planted by the religious, rooted out and destroyed by an English Hottentot—a *maître d'hotel* of the duke's, a Mr. Cole. Climate and soil of Berwickshire, and even Roxburghshire, superior to Ayrshire—bad roads. Turnip and sheep husbandry, their great improvements. Mr. M'Dowal at Caverton Mill, a friend of Mr. Ainslie's, with whom I dined to-day, sold his sheep, ewe and lamb together, at two guineas a piece. Wash their sheep before shearing—seven or eight pounds of washing wool in a fleece — low markets, consequently low rents — fine lands not above sixteen shillings a Scotch acre—magnificence of farmers and farm-houses. Come up Teviot and up Jed to Jedburgh to lie, and so wish myself a good-night.

"*Wednesday (May 9)*—Breakfast with Mr. —— in Jedburgh—a squabble between Mrs. ——, a crazed, talkative slattern, and a sister of her's, an old maid, respecting a Relief minister. Miss gives Madam the lie; and Madam, by way of revenge, upbraids her that she laid snares to entangle the said minister, then a widower, in the net of matrimony. Go about two miles out of Jedburgh to a roup of parks—meet a polite soldier-like gentleman, Captain Rutherford, who had been many years through the wilds of America, a prisoner among the Indians. Charming, romantic situation of Jedburgh, with gardens, orchards, &c., intermingled among the houses— fine old ruins—a once magnificent cathedral and strong castle. All the towns here have the appearance of old, rude grandeur, but the people extremely idle—Jed, a fine romantic little river.

"Dine with Captain Rutherford—the captain a polite fellow, fond of money in his farming way; showed a particular respect to my bardship—his lady, exactly a proper matrimonial second part for him. Miss Rutherford, a beautiful girl.

"Return to Jedburgh—walk up Jed with some ladies, to be shown Love Lane and Blackburn, two fairy scenes. Introduced to Mr. Potts, writer, a very clever fellow; and Mr. Somerville, the clergyman of the place, a man and a gentleman, but sadly addicted to punning. ‖ The walking party of ladies, Mrs. —— and Miss —— her sister, before mentioned. *N.B.*—These two appear still more comfortably ugly and stupid, and bore me most shockingly. Two Miss —— tolerably agreeable. Miss Hope, a tolerably pretty girl, fond of laughing and fun. Miss Lindsay, a good-humoured, amiable girl; rather short *et embonpoint*, but handsome, and extremely graceful; beautiful hazel eyes, full of spirit, and sparkling with delicious moisture; an engaging face, *un tout ensemble* that speaks her of the first order of female minds; her sister, a bonnie, strappin', rosy, sonsie lass. Shake myself loose, after several unsuccessful efforts, of Mrs. —— and Miss ——, and, somehow or other, get hold of Miss

---

* Dudgeon was the author of the once popular song—"Up amang yon cliffy rocks."

† It was at Coldstream that the famous scene described by Ainslie occurred. Ainslie suggested that they should cross the Tweed, and then Burns could say he had been in England. They did so, and were walking slowly along, when suddenly Burns, to Mr. Ainslie's great surprise, threw off his hat, knelt down, and lifted up his hands and in an attitude and tones of the greatest enthusiasm, looking the while back to Scotland, proceeded to repeat the last stanzas in the "Cotter's Saturday Night"—

"O Scotia, my dear, my native soil," &c.

‡ Brydone, the traveller, who was once tabooed for holding what is now the general opinion about the Mosaic account of the creation. His book of travels contains a very pleasant narrative of adventures in Sicily and Malta, including an account of an ascent of Mount Etna, and may even yet be perused with gratification.

§ Daughter of Dr. Robertson the historian.

‖ Dr. Somerville was father-in-law of the distinguished Mary Somerville, afterwards Madame Greg. A gentleman met her in her second marriage time, and after talk, said, "The most brilliant woman I ever met except Mary Somerville," and was told to his surprise she was Mary Somerville! Dr. Somerville's "Memoirs of Our Own Times" have been some time since published. He wrote also a "History of England" during the reigns of William and Anne. He never punned, it is said, after reading the above. He lived to a great age. We think we have read a reply to Tom Paine's "Rights of Man" from his pen.

Lindsay's arm. My heart is thawed into melting pleasure after being so long frozen up in the Greenland bay of indifference, amid the noise and nonsense of Edinburgh. Miss seems very well pleased with my bardship's distinguishing her; and after some slight qualms, which I could easily mark, she sets the titter round at defiance, and kindly allows me to keep my hold; and when parted by the ceremony of my introduction to Mr. Somerville, she met me half, to resume my situation. *Nota Bene*.—The poet within a point and a half of being —— in love; I am afraid my bosom is still nearly as much tinder as ever.

"The old, cross-grained, Whiggish, ugly, slanderous Miss ——, with all the poisonous spleen of a disappointed, ancient maid, stops me very unseasonably to ease her bursting breast, by falling abusively foul on the Miss Lindsays, particularly on my Dulcinea; I hardly refrain from cursing her to her face for daring to mouth her calumnious slander on one of the finest pieces of the workmanship of Almighty Excellence! Sup at Mr. ——'s; vexed that the Miss Lindsays are not of the supper party, as they only are wanting. Mrs. —— and Miss —— still improve infernally on my hands.

"Set out next morning for Wauchope, the seat of my correspondent, Mrs. Scott—breakfast by the way with Dr. Elliot, an agreeable, good-hearted, climate-beaten old veteran, in the medical line, now retired to a romantic, but rather moorish place, on the banks of the Rule—he accompanies us almost to Wauchope; we traverse the country to the top of Bochester, the scene of an old encampment, and Woolee Hill.*

"Wauchope.—Mr. Scott exactly the figure and face commonly given to Sancho Panza; very shrewd in his farming matters, and not unfrequently stumbles on what may be called a strong thing rather than a good thing. Mrs. Scott all the sense, taste, intrepidity of face, and bold, critical decision, which usually distinguish female authors. Sup with Mr. Potts—agreeable party. Breakfast next morning with Mr. Somerville—the *bruit* of Miss Lindsay and my bardship, by means of the invention and malice of Miss ——. Mr. Somerville sends to Dr. Lindsay, begging him and family to breakfast if convenient, but at all events to send Miss Lindsay;† accordingly, Miss Lindsay only comes. I find Miss Lindsay would soon play the devil with me; I met with some little flattering attentions from her. Mrs. Somerville, an excellent, motherly, agreeable woman, and a fine family. Mr. Ainslie and Mrs. S ——, junr., with Mr. ——, Miss Lindsay, and myself, go to see *Esther* [Easton], a very remarkable woman for reciting poetry of all kinds, and sometimes making Scotch doggerel herself—she can repeat by heart almost everything she has ever read, particularly Pope's 'Homer' from end to end; has studied Euclid by herself; and, in short, is a woman of very extraordinary abilities. On conversing with her, I find her fully equal to the character given of her. She is very much flattered that I send for her, and that she sees a poet who has put out a book, as she says. She is, among other things, a great florist, and is rather past the meridian of once celebrated beauty.

"I walk in *Esther's* garden with Miss Lindsay, and after some little chit-chat of the tender kind, I presented her with a proof print of my *nob*, which she accepted with something more tender than gratitude. She told me many little stories which Miss —— had retailed concerning her and me with prolonging pleasure—God bless her! Was waited on by the magistrates, and presented with the freedom of the burgh.‡

"Took farewell of Jedburgh, with some melancholy, disagreeable sensations. Jed, pure be thy crystal streams, and hallowed be thy sylvan banks! Sweet Isabella Lindsay, may peace dwell in thy bosom, uninterrupted except by the tumultuous throbbings of rapturous love! That love-kindling eye must beam on another, not on me; that graceful form must bless another's arms, not mine!

"Kelso.—Dine with the Farmers' Club—all gentlemen, talking of high matters; each of them keeps a hunter from £30 to £50 value, and attends the fox-huntings in the county. Go out with Mr. Ker, one of the club, and a friend of Mr. Ainslie's, to lie. Mr. Ker, a most gentlemanly, clever, handsome fellow, a widower with some fine children; his mind and manner astonishingly like my dear old friend Robert Muir in Kilmarnock; everything in Mr. Ker's most elegant; he offers to accompany me in my English tour. Dine with Sir Alexander Don,§ a pretty clever fellow, but far from being a match for his divine lady. A very wet day. . . . Sleep at Stodrig again, and set out for Melrose; visit Dryburgh, a fine old ruined abbey; still bad weather; cross Leader, and come up Tweed to Melrose; dine there, and visit that far-famed, glorious ruin; come to Selkirk, up Ettrick; the whole country hereabout, both on Tweed and Ettrick, remarkably stony.||

---

* Mrs. Scott of Wauchope, whose poetical correspondence will be found elsewhere in the Poetry.

† Isabella Lindsay, who so fascinated the bard, and who was a most amiable woman, was married to Mr. Adam Armstrong, who held some post under the Russian Government. She died young, leaving four children. Her youngest son was director of the Royal Mint at St. Petersburg.

‡ The usual "riddle of Claret" was presented to Burns; he insisted on paying it himself, but was overruled.

§ Sir Alexander Don's "divine lady" was Lady Harriett Don, sister of the Earl of Glencairn.

|| Dr. Clarkson, of Selkirk, along with two other gentlemen, were sitting in Veitch's inn at Selkirk when Ainslie and Burns arrived "like twa drookit craws." The travellers soon after sent Veitch in to ask them to take a glass with them. The Doctor objected, and asked Mr. Veitch what like the men were? Mr. Veitch said, "he could

"*Monday* (*May* 14).—Come to Inverleithen, a famous spa, and in the vicinity of the palace of Traquair, where, having dined, and drank some Galloway-whey, I here remain till to-morrow; saw Elibanks and Elibraes, on the other side of the Tweed.*

"*Tuesday.*—Drank tea yesternight at Pirn with Mr. Horsburgh. Breakfasted to-day with Mr. Ballantyne of Hollylee. Proposal for a four-horse team, to consist of Mr. Scott of Wauchope, Fittieland; Logan of Logan, Fittiefur; Ballantyne of Hollylee, Forewynd; Horsburgh of Horsburgh. Dine at a country inn, kept by a miller, in Earlston, the birthplace and residence of the celebrated Thomas à Rhymer—saw the ruins of his castle—come to Berrywell.

"*Wednesday.*—Dine at Dunse with the Farmers' Club —company, impossible to do them justice—Rev. Mr. Smith, a famous punster, and Mr. Meikle, a celebrated mechanic, and inventor of the thrashing-mill. *Thursday*, breakfast at Berrywell, and walk into Dunse to see a famous knife made by a cutler there, and to be presented to an Italian prince. A pleasant ride with my friend Mr. Robert Ainslie and his sister to Mr. Thomson's, a man who has newly commenced farmer, and has married a Miss Patty Grieve, formerly a flame of Mr. Robert Ainslie's. Company, Miss Jacky Grieve, an amiable sister of Mrs. Thomson's, and Mr. Hood, an honest, worthy, facetious farmer in the neighbourhood.

"*Friday.*—Ride to Berwick—an idle town, rudely picturesque. Meet Lord Errol in walking round the walls; his lordship's flattering notice of me. Dine with Mr. Clunzie, merchant; nothing particular in company or conversation. Come up a bold shore, and over a wild country, to Eyemouth; sup and sleep at Mr. Grieve's.

"*Saturday.*—Spend the day at Mr. Grieve's; made a royal-arch mason of St. Abb's Lodge. Mr. William Grieve, the eldest brother, a joyous, warm-hearted, jolly, clever fellow—takes a hearty glass, and sings a good song. Mr. Robert, his brother and partner in trade, a good fellow, but says little. Take a sail after dinner. Fishing of all kinds pays tithes at Eyemouth.

"*Sunday* (*May* 20).—A Mr. Robertson, brewer at Ednam, sets out with us to Dunbar.

"The Miss Grieves very good girls. My bardship's heart got a brush from Miss Betsy.

"Mr. William Grieve's attachment to the family-circle; so fond, that when he is out, which, by the by, is often the case, he cannot go to bed till he sees if all his sisters are sleeping well. Pass the famous Abbey of Coldingham, and Pease-bridge. Call at Mr. Sheriff's, where Mr. A. and I dine. Mr. S. talkative and conceited. I talk of love to Nancy the whole evening, while her brother escorts home some companions like himself. Sir James Hall † of Dunglass, having heard of my being in the neighbourhood, comes to Mr. Sheriff's to breakfast; takes me to see his fine scenery on the stream of Dunglass—Dunglass the most romantic sweet place I ever saw—Sir James and his lady a pleasant happy couple. He points out a walk for which he has an uncommon respect, as it was made by an aunt of his, to whom he owes much.

"Miss —— will accompany me to Dunbar, by way of making a parade of me as a sweetheart of hers among her relations. She mounts an old cart-horse, as huge and as lean as a house; a rusty old side-saddle without girth or stirrup, but fastened on with an old pillion-girth—herself as fine as hands could make her, in cream-coloured riding-clothes, hat and feather, &c. I, ashamed of my situation, ride like the devil, and almost shake her to pieces on old Jolly—get rid of her by refusing to call at her uncle's with her.

"Passed through the most glorious corn country I ever saw till I reach Dunbar, a neat little town. Dine with Provost Fall, an eminent merchant, and most respectable character, but undescribable, as he exhibits no marked traits. Mrs. Fall a genius in painting; fully more clever in the fine arts and sciences than my friend Lady Wauchope,‡ without her consummate assurance of her own abilities. Call with Mr. Robinson (whom, by the by, I find to be a worthy, much respected man, very modest; warm, social heart, which with less good sense than his would be, perhaps, with the children of prim precision and pride, rather inimical to that respect which is man's due from man)—with him I call on Miss Clarke, a maiden, in the Scotch phrase, *guid enough, but no brent new;* a clever woman, with tolerable pretensions to remark and wit, while time had blown the blushing bud of bashful modesty into the flower of easy confidence. She wanted to see what sort of *raree show* an author was; and to let him know that though Dunbar was but a little town, yet it was not destitute of people of parts.

"Breakfast next morning at Skateraw, at Mr. Lee's, a farmer of great note. Mr. Lee, an excellent, hospitable, social fellow, rather oldish—warm-hearted and chatty—a most judicious, sensible farmer. Mr. Lee detains me till next morning. Company at dinner; my rev. acquaintance, Dr. Bowmaker, a rattling old fellow. Two sea lieu-

---

hardly say; that the one spoke rather like a gentleman, but the other was a drover-like chap." So they refused to admit them. It was not till after three days that Clarkson discovered that he had *cut* Burns, and he never forgave himself for it till his dying day! While sitting in Selkirk inn Burns wrote a letter to Creech, including a clever copy of verses, entitled "Willie's Awa'."

* Burns seems to have taken some detours of considerable length to Inverleithen and Earlston, to see the "Bush aboon Traquair," Elibank, the Cowdenknowes, and other spots famous in the history of Scottish song.

† Sir James Hall of Dunglass was father of the famous Basil Hall.

‡ Mrs. Scott.

tenants; a cousin of the landlord's, a fellow whose looks are of that kind which deceived me in a gentleman at Kelso, and have often deceived me: a goodly handsome figure and face, which incline one to give them credit for parts which they have not. Mr. Clarke a much cleverer fellow, but whose looks a little cloudy, and his appearance rather ungainly, with an everyday observer may prejudice the opinion against him. Dr. Brown, a medical young gentleman from Dunbar, a fellow whose face and manners are open and engaging. Leave Skateraw for Dunse next day, along with Collector ——, a lad of slender abilities, and bashfully diffident to an extreme.

"Found Miss Ainslie—the amiable, the sensible, the good-humoured, the sweet Miss Ainslie—all alone at Berrywell. Heavenly Powers, who know the weakness of human hearts, support mine! What happiness must I see, only to remind me that I cannot enjoy it!

"Lammermuir Hills, from East Lothian to Dunse, very wild. Dine with the Farmers' Club at Kelso. Sir John Hume and Mr. Lumsden there; but nothing worth remembrance when the following circumstance is considered: I walk into Dunse before dinner, and out to Berrywell in the evening with Miss Ainslie; how well-bred, how frank, how good she is! Charming Rachel! may thy bosom never be wrung by the evils of this life of sorrows, or by the villany of this world's sons!*

"*Thursday* (*May* 24).—Mr. Ker and I set out to dinner at Mr. Hood's, on our way to England.

"I am taken extremely ill with strong feverish symptoms, and take a servant of Mr. Hood's to watch me all night; embittering remorse scares my fancy at the gloomy forebodings of death. I am determined to live for the future in such a manner as not to be scared at the approach of death; I am sure I could meet him with indifference, but for 'the something beyond the grave.' Mr. Hood agrees to accompany us to England if we will wait till Sunday.

"*Friday.*—I go with Mr. Hood to see a roup of an unfortunate farmer's stock; rigid economy and decent industry, do you preserve me from being the principal *dramatis persona* in such a scene of horror!

"Meet my good old friend Mr. Ainslie, who calls on Mr. Hood in the evening to take farewell of my bardship. This day I feel myself warm with sentiments of gratitude to the Great Preserver of men, who has kindly restored me to health and strength once more.

"A pleasant walk with my young friend Douglas Ainslie—a sweet, modest, clever young fellow.

"*Sunday* (*May* 27).—Cross Tweed, and traverse the moors through a wild country till I reach Alnwick—Alnwick Castle, a seat of the Duke of Northumberland, furnished in a most princely manner. A Mr. Wilkin,

* At this point Robert Ainslie left him for Edinburgh.

agent of his Grace's, shows us the house and policies. Mr. Wilkin a discreet, sensible, ingenious man.

"*Monday.*—Come, still through by-ways, to Warkworth, where we dine. Hermitage an old castle. Warkworth situated very picturesquely, with Coquet Island, a small rocky spot, the seat of an old monastery, facing it a little in the sea, and the small but romantic river Coquet running through it. Sleep at Morpeth, a pleasant enough little town, and on next day to Newcastle. Meet with a very agreeable sensible fellow, a Mr. Chattox, who shows us a great many civilities, and who dines and sups with us.

"*Wednesday.*—Left Newcastle early in the morning, and rode over a fine country to Hexham to breakfast; from Hexham to Wardrew, the celebrated spa, where we slept. *Thursday* (*May* 31).—Reach Longtown to dine, and part there with my good friends, Messrs. Hood and Ker. A hiring day in Longtown. I am uncommonly happy to see so many young folks enjoying life. I come to Carlisle. (Meet a strange enough romantic adventure by the way, in falling in with a girl and her married sister. The girl, after some overtures of gallantry on my side, sees me a little cut with the bottle, and offers to take me in for a Gretna-green affair. I, not being quite such a gull as she imagines, make an appointment with her, by way of *vive la bagatelle*, to hold a conference on it when we reach town. I meet her in town, and give her a brush of caressing and a bottle of cider; but finding herself *un peu trompée* in her man, she sheers off). Next day (*June* 1) I meet my good friend Mr. Mitchell, and walk with him round the town and its environs, and through his printing-works, &c.—four or five hundred people employed, many of them women and children. Dine with Mr. Mitchell, and leave Carlisle. Come by the coast to Annan. Overtaken on the way by a curious old fish of a shoemaker, and miner from Cumberland mines."

From Carlisle he went to Annan, and then to Dumfries and Dalswinton, where he saw some of Patrick Miller's farms, but as yet took none of them. He came thence by Sanquhar to Mauchline, and reached Mossgiel and his relatives on the 9th June, all at once, as if he had dropped from the clouds. Their words were quiet and few; their emotions too deep for their words or tears. "Oh, Robert!" his mother exclaimed. What these words said, and what they left unsaid! How often they had all sighed—

"O for him back again,
We wish we had him back again!"

And here, back again, "rantin', rovin' Robin" was once more. He called next on the Armours, and was received, he thought, with an excess of servility which disgusted him. He saw his little daughter, too, and of course Jean, with whom he again became intimate. His letters written this month to James Smith and William Nicol show him in a wretched state of mind—satiated with success, sick of Edinburgh and its *eclat*, worn out, probably, with the fatigues, and ashamed of the occasional excesses of his journey, intensely dissatisfied with the friends of Jean, if still in a manner enamoured of Jean herself, and gloomily pondering the uncertainties of the future—altogether in a fitting mood for committing suicide, or buying a copy of Milton to study the character of that great personage Satan! He chose, and it was safer surely, the latter alternative. Even Daddie Auld or Black Jock might have thought it better for Burns to purchase the devil's *simulacrum* than to go to himself!

Restless and unhappy, he did not remain long at this time in Mauchline; he disappeared as suddenly as he had arrived, going—some say to Edinburgh, others only to Glasgow—and re-appearing in a short time, having first sent home a lot of dresses of mode silk to his relatives. Mrs. Begg was sent to Ayr to assist in making them up for herself and her mother; and when she returned he had come back, and insisted on her putting her dress on that he might see how well she looked in it. For them at least he had no feelings but respect and affection, and how considerate as well as kind was this conduct on his part! It was either on this journey, or shortly afterwards, that he paid a flying visit to the West Highlands, and in passing he might see the relatives and the grave of Highland Mary. "Come like shadows, so depart," seems to have been his motto at this time. How he went to Inveraray we know not, but we find him there in huge wrath at being rejected from the castle by the Duke, and writing on the window the well-known epigram—

> "Whoe'er he be that sojourns here,
>   I pity much his case,
> Unless he come to wait upon
>   The Lord their God, his Grace.
>
> There's naething here but Highland pride,
>   And Highland scab and hunger:
> If Providence has sent me here,
>   'Twas surely in an anger."

We are reminded here of Alexander Smith, who once in a letter to us contrasted very humorously two visits of his to the western metropolis of the Highlands. In the first he lodged in the "worst inn's worst room" for some eighteen-pence, in a bed where he found himself never less alone than when alone; and in the second, after he had become famous, he was lodged like a prince in the grand mansion of the MacCallummore, and handed down the Duchess to dinner. Burns made only one visit to Inveraray. Thence he "recoiled into the wilderness," and reached Arrochar through a country whose "savage streams tumble down savage mountains, thinly overspread with savage flocks, which starvingly support savage inhabitants." On his way back he met with some "savage hospitality" to boot; and in riding, half seas over, a race with a Highlander who was wholly so, he and his famous mare, Jenny Geddes, came to the ground, and the bard was terribly bruised. In the too hospitable house at Lochlomond he is thought to have composed his lines on a "Highland Welcome." He tells his correspondent, in the same letter in which he records his misadventure, of a flirtation he was carrying on with a lady of good condition, but somewhat distant and cold to him when he approached the consummation of the matter. Of this lady little is known, except that nothing came of the affair, and that she was from Ayrshire. He returned in July to Mossgiel. While staying there he wrote an "Elegy" on the death of John MacLeod, Younger, of Raasay, with whose family Burns had become acquainted in Edinburgh, indited his famous autobiographical letter to Dr. Moore, and another "Elegy," on the death of Sir James Hunter Blair, an Ayrshire squire, and member of the banking house of Sir William Forbes. After he reached Edinburgh he inclosed this in a copy of verses which he wrote there to Miss Ferrier, afterwards Mrs. General Graham, a sister to Miss Ferrier—author of "Marriage," "The Inheritance," and "Destiny," three excellent Scotch novels—and aunt to the illustrious Professor Ferrier. Burns came to town on the 7th August; it was possibly on this transit that he had the grand reception at Covington Mains. He had need of it to maintain his spirits, for he was now again in a sad scrape. We said he had left Edinburgh outwardly unstained, but there was a girl in that city named Jenny Clow who bore him a hild,[*] and Chambers record that a writ of *In meditatione fugæ*, bearing date August 15, was issued against him, on which he had defiantly written some indecorous old verses. This serves to explain still more fully the gloomy state of his mind at Mossgiel, which he vainly sought to drown in the dissipation of the Highlands. If Burns sinned, he suffered; he was what old divines used to call a "sensible sinner." If his iniquities were much greater than those of other men, his remorse was infinitely deeper and stronger while it endured. If he did not sip at the cup of corruption, but drank of it deep and large, deeper and larger still were his draughts of the cup of misery and shame—yea, he wrung out the bitter dregs withal!

Burns had other business to do in Edinburgh, to transact with Creech, and to prepare for a new tour. Richmond had taken in another lodger, and Burns did not reside with him at this time, but with Willie Nicol, for whom he cherished a warm regard. Nicol was a coarse, irascible savage, with learning, wit, and talent, but without genius or taste; warm-hearted and friendly to his friends, furious and implacable to his foes; one of those men over whose graves friends feel thankful that they have escaped the

---

[*] See Appendix, No. III.

gallows! His conduct to Adam, the gentle and learned Rector of the High School—well known for his writings on Roman Antiquities, &c., better known, perhaps, for his exclamation, as he lay dying, "It is getting dark; you may go home, boys"—was distinguished by a rancorous and persevering cruelty. To Burns he was an uncongenial, troublesome, and dangerous associate; yet some coarse element in the poet's nature attracted him to Nicol, and he chose him as his companion in his northern tour.

We quote, as formerly, the account by Burns himself, down to September 16, when he again arrived in Edinburgh, appending, as before, a few *addenda*:—

"(*Saturday*), 25*th August*, 1787.—I leave Edinburgh for a northern tour, in company with my good friend, Mr. Nicol, whose originality of humour promises me much entertainment. Linlithgow—a fertile improved country —West Lothian. The more elegance and luxury among the farmers, I always observe, in equal proportion, the rudeness and stupidity of the peasantry. This remark I have made all over the Lothians, Merse, Roxburgh, &c. For this, among other reasons, I think that a man of romantic taste, a 'Man of Feeling,' will be better pleased with the poverty, but intelligent minds of the peasantry in Ayrshire (peasantry they are all below the Justice of Peace), than the opulence of a club of Merse farmers, when at the same time he considers the Vandalism of their plough-folks, &c. I carry this idea so far, that an uninclosed, half-improven country is to me actually more agreeable, and gives me more pleasure as a prospect, than a country cultivated like a garden. Soil about Linlithgow light and thin. The town carries the appearance of rude, decayed grandeur—charmingly rural, retired situation. The old royal palace a tolerably fine, but melancholy ruin, sweetly situated on a small elevation, by the brink of a loch. Shown the room where the beautiful injured Mary Queen of Scots was born—a pretty good old Gothic church. The infamous stool of repentance standing, in the old Romish way, on a lofty situation.

"What a poor pimping business is a Presbyterian place of worship; dirty, narrow, and squalid; stuck in a corner of old popish grandeur such as Linlithgow, and much more Melrose! Ceremony and show, if judiciously thrown in, absolutely necessary for the bulk of mankind, both in religious and civil matters. Dine. Go to my friend Smith's at Avon printfield; find nobody but Mrs. Miller, an agreeable, sensible, modest, good body, as useful, but not so ornamental, as Fielding's Miss Western—not rigidly polite *à la Francais*, but easy, hospitable, and housewifely.

"An old lady from Paisley, a Mrs. Lawson, whom I promise to call for in Paisley; like old Lady W[auchope], and still more like Mrs. C——, her conversation is pregnant with strong sense and just remark, but, like them, a certain air of self-importance, and a *duresse* in the eye, seem to indicate, as the Ayrshire wife observed of her cow, that "she had a mind o' her ain.'

"Pleasant view of Dunfermline, and the rest of the fertile coast of Fife, as we go down to that dirty, ugly place, Borrowstounness: see a horse-race, and call on a friend of Mr. Nicol's, a Bailie Cowan, of whom I know too little to attempt his portrait. Come through the rich carse of Falkirk to pass the night. Falkirk nothing remarkable, except the tomb of Sir John the Graham, over which, in the succession of time, four [three] stones have been placed.

"*Sunday, August* 26.—Camelon, the ancient metropolis of the Picts, now a small village in the neighbourhood of Falkirk. Cross the Grand Canal to Carron.*

"Pass Dunipace, a place laid out with fine taste; a charming amphitheatre bounded by Denny village, and pleasant seats down the way to Dunipace. The Carron, running down the bosom of the whole, makes it one of the most charming little prospects I have seen.

"Dine at Auchinbowie: Mr. Monro, an excellent worthy old man; Miss Monro, an amiable, sensible, sweet young woman, much resembling Mrs. Grierson. Come to Bannockburn. Shown the old house where James III. finished so tragically his unfortunate life. The field of Bannockburn: the hole where glorious Bruce set his standard. Here no Scot can pass uninterested. I fancy to myself that I see my gallant, heroic countrymen, coming o'er the hill and down upon the plunderers of their country, the murderers of their fathers; noble revenge and just hate glowing in every vein, striding more and more eagerly as they approach the oppressive, insulting, bloodthirsty foe! I see them meet in gloriously-triumphant congratulation on the victorious field, exulting in their heroic royal leader, and rescued liberty and independence! Come to Stirling.

"*Monday*.—Go to Harvieston. Go to see Caudron Linn, and Rumbling Brig, and Deil's Mill. Return in the evening.

"Supper—Messrs. Doig, the schoolmaster; Bell; and Captain Forrester of the castle. Doig, a queerish figure, and something of a pedant; Bell, a joyous fellow, who sings a good song; Forrester, a merry, swearing kind of man, with a dash of the sodger.

"*Tuesday morning*.—Breakfast with Captain Forrester; Ochil Hills; Devon River;† Forth and Teith; Allan

---

* We give in the Poems some trifling verses, written by Burns on his journey to Stirling, Falkirk, and Carron. Lockhart tells us a story, that when Nicol, along with Burns was approaching Carron Iron-works (he says riding, but they were undoubtedly in a post-chaise), he was constantly crying out, "Look, Burns! Good Heavens! Look, look! What a glorious sight!" "Sir," said Burns, "I would not look at your bidding, if it were the mouth of hell!"

† Burns diverged at Stirling to the valley of the Devon, leaving Nicol behind him for a day. He went there to visit Mrs. Chalmers,

River; Strathallan, a fine country, but little improved; Cross Earn to Crieff; Dine and go to Aberuchil; cold reception at Aberuchil; a most romantically pleasant ride up Earn, by Auchtertyre and Comrie, to Aberuchil; Sup at Crieff. *

"*Wednesday morning.*—Leave Crieff; Glen Almond; Almond River; Ossian's grave; Loch Fruoch; Glenquaich; Landlord and landlady remarkable characters;

the mother of Margaret Chalmers (afterwards Mrs. Lewis Hay), an Edinburgh acquaintance and special friend of Burns, who had met her at Dr. Blacklock's—to whom she commended herself by her fine voice. Margaret was now in Edinburgh; but her mother was at Harvieston, on a visit to Mrs. Hamilton the stepmother of Gavin Hamilton, Burns' Ayrshire friend. She was residing with Mr. Tait of Harvieston (the Archbishop of Canterbury is sprung from this family) presiding over his establishment till his daughter grew up. Her daughter, Charlotte Hamilton, was here also. Mr. Tait was a widower, and his deceased wife had been sister to Mrs. Chalmers and Mrs. Hamilton. Miss Mackenzie, an older sister of Margaret Chalmers, was here too, with her mother. It was altogether an interesting group; and if Burns regretted the absence of his musical friend, Margaret Chalmers, it was more than made up by the presence of Charlotte Hamilton. This

' Loveliest flower on the banks of the Devon "

had been once

" A sweet bud on the braes of the Ayr."

She was the younger sister of Gavin Hamilton; she is described by the poet (see his CORRESPONDENCE) in more than usually ardent terms, and not merely his first rapturous expressions, but his allusions to her in his subsequent writ'ngs, and notably the fact that a little before his death he wrote a song. his last song, about her, seem to prove that he cherished her as an ideal on his mind ever afterwards, and that even in that awful hour —

" Her dear idea gave relief and solace to his breast."

He accompanied her and her friends to the well-known Caldron Linn, on the Devon. He describes it in very general, and by no means enthusiastic terms; yet, he says he spent at it one of the happiest days he ever spent in his life. In fact, he thought more of her than the scenery, was fairly caught, and but for the unsettled state of his prospects, and perhaps her youth, might have proposed. At all events he left Harvieston for Stirling on the evening of that eventful day with a full, perhaps a sad and sore heart. We will find him in her company afterwards; but it was love at first sight, and like many of Burns' loves, was doomed to disappointment. The editor of the excellent Kilmarnock edition says it was Margaret Chalmers on whom Burns wrote his last song; but it is quite enough to say in reply that, while Margaret Chalmers was not that delightful day with the poet on the Devon, Charlotte Hamilton was. Besides, he calls her " fairest maid; " but Margaret Chalmers had no chance with Charlotte for beauty. Though never professed lovers, they became intimate friends; but that some estrangement occurred between them is evident from an expression in the song—

" Prithee leave that frown aside,
And smile as thou wert wont to do "—

and also from the fact that Miss Hamilton burnt all the letters which had passed between her and Burns, and many of Margaret Chalmers' too. More of her and her husband, Adair, in a little. Burns, everybody knows, wrote on her the beautiful song—

" How pleasant the banks of the clear winding Devon," &c.

At Stirling Burns, angry at the ruinous state of the old hall of the Scottish Parliament under the Stuarts, wrote some verses reflecting on the House of Hanover, which gave great offence and provoked some indignant comments—

Taymouth, described in rhyme; † meet the Hon. Charles Townshend.

"*Thursday.*—Come down Tay to Dunkeld; Glenlyon House; Lyon River; Druid's Temple; three circles of stones, the outermost sunk, the second has thirteen stones remaining, the innermost has eight, two large detached ones like a gate, to the south-east; say prayers in it; pass Taybridge; Aberfeldy, described in rhyme; Castle Menzies; Inver; Dr. Stewart. Sup.

"*Friday.*—Walk with Mrs. Stewart and Beard to

" Here Stuarts once in triumph reigned,
And laws for Scotland's weal ordained;
But now unroofed their palace stands,
Their sceptre's swayed by other hands.
The injured Stuart line is gone,
A race outlandish fill their throne—
An idiot race, to honour lost,
Who know them best despise them most."

He, himself, afterwards broke the pane.

* We, as belonging to Upper Strathearn, notice here with natural interest—Burns, after dining at Crieff and riding up the lovely valley of the Earn, approaching the dark noble ridge of mountains called the Aberuchill Hills, at the base of which stands the Castle of Aberuchill, and which seem abruptly to stop the valley and command the beauty of it to soar up into grandeur. That Burns admired this scene is certain, for he calls it a " delightfully pleasant ride." But he had, it seems, a cold reception at Aberuchill, by whom or for what cause it were vain now to inquire (but, see afterwards). He mentions Comrie. That beautiful village must have been then very different from what it is now. Its fine parish church, with its far-seen spire, was not erected. The monument to Lord Melville (old Hal Dundas), at present so romantic a feature, which looks like a bright finger relieved against the black hills beyond, was not built till 1811. And not a single shock of earthquake had as yet frightened the people from their propriety. But behind the village the Deil's Cauldron was then thundering (pity the author of the " Address to the Deil " had not visited it) above; the grey crag. where the monument came to be erected, was rising like a scalp over the woodland which begirds the cataract; and around were the noble semi-circle of volcanic mountains, with the giant Benvoirlich just peering into view, and the glen up which Kilmeny had gone, in far back years, to meet the visions of celestial day, expanding westward to Loch Earn. (See Hogg's " Queen's Wake.") Burns returned to sup in Crieff. We doubt if, in 1787, there was a good inn in Comrie; and perhaps had he entered the one there was, he might, like Nicol Jarvie, have found some tremendous Highlandman, equipped with wrath and whisky, who would have quarrelled with our poet, fought with him, perhaps murdered him, and then we would have wanted " Tam o' Shanter" and the sweetest songs in the world!

† Burns' verses on "Taymouth" and the "Fall of Fyers" are poor, stiff, stilted affairs, very different from his "Birks of Aberfeldy," "Loch Turrit," and the "Petition of Bruar Water." Ossian's grave and the glorious scenery of the Sma' Glen, Loch Fruoch or Freuchie, and Glenquaich, called forth no poetical response from him. At Taymouth he met with the Hon. Charles Townshend. This could not be the Townshend so gorgeously described by Burke:— " Before this splendid orb (Lord Chatham) was entirely set, and while the western horizon was in a blaze with its descending glory, in the opposite quarter of the Heavens arose another luminary, and for his hour became Lord of the Ascendant." This great man died in 1767, and Burke panegyrized him in 1774. It must have been some other gentleman of the same name, and we are not deep enough in the family history of the Townshends to determine who it was. It could not, of course, have been Tom Townshend, Charles' brother, of whom, in connection with Burke, Goldsmith thus wrote in his " Retaliation "—

" Though fraught with all learning, yet straining his throat
To persuade Tommy Townshend to lend him a vote."

Birnam top; fine prospect down Tay; Craigiebarns Hills; hermitage on the Bran Water, with a picture of Ossian; breakfast with Dr. Stewart; Neil Gow plays; a short, stout-built, honest Highland figure, with his grayish hair shed on his honest social brow, an interesting face, marking strong sense, kind open-heartedness, mixed with unmistrusting simplicity; visit his house; Marget Gow.

"Ride up Tummel River to Blair; Fascally, a beautiful romantic nest; wild grandeur of the Pass of Killiecrankie; visit the gallant Lord Dundee's stone.

"Blair; sup with the Duchess; easy and happy from the manners of the family; confirmed in my good opinion of my friend Walker. *

"*Saturday (Sept.* 1).—Visit the scenes round Blair—fine, but spoiled with bad taste; Tilt and Garry rivers; Falls on the Tilt; heather seat; ride in company with Sir William Murray and Mr. Walker to Loch Tummel; meanderings of the Rannoch, which runs through quondam Struan Robertson's estate from Loch Rannoch to Loch Tummel; dine at Blair. Company:—General Murray; Captain Murray, an honest tar; Sir William Murray, an honest, worthy man, but tormented with the hypochondria; Mrs. Graham, *belle et aimable*; Miss Cathcart; Mrs. Murray, a painter; Mrs. King; Duchess and fine family, the Marquis, Lords James, Edward, and Robert; Ladies Charlotte, Emilia, and children dance; sup; Mr. Graham of Fintry. †

"Come up the Garry; Falls of Bruar; Dalnacardoch; Dalwhinnie; dine; snow on the hills seventeen feet deep; no corn from Loch-garry to Dalwhinnie; cross the Spey, and come down the stream to Pitnain; straths rich; *les environs* picturesque; Craigow Hill; Ruthven of Badenoch; barracks; wild and magnificent; Rothiemurchie on the other side, and Glenmore; Grant of Rothiemurchie's poetry; told me by the Duke of Gordon; Strathspey, rich and romantic; breakfast at Aviemore, a wild spot; dine

---

* Burns, at Blair, again met with Josiah Walker, who was now acting as tutor in the Duke of Athole's family. We copy Walker's account of Burns at the Tilt, by far the best bit contributed by him to his Recollections of the Poet. "On reaching Blair, he sent me notice of his arrival (as I had been previously acquainted with him), and I hastened to meet him at the inn. The Duke, to whom he brought a letter of introduction, was from home: but the Duchess, being informed of his arrival, gave him an invitation to sup and sleep at Athole House. He accepted the invitation; but as the hour of supper was at some distance, begged I would, in the interval, be his guide through the grounds. It was already growing dark; yet the softened though faint and uncertain view of their beauties, which the moonlight afforded us, seemed exactly suited to the state of his feeling at the time. I had often, like others, experienced the pleasures which arise from the sublime or elegant landscape, but I never saw those feelings so intense as in Burns. When we reached a rustic hut on the river Tilt, where it is overhung by a woody precipice, from which there is a noble waterfall, he threw himself on the heathy seat, and gave himself up to a tender, abstracted, and voluptuous enthusiasm of imagination. I cannot help thinking it might have been here that he conceived the idea of the following lines, which he afterwards introduced into his poem on Bruar Water, when only fancying such a combination of objects as were now present to his eye:—

'Or by the reaper's nightly beam,
    Mild, chequering through the trees,
Rave to my darkly-dashing stream,
    Hoarse-swelling on the breeze.'

It was with much difficulty I prevailed on him to quit this spot, and to be introduced in proper time to supper.

"My curiosity was great to see how he would conduct himself in company so different from what he had been accustomed to. His manner was unembarrassed, plain, and firm. He appeared to have complete reliance on his own native good sense for directing his behaviour. He seemed at once to perceive and to appreciate what was due to the company and to himself, and never to forget a proper respect for the separate species of dignity belonging to each. He did not arrogate conversation, but, when led into it, he spoke with ease, propriety, and manliness. He tried to exert his abilities, because he knew it was ability alone gave him a title to be there. The Duke's fine young family attracted much of his admiration; he drank their healths as 'honest men and bonnie lassies,' an idea which was much applauded by the company, and with which he has very felicitously closed his poem.

"Next day I took a ride with him through some of the most romantic parts of that neighbourhood, and was highly gratified by his conversation. As a specimen of his happiness of conception and strength of expression, I will mention a remark which he made on his fellow-traveller, who was walking at the time a few paces before us. He was a man of a robust but clumsy person; and while Burns was expressing to me the value he entertained for him, on account of his vigorous talents, although they were clouded at times by coarseness of manners; 'in short,' he added, 'his mind is like his body—he has a confounded strong in-kneed sort of a soul.'

"Much attention was paid to Burns both before and after the Duke's return, of which he was perfectly sensible, without being vain; and at his departure I recommended to him, as the most appropriate return he could make, to write some descriptive verses on any of the scenes with which he had been so much delighted. After leaving Blair, he, by the Duke's advice, visited the Falls of Bruar, and in a few days I received a letter from Inverness, with the verses enclosed." The family wished much that Burns should have stopt a little longer, and even tried to bribe the driver to pull off a shoe from the horse; but he was incorruptible." It is a pity he did not halt, as Henry Dundas (Lord Melville to be) was expected; and had that king of Scotland's politics met the king of Scotland's poetry, we know not what he might have done for Burns. He was not a man to start at trifles, and, with many faults, was of a generous disposition. A very acute man, he would have seen Burns at a glance, his uses and possibilities as well as powers. We suspect William Pitt afterwards cooled whatever intentions Dundas might have had to Burns, as he pushed the bottle to Melville and said, "Very clever man Burns, true poet; his poetry, like Shakspeare's, comes sweetly from nature. Pity, &c., &c." Mr. Graham of Fintry. however, was at Blair, and became afterwards of partial service to our poet in his Excise schemes.

† Burns thought the day he spent at Blair Athole one of the happiest of his life. He was greatly struck with the children, whom he calls a "little angel band;" also, with two ladies, Mrs. Graham and Miss Cathcart. They were daughters of Lord Cathcart, and sisters to the Duchess of Athole. Mrs. Graham was married to Thomas Graham of Balgowan, afterwards the Lord Lynedoch of Barossa celebrity. She died in the bloom of beauty, five years after Burns saw her, and sorrow at this made her husband a soldier. Gainsborough had painted her as only he was able to do; but after her death the bereaved husband could not bear to look at the portrait, and sent it away to a picture-framer in London, to lie there out of his sight, as her beautiful self had been buried. It was discovered by Mr. Graham of Balgowan, and restored to light afterwards. Miss Cathcart too, an amiable and lovely creature, died early, and so did the Duchess of Athole—

"Sing mournfully, Oh! mournfully,
    The solitude of Binnorie."—*Wordsworth.*

at Sir James Grant's; Lady Grant, a sweet, pleasant body; come through mist and darkness to Dulsie, to lie [sleep].

"*Tuesday.*—Findhorn river; rocky banks; come on to Castle Cawdor, where Macbeth murdered King Duncan; saw the bed in which King Duncan was stabbed; dine at Kilravock; Mrs. Rose, sen., a true chieftain's wife; Fort-George; Inverness.

"*Wednesday.*—Loch Ness; Braes of Ness; General's Hut; Fall of Fyers; Urquhart Castle and Strath.

"*Thursday.*—Come over Culloden Muir—reflections on the field of battle; breakfast at Kilravock; old Mrs. Rose, sterling sense, warm heart, strong passions, and honest pride, all in an uncommon degree; Mrs. Rose, jun., a little milder than the mother; this, perhaps, owing to her being younger;* Mr. Grant, minister at Calder, resembles Mr. Scott at Inverleithen. Mrs. Rose and Mrs. Grant accompany us to Kildrummie; two young ladies—Miss Rose, who sang two Gaelic songs, beautiful and lovely—Miss Sophia Brodie, most agreeable and amiable—both of them gentle, mild—the sweetest creatures on earth, and happiness be with them!†

"Dine at Nairn; fall in with a pleasant enough gentleman, Dr. Stewart, who had been long abroad with his father in the forty-five; and Mr. Falconer, a spare, irascible, warm-hearted Norland, and a nonjuror; Brodie House to lie.

"*Friday* (*Sept. 7*).—Forres; famous stone at Forres. Mr. Brodie tells me that the muir where Shakspeare lays Macbeth's witch-meeting is still haunted, that the country folks wont pass it by night.

.   .   .   .

"Venerable ruins of Elgin Abbey (Cathedral), a grander effect at first glance than Melrose, but not near so beautiful. Cross Spey to Fochabers; fine palace (Gordon Castle, the seat of the Duke of Gordon), worthy of the generous proprietor; dine. Company:—Duke and Duchess, Ladies Charlotte and Magdeline,‡ Colonel Abercrombie and Lady, Mr. Gordon, and Mr. ——, a clergyman, a venerable aged figure; the Duke makes me happier than ever great man did; noble, princely, yet mild, condescending, and affable; gay and kind; the Duchess witty and sensible —God bless them!

"Come to Cullen to lie; hitherto the country is sadly poor and unimproven.

"Come to Aberdeen; meet with Mr. Chalmers, printer, a facetious fellow; Mr. Ross, a fine fellow, like Professor Tytler; Mr. Marshall, one of the *poetæ minores;* Mr. Sheriffs, author of 'Jamie and Bess,' a little decrepit body, with some abilities; Bishop Skinner,§ a nonjuror, son of the author of 'Tullochgorum;' a man whose mild, venerable manner is the most marked of any in so young a man. Professor Gordon, a good-natured, jolly-looking professor; Aberdeen a lazy town.

"Near Stonehive [Stonehaven]," he says, "the coast a good deal romantic. Meet my relations. Robert Burns, writer in Stonehive, one of those who love fun, a gill, and a punning joke, and have not a bad heart—his wife a sweet, hospitable body, without any affectation of what is called town-breeding.

"*Tuesday.*—Breakfast with Mr. Burns; lie at Lawrence-kirk; album; library; Mrs. ——, a jolly, frank, sensible, love-inspiring widow; Howe of the Mearns, a rich, cultivated, but still unenclosed country.∥

"*Wednesday.*—Cross North Esk river and a rich country to Craigow.

"Breakfast (Sept. 13) at Muthie, and sail along that wild, rocky coast, and see the famous caverns, particularly the Gairiepot; land and dine at Arbroath; stately ruin of Arbroath Abbey; come to Dundee through a fertile country; Dundee a low-lying but pleasant town;¶ old steeple; Tay

---

* Relations of "Man of Feeling."

† During all this journey Nicol was an awful incubus on Burns. He hurried him away from "Athole's honest men and bonnie lassies," from Kilravock and Kildrummie, and then again from Gordon Castle. The latter story stamps Nicol as a fellow totally unworthy of the companionship of Burns. Angry that Burns went to Gordon Castle without him, that Burns waited there a good while without him, and that Burns condescended to come and ask him to join him at the castle, the infuriated pedagogue at last led off his victim, otherwise he would have gone away without him, and pity he had not! It is said that the Duchess of Gordon had planned a meeting of Henry Addington (Lord Sidmouth) with Burns and Beattie, which might have been of material service to our poet. Addington was an admirer of Burns' genius, and is said to have forwarded to him certain lines, which are given by Allan Cunningham, but of the authenticity of which we have our doubts. Nor are we quite certain of the stories we have in *Chambers' Journal* about Nicol's talk with Burns at Banff, else we might have reproduced them. They have a decidedly apocryphal look.

‡ Lady Charlotte, mother of the Duke of Richmond. Magdeline, married to Sir Robert Sinclair of Murkle.

§ At Aberdeen Burns met with Bishop Skinner, son of the venerable Rev. John Skinner of Linshart, near Peterhead. Burns had passed his house unwittingly, and keenly regretted never having seen him, although he afterwards corresponded with that singularly patriarchal and gifted person, whose "Ewie with the Crooked Horn," "John of Badenyon," and "Tullochgorum," have given him such a high position among Scottish song writers; and who in purity and piety, although he was only a pastor, approached the ideal of a primitive bishop.

∥ Chambers regrets that Burns does not tell us more of his visit to his "Calf-country," the Mearns. We have been told that his cousin, James Burness, the writer in Montrose, father of Sir Alexander Burness, went out with his son to meet him at Marykirk and accompany him to Montrose, when Robert Burns said to him—"I have been at our paternal farm in the Mearns, and showed our cousin some little things I had written by the way, which I mean to publish;" but the former streekit himself up, struck his stick on the floor, and said, "Fie, fie, man, are ye gaen to affront your respectable freends by printing sic godless nonsense? na, na, gie me them, and I'll put them in the fire." To this it is said the poet often alluded while in Montrose and afterwards, and never altogether forgave his old relative. This anecdote was communicated to our informant by one of the Burness family, living recently in Montrose.

¶ Dundee he calls "a low-lying but pleasant town" We are able, through the kindness of a worthy and intelligent widow lady residing in Dundee, Mrs. Home Scott, to supply some new information in reference to the night Burns spent in Bonnie Dundee. Mr. Jobson of the Commercial Bank was at this time one of the principal, if not the

Frith; Broughty Castle, a finely-situated ruin, jutting into the Tay.

"*Friday.*—Breakfast with the Miss Scotts; Miss Bess Scott like Mrs. Greenfield; my bardship almost in love with her; come through the rich harvests and fine hedgerows of the Carse of Gowrie, along the romantic margin of the Grampian Hills to Perth—fine, fruitful, hilly, woody country round Perth.

"*Saturday Morning.*—Leave Perth; come up Strathearn to Endermay; fine, fruitful, cultivated Strath; the scene of 'Bessie Bell and Mary Gray' near Perth; fine scenery on the banks of the May; Mrs. Belshes, gawcie, frank, affable, fond of rural sports, hunting, &c.; lie at Kinross; reflections in a fit of the colic.

"*Sunday (Sept.* 16).—Pass through a cold, barren country to Queensferry; dine; cross the ferry, and on to Edinburgh."

There are various other rumours floating in Dundee about Burns. One, although it cannot be exactly credited, is so curious that we are tempted to relate it. A venerable and singularly worthy old lady, ninety-six years of age, but in wonderful preservation, insists on it that she remembers Burns. She says she was then a little girl or "gilpie," doing "chares" in the house of a farmer, residing in a place, near Dundee, called Clepington; that Burns came to her master's house and stopt all night; and that she "washed his sark." Of this she is perfectly assured, although in 1787, being only four years of age, she could hardly have been competent to such a feat; and as a gentleman humorously remarked, had been more likely to have fallen into the washing tub and been drowned. Still it is the one bit of romance in all her history, and it were cruel to disturb her in her long life-dream.*

From Dundee he would, after sleeping probably in the Vault Inn and breakfasting with the Scotts, ride to Perth. He makes a blunder in his Journal: he says that he came along the romantic margin of the Grampian hills to Perth; but the hills to the north of the Carse of Gowrie are not the Grampians, but only a spur from the Sidlaws. From Perth he went to Invermay, or "Endermay," as he calls it, where lived the Belshes family, to whom he had an introduction, and which was the scene of the old song, "The Birks of Invermay." We remember the late amiable and truly gifted Jamieson, United Presbyterian minister of Methven, telling us of a Perthshire gentleman in Paris who was sitting in his hotel, sad and home-sick, when he suddenly heard two children singing on the street, "The Birks of Invermay." It saddened him more at first; but the sadness brought tears, which carried away the sorrow. Mr. Jamieson did not tell, probably did not know, who the children were, or how they came there, or their future fate. Burns says, "The scene of Bessie Bell and Mary Gray, near Perth," but does not say that he visited the traditionary spot, which lies on the opposite side of the valley from Invermay. He could hardly have seen both places, dined with the Belshes, and reached Kinross, all in one day. He had a fit of colic at Kinross, and some serious reflections therewith—perhaps bearing more on the far past than on this recent journey, which seems to have been one of unmingled and innocent gratification. He arrived at Edinburgh on the 16th of September.

Returned to the metropolis, Burns threw himself with great enthusiasm into Johnston's projected "Museum of

principal, citizens in Dundee. He was in good circumstances, and possessed of much and varied intelligence. Before, but still more after his marriage, his house was open to all guests of distinction who visited the town—actors, painters, and other celebrities. This gentleman entertained Burns. It is doubtful if he slept in his house, as Jobson was then a bachelor, and might not have proper accommodation for him and for the horse on which he had likely rode from Arbroath. (He had come part of the road from Montrose by sea, visiting the caverns at Auchmithie, and had landed at Arbroath.) But he supped with him. Suppers at that time took place at eight in the evening, and likely, according to the manner of the times, the wee short hours would be reached before the party separated. Probably some of the leading citizens might be invited to meet the lion. Mr. Jobson used to speak to his daughter (Mrs. H. Scott, and to a son of his, who ultimately settled in England and died there) of Burns' great modesty of manner, the extraordinary charm and power of his conversation, and the almost preternatural lustre of his eyes. Burns, in his brief notes, says, "Breakfast with the Miss Scotts; Miss Bess Scott like Mrs. Greenfield; my bardship almost in love with her." These Miss Scotts were two unmarried but young ladies residing in Dundee. Their father had been parish minister in Auchterhouse, near Dundee, but was dead. They had a house together, and were remarkable for their accomplishments and general superiority of mind and manners. Miss Scott was more a blue than a beauty; Bess was more of the beauty. Miss Scott had many offers of marriage from gentlemen of high standing, both citizens and strangers, but declined them all, and lived long single and very highly respected. Bess was, at the time when Burns came to Dundee, engaged to Mr. Jobson, and it was very natural in him to carry the poet in the morning to breakfast with the ladies, and see his sweetheart. Mr. Jobson married Bess Scott shortly after, and our kind and accomplished informant, Mrs. H. Scott, is her daughter, a lady full of all sorts of information about the *élite* of the society of her younger days—the Siddonses, Murrays, Kembles, and others, including Robert Ainslie, the friend of Burns. Who the Mrs. Greenfield mentioned here by Burns as very like the younger Miss Scott was, we are not exactly sure, unless she were the wife of the Mr. Greenfield whom we spoke of before as having to abscond from Edinburgh.

* This allusion to the Clepington led to the supposition that as a Mr. Jobson once possessed that estate and house, it was probable that he was the same with Miss H. Scott's friend, and that hence came the floating tradition of Burns being there. This idea was suggested to us by W. Neish, Esq., a Forfarshire proprietor (of Tannadice) of great intelligence, who has taken a special interest in this edition, and communicated to us full copies of Burns' letters to his brother William (see GENERAL CORRESPONDENCE). We found, however, on inquiry, that it was a different Mr. Jobson who in the year 1805, eighteen years after Burns' visit to Dundee, became proprietor of the Clepington—one Mr. David (known by the sobriquet of Bonnie Dauvid, from his fat, fair, and florid looks).

There is a floating rumour that Burns slept all the night he was in Dundee in a tavern called the Vault or "Vowt," then and long afterwards the principal inn of Dundee; but after inquiries, pursued with the most sedulous diligence by our friend, Mr. William Smith (of Newport) nothing very distinct or definite could be discovered—nothing but the fact that this was the constant tradition of the house, and that a room called Burns' room used to be pointed out, which no longer exists.

Scottish Song," got into a stream of correspondence with old Skinner of "Tullochgorum" fame, and with still greater ardour wrote letters and sent songs to his Harvieston friends (Margaret Chalmers having now joined the pleasant party there), and no doubt inclosing his heart in his epistles. He had wished to see Mr. Miller's farms in August; but it was now too late for this, and he determined to spend a portion of the remaining part of autumn in the north. He went in company with Dr. John M'Kittrick Adair, to whom he had been introduced by his Ayrshire friends, a physician afterwards settled in Harrogate. The travellers went by Linlithgow, Carron, and Stirling, to Harvieston. Adair says in August; but this is evidently a mistake. It must have been much later in the autumn. At Stirling they met Nicol, and had one joyous night with him. Burns, whenever he was called to sing, used to repeat a piece of poetry instead. They went the next day to Mrs. Hamilton's; Adair remarking rather needlessly that Burns, who had visited the place last summer, was acquainted with the younger people before. If Burns had any designs on Charlotte, he must, to use the vulgar expression, have put into Adair's hands a stick to break his own head; for he introduced him to her, and he became speedily her declared admirer, and soon after her accepted lover. They found the family engaged in a great washing, and in *deshabille*, but were graciously received; and after the gentlemen had retired to rest, Mrs. Hamilton, who slept in a room divided from theirs by a thin partition, overheard them discoursing for a long time ere they slept on the charms of Charlotte. Detained at Harvieston by heavy storms and floods, after the weather cleared they spent the time in very pleasant excursions. They revisited the Cauldron Linn and Rumbling Bridge, the ladies wondering at Burns' indifference to the scenery; he, in fact, being more, as upon a former occasion, engrossed in admiring them. Had he gone alone, he might have been inspired to write something worthy of those delightful spots. Dr. Adair is quite wrong in saying that Burns had no taste for the picturesque. But he did not like to be forced to admire, far less to be forced to versify his admiration. And to him, and probably to Adair, too, metal more attractive was near. He visited, also, Castle Campbell, or the "Castle of Gloom," and went afterwards to the two Ochtertyres. The laird of the one in Menteith was Mr. Ramsay, a man of some literature, fond of poetry, full of antiquarian lore, and afterwards a great friend of Sir Walter Scott. From hence he rode through Strathallan to the other Ochtertyre in Strathearn; then, as now, a plain house hung in the midst of a gallery of woods and gardens, with a placid lake below, and dark mountains rising behind and carrying off the view toward Loch Turrit—a loch lying dern and dreary under the frowning shadow of Ben-chonzie and Cair-na-chozie. It is supposed that Burns visited Sir William Murray, partly because he was a cousin and friend of Mr. Graham of Fintry, a Commissioner of Excise, whom the poet, beginning to look in that direction, was anxious again to meet, or at least to influence. Burns enjoyed Ochtertyre exceedingly. Sir William's lady, Lady Augusta, was a fine-looking woman in the prime of life. We have heard of a farmer on the estate, after paying his rent at the mansion, brought into the drawing-room to get a glass of wine, and to see, as a great treat, Lady Augusta, the celebrated beauty, newly married at the time. He was asked afterwards what he thought of her, and his answer was, "Toots, she's naething to oor Kirsty," his own comely but homely spouse. Burns visited Loch Turrit, then a much grander solitude than now — unprofaned by *pic-nics*, and meet mountain-chamber for the steps of a solitary poet. The tradition (a small disenchanting one) of the House of Ochtertyre avers, that being a little exhausted by his walk, which is long, rough, and uphill, he went on returning to the butler's room, asked a glass of his best whisky, and wrote, "Blythe, blythe, and merry was she;" the genuine impulse to write which, however, was given by the sight of Miss Euphemia Murray of Lintrose, the "Flower of Strathmore," a young cousin of Sir William's, a fair-haired, lively girl of eighteen, afterwards married to Mr. Smythe of Methven Castle. He wrote his lines on scaring wild fowl at Loch Turrit, he tells us in the Glenriddell MS., during a solitary forenoon's walk from Ochtertyre House, and few verses are more characteristic of Burns. Indeed it may be called his Ode to Independence. The following lines, we venture to say, rushed on his mind in the shadow of the great silent mountains, and by the side of the lonely lake:—

> "Swiftly seek, on clanging wings,
> Other lakes and other springs;
> And the foe ye cannot brave,
> Scorn at least to be his slave."

There are many fine scenes and castles in the neighbourhood, such as Abercairney, Braco Castle (lying sublime and lonely by its hermit and homeless stream, and at the termination of that long ridge of sterility and silence, stretching between Ardoch and Comrie, called the "Langside"—a castle where dwelt a lady, after whom our old teacher, Sir Daniel Sandford, most brilliant of men, in his youth sighed, and sighed in vain; Ardoch being his headquarters during his hapless courtship), Lawers, Dunira, and Loch Earn; but we know not if Burns ever visited any of them. To the magnificent Drummond Castle (which we always think was in Scott's eye when he painted "Tullyveolan"), then occupied by Captain Drummond, afterwards Lord Perth, Burns was not invited, owing to his lines on the inn window at Stirling, formerly quoted.

Lord Perth was at this time a new convert from Jacobitism, having just got back the forfeited estates of his family again; and resented the verses the more on that account, which was rather paltry.* So Burns was not asked to visit the grand old house, throwing its tall, bold shadow westward toward the mountain, Turleum (which stands directly opposite, with all its fine wave of woods flowing to the very summit), with the beautiful lake on the north, the long stately avenue (see it described in "Waverley"), the gorgeous garden, and the green Ochils, terminating the southern prospect. Burns returned to the other Ochtertyre, after visiting, it is probable now, the scene of the tragedy of Bessie Bell and Mary Gray, which lay on the estate of Mr. Graham of Balgowan, whom he seems to have called on. In returning to Mr. Ramsay's, he must needs pass through Strathallan again.†

At his seat (which he could easily have reached on horseback from Greenloaning in a few hours) Burns remained two days, and Mr. Ramsay thought his conversation the best he had ever heard. He advised him to write a play like the "Gentle Shepherd," and also "Scottish Georgics." We doubt if either of these plans would have exactly suited Burns. He had not much plot-producing skill, although he had decided dramatic talent, so far as character was concerned. Nor could he have sustained descriptive enthusiasm, like Thomson, through a long poem. James Graham of the "Sabbath," who of all Scottish men in the nineteenth century, unless we except Wilson and Aird, loved Nature most and painted her best—at least, in those nooks and corners into which she retires, and to which he seemed to have followed her on his hands and knees—wrote "British Georgics" on

---

* Perhaps here, too, we find the cause of Burns' cold reception at Aberuchill. It belonged to the Drummonds.

† Here we may intercalate a piece of information about him we have received from a very respectable farmer—Mr. Finlayson of Dam of Quoight, by Greenloaning. This gentleman had an uncle, named Peter Finlayson, of Nether Meal Mill, near Greenloaning, who was with one of his customers in a small inn at Greenloaning, kept by a person named Towers. About the gloaming there dropt in a decent-looking countryman, with a strong south country accent. "On his taking a seat, he was presented with a glass of whisky, of which he took a moderate sip, and was returning it, when Finlayson said, 'Take it out, sir,' which Burns, for it was he, did; and then 'dunted' and called in his gill or noggin, and helped Finlayson and his friend to a return glass, which was only tasted by them, when Burns cried, 'Take it out as ye made me do,' to which they replied that they had some before. Nevertheless the party became very social. Burns' conversation was electrifying, and they sat very late. He told them who he was, but not till they were parting; and Peter Finlayson had often read his poems and songs in the *Edinburgh Courant*, a paper which was then in being, and where his poems occasionally did appear, although he had not read his book. He told them he had been at Ochtertyre; and they plied him with questions, which he dexterously parried till the very close of the evening." There is not very much in this story, but it is quite possible it fits in with this part of his history; and our informant assures us that it was narrated to him by his uncle forty years ago, and he was often urged to give it publicity.

---

this plan; but the book, in spite of some inimitable touches, totally failed, and is now nearly forgotten. Ramsay told Burns some traditions about Omeron Cameron (see CORRESPONDENCE), but Chambers wisely adds, "It was not for Burns, but for that noteless youth he met at Sir Adam Fergusson's, to accomplish such feats." Scott's "plays" are certainly not feats of genius; but of course if he refers to his novels, he is right. Ramsay more sensibly advised Burns to employ his imagination in the cause of truth and virtue, and in the main he followed his advice. On the whole, Ramsay did not resemble certain Edinburgh critics of the time, who reminded Burns of those spinsters in the country who "span their thread so fine that it was fit for neither weft nor woof."

At Clackmannan he met with a fine old gentlewoman of ninety, of whom Ramsay had forewarned him—Mrs. Bruce, calling herself of the blood of the Bruce, tall, dignified, dwelling in the ancient tower of Clackmannan, which overlooks the Forth, wearing a tartan scarf, and with the white rose of the Stuarts at her breast. She greatly impressed the imagination of the poet. When he asked her if she was sprung from the family of Robert Bruce, she replied that Robert Bruce was sprung from her family! She possessed the helmet and two-handed sword of the hero; and conferring the order of knighthood with it on Burns and Adair, she said she had a better right to confer it than *some folks*. She gave as her first toast after dinner, "Hooi uncos"—away strangers—a word used by shepherds to direct their dogs to drive away the sheep. She died in 1791, and the sword and helmet fell into the hands of Lord Elgin, and in his mansion of Broomhall are still preserved. Her connection, however, with the Bruce of Bannockburn is not, we believe, founded on fact.

Burns again (it is somewhat obscure in his Correspondence) visited Harvieston, and found that during his absence Dr. Adair had been using his time well by pushing his addresses to the beautiful Charlotte. They returned together to Edinburgh by Kinross and Queensferry. He visited Queen Mary's Isle at Loch Leven, also Dunfermline Abbey Church, and when he saw the two large flagstones which mark the grave of Robert Bruce, he knelt down and kissed the spot so sacred to memory. It is indeed holy ground! A clergyman, who preached there some years ago a public sermon, says "that he never felt so excited in his life as when remembering as he went on that the hallowed dust of the Bruce of Bannockburn was beneath his feet!" With characteristic volatility, however, Burns made Adair ascend the "cutty stool," and read him a ludicrous reproof (we once witnessed a similar scene between two clergymen, now dead, in the parish church of Inverleithen), founded on that he had received in Ayrshire from Daddie Auld, when he was one of seven (Chambers say five) who mounted the seat of shame together.

Burns came back to Edinburgh on the 20th October, 1787, ill of a heavy cold he had contracted during his journey. Here our story parts from Dr. Adair, who returned to England, where he had a great many fashionable acquaintances, and became a popular physician in Harrogate. He was married to Charlotte Hamilton on the 16th November, 1789. His lovely wife, who seems to have been amiable, beautiful, and even gifted (Burns speaks of her "eye beaming with mind") fell into ill-health and died prematurely in 1806. She had, as we saw previously, burnt a number of Burns' and Miss Chalmers' letters. Dr. Adair volunteers a statement that his marriage with Charlotte Hamilton was happy, and we do not deny it. But it were to inquire too curiously if she, far away and hearing sad tales of her immortal friend, never heaved a sigh, and along with it felt a wish, that she had either—

"Never met or never parted"

from one who so long and fondly cherished her memory, and who was yet to see that beauty which he had admired at the Cauldron Linn glassed to his imagination in the waters of the Black River!

Burns, returned, began again to think of Dumfriesshire as a place to set up the staff of his rest; but ere he took any definite step he settled down in Edinburgh for some months; lived in the house of William Cruickshank, one of the High School teachers; and got his daughter Janet, a girl of twelve, to learn his songs by heart and play them on the piano, and rewarded her for doing so by writing some beautiful verses in her praise. Jenny Cruickshank, who became a fine girl, married a Mr. Henderson, a lawyer in Jedburgh; and a lady, her daughter-in-law, showed Chambers a china punch bowl which Burns, according to tradition, had broken in one of his *bouts* in her father's house in St. James' Square. (Ah! that measureless liar, Tradition! If we could believe it, we saw a year or two ago in the North of Scotland the very china saucer out of which Byron, in one of his boy rages, bit a piece, and there was the piece, too*). He threw himself into Johnson's plan of collecting songs with all his heart, and wrote many for him without money and without price. He got into a correspondence with James Hoy, librarian at Gordon Castle, a great enthusiast in Scottish song. He received a nice letter from his old master, Murdoch, now in London, and he wrote regularly to his two Harviestoun flames; for he seemed, like Squire Thornhill in the "Vicar of Wakefield" with Olivia and Sophia Primrose, to have loved them both at once, although, Mrs. Johnstone thinks, he used the one as a stalking-horse to the other, and that his real affections were centred, like a true poet's, in the one he never had a chance of getting—Charlotte. Both were very superior women. Margaret Chalmers was short in stature; and although her portrait represents a highly-bred, refined, and dignified face, she had little beauty. But she had great spirit and ability, and whether loved or not, loving or not, she had undoubtedly much influence on Burns; a refining and softening influence, so long at least as she was with him. That this would have been permanent, had they come more closely together, we cannot say. Burns' manners were swayed perpetually by his passions, which were terribly strong, and by his impulses, which were exceedingly capricious. And it is so, we suspect, with most self-taught men of genius. About this time he visited Dalswinton, but did not instantly take a farm. In a letter to Miss Chalmers he talks about it and about it, and seems exceedingly uncertain as to his future prospects. But his Muse has not been idle. He has written a song on Charlotte, "The Banks of the Devon," and expects she will be highly pleased with it, and so no doubt she was. He had inscribed some trifling Jacobitish verses to William Tytler, the well-known defender of Mary Queen of Scots. And he had written a manly letter to Sir John Whitefoord, one of his Ayrshire patrons, vindicating his own character against the calumnies by which he had been assailed, especially in reference to the affair with poor Jean Armour, and to his presumed religious opinions. Besides the business of the farm, Burns had the annoyance of a reluctant and dilatory publisher, who was in no hurry to settle accounts with him for his very successful poems. Robert Chambers, himself a publisher, gives a statement of the Creech affair which is not very luminous, and we do not presume to understand the mystery better than he. He is right, however, when he says that Burns, instead of getting angry, should have put the affair into the hands of a legal deputy. But when he speaks of him repairing to Mossgiel, and writing fresh poems in the style of "Halloween" and "The Cottar's Saturday Night" he shows a misapprehension, as he did formerly, of the source of Burns' inspiration. "Halloweens" and "Cottar's Saturday Nights" do not come at the magic of mere money. Burns' heart and passions were his muses. His account was not yet to be settled for four months. In spite of Creech's delay Burns had now determined to leave Edinburgh, when another Will-o'-the-wisp shot across his path, and had well-nigh changed its course for ever and a day.

* We have heard since that evidence is soon to be produced by Dr. Thom of Stonehaven in proof of this tradition.

CHAPTER X.

BURNS AND CLARINDA—LAST DAYS IN EDINBURGH—MARRIAGE.

AGNES Craig, the heroine of this part of Burns' life, was no ordinary person, was of no common origin, and had no ordinary antecedents. She was the grand-niece of Colin MacLaurin, the celebrated mathematician; and he was brother of MacLaurin the divine, whose sermon, "Glorying in the Cross of Christ," has been called the most eloquent in the English language. She was the full cousin of Lord Craig, who wrote the pathetic paper on Michael Bruce in the *Mirror*, and the daughter of a respectable Glasgow physician. She was herself a lady of considerable accomplishments—wit, poetical feeling, warm temperament, and a style of beauty approaching the voluptuous. Her history had been singular. Her husband, James MacLehose, had gained her, it was rumoured, in a peculiar way. Falling in love with her, he determined to woo her in a fashion of his own. Ascertaining that on a certain day she was to travel to Glasgow from Edinburgh by stage coach, he took all the other seats in the coach, and had her to himself for forty miles; and played his game so effectually that by the time they reached Glasgow they were engaged. Such, at least, was the *on dit*, according to Mrs. Johnstone. Married in 1776, she being only seventeen, they were not happy, and MacLehose went out to the West Indies; and occupied in business and pleasure, took little thought of his wife and children. She came to reside in a kind of semi-widowhood, an unprotected female, in Edinburgh. Mrs. MacLehose had expressed to Miss Nimmo, an elderly lady, an acquaintance of Miss Chalmers, an ardent wish to meet with Burns; and at her house accordingly they met on the 11th of December, 1787, and probably he felt this when he wrote afterwards—

"O May, thy morn was ne'er so sweet
As the mirk night of December"

Their attachment, such as it was, seems to have begun on both sides, and at once. It is very difficult to settle its exact nature. It was neither love nor lust. It was in both strongly dashed with vanity, and from first to last there was need of danger signals and red lights. Yet they escaped, it would seem, as by a hair's breadth; or, as Mrs. Jameson says, "were saved so as by fire."

The Correspondence will tell the tale, and on this point, and this chiefly, is valuable. And although there are some very fine passages, the letters, as a whole, are as ridiculous rubbish as two intelligent persons, who were at the same time perfectly sane, ever addressed to each other Foolish, wicked James MacLehose never, we believe, in the first heyday of his courtship addressed such trumpery to Agnes Craig as "Sylvander"—*i.e.*, the greatest poet, and potentially one of the greatest men of his age—did here to "Clarinda." "Thank God," says Matthew Lewis, "even our passions pass away," however much, while they last, they may do to stunt intellectual stature, and to give the animal or the fiend the ascendency over the man. Sometimes indeed, on the other hand, passion, aye when it approaches the brink of insanity, gives a lurid grandeur to the character and an unnatural life to the intellect. So it did to Schiller and to Hazlitt. But of the infatuation of passion there was none in Burns' feeling for "Clarinda." Compare, in order to prove this, Hazlitt's "Liber Amoris" with "Sylvander's" letters. In the one you have the utmost misery, abandonment, and defiance of a desperate affection, and you hear in every page the eloquence of a broken, bursting heart; in the other you have every variety of falsetto and fudge—the happiness that of a drunken night's dream: the misery, on his side at any rate, more imaginative than real. Yet strange that when Burns passes from prose to poetry his right hand regains its cunning; and one or two of his songs—"My Nannie's Awa" and "Ae fond kiss and then we sever"—if not sincere, show a power of simulating sincerity almost miraculous. Scott finds the essence of a hundred love tales in the following stanza:—

"Had we never loved so kindly,
Had we never loved so blindly,
Never met or never parted,
We had ne'er been broken-hearted."

In reference to the letters given in the Correspondence, we may make a few observations, filling up gaps in the history they tell.

1. Clarinda lived in a house on the western pavement of Potterrow, a street now taken down in the march of improvement. We visited it in 1876. We are told that

Burns used to pace along the east pavement and look up to the window, where, in what was called the General's Entry (from General Monk), Clarinda lived. We could not gaze without deep interest on the spot where the brawny poet, still in the pride of his popularity, clad in buckskins, with his riding whip in his hand, stalked along and turned up his glowing looks to his cynosure, if haply he might catch a glance from her eye or a smile from her lips; and entering in we could not look without emotion at the little old-fashioned room, where, as with Mary Campbell, though in less romantic circumstances and scenery, he spent one day of parting love ere they were separated for ever, and by a yet ghastlier gulf than that of death.

2. Nothing is known about the cause of the accident which befell Burns but what he tells us—that his carriage was overturned by a drunken coachman, and his knee terribly bruised. This prevented him fulfilling an engagement with Clarinda, and gave him time for serious reflection and female correspondence. He did not confine on this any more than on other occasions his attentions to one lady, for we find him writing to Miss Chalmers too, expressing a wish that she and Charlotte Hamilton were with him to soothe his tedium and sorrows. He took, he tells us, tooth and nail to the Bible, and pronounces it a glorious book. He indited, at the suggestion of Charles Hay, advocate, a poetical elegy on the death of Dundas, the president of the Court of Session, of no great merit. He writes a funny letter to Francis Howden, jeweller, along with a silhouette portrait, in which he tells a familiar story ill—"Everybody has heard the auld wife's observation when she saw a poor dog going to be hanged. 'God help us, that's the gait we have a' to gang.'" This has no point. The real story is, that an ancient maiden, when she heard of a young lady being married, exclaimed, "That's the gait we maun a' gang." Howden used, to tell a story about Burns and Dr. Gregory. "Well, Burns, what sort of man was your father—a tall man?" "Yes: rather." "A dark-complexioned man?" "Yes." "And your mother?" "My mother was not a man at all." This, poor as it was, extinguished Gregory for the nonce by turning the laugh against him. He had his revenge when he wrote his critique on Burns' poem "On a Wounded Hare," and Burns cried out, "Gregory crucifies me!" Gregory attended Burns while ill with his accident, assisted by Alexander Wood, "Lang Sandy Wood" (see him admirably hit off by James Hogg in "Geordie Dobson's Expedition to Hell"), and gave him a present of Cicero's select Orations done into English, which he highly appreciated.

3. It is hardly worth while following all the ups and downs of this eccentric flirtation between Burns and Clarinda—their capping verses together; Burns alluding to this, and to Clarinda, in a letter to his old friend Richard Brown, calling her a young widow, and speaking of suicide (in terms which showed that nothing was farther from his thoughts); her trying to turn the affair into a religious courtship, and to elicit from him his theological opinions (whence comes in one letter Burns' Creed, a very interesting document, if not very orthodox); her allusion to a noted divine of the day, a Mr. Kemp, whom she wishes Burns to meet, and who, according to Mrs. Johnstone, got latterly into grief by the report that he extended his affections from the souls to the persons of his female devotees—a report the truth of which she leaves uncertain; the clandestine visits Burns at her request paid her; the dangers he repeatedly evaded of the moth approaching too near the candle, their interviews becoming more fascinating and perilous as his departure drew near; and, in fine, his leaving her for a season to meet again in 1791 and then to part for ever. We think every true admirer of Burns will be glad when this strange interlude in his history is over, and may sometimes regret that it has been brought out so much in detail before the public eye. In 1791, as we will hear again, Clarinda's husband, quite unexpectedly, invited her to Jamaica; she went, but was soon glad, from her experience of him and of the climate, to come back again. She was jealous of Burns, of his attentions to Peggy Chalmers, and very angry at his marriage with Jean. She died on the Calton Hill in 1841. Poor lady! she remembered Burns long and warmly. Thus she writes in her journal forty years after: 6th December, 1831—"This day I never can forget, parted with Burns in the year 1791, never more to meet in this world; Oh, may we meet in heaven!" She was of the same age with Burns, and survived him forty-five years. Chambers says, "I have heard Clarinda at seventy-five express the same hope to meet in another sphere the one heart she had ever found herself able entirely to sympathize with, but which had been divided from her on earth by such pitiless obstacles." This was in her very beautiful and natural, but leads to some odd thoughts and perplexed questions. Dr. William Anderson used to speak of the lover, Burns, meeting his "Mary" in Heaven; and the title of Burns' famous song, and an expression in one of his letters, would suggest that Burns expected this too. But Jean, his long tried and devoted wife, might be named as having also a claim to

"A blest and a blythe meeting there"

in the "Land of the Leal." The "Fairest Maid on Devon Banks" was in his mind's eye when he was about to leave the earth. Some enthusiasts might say that in that world of purity and peace, where they, being disembodied spirits, neither marry nor are given in marriage, all these angels might be with him and minister to him; but we shall say nothing on the subject.

During all this time he was not forgetting his friend Johnson, whose second volume appeared in February, 1788, containing some of Burns' finest songs, such as "MacPherson's Lament," and a few sentences in the Preface are from his pen. He had inserted in the "Museum" Clarinda's verses, "Talk not of Love," and a "Canzonet on a Blackbird," the production of the united hands of the two lovers. He had been feeling his way, too, toward a situation in the Excise, and his name had been enrolled in the list of expectant officers. He had been helped in this by Lang Sandy Wood, a kindred spirit, who notably resembled Burns in his liking for animals, and was seldom seen in Edinburgh on his professional visits without a pet sheep following him. It would be thought strange if the amiable "Rab" were seen with such a friend on his journeys of mercy through the Modern Athens now-a-days! Wood strongly backed the poet in his humble ambition to "gauge ale firkins!" Burns left Edinburgh on Monday the 18th of February, 1788. He went first to Glasgow to meet his old friend Richard Brown, and perhaps enjoy with him some exceptionable talk, as Lord Jeffrey would say; thence to Paisley; thence to Dunlop House, where he stayed two days; thence to Kilmarnock, writing to Clarinda at every stage, vowing eternal friendship, and so forth. On Monday the 25th he seems to have gone to Dumfriesshire along with Mr. James Tennant of Glenconnar to view and judge Miller's farms, with one of which he was greatly pleased, and it he afterwards took. We next find him at Mossgiel, where he found matters with Jean in a very strange way. It must be remembered that the marriage between him and Jean Armour might be considered cancelled by her conduct and that of her parents. When Burns returned triumphant the Armours fawned on him, and, as Burns tells us, made him very welcome to visit his girl, no doubt expecting that the renewed intimacy might lead to marriage after all. At this point, we imagine, Burns should have planted his foot, and never entered her house again. With a man of his temperament and former habits of familiarity visiting Jean was equivalent to falling into a scrape. This he felt when too late; and there can be little doubt that the disgust he expresses at her friends' obsequiousness was aggravated by his yielding to a seduction which he despised. Their conduct was that of the spider.

"Wilt thou walk into my prlaour, said the spider to the fly."

And he walked in accordingly. What might have been expected followed—Jean became *enceinte*, and still no word of marriage. Nay, Burns was, and they certainly knew he was, in full cry after other ladies. This provoked the Armours excessively, and they cast out their daughter in the depth of winter; and she might have been miserably ill off had it not been for Mrs. Muir, wife of the owner of "Willie's Mill," who took her in, and treated her with great kindness before and after her *accouchement*, in this acting *pro* Burns.

Let us try to judge fairly while summing up the particulars of this strange matter:—1. The conduct of the Armours deserved all the condemnation of Burns. They had exposed their daughter to danger from mercenary motives, and had afterwards treated her very harshly—Mrs. Armour, indeed, so far relenting as to wait on Jean during her confinement. 2. Jean is more to be pitied than blamed. There was indeed a strong temptation to renew her intercourse with such a lover as Burns, but she should have resisted it. It would, we believe, have been far better for her had she never seen Burns again. 3. Burns, for his part, should be both pitied and blamed. If he still loved Jean with that wild, animal affection he had for her, it was wrong in him to seek her company. At all events, he saw very well where the danger lay, and "surely in vain is the net spread in the sight of any bird." His duty had been to have avoided the house entirely, unless he had had a distinct purpose of marriage. But notice, 4, how the case was now complicated on his return from Edinburgh. He found Jean cast out to the naked elements, in a condition calling for all his manly sympathy. This pointed to marriage as the only remedy. In opposition to this there were certain considerations:— 1st. He had learned, and it was not his fault that he had done so, to appreciate a higher style of woman, and could not but contrast Jean with Miss Hamilton, Miss Chalmers, and others he had met and admired. 2nd. Jean must have lowered herself to a certain degree in his estimation by her recent conduct, and he must have shrunk from the thought of connecting himself with a family which had used him so ill. And then, 3rd, there was "Clarinda" entertaining the hope that she might yet win and keep him. Such was the many forked dilemma in which Burns was placed; and it says a great deal for him that he determined to give to poor Jean the benefit of whatever doubts he might have as to the propriety of his conduct. It was mainly, we think, compassion which caused him make what was, in many points, a sacrifice. If so, it was virtue rewarded, for she turned out in many things an excellent helpmeet for him; and much of the real sunshine of his later life, besides that which broke on him fitfully from the smile of the Muse, came from the face of his faithful, industrious, and loving wife. He found for her a lodging in Mauchline, where she remained till he acknowledged her to be his wife—not formally at first, but according to Scotch fashion, by calling her "Mrs. Burns" publicly, in company and in correspondence. A friend of ours remembers well seeing in Mauchline the room and the bed where Burns and Jean first slept after their marriage was acknowledged.

Burns left Mauchline for Edinburgh on the 10th of March. A few days after he writes Miss Chalmers that he had taken Ellisland. Patrick Miller, brother of the Lord Justice Clerk, had lately become possessor of an estate which had once belonged to the family of Comyn, whose chief, the Red Comyn, had been stabbed by Bruce at Dumfries. On this estate of Dalswinton there were several farms, two of which were rich haugh ground bearing wheat, and the third, Ellisland, not nearly so rich. Burns, as Allan Cunningham's father told him, made a poet's choice, not a farmer's. Now it seems most beautifully situated, the river Nith flowing with measured majesty through bold banks and red scaurs, which are surmounted by the richest woodland; arable and pasture fields behind; Dalswinton and its deep groves on the other side of the stream; Friars' Carse a little way to the north-west; the house clean and plain — quite a model farm-house now as well as then—standing over the river, and before the barnyard where Burns produced his "Mary in Heaven;" altogether the sweetest, most romantic, and congenial piece of scenery which has any permanent connection with the history of Burns. Lochlea and Mossgiel have both features of interest, and around both, as well as around the cottage of his birth, are entwined more peculiar associations; but none of them can for a moment be compared for beauty with Ellisland. Could a poet fail to be happy here is a question which at once suggests itself at the first sight of the place. Assuredly there are other things necessary to happiness besides a beautiful locality; but it constitutes one element in a poet's life, which is by no means to be despised, and which it took a good deal in Burns' environment otherwise to counteract. We remember a man of great powers of mind, warm political feelings, and poetical temperament, unfavourably situated in a northern town, where he had a great deal of factious opposition to encounter which embittered and shortened his career, exclaiming, "Were it not for that glorious river (one of the finest of Highland streams) how wretched I should have been here!" And miserable as Burns often was at Ellisland, we believe he would have been more so had he not had the red scaur on which to stride, and the river to contemplate, now with calm emotion when it was calm, and now with a "stern delight and strange" when its waters were swollen and stormy, and his spirit required not so much solace as sympathy.

His landlord is said to have been kind to Burns in his bargain, giving him a lease of seventy-six years at an annual rent of £50 for the first three years, and £70 for the remainder, with other promised advantages. Miller was himself a remarkable man, of a mechanical genius, and was at this time employed in trying to propel vessels by means of paddles. He even built a vessel with paddles and a small steam-engine, and tried it on a lake near Dalswinton. The attempt was successful, but Miller did not persevere although it was his boat when lying neglected at Port-Dundas that suggested to both Fulton and Henry Bell their better-considered mechanisms, by which the Hudson and the Clyde were to be peopled by those grand imperious vessels, which do not supplicate but force their way through the waves, and which, when traversed and opposed, wrestle like demons of kindred power and greater mastery with the angry billows. We remember seeing a mythical story of this Dalswinton voyage and its crew, said to consist, among others, of Burns and of Brougham, then a boy student out from Edinburgh; and it had been a capital subject for a Savage Landor to describe their forgathering, their talk during the day, and above all their symposium at night, and would remind one in some points of the scene described by Scott in his "Fair Maid of Perth"—the boy Crawford, the Tiger Earl, out-talking and out-drinking such an auld-used hand as Sir John Ramorny! But the story is, we suspect, a mere fable.

On the 13th March Burns concluded his arrangement with Miller, and on the 20th of the same month he completed his reckoning with the much-revolving and slow-rendering William Creech. There are here some puzzling contradictions in statements of facts. On the one hand, Burns himself says to Dr. Moore, "I believe I shall clear about £400, some little odds; but even part of this depends on what the gentleman (Creech) has yet to settle with me." Currie, again, declares at the close of his memoir, that Burns received a clear profit of £900. William Nicol wrote to Mr. Lewars, after the poet's death, that Burns told him that he received £600 for the Edinburgh edition, and £100 after for the copyright. Heron, again, says that the whole sum paid to the poet for the copyright, and for the subscription copies of this book, amounted to nearly £1100. Out of this the expenses of printing the edition for the subscribers must be deducted. The probability is that Burns only realized £400. For whatever the round sum he got, there would be deducted from it not only the printing expenses, but certain debts which we are told the poet had contracted in Edinburgh, and thus there would be left only £400, and a little odds, as he admits there was. During this process of arrangement Burns describes himself as nearly crazed, and actually fevered. No wonder.

On the 24th March, 1788, he left Edinburgh permanently, doubtless with mingled emotions of gratitude, grief, and perplexity, with life absolutely to begin again at the age of twenty-nine. He went first to Glasgow, and thence by a rapid movement to Dumfriesshire. While in Edinburgh he must have heard that Jean had born him twins, both of whom soon died. On the 30th of March we find him riding across a track of melancholy moors between Glasgow and Ayrshire on a Sabbath

LIFE OF BURNS.

day, and composing some stanzas, which he afterwards interwove into the "Chevalier's Lament," and which bear a strong testimony to the dreary state of his mind. It might have been called Burns' Lament, not alas! his last one: for the rest of the life of this most blithesome (at times) of the sons of men, and who sometimes drank out larger draughts of intellectual, social, animal, and moral pleasure, than any other man—to whom, indeed, the word enjoyment meant something else than to most of his kind—meant rapture or ecstasy—was to be one long lamentation seldom briefly and irregularly interrupted by what ought to have been in happier circumstances the normal tenor of his existence. He went next to Ayrshire to receive instructions for an exciseman; and Mr. James Findlay, Tarbolton, had a charge from the worshipful Excise Commissioners "to instruct the bearer, Robert Burns, in the art of gauging casks, and fitting him for surveying victuallers, rectifiers, chandlers, tanners, tawers, &c.; and after Robert Burns has been six weeks thus engaged, certifying that he hath cleared his quarters both for lodgings and diet, and that he has actually paid each of you for his instructions and examination, and that he hath sufficient at the time to purchase a horse for the business." A more humiliating document our country does not possess amidst all her records, from the Ragman's-roll downwards! The brightest, and not by many, many degrees the worst man in Scotland, doomed to such drudgery as preliminary to drudgery of a similar sort ranging over his whole future life! And how few *felt* the appalling anti-climax of the author of the "Cottar's Saturday Night" studying gauging for six weeks at Tarbolton under the eye of a supervisor, James Findlay by name. Nay, we question if he felt it fully himself; had he done so, we would not have answered for the consequences. Nevertheless he had some real happiness even then, as all men may reach at any time by virtuous action. He had before refused to Gavin Hamilton to be security for his brother, but had truly said that the language of refusal was to him the most difficult of all language. It was his misfortune, not his fault surely, that his lips could not easily fold around the monosyllable "No." Now, however, he gave his brother Gilbert, who was in difficulties and had the support of poor old Mrs. Burns on his shoulders, £180, about the half he had himself. It was strictly more a gift to his mother than to his brother, and given at interest. The rest of the sum he put into his farm, with as little result ultimately as if he had thrown it into the Nith.

Jean was with him while he was receiving his instructions in the Excise mysteries. Chambers says she preferred another to Burns, and we hardly wonder at it. She was, we think, incapable of appreciating him fully in himself, or of seeing him except in the reflex light of the admiration of others. And she knew his faults so thoroughly. Indeed, our astonishment is that, all things considered, the marriage turned out so well. As there was little love to begin with, the wonder was that, like Slender's, it did not decrease on better acquaintance. With a little money, however, a little experience, Jean less "glaikit" than she had been, and Burns a sadder and thinking himself a wiser man, "they," as one in "Caleb Williams" has it, "turned in together, and thought they would rub on main well with one another." And so in a manner they did, and the longer the better.

Chambers closes his account of what may be called the Edinburgh section of Burns' life with some remarks breathing a good spirit, but hardly germane to the matter. His talk of Burns as being a prophet, a Prometheus, and sustaining such a character in Edinburgh, is more suited to the high-wrought, self-reflecting nature of a Carlyle than to his own sober and sensible style of thought. We think Burns far greater, though not better, in Dumfries, writing his songs or cherishing his solitary ideals, rejected by the select society of the place, walking out lowering and lonely to Lincluden Abbey, or taking the shady side of the street, than when he was the pet of the Edinburgh public. All we can say of him then is that in Edinburgh his head was not turned nor his self-possession lost. It may be said that it was the Sun, and not the Wind, which made the traveller loosen his cloak. But what were the soft airs and warm glances of his Edinburgh experience, as a trial of manhood, compared with the forces of the Sun of Sahara and the Simoom, which united latterly against his naked head? Yet them he withstood. He died, indeed, but died not yielding to them, but yielding to his own passions and appetites; for, like Byron's wounded eagle,

"He nursed the pinion that propelled the steel."

None but himself was able to destroy himself. He had undoubtedly a contempt for pensions, but it does not seem to us a wise contempt. Did a pension necessarily compromise independence? Were all pensions bribes? He thought a pension a "collar;" but was it not sometimes a becoming badge, such as he had given to his own "Cæsar?"

"His lockit, lettered, braw, brass collar,
Showed him the gentleman and scholar."

In his wild spirit of independence Burns would have spurned even "fairy gold," had it fallen at his door. There was but one man living then in Britain Burns' superior—namely, Edmund Burke, his equal in genius, and incomparably his superior in acquirements. He accepted a pension, and the most eloquent and powerful of his writings—his "Letter to a Noble Lord" and his "Letters on a Regicide Peace"—arose to the tune of Government ingots. He felt he had a title to what he received, and that gave him a proud honesty in using it; and within his pension, as within a bank, the noble stream of his genius flowed on with equal dignity and with greater power than before.

CHAPTER XI.

ELLISLAND.

LLISLAND was in the full flush of summer when, on the 13th of June, 1788, Burns took possession. It needed all the music, and flowers, and foliage of the leafy month, to cheer up to his eye the circumstances amidst which he came to it. There was an old steading to be taken down; there was a new house to be built; Jean, with her sole surviving child, was far off in Ayrshire, and was not expected in a hurry. All was annoyingly and disappointingly new. He was alone. His Muse at first was shy, and his prose journal and his correspondence became his only safety valves. He speaks of the "foggy atmosphere of his soul," as if his years were now "all winters," to use that gasp of poor Byron's. He praises Jean to Mrs. Dunlop, determined to make the best of his bargain. He gives a great many reasons for his marriage, besides "rooted attachment," which itself might have been sufficient—reasons, however, which the reader, remembering his quite recent flirtations with Clarinda, is not very much disposed as a whole to believe. He has now reached the poet's dream—"Love in a Cottage;" but, alas! the cottage is smoky—

> "The red peat gleams a fiery kernel,
> Encircled by a fog infernal,"

and he is far from his Love. Her absence, however, made his heart grow fonder, and he poured out the exquisite song, "Of a' the Airts the Wind can Blaw," showing how, while prose could only lamely argue out his case in the matter of the marriage, poetry could create passion where it was not, or stir up the last fading embers into a youthful blaze. One might imagine in reading "Of a' the Airts," and "Were I on Parnassus' Hill," that they were the effusions of a boy lover. It casts a curious light on song writing, as the outcome of the sincerity or depth of love, to know that the best verses in "Of a' the Airts" (Oh! blaw, ye westland winds, blaw saft, &c.), are not by Burns at all, but by one John Hamilton, a music-seller in Edinburgh. But these songs of Burns show that he was trying to recall the old love of his espousals, and to reconcile at once himself and his wife to their inevitable lot.

While thus musing and rhyming in solitude, he sometimes employed his leisure in wandering through the grounds of Friars' Carse—an estate lying northward from Ellisland, belonging to Captain Riddell of Glenriddell, a man of antiquarian and literary taste, and of a social turn. His mansion was once a monastic establishment, and stands on a rocky promontory overlooking the Nith, with a long strip of alluvial soil [carse] stretching eastward through shrubberies—hence the compound word Friars' Carse. Here Burns, furnished with a key, often wandered, not, however, as Robert Chambers describes him, with "hope green in his bosom," but with pensive and melancholy thoughts, which he expresses without disguise in his journal, but which, toned down, took the form of his "Verses written in Friars' Carse Hermitage," a rural cot Riddell had constructed near the house. These bear the date of 28th June, but were altered and a little expanded afterwards.

Burns was now, if we believe Allan Cunningham, a "busy and a happy man;" presiding over the building of his new house and steading. That he was busy is unquestionable; but as the business and other circumstances were not congenial, we doubt the happiness. He worked on, however, energetically, "digging foundations, collecting stones, seeking sand, carting lime, and even laying on the stones of the house." The result was, as we can vouch, a pleasant humble cottage near the red scaur he loved; with a sitting room on the east, looking down on the stream and valley; a west room called the Spence, where guests of distinction, like Sir Egerton Brydges, would dine with Burns; a kitchen and a bedroom lying between, and a garret. A well was in a bank below; and a barn, stackyard, byre, and stable were behind.

At Communions of old time, and not indeed very long since, there was a general washing and clearing of reputations, like the Whitsuntide cleanings; and on the Monday after the town or village looked, to use Andrew Fairservice's language (in "Rob Roy"), as "crouse as a cat when all the flaes are kamed aff her;" and the streets presented a kind of jaunty, jail-delivery aspect, partly because the old sins were condoned, and partly because new ones might now be contracted with impunity till the next year! One of these annual atonement days now

ELLISLAND.

reached the village of Mauchline on the 5th of August, 1788; and Robert Burns and Jean Armour compeared before the Session for the last time, were rebuked for their past irregularity, their marriage formally acknowledged, the parties solemnly exhorted to adhere faithfully to each other as man and wife, and the amount of the fee usual on such occasions for the poor left to the generosity of "Mr. Burns." "Mr. Burns," it is added, gave a guinea note on behalf of the poor. Thus under difficulties was the complete consummation of the marriage between this immortal pair attained at last, and Burns might and did exclaim—

"I hae a wife o' my ain."

Extremely miserable at Ellisland, as some of his letters prove him, Burns was rather often repairing to Ayrshire to meet his Jean, and to string again his lyre, which had become somewhat "becobwebbed" in the hut on his farm. One of these productions was a "Fête Champetre," written on the occasion of a gay supper or ball given by Mr. Cunningham of Enterkin, who, it was said, meant it for an electioneering feast, as he intended to canvass Ayrshire, an intention he afterwards relinquished. It was the first specimen of a style which Burns often practised afterwards, and in which, as in most styles, he excelled, but which was hardly worthy of his genius, it being thoroughly artificial—its inspiration, party spirit; and its result, clever personality; and on its point, as on a bright prong, many insipid and worthless characters are suspended and immortalized. Soon after this he was advised to try English instead of Scotch verse, and produced the first of three Epistles to Mr. Graham of Fintry, which are certainly not the most felicitous of his writings, but forced and powerless. When a Highland woman got excited in conversation she began to talk good English instead of Gaelic, and then it was said, "Ye have gotten to your English." So Burns sometimes, as in his "Vision" and the close of his "Cottar's Saturday Night," got to his English, and was never better, or so good. But in these "Epistles to Graham," and some other productions, he began with his English, and conspicuously failed. Yet the following are manly lines:—

"Ere my poor soul such deep damnation stain,
My horny fist assume the plough again,
The piebald jacket let me patch once more;
On eighteen pence a week I've lived before."

Still wearying for his wife, he writes a letter to Miss Chalmers in her praise. He says, "I have not got modish manners, polite tattle, and fashionable dress." One might think of the fox and the grapes; but he adds, "I have got the handsomest figure, the sweetest temper, the soundest constitution, and the kindest heart in the country." This cluster of superlatives seems a little overdone, and, as formerly, distance is lending enchantment to the view.

Yet he did undoubtedly like Jean better after she was made "an honest woman," and when, like many Scotch women of humble life, who were erratic before, she was likely to prove, and did prove, an excellent and devoted wife. At last, after Burns had been compelled to enter his new house before it was plastered, and to suffer all that damp and disarray could add to his previous discomfort, came bleak December with its horrors and its memories, and in stept Jean, like a winter sun-glint, to minister a little light and comfort. The new house was not fit for her as yet, and she had to go to a neighbouring farm, which stood on what is called the Isle—a piece of ground once encircled by the Nith, in the immediate proximity of the old churchyard of Dunscore, which contained the tomb of Grierson of Lagg, the noted persecutor; and as it was thought at that time haunted, it was at present without a tenant. In this "ruined grange," as Shakspeare has it, Jean Armour, now Mrs. Burns, was installed mistress. It was rather a gloomy and ominous place she had reached, but it was her home—the first she could really call her own. Burns was with her, and her flitting had come safely the week before, including a fine four-posted bed, presented her by Mrs. Dunlop. A west-country servant, Elizabeth Smith, daughter of an exemplary parent, who had charged Burns to look after her morals, and

"On the Questions tairge her tichtly"

(and she used to say that he did so faithfully), had arrived. Not a mile up the stream the new house of Ellisland was getting ready for his wife's reception; and we have no doubt that, composed if not gleeful, she accepted the circumstances of her situation, and had no prophetic glimpse of the haggard destiny which here and elsewhere lay before her lord and herself.

Her coming seemed to rouse the old soul of song within him. He had written previously one on Captain Riddell's marriage—"The day returns, my bosom burns"—and an elegy on the death of a promising son of Fergusson of Craigdarroch. But these, though good, bore no proportion to the two charming songs, both dated Ellisland, the 17th of December—"Auld Langsyne" and "Bonny Mary"—

"Go fetch to me a pint of wine"—

both pretending to be old, but both stamped in the fresh burning mint of his own genius. It was, for the nonce, a happy and half-inspired man who, on one day (the 1st January, 1789) wrote that letter to Gilbert Burns, so honourable to his heart and filial piety, and that other letter to Mrs. Dunlop, so characteristic of his sensibility, native taste, and imaginative power. Surely, we say, habitual happiness would have made this man always good and true to himself; or surely, at least, elements could have been mingled in his cup which might have made it a sweeter and a holier one. What might not fuller recognition, better society, a more congenial employment, a little more money, along with this new domestic comfort, have done for him, to save him from temptation and to minister to him peace! Such thoughts will pass through our minds, useless as they may be deemed; he was so worth saving, not so much as a poet, in which he has in spite of everything gained the highest honours, but as a man.

A month previously, on occasion of an attack being made on the memory of the Stuarts by the Rev. Mr. Kirkpatrick of Dunscore, he wrote an indignant and eloquent letter to the London *Star*, a paper conducted by John Mayne (author of "The Siller Gun"), a native of Dumfriesshire. It seemed the last expression of Burns' Jacobite loyalty. We meet with that very seldom, if ever afterwards, either in his prose or verse.

He began very soon to have doubts as to the success of his farm, and this made him exert every influence to get an Excise appointment in the district where it was situated. His acerbity seems in a short time to have returned, as we judge from a letter to Dugald Stewart, in which he speaks of a projected work, entitled "The Poet's Progress," and gives as a specimen a character of Creech, whom he regarded at that time with great bitterness and aversion. It is a mercy for Burns that this poem was never carried further, since, in the first place, it would have been another effort in that style of laboured and heavy satire which he had begun in his Letter to Graham of Fintry, and which, when compared to his earlier effusions, resembles the sluggish flight and blunted blow of a heron beside the rapid swoop and sharp decisive stroke of an eagle; and because, secondly, to Creech it would have been, on the whole, unfair. All his fellows in trade maintained that Creech was incapable of wilful injustice, though not incapable of remissness, craft, and negligence. But the fact is that Burns, whenever unhappy in himself or in his environment, threw out and partially relieved his misery by fierce and unprovoked attacks on others, and this he was most apt to do when unduly excited. He was, besides, haunted by an ambition to be a great satirist, one of the most wretched of literary callings; and for which, if his wit and humour fitted him, his naturally kind disposition and his solid judgment were as certainly disqualifications. His misery more than his will consented to write bitter things, and his irregularities coincided. But whenever he was comparatively happy, and this was not infrequent, and when his intellect was in its average state of manly clearness, he deplored what he had written; and such is very nearly the way in which we account for his obscene verses. In heated passion he wrote; in hours of calm reflection he regretted them. In Byron it was not quite the same. He had not such warm and generous feelings as Burns—was more permanently and less reasonably soured—did not, however, commit himself so much as the Scottish poet either in severity or in smut, but went to the unhappy work with more coolness and deliberation. We can never conceive Burns thrusting his character of Creech under the Bibliopole's chair, as Byron did, under Rogers', his Satanic philippic on that poet. Burns' "Creechiad, or Progress of a Poet," was never completed. The letters to the bookseller—some of them intemperate enough—were submitted to the eye of Miss Chalmers, who got them destroyed, and long before the Poet's death the two were reconciled. Dr. Currie speaks somewhat doubtfully of the rides Burns took while still Jean was in the West, as exposing him to danger; and Professor Wilson has most unmercifully ridiculed the idea of there being no safety for Burns in Sanquhar, and of it being impossible for him to pass the door of a public-house in Thornhill; and says that if this were the case, he should have been shut up in a lunatic asylum. And here Wilson is substantially right. Burns, though far too social, and though he might have what is proverbially called a "spark in his throat," a complaint very common in his day, was by no means in danger of becoming a victim or habitual debauchee. To say he never drank alone is not true, since in his letters he speaks several times of doing so, even to intoxication (see letter from Ecclefechan); but that he often debauched himself by himself or in his own house is not proven, and is not very likely. Like Falstaff, "villanous company" was his undoing, and often company not very select; an honest Boniface, a "pursy" old landlord, "waddling upstairs" with his huge "jeroboam" in his shaky hand; a bagman from the south or a pedlar from the north; a hedge schoolmaster or a landlady like that accommodating she of "Tam o' Shanter"—any of these were good enough "to drink with," and he extracted from them humour and character, and various poetical material. Now and then, no doubt, in his rides to Ayrshire he found reunions collected for him, and receptions given, which implied a late sitting and a late rising, with a dreadful headache, and, as he confesses to his brother William, with an addled brain. But nothing that would then be considered very serious happened; and for such excesses as he committed and confessed to Jean, she would give him a gentle shrift. Once or twice he met with strange adventures, one of which will be found described by himself in reference to the funeral retinue of Mrs. Oswald of Auchencruive, driving him out from a snug room, fire, and smoking bowl, through moors, mosses, and snow drifts, to New Cumnock. The defunct lady, we believe, was as much to blame for his exclusion from the inn as for the other charges brought against her in the portentous ode beginning—

LIFE OF BURNS.

"Dweller in yon dungeon dark."

In February he visited Edinburgh to receive £50 which Creech was owing him for sales effected since the final settlement, and with which Burns seems to have been satisfied. His younger brother, William, had at this time called at the Isle, and been kindly received. Burns addressed to him some very brotherly and sensible letters (to be found fully in CORRESPONDENCE). He was a saddler first in Newcastle and afterwards in London, and died in the latter place in July, 1790. He lies in Paul's Churchyard. He seems to have been a quiet, steady, commonplace, un-Burnsian, but worthy kind of man.

Burns did not call on "Clarinda" when in Edinburgh. That she expected and wished for him we gather from the fact that she tells Ainslie that she was determined to avoid her windows when he was in town, lest she should catch even a glimpse of him from them! She wrote him soon after in upbraiding terms about his marriage; and he replied in a tone half savage, half soft, vindicating himself vigorously, reproaching her gently, throwing out hints about his severe struggles, and pointing back to the "mirk night of December,"

"When sparkling was the rosy wine, and private was the chamber,"

with a finger which seemed to tremble at the recollection, rather with joy and glad reminiscence than with regret. He began at this time to bear the penalties of successful authorship, partly by having books or MSS. submitted to his opinion or revision, and partly by finding himself patronized by men who were his inferiors in everything but popularity and a better account at their booksellers than his. Yet Dr. Moore's letters, while a little too consciously condescending in their tone, are both friendly and discriminating. Still, in advising him to give up the Scottish language in his compositions, he shows that he had no conception that Burns was a national poet—the national poet of his country. Burns was not only the greatest British poet living, but Scotland was his special province, and her language on his lips was royal.

In poetry he was doing little, and that little of no great importance or sufficiently characteristic—a few trifles, such as his rhymed sketch of Charles James Fox; "Delia," which, though doubted to be his, he unquestionably sent to the London *Star*; his clever octosyllabics "To James Tennant of Glenconnar," an old and tried friend of the poet's and his family, whom we have seen helping him in his choice of Ellisland;* his lines on a "Wounded Hare," which are more creditable to his humanity than to his poetic powers, although, if the *lout* was cruel to the hare when shooting her with young, Dr. Gregory was equally so in his savage hypercriticism on the poem—a critique

* The late Charles Tennant, Esq., of St. Rollox, was a son of his.

done with true professional *animus*, as if to show he had seldom such a fine subject for his scalpel; and his "Address to the Toothache," worthy of the days of the "Louse" and the "Haggis," and which we know has been read for consolation by the martyrs of the malady, and has given to sad despair

"A gloomy smile."

Some of these he despatched to Creech, who talked of publishing a new edition of the poet's works, but paid him nothing for these additional pieces in the meantime.

A few miles from Ellisland, to the north-west, lies a fine undulating country, stretching toward the little village of Dunscore; on the south are the hills of Irongray, a bold and rugged range; in the valley at their feet, in the centre of a wood, stands the monument erected by Sir Walter Scott to Helen Walker, the prototype of Jeanie Deans, where we have been; and in the midst of them lies Craigenputtock, the property and once the dwelling-place of Thomas Carlyle—a gloomy place, we are told, with its dark firs around and melancholy moors behind, reminding visitors, who are also readers, of the pine-shadowed and moated castle where Maturin describes his dark Knight of the Forest keeping his state, and conversing at the portals with those doomed ones who came to consult him and inhale all hell through his half-shut visor, as

"Rolls the rich thunder of his awful voice"

in that

"*Infernal* colloquy sublime,"

and who remained his vassals and victims forever more! It was of Dunscore auld kirk that Carlyle said to Emerson, when the latter was sounding him on religious subjects, "Christ died on the Cross, and that built Dunscore kirk in the valley down there, and brought you and me together." They were standing on a hill behind Monyaive. In that kirk, in Burns' day, there laboured a Mr. Kirkpatrick, a Calvinistic clergyman of the old school, whose public teaching was in inverse ratio and dismal antithesis to his private benevolence. He was a blameless and good man; but his doctrine made Burns, not unaccustomed to the habit, to "blaspheme an octave higher," and to cry out "From such conceptions of my Creator good Lord deliver me." He seems to have had a wicked pleasure, while Mr. Kirkpatrick was preaching, in silently tearing asunder the webs of argument the preacher had been laboriously weaving, and would come home often on the tiptoe of triumph at his success. One remembers Theodore Parker listening for years to Lyman Beecher! There is a story about the minister having rather maltreated the poet. Burns, highly to his credit, had got up a library in the parish. Sir John Sinclair had begun to prepare his great statistical work on Scotland, and had applied to Mr. Kirkpatrick, as he did to hundreds of parish ministers, for information. In his reply, we have been told that Kirkpatrick deliberately suppressed the fact of Burns having instituted a library at Dunscore; and that Burns, in indignation, wrote Sir John on the subject. We find no such letter among his Correspondence, although in Mr. MacDowell's interesting notices of Burns' closing days there is a reference to a letter from Captain Riddell to Sinclair on the matter. If Kirkpatrick did omit to mention it out of spite to Burns, it was mean; but then we must remember that he was not only a Calvinist, but a heresy-hunter! and this should cover a multitude of sins.

At this time occurred the famous case of Dr. William MacGill of Ayr, who was tried for Socinian error, and in defence of whom Burns wrote the "Kirk's Alarm," a piece of very considerable point; although he was only half-hearted in his satirical poems—showed rather the power than the will to sting, and wanted something of the savage gusto of a Swift or a Byron. MacGill was a very respectable but odd man; he escaped by making sundry concessions to his adversaries, and died reputed a saint, if not an orthodox divine, at the age of seventy-six. Late on in summer Burns took possession at last of Ellisland. He did so in a peculiar and poetic fashion. He told his servant, little Elizabeth Smith, to take the family Bible with a bowl of salt, placing the one above the other, and walk on from the Isle to the new house, and take care to enter before any other person. This was the old *freit* to secure good luck. He and his wife followed—a peculiar couple—he strong, swarthy, somewhat stooped, striding manfully along; his wife, tall, fair, and though not remarkably beautiful, rather handsome; with little Betty, the Bible, and the salt: the whole procession advancing picturesquely, perhaps with involuntary laughter on his part and a look of puzzled pleasure on Jean's, along the brushwood banks of the Nith to their common home. Did the salt spill as the party were entering, and did he read in this the disturbance of the *freit*, and an omen of the dark future? Burns, superstitious from his constitution, habits, and education, was fond of visits to the Witch of Endor Cavern, to inquire as to the *to come;* although, to his knocking at the door of Destiny, there was but the old reply—the echo of the sound he himself had made, or a voice like that of hollow laughter, shivering and dying away in the distance!

Burns had now some critical correspondence with Miss Helen Maria Williams (see Boswell's Johnson) anent a poem of her's, long since forgotten, on the Slave Trade; and with the brothers Stuart, three remarkable Scotchmen connected with the London Press, one of whom enjoyed the applause and friendship of Coleridge and inherited the hatred and rampant abuse of William Cobbett. On the 18th of August his wife bore the poet another son, whom he called Francis Wallace, in honour of Mrs. Dunlop. He now saw, more forcibly than ever, the necessity of having two strings to his bow, and applied to Mr. Graham to be appointed excise-officer of the country district where he lived. He meant to make his farm principally a dairy farm, with which branch his sisters were most conversant, so that, while they and his wife might manage the cows and milk, he might attend to his excise duties. One of the Stuarts had known Robert Fergusson, and his allusions to him called forth some plaintive letters from Burns anent his case, with a kind of prophetic murmur in them, as if the fate of the admired might be soon that of the admirer. Indeed, his too intense sympathy with him was itself an unconscious prediction of this.

Yet now let all gloom for a season be dismissed! From o'er the hills and far away let two kindred spirits arrive (like spate-swollen tributaries, the Cairn and the Scaur, to join the Nith) to mingle with the Burns river, relieving its monotony, and making it resound with the joy of waves! Let William Nicol, Allan Masterton, and Robert Burns compear together, and let Moffat be the meeting place of the three friends, determined for one night to be as happy as the dreams of avarice or the realities of royalty! There are some perplexities about the date and place. Allan Cunningham says it was the heating of the house of Laggan, a small estate which Nicol had purchased in the parish of Glencairn. But the inexorable evidence of documents seems to prove that Nicol had not entered on his estate till 1790, a year after this jovial meeting. Burns speaks of Moffat as the scene; but if so, how came Nicol to brew a "peck o' maut" there? a process which would have been natural enough at the farm town of Laggan. At all events the orgy took place; and however strange it may seem now in the eyes of Good Templarism or of sober sense, there can be no doubt it was a joyous one; not a coarse Bacchanalian carousal but "the feast of reason and the flow of soul." They were all superior men, and their talk that night, be sure, was not "of bullocks." It was quite a *Noctes Ambrosianæ*, and since all three, the Laird of Laggan's many hills, the fine-hearted teacher of English in the Edinburgh High School, and the Poet of all time, are dead, and such symposia are past, we presume for ever, let us not be too severe on its memory. Let us charitably believe that all went to bed sober; and though it was sung—

> "Wha last beside his chair shall fa',
> He is the king amang us three,"

that the feast ended as it began, in a republic, not a monarchy. Now it seems, through the vista of eighty-nine years, a feast of Valhalla—the "maut" and the symposiasts are alike shadows, and it is the ghost of a moon which sheds her evasive light and lifts her hollow horn over the ghastly revellers. The "ae nicht" was not followed by a second till some years afterwards, when we

FRIARS CARSE.

WILLIAM MACKENZIE, LONDON, EDINBURGH & GLASGOW.

find the three in Dumfries together for a week and more at the old work.

This autumn, too, occurred the contest of the "Whistle." Burns' account of the tradition from which it sprang will be found along with the poem. Charles Sharpe exposes some errors in it; but the whole story is evidently mythical, remotely founded on fact. The contest this year was to be between Captain Riddell of Glencarse, Mr. Fergusson of Craigdarroch, and Sir Robert Lawrie of Maxwelltown, then M.P. for Dumfriesshire. Fergusson gained the day. Burns was present, being invited to attend the party to see that the gentlemen drank fair, and to write a poem on the subject. An eye-witness, William Hunter, told Chambers he remembered the whole transaction, being then a servant at Friars' Carse. Burns took no part in the proceedings, sat by himself drinking only a little brandy, was quite sober, and left on his own feet after they were carried to bed. He wrote at a side table the verses, and read them over and over to the gentlemen to their great amusement. So far well. But think of Burns being present as a kind of flunkey or waiter at such a scene, and compelled to draw inspiration from it! His position at "Willie brewed a peck o' maut" rises to judicial sobriety and dignity compared to this. The ebony whistle remained with Mr. Fergusson of Craigdarroch, son of the victor, M.P. for the county of Kirkcudbright. Will it be believed that the author of these pages, along with another clergyman from the neighbourhood of Dumfries, called in June, 1865, on an English family which had taken Friars' Carse for the season—people genteel in appearance, in respectable circumstances, and exceedingly polite, tradespeople hailing from London; and when we asked to see the room where, according to Robert Burns, the "Whistle" contest took place, we found they had never heard of it, and had never heard of Robert Burns! Such are—

"The glory and the nothing of a name."

This autumn Burns composed his "Mary in Heaven," or rather, like many of his poems, it came upon him in remarkable circumstances, observed by his wife, and afterwards recorded by Lockhart and his other biographers. How forcibly they were recalled to us when, after our visit to Friars' Carse and our unique adventure there, we strolled in the fine sunset to the barn-yard behind Ellisland, and the whole scene and a portion of the agony, too, were reproduced as we repeated the lines—

"O, Mary, dear departed shade,
Where is thy place of blissful rest?
See'st thou thy lover lowly laid?
Hear'st thou the groans that rend his breast?"

In such hours as those, which so rarely occur in life, when the heart is forced back by intense realization of the woes of others on perished passages of its own past, it knoweth its own bitterness, and feels it partly relieved and partly increased, and that such a mingled feeling is far more precious and far more dear than the most exquisite enjoyments. Bruise down joy sufficiently, and it yields sorrow; and bruise down misery sufficiently, and it yields deep, though pensive and peculiar joy; and whatever be the case with the joy which ends in sorrow, with that which arises from it no stranger can intermeddle. It is beyond the name of pleasure; it is too deep for tears.

Burns was labouring under a cold, but still in fair spirits, and busy at his harvest work. As the evening drew on he appeared to get very sad about something, and instead of entering the house went to the barn-yard, and continued there in spite of his wife's reminding him that it was frost; wandering up and down, throwing himself on a mass of straw and fixing his eyes on the starry firmament, especially on one bright planet which shone like another moon.* At length he came in, called for his desk, and wrote "To Mary in Heaven." Chambers is at great pains to show that this took place on the 20th of October, 1789, that being a late season, and that this supplies the date of Mary's death. He proves what is more remarkable, that Venus was not then a morning, but an evening star, and not the "star that ushers in the morn." Perhaps Burns took a poetical license. Chambers wonders how Burns can, after he had met with Charlotte Hamilton, Margaret Chalmers, and Clarinda, revert so fondly to this simple country girl. But he forgets they were still living, Mary was dead. They were brilliant figures which crossed his stage; she was his betrothed wife, dear to him as the ruddy drops that visited his sad heart, and torn by a malignant fever, as by the hand of a demon, from his very arms. He loved to observe anniversaries, and here was seemingly the third one of his great loss; and in the transfiguring mood of his imagination, stirred by the unspeakable charm of autumn eve, he must shrine his loved one in heaven. It might be, too, that a tinge of remorse was in his bosom, else why should he talk, three years after her death, of his anguished bosom and heavy groans? In quite a different vein he wrote the next day to kind old Blacklock, and soon after we find him much in the society of a man who did a great deal to get Burns to forget his poverty and remember his misery no more—the redoubtable Captain Grose. Francis Grose, an Englishman, had seen better days, but had been compelled to live by his wits, and had—

"Ta'en the antiquarian trade,"
I think they call it."

He was a wit, scholar, humorist, and *bon vivant*, in

* Sir John Steel has thus represented him, in his magnificent statue of Burns, preparing for New York and Dundee.

person fat and little, had come to Friars' Carse to collect antiquities, and was a great favourite with Captain Riddell and his circle. He was getting up a work on Scottish antiquities, to which Burns, as we shall see, made a most important poetic contribution. At table Grose was fully a match for Burns in fun and anecdote; but Burns in his poems, and sometimes in talk, too, possessing the power of imagination, which Grose had not, could and did, by a single flash, at once illuminate and eclipse him. See his verses on Grose's peregrinations in Scotland in his oldest and best satirical vein. It was much the same with Patrick Robertson and Christopher North. Both were witty, one only a man of genius. Both were stout men; but Robertson was coarse and flabby. "You are getting enormously fat, Professor Wilson." "Yes," was his reply, "but not like many fat people, *loathsome*."

Meanwhile, our Poet had become, as he says, "a mighty exciseman before the Lord," doing his drudgery and scrub work with immense energy. John Newton said once, that if the angel Gabriel were appointed a shoe-black on earth he would be the best shoe-black in the parish; and so Burns, reduced to stoop and slave, must stoop with dignity and slave with diligence. He had the charge of ten parishes, and rode often two hundred miles a week. He was severe in general on the smuggler; but he knew how to temper justice with mercy. Professor Gillespie saw him once entering the house of a poor widow who sold whisky, to give her the hint to put her barrels out of the way, as the supervisor was coming. On another occasion he stept into a house where the wife was shrewdly suspected of selling a contraband dram, and sought for a gill and some bread and cheese; and after discussing them, he asked her, "Well, Jean, what's to pay for the whisky?" to which she archly replied, "Oh, naething ava for the whisky, but there's saxpence for bread and cheese." "Sin on, and fear not," was his laughing rejoinder as he left the house.

Once, according to the late esteemed Mr. Rodgerson, United Presbyterian minister of Thornhill, he was fairly *done* by a smuggler. A cart came to the inn at Thornhill with a number of barrels, on which Burns instantly *pounced*. The smuggler came up, and with tears in his eyes told a distressing story of a poor starving family, and so forth. Burns was quite melted, let the man off, and even gave him a pound. He had no sooner left than the barrels were examined, and lo! were filled with water. He found his continual riding over hill and dale rather laborious, although conducive to health and to that wayward and excursive tone of mind which a poet loves. Nor was this mode of life without its pleasant relaxations. There were respectable people here and there to whom his approach was an advent, who appreciated his genius, and admired his social qualities and conversational powers. One of these was the Rev. Mr. Jeffrey, minister of Lochmaben. He had a lively blue-eyed daughter. She had received him one night at the manse after a long ride very kindly; had given him a dish of tea or whatever might best contribute to his comfort. He brought down the next morning to breakfast one of the sweetest of his smaller lyrics—

"I gaed a waefu' gate yestreen,"

which we may be excused for saying we heard sung by an uncle of our own and namefather—the late Mr. George Barlas, of Glasgow, a *non-professional*—in tones of melting sweetness and manly pathos, which no stage ever excelled, and which delicious tears praised more eloquently and sincerely than could a thousand plaudits!

This blue-eyed lassie married a Mr. Renwick in New York, and afterwards gave a Scotchman a charming picture of Burns coming in to her father's house on cold rainy nights after long riding among the moors—of his manly and luminous talk, his easy and affable manners, and added, she "never could fancy that Burns followed the occupation of the plough, because everything he said or did had a gracefulness and charm that were in an extraordinary degree engaging." It is well when people are thankful for the gift of earthly immortality, and prove this by speaking with respect as well as gratitude of the donor.

And now 1790 had arrived and brought with it various verses, a Sketch, addressed to Mrs. Dunlop, and a Prologue, spoken at the Dumfries theatre on New-year's evening, communicated by him to Mr. Sutherland, a friend of David Campbell, of Ayr. But it brought also carking cares connected with business, bad prospects for his farm, and a gloomy state of mind. He had, he says, a bad tract of health most of the winter. Consequently, the first letters of the year are darkened by the heaviest hypochondria. It is sad to think that when a life is to be so short it should be so miserable. Burns did not attain even to a short life and a merry one. The gloom was still on him when in February he wrote a reply to a letter from Clarinda, in which he speaks of incessant headache, depressing spirits, a deranged nervous system, hints at grievous error and imprudence on his own part, and ends with a song—"Lovely Nancy!" He came in now and then to Dumfries to attend the theatre. And we soon find him in Johnson's "Museum" pouring out some of his most exquisite ditties — "Tam Glen," "Bonnie Ann" (addressed to Annie Masterton, a daughter of his friend Allan Masterton), and "My Heart's in the Highlands." The third volume of this Miscellany was now published with a characteristic preface by Burns.

A heresy-hunt was instituted by some nameless bigots of the day against a man, Heron of Kirkgunzeon, equally unknown till he signalized himself by binding down a man that was to be ordained to the Confession of Faith, "so far as it was agreeable to reason and the word of God." This raised Burns' wrath, who calls it a farce got up by the clergy; but he did not think it worth while to express his feelings about it in rhyme. He wrote instead such trifles as Elegy "On the Death of Peg Nicholson," a mare—called after the attempted assassin of George III.—which Willie Nicol had given Burns; and some clever verses addressed to a gentleman who had presented him with a newspaper, and offered to continue it free of expense, in which occur glimpses of rare sagacity and felicitous expression, such as—

"And how the collieshangie works
Between the Russians and the Turks;"
"If Denmark, ony body spak o't;"
"If sleekit Chatham Will was leevin,
Or glaikit Charley got his nieve in;
How Daddie Burke the plea was cookin';
If Warren Hastings' neck be yeukin'."

What admirable discrimination in these words—" Sleekit Chatham Will," more rogue than fool; " Glaikit Charley," careless, rollicking Charles James Fox; " Daddie Burke," prudent, profound, fatherly, as well as all-learned and all-brilliant, Edmund Burke. Burns saw men at a glance, and the glance was followed up like lightning by the single, searching, thunder word. This made him potentially as great a critic as a poet—a Hazlitt as well as a Byron. This insight he carried into his estimate of his species, of character, and of life. " Mankind," he says, " are by nature benevolent creatures, except in a few scoundrelly cases. I do not know that avarice of the good things we chance to have is born with us; but we are placed here amid such nakedness, hunger, and poverty and want, that we are under a cursed necessity of studying selfishness in order that we may exist. Still there are in every age a few souls that all the wants and woes of life cannot debase to selfishness, or even to the necessary alloy of caution and prudence. If I ever am in danger of vanity, it is when I contemplate myself on this side of my disposition and character. God knows I am no saint. I have a whole host of sins and follies to answer for; but if I could—and I believe I do it as far as I can—I would wipe away all tears from all eyes. Even the knaves who have injured me, I would oblige them; though, to tell the truth, it would be more out of vengeance, and to show that I was independent of and above them, than out of the overflowings of my benevolence."

Passing over some electioneering ballad writing, a thing Burns always does well, although it is seldom worth doing, we meet with a piece of real poetry, written about a man of whom hardly anything is known except that he was a jolly companion—one who loved his friend and his bottle —Matthew Henderson, Esq. On his unknown grave and obscure name Burns lavishes roses and *immortelles* in a very shower, one would say, of wasted feeling and beauty, were not the beauty so rich, and the feeling, though a little exaggerated in expression, so sincere. It might have been an elegy for Fox or Mirabeau, the idol of a nation, instead of for Matthew Henderson, the idol of Fortune's tavern. How powerful the genius which could almost match Lycidas in commemoration of a kindly *bon vivant*, to whom Burns bore probably the relation of "Tam o' Shanter" to "Souter Johnny!"—

"Tam lo'ed him like a vera brither."

We get from various quarters accounts how matters were going on in Ellisland this year (1790). They are somewhat contradictory, and it is difficult to strike an average. Some find nothing but extravagance on the part of the servants, and carelessness on that of the masters— "the lasses constantly employed in baking scones, and the lads eating them warm with ale." Others speak of Mrs. Burns as a prudent manager. One, William Clarke, who was a ploughman to Burns for six months, gives his master a good character on the whole—as hasty, but kindly; often from home, but attending pretty well to his farm when at home; never once intoxicated to Clarke's knowledge, or unable to attend to business; once terribly angry when he saw a servant woman nearly choking one of the cows by not cutting the potatoes small enough; not flush of liquor to servants, as other masters Clarke had known, though he sometimes gave them a dram for extra work; and the following, at least, was pretty certainly correct:— Usually dressed in a broad blue bonnet, a drab or blue long-tailed coat, corduroy breeches, dark blue stockings and cuitikins (short leggins), and with a "maud" on his shoulders when it was cold—just the Scottish farmer of the period, *cap-à-pié*.

We quote the descriptions of visits paid to him by Ramsay of Ochtertyre and Sir Egerton Brydges, the last of which especially is full of true, fresh enthusiasm :—

"Seeing him pass quickly near Closeburn, I said to my companion, 'That is Burns.' On coming to the inn, the ostler told us he would be back in a few minutes to grant permits; that where he met with anything seizable, he was no better than any other gauger; in everything else that he was perfectly a gentleman. After leaving a note to be delivered to him on his return, I proceeded to his house, being curious to see his Jean, &c. I was much pleased with his *uxor Sabina qualis*, and the poet's modest mansion, so unlike the habitation of ordinary rustics. In the evening he suddenly bounced in upon us, and said, as he entered, 'I come, to use the words of Shakspeare, "stewed in haste."' In fact, he had ridden incredibly fast after receiving my note. We fell into conversation directly, and soon got into the *mare magnum* of poetry. He told me that he had now gotten a story for a drama, which he was to call 'Rob Macquechan's Elshon,' from a popular story of Robert Bruce being defeated on the Water of Cairn, when the heel of his boot having loosened in his flight, he applied to Robert Macquechan to fit it, who, to make sure, ran his awl nine inches up the king's heel. We were now going on at a great rate, when Mr. S[tewart] popped in his head, which put a stop to our discourse, which had become very interesting. Yet in a little while it was resumed; and such was the force and versatility of the bard's genius, that he made the tears run down Mr. S[tewart]'s cheeks, albeit unused to the poetic strain. . . . From that time we met no more, and I was grieved at the reports of him afterwards. Poor Burns! we shall hardly ever see his like again. He was, in truth, a sort of comet in literature, irregular in its motions, which did not do good proportioned to the blaze of light it displayed."

Thus speaks Sir E. Brydges:—"I had always been a great admirer of his genius and of many traits in his character; and I was aware that he was a person moody and somewhat difficult to deal with. I was resolved to keep in full consideration the irritability of his position in society. About a mile from his residence, on a bench under a tree, I passed a figure, which from the engraved portraits of him I did not doubt was the poet; but I did not venture to address him. On arriving at his humble cottage, Mrs. Burns opened the door; she was the plain sort of humble woman she has been described. She ushered me into a neat apartment, and said that she would send for Burns, who was gone for a walk. In about half an hour he came, and my conjecture proved right—he was the person I had seen on the bench by the road-side. At first I was not entirely pleased with his countenance. I thought it had a sort of capricious jealousy, as if he was half inclined to treat me as an intruder. I resolved to bear it, and try if I could humour him. I let him choose his turn of conversation, and said a few words about the friend whose letter I had brought to him. It was now about four in the afternoon of an autumn day. While we were talking, Mrs. Burns, as if accustomed to entertain visitors in this way, brought in a bottle of Scotch whisky, and set the table. I accepted this hospitality. I could not help observing the curious glance with which he watched me at the entrance of this signal of homely entertainment. He was satisfied. He filled our glasses: 'Here's a health to auld Caledonia!' The fire sparkled in his eye, and mine sympathetically met his. He shook my hand with warmth, and we were friends at once. Then he drank 'Erin for ever!' and the tear of delight burst from his eye. The fountain of his mind and his heart now opened at once, and flowed with abundant force almost till midnight.

"He had amazing acuteness of intellect as well as glow of sentiment. I do not deny that he said some absurd things, and many coarse ones, and that his knowledge was very irregular, and sometimes too presumptuous, and that he did not endure contradiction with sufficient patience. His pride, and perhaps his vanity, was even morbid. I carefully avoided topics in which he could not take an active part. Of literary gossip he knew nothing, and therefore I kept aloof from it; in the technical parts of literature his opinions were crude and uninformed; but whenever he spoke of a great writer whom he had read, his taste was generally sound. To a few minor writers he gave more credit than they deserved. His great beauty was his manly strength, and his energy and elevation of thought and feeling. He had always a full mind, and all flowed from a genuine spring. I never conversed with a man who appeared to be more warmly impressed with the beauties of nature; and visions of female beauty and tenderness seemed to transport him. He did not merely appear to be a poet at casual intervals; but at every moment a poetical enthusiasm seemed to beat in his veins, and he lived all his days the inward if not the outward life of a poet. I thought I perceived in Burns' cheek the symptoms of an energy which had been pushed too far, and he had this feeling himself. Every now and then he spoke of the grave as soon about to close over him. His dark eye had at first a character of sternness; but as he became warmed, though this did not entirely melt away, it was mingled with changes of extreme softness."

He began to be now flattered by Mr. Graham with the hope of a supervisorship. This would have brought him in £200 a-year (a sum about equal to £400 now), although attended by great drudgery; and in this case we should have heard less of the ruin and poverty of Burns. But even this beggarly promise of a Boreal morn never came to day. Dr. James Anderson (not to be confounded with Dr. Robert Anderson, editor of the "British Poets," and an early friend of Thomas Campbell), editor of a periodical called "*The Bee*," asked Burns through Blacklock to contribute to it. Blacklock did this in a rhymed epistle, and Burns hurled back his *No* in a torrent of honest execration, not at Blacklock, but at his own business, "the friction of holding the noses of the publicans to the grindstone of *the Excise*."

At this time his brother William died in London, and Robert paid the expenses of his illness and funeral. Robert Ainslie visited him on the 15th October, and found the *kirn* of the year going on; and found, besides Burns and his wife, a sister of Burns, and a sister of Mrs. Burns, three male and female cousins, and some neighbours who had been harvesting. Ainslie describes it as a humble enough affair, although he enjoyed in the evening, *more suo*, dancing and kissing the lasses at the end of each dance. He thought Burns happy in a situation which yet he was preparing to leave, and of which he gave Ainslie some rather disagreeable particulars. He wrote this for the benefit of Clarinda, who eagerly swallowed all she heard of her lover, although the hope of her ever being hers did not now, we presume, visit her wildest dreams.

Having talked with Grose about Alloway Kirk, the poet had told him to make a drawing of it, because it was the burying-ground of his father, and was believed to be haunted by ghosts and witches; and Grose had promised to print a weird story for him in his book if he would write it. And hence came the immortal tale of "Tam o' Shanter." The circumstances are familiar to everybody—the poet spending a day in autumn (always his inspired season, even, as Thomson says, "inspiring autumn comes!") by the banks of the Nith; approached at evening by his wife and her two weans; her stopping back, however, as she sees he is crooning to himself in one of his poetic moods, and cowering along with her two little boys in the broom while waiting for him; his reappearance in a state of half-frenzied excitement, in what Burke would call an "agony of glory," with the big tears falling over his cheeks, and reciting to himself

"Now, Tam! ah, Tam! had thae been queans,"

and so on. We can never reconcile this ravished hour of triumphant genius with the picture MacDiarmid adds of the poet writing down his verses on a sod-dyke, although we have little doubt that the second part of the statement is true, that he repeated them at his fireside with great glee; but we fancy they were transcribed in the house, probably after recitation. Not a few such rapid improvisations of first-rate poetry or prose are found in literary history. There are many passages which appear to heave and hurry on with a celerity and totality of motion that suggest the idea of inspiration or abandonment—seem as if they were copied out from some fiery scroll unfolded suddenly before the Man of Genius by an invisible hand ere it has vanished away. Such passages we find in Milton, notably in the "Areopagitica;" in many of Jeremy Taylor's glowing and gushing similitudes ("So have I seen"); in some of the grand swells of Burke's "Regicide Peace," and "Letter to a Member of the National Assembly;" in Curran and Grattan *passim;* not unfrequently even in Charles Phillips; in some of the high-wrought climaxes of Chalmers and Irving, where the effort indeed rather overwhelms the ease, and the power is born in pain and labour; in the splendid peroration of Hall's "Sermon on the Present Crisis;" in many parts of Wilson's "Tales" and "Noctes;" in a few of Carlyle's and Ruskin's descriptions; and in De Quincey's "Suspiria de Profundis," especially his transcendent "Ladies of Sorrow." These are all in prose; but there are many in verse, too, such as the close of Milton's sixth book of "Paradise Lost;" much of "Lear," "Macbeth," and "Timon of Athens;" Christopher Smart's marvellous "David;" a poem or two of Crashaw's; Coleridge's "Ode to France;" Shelley's "Cloud," and the first canto of the "Revolt of Islam;" Wordsworth's "Ode to Sound" (a little too elaborate); Wilson's "Address to a Wild Deer;" Byron's fourth canto of "Childe Harold" throughout, and some portions of "Don Juan;" Campbell's "O'Connor's Child;" Smith's "Barbara" and "Garden and Child;" Keats' "Nightingale" and "Hyperion;" Mrs. Browning's "Lady Geraldine's Courtship;" the close of Aird's "Devil's Dream;" Dobell's "Chamouni," and some parts of his "Roman;" Bailey's description of himself as a student in "Festus," and many others. Here all differ from Tam o' Shanter, and differ from each other in many points, but agree in the wonderful manner in which they are all not sought, sent for, or sweltered out, or pumped up, or forced down, but come spontaneously in and from the poetic soul—as if brought at one time on the pen of the lightning writing on a black sky, and compelling the poet to write as fast and furiously below, and as if breathed at another from the silent and holy midnight more calmly and slowly into the lowly and listening ear, in which way it was that the soul of Wordsworth received the serenest and deepest of his inspirations! Campbell, in his "O'Connor's Child," describes his high-wrought heroine, in accounting for the frenzy which made her utter the *malison* of heaven against her cruel brothers' rage, that she durst not

"Have spoke
The curse which severed Nature's yoke
But that a *Spirit* o'er her stood."

It were difficult to settle to what order the Spirit which inspired "Tam o' Shanter" belonged. "Puck" might have given the light raillery of the opening part; "Ariel," though of a loftier mood, was hardly competent to the deep and terrible imagination found in the elements on the "haly table." The Spirit assuredly was a "Proteus," by whatever other names it might be known in heaven, earth, or hell; and was like "Puck" in this respect, that as he

"Put a girdle round about the globe
In forty minutes,

so the Genius of the Hour in "Tam o' Shanter" ranges with incredible speed and ease, in the very twinkling of an eye, "from gay to grave, from lively to severe"; and in some two hundred and thirty lines includes every species nearly of literary excellence—the humorous, the picturesque, the sententious, the grotesque, the sublime, the playful, the horrible and awful, all expressed in the most terse and felicitous language—every word a thing, every line a picture; and while the unity of the whole might be the despair of Art, it is felt to be the mere unconscious result of Nature. Shakspearean, it has been called; but we question if Shakspeare has any where so much that is Shakspearean lying in the same compass: it is Shakspeare in shorthand. The "haly table," though the most powerful, is not the most perfect part of the poem; but in it here and there you feel as if the wild wing of the inspiration flagged.

Grose printed "Tam o' Shanter" in April, 1791, calling it a "pretty tale!"* but died in Dublin almost immediately after its publication. Moore praised it languidly; Tytler gives it a far more generous encomium. Burns felt, as poets often do correctly, that he had produced his masterpiece. The Ayrshire people found time, after having their long laugh out, to identify the characters—"Tam" with Douglas Graham of Shanter farm, between Turnberry and Colzean; "Kate" with his wife, Helen MacTaggart, much given to superstition; and "Souter Johnny" with a crony called John Davidson, a tanner, who believed there was nothing like leather except whisky.

After a long symposium in the town of Ayr on a tempestuous night, Graham, riding home, lost his bonnet near the Brigg of Doon, which contained all the money he had made at the market. Afraid of a scold, he invented and told Helen some cock-and-bull story about being frightened by witches near Alloway Kirk; but nevertheless returned to the place in search of his bonnet, which he found, along with his money, in a plantation. Burns knew this couple when at Kirkoswald, in the churchyard of which the reader may see an inscription recording the memory of "Tam" as a very religious man, who was not, after all, "drooned in Doon" or caught by demons, but died in the odour of sanctity, if not with the reputation of eminent sobriety. In March of this year a posthumous child was born to Mrs. Henri, a daughter of Mrs. Dunlop, married to a Frenchman, who had died; and this event delighted our poet, and awakened his muse. "This pledge o' meikle love" removed while very young to France. Mrs. Henri died, and the paternal grandfather had to flee from the French Revolution to Switzerland, where the boy was brought up by a Mademoiselle Susette, a domestic, who was the means of preserving for him the family estates.

In due course came 1794; and we find Burns writing a stern Hymn to Poverty, still his close companion and cold mistress, in the shape of a letter to Peter Hill, inclosing a part payment of an account for books. Chambers gives a list of the books, and says, "It thus appears that Burns loved Smollett, Fielding, the English dramatists, and books of liberal divinity." One is amused to find amongst these liberal books the "Marrow of Modern Divinity," Cole on "God's Sovereignty," Newton's "Letters," and the "Confession of Faith"—books of the very highest Calvinistic type, and which might have filled very creditably a shelf in the library of "Daddie Auld" or Mr. Kirkpatrick. We wonder if Burns left any notes or queries upon their margins. In John Newton he would have found some sentimental matter, transfiguring his own amorous feelings—John Newton being a converted Burns. But old Elisha Cole must have been a chokepear; and the statements of the "Confession" as to elect infants and reprobation would find a feeble echo in the warm and all-embracing charity of Burns' heart.

Poor Miss Burnet, his Edinburgh idol—an idol he had seen for a long time now at a distance, and dared not approach—died; and Burns, as he truly says, "hammered at" a poor poem about her. His real poem was the sentence already quoted when he first saw her; and he did not, nor perhaps could, write on her what Coleridge did not very long afterwards on a kindred spirit called prematurely home:—

> "They surely have no need of you
> In the place where you are going;
> Earth hath its angels all too few,
> While heaven is overflowing."

Some people write best on Nature in winter—memory and absence bringing out its beauties then more forcibly, along with a certain pathetic feeling, like the sweet, soft tone which a slight illness gives to the heart, not felt in robust health. Perhaps it is on this principle that Burns' letter to Dr. Alison on Association and his "Lament of Mary Queen of Scots"—both written in February—are so exquisitely beautiful. But it would be difficult to conceive Burns writing poorly on Mary or on Beauty. Still this was, after all, a fictitious woe; but the death of Lord Glencairn, Burns' kindest and truest patron, was real sorrow. That admirable nobleman died at Falmouth on his way home from Lisbon, where he had gone in a vain search for health. Burns was deeply grieved, named in a year or so a son after him, and wrote the touching lament—

> "I'll remember thee, Glencairn,
> And a' that thou hast done for me."

He even meant to cross the country, had he known the day of the funeral, to drop a tear at his benefactor's grave. Few poets have ever had such a patron, and certainly no patron in Scotland had ever such a poet—not merely in genius, but in gratitude. It seemed a year of misfortune. Soon after Lord Glencairn's death Burns fell and broke his right arm; and may it not be ranked as a third calamity that Janet Little, a poetical milkmaid, came to visit him? Such humble contemporaries, however, he seems to have treated in a kind and considerate manner. This was in March. In April Mrs. Burns presented him

---

* Grose, it is to be hoped, was a better soldier and antiquary than a critic.

with a son, and he, probably in accordance with an old promise, gave the name to his irascible, but hearty and learned friend, Willie Nicol. He soon after, though his broken arm was healed, bruised his leg, and to crown all, he determined to leave Ellisland. And it was amidst this complication of disagreeables that he wrote his third Epistle to Mr. Graham of Fintry, a clever copy of verses, sententious, laborious, querulous, but neither plaintive nor powerful.

A letter he wrote to his friend Cunningham of Edinburgh in defence of a schoolmaster at Moffat, one Clarke, (of whom afterwards), who was accused of inhumanity to his boys, is savagely strong in its expressions, and points, according to Chambers, to a begun exacerbation in his tone of feeling. But we find many similar outbursts in his letters before he came to Dumfriesshire at all. Still there runs through all his Ellisland correspondence a certain current of bitterness and disappointment which it is not difficult to understand. He was not keeping his farm, and hence his farm was not keeping him. He was not the better, but the worse, of having two strings to his bow. The exciseman and the farmer were perpetually jostling. There is no evidence that his irregularities were getting habitually worse; but he was greatly exposed to company, and was professionally and otherwise often in inns. He seems, too, as his friend Ainslie noticed, to be now often among the great, and that not on equal or anything like equal terms; but was sometimes at their feasts, brought in to amuse them, and his noble genius was degraded into a menial at their tables. This, on reflection, must have made his proud spirit very miserable. It could not be pleasant to awaken at once with a burning head and a sense of degradation, equally ardent. His best patron, Glencairn, was dead. His poems were going into new editions, for which he was rewarded by a few extra copies by the sly, stingy Creech. Chambers speaks of a system of severe criticism being directed to his writings, which he could not brook. This is a common case with authors at a certain stage of their progress. If the first book of a writer has been a great success, the second is usually thought a failure. It appears amid a greater glare of notice and expectation. It is uniformly, if unreasonably, expected to be a vast stride ahead of its predecessor; and if not, the disappointment is commensurate. If, on the other hand, the author is for a long time silent, it is said that his vein is exhausted—"We have got all that's in him." Then whatever faults are known to exist in the man, are made makeweights against the merits of the poet or author. We know that at one time of Byron's life he was so disgusted by this kind of treatment that he threatened to quit the arena altogether, to burn all his works and write no more, and was with difficulty dissuaded by his friends. Burns for a year or two had written little, and that not his best, and his enemies exclaimed, "He is a waning star, we thought him too bright to last;" and the common, though then exaggerated, rumour of his habits strengthened this spirit of depreciation. No doubt "Tam o' Shanter" came as a blow in the face of such judges, exhibiting, as it did, all his powers as bright as ever, and blended into one glorious focus—incomparably the best of his productions, in point both of art and of genius. But that masterpiece was for a good while little known; and even it did not escape the down-taking process of Dr. Moore, and perhaps of others, of whom Burns was aware, though we are not. At all events, how eagerly he grasps at the praise of Tytler and other generous critics on his favourite "Tam!" We believe he was inclined, like Byron, to give up writing, and would have done so, all but his songs; but they came from his heart, and that could not be shut. It produced an irresistible outflow. He could as well cease to breathe as to pour forth the passions of his bosom and the sentiments of his soul in song. We sometimes think that either now or a year afterwards Burns, as he was urged to do, should have issued a second volume of poems, with "Tam o' Shanter" in the van. If smaller than his first, it would still have been of great merit, would have become very popular, shown the public that he was still Burns, the unequalled poet of Scotland, and its success would have cheered, perhaps bettered him.

He had resolved now to leave Ellisland in December. The place was getting gradually hateful to him. It was sown with the salt of lost time and money. It was haunted by not a few saddening and humiliating memories. The Nith had not the music in his ear it had three years before, and every murmur of its waters seemed to say, "Let us go hence." But ere he left the farm for ever, some little adventures relieved the monotony of his life, if they did not increase its happiness. Two English gentlemen—"Pilgrims of his Genius"—came to see him; found him angling in the river with a huge foxskin cap on his head, a greatcoat fastened round him by a belt, from which depended an enormous broadsword; made a night of it with him; went away maudlin; and left him miserable. This story Carlyle doubts, but it is very like Burns in one of his vagaries and reckless moods. There was now and then a dash of affected oddity about him. He had got the notion (as Thomas Aird always insisted, and Jeffrey hints at it, too, in his Review) from the lives of the English dramatists and poets of Charles II. and of Queen Anne, that oddity and wildness were essential to a wit. In the same spirit he inscribed on the collar of his dog, "Robert Burns, Poet." But this spice of absurdity bore no more proportion to his wisdom and genius than Falstaff's bread did to his sack; and would to God, he had had no greater sins for which to answer! The Earl of Buchan invited him to perpetrate a greater folly still, by walking across the country in harvest time and down the Tweed to assist at the crowning of the bust of Thomson at his native Ednam. Burns, however, refused, and sent a copy of middling verses instead. A bright, transient ray now shone on him in the shape of a lively young Englishwoman—the first English lady that seems ever to have made any impression on his susceptible bosom, so slender had hitherto been his opportunities of making the acquaintance of England's graceful daughters—one Deborah Davies, who was on a visit to the Riddells. She was of small stature, but very handsome. Her lot was unfortunate—to be jilted by a Captain Delany, and afterwards to droop and die.

He now, too, made acquaintance with Mr. Charles Sharpe of Hoddam, an exquisite musician and player on the violin; and a correspondence took place between them, which has been lost. At the roup of his last crop a scene of debauchery took place, which we leave Burns to describe himself in his letters. Roups and sales in Scotland at this time, as Sir Walter notices in his "Guy Mannering," were often very riotous scenes, owing to the free circulation of whisky. To Mr. Maxwell of Terraughty, a leading man in Dumfriesshire, he wrote some verses. Maxwell was descended in the fifth degree from Lord Herries, Queen Mary's friend, honourably mentioned in "The Abbot," and died so late as 1814. Is it not rather curious that Burns' last song composed at Ellisland was his "Song of Death?" a powerful, but surely a most gloomy production; no shout from the wounded and the dying in a patriotic and triumphant army—"O, Death, where is thy victory?"—but a mock-heroic challenge, sinking into a hollow groan of empty defiance. It is death without the faintest gleam of prospect beyond.

He left Ellisland without much regret, for it had long been a losing concern, and but for his Excise income would have ruined him. He got no supervisorship; but it was arranged that he would perform duty at Dumfries as a common exciseman for £70 a year, an increase on his salary of £20. And as he kept now no horse, and still expected to rise in his profession, it was thought a change for the better. Miller at the time when Burns parted from Ellisland sold it to a Mr. Morine, and some time in November Burns and his family removed to Dumfries.

We saw Ellisland in December, 1877, for the third time, we think, on a fine morning, on our way from Dunscore to Dumfries, with the beautiful winter light, so spiritual in its clearness, shining on the distant hills to the west; while the sky was crossed by a rainbow, broken and invisible in the centre, but with its two arms exceedingly brilliant—one of them resting on the barn-yard where Burns passed his hour of love agony. It seemed very significant of his tearful, bright, and fragmentary existence. Farther down we got a glimpse of Dalswinton, with its skeleton woods, and of the Isle, Friars' Carse, and the miserable erection which has now taken the place of the Hermitage we had left behind. It was market day, and a multitude of peasants were trudging into Dumfries, much as it probably was in 1791. But one was wanting—the bright-eyed, swarthy poet, walking beside the cart containing his furniture, on which are exalted his wife and children, who seems, as he now fixes his dark gaze on the approaching town, and anon reverts it to the receding farm, with all its sere woods and dismal recollections, to mutter to himself, not as of yore—

> "As I gaed up by Glenap,
> I met an aged woman,
> Who bade me keep up my heart,
> For the best o' my days were coming;"

but,

> "Och, I backward cast my e'e
> On prospects drear;
> And forward, though I canna see,
> I guess and fear."

DUMFRIES.

CHAPTER XII.

BURNS IN DUMFRIES—HIS DEATH.

HIS chapter is to be a long one, for we cannot tell where logically to break it in two. Burns has got now on the inclined plane leading down to the grave. Either before or immediately after his removal to Dumfries he had paid a visit to Edinburgh, and had one more interview with Clarinda. She had been occasionally corresponding with him, and had been gradually reconciled to the belief that they were never to be one. Her anger at his marriage had subsided, and she wished to see him once more before going to join her husband in Jamaica. We suspect that Burns did not care much for this; that his feelings for her were not so strong as hers for him; and that he felt that an interview would be extremely embarrassing and painful—how much so we cannot tell, unless we knew the exact terms on which the two lived and loved together. But he could not deny her request, and they met accordingly on the 6th day of December, 1791. Perhaps the taste is a little prurient which would like to know the particulars of the interview. Let us say, as Byron of Numa and Egeria—

"The purple midnight veiled that mystic meeting
With her most starry canopy, and seating
Thyself by thy adorer—what befell?"

Grant it a scene of perfect purity, and even delicacy—there would be passionate words, perhaps bitter recriminations, burning tears, and "again and again reverberated, everlasting farewells." Jamie in "Auld Robin Gray," and his lover, took but "ae" kiss, and then separated for ever. Burns and Clarinda probably took more, but there came a last one—

"Ae fond kiss, and then we sever."

Burns vented his chagrin, or whatever his feeling was, in lyric after lyric, each more beautiful and passionate than another, and they became a safety valve. Clarinda's feelings were deeper and more silent. On January 25, 1792 (Burns' thirty-third birthday), she wrote him her last letter bidding him farewell in anticipation of her immediate voyage. It has the *religiosity* which characterized her; perhaps we might use a better, perhaps a worse name:—"Seek God's favour; keep his commandments; be solicitous to prepare for a happy eternity. Then I trust we will meet in never-ending bliss." She did not sail till February, and, curiously enough, she set out in that very *Roselle* in which Burns intended to have sailed for Jamaica five years before. It was doomed to bear in it for once, and very nearly twice, the cargo of a broken and miserable heart.

Burns had no time to spend in idle lamentations, nor do we think his inward wound was so deep as in the case of Mary Campbell. He soon plunged into other pleasures in addition to the cares of his calling. He got acquainted with Maria Riddell, and, as usual, there was a mutual fascination, which never went any farther, but in a while withered into an estrangement. Maria Woodley was the daughter of the Governor-general of Berbice, and had married Walter Riddell, younger brother of Glenriddell, who had come home lately from Antigua, where he had an estate. They settled at a place called The Holm (once the seat of Andrew Crosbie, better known as "Counsellor Pleydell," in "Guy Mannering"), four miles south of Dumfries, which Mr. Riddell named Woodley Park, after his wife. She was a highly accomplished and very clever woman, perhaps the most accomplished lady Burns had ever met—a lover of poetry, herself a poet, and extremely fond of books and of literary society. She was very young—only eighteen; already a mother; and like most natives of her burning clime, ardent, susceptible, and not a little capricious. Burns knew her through the Riddells of Friars' Carse, and became soon a frequent visitor of Woodley Park, and, as usual, imagined himself in love with the lady of the house, who treated him with great distinction, and often called at his dwelling. As she had a book preparing for the press on the "Natural History of Madeira and the Leeward Islands," she consulted Burns, who sent her, with a letter of introduction to his old friend Smellie, like a gazelle into the den of a bear. He received her, however, very graciously. About this time Burns paid an account he had owed for two years to Robert Burn, architect, of £5 10s., for erecting a monument to Robert Fergusson. Burn, who was all but the poet's namesake, had some of his wit; for he returned

k

the account, adding, " I will be happy to receive orders of a like nature for as many more of your friends that have gone hence as you please!"

Burns' first house was in the Wee Vennel, as it was called, now Bank Street. It is the first flat of a two-storied house, and consists now of two rooms inhabited by different families — the one having been, we are told, Burns' study, while the other is much larger, and might have formed a very respectable parlour or dining-room in those days. It originally consisted, we think, of three apartments—study, bedroom, and parlour. On the ground floor in Burns' day was John Syme's office for the distribution of stamps, where now our worthy friend Mr. Hamilton, corn merchant, has his business room. There does not seem to be much alteration either in the approach or the interior; and we said to ourselves as our friend and we climbed up the stair, how often has Burns done this, and how interesting such a common-place sound as we are making must have been in the ear of Jean, wearying for the return of her lord, and saying, when it was at last heard—

> " His very foot has music in 't
> As he comes up the stair ! "

We pass now to a curious incident, which has much exercised the biographers of Burns. A superintendent, a kind of " Frank Kennedy," was stationed in Annan to watch the smuggling trade, then carried on with great activity along the Galloway coast. Burns was one of the party employed to watch a suspicious-looking brig which appeared in the Solway Frith. As it seemed too strong and well-armed to be attacked rashly, Lewars, a brother exciseman, went off for a party of dragoons to Dumfries. Burns and his companions waited impatiently for their return, and one of them expressed a wish that the Devil had Lewars for his slowness in returning, and that Burns might indite a song on the laggard. Burns said nothing, but after a few strides along the wet marsh, came back roaring out the clever ditty, " The Deil 's awa' wi' the Exciseman." By-and-bye Lewars arrived with his troop, the brig was boarded, Burns being the first man ; and the next day, when the vessel was sold in Dumfries, he purchased four carronades (at £3) and presented them to the French Legislative Assembly—not the Convention, as Lockhart says, which had not then existence. We were still at peace with France, although possibly, ere these carronades reached, war might have begun. It was a fine erratic impulse on the part of the poet, and showed with what evident sympathy he was watching the rising of the Day-Star of Liberty, soon to be quenched in darkness and in blood. He had arrived at the first stage of sympathy with the French Revolution, which almost all the poetic souls and liberal politicians of the period reached—Coleridge, Southey, Wordsworth, Godwin, Cowper, Mackintosh, Fox, Hazlitt, Canning—all except Burke, whose prophetic eye saw the red flower of massacre and anarchy within the white and beautiful bud which concealed it, and

> " Heard the thunder ere the tempest lowered !"

Significant that all these except Fox, Godwin, and Hazlitt, turned more or less against this " Grand Phenomenon," which they had so warmly admired and so eloquently praised! Burns is hardly a case in point, and his conversion to Conservatism was not that of his whole heart.

Our poet at first seems rather to have liked Dumfries. He had more there to divert him from his own sad thoughts. An evening walk by the Nith did not always soothe him to peace. The theatre or a night at the Globe always seemed to do, and he had no time the next morning, as at Ellisland, to nurse his headache or indulge his remorse. Another vision of beauty and grace transported him (Miss Lesley Baillie, afterwards Mrs. Cumming of Logie, who died in 1843), recalled the perished days of Margaret Chalmers and Charlotte Hamilton ; and he accompanied her, though he could ill spare time, thirteen miles on her southward journey, dined with her, and made a ballad on her as he returned.

George Thomson of Edinburgh having, along with a company of musical amateurs, projected a collection of Scottish airs and tunes on a new and *recherché* scale, asked the aid of Burns, which was enthusiastically rendered ; Burns stipulating for no fee or reward, and not even expecting at first what was to be the richest of all his rewards—the privilege of setting the heart of the Scottish nation to everlasting song, and doing for Scottish feeling what he had done for Scottish manners, customs, and religious rites.

In August this year came out, along with the heather blooms, the fourth volume of "Johnson's Musical Museum," which Thomson's book was to eclipse, but in which appeared some of Burns' most charming songs— " Craigie Burn Wood," " Oh meikle thinks my love o' my beauty," the " Banks o' Doon," " Flow gently, sweet Afton," and perhaps best of all, that dainty and delicious strain—

> " O luve will venture in where it daurna weel be seen,
> O luve will venture in where wisdom ance has been;
> But I will down yon river rove, amang the woods sae green,
> And a' to pu' a posie to my ain dear May."

On the 21st of August, 1792, Mrs. Burns had a daughter, who was named Elizabeth Riddell, in honour of the laird of Friars' Carse, and was not destined to a long life. Chambers speaks with a kind of surprise of Burns' being seen in the summer gloamings dandling his little daughter in his arms, and singing to her. One minds the story of the poor negro who, when he heard of God sending His

BURNS STATUE, DUMFRIES.

ENGRAVED BY W. ROFFE FROM SKETCH MODEL BY MRS D. O. HILL.

WILLIAM MACKENZIE, LONDON, EDINBURGH & GLASGOW.

Son to redeem the world, cried, "It be just like Him." So this little anecdote "be just like" Burns, the most affectionate of fathers. Smellie and Maria Riddell had become great friends. He praised and patronized her volume; and she got the great eccentric naturalist to visit Dumfries, where he figured as a most extraordinary "lion"—attended assemblies, and was, along with Burns, entertained by the magistrates. Bozzy was not a prouder man when he brought Dr. Johnson and Jack Wilkes together, than was Mrs. Riddell when she accomplished a reunion between such a pair as Burns and Smellie; although as Bozzy received sundry knocks from both his friends as a reward for going between them, so Mrs. Riddell got one coarse compliment, at least, from Smellie, which we would rather not transfer from Chambers' page to our own. It was characteristic of the times, and of the rude "Orson" who uttered it; but not, we trust, applicable to the lady. Chambers says that in those days a woman even of refinement had to stand a great deal from her male friends. But unlike Smellie, Burns, unless when intoxicated, was incapable, we think, of insulting a lady like Maria Riddell.

And now commenced that correspondence with Thomson which, with the delightful lyrics sprinkled through it, and the comments from the pen of Burns, forms such a pleasant portion of his writings. How charming, at the turning of every page, to come upon those old familiar faces of song —"Highland Mary," the "Lea Rig," "Duncan Gray," and "Auld Rob Morris." He found time, too, to write some trifles upon Miss Fontenelle, a *petite* actress of the day on the Dumfries stage, such as the "Rights of Woman," "An Address," &c.

Burns had at this time fallen into a grave error. A young woman, residing with her sister, Mrs. Hyslop of the Globe Tavern, bore him a daughter. Some suppose that it was while Mrs. Burns was in Ayrshire visiting her friends that this unhappy affair occurred. Everybody remembers that Jean took home the child, laid her in a cradle beside her own infant, and when her father, who visited her, asked in astonishment if she again had twins, answered "It's a neebor's bairn who is unwell," and brought up the child as her own. The child's name was Elizabeth, as that of all the three daughters of Burns was. She became a Mrs. Thomson, of Pollokshaws, and bore a striking resemblance to her father. People will judge of Burns and Jean in this matter according to their own temperament and habits of thinking. Burns' conduct may be palliated, but cannot be defended; he would not have defended it himself, and many will deem the palliations pled from his passions, his habits, and his wife's absence, very poor ones. Let us simply say, "None else is judge but God!" But Jean's conduct, in our idea, rises to the sublime. She acted to the child in the cradle, to her husband, and to the guilty mother in the very spirit of Jesus Christ. And how her conduct led, undesignedly, to deeper retribution! Burns suffered severely in his own conscience, but it was Jean's action which barbed the arrow that pierced his vitals. How could he sleep while she was in unmurmuring silence rocking the cradle of that child of sin?

Robert Chambers says, in allusion to Burns' feelings of remorse and misery, "Is there really in the world anything greatly to discompose a man besides the Promethean vulture of a sense of his own errors?" This may to some extent, though not entirely, solve the mystery of Burns' misery, but not that of thousands of other men. Surely Chambers has forgotten the names of Pascal, Johnson, Foster, Carlyle, among philosophers; Young and Cowper among poets; Robert Hall, at one period of his life, among preachers; the whole martyrology of the world; Paul exclaiming, "O wretched man that I am;" and innumerable more names recorded in history of men and women of spotless life and noble character who have been unhappy. One name occurs to us—mentioned in Thomas Erskine of Linlathen's "Memoirs"—Madame de Broglie, daughter of the great Madame de Stael, a lady of virtue, parts, easy circumstances, fortunate family relationships, and yet weighed down by constant melancholy, desiring to die, and glad exceedingly when she had found the grave. Errors in life are common; but while they spread down for some men a Promethean pillow of thorns, on many, perhaps on more, they have little effect. A more sensible question has been asked, "Who is happy?" although many try to believe they are so who are most miserable in spirit. How many shrink back from looking into their own hearts as men used to shrink from looking into a mirror when alone, afraid that they might see there, instead of their own face, that of a fiend, or worse still, that of the image of themselves as they were in innocent childhood or happy youth, now gone for ever!

Burns certainly was not happy at this time, and seems to have often (what a sad and suggestive expression!) forgot himself! He was a good deal exposed to temptation. Dumfries was then a small, social, hearty town—a town like those so graphically described by Christopher North:—"The whole town tipples; there are club-rooms in every lane; the flow of ale is perpetual, perpetual the puffing of pipes; the system of soaking knows no change of seasons. All classes drink—the schoolmaster, the curate, the private saint, the publican and sinner, the tax-gatherer, the exciseman, the half-pay officer, the rough-rider, &c., &c." In Dumfries there were three great howffs—the King's Arms, the George, and the Globe—all, we believe, still extant. The Globe was Burns' favourite haunt. It is a snug little inn—to gain which you must pass through a close and ascend a stair, which was very convenient for those "drouthy cronies" who did not like to be seen entering a hostelry, however respectable in its character, as it has always been—where you can still sit down in Burns' leathern chair in the corner, and see the words, "Lovely Polly Stewart" and other ditties, scrawled by him on the window-pane. Many strangers were then passing through Dumfries on their way from England to the north of Ireland; and perhaps for a hundred in our hero-worshipping days who pause to visit his grave, or call on his two houses, or drink his memory in the Globe or King's Arms, ten might then stop to see the living dog, so much better than the dead lion. "Is Burns still here? Is he at home? Do get me a sight of our great national poet. Send for him with my compliments (Mr. So So), and say I shall be so proud if he will step over and drink a single glass with me. I take no refusal." And Burns good-naturedly comes, and takes one glass, and then another, and another; and the afternoon becomes evening, and the evening midnight, and the rest can be imagined. The traveller goes to bed in the inn, rises in time for the stage-coach, has a headache, which he charitably imputes to the great poet who made him sit too late with him; but by the time he reaches Portpatrick is quite well, and tells all the people he meets of his glorious "Night with Burns." Burns reels home, gets a curtain lecture, sleeps a few uneasy hours, and rises miserable to his miserable drudgery. Once, we are told, returning from some such orgy, he met his neighbour, George Haugh, the blacksmith, going forth to his manly toil "until the evening," and contrasted himself with him—the one repairing to his healthful labour, the other to his brief and troubled repose. This state of matters, although only of course occasional, was not infrequent, and could not be expected with a man of his temperament to last very long.

Poor "Clarinda" had come back to Scotland. She found a cold reception from her husband. There would be little but a bandying of reproaches. Very likely he had heard of her intimacy with Burns; her admiration for him she would scorn to conceal, and he had been openly and grossly unfaithful to her. He used her ill, at all events, and she suffered besides from the climate. She resolved to come home, and did so in August, 1792. Burns had written her twice through her friend, Miss Peacock, but both letters had miscarried. He now, on the 6th of December, the fatal anniversary, wrote Miss Peacock again, "Clarinda's" return being not yet known. When he knew of it, he wrote to herself an elaborately-frenzied letter. It would seem as if these two lovers could ne'er be sundered. Like the curve seeking the asymptotes, for ever in vain, so perpetually fruitless was the pursuit going on between them.

But now the times had become portentous and electric. It was the hour fully come—memorable for evermore in the annals of men—when, in the language of a poet, kindred to Burns in enthusiasm for liberty, if not so masculine and brawny in his power—

"Great France sprang forth,
And seized, as if to break, the ponderous chains
Which bind in woe the nations of the earth;"

and when her effort was welcomed with a shout of applause from all the most ardent and aspiring spirits in Europe. Wilder events, the imprisonment of the king and the formation of a republic and a revolutionary army in France, had succeeded. In Britain Paine's "Age of Reason" had struck at the root of despotism, with the force and will of the axe of a backwoods-man at some old pine of the forest, and the blow echoed through the universe. Societies of Friends of the People—in spite of Burke, in whose "Reflections on [or Reply to] the French Revolution" Vesuvius seemed to answer Etna—were formed. The Government got alarmed, prosecutions for sedition became the order of the day, and war with the infant republic was imminent. Burns' heart—a heart overshadowed and withered under the pressure of poverty, pride, and a galling sense of injury and neglect, leaped up when he saw the beautiful rainbow of the French Revolution bridging the sky; and in his usual outspoken and fearless manner he expressed his gladness. He ordered a Radical paper, started in Ayr by one Captain Johnstone—the same paper spoken of by Hector MacNeil in his "Will and Jean," when his hero and others

"Clubbed and gat the *Gazetteer*."

He threw off a political song—

"Here's a health to them that's awa'."

He uttered a few fierce speeches, and gave some rather daring toasts in private. It would seem as if he had a presentiment of some coming calamity, as on the 6th December, the same day he had written to Clarinda, he penned a dismal letter to Mrs. Dunlop, announcing a visit to Ayrshire, and his intention to see her. He spent four days at her house, and on his return he got an intimation that the Board of Excise were about to inquire into his political opinions and conduct, and to reprimand, if not to dismiss him, on account of them. This plunged him into a terrible state of apprehension that total and irreversible ruin lay before him and his family. He wrote a letter to Mr. Graham of Fintry, and although some expressions in it are so excessively exaggerated that you are led to suspect other influences at work besides alarm, there can be no doubt that there was real danger, and the report spread that he was dismissed; indeed, he says he would have been so but for Mr. Graham's intercession. Erskine of Mar (descended from the rebel earl, but himself a great Whig), hearing that Burns was cashiered, wrote to Mr.

Riddell offering to head a subscription for him. Burns in reply wrote (13th April, 1793) his noblest letter—that one at any rate in which his characteristic qualities of manly freedom and stubborn independence come out most strongly. His conduct was in the last degree imprudent, and in some measure unreasonable. He had sold his birth-right for £50, and was it not now rather late to quarrel with the bargain? As a gauger and government servant he had no business to take part in political agitation; the fault lay in his position, or rather in the poverty which rendered that position involuntary and inevitable.

This dreary December merged in 1793. Mrs. Dunlop presented him with a cup which had been a family piece among the descendants of Sir William Wallace. This was soon employed in ladling out cold punch, which effectually overthrew some of his visitors; he having previously told her on the second of the month that he had given up "hard-drinking." It had now become a daring feat in any clergyman to baptize Burns' children. Mr. MacMorine of Caerlaverock, an able, worthy, free and easy man, had promised to Burns to come one day and sprinkle little Elizabeth Riddell, Burns' babe, and when he came, found a curious group; Burns was seated beside two companions, not of the most respectable appearance, and they had all evidently been up the whole night. Burns, however, was sober, or at least speedily sobered himself, and arranged matters for a ceremony about which he had forgot. The baptism passed off fairly, but MacMorine, we suppose, left humming the line—

"We'll gang nae mair to yon toun."

Some suppose that these were the "two worthy men" Burns refers to in a letter as having partaken too liberally of his "Wallace Cup."

Still the new year began well with Burns in a literary point of view, with "Poortith Cauld," written for and on a Miss Jane Blackstock, afterwards a Mrs. Whitier of Liverpool, for whom he seems to have had one of his passing *penchants*. On his birthday, the 25th of January, he wrote a sweet sonnet on a thrush singing in his morning walk, and next day "Lord Gregory." The story of this fine ballad is old. Peter Pindar, the popular poet of that day, had written some very good verses on it; but Burns certainly excelled him. There are some touching lines on a similar story—that of a maiden seduced by a lord and going to his door to die, to be found in the "Roman" by our dear deceased friend, Sidney Dobell, entitled a "Winter Night," which we never have been able to read without tears. Less powerful and condensed than Burns', it is more pre-Raphaelitically simple and minutely true. We venture to quote some passages of it in a note.*

"Clarinda" again turns up for the penultimate time. Burns, we said, through accident, had not heard of her return to Scotland for a long while after it had occurred;

---

* " And she stood at its father's gate,
  With her baby at her breast;
  'Twas about the hour of rest,
  There were lights about the place.
  The old moon began to sink
  (Long like her upon the wane);
  It grew dark, she drew her hood
  Close about her pallid face.
  At the portal door she sate,
  Where she will not sit again.
  ' Little one,' she slowly said,
  Bending low her lowly head,
  ' In all this wide world only thee
  And my shame he gave to me.
  When thou camest I did think
  On that other gift of his.
  Hating that, I dreaded this;
  Thou art fair, but so was he—
  'Tis a winning smile of thine,
  Ah what fatal praise it is!
  One such smile once won all mine.
  Little one I not repine;
  It befits me well to wait
  My Lord's will, till I be dead;
  Once it was a gentler will.'

  . . . . .

  ' Little one,' she said, ' the cot
  Where I bore thee was too low
  For a haughty baron's bride.
  Little one, I hope to go
  Where the palace halls are wide.
  When thou prattlest at his knee,

  Wilt thou sometimes speak of me?
  Tell him on some eve,' she said,
  ' Where thou knowest I shall be.
  When he hears that I am grand,
  In those mansions ever fair,
  Will he hope to meet me there
  As a lady of the land;
  And think no more in scorn
  Upon thee and on the dead?'
  Furious blasts arose, and
  Grown gross
  With the licence of the hour,
  They smote the mother and the child!
  Dark night grew darker, not a smile
  Came from one star. The moon, long since,
  Had sunk behind the mountain.
  At the mirkest, somewhat stirred
  The sere leaves where the mother sate.
  For a moment the babe cried,
  Something in the silence sighed,
  And the night was still. O Fate!
  What hadst thou done? O that hard night
  Which morn must see! When winter went
  About the earth at dawn, he rent
  His locks in pain, and cast grey hairs
  Upon it as he past. So when
  Maids, poor mother, wail thy lot,
  Mournful at the close of day
  By that legendary spot,
  Oft they tell us, weeping, how
  Hoar frost lay on thy pale brow
  When they found thee, and was not
  Paler than the clay."

but when he learned she was in Edinburgh he wrote her a letter full of ravings about wounded pride, ruined peace, frantic disappointed passion, and adjured her to write him no more—words which she began to rate at their true value. One gets tired of the eternal popping up (so it was on Burns' part at least) of this equivocal and ridiculous passion in a history where there is so much of real suffering and sorrow. We turn with far more interest to his correspondence with Thomson, and to the care and enthusiasm he was bestowing on his songs. We remember that when Hannah More expressed her wonder to Dr. Johnson how the author of "Paradise Lost" could write such poor sonnets, the Doctor replied, "Milton, madam, could cut out a Colossus from a rock, but could not carve heads upon cherry stones." But Burns could do both. Hogarth was never more Hogarth than when drawing heads upon his thumb nail; and so Burns, our Scottish poet, carved immortal passions and poetry, faces of surpassing beauty and forms of unequalled grace, upon his cherry stones—his smallest ballads and bits of ballads. We are sorry to find him underrating "Mary Morrison," calling it nothing remarkable, while he praises a most bombastic effort, "Raving winds around her blowing," as his best verses. But Burns, to do him justice, very seldom indeed errs in his estimate of his own works. We find him applying about this time, on the strength of a burgess ticket he had got when he first visited Dumfries in 1787, asking cheaper education for his children at the public school; his request was complied with at once and gracefully by the magistrates, and his sons were getting a good education at the time their father died. A new edition of his Poems was issued about this time. He does not seem to have derived any profit from it; but he took the opportunity of sending copies to some of his friends, such as Patrick Miller and the new Lord Glencairn. One evening he was sitting in the inn at Broomhill with two friends, when a poor soldier passed the window. Burns, on a sudden impulse, called him in and inquired the story of his adventures, afterwards fell into a fit of abstraction, and in fine, produced the song "The Soldier's Return," which became not only popular with the general public, but raised his repute for loyalty, which had rather sunk in the land. Yet, when he heard of Dumourier deserting the army of the Republic, he broke out into the fiery lines—"You're welcome to despots, Dumourier;" nor was this his only rhymed and spoken offence. When at some feast or other Pitt was proposed as a toast, Burns was for substituting George Washington as the greater man; and when the other was preferred, he let his glass stand untasted before him and preserved a sullen silence. He wrote a song of a somewhat equivocal character—"The last time I came o'er the muir"—although we think the evidence by no means clear that it was prompted by a disreputable passion for Mrs. Riddell. What passion is in it was probably excited by the fumes of the port wine, and perished in those, or was absorbed into and evaporated by the song.

At Whitsuntide Burns and his family removed to a self-contained house in what was then known as Millbank Brae, but is now called Burns Street. It is at present the dwelling-house of the keepers of a Ragged School which stands on the south of it—a most respectable couple, Malcolm by name.

In December, 1877, we visited this house, passed through all the rooms, but paused with special emotion in the room where he died. The bed is under the wall, and on the very spot of Burns' deathbed. Many thoughts passed through our mind, chiefly of sadness, tinged with a little exasperation. All very well, we thought, to talk of posthumous honours, and universal influence, and enviable immortality. What are all these to the poor inhabitant that once occupied this miserable corner? What availeth to him that the enormous blunder, and misconception, and cruelty perpetrated on him living, ceased with his death, and that since whole trade-winds of "mouth-honour breath" have passed over him? that he asked for bread, and received a forest of statues and busts? Who can tell whether these are known to him in his present state of existence; or if known, that they can give him any pleasure? How much a very little of all this paid him in advance would have soothed his wounded spirit, consoled him in the prospect of death, of leaving his widow destitute and his children abjects! The cry of a dying minister to his wife yet rings in our hearing after many years, "You will be a widow, and a poor widow!" and that cry might have been the cry of Burns. But it is the way of the world, and a miserable way of a hard and heartless world it is; since for the sums given and the incense offered up after death, the donors were recouped by the gratification of their vanity, and perhaps by the calming of their remorse—if remorse they were able to feel; and probably not a shilling paid implied any self-sacrifice. But Burns was "a proud man, and a dissipated man, and a man to whom it was difficult to do any real service." If this had been said after any sincere trial to do him good, it might have been something to the purpose. But the priest and the Levite had passed by on the other side, and the offices of the good Samaritan were performed, not to the living man, but to the cold and senseless corpse! Perhaps such thoughts might come in more logically afterwards; but we prefer recording them now, as we still seem to stand by Burns' deathbed in this upper room of the Old Mill Vennel of Dumfries. Well do we remember many years ago, in the company of Thomas Carlyle and Thomas Aird, passing this house, and the mood in which we passed it was that of silence—the silence of pity, love, and a shade of awe; and how the feeling, awakened but not expressed—an hour afterwards, in a walk through a deep-wooded, moonlit lane leading up from the Nith—became in Carlyle inspiration, as he sounded on his way in a stream of talk so wild, holy, and melancholy, that it seemed as if the great inspired soul of Burns were incarnate in his person and speaking through his lips!

Chambers proves that Burns at the time he entered his new house was by no means rich, and quotes a letter of his to some unknown friend earnestly begging the loan of three or four guineas, and complaining bitterly of the times. Yet he would take no money from Thomson for his songs, and even fiercely rejected an offer of it again and again made by him. He seemed to think that song-writing must be a labour of love, and that the idea of cash connected with it would deprive it of all spontaneity. He could not turn his blood into ducats; and songs or rhymes were to him, to quote Shakspeare's beautiful words again, as the "ruddy drops which visited his sad heart." William Motherwell got ten shillings for "Jeanie Morisson," the most natural and pathetic of recent Scottish lyrics. Thomas Aird got two guineas (!) for his "Devil's Dream on Mount Acksbech," one of the grandest flights of modern imagination. But Burns got nothing whatever for what has been truly called a world of songs, and a world as varied as vast—nothing but the solitary joy and triumph of the Demiurge. Neither he nor his family could dine on "Scots wha hae" or a "Man's a man for a' that;" and in vain might he say with Milton—

" Ever against *eating* cares,
Lap me in soft Lydian airs."

One cause of his peculiar poverty at this time was that, owing to the war, an extra income derived from the unloading of foreign vessels was stopped.

We are now as far as 1793, and find Syme and Burns on an excursion to Galloway, a country well worth a more thorough exploration than he had then time to give it, with its fine meandering rivers, its gloomy moorlands, alternating with rich reaches of arable ground and alluvial scenery; the storm of mountains surging above Newton Stewart, the beautiful bay of Wigton, the exquisite coast scenery around Ravenshall, where you find a combination of different trees as varied as Spenser's "Wood of Error," with rocks, and caves, and creeks, bold promontories plunging into the blue sea on the one hand, and high bleak mountains piercing the blue sky on the other (Guy Mannering's country), the famous Castle Kennedy, and the Mull of Galloway planting its foot into the ocean with an air of such blunt and bold defiance! We quote all John Syme's account of the journey, and a supplementary bit from Mr. Carson:—

"I got Burns a gray Highland shelty to ride on. We dined the first day, 27th July, 1793, at Glendonwyne's of Parton—a beautiful situation on the banks of the Dee. In the evening we walked out, and ascended a gentle eminence, from which we had as fine a view of Alpine scenery as can well be imagined. A delightful soft evening showed all its wilder as well as its grander graces. Immediately opposite, and within a mile of us, we saw Airds, a charming romantic place, where dwelt Lowe, the author of 'Mary, weep no more for me.' This was classical ground for Burns. He viewed 'the highest hill which rises o'er the source of Dee,' and would have stayed till 'the passing spirit' had appeared, had we not resolved to reach Kenmure that night. We arrived as Mr. and Mrs. Gordon were sitting down to supper.

"Here is a genuine baron's seat. The castle, an old building, stands on a large natural moat. In front, the river Ken winds for several miles through the most fertile and beautiful *holm*, till it expands into a lake twelve miles long, the banks of which, on the south, present a fine and soft landscape of green knolls, natural wood, and here and there a gray rock. On the north the aspect is great, wild, and I may say, tremendous. In short, I can scarcely conceive a scene more terribly romantic than the castle of Kenmure. Burns thinks so highly of it that he meditates a description of it in poetry; indeed, I believe he has begun the work. We spent three days with Mr. Gordon, whose polished hospitality is of an original and endearing kind. Mrs. Gordon's lap dog, *Echo*, was dead. She would have an epitaph for him. Several had been made. Burns was asked for one. This was setting Hercules to his distaff. He disliked the subject, but to please the lady, he would try. Here is what he produced—

'In wood and wild, ye warbling throng,
Your heavy loss deplore!
Now half extinct your powers of song,
Sweet Echo is no more.

Ye jarring, screeching things around,
Scream your discordant joys!
Now half your din of tuneless song
With Echo silent lies.'

"We left Kenmure and went to Gatehouse. I took him the moor-road, where savage and desolate regions extended wide around. The sky was sympathetic with the wretchedness of the soil; it became lowering and dark. The hollow winds sighed, the lightnings gleamed, the thunder rolled. The poet enjoyed the awful scene; he spoke not a word, but seemed rapt in meditation. In a little while the rain began to fall; it poured in floods upon us. For three hours did the wild elements rumble their belly-full upon our defenceless heads. Oh! oh! 'twas foul. We got utterly wet; and to revenge ourselves, Burns insisted at Gatehouse on our getting utterly drunk.

"From Gatehouse we went next day to Kirkcudbright, through a fine country. But here I must tell you that Burns had got a pair of jemmy boots for the journey, which had been thoroughly wet, and which had been dried in such manner that it was not possible to get them on again. The brawny poet tried force, and tore them to shreds. A whiffling vexation of this sort is more trying to the temper than a serious calamity. We were going to St. Mary's Isle, the seat of the Earl of Selkirk, and the forlorn Burns was discomfited at the thought of his ruined boots. A sick stomach and a headache lent their aid, and the man of verse was quite *accablé*. I attempted to reason with him. Mercy on us, how he did fume and rage! Nothing could reinstate him in temper. I tried various expedients, and at last hit on one that succeeded: I showed him the house of [Garlieston?], across the Bay of Wigton. Against [the Earl of Galloway?], with whom he was offended, he expectorated his spleen, and regained a most agreeable temper. He was in a most epigrammatic humour indeed! He afterwards fell on humbler game. There is one . . . . whom he does not love; he had a passing blow at him—

'When ——, deceased, to the devil went down,
'Twas nothing would serve him but Satan's own crown;
Thy fool's head, quoth Satan, that crown shall wear never:
I grant thou'rt as wicked, but not quite so clever.'

"Well, I am to bring you to Kirkcudbright along with our poet without boots. I carried the torn ruins across my saddle in spite of his fulminations, and in contempt of appearances; and what is more, Lord Selkirk carried them in his coach to Dumfries. He insisted they were worth mending.

"We reached Kirkcudbright about one o'clock. I had promised that we should dine with one of the first men in our country, J. Dalzell. But Burns was in a wild and obstreperous humour, and swore he would not dine where he should be under the smallest restraint. We prevailed, therefore, on Mr. Dalzell to dine with us in the inn, and had a very agreeable party. In the evening we set out for St. Mary's Isle. Robert had not absolutely regained the milkiness of good temper, and it occurred once or twice to him, as he rode along, that St. Mary's Isle was the seat of a lord; yet that lord was not an aristocrat, at least in his sense of the word. We arrived about eight o'clock, as the family were at tea and coffee. St. Mary's Isle is one of the most delightful places that can, in my opinion, be formed by the assemblage of every soft but not tame object which constitutes natural and cultivated beauty. But not to dwell on its external graces, let me tell you that we found all the ladies of the family (all beautiful) at home, and some strangers; and among others, who but Urbani! The Italian sang us many Scottish songs, accompanied with instrumental music. The two young ladies of Selkirk sang also. We had the song of 'Lord Gregory,' which I asked for, to have an opportunity of calling on Burns to recite his ballad to that tune. He did recite it; and such was the effect, that a dead silence ensued. It was such a silence as a mind of feeling naturally preserves when it is touched with that enthusiasm which banishes every other thought but the contemplation and indulgence of the sympathy produced. Burns' 'Lord Gregory' is, in my opinion, a most beautiful and affecting ballad. The fastidious critic may perhaps say some of the sentiments and imagery are of too elevated a kind for such a style of composition; for instance, 'Thou bolt of heaven that passest by,' and 'Ye mustering thunder,' &c.; but this is a cold-blooded objection, which will be said rather than felt.

"We enjoyed a most happy evening at Lord Selkirk's. We had, in every sense of the word, a feast, in which our minds and our senses were equally gratified. The poet was delighted with his company, and acquitted himself to admiration. The lion that had raged so violently in the morning was now as mild and gentle as a lamb. Next day we returned to Dumfries; and so ends our peregrination. I told you that, in the midst of the storm on the wilds of Kenmure, Burns was wrapt in meditation. What do you think he was about? He was charging the English army, along with Bruce, at Bannockburn. He was engaged in the same manner on our ride home from St. Mary's Isle, and I did not disturb him. Next day he produced me the following address of Bruce to his troops, and gave me a copy for Dalzell—

'Scots, wha hae wi' Wallace bled,'" &c.

Mr. Carson says:—"The only friends of the host and hostess invited to meet the travellers, Burns and Syme, at Kenmure, were the Rev. John Gillespie, the highly-esteemed minister of the parish (Kells), and myself.

"On the evening preceding their departure, the bard having expressed his intention of climbing to the top of 'the highest hill that rises o'er the source of Dee,' there to see the arbour of Lowe, the author of the celebrated song, 'Mary's Dream,' Mr. Gordon proposed that they should all sail down the loch in his barge *Glenkens*, to the Airds Hill below Lowe's seat. Seeing that this proposal was intended in compliment by the worthy host both to the bard and to Mr. Gillespie, who had been the patron of Lowe, the gentlemen all concurred; and the weather proving propitious next morning, the vessel soon dropt down to the foot of Loch Ken with all the party on board. Meanwhile, Mr. Gordon's groom led the travellers' horses round to the Boat-o'-Rhone, saddled and bridled, that each rider might mount on descending from the poet's seat; but the barge unfortunately grounded before reaching the proposed landing-place—an obstruction not anticipated by any of the party. Mr. Gordon, with the assistance of an oar, vaulted from the prow of the little vessel to the beach, and was soon followed in like manner by Mr. Syme and myself; thus leaving only the venerable pastor of Kells and the bard on board. The former, being too feeble to jump, as we had done, to land, expressed a desire to remain in the vessel till Mr. Gordon and I returned; upon hearing which, the generous bard instantly slipt into the water, which was, however, so deep as to wet him to the knees. After a short entreaty he succeeded in getting the clergyman on his shoulders; on observing which Mr. Syme raised his hands, laughed immoderately, and exclaimed: 'Well, Burns, of all the men on earth, you are the last that I could have expected to see priest-ridden!' We laughed also, but Burns did not seem to enjoy the joke. He made no reply, but carried his load silently through the reeds to land.

"When Mr. Syme's account of this excursion with the bard into Galloway appeared in Dr. Currie's first edition of the 'Life and Works of Robert Burns,' the Glenkens people, who were actors in this part of the drama, were very much surprised to find the above incident not even alluded to; but we plainly perceived that Syme had only taken a few incidents of the journey as pegs to hang other drapery upon. We were all fully satisfied that it was by the bard's wading in the loch that his new boots were so thoroughly wet, and that the choler or independence next day manifested by him to Syme was only the result of his wounded feelings at having been made such a laughing-stock by his friend for merely rendering the assistance due by common humanity to old age or infirmity, which Mr. Gordon and myself charged ourselves afterwards for having overlooked in that instance."

And thus the first rude draught of the grandest War Ode in the world was produced. No doubt Burns, in a letter dated September that year, speaks to Thomson of having in his evening walk along the Nith thrown off what he calls a kind of Scottish ode—"Scots wha hae;" and Chambers rather perplexes than clears up the matter in his remarks. John Syme was a man of honour and a genuine enthusiast, and would not, in his letter to Dr. Currie, have given a false report of what he had witnessed; nor could he have forgotten at that date such a remarkable circumstance. In the solitude of Galloway Burns, we believe, produced and gave to Syme the first rude draught; on the banks of the Nith he expanded it to its perfect and final form. "Scots wha hae," we venture to say, could not have been conceived except in a thunderstorm and on the dreary moors—the place is the same still, all wanted is the poet—between Kenmure and Gatehouse. The song tuned itself to the thunder, and might, as Carlyle says, "be sung by the throat of the whirlwind." Every line is electric; and the eye of the poet meeting the blackness of the sky, with fierce flashes falling across it, like spilt shafts from the quiver of Death, and vibrating as they fell, must have been a sight to dream of, not to see. The excitement was of that fearful and half-frenzied sort which sought relief and gained the gate of slumber through the power of a coarser intoxication. Burns at Gatehouse got "utterly drunk." It is not to be defended—it will be sternly condemned; but it is hardly, at that time and in a man like Burns, to be wondered at. Thus Edmund Kean could get no other relief, after "Othello" or "Lear" had awakened a delirium which ran through his brain and nerves like molten lead. Thus Fox and Sheridan rounded off some of those tremendous philippics against the tyrants of India and the Continent, which are matched only in those by which Demosthenes

" Shook the Arsenal and fulmined over Greece,
To Macedon and Artaxerxes' throne!"

In his age perhaps only one man of Burns' order of mind and genius—namely, Burke—was much more temperate than Burns.

Peter Pindar, alluded to above as the author of another poem on Lord Gregory, and considerably overrated by Burns, does not deserve, on the other hand, the cold water cast by Chambers on his claims. He calls him a man of moderate abilities, speaks of his ribald recklessness, and so forth. Macaulay somewhere expresses a much higher opinion of him. Dr. Wolcot was no common man. His appearance and enormous brow proved it, apart from his works. His patronage of Opie, the painter, testified to his discernment as well as heart. His witty tales will last as long as the English language. He was a coarse man, and many of his writings are as coarse as they are all eminently clever. But in political integrity he rivalled Burns himself. He is a star that has somewhat receded from his pride of place, but he remains in the firmament still. His lowest praise is that he was a piercing thorn in the king's side. In a letter to Horne Tooke, Junius applies this as a compliment to Wilkes; and such as it was, it was equally deserved by Peter Pindar.

More truly, Chambers notes with wonder Burns' extreme fertility of song-writing this season. Gagged and muzzled in politics, told that it was his business to obey and be silent, not to think or speak, he found no outcome for his fancy and no channel for his feeling but song. Among the beautiful songs he produced this autumn, besides his final version of "Scots wha hae," we notice his "Auld Lang Syne," a song which for many years has been sung at the close of every festive gathering on the New-year, and often at other seasons, throughout the world; and the myriads then standing up and grasping each other's hands, and who for the nonce are "brithers for a' that," are standing up in honour and recognition of

l

Burns. Burns has added one innocent, universal, and unselfish joy to the list of the world's pleasures; and surely the universal poet, who is the universal benefactor too, is twice blessed!

Many were now disposed to say—Let the poet confine himself to his art, and leave politics alone. Thus do they often say to men of eminence, as if excellence in one department disqualified them from interfering in another; and because an extraordinary man is only, after all, an ordinary citizen, he has no right to speak at all on subjects which, as a citizen, interest him! Burns, the greatest of Scotland's poets, was not, perhaps, the profoundest of politicians; but was this to seal his lips? The mere feeling of such a man on political matters, the mere side he takes, is itself a matter of importance as a weight in the scales with that of many ordinary citizens. Burns felt this himself, and felt besides an ardent interest in the political questions of the times. Hence, even after his rebuke by the Excise and his enforced silence, he was now and then nearly getting into scrapes by his outspokenness. He had taken a great part in a public library which had been established in Dumfries, was presented by the committee with a share in it free of entrance-money and of the quarterly contribution, in honour of his literary reputation, and elected a member of committee. And he presented four books to it —" Humphrey Clinker," "Julia De Roubigne," "Knox's History of the Reformation" (a special favourite of his), and " De Lolme on the British Constitution." This volume, chiefly owing to the praise of Junius, who calls it a treatise " deep, solid, and ingenious," was then counted a book of great authority. On the fly-leaf Burns had written—" Mr. Burns presents this book to the library, and begs they will take it as a creed of British liberty until they find a better." Early in the morning after it had been presented he called on Mr. Thomson, the provost of Dumfries, ere he was up, and asked to see the volume, as he was afraid he had written on it something that might bring him into trouble. It was brought; and having got some paste, he proceeded to paste over it the fly-leaf, so as to conceal it. It could, however, be seen by holding up the leaf to the light. Poor Burns! In politics as in charity he needed to learn the lesson not to tell his left hand what his right was about, and when he tried to deceive he made only a bungling hypocrite. On another occasion he called on his neighbour, George Haugh the blacksmith, and gave him Paine's "Common Sense" and "Rights of Man," and told him to keep them for him, since if found in his possession ruin would follow. On another occasion still (we were told by a clerical gentleman in Dumfries) Burns and a few other Republican friends were met, as they met occasionally, in a room in an inn to discuss politics, when the cry got up that the magistrates and their myrmidons were at hand, and they all leaped out of a window and made an abrupt and narrow escape. At that time a cloud of suspicion and espionage rested over all the land, but seemed thickest over Dumfries. We may liken it to that cholera cloud which, in 1832, Dr. Robert Knox described to us as hanging above the Queen of the South, and which he and his brother, who were travelling toward the town, and felt themselves (the brother particularly) getting ill as they approached, avoided by riding in another direction, till gaining Lochmaben they became quite well, and heard the next morning that the pest had come down over the place like a blanket, in the evening, and slain its hundreds. Alas! Burns had not the power that others possessed of removing from the sphere of danger, but must wait gloomily where he was till the advent of better times.

It was about this time—surely one of the darkest points in his whole history—that Burns, as he tells Mr. MacMurdo, to whom he was paying the debt of a few guineas (after which "he didn't owe a shilling to man or woman either"), began to form a collection of licentious songs, known as the "Merry Muses," and which is certainly the biggest literary blot on his memory. We own to having read these unworthy productions; and while we admit the plea that many of them are not, as a whole, from the pen of Burns, that those which are manifestly his are the purest, and that to his hand we trace all those strokes of quirky humour and naïveté which are found in the most and worst of them, we freely grant that the "Merry Muses" may be called, what Leigh Hunt calls Cotton's "Virgil," a "beastly book," and is rank throughout with the very miasma of uncleanness. We believe that most of what Burns wrote in it was written while in a state of intoxication. Than the gentleman who showed us the copy— the late Robert White of Newcastle, author of "Otterburne" and "Bannockburn," works both of high antiquarian value—a purer, sincerer, simpler being, or one who more admired Burns, never existed. Deep sorrow, rather than anger, was in both our hearts as we went over it together. White told us he knew an innkeeper (he mentioned his name, but we, who had no thought then —it was in 1872—of writing a life of Burns, neglected to take it down) whose house the bard frequented, who said that up to a certain point he was most delightful society, but beyond that he would often spend the rest of the evening in singing obscene songs; at a certain stage the poet and the man were spirited away—the Burns evaporated, the Brute only remained. White mentioned this to us repeatedly, and it was undoubtedly true. Chambers gives what is, we suppose, an accurate enough account of the way in which the collection came to see the light, after Burns' death, through the cupidity of a bookseller. He calls it a "mean-looking volume." This was true of the copy White showed us; but we once saw, for a mere minute or two, a better got-up edition (not for sale, however), in two volumes, in the shop of the late Maurice Ogle, publisher, Glasgow. This miserable book may probably be still creeping, like the plague in Constantinople, in obscure regions of the country. But its very vileness prevents it from being noxious; it kindles no feeling but disgust, awakens no passion but anger, or rather grief—disgust at the volume itself, grief for the author.

While on this ungrateful subject, we may as well quote what Byron says of Burns' letters, which had been shown him by Allen, Lord Holland's librarian—a man of vast and curious erudition:—"Allen has lent me a quantity of Burns' unpublished and never to be published letters. They are full of oaths and obscene songs. What an antithetical mind! tenderness, roughness, delicacy, coarseness, sentiment, sensuality, soaring and grovelling, dirt and Deity, all mixed up in one compound of poor clay." This is from his Journal; but in his Letter to Bowles he says farther—" I have seen myself a collection of letters of another eminent—nay, pre-eminent—deceased poet, so abominably gross and elaborately coarse, that I do not believe they could be paralleled in our language. What is more strange is, that some of them are couched as postscripts to his serious and sentimental letters, to which are tacked either a piece of prose or some verses of the most hyperbolical obscenity. He himself says that 'if obscenity (he uses a much coarser word) were the sin against the Holy Ghost, he most certainly could not be saved.'" We have not seen the letters referred to, but perhaps Mr. White's statement points out one way of explaining them —the sentimental part might be written before dinner, and the postscript added after. This is an explanation, though, of course, not a sufficient palliation of the offence. Burns, writing to Mrs. Dunlop, Dr. Moore, and Dugald Stewart, could not have written obscenely; since he would not, one would think, have allowed himself to write to them if he had been in this state. Writing to others whom he respected less, he might have permitted wine and passion to have their way; and then, as when he was with the innkeeper, the Burns vanished, the Brute survived (and is there not more or less of the brutal nature in all men?), and hence came the "hyperbolical obscenity."

During the summer of 1793 Burns was little at Woodley Park; Mrs. Riddell was away in London for some months, and afterwards her husband was called suddenly on business to the West Indies, and when he returned found her alone in the mansion house. Here Burns, according to the etiquette of the times, and perhaps also owing to his peculiar reputation, was not permitted to visit her, but would have occasionally entered her box at the theatre had it not been for what he calls "lobster-coated puppies," *i.e.*, officers belonging to a regiment in Dumfries, and with whom it was the fate of the bard more than once to come into collision. He suspected that they had spread reports against his loyalty to the Board of Excise; they feared his power of scathing sarcasm, and cowered at the flash of his dark eye. They not only came between him and Mrs. Riddell, but on another occasion Miss Benson, afterwards Mrs. Basil Montagu, met his displeasure for mingling with these "epauletted puppies," as he called them, and seeming to neglect him. They got a handle against him, when one evening heated with wine in a private company he gave as a toast—" May our success in the present war be equal to the justice of 'our cause!'" At these words a captain present chose to be so seriously offended that a quarrel was the consequence, and Burns the next morning had to write a letter which was equivalent to a humble apology. Worst of all, Mr. Riddell having returned, and Burns having resumed his visits to Woodley Park, he one day committed himself by a nameless insult to his fair hostess, in remorse for which he next morning indited a letter to her purporting to be written in the abode of the damned; this produced a breach between them, which gradually widened into a great gulph fixed till very near his end, and Burns took his revenge by certain bitter lampoons, which did as little honour to his gentlemanly feeling as to his genius. Rejected at Woodley Park, he continued his visits to Tinwald Downs, where John Bushby was landlord—a remarkable person, who had risen from the ranks to opulence, was a solicitor, a banker, a country gentleman, kept open table, and had Burns often among his guests. It is said that Burns sometimes preferred dining in the room of the housekeeper, a decent lady reduced in circumstances, and afterwards was brought up along with a new batch of claret, like a bag-pipe player, to amuse the company. Chambers hints that Burns liked this: he might at times, at other times he stormed. The story at least is told that when once brought up stairs and to table, like Samson to make the people sport, he showed what terrible sport a Samson could make by pouring out a torrent of invective, flaked by oaths, shaking the pillars of the house, and rushing out in unceremonious haste and recalcitrating fury! This perhaps is a mythical, but decidedly improved version, of Chambers' tales about Burns being snared by Bushby into swallowing a piece of pudding boiling hot, while Bushby laughed till the tears were gushing out at his eyes in emulous sympathy with those produced by heat in the eyes of Burns; and Burns got angry, and this little bit of hot pudding led to a long coolness between them—an incident altogether more characteristic of the "Bashful Man" in fiction than of a being like Burns in reality. At all events Burns and Bushby ceased to be friends, and the poet visited the offences of the sire on the son in his lines "Æsopus to Maria," in which he lashes Bushby

Maitland as an advocate, and a man reputed much inferior to his father in intellect.

Amidst all this tempest of quarrel, contrition, and chagrin, the year 1794 dawned on our impolitic poet. It dawned darkly upon him personally and in public estimation; but we know not if his mind was ever stronger, prouder, yet tenderer than then, and if ever soured sensibility, feigned pride, and irritated passion produced through the compound stimulus they gave to genius (with the one exception of Byron's writings in Venice, "Childe Harold," "Manfred," and "Don Juan") such works as his noble letter to Cunningham, dated the 25th February, "The Lovely Lass of Inverness," the "Red, Red Rose," and above all, the "Vision of Liberty," decidedly, in the brevity of its compass, the concentration of its power, and the vividness of its imagery, one of Burns' very noblest strains. It is a *torso*, ranking not in size but in merit, with "Cambuscan" in Chaucer, with "Hyperion," "The Excursion;" greater in its mutilation, even as the splinter of a statue gives a better idea of the infinite than a statue itself. It was inspired by a visit to Lincluden Abbey. Burns often there

> "Turned from men his lonely feet,"

especially when evening was resting on the landscape, and he could glide out like a ghost to meet with the loneliness and lurid grandeur of the Abbey, carrying a ruin to ruins, as if to compare the fissures in a broken heart with the larger inroads of time upon one of the sublime structures of the past. Where, indeed, can the unhappy repair to escape from their own sorrows, or from the unthinking glee or constitutional cheerfulness of others, more fitly than to those spots where naked Nature dwells alone, or adopts and fondles the fallen fanes of Religion and the broken masterpieces of Art? She will not then and there seem to insult them by her laughing luxuriance, her foliage fluttering, as if in vain display, with the glossy gilding of her flowers and the sunny sparkle and song of her waters. But she will uplift a mightier and older voice. She will soothe them by a sterner ministry. She will (as says De Quincey in his sublime *Suspiria de Profundis*) "teach them old truths, abysmal truths, awful truths." She will answer their sighs by the groans of the creation travailing in pain; suck up their tears in the sweat of her great agonies; reflect their tiny wrinkles in those deep scars and stabs upon her forehead, which speak of ages of struggle and contest; give back the gloom of their brows in the frowns of her forests, her mountain solitudes, and her waste midnight darkness; perhaps infuse something, too, of her own sublime expectancy (the "earnest expectation of the creature") into their spirits, and dismiss them from her society, it may be sadder, but certainly wiser men. How admirably is Nature suited to all moods of all men!

In Spring she is gay with the light-hearted; in Summer gorgeous as its sun to those fiery spirits who seem made for a warmer day; in Autumn she spreads over all poetic hearts a mellow and unearthly charm; and even in Winter she attracts her own few but faithful votaries, who love to see her severe charms then unveiled, and enjoy her solemn communion none the less that they enjoy it by themselves. To use the words of the late John Wright of Ayrshire, a true poet undeservedly forgotten, addressing the Spring specially, but it applies to all Nature—

> "Thou op'st a storehouse for all hues of men:
> To hardihood thou, blust'ring from the North,
> Roll'st dark; hast sighs for them that would complain;
> Sharp winds to clear the head of wit and worth,
> And melody for those that follow mirth;
> Clouds for the gloomy, tears for those that weep;
> Flowers blighted in the bud for those that birth
> Untimely sorrow o'er; and skies where sweep
> Fleets of a thousand sail for those who plow the deep."

Two or three days after our first visit to Burns' house we went along with Thomas Aird, on the evening of a burning Sabbath day, leaving Dumfries while the full moon had newly risen and was resting on the top of the Crichton Asylum, to Lincluden; the Nith talking to us all the while in her gentlest mood of soliloquy, and when we reached the pile, the moon appearing in the eastern window, acting as our guide into the interior, and shedding her "holier day" with an effect wholly magical and indescribable upon the sides and secret places of the ruin.

> "It was a night so still and fair,
> We scarce would start to meet a spirit there."

But the "stern and stalwart ghaist" whom Burns encountered could only appear in the light of the "cauld blae north," and to the music of the "hissing eery din" produced by its fantastic and capricious fires—

> "Like fortune's favours, tint as win'."

Burns eldest son used to point out the spot where his father loved to rest and muse on two lovely landscapes, which can be seen from a little mount to the south, as if set in the windows of the ancient building.

In one of the panes of the Globe Tavern, as already hinted, may yet be seen, scrawled in Burns' handwriting, the stanza—

> "O lovely Polly Stewart!
> O charming Polly Stewart!
> There's not a flower that blooms in May
> That's half so fair as thou art!
> . . . . .
> Worth and truth eternal youth
> Will gie to Polly Stewart."

This young woman was reared in good circumstances in a

place near Ellisland, and married to a wealthy gentleman. She came, however, to grief, lost her way in life, lived in a poor position in Maxwellton, near Dumfries, and died in France. Alas for poetical prophecy! Alas for the poetical prophet himself! who while free to drink jorums at the Globe, and to scribble down the names of heroines on its windows, was sinking out of the sight and the respect of that upper class which, perhaps, he had done but too much to conciliate. The Riddells of Friars' Carse followed the example of the Riddells of Woodley Park in cutting Burns. Glenriddell himself died soon after, and Burns sang his loss; and as he had in his possession some MS. * books of Burns', especially one collection of his minor pieces, Burns felt a natural desire to reclaim them, the more as much of it was unfit for the public eye. In doing this he applied to a sister of Mr. Riddell's, and his letter to her shows how sore he felt about the numerous rumours which were then being circulated against him. Burns had now come round to the second *Nadir* in his life; 1794 was indeed the darkest year in his dark sojourn on earth. His expected promotion in the Excise was now, as it turned out, arrested for ever. Even the secret solace of song-writing was for a time closed this spring. Many doors in Dumfries and its neighbourhood, which had been thrown wide open, were now shut in his face. Insinuations of the darkest kind, probably darker than the truth, were circulating busily against his morals, his religious opinions, the *jeux d'esprit* he was inditing, and the company of his private hours. And now occurred the melancholy incident communicated by David MacCulloch of Ardwell—recorded by Lockhart and commented on so plaintively by Carlyle—of Burns on a grand ball night in Dumfries (perhaps in honour of the king's birthday) walking along the shady side of the street alone, while the opposite side was gay with parties of ladies and gentlemen who had assembled for the ball; and how when the young MacCulloch proposed they should cross the street and join them, Burns replied, "Nay, nay, my young friend, that's all over now," and proceeded to quote some lines from Grizel Baillie's ballad—

> "His bonnet stood ance fu' fair on his brow,
> His auld ane looked better than mony ane's new;
> But now he let's wear ony gate it will hing,
> And casts himsel' dowie upon the corn bing;
>
> Oh! were we young, as we ance hae been,
> We sud hae been galloping down on yon green,
> And linking it o'er the lily-white lea;
> *And were na my heart light I wad dee!*"

Sad, too, his taking MacCulloch home and entertaining him with punch, and Jean's singing his own songs till the hour of assembly came, when he was left alone in his house to brood bitterly on past and present. The whole is characteristic of the proud and self-contained poet. Field-

* Glenriddell MS. See APPENDIX, No. v.

ing when in deep waters was happy on a mutton chop and a bottle of champagne, as happy as his nature could possibly be. But Burns was not a Fielding; he had a deeper moral constitution, a prouder spirit, and a keener sense of right and wrong. The iron had entered into his soul, and his main sense of suffering was, not that he was rejected and despised of men, but that he knew he in some measure deserved it. We remember no parallel instance of the universal rejection of a gifted and admired man, except that of Byron in 1816. But Byron possessed the money power, and used it in accomplishing a Parthian retreat from his angry country. Burns' poverty compelled him to remain, else unquestionably he would have fled Dumfries, and shot barbed arrows behind him at every step of his departure. As it was, he persisted in the duties of his calling, consumed his own smoke as successfully as possible, and tried to hope and do the best he could. But we can conceive few more painful spectacles than that of this great, unhappy, indignant being pacing along the banks of the Nith or going out to Lincluden, perhaps, as of old, with a pocket edition of Milton in his hands that he might study the character of Satan, and with something of Satanic pride, misery, and remorse in his heart. Retreat from men, however, was a greater punishment to Burns than to Byron, for the former was a sincere lover of his kind, and valued their love even more than their admiration. We find him in June this year in Galloway on a visit to Heron of Kerroughtree, along with David MacCulloch, who promised to accompany him there; and in Castle Douglas penning a melancholy letter to Mrs. Dunlop, and complaining of a flying gout. And here, positively for the last time, turns up the "unspeakable" Clarinda, to whom Burns, sitting like a solitary hermit in a solitary inn, with a solitary bottle of wine, wrote a characteristic letter. In it he proclaims his pride; he rejoices in her recovered health; tells her that he constantly gives her health, when asked for the toast of a married lady, as Mrs. Mac ——; and incloses as a *bonne bouche*, a "Monody on a Lady noted for her caprice"—his old flame and new foe, Maria Riddell.

He, John Syme, and young Maxwell the surgeon, held meetings of a quasi-seditious kind, with locked doors and bated breath, a few bold toasts, and free and easy songs. From these orgies, however, there issued nothing of consequence except some epigrams of little value in reply to others of none, and one rather spirited song, "The Tree of Liberty." In autumn he resumed his song writing, and as poets, according to "Festus," must have a lay figure, he found the inspiration of many a sweet and many a silly ditty in *Chloris*, the last of his many fancy-loves. Her real name was Jean Lorimer. She was the daughter of a substantial farmer a little way from Ellisland, nearer Dumfries, and also a tea and spirit dealer in Dumfries and Kemmis-hall. Burns first came in contact with him professionally as an exciseman, but was afterwards a great favourite and frequent visitor of the family. Once arriving unexpectedly, and entering by the back-way, he found Mrs. Lorimer busy making candles for her home use—they were then an exciseable commodity. He said simply, "Faith, Ma'am, ye 're thrang the nicht!" and passed in. Jean, her daughter, was a beautiful creature with fine flaxen hair and a handsome figure. A Mr. Gillespie—a brother exciseman settled in Dumfries—wooed her, being backed in this by Burns; but in vain. A splendid spendthrift called Whelpdale, from Cumberland, who had taken a farm near Moffat, got acquainted with Jean, then only eighteen years of age, proposed elopement to Gretna Green, threatening to hang or drown himself if she would not consent, gained his point, and they returned to Barnhill man and wife. Soon, however, his debts forced him to decamp, and she did not see him for twenty-three years! She returned to live with her parents, and it was then that Burns became intimate with her. Whether he really loved her, or not, cannot now be very accurately ascertained. It is certain that his wife was intimate with the Lorimers as well as he; but it is certain also that he wrote a great many verses, very sweet and tender, belauding her charms. The frequent visits he paid to her abode were in her unprotected state extremely imprudent, and no doubt his enemies would put the worst construction on them; but this perhaps he knew not, or if he did, treated it with contempt. Her after fate was tragical. Her father failed, and she had from poverty to become a governess, and continued so for years. Returning, in 1816, from a visit to her brother in Sunderland, she heard at Brampton that her husband had left the village only a few hours before she called. He was afterwards imprisoned for debt at Carlisle, and Jean went to see him. When they met she could hardly recognize him, till he cried out "Jean;" he was so changed, slightly paralytic, a mere wreck. They met only once afterwards, and then parted for ever. After this she fell gradually—committed a *faux pas*, became a mendicant, then got a situation as a housekeeper in Newington, and ultimately died in a humble lodging in Middleton's Entry, Potterrow, not far from "Clarinda's" house. This was in 1831. Her husband, who latterly lived in Langholm, survived her a few years. She never ceased to retain her elegance of form and the remains of beauty, nor to be proud of having been sung by Burns, as "Chloris," in eleven or twelve songs.

Nothing else of importance occurred in his history this year, which had gradually brightened a little around him, but a proposal from Mr. Miller, junior, of Dalswinton, and Perry of the *Morning Chronicle*, afterwards the patron of Hazlitt, and the generous friend of many literary men, that Burns should remove to London, and write regularly at a good annual stipend for the *Morning Chronicle*. This offer he declined. Was it a pity he did not accept it? There are here various opinions; and first, of his going to London. Had Burns been as young as his years, and had he acquired thorough self-control, this had been a desirable measure. London in 1794 had no man his superior in general mental power, except Fox or Burke; in poetical genius no rival at all, unless Cowper, who was nearly off the stage, and fated to write little more. Coleridge, Southey, and Wordsworth were yet in blossom. Godwin, Thomas Paine, Holcroft, and others were mainly political writers, although Godwin's "Caleb Williams" had just appeared. On the whole, although Peter Pindar, Sheridan, and Colman were the wits of the day, and very popular, there was ample field for Burns. He could have probably got into better society than in Scotland; and from the time of his death, and long afterwards, regrets were expressed that he had not been introduced among the more liberal yet refined society of England, where indeed peccadilloes and peculiarities might have had a large margin, but where, even then, there was a demand for greater regularly and decency of outward deportment and converse, although there were some men, like Sheridan, who set habitually both morals and decorum at defiance. But while they were chartered libertines, we doubt if Burns would instantly have obtained a similar privilege; we doubt, too, if he would have subsided easily into a hard-working literary man, and he would have been exposed besides to many temptations. Then his constitution was to some extent injured, and Nature had begun to signal through all his veins that she was angry with him and must soon call him to account. We fear his career in London would have been very short; seven or eight years before it might have been otherwise. As it was, and on the whole, he was wise in refusing to go to London; although he did not act with equal wisdom in refusing the pay which Perry so generously offered him for contributing regularly to the *Morning Chronicle*. This, in the first place, would have secured him a valuable addition to his income; secondly, given him work to do, the fact of which being paid for would have acted as a stimulus to do it well; and, thirdly, it would have created for him a much wider public, and would have probably procured more enthusiastic readers and more generous patrons.

One reason why Burns refused to go to London and bind himself down to be a regular contributor to Perry's journal was, that he began to entertain hopes of promotion in the Excise. Chambers is at pains to prove that Burns, by fines, &c., made up his income to nearly £90 per annum, a sum fully equivalent to £160 at present; that he often received presents of rum, oysters, game, &c.; that he had thus a good deal of roughness in his *ménage;* that his house was tolerably well furnished, with mahogany table,

&c.; that he had a maid-servant, and sat with his Jean in the parlour; that there was often very good society with him; that he liked to see his wife well dressed, and gave her the first gingham gown ever seen in Dumfries. Burns speaks, when the "Mousie" is accused of stealing from his corn, of "getting a blessing wi' the lave and never missing it." There were two worthy clergymen, long since dead, one of them specially known to us, who were conversing about their respective incomes: one of them had £300 a year and a vixen, quite a "Xantippe," for his wife; the other £50 with a kind, sunny, excellent spouse. "I have £300 a year," said Mr. C.; "how much, brother G., have you?" "£50 and a blessing" was the naïve reply. We fear the blessing (we do not, however, refer to Jean) was denied to Burns. Amidst comparative competence and comfort he was not happy, but restless, discontented, and too ready to seek solace in excesses, where it ought not to be sought, and cannot be found. Yet he began 1795 well. January brought with her as her "first foot" that noblest of his songs, "A Man's a Man for a' that." It was the true "Psalm of Life," and at it, as at the blast of a trumpet, many of his spectres vanished. He says, in a preliminary letter to Thomson, "A great critic on songs (Dr. Aiken) says that love and wine are the exclusive themes for song-writing; the following is on neither subject, and is consequently no song." But Burns has selected here a nobler subject than either love or wine. It is manhood, and his poem, for it is rather a poem than a song, may be called the triumph or Apotheosis of Manhood. Shakspeare makes one of his characters define a man as a "forked radish," another, as a man made out of a "cheese-paring." Burns goes in opposition to such mean and disenchanting views of humanity on the one side, and to Daddy Auld's and Thomas Boston's dismal notions on the other. Burns glories in humanity *per se*, in its aboriginal elements. He is naked, and not ashamed. He believes (with all deductions) in the Divinity of human nature—in it, within and without, as the God-Man, of whom the Christ is the starry Head. And the God within us is propelling slowly but surely the coming time

"When man to man the warld o'er
Shall brithers be for a' that."

The sentiment and the song together form at once a burst of the clearest prophetic insight, an act of the noblest self-assertion, and a strain of the truest poetry, and are being fulfilled every moment in the advancing wisdom, the decreasing selfishness, the enlarging benevolence, and the approaching unity of Man.

Things otherwise began to mend. The political ferment subsided, and there was less danger of "raxed necks coming into fashion," as "Pate in Peril" says in "Redgauntlet." Burns' political sins, he says, were forgiven him. A coldness which had estranged him from Captain Hamilton of Allershaw, his landlord and warm friend, was terminated by a kind letter from him in acknowledgment of the receipt of three guineas Burns sent in part payment of rent. Mrs. Riddell and he were so far reconciled as to exchange songs, books, and literary courtesies, though in a formal "Mr. Burns to Mrs. Riddell" kind of way. All this shows that after an estrangement he and the Dumfries public were coming again to terms.

Acting as supervisor in lieu of another, Burns got snowed up at Ecclefechan in a storm, which seems to have been almost unparalleled in Scotland; houses being covered up to the second storey, and wreaths accumulated amid the Campsie hills to the depth of one hundred feet. His Correspondence contains a very laughable account of the poet's plight in what he calls the "wicked little village," a village closely connected with his own history—since Nicol, his ancient friend, Currie, his first biographer, and Carlyle, his most powerful panegyrist and advocate, were all born there.

We find next the bard in a position not much more creditable to him than when he drowned his snow-sprung sorrows in the flowing bowl at Ecclefechan—engaged in doing the squib work and letting fly the miserable crackers of a south-country election of the period. The death of General Stewart in January created a vacancy in the representation of Kirkcudbrightshire, in which two candidates presented themselves—Mr. Heron of Kerroughtree, an excellent man, and Mr. Gordon of Balmaghie, supported by Murray of Broughton and the influence of the Earl of Galloway. Burns mingled in the fray, moved more by dislike to John Bushby and the Earl of Galloway than by political feeling. Hence came his two ballads. From a letter he wrote to Heron along with them, it appears he had some hope of promotion, for which he asks his aid. He wishes to rise to the office of a collector, which implied more money—from £200 to £1000—and almost complete leisure. The first man in Scotland humbly confines his ambition to a life of literary leisure with a decent competency; and he hints very gently that perhaps Mr. Heron might help him toward this by his political influence. He might as soon have asked for his estate of Drumlanrig at once. Heron triumphed, and Burns wrote a third ironical ballad, entitled "John Bushby's Lamentation." In the second and third ballads he had attacked Muirhead, the minister of Urr, a man of ability and scholarship, who had been a wit about town in Edinburgh among the Gilbert Stuarts and Dr. John Browns of that day (some notices of him will be found in the Life of the great scholar, Dr. Alexander Murray, recently published); full of family pride, and fond of talking of his genealogical tree, and who had been sarcastically described by Burns—

"Muirhead, as good as he's true,"

And as one

> "Whase haly priesthood nane can stain,
> For wha can dye the black?"

Muirhead was not a man to sit silent under the attack of any one—not even of Burns. It was not uncommon for satirists, both in prose and verse, to take some passage from a classical author, and to found on it their attack, by translation or paraphrase more or less free. Camille Desmoulins, during the Reign of Terror, had based some of his most brilliant and scathing diatribes on Tacitus. Muirhead printed in Edinburgh a *brochure* founded on the following lines of Martial (*Martialis*, lib. ii. ep. 66):—

> "Et delator es et calumniator,
> Et fraudator es et negotiator,
> Et fellator es et lanista: miror
> Quave non habeas, Vacerras, nummos?"

Then followed a free translation—

> "Vacerras, shabby son of w——,
> Why do thy patrons keep thee poor?
> Bribe-worthy service thou canst boast,
> At once their bulwark and their post!
> Thou art a sycophant, a traitor,
> A liar, a calumniator,
> Who conscience (hadst thou that) would sell,
> Nay, lave the very sewer of hell
> For whisky! Eke, most precious imp,
> Thou art a rhymster, gauger, pimp.
> Whence comes it then, Vacerras, that
> Thou art as poor as a church rat?"

It is a very clever epigram, doubtless; and because its two severest words, "whisky" and "poor," were founded on fact, Burns felt it severely, and took his revenge afterwards in his "Excellent New Song"—

> "Here's armorial bearings
> From the manse of Urr;
> The crest a sour crab apple,
> Rotten at the core."

This shaft was aimed at Muirhead's weakness about his family, which was all right; but Burns had no business with his heart, never a fair mark, and from which the keenest arrow rebounds. Muirhead survived the poet twelve years (he died 1808, in the sixty-eighth year of his age and thirty-eighth of his ministry), long enough, we trust, to forgive Burns, and to regret his angry collision with him in his sad declining days.

In spite of such severities and their effect on the public mind, which is said to have been very great at the time, Burns was steadily rising from the low pitch which he had reached in 1794. Partly from his changed tone of mind, and partly as a popular stroke, he joined the volunteer corps which had been formed in Dumfries, and to which his friends, Maxwell and Syme, had from prudential motives annexed themselves. Some of the haughtier Tories tried to prevent Burns from joining this corps, on account of his former imprudences. But among them he appeared, and was seen by Allan Cunningham, then a boy, with his very swarthy face, his ploughman stoop, his large dark eye, and his indifferent dexterity in handling his arms. But while many could handle their arms better than Burns, none but he could write what he now wrote, "The Dumfries Volunteers," a song discovering the same genius, although with a fainter breath, which had fanned the banners of Bannockburn. But while people sang and shouted at this song in hundreds of Scottish villages, country sides, and many populous cities, all its author received for it was a reluctant pardon for his past offences from the Dumfries gentry, a permission to enter and continue among the volunteers, and to get *fou* as often as he could afford it in their ranks! A gentleman told a friend of ours that the only time he ever saw Burns was in Thornhill on a market day, lying in his full volunteer uniform, totally incapable, in the mud of the main street; no one taking the trouble to lift him up or cover him from the public gaze. Had Burns been a Frenchman on the Republican side, how different would have been his treatment! he would have given France another and a nobler Marseillaise Hymn to sing; and with what sympathetic music his strains would have accompanied the march of the Tricolor, forcing its terrible way to victory over heaps of dead, or floating over cities, forests, fields, and provinces on fire, or swaying dubiously above the tide of deep and desperate battle! Their Laureate would not have been left, nay, never would have fallen, in the mire. There never yet was a Tory Tyrtæus. Burns was essentially a Republican poet, and even in his song, "The Dumfries Volunteers," the old spirit comes out in the lines—

> "But while we sing 'God save the King,'
> We'll ne'er forget the People."

In the course of 1795 there was a renewal of a scheme which had been under consideration some years before—that of appointing Burns to a decent office in Leith, with easy duties and emoluments amounting to £200 a year. This was a project of Graham of Fintry; but, says Professor Walker, it was frustrated by the imprudence of the poet himself. We do not know whether he refers to any new special act or to his general character. No such arrangement, even if proposed again, was ever effected. Burns continued all the rest of the year to write songs for Thomson, to take his ease in the old Globe Inn, or to hold literary "symposia" with John Syme, a man of no ordinary abilities and of very social habits, a "No Song no Supper" person, who often entertained the poet at his house at Ryedale, beyond the Nith. He tells some story, which Chambers tries to prove exaggerated, about Burns in an exalted mood drawing his sword-cane and threatening to kill Syme, till checked by his exclaiming "What! wilt thou thus, and in mine house?" and that the repentant poet in remorse dashed himself down on the floor. The "sword-cane" adds a romantic air to this story, and perhaps, more than anything else, has led to doubts as to its authenticity. Had it been a poker, men might have readily believed that one whose eyes, according to Syme, were "coals of living fire" in repose, might in his altitudes have threatened to knock him down therewith. Such things have happened in better regulated families than that of Ryedale. Burns did certainly wear a sword-cane, and, according to Chambers, touched it in his ire; but how does this merely touching it with his finger account for his thereafter dashing himself down on the ground in an agony of shame? We incline to believe that Syme was, in the main, accurate both in his account of Burns composing "Scots wha hae" on the moors of Galloway, and of his getting into a towering passion when his host began, in his own house and over his own wine, to act the Mentor to the irritable poet, by this time, doubtless, considerably excited; while Syme might perhaps, from the theatrical tone of his words, appear to his guest to bear a striking similitude to Satan reproving sin.

This year the graceless Duke of Queensberry, of whom Burns had previously written

"How shall I sing Drumlanrig's Grace—
Discarded remnant of a race
Once great in martial story?
His forbears' virtues all contrasted,
The very name of Douglas blasted—
His that inverted glory,"

capped his previous infamy by cutting down all his wood, fit for being sold, in Drumlanrig and Neidpath, to furnish a dowry for the Countess of Yarmouth, supposing her to be his daughter. (George Selwyn, the famous wit, also left this lucky lady a fortune under the impression that she was his! Truly a miscellaneous composition.) Burns, who had often occasion to pass that way, was of course indignant at the devastation, and wrote his famous verses on the destruction of the woods of Drumlanrig on the back of a window in a toll-house hard by. It is difficult to believe, looking at these woods now casting their solemn weight of shadow on the immemorial castle, that they had ever been touched by a sacrilegious hand; "but," says Dr. Ramage, in his interesting book on Drumlanrig and the Douglasses, "it will take a century to replace them." Wordsworth champions the cause of injured Neidpath, and aims at the devastator a smooth stone from the brook in the shape of a sonnet—

"Degenerate Douglas! oh, unworthy lord,
Whom mere despite of heart could so far please,
And love of havoc (for with such disease
Fame taxes him), that he could send forth word
To level with the dust a noble horde,
A brotherhood of venerable trees,
Leaving an ancient dome and towers like these
Beggared and outraged! Many hearts deplored
The fate of these old trees; and oft with pain
The traveller at this day will stop and gaze
On wrongs which Nature scarcely seems to heed.
For sheltered places bosoms, nooks, and bogs,
And the pure mountains, and the gentle Tweed,
And the green silent pastures, still remain."

Burns flings a flake of that "wil'fire" of which he speaks—

("Was't *wil'fire* scorched their boughs?'")—

to blast and scorch the Vandal.

"The worm that gnawed my bonnie trees,
That reptile wears a ducal crown."

In spite of the combined assaults of the two mighty poets, and the indignation of the public, William, Duke of Queensberry, sat down infamous and contented, and lived on till 1810, dying at the great age of eighty-five, without legitimate children, but bequeathing Drumlanrig estate to Henry, third Duke of Buccleuch.

Burns was now living in Dumfries a life very differently described by different observers, and of which it is difficult to form an accurate average estimate. On the one hand, he was not idle; but along with his various engagements, professional, domestic, and literary, was rather busy, although by no means hard wrought. He occasionally assisted his children in their lessons. He was generally *himself* in the forenoons. James Gray, the teacher, paints the poet's life in rose colours; but he was a simple, warm-hearted enthusiast, one of that class of hero-worshippers who can, in reference to their idols, see no iniquity in Jacob, and no perverseness in Israel. It is told that when the famous convivial and privileged eighteenth century divine, Dr. Webster, was reeling home one night or morning past the Tron Church, a gentleman met him and said, "Ah, Dr. Webster, what would the Whigs in St. Giles' say if they saw you in this state?" "Deed," quoth the Doctor, "they wadna *believe their ain een.*" So, had Gray seen Burns ever so bad, he would not have believed his senses. This, at least, James Hogg avers of him; and Hogg knew Gray well. Mrs. Burns very naturally makes the best of it, and describes her husband as tolerably sober when he came home at night; and this was no doubt, as a rule, the case. Findlater, the supervisor, always speaks kindly and tenderly of him. On the other hand, to be perfectly candid, there were floating rumours of a very dark kind, and affecting his *morale* in other points besides drinking. It was broadly hinted that his society did no good to young men; and that young women, too, had to avoid it or risk their character, and had to visit Mrs. Burns by stealth. Thomas Aird—one of the most virtuous and generous of men, who had lived forty years in the locality, who had even a pet fancy that no bitter assailant of Burns had ever come to a good end, and who in his Mount of Communion in the "Old Bachelor," has given a good poetic photograph of him—told us he knew stories about Burns he never would reveal, and often deplored that "raging animalism" which was the fountain of his errors and his misery. We are anxious to avoid all one-sidedness and all mere sermonizing on this matter; but we should remember, that while *Premat atra Nox* ("Let the deep night conceal these errors") is a noble charitable motto for such men as Aird and Wilson to use, it could not be expected to be that of Dumfries in Burns' day, or to be altogether that of his professed and honest biographer in ours. As we have repeatedly said and will say again, we believe Burns to have been a noble being in spite of his errors; but we believe his errors to have been very great, and that it is the part of a real biographer to admit this, and to register everything of importance in reference to such a man, that he believes true, even if against his hero, as did Boswell to Johnson (see what Boswell says of Johnson's moral errors in the close of his Life), while maintaining on the whole the worth of the character, and while drawing as an inference of broad application and most mournful truth, "Lord, what is Man!" and enforcing the lesson implied in the words of Burke, "to love all human-kind, and to fear ourselves." Chambers quotes Burns' words—

"A towmond of trouble, should that be my fa',
A night of guid fellowship southers it a'"—

as if this were Burns' sober and habitual estimate of the balance of existence. Robert Hall says justly "that the greatest sensualist would prefer a small addition to his fortune to the most exquisite repast," and Burns, unless in a moment of caprice or irritation, could never have believed in such a monstrous moral misproportion as is implied in these two lines. Over the sky of his strong judgment gusts of passion and clouds of sophistry were continually rushing, but ever behind them the clear stern azure was sure to arise in its calm immortality :—

"It trembled, but it could not pass away."

In the Autumn of the year he lost his daughter, who, after a long illness, died at Mauchline. It was a heavy blow to his kind parental heart that he could not leave his duties and attend her to the grave. His own health was now beginning to break down. A person called on him in the spring of 1795 and found him ailing, and exclaiming, as he rubbed his shoulders, "I am beginning to feel as if I were soon to be an old man." Byron was still younger when he said, "I am beginning to have a dreary sort of old feel about me." A year before he had spoken to Mrs. Dunlop of a flying gout as inflicting punishment on him for the sins of his youth. To these forebodings of his fate his own folly possibly added that accidental complaint which Currie speaks of as confining him from October, 1795, to January, 1796. The confinement and regimen could not indeed have been very strict, since we find him spending a night in November in an inn with Professor Walker.

"Circumstances," says the professor, "having at that time led me to Scotland, after an absence of eight years, during which my intercourse with Burns had been almost suspended, I felt myself strongly prompted to visit him. For this purpose I went to Dumfries, and called upon him early in the forenoon. I found him in a small house of one storey. He was sitting on a window-seat reading, with the doors open, and the family arrangements going on in his presence, and altogether without that appearance of snugness which a student requires. After conversing with him for some time he proposed a walk, and promised to conduct me through some of his favourite haunts. We accordingly quitted the town, and wandered a considerable way up the beautiful banks of the Nith. Here he gave me an account of his latest productions, and repeated some satirical ballads which he had composed to favour one of the candidates at the last borough election. . . . He repeated also his fragment of an 'Ode to Liberty' with marked and peculiar energy, and showed a disposition, which, however, was easily repressed, to throw out peculiar remarks, of the same nature with those for which he had been reprehended. On finishing our walk he passed some time with me at the inn, and I left him early in the evening to make another visit at some distance from Dumfries.

"On the second morning after," continues the professor, "I returned with a friend who was acquainted with the poet, and we found him ready to pass a part of the day with us at the inn. On this occasion I did not think him quite so interesting as he had appeared at his outset. His conversation was too elaborate, and his expression weakened by a frequent endeavour to give it artificial strength. He had been accustomed to speak for applause in the circles which he frequented, and seemed to think it necessary, in making the most common remark, to depart a little from the ordinary simplicity of language, and to couch it in something of epigrammatic point. In his praise and censure he was so decisive as to render a dissent from his judgment difficult to be reconciled with the laws of good-breeding. His wit was not more licentious than is unhappily too venial in higher circles, though I thought him rather unnecessarily free in the avowal of his excesses. Such were the clouds by which the pleasures of the evening were partially obscured, but frequent coruscations of genius were visible between them. When it began to grow late he showed no disposition to retire, but called for fresh supplies of liquor with a freedom which might be excusable, as we were in an inn and no condition had been distinctly made, though it might easily have been inferred, had the inference been welcome, that he was to consider himself as our guest; nor was it till he saw us worn out that he departed, about three in the morning. . . . . Upon the whole, I found this last interview not quite so gratifying as I had expected; although I had discovered in his conduct no errors which I had not seen in men who stand high in the favour of society, or sufficient to account for the mysterious insinuations which I had heard against his character. He on this occasion drank freely without being intoxicated, a circumstance from which I concluded, not only that his constitution was still unbroken, but that he was not addicted to solitary cordials; for if he had tasted liquor in the morning, he must have easily yielded to the excess of the evening."

Professor Wilson has commented severely on Walker's narrative, and it has certainly a petty, patronizing air. But our readers should recall to mind who and what Walker was, and his relation to Burns: he was a violent Tory, while Burns had but recently escaped from the suspicion of Jacobinism. He was a man of a formal and finical cast of mind. It was almost a risk in him—looking forward as he did to promotion in the Revenue service, a promotion he ultimately got in the Custom House of Perth—to visit and spend an evening with such a tabooed character as Burns. And then he could not be expected to look at the shabby-seeming, deboshed gauger, throwing out political inuendoes, quoting bitter pasquinades, and calling for fresh supplies of liquor at three in the morning, with the same eyes as eight years before when he saw him lying entranced on the mossy couches of the Tilt, or sharing in the refined hospitalities of Blair Castle; or with the same eyes as Christopher North, writing in the year 1841, when the grief and guilt were both past, and the glory remained. There cannot be a doubt that a certain degree of degradation came across this great spirit in these latter years. This we gathered from the late amiable and child-like Dr. Wightman of Kirkmahoe, a man of a very different type from Josiah Walker, equally sincere, and far more enthusiastic. He told us that when he knew Burns he had become desperate and at bay, and it was a great affliction to be in his company. His talk was fierce, lurid, too often loose, profane, and unhappy. The noble vessel, as we would put it, had got on fire; its guns were going off, and it became positively dangerous to approach it. This Dr. Wightman said infinitely more in sorrow than in anger. It was corroborated by the statement, or rather by the silence, of another gentleman in Dumfries, a Mr. Thorburn, who had also met Burns, and who, while saying very little, gave us the same impression. This applied more to the years 1794 and 1795 than to his closing days, in which there were occasional indications of a great though fitful amelioration. Our readers are invited to compare such statements, for which this biographer vouches, with the picture of Burns' private manners Chambers has given, from the pen of Mr. Pattison of Kelvin Grove (Chambers, vol. iv. p. 173), which is exceedingly charming, and though no doubt coloured a little by a boy's vivid fancy, is in the main, we believe, true. Never, save in Shakspeare, was there volatility like that of Burns. Shakspeare could in an incredibly short time create a "Hamlet," a "Prospero," a "Falstaff," and a "Sir Toby Belch." Burns could be a "Lord Glencairn," a "Robert Ainslie," a "Smellie," a "John Rankine," or a "tinkler caird" in the course of twenty-four hours.

Ere this year closed Burns favoured the young actress, Miss Fontenelle, with an Address for her benefit night; wrote Collector Mitchell a rhyming epistle soliciting the loan of a guinea, and hinting that he had narrowly escaped death; and when, in a Reign of Terror which came upon Scotland, Henry Erskine was beat by the Lord Advocate as candidate for the position of Dean of Faculty, poured out the vexation of his heart, which was that of the community at large, in a copy of truculent and not over-decent verses ycleped the "Dean of Faculty." It was under this mortification that honest Henry went at night and hewed off with an axe the brass plate on his door which bore the lost title. But his chagrin soon gave way, and he retired to the country; and when found one day busy in a potato field, and a gentleman said to him, "So you are enjoying *otium cum dignitate*," replied, "Yes, *diggin a taty*." It would be long ere Pious Bob (as Burns nicknames the Lord Advocate) forgave the poet.

In January, 1796, the last January Burns was ever to see, he committed a great imprudence, which was punished as just but remorseless Nature punishes all such offences. The story told by Currie and Chambers is, that Burns tarried to a very late or early hour in the Globe Tavern, drank too much, fell asleep on his way home in the snow; and that, owing to the particular condition to which the use of a severe medicine had reduced his body, a fatal chill penetrated his bones, and was succeeded by a rheumatic fever from which he never thoroughly recovered. We add another version of the story communicated to us by the late Dr. William Anderson of Glasgow, a man whose probity was as conspicuous as his genius. He said that Burns went from the Globe Tavern to a house of ill fame, and there behaved so disgracefully, being of course intoxicated, that he was spurned out, and fell on a hedge opposite the door. The ground was covered with snow; and when he awoke and went home, he found the fatal chill and the accidental disease to boot. To this version of the story, which Dr. Anderson firmly believed, and which he appeared to have on good authority, our chief objection is that it contradicts Currie, who makes the accidental disease precede, not succeed, that fatal visit to the Globe. We therefore have doubts of its truth, and even were it true it would not materially alter our opinion of Burns; it would not increase our surprise, though it might deepen our sorrow. It was not Burns who left the Globe that night, and who probably had no consciousness of what befell; it was a blind-besotted vassal of an infernal will! But it was Burns, alas! who awoke and experienced horrors such as few but he have ever felt in their dread and disgraceful complexity. Burns received in himself the reward of his error which was meet, and let us trust, forgiveness afterwards from the Father who will by no means clear the guilty and remorseless, but accepts the penitent child.

Chambers says it was not the pressure of poverty, or disrepute, or wounded feelings, or a broken heart, in which lay the determining cause of the sadly shortened days of our great national poet. All true; but no doubt these combined with this unfortunate accident in bringing him to an untimely grave. It was only a complication of calamities, some sapping within, others assaulting from without, which could, at such an early age and in such a short time, have destroyed the great soul and powerful body of Burns. All these united in his ruin, and there was fatality besides:—

> "It was that fatal and perfidious bark,
> Built in the Eclipse and rigged with curses dark,
> That laid so low that sacred head of thine!"

From his melancholy bed Burns rose on the 28th January, and attended a Mason Lodge meeting, and recommended for entry as an apprentice Mr. James Georgeson, a Liverpool merchant. He wrote an unhappy letter to Mrs. Dunlop, deploring his situation and her silence. He tottered out sometimes to the street, where one day meeting his old neighbour, Mrs. Haugh, after a long talk about his state of health, he parted with the words, "I find that a man may live like a fool, but he will scarcely die like one." His commander in the volunteers—Colonel De Peyster, a remarkable man, who had served in Canada, borne the Royal Commission for eighty years, resumed in Dumfries, where he retired, the command of a troop (we figure him another Syme or Timothy Tickler of the "Noctes"—seven feet high, straight as a statue, his cheek a rose, his hair a snow-drift, his bearing that of one of Nature's noblest chivalry), and who died in his ninety-seventh year—was one of Burns' staunchest friends, sent some kind inquiries in reference to his health, and received from the poet a characteristic epistle, showing the old Adam, which was in his case the love of wine and woman, reporting itself in the midst of "bolus, pills, and potion glasses"—the ruling passion surging up strong in the very jaws of Death! On the 3rd January he had indited his lamentable epistle to Mrs. Dunlop; in February (probably one of the first days of it) he wrote for Thomson the lively song, "Hey for a lass wi' a tocher!" Currie describes his state as most deplorable:—"His appetite now began to fail, his hand shook, and his heart faltered on any exertion or emotion. His pulse became weaker and more rapid, and pain in the larger joints and in the hands and feet deprived him of the enjoyment of refreshing sleep. Too much dejected in his spirits, and too well aware of his real situation to entertain hopes of recovery, he was ever musing on the approaching desolation of his family, and his spirits sank into a uniform gloom." The last clause is hardly true. His spirits might be artificial, but he *was* in spirits when he wrote that knowing, knavish, lively ditty, "Hey for a lass," &c. Burns had taken the part of Mr. James Clarke, who had been schoolmaster in Moffat, when unjustly accused of undue severity to his boys. They had had, he says, "many a merry squeeze together," and Burns had lent him money. Clarke *was* now reported to be prosperous in Forfar as a teacher; and the poet was driven by the excessive badness of the times—the dearth of oatmeal keeping the lower orders on the brink of rebellion—and the increased expenses of his establishment, produced by his illness, to apply to him for his own. Clarke inclosed £1 in a very sympathetic letter, explaining why he could not send more till afterwards—a letter which perhaps did Burns more momentary good than £10 would have done. Moving one day through the street—the reality at thirty-seven of his own picture of old age, when it comes

"Hoasting, hirpling o'er the field"—

he met Miss Grace Aiken, a young daughter of his old friend, Robert Aiken. She knew him not till he spoke; then she prest him to go with her to Mrs. Copland's, where she was staying; and they spent a quiet, pleasant evening in that highly respectable and hospitable house, the subject being, doubtless, Ayr, Ayr, Ayr, all the time. Chambers thinks Mrs. Copland's welcoming Burns a proof that the Respectables of Dumfries were now ready to receive him into their dwellings. Alas! what family so callous and cruel as to have refused the poet admission now, with his hollow cheek, crinkling cough, stammering step, eyes burning bright, like gems set in the head of his own "Death?" Surely every house in Dumfries, we think, would then, when too late, have been thrown open to him. Chambers says "the provincial clergy had forsaken him to a man," nor do we hear of them returning when he needed their help. Perhaps they had not forgiven his

> "Three priests' hearts, rotten, black as muck,
> Lay stinking, vile, in every neuk."

He was none of their charge. Burns had latterly attached himself as a hearer to a Secession meeting-house, where then preached a Mr. Inglis, who, according to the poet, believed what he said and practised what he preached. Of him we have ascertained only that he laboured in the congregation of Loreburn Street for forty-two years, died in 1826 in his eighty-fifth year, and hailed from Leslie, in Fife. He was succeeded by Mr. Clyde, father of the accomplished Dr. Clyde of the High School, Edinburgh, and he by our excellent friend, Rev. David Scott. We may here mention that Dr. Ferrier of Paisley, one of the most eloquent and able ministers of the Secession body, used to tell that he once encountered Burns in an inn. They began to dispute on the subject of promiscuous dancing, and took different sides. Both were powerful talkers; but Ferrier, who knew Burns, at last levelled him by quoting his words from the "Holy Fair" —"As you have said, sir,

> "Mony jobs that day begin
> May end in houghmagandie
> Some ither day."

Burns felt the home-blow, laughed heartily, and they became for the rest of the evening the best of friends.

But now the poet was manifestly going down, and that in the sight of a Scotland which had received him as it had never received a poet before nor has since. His works were read in every hamlet, and his songs sung in every cottage; and he was dying, poor, neglected, and miserable. Partly, of course, the fault was his own. Nor was his case so well known as it would become now in a single week. We think, however, it was better known than is generally suspected; but he had far less sympathy than he ought to have had. Many would have been kind to him had he crossed their path, and welcomed even a visit from him; but they did not go out of their way to seek him. There was now no nobleman, as Lord Craig says of Michael Bruce, to come to his dwelling, and bid him be happy. Mrs. Dunlop at last became cold and silent, and her silence, we believe, was never explained to the poet before death, although Currie says it was; to his family after it she was eminently kind. Now it is remarkable, and has not, we think, been noticed before, that in his letters to her he was no hypocrite, but spoke out sometimes as frankly about his errors as to any of his correspondents.

May at last arrived, a May for once worthy of its old fame and of Buchanan's exquisite Ode on the 1st of May; but, alas! Burns might exclaim with Bruce—

> "Now Spring returns, but not to me returns
> The vernal joy my better years have known."

The breeze blew around his faded form and hollow features, flattering him with hopes which it was unable to fulfil. His pay is not to be materially reduced, but he receives no satisfactory assurance to the contrary; and this, of course, adds to his misery. His family had made him, as he says, a broadened mark for misfortune; and Misfortune's motto was, Spare no arrows. The duties necessary for receiving his pittance of pay were performed by one Stobie, a young expectant for Excise promotion; to his name be everlasting honour! for he who did a little could and would, if necessary, have done more. Findlater defends the Board by saying that Burns was no worse treated than others in similar circumstances, of which apology let us only say—

> "Come, then, expressive Silence, muse its praise!"

Still the old poet and lover's spirit was in him, would not be subdued, and burst out in a song called "Jessie"— a song as sweet as if inspired by real passion, although it could only have been deep respect and gratitude which were rising in his bosom as he wrote. The object was Jessie Lewars, sister of his brother exciseman, and one altogether worthy of ministering to the later hours of a Burns. Seemed she not, while bending over his bed, though he was a sinful man,

> "Like an angel o'er the dying
> Who die in righteousness?"

And it was fine to see Burns sitting, weary and wasted like a ghost, at this young lady's piano, and at her request composing better verses to a favourite tune—

> "Oh, wert thou in the cauld blast,
> On yonder lea, on yonder lea?"

words which were afterwards set to music by Felix Mendelssohn. And was there ever compliment paid to woman more delicately beautiful, worth hecatombs of flattery, than in the words—"Jessy,"

> "Although thou maun never be mine,
> Although even hope is denied:
> 'Tis sweeter for thee despairing,
> Than aught in the world beside—Jessy!"

And he covered goblets and sheets of paper with similar poetic expressions of regard and gratitude, all rose-edged, as he thought compliments to ladies should ever be, with the language of love. He predicted her matrimonial felicity. One of her swains, Bob Spalding, "had not as much brains as a midge could lean its elbow on—James Thomson is to be the man." And it was so. She became a happy wife, a resigned and industrious widow; and the blessing of Burns never forsook her in life, and still pursues her memory.

He lifted up for the last time his satirical pen, and

wrote an "Excellent New Song" in favour of Heron, who was standing again for Parliament to represent Kirkcudbright. Burns did not live to see his triumph. In this song he had a parting blow at his old enemy, Muirhead of Urr. As the 4th of June approached, Mrs. Walter Riddell, who must have been ignorant of the real state of his health, wrote him urging him to come to a birthday assembly to show his loyalty, and seeking from him the copy of a song he had newly composed; and he replied in a most melancholy tone, asking her in turn for the song, "Let us all be Unhappy Together." Seven weeks after he wrote again to Clarke in Forfar, craving, how reluctantly! another instalment of the debt due him, and owning that the thought of his widow and little ones made him "weak as a woman's tear." And on the 4th July, ere he started for the Brow, he wrote to Johnson humbly begging, in his wife's name, a spare copy of the "Scots Musical Museum" to present to a young lady—probably Jessie Lewars.

To the Brow, on the Solway, ten miles from Dumfries, he went in search of health. We passed it in 1843 in the company of Thomas Aird, Dr. John Carlyle, Dr. Browne of the Crichton Asylum, and there was a brother of Tennyson's among the party. The memory of poor Burns imposed the silence of sorrow on us all as the omnibus, in which we had been visiting Caerlaverock Castle, drove through. The Brow was then a little village; in Burns' day it consisted of only a few houses. The principal was a small inn, kept by a Mr. Davidson, who gave the "chaumer end" of his hostelry to Burns as a lodging. There was a chalybeate spring near. The Brow was then a station between Carlisle and Dumfries, past which great herds of cattle were pouring southwards, their drovers (like Robin Oig and Henry Wakefield) finding a home in the *hospitium*, and perhaps, in their cups and quarrels, disturbing the bard's equanimity and repose. But near him was the Solway, and to its side he would repair for solitude, if not solace. He might there have written as sweet a poem as Shelley's "Stanzas written in dejection at Naples," although the skies here were less blue and the foam of the ocean less bright—

"Like light dissolved in star showers thrown."

But here assuredly he might feel the wish

"To lie down like a tired child
And weep away this life of care."

He had one comfort, however, beyond the noble Alastor, who could not believe the Bible. Burns could, although he might not credit all that Daddy Auld and others found in it, or thought they found. But he had taken an old pocket Bible with him from Dumfries, and spent much of his time, it is said, in reading, and we can guess what he would read in its blessed pages.

Davidson was kind to Burns; but the only two viands he could swallow were *parritch* and port wine. The former was easily procured, but the latter was not found in the Brow cellar; and one day the Poet of Scotland might be seen walking with great difficulty—many gasps and rests — carrying in his hand an empty bottle, a mile away to Clarencefield, to see if John Burney, who kept an inn there and was married to a daughter of Davidson's, had not some for sale. He asked for a bottle of port wine, placing the empty bottle on the counter, but whispering to Burney that the muckle Deil had got into his pouch, and proffering his favourite *seal* in pledge (see it described in General Correspondence in a letter to Cunningham, March, 1793). The landlady, as Burns was unfastening the seal from the watch, stamped indignantly on the floor; and the husband, taking the poet into his arms, and giving him the wine, pushed him gently out of the door, and ended abruptly this scene of pain and shame, weeping, it is said, as he did so.

Mr. MacDougall, who tells the story very plaintively in his pleasing little work on "Burns in Dumfriesshire," intimates his belief that Burns might easily have got port wine by a word to Mrs. Riddell or any of his great friends in Dumfries, of whom he had still a few. But Burns was too proud to beg, especially in such a matter as this. He was not like a character described by Wilson in his famous lecture on the Miser, who, when the reckoning was being called for, shammed drunk, and kept his hand on his purse. Burns' motto was usually, "I pay for all." He would have sacrificed a shopful of seals rather than have borrowed a penny to discharge his *lawing*. The depths of poverty only revealed in him new pride; and if this was a fault it was a fault quite inseparable from his character—it was a bit of the genuine Burns. Mrs. Walter Riddell was in the neighbourhood, and hearing of Burns being at the Brow, invited him to dinner, and sent her carriage for him. "I was struck," says this lady in a confidential letter to a friend written soon after, "with his appearance on entering the room. The stamp of death was imprinted on his features. He seemed already touching the brink of eternity. His first salutation was: 'Well, madam, have you any commands for the other world?' I replied, that it seemed a doubtful case which of us should be there soonest, and that I hoped he would yet live to write my epitaph.* He looked in my face with an air of great kindness, and expressed his concern at seeing me look so ill, with his accustomed sensibility. At table he ate little or nothing, and he complained of having entirely lost the tone of his stomach. We had a long and

* Mrs. Riddell became a widow about the close of the eighteenth century. She removed to London, and married an Irish gentleman about Court, named Fletcher, and died in State Apartments at Hampton Court in 1820.

BROW.

serious conversation about his present situation, and the approaching termination of all his earthly prospects. He spoke of his death without any of the ostentation of philosophy, but with firmness as well as feeling, as an event likely to happen very soon, and which gave him concern chiefly from leaving his four children so young and unprotected, and his wife in so interesting a situation —in hourly expectation of lying in of a fifth. He mentioned, with seeming pride and satisfaction, the promising genius of his eldest son, and the flattering marks of approbation he had received from his teachers, and dwelt particularly on his hopes of that boy's future conduct and merit. His anxiety for his family seemed to hang heavy upon him, and the more perhaps from the reflection, that he had not done them all the justice he was so well qualified to do. Passing from this subject, he showed great concern about the care of his literary fame, and particularly the publication of his posthumous works. He said he was well aware that his death would occasion some noise, and that every scrap of his writing would be revived against him to the injury of his future reputation: that letters and verses written with unguarded and improper freedom, and which he earnestly wished to have buried in oblivion, would be handed about by idle vanity or malevolence, when no dread of his resentment would restrain them, or prevent the censures of shrill-tongued malice, or the insidious sarcasms of envy, from pouring forth all their venom to blast his fame.

"He lamented that he had written many epigrams on persons against whom he entertained no enmity, and whose characters he should be sorry to wound; and many indifferent poetical pieces, which he feared would now, with all their imperfections on their head, be thrust upon the world. On this account he deeply regretted having deferred to put his papers in a state of arrangement, as he was now quite incapable of the exertion. . . . . The conversation," she adds, "was kept up with great evenness and animation on his side. I had seldom seen his mind greater or more collected. There was frequently a considerable degree of vivacity in his sallies, and they would probably have had a greater share, had not the concern and dejection I could not disguise damped the spirit of pleasantry he seemed not unwilling to indulge."

Burns took tea one night at Mr. Craig's, the parish minister. His daughter, Agnes Craig, "Clarinda's" namesake, was an accomplished young lady (married afterwards to Henry Duncan, the well-known minister of Ruthwell, the originator of saving banks, and author, besides other works, of three novels once popular—the "Cottager's Fireside," the "Young South Country Weaver," and "William Douglas, or the Scottish Exile"). She took an uncommon interest in the Poet, was amused when he described himself to her as a poor plucked pigeon; and when the setting sun was shining in upon him too strongly, and she hastened to take down the blind, he cried out, "Let the sun shine in on us, my dear young lady; he has not now long to shine on me!" This story has been told of him and Jessie Lewars, when still nearer his end, at Dumfries, and the lines are attributed to him (our informant is Mr. David Clarke, Thornhill, an enthusiastic admirer of our poet)—

"Draw up the curtain, Jessie,
And lift my head a wee;
And let the bonnie setting sun
Shine in on you and me!"

Thus Rousseau desired to be lifted up in his bed, that he might look once more at the skies. Thus Mirabeau, beholding the sun in the spring heaven from his dying couch, said, "If he be not God, he is his cousin german!" All Sons of the Morning love the sun, rising, shining, and setting in glory.

Burns, it is said, had slightly improved at the Brow. Through sea bathing his pains were lessened, though his appetite did not get better. He made one effort more to re-string his lyre. Some link of association, it might be the power of contrast, brought back to him, as he wandered along the Solway, the recollection of that happiest day of his life which he spent at the Caldron Linn; and he was impelled to enshrine the sweet sad memory of Charlotte Hamilton in the song, "Fairest Maid on Devon Banks." He speaks, as alluded to before, of her "frown" as if some jar had broken in recently on their friendship. But he anticipates seeing her angelic smile again; perhaps he means beyond the gulf of death. And thus closed the minstrelsy of the Sweet Singer of Scotland—charmingly, characteristically, and for ever. On the altar of Woman, his life-long goddess, he threw this last grain of incense, with faltering hand, and then turned him to matters more severe, solemn, and imperiously pressing.

Amidst his meditations and preparations for the Great Future which was near, he is recalled rudely to the cares of this world. A letter is handed in to him, and he knows instantly, with sure presentiment, that it is from a dun. We see his hand trembling as he with difficulty breaks the seal. It is a letter from Mr. Matthew Penn, a solicitor in Dumfries, seeking payment of a bill due to one Williamson, draper, of £7 9s., for his volunteer uniform. It contained no threat, and had Burns been strong he would have felt it little; but as it was, it shook him soul and body, and he wrote two letters, one to James Burnes of Montrose, seeking £10, and the other to George Thomson, seeking £5. Both were instantly responded to; but the shock had been given, and he trembled less at a grave than at the horrors of a jail.

On the 18th of July he returned to Dumfries in a spring cart, which stopped at the foot of the Millhole Brae.

When alighted he trembled like an aspen leaf, and tottered with difficulty into his own house. He was laid in the room on the south, on the second floor. A tremor, says Dr. Currie, pervaded his whole frame; his tongue was parched, and his mind sunk into delirium when not roused by conversation. According to Dr. Carruthers of Inverness, who derived his information from Maxwell, the case was the most painful and complicated one the physician ever attended, partly through Burns' inability to control himself, and allow the regimen and medicines fair play. This, however, might refer to him before he went to the Brow. On the day he arrived he penned his last letter to his father-in-law. Such a letter from Burns! It resembles an epistle from the dead to the dead—beginning, "My dear Sir," and ending, "Your son-in-law." Alas! the feud had never been made up, and Burns in this dread hour durst not simulate affection he could not feel. He must now be permitted to die in peace. His four little boys were sent to Leuchars' house. Findlater, who previously forwarded him £5, came occasionally to soothe his last hours. Jessie Lewars often moistened his lips, and ministered to his other necessities, now numbered, and would be rewarded by a pressure of the hand, and a look of gratitude from those eyes of flame soon to soften into the dimness of death. Jean was in bed, owing to her peculiar condition; but she rose ever and anon and stole over to look at her expiring lord. One of the corps of Volunteers called, and the last spark of Burns' matchless humour leaps to his eye as he says, "Don't let the awkward squad fire over me."

The sun of July 21 has risen and kindled his beacon-red on the top of Criffel, and the bright serpent of the Nith has uncoiled in his beams, while all unconscious of the summer day the Poet is lying in deep delirium. His children are now brought in to see their Sire ere he depart. Look at him as he tosses and writhes! Is that poor pallid being, livid with long confinement, unshaven, worn to a skeleton, with black masses of hair prematurely tinged with gray, with frenzy in his gestures and fever in his eye—is that the Boy-poet of Doon; the Star of Edinburgh; the inspired author of the "Cottar's Saturday Night;" the Rhapsodist and Dramatist; the Homer and Shakspeare of Scotland? Even so. He has been hitherto silent; but now he speaks, and his last word reveals his last thought. And of whom is his last thought? Is it of his long-lost and deeply-loved father? of his patron, in whose grave his heart is lying, Glencairn? of the wife of his bosom, soon to be again a mother and a widow? of one of his many loves, the Mary of his youth? the star-like Miss Burnet? the lovely Charlotte Hamilton? his admired and adoring "Clarinda?" No, it is of the mean haberdasher who has threatened him with a jail; and the last word of this Bard of Humanity is that of the last stern prophet of Israel—Malachi—a curse! But now he swallows a cup of medicine which had been put into his hands, and throwing out his arms, as if he were plunging into an ocean visible to him alone, he falls forward from the top to the bottom of the bed, and—

"He is gone!
It once was Lara that thou look'st upon."

Conceive the wild wail of sorrow that breaks out in the chamber—the poor children crying as if they would weep out their very hearts, and the low sob of his wife, and see amidst all this, serene and silent as a spirit, Jessie Lewars approaches the bed and shuts

"The Poet's ardent eyes."—(*Roscoe*).

Scarcely was he cold when the pent-in sorrow, first of Dumfries, then of Scotland, then of the world, burst out like a sea. Since to *him*, at least, "it could do no good on earth," it came forth the more speedily and the more generally. Had it been an instant sooner—had it but given one gleam of hope to pierce the dim haze of delirium which wrapt the dying Poet—it had been out of this world's way, it had been something like a sin. He *must* die in utter darkness as to the future of his wife and children. Was this a just Nemesis persecuting him to the last gasp? We hardly think it was. But he had a glimpse in his own prophetic soul some time before, when he told Jean he believed that, in a hundred years, he and she would be more *respeckit* than now. How characteristically Scotch and *Burnsian* was the word "respeckit"—*respeckit like the lave*—not applauded, dosed in his dust with flattery, but "respeckit." This is what every Scotch heart loves when it comes, desiderates when it does not. "He was weel respeckit" is still the warmest encomium an honest Scotchman can pronounce over the grave of a good and honourable brother man. Dumfries had now, as her first duty, to bury him; and with true, though belated sympathy, she performed the task, and in a good spirit. He had sung, "For man is a sodger, and life's but a faucht;" and surely he had been a brave, if hapless, soldier himself. Carlyle says, "Edward Irving fell, if not victorious, yet unconquerable." But poor Burns was a beaten man, though vigorous and gigantic had been his struggle; and he now lay low, but mighty still. He deserved, at all events, military honours, and he was buried with them. The Volunteers, of which corps he was a member, the Fencible Infantry of Angusshire, and the regiment of cavalry of the Cinque Ports, offered their assistance. On the evening of the 25th July his remains were carried to the Town Hall, and on the following day—a party of the Volunteers in front with their arms reversed, the main body behind supporting the coffin, on which Burns' hat and sword were laid; behind, a numerous body of attendants, and the Fencible Regiment lining the streets—the funeral procession moved along to the South-

BURNS' MAUSOLEUM,
DUMFRIES.

LIFE OF BURNS.

ern Churchyard to the sublime music of the Dead March in "Saul:" and arrived there, three volleys (*straggling*, as the dying Poet anticipated, and as Allan Cunningham, who was present, observed) attested Burns' wedding with the grave, and the arrival of—

> "The long, long silence, and the wormy shroud,
> And the *Amen* carved on the lonely tomb."

Nineteen years afterwards, at the instance of Mr. William Grierson of Boatford, who wrote a graphic sketch of the poet's interment (the enthusiastic father of an equally enthusiastic and indefatigable son, Dr. Grierson of Thornhill, an eminent antiquarian, and who has collected a great number of relics of Burns, some of which he has kindly furnished to us *), a movement for a monument began; and when the present mausoleum was finished, the corpse of the Poet was raised on the 16th September, 1815, and found in admirable preservation—the hair still abundant, the teeth firm and white; but when a shell or case was inserted below the coffin, the head separated from the trunk, and the whole body, with the exception of the bones, crumbled into dust, which was carefully collected and placed in a new coffin, and laid beside his two boys, Maxwell and Francis Wallace, who were also buried there. The mausoleum is an elegant Grecian temple, designed by Mr. T. F. Hunt of London, adorned within by a mural sculpture by an Italian artist, Turnerelli, representing his own ideal of "Coila" finding her Poet at the plough, and casting her inspiring mantle over him. Many eminent citizens of Dumfries are buried in the same cemetery with Burns; but the one approaching him most closely in genius is unquestionably Thomas Aird, who was laid in that God's acre on the 1st of May, 1876—a man of as true and original, if less varied, powerful, and popular genius, utterly free from Burns' errors, but possessing a heart as warm, and a simplicity and sincerity of character proclaiming the author of the "Devil's Dream on Mount Acksbech" and of the "Old Bachelor in the Old Scottish Village" not unworthy as a poet, and more than worthy as a man, to repose near the author of the "Vision" and the "Cottar's Saturday Night."

Scotland, England, and the world almost simultaneously proceeded to do justice to Burns' memory. Appeals were made by Lewars and Syme for the pecuniary relief of his family, and not in vain. He had, to his infinite credit, left only a little debt—not more than £30. But even this was a burden too heavy for his family to bear, and James Burnes, George Thomson, and Gilbert Burns all made efforts in different ways to clear it off. Syme, Maxwell his physician, and Alexander Cunningham of Edinburgh commenced a subscription, and projected an edition of his works and life. After some hesitation as to the choice of a biographer—Dugald Stewart being first thought of, then Mrs. Walter Riddell, and then John Syme—Dr. James Currie of Liverpool, an accomplished and warm-hearted man, was selected for the task. The subscription went on slowly. Subscriptions even for the most proper and popular objects are often failures from sheer want of pushing. The mass are usually quite passive, and the impulse to continue, as well as the initiative to start, must come from a few individuals. Sometimes one fashionable name determines the fate of a testimonial or subscription. This for Burns at the end of a year did not amount to more than £700. The Life was more successful. Dr. Currie got into his hands, though in a confused state, a mass of valuable material, including the Thomson Correspondence, which that gentleman generously gave up to him. The book was published by subscription. It appeared in May, 1800, was received with universal approbation, and realized about £1400 to the family. Mrs. Burns was now in comfortable circumstances, and continued to live in her husband's house. It may be mentioned here that on the morning of the poet's funeral she was taken with the pains of labour, and about the time that he was being committed to the dust his posthumous child was ushered into the world—"Every moment dies a man, every moment one is born." The child was called Maxwell, after Burns' kind and skilful physician, but did not long survive. A curious story is told that Mrs. Burns, shortly after his birth, had a dream that her husband appeared at her bedside, and said he had been permitted to return to behold his child—looked in at the mother and child, and then vanished. This probably arose in Jean's mind from her regret that he had not lived to see this Benoni, the Son of Sorrow; but it might be a true rendering of his yearning even in the world of spirits for a sight of his own babe, born in circumstances so intensely peculiar and painful. Jean lived in Dumfries much respected till March, 1834, when she died, and was buried beside her husband. It was then that a cast of the poet's skull for a phrenological purpose was taken by Bailie Frazer, and submitted to Mr. George Combe, who passed over it a characteristic and oracular verdict, asserting very truly that if Burns had been a nobleman, liberally educated, and employed in pursuits suited to his powers—been, in short, everything he was not—he would have become a very different and superior being; but where meanwhile would have been "Hallowe'en," the "Twa Dogs," "Tam o' Shanter," and the thousand and one songs? Jean was very much pestered by visitors, many of whom called to procure relics of the Poet, till at last she is said good-humouredly to have told one of them that she had nothing to give him unless he took herself. She was certainly the Relic of Burns. She had some offers of marriage of a

---

* See APPENDIX VIII.

respectable kind, but she steadily refused. She felt herself wedded to the dead, and that her individuality would have been lost had she ceased to be the widow of the great Poet of Scotland.

Burns, by Jean Armour, had five sons and four daughters. Jean, the eldest daughter, was a twin, and she and her brother, Robert, born 3rd September, 1786, died in the course of fourteen months. Twin daughters, born on the 3rd March, 1788, died soon after. Elizabeth Riddell, called after Mrs. Captain Riddell of Glenriddell, was born 25th November, 1792, died at Mauchline, 1795, and was buried there, Burns being unable to attend the funeral. Of the Poet's five sons, Francis Wallace, the second son, named in honour of Mrs. Dunlop, was born 18th August, 1789, died 9th July, 1803, aged fourteen. Maxwell, the youngest son, was born on the 26th July, 1796, and died in April, 1799, aged two years and six months. Robert (twin), born 3rd September, 1786, studied three sessions in Edinburgh and Glasgow, obtained a situation in the Stamp Office, London, 1804, got in 1833 a superannuated allowance, came down to Dumfries, saw his mother, whom he had not seen for twenty-six years, and fixed his residence in the Queen of the South for the rest of his life. He remembered his father, who put the "English Poets" into his hand to read, but never mentioned to him his own verses. He was intellectual, a capital mathematician, wrote a song—once a favourite—

"Have ye seen in the calm dewy morning?"

and resembled his father much, alike in his strength and weakness. He lies in the mausoleum. William Nicol Burns was born in Ellisland on the 9th of April, 1791, sailed to India when sixteen as midshipman, became ultimately a colonel; in 1843 retired from the army and came to reside at Cheltenham with his brother, James Glencairn, where he died in 1872, aged eighty-one. James Glencairn was born in Dumfries 12th August, 1794, sought, too, his fortunes in India, became major, and then lieutenant-colonel, returned to Britain and settled along with his brother William in Cheltenham, and died there in 1865, aged seventy-one. Both brothers, too, lie in the mausoleum. They were entertained at the great Burns Festival on the Doon in 1844. Gilbert Burns, Robert's younger brother, went from Mossgiel to the farm of Dinning in Nithsdale; thence to the farm of Morham Muir, near Haddington; thence, becoming factor to Lord Blantyre, he established his residence at Grant's Braes, near Lethington, where he died in 1827, aged sixty-seven. He lies in Bolton Churchyard, East Lothian.

Burns had three sisters, Agnes, Annabella, and Isabella. Agnes married a Mr. Gall, and died in Ireland. Annabella died unmarried at her brother Gilbert's house at Grant's Braes. Isabella married a Mr. John Begg, who became a land steward in Lanarkshire; and after his death she resided first at Ormiston and then at Tranent, till she herself died in 1858, leaving a large family.

We pass now to a chapter or two of criticism.

CHAPTER XIII.

BURNS AS A MAN, LOVER, CONVERSATIONIST, AND RELIGIONIST.

E cannot close this account—meant, at least, to be a fair and sternly accurate, although meant also to be a favourable, friendly, enthusiastic history of Burns' life—without attempting a summary, however difficult, of his character as a Man. And yet the difficulty is perhaps more apparent than real. Such sharp-pointed sentences as that of Byron about Burns being a compound of "dirt and Deity" do not help us much. Dirt and Deity mixed is a very good general definition of man. Burns, to be sure, had these elements in larger proportions than others, just because he was a larger man—a Big Brother. But if he had more dirt, he had more Deity too. To decide the preponderance of the one over the other is the difficulty of the moral critic, even as to produce a proper subordination of the lower to the higher principles is the greater difficulty of the moral man.

To no one, unless to Shakspeare or Goethe, was Nature kinder than to Robert Burns. True, she found her favourite in an "auld clay biggin'," hearing

" The restless rattons squeak
     Ayont the riggin' '—

found him a poor man's son, and destined to partake of his father's poverty all his life. This Nature knew; but unmoved by this, she showered on him with prodigal hand her choicest gifts—gold, frankincense, and myrrh: the gold of genius, the frankincense of a large and loving heart, and the myrrh of keen, acrid, yet aromatic and genial wit. Withal she gave him strong intellect, uncommon and common sense, and a brawny constitution, which seemed built to last a hundred years. But she did not apparently intend him to change his position in life. She

" Damned his fortune to the groat;"

but in requite,

" She graced him with a random shot
     O' countra Wit."

What more could Nature have done for him? unless, indeed, the gift of self-control be hers to give, and not rather a habit which the man must acquire for himself. In that he failed, signally, although not perhaps quite so much as many have supposed. Let us remember that if his vices were great, his virtues, too, were great; and that when he died at thirty-seven, there were still vast possibilities before him. He says himself that

" Aft a ragged cowt 's been known
     To mak a noble aiver."

How many, after sowing their wild oats, become consistent and useful men! He pursued his sowing a little longer than most men of this class certainly; still he died young, and when personal reformation and a long consecration, even, of his wondrous powers might still, had he lived, have been before him. His natural tendencies were good, but distorted by circumstances and position. We by no means intend by this that these were entirely to blame, and not partly himself. But while we condemn Chambers for always pointing to Burns' *Moimême* as the cause of his evils, we own much force in it withal. Circumstances and position are never deserving of blame, any more than they are susceptible of punishment. They are very much what a man makes them to be. Burns might have triumphed over them, and we might by this time of day have been paying him the same pure and unmingled homage we pay to Milton or Wordsworth. But would he, after all, in this case have been quite so dear to us as he is? Would he have been so near to us either? Pour water into a bowl, and it brings a coin previously invisible into sight, and brings it close to our eye too. We see it, and we see it well. And so with the tears of sympathy and sorrow. They interpose a new and softer medium between us and a man. We see him more clearly, and we learn to love him more warmly.

Let us try in a sentence or two to sum up those causes which produced the sad failure of Burns. Poverty from first to last—he never had, for a month together, a hundred pounds he could call his own; hard moiling labour; a bilious constitution; an incipient heart disease stretching like a precipice below his life all his days; the strongest animal organization and passions withal, since Mahomet; imperfect education; society (of necessity) uncongenial and below him, an irascible temper, a highly nervous temperament, many misfortunes and disappointments, niggardly patronage; "the oppressor's wrong, the proud man's contumely, the insolence of office, and the spurns which patient merit of the unworthy takes," and which impatient merit gives back with usury; an age when flunkeyism was rampant and independence had not yet left the side of "the violated goddess," who, according to Smollett, "brought forth a Creed too narrow, and a Church too divided and too much secularized; a haughty nobility; a rude though picturesque populace; a middle class virtuous but untrained; a society in many parts of which intemperance and loose morals prevailed to a terrible extent— these were the links, and not all the links either, of the chain which fixed the strong man to the ground or crippled him when he moved above it; these the causes which combined with his own recklessness and want of self-control in rendering him unutterably miserable, hurrying him into folly and sin, and in fine, cutting him prematurely off after a life short in years, long in wretchedness —like a piece of music lengthened out by its dying falls and quavers of anguish. And yet, in spite of all this, it could not be denied that, apart from his unrivalled genius, he was a man of a generous, affectionate, liberal, noble nature—a painstaking ploughman, a diligent farmer, a pattern exciseman, a devoted father, a kind husband, a good neighbour, and in his dealings, as well as in his feelings and opinions, a thoroughly honest man. His cattle on one occasion, we have been told, had found the gate of his neighbour farmer's clover field unbarred, had entered, and committed considerable depredations. Burns did not like to offer, what would certainly have been refused, any recompense for the trespass. Yet his conscience would not be at ease till he threw open one of the fences of his own field, and allowed his neighbour's cattle to take their master's revenge. Of course, there were lower and stormier elements in the man which come out, like characters written in milk, when exposed to fire—the fire of insult, or of softer temptation. But we cannot judge of the whole of any man from transient moods and hurried ebullitions.

Our readers may, perhaps, have seen Sam Bough's engraving of the Bell Rock Lighthouse in a storm. What a fierce, torn, terrible sky! What a strange, dusky, uncertain gloom pervades it! And how the light is so directed and concentrated as to pierce the great darkness, and to rest on the lighthouse and a little bit of the angry sea! With what feelings you contemplate the lonely column standing up in the midst of these frantic waves, which are lashing and dashing, rising, rolling, and uttering, you know though you cannot hear, a thousand furious outcries like those of exasperated and tormented demons. Just one thing is wanting to the grandeur of the scene. You have no fear for the safety of the lighthouse. You feel it can stand a hundred such storms, and that to stand one is to stand for ever. It would be different were there the slightest sensation of doubt, did you see it actually on the first night it had ever encountered such a tempest. Then you might be inclined to pant, to pray, to cheer it on, as if it were a human being. And would you not admire and love it more on account of the dubious struggle? And when you witness a man like Burns assailed by a thousand blasts of passion and appetite, your interest and your regard for him strengthen immensely, and you now see in him an emblem of—

"Poor Humanity's afflicted Will
Struggling in vain with ruthless Destiny."

No doubt he fell, but assuredly he struggled not to fall; and ere you condemn and wonder at his weakness, try to estimate the strength of those wild waves and blasts which assailed him; and while you blame him more than them, weep at the thought that between them such a ruin was wrought, and such a glorious wreck remains!

Had he stood, and become a man of marble firmness like his father, what a triumph! And had he attained his father's years he might, for Burns' moral constitution was originally strong and sound. But during his short life he never gained a victory over that more than Protean volatility which characterized him. He was everything by turns, and nothing long. He yielded, as a rule, to every impulse, good or bad, high or low, which assailed him. He was at the mercy of innumerable moods, as diverse from each other as Heaven from Hell. He began life as a Jacobite in politics; he ended it as a Jacobin. He often loved, or seemed to love, several females at the same time; and no sooner had one forsaken him than he had another ready to supply her place. His opinions of men, too, were continually fluctuating. His genius partook of the same uncertainty, and so did his taste and his moral frame. From divinest poetry to sheer doggerel, and worse, how frequently did he descend, and that in the compass of a single page! All this arose partly from his circumstances in life, so unworthy of his genius, partly from his imperfect education, and partly from that seven-times heated fervour, increased by youth, passion, and excess, which burned in his veins. Age, along with a better regulated life, would have abated if not altogether removed this. As it was, the contradictions were never reconciled; the controversies raged even to the hour of death, and despair over the unresolved problem of his history must always mingle with and shade the delight with which we peruse the miracles of his genius. Still he had a noble nature, nobler in its mysterious ruins than others in their cold colossal integrity of moral character, in that faith which, though not altogether "alone," is dead, or in that perfection of life which might be called divine, were it not that it knows itself, and avows itself, to be perfect, boasts and blabs, and is so unlike the silence with which our God conceals His benevolent operations and character, veils His face, and will, neither to blasphemous calumny nor to flattering advocation, reveal His purpose of Universal Love and His plan of Universal Happiness.

We will not retread the ground on which many critics and biographers have dwelt so long. Burns' errors in the use of stimulants were great, although not exactly habitual. They were intensified by his temperament; they were often forced on him by temptation; they were the habits of his age; they were shared in by some of the greatest of his contemporaries, such as Pitt, Fox, Sheridan, Porson, and at one time of his life, Dr. Johnson; they were common in Scotland among clergymen, even highflyers like Webster; whose example, however, in our more temperate time, cannot mightily seduce, although it may serve as a warning still. Alas! instead of the intemperate habits and customs of our fathers, there have come in even greater uncharitableness, gossip, envy, detraction, mean avarice, hypocrisy, selfishness, cant, and falsehood, than those which Burns lashed with a whip of scorpions. If one devil has (partially) gone out, seven less offensive but even wickeder have entered in, and the last state of society is in some classes worse than the first. We attach no blame to Temperance Societies, which have done immense good; but Burns lived before their day, and has not a word that can reflect on their wise and benevolent supporters. On his other faults delicacy forbids us to dwell more than we have already done. They were peculiarly his weaknesses, but they were not, on the whole, systematic nor seductional, and very seldom were they committed in cold blood. We leave, and we have not sought to disguise them, in trembling hope on the

"Bosom of his Father and his God."

Nay, we cast them on the smokeless altar of the great Christian Sacrifice, as Burns himself devoutly did in many a lucid and penitential hour, in many a sincere and profoundly sorrowful page.

Whom did Burns chiefly love is a more pleasing but still a somewhat puzzling question. We have some doubts if he ever loved one with his whole being. Jean Armour, as we have hinted more than once, he loved sincerely, warmly, at one time passionately; but it was calf love, not the result of profound sympathy, nor of the highest kind of esteem either, although he respected her highly in later days. And so perhaps with Mary Campbell. He loved her with strong, superficial, half-animal passion on earth; he loved her best as "Mary in Heaven!" He could not affect, and had not profound fellow-feeling or kindred tastes with her, nor she with him; and had he married her, says Wilson, he would have broken her heart. His feeling for "Clarinda" we have already characterized rather sternly. His Jean Lorimers *et hoc omne genus* were burnished butterflies, amusing his noontide leisure. Miss Alexander burst on him like a splendid vision, and faded away, although she might perhaps in happier circumstances have fixed him. Maria Riddell he regarded with feelings as changeful and capricious as that lady herself. Charlotte Hamilton comes nearest of all his flames or semi-flames to the ideal of his Other Self. Jessie Lewars was a dream, a dream such as "waves before the half-shut eye" of Death. But, we repeat, he never had his whole nature reflected in a female as in a mirror; and perhaps the thought of this is Utopian—at least in the history of poets it has not been common. If they get even a shred of the Divinity, it is much. Milton got his full wish in the matter, in his second wife, for a year; Shakspeare seemingly not at all. Shelley got his heart's desire in Mary Godwin, and was not satisfied, if it, indeed, be true that the Lady Emilia V——, the heroine of that divinest of rhapsodies, "Epipsychidion," came between them for a season. Godwin obtained the most magnificent woman of her time—physically, mentally, spiritually—in Mary Wollstonecraft, and the Gods took her away soon, because he was not worthy of her, though the express image of his own noble creation in "St. Leon," Marguerite de Damville. In still later times there have been the favourable examples of Wordsworth, Wilson, Southey, Moore, Croly, Browning, Tennyson, Dr. Chalmers; and, on the other side, of Sir Walter Scott, Coleridge, Lord Lytton, Byron, Campbell, Landor, and Dickens. On the whole, we may consider Burns well off, so far as domestic circumstances went, in Jean Armour, a lealhearted woman, a model mother, and an affectionate and devoted wife.

Much has been said by his biographers about Burns' power over females, which is said to have amounted to sorcery. What was the cause of this? Not beauty, as in the case of Byron; for although Burns was altogether no "vulgar boy," in mere appearance he was little better than a "lout," with the fine eyes and with brawny limbs. It was partly his talk, which he softened and sweetened down to their level. With the accomplished and wellinformed, the feeling and poetry of his songs and verses did much; but with them, too, with others, with all, it was greatly the passion that was visibly in him, the excessive power of the love-feeling. Women loved Burns because he loved them; and was, besides, no ordinary swain, but a king of men and a poet of poets. Danaës do not always need a shower of gold to recognize a Jupiter. Byron had something of the same power—less pure, indeed, for he idolized himself even more than he did woman; but perfumed more by sentiment, and pointed by a coronet. In Shelley and Jean Paul the sentiment predominated, and the love interchanged was Platonic, but the fascination was similar. No doubt there are other considerations. Women like praise as well as appreciate love, and like praise best in its best form—poetry; and this is what the poets alone can worthily give. And this is what Burns, of all poets, was best fitted to give. But his power of giving it lay not in his genius alone, but in his enthusiasm for the woman combined with it. The conditions of success may be named :—1st, he was an extraordinary man; 2nd, he possessed an extraordinary love for the female sex; and 3rd, he was able to render it into matchless song. Had Miss Alexander, the "bonnie Lass of Ballochmyle," received the song in her honour after Burns had become the man of the country, and ere he began to decline, we are almost inclined to believe that the wild dream of his song might have been realized. But probably this is idle speculation.

Burns' conversation was one of the truest, if not the truest, reflection of his powers. John Sterling says, "No man was ever so born a poet but he required to be regenerated into a poetic artist." It is still more certain that no man was ever so born a converser but that he required to be regenerated into a conversational artist. Fluency is a gift; but conversation, in the true sense of that term, is more an acquirement. Johnson was naturally fluent and sonorous enough, but his temperament would often have inclined him to be sullenly silent were it not that he had determined to talk, and, as he said, to "talk his best." Burke, although, as Johnson said of him, "he talked because he had a full mind," yet seems resolutely to have set himself to practise conversation. And Burns, in his early conversations with his father, and brother, and teacher, in his disputes with the Calvinists of the West, and in his Tarbolton Debating Societies, was cultivating with the greatest care that power of conversation by which he was afterwards to astonish Edinburgh. He studied, it is said, even emphasis and modulation of voice. His conversation was not, as many seem to imagine, that of a mere rough, rich mind, crumbling down in unconscious utterance of his unpolished thoughts and untutored feelings. Burns was at once a consummate master of talk, and a man of impetuous impulse and teeming genius. He was not a machine of words, conversing at all times with equal ease. He was often, it is said, for long evenings silent, leaning his brow on his hand, and with his thoughts far, far away, in memory, or remorse, or love, from the societies around him; but at other times, when the social feeling came upon him, or when the fascination of female eyes excited him, or when he felt himself among his rivals in conversational power, or when the sight of some pompous charlatan or haughty lordling aroused his displeasure, he became like a man inspired, and threw out, partly with his eyes and partly with his lips, beautiful, or quaint, or sententious, or wild, or humorous, or pathetic thoughts in a torrent, accompanied by words stronger and often more select than would have occurred to him at his desk or anywhere else, if in a less excited state; pointed by a manly yet artistically-managed elocution, and diversified by anecdotes, compliments, and poetic quotations. It were of no use to deny that there were often oaths, too; but first we cannot say, as Dr. Johnson says of Colley Cibber, that in conversation he had only half original matter to supply, the other half being oaths solely. Oaths, unfortunately, were too common then and long after; for we have heard them in volleys at least twenty years ago from persons seemingly of the first respectability, although now they linger only on the lips of some eccentric individual, who swears still because he has been swearing for sixty or seventy years. Johnson's famous saying about a person on meeting Burke under a shed to shun a shower, and pronouncing him, from his talk, an extraordinary man, would not have applied to Burns, for he under the shed would probably have remained silent, if his chance companion had not been congenial; but no one would have spent a night with him in his happier moods without being astonished at the versatility, the naturalness, and the strength of his genius. Latterly his deepening dissipation and the fierce exasperation of his mind rendered his conversation less uniformly delightful, while probably increasing its power.

Burns was indeed a man of many moods, but his general feeling was that of sombre melancholy—the lightning of his eye flashing above the dark thunder cloud of his face, which in its normal state received from it no illumination, but continued sombre and swarthy, though calm. Thus he looked, we think, generally at the plough, where he did not always walk in glory and in joy—always in glory perhaps, since it was glorious to be a Burns even in silence and in gloom; but seldom in joy, except when he had the sight of a "mousie" running away from his plough, or of a sudden sunbeam of brief, bewitching beauty from the October sky appearing and retiring again, or had some stirring thought of patriotism, or some warm memory of woman; and then he became a poet, inspired beyond the guess of folly, rich beyond the dreams of avarice, happy beyond the bliss of love. Thus men saw him in society, as Wilson describes so beautifully, with his large black eyes subdued into profound and melancholy thoughts. There were even darker moods than these, as when he indited the "Lament," or tossed in his bed in sleepless anguish because of blighted hopes, or follies and sins having "brought forth death," and felt that

"Deep and shuddering chill
Which follows fast the deeds of ill."

But how easily and rapidly did he, in general, rebound

LIFE OF BURNS.

into gladness! The sight of a "bosom crony" on the street, the smile of a maiden in the evening from her cottage door, the advent of a new book to the village library, a solitary walk by the river side, an assignation with a beloved female in the glen of green bracken, a starry night, with the "cauld blue north" sending up her streamers, the sound of psalms from a godly household in the gloaming, or the sight of a column of smoke curling from a cottage "lum" in the grey dawn; let him see or hear any of these, and the gloom which had rested on his brow lifted from it like a cloud, and he was glad, and glad profoundly, and glad long. This gladness was of various kinds and degrees, and might be called by various names. Uproarious mirth, deep sober joy, social madness, reinless passion, wild abandonment to the Spirit of the Hour, were all his by turns; but perhaps his most common and characteristic feeling of a lightsome kind was *glee*. The polar opposite of his gloom was gleesomeness, which, in default of a better definition, we may call the Spirit of Song—the spirit in which some men are disposed to sing songs, others to write songs, and others to listen enraptured to songs read or sung. Glee is incompatible usually with excess, though dependent greatly on excitement. Could Burns but have stopped at glee, ere it became extravagance, or got mixed up and poisoned with passion! But, alas! he often could not, and his feelings becoming delirium in the evening, prepared for him a fearful reaction in the morning. But no poet, perhaps no man that ever lived, felt more thoroughly the spirit of glee than "blithe-hearted Burns," as Landor calls him in the lines—

"Though water is my daily drink,
　Had I met thee, blithe-hearted Burns,
We should have roared out toasts by turns;"

and he has not only filled, but overcharged his best songs with it, and they shall recreate the feeling in human bosoms for ever more! And the best word for the inspiration which prompted his masterpiece, "Tam o' Shanter," is not, after all, poetic enthusiasm or the glorying of creative power, so much as it is boundless glee. It was this which brought tears to his eyes as he began to recite the part of the marvellous poem in which glee came to its culmination—

"Now Tam, O Tam, had thae been queans," &c.

As to Burns' religion, he was a Broad Churchman born out of due time. He disliked the severer dogmas of Calvinism; on some of the mysteries of Christianity he was silent, neither accepting nor rejecting them. His hatred of hypocrites and hypocrisy, fanatics and fanaticism, cant and canters, made him often say wild things about religion, if not exactly against it; but he valued it in its ordinances sincerely celebrated, in its professors and preachers when genuine, in its virtues when merciful and unostentatious, in its Founder on the human side of His character. His views on the other fluctuated; but we hope the divinity of Christ latterly commended itself to his view. His first confession, "Christ was from God," seems gradually to have slid into the fuller truth, "He was the Son of God;" and the mildness of the religion of Jesus — its forgiving love and brotherly kindness, its hatred of hypocrisy, oppression, cruelty, cant, and self-righteousness—rendered it very dear to him. He thought, rightly or wrongly, that Christianity did not require a personal Devil, an eternal hell, a bloody vicarious atonement, or perhaps even a scheme of miracles, prophecy, and eschatology, to support its claims or develope its idea; that these rather detracted from its power, which is a power over the heart and the higher principles of humanity. If many said then, and would say now, that this was only to be an almost Christian, Burns would have taken up the title, and bound it as a crown unto him, and said, I would rather be an almost Christian than a Christian bigot or a Pharisee, which were to be in my judgment no Christian at all. I cannot be a Paul; I may be only a doubting Thomas; but Thomas loved before he was able to believe, and after believing he did no more—although his reverence was increased, and he said, "My Lord and my God." His father's creed was very much his son's, only William Burness was able to defend and glorify it by a thoroughly consistent life. A strait creed might have done Burns good, but only as a strait-waistcoat does a maniac—it would have restrained, not changed him; in such an intellect, temperament, and environment as his, such a creed could not, without a miracle, have become incarnate. It would not have made him really better, and we tremble at the thought of the curb of a charger like him breaking, and of his plunging again into the wilderness. It would not, probably, have made him much happier, it might have made him, especially had it improved his morals, less miserable; but he had been at best a caged eagle. Byron thought had he lived *he* might have become a monk; but Burns' strong common sense and hereditary Scottish prejudice would never, we think, have allowed him even to seem to bolt Popish tenets, and he was too religious to need any high-spiced ceremonial and vaulted cathedral for his devotion. Scottish family worship and "the dim religious light" of an auld clay biggin' were enough for him; nay, Nature in a breezy autumn morn, a spring morning, or a stormy winter day, when the blast was bending the trees and raving over the plain, was to him a fitting temple where he could offer up that vague, vast, wordless worship which, perhaps, in a mind like his, soaring ever in its loftier mood toward Immensity and the Supreme God, was the best.

We have often said that Shelley just inverted the

grandest truth in Christianity, and instead of God is Love, said "Love is God." Burns did the same. As love was, in one or other of its forms, the great pervading passion of his life, so it was the secret of his devotion; and his conception of God was that of love universally diffused, and animating more or less all being—the poet himself being only a leaf in that infinite forest in which the Breath of Love was moving continually. And Jesus Christ, as his letters often declare, he considered to be the best and fullest representative and channel on earth of that all-embracing and everlasting Love. This, if by no means the whole of Christianity, was an important part of it, and one which he turned into practice. He loved much; and we have Christ's own authority, that "to him that loveth much, much shall be forgiven." Peace, then, be to us, not him, for "he sleeps well." He was a truant child; but the sleep of the truant child is often deeper and sweeter than that of the diligent scholar. And this deep sweet sleep Burns now enjoys—soothed by the murmur of the Nith, and shadowed by that great blue sky of immensity where he delighted to worship, and where he worships still by silence.

CHAPTER XIV.

BURNS AS A PROSE WRITER AND NATIONAL POET.

WE have, in a chapter further on, characterized Dr. Waddell's "Life of Burns," and spoken highly of many parts of it, and of its pervading spirit. We have hinted, however, that there is a good deal in it from which we differed, and notably from his view of Burns'. prose works. He fights hard for his Correspondence, and compares his letters advantageously with those of Cowper, Byron, and others. Here we deem him mistaken. Of his letters we would say—Wonderfully good, considering when, where, and how they were written. But they must not be compared to his poetry, because much of his poetry was written under similar disadvantages to his letters, and is far better. He wrote many of his letters in great haste on deal tables, moist with beer and begrimed with tobacco; on chests of drawers, in the worst inn's worst room, amid bad or boisterous company; sometimes himself half-seas over or more; and so with many of his poems and songs. But as there are men who can leap well when unable to walk or stand, who can sing when they cannot speak, so with Burns. He was, as a rule, better at poetry than prose. His letters are often, indeed generally, loose, careless to a degree, extravagant, forced, their humour riotous without being rich, their eloquence fantastic and flighty, like the boozy boisterous talk of a clever vain man showing off—untrue, as a whole, to his deepest nature, the most untrue discovery he ever made of himself anywhere. Undoubtedly there is much about Burns' Correspondence that is good, nay, much that is transcendent. Besides his letters to Mrs. Dunlop, which Carlyle says are all excellent, there are passages in his letters to Dr. Moore, to Dugald Stewart, to Cunningham, as good as anything he ever wrote. Dr. Robertson said they gave him a higher idea of Burns' power; but what struck him seems to have been their multitude, their variety, and their command over English, which was not the Poet's mother tongue. Had Jenny Lind taken to preaching, and preached some excellent sermons, the first impression would have been that of greater wonder than at her songs. But just as the most untrue outcome of a very true man, Burns, was his Correspondence; so the truest thing from a partially untrue man, Byron, was his. We care less for the mere intellectual power of Byron's letters—which Dr. Waddell rather underrates, forgetting that they contain (see especially his letters from Switzerland) the germs of many of the most striking passages of his finest poems—than we do for the sincerity of their tone. The man is in miserable earnest throughout, and this is their charm. This applies also to a number of Burns' later letters, but not to all. We imagine that many of Burns' and Byron's best letters (in this sense) have never been published, nor ever will. Artistically and morally, Cowper's Letters are better than either, although not so powerful or peculiar. To uplift Burns' letters as a whole to the highest rank, beside Madame de Sevigné's, Gray's, Lamb's, Cowper's, Byron's, or (prospectively) Carlyle's, is, we think, a hopeless task, and augurs rather enthusiasm than critical accuracy.

To pass to his poetry: Burns' powers consisted of great perspicacity; of rude, massive, untaught logic; vivid imagination and fancy; a fertile though coarse wit; a humour of the truest vein; lyrical impulse and music; a racy, varied, and powerful diction—all inspirited by a constant play of passionate enthusiasm, and pulsing to the motions of a hot and half-maddened blood. Like most great poets, he combined something of the animal, of the man, and of the woman, with rather much of the first, and with a strong dash of the "Deil" besides. His genius did not lie in him separate from his general idiosyncrasy, like the bag of honey in the bee; it is the result of all his powers and passions, as the sun's crown of rays is the result of all the light and radiance of the orb. And yet his addiction to poetry did not, as some pretend, arise entirely from the warmth of his temperament. He might, indeed, in certain conceivable circumstances, have not been a rhymer; in no conceivable circumstances could he have failed to be a Poet. Had he been a statesman, he would have been a poetical statesman like Burke; or a warrior, have written in fire another Napoleonad; if a divine, he had been a divine like Jeremy Taylor, with something of South superadded; or if he had been a philosopher, he would have wreathed around his speculations richer flowers than even Brown or Wilson has done. But a Poet, *i.e.*, a man of lofty genius, insight, heart, and passion, he of necessity and by nature was.

Burns' place as a Poet has been fixed by the consent of the world. That verdict declares that he is only a little lower in faculty, though greatly inferior in actual development and result, to the very highest poets on earth—the Homers, the Dantes, Shakspeares, and Miltons. Both Burns and Byron possessed, we think, native power to have approached very near those demigods of fame. But many circumstances prevented either of them from reaching an eminence to which they might both have been elevated by their genius.

But Burns was the greatest National Poet that ever lived, if not the only thoroughly National Poet that ever lived. We define a national poet one who reflects most of a nation, who is its broadest and brightest mirror, who reflects in his song both those points in which the nation is generally one with others, and those in which it stands by itself—reflecting the first in virtue of his being a poet, and the second in virtue of being a national poet. And not only must he reflect national character, intellect, and peculiarity in his song, but in himself. He must not be a dead, but a living image of his country. He must not only be a national poet, but himself a microcosm of his nation.

Burns was the National Poet of Scotland. He reflected that country as a whole. He sang its scenery as no one but himself could sing it; if not with the lingering minuteness of detail, or with the large, life-long knowledge of all its features possessed by Sir Walter Scott, yet with a powerful dash, a passionate love, a gusto, an enthusiasm of touch, only competent to his own burning genius. His power in this point, as in many others, lay in abandonment to the impulses that came upon him, and momentary absorption in the objects he was describing: we say momentary, for in this point he differed from Wordsworth, who was immersed in Nature as the river in the ocean, who became, as he so often describes himself, one with it, and continued so—a portion of the tempest, a presence in the calm, a motion among the careering elements. Burns threw himself in the wave, mingled with its headlong transport, shared in its tumultuous joy; but speedily regained the shore, and returned to his manly self again. In such moods—but let him describe them himself—

" I saw thee seek the sounding shore,
  Delighted with the dashing roar;"

'· Or when the deep green-mantled earth
   Warm cherished every floweret's birth,
   And joy and music pouring forth
     In every grove,
   I saw thee eye the general mirth
     With boundless love."

He sang Scotia's manners and customs; and by doing so, preserved some of them in life, saved others from oblivion, and shed a glory and consecration on all—its Kirns, its Hansel Mondays, its Rockings, its Hallowe'ens, its Holy Fairs, its Ordinations, its Family Worship, when

" The Sire turns o'er, wi' patriarchal grace,
  The big ha' Bible, ance his father's pride."

He sang its follies and its sins, its Nanse Tinnoch's hostelries, and its Poosie Nansie's revels, humorous "gangrel" bodies, and "Jolly Beggars"—sang them because, though erroneous, they were human, because there was something good to be extracted even from them, and because they were a portion of Scotland — ay, of moral and religious Scotland — and because he, as Scotland's Poet, must paint its blemishes as well as its beauties. He sang its good things of this life—its "souple scones," its "hamely parritch, chief o' Scotia's food," its "curny ingans mixed wi' spice," its herrings and its haggisses, its "tippenny" and its "usquebae." He sang its grand heroic warfares and grand heroic men in the old War of Independence; and he did not write any great poems or songs on the noble struggle of the Covenant or Covenanters, when one sneered at it and them, he replied—

" The Solemn League and Covenant
  Cost Scotland blood, cost Scotland tears,
  But it sealed Freedom's sacred cause;
  If thou 'rt a slave, indulge thy sneers."

And need we say he sang with deep sympathy the ill-starred Jacobite rebellion; and his "Drummossie Moor" and "Chevalier's Lament" rank among the sweetest of the Jacobite Melodies, and the Jacobite Melodies are among the most beautiful of the songs of Scotland. He sang of the loves and griefs of Scotland's peasantry—their privations and poverty, their misfortunes "great and sma'," their wrongs from cruel factors and haughty landlords, the gashes made by disappointment and death in their hearts; but he sang, also, their love-assignations,

"Beneath the milk-white thorn that scents the evening gale,"

their courtships, their marriages, their family joys, their "wee things toddlin'" to meet their sires on their return from toil, and all the other blessings which sweeten the bitter draught of being to the poor, and make their cup often mantle with a higher and purer joy than crowns the richest feasts of kaisars and of kings. He sang Scotland's proud, independent spirit—that spirit which has kept her from her earliest days an unconquered and unconquerable land, and which preserves still, amidst all her intimacy of intercourse with England, her integrity of purpose, her patriotic feeling, her strong individuality, her *perfervidum ingenium*. He sang her superstitions—her "ghaists," her "brownies," her "fairies," her "witches," her grisly ideas of Death, and, above all, her "muckle black Deil," in all his guises and under all his names—

"Whatever title suit thee—
Auld Hornie, Satan, Nick, or Clootie."

And he sang his country's religion, not, perhaps, her special dogmatic creed—a yoke our fathers might, but which their sons may not, much longer be able to bear, since in Europe they bear it alone—but her profound belief in God, Truth, Immortality, Christ, and His love. That belief was Burns', and was that of Burns' Bible; and it breathes in this stanza, as well as in the rest of the immortal poem to which it belongs—

"O Thou! who pour'd the patriotic tide
That streamed through Wallace's undaunted heart,
Who dared to nobly stem tyrannic pride,
Or nobly die, the second glorious part
(The *Patriot's God peculiarly Thou art*,
His friend, inspirer, guardian, and reward!),
O never, never Scotia's realm desert,
But still the Patriot and the Patriot Bard
In bright succession raise, her ornament and guard."

But Burns was not only in his song, but in himself, a mirror of Scotland. He had most of the merits, and most of the faults, of his countrymen. He had, as we have seen, the perfervid genius so often attributed to the Scotch. Edward Irving, in a letter to Dr. William Anderson of Glasgow, says, "I am accustomed to say that a Scotchman's hand is twice as near his weapon as another man's. They used to say in the middle ages, '*Nemo Scotus sine pipere in naso*.' It is a proverb on the Continent, 'Fiery as a Scotchman;' and the *perfervidum ingenium Scotorum* is well known. My notion is, that in the Commonwealth of Nations the Scotch have been purposed to set forth the indomitableness of man under all outward assaults and oppressions—the adamantine resistance, the asbestos unconsumableness." This belonged, above all Scotchmen of his period, to Burns. But along with this fervour he had a little Scotch pawkiness—inherited probably from his ancestors, who lived not a great distance from Aberdeen—a certain canny common sense, and acted sometimes on his own advice—

" Still keep something to yoursel'
You scarcely tell to ony."

Then he had all the proverbial pride of a Scotchman; and he had a Scotchman's strong intellect. He was no namby-pamby rhymster, no mystical dreamer; but what he calls a "carl stalk" of penetration, sense, and untrained logic runs through all his poems and all his prose works, too, and was, we are told, conspicuous in his conversation. He was a natural sage—if you will, a Socrates of the smithy. Dr. Blair says, as derogation, that Burns' politics always smelt of the smithy; but we have heard long ago conversations at the village smithy where Hugh Blair would have had to play a very secondary part, so full were they of native sagacity and sarcastic wit. It was a smith, by the way, who gave that capital definition of Metaphysics—better than anything in Blair's Lectures—"If ye hear a chield in the pulpit that ye dinna understand, and have a gey rough guess that he disna understand himself, that's Metapheesicks." Then Burns had all the Scottish humour, and tenderness along with it: humour proved by a hundred pieces of poetry—"The Twa Dogs," &c.—rich, rough, natural, bright, but harmless as sheet lightning; and tenderness, proved, need we say, by those songs in which he has set every mood of the Scottish mind, but especially its grief and its love, to a music sweet as the murmur of the summer brook and the sigh of the breeze through the cones of the ever-green pine of his own mountains. Except in Shakspeare there is no tenderness like that which breathes in the songs of Burns. Then he had a Scotchman's attachment to his country. He was of a pious and worshipping temperament—in one word, he wrote the "Cottar's Saturday Night." We deny not that he had some of his country's faults too—nay, it might be maintained that these faults, while they weakened him as a man, strengthened him as a poet. But we do not and have not palliated them. They do not deserve to be spared, since they spared not him; and many will cry, Curse on the evil influences which laid him low, and at thirty-seven broke one of the hardiest of constitutions and ruined one of the noblest of intellects. But whatever they were, they were counterbalanced by his truthfulness, his kindliness, his honesty, his sincerity, his enthusiasm, his extraordinary industry as a poet, a ploughman, and a gauger, by the tenacity of his friendship, and the warmth of his love. And if he possessed some of the faults usually ascribed to Scotland, and which, of course, characterized it as a country a hundred years ago far more than now, he wanted others which are sometimes imputed to us—unjustly, at least, to our nation as a whole—hypocrisy, formalism, bigotry, love of money, rooted prejudice, intense clannishness, and an inordinate love of ourselves. Burns had not one iota of these feelings, and could only understand them through the medium of the contempt he felt for them, and which he has recorded in some of his immortal satires—the "Unco Guid," and so on—which reveal in him a power of withering scorn not less remarkable than his melting pathos, simple beauty, and high-toned sublimity.

We know no poet who in nationality can be compared to Burns. Shakspeare was not the poet of England, but of the universe. Moore was too refined, too delicate, too much of a curled darling to be the poet of Ireland; he turned the "wild harp of Erin into a musical snuff-box;" and sturdy Pat likes sterner stuff than Tom Little, with all his wit and all his genius, could supply. Béranger was the poet of Paris, not of France. Goethe was the poet of Germanism, not of Germany; with Germany, the country, he had little sympathy. Dante, Petrarch, Ariosto, and Tasso were all Italian poets; none of them was the poet of Italy. Campbell has written beautiful things about Scotland, but his larger poems are on general subjects; and his very best poem and best song—"O'Connor's Child" and the "Exile of Erin"—are on Ireland. Tennyson is the poet of the Court and the cultivated classes in Britain, not of Britain. Sir Walter Scott—never let Scotland forget her obligations to his illustrious shade! perish the thought of sacrificing one great Scottish author at the shrine of another!—was yet not so much identified, either in his works or in his life, in his politics or his position, with Scotland as Burns. And we may even, we have said, go farther, and say that we know no thoroughly national poet but Burns in the world—none answering to the ideal in the past, none in the present; and as national peculiarities are fast fading away, none likely to rise in the future. And might not the Muse who appeared to him in that matchless "Vision" be figured to feel this herself, rising to the conception, as she proceeded to crown him, not the Bard of Coila alone, but the great National Poet of Scotland to all time—

"And wear thou *this*, she solemn said,
And bound the holly round my head;
The polished leaves and berries red
Did rustling play;
And, like a passing thought, she fled
In light away."

CHAPTER XV.

BURNS AS A SONG-WRITER.

T has been justly said, that in Burns' Epistles and Poems you see more of his general powers of mind—in his Songs more of his passions; that the one class discovers more of his head, and the other more of his heart. This arises partly from the different nature of the compositions, and partly from the different times of his life at which his poems and songs were respectively written. Song-writing does not require nor permit such an exertion of intellect as satire or didactic poetry, or even poetic narrative. Nature, feeling, melody, and above all, thorough sincerity and simplicity, are its chief requisites. Burns' songs, accordingly, are richer in feeling than in thought. They catch and crystallize some one simple emotion — some single swelling in a torn heart, some little incident in personal or domestic life—a feeling that has passed like a breeze over a solitary wanderer at eventide, a mood which has swept over his pillow like a meteor—

" Some natural sorrow, love, or pain,
Which has been, and may be again."

Such is the plain but profound material of songs. A song is just an unmeasured sonnet, and aspires to the same simple unity. It is essentially a drop—whether a drop of joy or grief—from a poet's eye, or of blood from his vitals, or of a thunder-shower from the laden sky of his imagination. Such glorious or gloomy drops are Burns' songs: it is a very shower of them he pours forth—some luxurious as lovers' tears; some rich as a patriot's gore; some simple as the dew; and some magnificent as a cloud on which swims the rainbow. But all are true, all clear, and all more or less beautiful.

Strength is not so requisite in songs, though the strong man will be seen in his singing as well as in his more elaborate speech; but he will sing best when ungirt and unbending. And thus, even when his songs passed into the higher form of the ode, as in "Scots wha hae" and " A man's a man for a' that," always sung Burns, who knew that the true spirit of a song-writer is not effort nor study, but abandonment; and that whenever a strong tide of feeling was flowing beside him, he had only to cast himself fearlessly upon it to reach the shore of success. The swimmer who would ride in triumph on the storm of song must strip him of his intellectual harness, and of the gorgeous robes of his imagination, and wear only a simple garland on his brow; and many who had no such robes to resign, and no such harness to unloose, have yet, by trusting entirely to naked Nature, gained their object. This explains the fact, that while no Scottish poet since Burns has approached him by a thousand degrees in this other department of the art, some, such as Tannahill, Lady Nairn, Robert Gilfillan, and James Ballantine, have uttered melodies not much inferior to his. Burns is, in fact, the greatest of Scotch song-writers, chiefly because he was before the rest in the field, and because his songs are more numerous and more varied. This seems to prove that good song-writing is more an affair of warm heart, considerable ingenuity, and a good ear, than of transcendent genius. Sandy Rogers wrote " Behave yoursel' before folk," and William Miller " Wee Willy Winkie," and neither of these has ever been surpassed by Burns. Song-writing, too, must, more than any other species of poetry, appeal to *universal* feeling; and because thousands who have no liking for strong sense, or pointed wit, or lofty imagination, can relish simple pathos or broad humour, the authors of songs have very wisely accommodated themselves to the popular taste. Wordsworth, in his once famous letter to James Gray about Burns, says that his earlier verses are more valuable than his later, and others have gone the length of asserting that his genius, as well as *morale*, fell wofully off in Dumfries. We think the truth to be this, not that his intellect became weaker, but that his heart became morbidly larger. When he entered the Queen of the South he might have said, " Hail thou Fever that shalt henceforth be my existence! I shall never be calm enough again for such broad, bright pictures, sententious moralizings, and lively narratives, as I produced in earlier days—to short bursts of song or satire, relieving, the one my burning heart, the other my disappointment and chagrin, shall my genius be now and for ever confined." And so, accordingly, it was. His power remained, but his impatience of temperament and his melancholy plight rendered its strong continuous exercise impossible.

Song-writing, latterly Burns' only true solace, has become perhaps his most generally admitted claim to fame. What unquenchable life is possessed by these simple melodies! "Like rivers they are wandering at their own sweet will through many lands, and like winds of balm they are sweetening the very air of the world." Listen to yonder solitary Lowland lass singing in the harvest-field (it is long since Wordsworth heard her Highland compeer, and complained, "Will no one tell me what she sings?"), you can tell what she is singing, it is one of the songs of Burns, perhaps his "Lea-rig." Hear yonder ploughman chanting to himself as he draws his straight clear furrow; the song is Burns' "Caledonia," and as he sings, you see the sentiment in his kindling eye, "Burns was once a ploughman like myself." From the city loomshop, at the hour of dawn, you hear a loud cheerful stave; you hearken, and find it to be "My heart's in the Highlands, my heart is not here." From the giddy summit of a rising mill-stalk there descends a voice; it is a mason lad singing Burns' "Farewell to St. James' Lodge,"

"Adieu, a heart-warm, fond adieu,
Dear brothers of the mystic tie."

Or you, a Scotchman, are pacing in a melancholy vein, thinking perhaps of home, the streets of a southern city on an Autumn eve, when, hark! a strain of dulcet melody from a female voice, mingling with the thrilling notes of a harp or piano; it is an English lady setting "Mary in Heaven" to the exquisite modulations of her Southland tongue. How often under the frowning battlements of Sebastopol did little clubs of brave and true-hearted Scotchmen sing together, and feel the trumpet-like inspiration of—

"Scots wha hae wi' Wallace bled;"

words which we heard O'Connell, too, in the very pride of his triumph quote, and by quoting send an electric shock to the hearts of thirty thousand Scotchmen assembled within sight of Burns' monument on the Calton Hill! And what festive meeting of the Scotch, need we say again, met on the beginning of each year—whether in Caledonia herself, or in the backwoods of America, or anywhere else in the wide world—can part without "Auld Lang Syne?" nay, did not the noble Robert Moffat teach the tune of that matchless melody to the Hottentots themselves, and sing it with them for long hours under the soft bright moon of an African night? This is true fame.

Would, we have often breathed the wish, that the Poet could look up from his grave and witness the estimation in which his genius is now held! In this case he would not turn so much to monuments to his memory, or editions of his works, or to the clubs and assemblies meeting on the day of his birth; but the sound of his immortal songs echoing from bank to brae, from town to farm of his beloved land, would be a welcome music in his ear, and he would rejoice to find his purer and better songs circulating most widely, and continuing, as he would say, to "beet the weel-placed lowe o' virtuous love," to stir the blood of manly enthusiasm and enterprise, and to increase that glow of patriotic emotion which can upon occasion teach Britons to front the dangers, make light of the privations, and exhibit a stern and stormy gladness amidst the darkest horrors of war.

Apart from the popularity of his songs, their artistic merit is very great. The best of them are beautiful poems. And even in the worst and feeblest there are rarely wanting little delicate traits and stray images, or touches of tenderness, which redeem the surrounding sterility; and you think of one of those Scotch moors where the desolation is relieved by a single sparkling well, or by a clump of yellow gorse, or by the green margin of a stream finding its stealthy way through the wilderness. In all of them we find the genuine spirit of the Lyric Muse, which is, and ought to be, ever in extremes: its joy, rapture; its grief, despair; its love, agony; its admiration, enthusiasm; its tenderness, passion; its words, oaths; and yet the language used by which is generally as simple as it is strong—"simple as the water, strong as the cataract." Besides the songs to which we alluded to above, there are others by Scott, Hogg, Cunningham, and Campbell, quite equal perhaps to any of Burns'; but taking his songs as a whole, they are the finest extant. The Border Ballads and the early songs of Scotland can alone stand comparison with them. Not the least remarkable of their characteristics is their infinite variety of subject and of mood. The whole heart of Scottish Life is reflected in them, even more than in his Poems, as well as the Poet's own entire history. Scottish love and courtship, domestic felicity and infelicity, jealousies and rivalships, humours, eccentricities, and mishaps, virtues and vices; loyalty to King George and loyalty to Prince Charlie; the scenery of both Highlands and Lowlands; all the seasons of the year and all the divisions of the day; the joys which surround the cradle, the mirth which rings around the marriage, and the grief that weeps by the deathbed and the grave; beauty and deformity; the hopes, disappointments, and despairs of his own bosom— are all included in the Shakspearean songs of Burns, who has discovered the vast width of his sympathies more in these than in any other of his writings.

Not more certainly was Shakspeare the greatest Dramatist, Milton the greatest Epic Writer, and Wordsworth the greatest Reflective Poet, than Burns was the greatest of all Lyrical Bards. In his writings you find every note of the Lyric Muse sounded, every chord of that greater lyre, the human heart, touched with equal mastery, and with a skill in which untaught Nature far exceeds the efforts of Art. The very essence of love and of chivalry may be found in a hundred of his ditties. Patriotism has inspired his "Scots wha hae," and the spirit of a thousand battles for liberty has breathed through the words, "Let us do or die." Revelry in its wildest, maddest shape, animates his "Jolly Beggars" and "Willie brewed a Peck o' Maut." Manly independence glows in many a noble verse; witness this—

> "I hae a penny to spend,
>   There—thanks to naebody;
> I hae naething to lend,
>   I'll borrow frae naebody."

The love of Nature colours many of his songs besides "Highland Mary," where he shows a passion for her charms only inferior to that for his lost love—

> "Ye banks, and braes, and streams around
>   The Castle of Montgomery,
> Green be your woods and fair your flowers,
>   Your waters never drumlie."

And humanity itself—the love of the whole human race—comes out in the words—

> "Its coming yet for a' that."

The proof of the purpose and power of Burns' songs, that they were designed to be the expressions of the universal human heart, is that thay have become so. They are not confined to Scotland or to Britain. They are sung in every land; and are as familiar and enthusiastically welcome among the Rocky Mountains as among the streams and lakes of Coila, among the burning sands of Arabia as among the heather bloom and green bracken of Caledonia, under the Southern Cross of Australia and Queensland as under the morning star rising over Criffel, or the evening sun seen from Ayr setting behind the dark mountains of Arran. There is scarcely another Son of Song in the world of which this can be said.

CHAPTER XVI.

THE INFLUENCE OF BURNS ON SCOTTISH POETRY AND SONG.

 WE add a few words on this subject to complete what we have said before. It is exceedingly difficult to settle the exact place of, as well as to compute the varied influences wielded by, a great original genius. Every such mind borrows so much from his age and from the past, as well as communicates so much from his own native stores, that it is difficult to determine whether he be more the creature or the creator of his period. But ere determining the influence exerted by Burns on Scottish song and poetry, it is necessary first to inquire what he owed to his predecessors in the art, as well as to the general Scottish atmosphere of thought, feeling, scenery, and manners.

First of all, Burns felt, in common with his "forbears" in the genealogy of Scottish song, the inspiring influences breathing from our mountain-land, and from the peculiar habits and customs of a "people dwelling alone, and not reckoned among the nations." He was not born in a district peculiarly distinguished for romantic beauty—we mean, in comparison with some other regions of Scotland. The whole course of the Ayr, as Currie remarks, is beautiful; and beautiful exceedingly the Brig of Doon, especially as it now shines through the magic of the Master's poetry. But it yields to many other parts of Scotland, some of which Burns, indeed, afterwards saw, although his matured genius was not much profited by the sight. Ayrshire—even with the peaks of Arran bounding the view seaward—cannot vie with the scenery around Edinburgh; with Stirling—its links and blue mountains; with "Gowrie's Carse, beloved of Ceres, and Clydesdale to Pomona dear;" with Straths Tay and Earn, with their two fine rivers flowing from finer lakes, through corn-fields, woods, and rocks, to melt into each other's arms in music, near the fair city of Perth; with the wilder and stormier courses of the Spey, the Findhorn, and the Dee; with the romantic and song-consecrated precincts of the Border; with the "bonnie hills o' Gallowa'" and Dumfriesshire; or with that transcendent mountain region stretching up along Lochs Linnhe, Etive, and Leven—between the wild, torn ridges of Morven and Appin—uniting Ben Cruachan to Ben Nevis, and including in its sweep the lonely and magnificent Glencoe—a region unparalleled in wide Britain for its quantity and variety of desolate grandeur, where every shape is bold, every shape blasted, but all blasted at such different angles as to produce endless diversity, and yet where the whole seems tortured into a certain terrible harmony; not to speak of the glorious isles

"Placed far amid the melancholy main"—

Iona, which, being interpreted, means the "Island of the Waves," the rocky cradle of Scotland's Christianity; Staffa, with grass growing above the unspeakable grandeur which lurks in the cathedral-cave below, and cows peacefully feeding over the tumultuous surge which forms the organ of the eternal service; and Skye, with its Loch Coriskin, piercing like a bright arrow the black breast of the shaggy hills of Cuchullin. Burns had around him only the features of ordinary Scottish scenery, but from these he drank in no common draught of inspiration; and how admirably has he reproduced such simple objects as the "burn stealing under the lang yellow broom," and the "milk-white thorn that scents the evening gale," the "burnie wimplin' in its glen," and the

"Rough bur-thistle spreadin' wide
Amang the bearded bear."

These objects constituted the poetry of his own fields; they were linked with his own joys, loves, memories, and sorrows, and these he felt impelled to enshrine in song. It may, indeed, be doubted if his cast of mind would have led him to sympathize with bold and savage scenery. In proof of this, we remember that, as formerly mentioned, although he often had seen the gigantic ridges of Arran looming through the purple evening air, or with the "morning spread" upon their summer summits, or with premature snow tinging their autumnal tops, he never once alludes to them, either in his poetry or prose; and that although he spent a part of his youth on the wild smuggling coast of Carrick, he has borrowed little of his imagery from the sea—none, we think, except the two lines in the "Vision"—

"I saw thee seek the sounding shore,
Delighted with the dashing roar."

His descriptions are almost all of inland scenery. Yet, that there was a strong sense of the sublime in his mind is manifest from the lines succeeding the above—

"And when the North his fleecy store
Drove through the sky,
I saw grim Nature's visage hoar
Struck thy young eye."

Perhaps his mind was most alive to the sublimity of *motion*, of agitation, of tumultuous energy, as exhibited in a snow-storm, or in the "torrent rapture" of winds and waters, because they seemed to sympathize with his own tempestuous passions, even as the fierce Zanga, in the "Revenge," during a storm, exclaims—

"I like this rocking of the battlements.
Rage on, ye winds; burst clouds, and waters roar!
You bear a just resemblance of my fortune,
And suit the gloomy habit of my soul."

Probably Burns felt little admiration of the calm, colossal grandeur of mountain scenery, where there are indeed vestiges of convulsion and agony, but where age has softened the storm into stillness, and where the memory of former strife and upheaving only serves to deepen the feelings of repose—vestiges which, like the wrinkles on the stern brow of the Corsair,

"Speak of passion, but of passion past."

With these records of bygone "majestic pains," on the other hand, the genius of Milton and Wordsworth seemed made to sympathize; and the former is never greater than standing on Niphates Mount with Satan, or on the "hill of Paradise the highest" with Michael, or upon the "Specular Mount" with the Tempter and the Saviour; and the latter is always most himself beside Skiddaw or Helvellyn. Byron professes vast admiration for Lochnagar and the Alps; but the former is seen through the enchanting medium of distance and childish memory; and among the latter, his rhapsodies on Mont Blanc, and the cold "thrones of eternity" around him, are nothing to his pictures of torrents, cataracts, thunderstorms; in short, of all objects where unrest—the leading feeling in *his* bosom —constitutes the principal element in *their* grandeur. It is curious, by the way, how few good descriptions there exist in poetry of views *from* mountains. Milton has, indeed, some incomparable ones, but all imaginary—such, at least, as no actual mountain on earth can command; but, in other poets, we at this moment remember no good one. They seem always looking up *to*, not down from, mountains. Wordsworth has given us, for example, no description of the view from Skiddaw; and there does not exist, in any Scottish poetical author, a first-rate picture of the view either from Ben Lomond, Schehallion, Ben Cruachan, or Ben Nevis.

After all, Burns was more influenced by some other characteristics of Scotland than he was by its scenery. There was, first, its romantic history. *That* had not then been separated, as it has since been, from the mists of fable, but lay exactly in that twilight point of view best adapted for arousing the imagination. To the eye of Burns, as it looked earnestly back into the past, the history of his country seemed intensely poetical—including the line of early kings who pass over the stage of Boece' and Buchanan's story as their brethren over the magic glass of Macbeth's witches, equally fantastic and equally false; the dark tragedy of that terrible thane of Glamis and Cawdor; the deeds of Wallace and Bruce—the battle of Flodden; and the sad fate of Queen Mary: and from most of these themes he drew an inspiration which could scarcely have been conceived to reside even in them. On Wallace, Bruce, and Queen Mary, his mind brooded with peculiar intensity—on the two former, because they were patriots; and on the latter, because she was a beautiful and unfortunate woman; and his allusions to them rank with the finest parts in his or any poetry. He seemed especially adapted to be the poet-laureate of Wallace—a modern edition, somewhat improved, of the broad, brawny, ragged bard who actually, it is probable, attended in the train of Scotland's patriot hero, and whose constant occupation it was to change the gold of his achievements into the silver of song. Scottish manners, too, as well as history, exerted a powerful influence on Scotland's peasant-poet. They were then far more peculiar than now, and had only been faintly or partially represented by previous poets. Thus (peculiarities mentioned in Chapter xiv.), the christening of the *wean*, with all its ceremony and all its mirth—Hallowe'en, with its "rude awe and laughter"— the "Rockin'"—the "Brooze"—the Bridal—and a hundred other intensely Scottish and very old customs, were all ripe and ready for the poet, and many of them he has treated, accordingly, with consummate felicity and genius. It seems almost as if the *final cause* of their long-continued existence were connected with the appearance, in due time, of one who was to extract their finest essence, and to embalm them for ever in his own form of ideal representation.

Burns, too, doubtless derived much from previous poets. This is a common case with even the most original. Had not Shakspeare and Milton been "celestial thieves," their writings would have been far less rich and brilliant than they are; although, had they not possessed true originality, they would not have taken their present lofty position in the world of letters. So, to say that Burns was much indebted to his predecessors, and that he often imitated Ramsay and Ferguson, and borrowed liberally from the old ballads, is by no means to derogate from his genius. If he took, he gave with interest. The most commonplace songs, after they had, as he said, "got a brushing" from his hands, assumed a totally different aspect. Each ballad was merely a piece of canvas on which he inscribed his inimitable paintings. Sometimes even by a single word he proclaimed the presence of the master-poet, and by a single stroke exalted a daub into a picture. His imitations of Ramsay and Ferguson far surpass the originals, and remind you of Landseer's dogs, which seem better than the models from which he drew. When a king accepts a fashion from a subject, he glorifies it, and renders it the rage. It was in this royal style that Burns treated the inferior writers who had gone before him; and although he highly admired and warmly praised them, he must have felt a secret sense of his own vast superiority.

We come now shortly to speak of the influence he has exerted on Scottish poetry. This was manifold. In the first place, a number were encouraged by his success to collect and publish their poems, although few of them possessed much merit; and he complained that some were a wretched "spawn" of mediocrity, which the sunshine of his fame had warmed and brought forth prematurely. Lapraik, as we have said, was induced by the praise of Burns to print an edition of his poems, which turned out a total failure. There was only one good piece in it all, and that was pilfered from an old magazine. Secondly, Burns exerted an inspiring influence on some men of real genius, who, we verily believe, would, but for Burns, have never written, or, at least, written so well—such as Alexander Wilson, Tannahill, Macneil, Hogg, and the numerous members of the "Whistle-Binkie" school. In all these writers we trace the influence of the large "lingering star" of the genius of Burns. "Wattie and Meg," by Wilson, when it first appeared anonymously, was attributed to Burns. Tannahill is in much of his poetry an echo of Burns, although in song-writing he is a real original. Macneil was roused by Burns' praises of whisky to give another account in his "Scotland's Scaith; or, the History of Will and Jean." And although the most of Hogg's poetry is entirely original, we find the influence of Burns distinctly marked in some of his songs—such as "When the Kye come Hame."

But there is a wider and more important light in which to regard the influence of our great National Bard. He first fully revealed the interest and the beauty which lie in the simpler forms of Scottish scenery, he darted light upon the peculiarities of Scottish manners, and he opened the warm heart of his native land. Scotland, previous to Burns' poetry, was a spring shut up and a fountain sealed.

"She lay like some unkenned-of isle
Ayont New Holland."

The glories of her lakes, her glens, her streams, her mountains, the hardy courage, the burning patriotism, the trusty attachments, the loves, the games, the superstitions, and the devotion of her inhabitants, were all unknown and unsuspected as themes for song till Burns took them up, and less added glory than showed the glory that was in them, and showed also that they opened up a field nearly inexhaustible. Writers of a very high order were thus attracted to Scotland, not merely as their native country, but as a theme for poetry; and, while disdaining to imitate Burns' poetry slavishly, and some of them not writing in verse at all, they found in Scottish subjects ample scope for the exercise of their genius; and in some measure to his influence we may attribute the fictions of Mrs. Hamilton and Miss Ferrier, Scott's poems and novels, Galt's, Lockhart's, Wilson's, Delta's, and Aird's tales and poetry, and much of the poetry of Campbell, who, although he never writes in Scotch, has embalmed, in his "Lochiel's Warning," "Glenara," "Lord Ullin's Daughter," some interesting subjects connected with Scotland, and has in "Gertrude of Wyoming," and in the "Pilgrim of Glencoe," made striking allusions to Scottish scenery. That the progress of civilization, apart from Burns, would have ultimately directed the attention of cultivated men to a country so peculiar and poetical as Scotland cannot be doubted; but the rise of Burns hastened the result, as being itself a main element in propelling civilization and diffusing genuine taste. His dazzling success, too, excited emulation in the breasts of our men of genius, as well as tended to exalt in their eyes a country which had produced such a stalwart and gifted son. We may, indeed, apply to the feeling of pride which animates Scotchmen, and particularly Scotchmen in other lands, at the thought of Burns being their countryman, the famous lines of Dryden—

"Men met each other with erected look,
The steps were higher that they took;
Each to congratulate his friends made haste,
And long inveterate foes saluted as they pass'd."

The poor man, says Wilson, as he speaks of Burns, always holds up his head and regards you with an elated look. Scotland has become more venerable, more beautiful, more glorious in the eyes of her children, and a fitter theme for poetry, since the feet of Burns rested on her fields, and since his eyes glowed with enthusiasm as he saw her scenery, and as he sung her praise; while to many in foreign parts she is chiefly interesting as being (what a portion of her has long been called) the Land of Burns.

The real successors of Burns, it is thus manifest, were not Tannahill or Macneil, but Sir Walter Scott, Campbell, Aird, Delta, Galt, Allan Cunningham, and Professor Wilson. To all of these Burns, along with Nature, united in teaching the lessons of simplicity, of brawny strength, of clear common sense, and of the propriety of staying at home instead of gadding abroad in search of inspiration. All of these have been, like Burns, more or less intensely Scottish in their subjects and in their spirit.

p

When we subtract some half-dozen pieces, either coarse in language or equivocal in purpose, the influence of Burns' acknowledged poetry may be considered good. It is doubtful if his "Willie brew'd a peck o' Maut" ever made a drunkard, but it is certain that his "Cottar's Saturday Night" has made many careless earnest, edified the godly, and induced some to erect family altars. It has been worth a thousand homilies. And taking his songs as a whole, they have done much to stir the flames of pure love, of patriotism, of genuine sentiment, and of a taste for the beauties of nature. And it is remarkable that all his followers and imitators have, almost without exception, avoided his faults while emulating his beauties; and there is not a sentence in Scott, or Campbell, or Aird, or Delta, and not many in Wilson or Galt, that can be charged with indelicacy, or even coarseness. So that, on the whole, we may assert that, whatever evil he did by the example of his life, he has done very little—but, on the contrary, much good, both artistically and morally—by the influence of his poetry.

BURNS STATUE, GLASGOW.

ENGRAVED BY G. J. STODART, FROM THE STATUE BY G. E. EWING

WILLIAM MACKENZIE, LONDON, EDINBURGH & GLASGOW.

CHAPTER XVII.

HISTORY OF BURNS' FAME.

E have sometimes thought that even were Burns' poetry to perish, with the exception of the fragments contained in the criticisms which have been written on his genius, these would serve to preserve his memory for ever, and to give an impression of his powers scarcely inferior to that suggested by his whole works; nay, that even were it possible that only the criticisms themselves should survive, they would at once immortalize his name and that of their authors. It is a true sign of wit when it begets wit in others, and that genius must be transcendent which raises gifted men to surpass themselves in its praise, and makes ordinary men for a season seem half inspired. A collection of the eloquent panegyrics which have been passed on the Ploughman Poet in prose and verse by writers of every grade and country—in Scotland, England, Ireland, America, Germany, France, and the British Colonies—would form a monument nearly as large, and far more lasting and brilliant, than any of the mausoleums which have been erected to his memory. Extraordinary, too, has been the unanimity of his critics. While differing widely in their estimates of his character and *morale*, they have, without almost a single exception, expressed a lofty idea of his powers of mind and of the excellence of his poetry. Here, as on the subject of Shakspeare, and on scarcely any other, have Whigs and Tories, Infidels and Christians, bigoted Scotchmen and bigoted sons of John Bull, the high and the low, the rich and the poor, the prosaic and the enthusiastic lovers of poetry, the strait-laced and the morally lax, met and embraced each other. And hence, perhaps, the number and the excellence of the essays which have been written about his genius. Nothing so fatal to criticism as timidity and want of confidence. But all the critics of Burns have felt themselves sustained and cheered on by general sympathy, and by knowing that the opinions they expressed were only the echoes of a universal and warmly-cherished sentiment.

Besides the merit of the poems, several other causes have contributed to this unanimity. In the first place, there had arisen shortly after Burns' death a strong conviction that, with all his errors, he had been, on the whole, a neglected and ill-used man; and sympathy with his unhappy fate led to a generous estimate of his poetry. Ebenezer Elliott says that the public

" Gave him more than gold,
They read the brave man's book."

Yes! but they read it with more interest and admiration, because they knew that it was the production of one who had died little better than a pauper in a second-rate Scottish town. Then they remembered his age. And then he had done so little in proportion to his powers. These odes, epistles, stories, and songs—what were they compared to the *man* manifested in them? Nothing, in one sense; in another, they seemed dearer on account of their smallness, and were valued and cherished as you could conceive would be the first fair blossoms of a garden, where spring had never come to summer.

There had, too, been floating through the land an idea of Burns as having in him a general gigantic power, apart altogether from his poetical faculty. Wherever he had gone he had by his eyes, by his manly, fearless manners, by his authoritative but not presumptuous air, by his rich and powerful conversation, as well as by his pregnant silence, exerted on all he met a certain indescribable impression that here was—strangely disguised, indeed, ill-accredited, and partially weakened—one of the kings of men, not the less so that he seemed a king uncrowned and in part degraded. This impression was as universal as it was indescribable. It was felt at the penny wedding, where some rude fellows becoming noisy, the Poet threatened to hang them up in song like *potato bogles*, and they instantly shrunk into silence. It was felt in the mason clubs and the coteries of the kirkyard in the West, as well as by the most select companies in Edinburgh, taking to ladies, as we have seen, the form of fascination. With this commanding and royal nature even his foibles, caprices, and errors seemed somehow to consort. They resembled the errors and foibles of a powerful and popular monarch. There was, besides, a self-assertion about him which added to, instead of detracting from, the effect. He was " great, and knew how great he was." He said that when he died he desired to be buried at full length, and to have every inch of ground to which he was entitled. He became thus, as well as through that wondrous *readiness* of speech, wit, and verse which he possessed, and which has seldom been combined with such original genius and masculine talent, a *Fourth Estate* within a wide sphere, and suggested the possibility of the very highest achievements. And although his short life prevented the fulfilment of this promise, and although many who knew him might be tempted to cry as they took up his works—Is this *all* Burns has left the world? they would soon add, Yes; but it is the *all* of *Burns*, and must be welcomed with thankfulness and embalmed with joyful tears: "Kings' chaff is better than other people's corn." Previous to his death such a feeling had been floating through the land, and was found strongest in those who knew Burns best. After it, although the mere eleemosynary gifts to him in the shape of subscriptions were but small, the rapid sale and kind reception of Currie's edition of his "Life and Letters" showed how a deep-rooted love to him had been slowly accumulating in the country, and found this opportunity of expressing itself. The history of Burns' fame may be read in the sale of his works; in the many editions of all shapes, and sorts, and sizes which they have passed through—a point in which Burns emulates John Bunyan; and in the number of critiques and biographies of the author which have appeared, vieing in this with Goethe, and surpassing Lord Byron and Sir Walter Scott.

The names of his biographers and critics being Legion, we will only select a few, not merely for individual appraisement, but to show how his fame has grown, at once in its depth and in its width, in the full assurance of its faith, and in the warmth and discrimination of its love. And here, while professing to be free, we disclaim all invidiousness; we shall say exactly what we would have said had we not been ourselves writing a Life of Burns: indeed, a good deal that follows was written long ago. Dr. Currie's Life is for its day, and from a man in Currie's position, admirable. Carlyle hints that he is a little patronizing to Burns, but, as Scott says of Reuben Butler and his occasional pomposity, "the man was mortal and had been a schoolmaster." And so Currie was a popular medical doctor in a large and wealthy town, and he belonged to a literary set who, if De Quincey may be believed, gave themselves *plusquam* provincial airs, and formed a little senate with Roscoe as Cato, and Currie for his Master of the Horse; were disposed to dogmatize on political as well as literary matters; and the leader of whom, Roscoe, a most respectable and eminent man, but no more to Burke than I to Hercules, ventured to challenge *him* on the subject of the French Revolution, and was treated somewhat as W. Crabbe Robinson tells us Cribb, the champion of the ring, treated a young fellow near Cambridge who knew him not, but had a little altercation with him, and offered to spar, when the great boxer laid his hand gently on his shoulder and whispered, "I'm Cribb," and there was no more of it, save gratitude on the part of the youth, who treated Cribb to a jug of ale for not having broken his bones! Currie, if not the most gifted and renowned of the clique, showed himself one of the most sensible of them in his treatment of Burns. He came to Dumfries when the Poet had newly gasped his last, when all sorts of contradictory and exaggerated rumours were floating about his character, and when his MSS., like his character, were one mass of confusion; and out of this twofold chaos the Liverpool doctor formed a Cosmos, treating Burns as a man with a mixture of truth and tenderness which is only beginning to be appreciated, and praising his genius with much eloquence, sincerity, and discrimination—taking the age, and its canons and style of criticism, into account. Then there was his Life by the unfortunate Heron, the Richard Savage of Scotland, without his power, whom Burns seems to have admitted into some of his confidences, and who felt a very natural desire to pull the Scottish Poet down to his own level. An attempt unsuccessful; for although Burns was often foolish and worse, his genius and his pride combined to preserve him from the habitual folly, vice, improvidence, and vanity by which poor Heron's considerable ability and extraordinary industry were neutralized. Of Walker we have spoken repeatedly. He committed two great blunders in the course of his long, harmless, useful, and laborious life; he published a bad poem, and he wrote a middling life of a good poet. "The Defence of Order" was mercilessly and somewhat heartlessly mangled by Lord Brougham in the *Edinburgh Review;* and his "Life of Burns," more recently, quivered under the knout of Christopher North. Hogg's Life of our Poet we read recently; it is excessively twaddling, uncritical, full of unvivified gossip, and is, unless from its connection with Motherwell's edition of the Poems, nearly forgotten. Lockhart's "Life of Burns" came out in *Constable's Miscellany*, and excited great expectation. He was limited, however, in space, and perhaps in time. It is too short, and resembles rather a thickly and strongly chiselled inscription to his memory on his tombstone, than a careful and complete account of his life or estimate of his character; or it may be called a *bust* of Burns, and, like all busts, while showing the intellect, it omits the heart. It does not seem the result of much personal investigation. It contains, however, many admirable passages, and its writing, as always with Lockhart, is sharp, clear, masculine, and decisive. It was with Burns the Man, strong, sarcastic, proud, and fearless, with his appetites and passions as well as with his powers, that Lockhart sympathized; he cared not so much for Burns the Poet, and still less for Burns the Lyrist. He had been himself an exquisite lyrist in his youth, as his Spanish Ballads prove; but that power had died out of him long before he lifted the iron pen of his middle life to write his Burns, Scott, and Napoleon. Lockhart's text was eclipsed by the rich marginal comment of Carlyle's paper on it in the *Edinburgh Review*. Hamilton Paul's Life hardly deserves notice. Its one good point is its zeal for Burns—a zeal seldom according to knowledge. He defends Burns' most exceptionable words, deeds, and writings, instead of first recording them, admitting their evil, and then contending that there was nevertheless a balance of good on the Poet's side which justified his claims to be counted a worthy man in the main, as well as a most admirable writer. Gibbon says, "The wretched Travis still writhes under the lash of the merciless Porson; and it might have been expected that the same could be told of poor Paul under the scourge of knotted scorpions wielded by the late Dr. Andrew Thomson of St. George's, Edinburgh, in his *Christian Instructor;* but we believe he felt it very lightly, and lived and died in the hospitable manse of Broughton a happier man than his over-tasked, over-excited, one-sided, prematurely removed, though honest, fearless, and formidable assailant.

Allan Cunningham's "Life of Burns" is a very characteristic and ably written production, full of new facts in the poet's history, conceived in a spirit of thoroughly brotherly appreciation; worthy of a master mason, a self-taught bard, and a double-dyed Scotchman; an interesting, rambling, genial book, perhaps written in too gay and easy a style, as if the author were recounting the incidents of a comedy, and not a deep and painful tragedy; and you cannot apply to Cunningham's "Life of Burns" (nor yet to Chambers'), the lines of Wordsworth on a picture of a Shipwreck by Sir George Beaumont—

"Oh! 'tis a passionate work, but wise and well,
Well chosen is the spirit that is here,
The hulk that labours in that deadly swell,
That sky in anger, and that rueful shore!"

Yet Robert Chambers' Life, though its tone of criticism be not very lofty, nor its taste always the best, is a very praiseworthy production. If not *the* Life of Burns, it contains a most valuable mass of materials for it. It collects in four volumes, as in four baskets, almost all that can be gathered of the poetry, prose, correspondence, and the incidents of his story. His mode of estimating Burns was generally sound and judicious. We have been compelled in our own effort often to differ from him, but cheerfully admit the general spirit of impartiality, fairness, and kindliness, which distinguish the Memoir. Robert Chambers, whatever might be his deficiencies, was a sincere lover of truth, an eminently candid and conscientious man. But apart from the want of much enthusiasm and of fine instinct, his temperament was entirely opposed to that of Burns. No one can doubt this who has ever seen him—the genuine, "auld-farrand, canny" Scotchman; the half of a Sir Walter Scott, with Scott's research, common sense, Scottish sympathies, his kindliness, and his calm, but without his rapt Minstrel feeling, his commanding and creative genius. The only time we ever met Chambers, he spoke to us warmly of Scott; and alluding to something we had said in a lecture on him, told us that he, too, read all the Waverley Novels through every year, or nearly so; and while he was talking thus, we were all the while struck with his extraordinary resemblance in person and manners to our conception of Sir Walter. But, at the same time, we felt assured that he was never fitted to be the biographer—*i.e.*, the final or thorough-going biographer—of Burns : Burns, who could and did commit more follies in a week than Chambers in a long life-time, and would and did condense more wit and curdle more genius into a single night than Chambers into a decade. This vital divergency between the two men will for ever prevent Chambers' Life taking up the lofty and lonely place to which its elaborate painstaking, its general fairness, and its good, manly composition would have entitled it. The Rev. Dr. Hately Waddell has gone rather too far on the other extreme. His work is a long and powerful prize poem, written with immense fellow-feeling, energy, and eloquence. It has been preceded by very diligent and extensive inquiry; and although you sometimes think of the philosopher who, when the facts were against his theory, said, "So much the worse for the facts," Dr. Waddell always means to tell the truth. But the whole (he will permit us to say, both out of respect to him and from a wish to imitate his love of truth-telling) is pervaded by a spirit of enormous exaggeration. His imagination creates stilts, on which he mounts Burns a hundred miles higher than his level; his conception of him is epic, not historical or biographical; his language in panegyric would need some modifications were it applied to an angel; and although some passages in the book are among the most powerful and eloquent of the present day, we cannot compliment Dr. Waddell either on the judgment which overruled the composition of the whole or arranged the order of the parts. A more complex and confused book does not exist in our literature, nor a more earnest and animated one; and as a piece of Hero Worship, it must hold its place as unique and eclipsing all others, so that, even when compared with Wilson's *Éloge*, it seems another

"Morn risen in mid-noon."

Besides biographers, all or most of them possessing much merit, there have been many criticisms, surpassing the Lives alike in excellence and in popularity. The first of these of much mark was Lord Jeffrey's, which owed both its power and its weakness to the intense dissimilarity between the critic and the poet. Jeffrey's fine critical instinct could not despise the manly and natural poetry of Burns; but his fastidiousness, as also in the case of Wordsworth, rendered him too sensitive to its rude environment; he liked the honey, but saw little beauty or order in the rough honeycomb. Although a kindly and genial, he was an artificial man — the pet of the very drawing-rooms which Burns some twenty years before had made to tremble at his stalwart stride, leaving, as Cunningham has it, the red earth of the plough on their carpets; and he could not endure either the unkempt manhood of the Peasant or the rustic coarseness of the Poet. He even tried to trip up Burns' heels, forgetting that, falling at the plough, where could he fall but on the fresh, soft, strong earth; and how could he rise but in the attitude of an Antæus? The one great point he made against Burns was when he accused him of sometimes affecting the oddities and copying the vices of the wits of the previous age. But the attack was altogether petty, and unworthy of the better nature and nobler qualities of Jeffrey. We must say, too, that Jeffrey seldom did justice to the genius of Scotland. He was niggardly in his editorial praise of Professor Wilson, of Lockhart, of James Hogg, of Chalmers, of Scott as a poet. To Campbell alone, among Scotchmen, and to Alison has he done justice — heaped up, pressed down, and shaken together; and he reserved even richer encomiums for Dickens and Crabbe and Macaulay. Edward Irving he never mentions at all, nor, among English writers, Hall or Foster. When Carlyle's review of Lockhart's "Life of Burns" appeared in the *Edinburgh* it was attributed by some to Jeffrey, although internal evidence was against this, both in its style and its sentiment. The style was High German (considerably clipped, we know now, by Jeffrey's nimble scissors), and the sentiment singularly generous and noble. There were four conceivable ways of treating Burns—Impeachment, Monody, Calm but Loving Criticism, and Glorification. Jeffrey had followed the first course; the time for the third was not yet come; Dr. Waddell was alone fully competent for the fourth; Carlyle became the organ of the second, and his is surely one of the finest prose monodies in the world! It sounds like a coronach among the mountains—how full of love and sorrow, of blame and pity; blame so severe and measured, pity unlimited and "yearning, like a God in pain;" and its exaggeration of the powers and virtues of the man is forgiven in your feeling of the unutterable charity shown for his faults and sympathy with his fate. It is the most eloquent and human thing Carlyle ever wrote, unless it be his paper on the death of Edward Irving, which belonged also to the early part of his literary history, when his genius was as yet unperverted by prejudice, when his disappointment at humanity had not soured into misanthropy, and his young enthusiasm for this "Divine Temple of Heaven and Earth" had not sunk into that disgust at the "dog-hole" and beggarly world which he now habitually calls it. Yet in Carlyle's pleading, powerful though it be, he seems sometimes to have another Burns in his eye—a Demon of the Brocken mist magnified. What he says about Burns' actualities is better than what he says of his possibilities. If Burns did all Carlyle says, there was little need of more. What were twenty epics like, say Southey's, compared to a few such tales as "Tam o' Shanter," and songs like "Scots wha hae?" Goethe's power is widespread over twenty or thirty volumes, but the real gist of his matter lies in much less compass—in some pages of "Werter," some chapters of "Wilhelm Meister," "Faust," a few ballads, odes, and many fragments of conversation. And so with most writers, you must subtract a vast quantity of rubbish. Shakspeare and Scott least require this; and with Burns, if he has done comparatively little, a large proportion of it is good. By that little, too, Burns made himself the God of a Nation; a small, but distinct, intelligent, clannish, and growing people, each one member of which can carry all its Poet's songs and verses in his pocket, yea, in his memory. This apart from the power and charm Burns has exerted on other nations, which is very great. Then Burns is the Poet of Love, and as long as that strange, delightful, but delusive passion exists, so long will he reign. Here again is an enviable power, which a hundred Iliads could not have given him. Perhaps we mourn too much over his early fate, as well as his slight achievements. To himself the loss was no greater than to other men; to us, since he has done so much and taught us so much both by life and death, it was not so great as is supposed. He had done his work. Morally, he has become our "frightful example" for ever, and perhaps done more good in this way than evil was done by his errors. His virtues, too, were clearly if not completely shown ere his death.

There is great talk in Carlyle and others about Burns' intellect. But we doubt if it, although very strong, was at all equal to his passion and poetical temperament, and their excessive strength weakened it in some degree. After all we hear of Robert Burns' logic, it was Gilbert, his brother, who always took the lead in discussion, and was thought superior to him. Passion, soured by poverty, roused to fury by imagination and social indulgence, and only partially fed by intellect and restrained by common sense, was the staple of Burns' character, the master current of his being, the source at once of his rise, his ruin, his songs and poetry, his moral suicide, his perpetual power while living, his everlasting fame after death. He was, though not a Seraph, a Burning One, the flame neither celestial nor terrestrial, but human, the red radiance of the Earth, like that of newly made Man when he rose from the ground out of which he had been taken.

Hazlitt, in his "Lectures on English Poetry," has some beautiful remarks on Burns' genius and character, giving, as is usual with him, the essence of volumes in a few sentences:—"Shakspeare says of a man that he seemed made after supper, and of a cheese-paring. Burns, the poet, was not such a man. He had a strong mind and a strong body, the fellow of it. He had a real heart of flesh and blood beating in him. You can almost hear it throb. He was as much of a man, not the twentieth part so much of a poet, as Shakspeare. He had an eye to see, a heart to feel—no more. His pictures of goodfellowship, of social glee, of quaint humour, are equal to anything—they are up to Nature; they cannot go beyond. The sly jest collected in his laughing eye at the sight of the grotesque and ludicrous in manners, the large tear rolled down his manly cheek at the sight of another's distress. His virtues belonged to his genius, his vices to his situation, which did not correspond to his genius." Wordsworth has written a long, ingenious, but wirespun and coxcombical letter in defence of Burns to James Gray of the High School. Professor Wilson's Essay, prefixed to the "Land of Burns," hovering between a life, a criticism, and an apology, is one of the most magnificent panegyrics extant. It gushes on like a great river, now gliding at its own sweet will, now sporting in shallows, and now rushing red with poetic fury, till—down leaping from its crag, like a "god to suicide," deafened as well as drowned—Foyers cries for quarter in the fell uproar! It is by no means, however, a fair or impartial character of the man, and reveals Wilson rather than Burns. Delta in one of his best poems magnified Burns' genius and defended his memory. Thomas Aird has often, in his "Old Bachelor" and elsewhere, touched in the most genial spirit on points in Burns' history and poems; and his defence of the Burns' Festival in 1844, transferred from his paper, the *Dumfries Herald*, to *Blackwood's Magazine*, was worth all the speeches at that entertainment put together. Thomas Campbell has some exquisite sentences of criticism on Burns in his "Specimens of English Poetry." Alexander Smith's Life is sketchy and hurriedly written, as well as short; but has some of its author's felicitous strokes and beautiful figures, and the figures of the poet of the "Life Drama" have seldom been surpassed. Having himself risen from the ranks, he is the better able to sympathize with Burns' position; and his own fine sensuousness of spirit and language leads him to appreciate more warmly in Burns' songs—

"The bloom of young desire, and purple light of love."

We need not quote Byron's one affecting and eulogistic line on Burns in his "English Bards." Charles Lamb and Coleridge have charming allusions to the great ploughman, and could in different styles have produced unequalled criticisms on his writings and life. We notice only two more on the subject—a very sensible estimate of Burns by the Rev. James White; and a kind of drama, or rather succession of dramatic scenes, by our friend Dr. Hutcheson Stirling—"Burns in Drama"—an exceedingly clever and characteristic *brochure*, some of the scenes in which, such as the Tailor in the Auld Clay Biggin, Jean and Burns Courting at the Bleaching Green, and Ainslie, Burns, and Jean at Ellisland, are rendered with the hand of a master, and must be read and enjoyed by hundreds to whom the "Secret of Hegel," and "Regarding Protoplasm," are a spring shut up and a fountain sealed.

Apart from literary recognitions, no sooner was Burns dead than there arose, we have seen, a stir of sympathy, subscription, and stone-cutting throughout the land. Then followed great gatherings in his honour—one of the most notable of which was the Festival on the banks of the Doon in 1844; and without inquiring too minutely into the history of that demonstration, or speaking of certain circumstances which somewhat marred its harmony, we may say that it developed a great deal of genuine feeling for Burns, which Professor Wilson caught up, and with his large and generous hand flung abroad (in *Blackwood*, where his speech appeared) over all the country. More thoroughly spontaneous was the Centenary celebrations of 1859, where all ranks, high and low, all creeds and denominations, all varieties of opinion and of caste—nobles, cotters, cotton lords, artizans, churchmen, dissenters, teetotallers, men of mason lodges, and many Englishmen, Irishmen, and foreigners—commemorated the birth of Burns, not in riot and revelry, but in calm, sober, though merry and multitudinous assemblages. Then it was publicly said, and the saying was enthusiastically responded to, Scotland has this day proclaimed an act of oblivion to her Poet's errors. She may remember them, ought to remember them to-morrow, and be instructed and warned by them; but to-day she cries out in the language of the Poet, a little altered—

"Seek not, at least not now,
To draw his frailties from their dread abode."

To-day let there be solemn silence in reference to all that was unworthy in his life, and loud, reverberated, and enthusiastic applause as to what was noble in his character and immortal in his song. We can only allude to the statues in Glasgow, New York, Kilmarnock, Dumfries, and Dundee—some of them, like Sir J. Steel's already spoken of, entirely worthy of poet and sculptor—which are seeking to stereotype in everlasting bronze the feeling with which Scotland, Britain, and the world regard his memory.

CONCLUSION.

THUS we close our Life and Criticism of Burns. If we have not succeeded in digging out a great many new facts or documents, we have found some of both; we have, we venture to hope, maintained a freshness of treatment throughout, and have followed slavishly no model. We have tried, whether successfully or not it is for the public to decide, to steer a medium between a partial apology and a ruthless and unsparing dissection. We have sought to blend pity and blame, admiration and love—the latter preponderating—as the true libation over his dust. We are, at least, certain of this, we have fulfilled the intention which we expressed in our first page—we have written it with the heart; and with the heart, too, we close by dedicating this biography to the memory of our late dear and devoted friend, Thomas Aird, who long lived in Dumfries, possessed a lofty genius, which he, next to its consecration to God, laid on the same altar with Scotland's supreme poet—that of the land they both loved so dearly; and who now slumbers not far from the fiery dust of Robert Burns.

GEORGE GILFILLAN.

DUNDEE, 15*th April*, 1878.

APPENDIX.

No. I.—Burns' Cottage.

We publish a letter we received from a gentleman in Stirling of respectability and enthusiasm on the subject of Burns :—

"Dear Sir,—Will you permit me, as a stranger to you personally, to say that it is with infinite satisfaction I observe you are about to publish a Life of Burns. From your pen I know what it will be, and I shall eagerly look for it. But there is one point which I venture to urge upon you—viz., to advocate the purchase of Burns' Cottage, with a view to its being made public property, as in the case of Shakspeare's house. As all the thinking world knows with pain, the cottage is at present a second-rate dram shop, which should be allowed to remain so no longer. I am sure you will be ready with your pen and influence to urge the purchase of the cottage at once. Knowing, as I do, the grand-daughter (Mrs. Gresitt) and the nieces of Burns intimately (the Beggs), I am in a position to say that they feel deeply the position in which the cottage stands. I send you herewith copy of a letter which I wrote in the *Daily Mail* of 14th February last, which favour me by perusing. You will gather from it what I, in common with all admirers of Burns, so much desire."

We only add that we cordially approve of Mr. Dick's proposal, and trust that it will be energetically and generally taken up by the public. Not from a Good Templar or Temperance point of view at all, but on general grounds, it is a pity that the birth-cottage of our great Scottish Poet should be a public house, as if for the purpose of forcing on the memory of men facts in his history which we say not can or should be forgotten, but which it is not pleasant to have *thus* recalled, especially in reference to a cottage where his first innocent days were spent, and which was not a public house from the beginning. We trust that, in pursuance of these hints, the cottage will soon cease to be a public house and become the Public's House.

No. II.—The Monument to Burns' Parents.

In the text, here and afterwards, we describe our emotions at beholding the stone erected by Burns to his parents. We were not aware then, nor till lately, that the original stone has long been destroyed and carried away piecemeal, and another substituted of somewhat finer proportions by David Auld of Dunbrae. Still, the association remains. Chambers thus writes about Alloway Kirk :—"The church has long been roofless, but the walls are pretty well preserved, and it still retains its bell at the east end. The inner area is now divided by a partition wall, and one part forms the family burying-place of Mr. Cathcart of Blairston. The 'winnock bunker in the east' is a conspicuous feature, being a small window divided by a thick mullion. The old oaken rafters of the kirk have mostly been taken away. The old road by which Burns supposed his hero to approach Alloway Kirk lay considerably west of the present. The ford and the well are still, we believe, pointed out; but the cairn and the thorn have vanished. The area of the churchyard is now crowded with tombs and monuments—many belonging to fashionable people who have determined to make that classic spot their 'God's Acre.'"

No. III.

We here print for the first time a document drawn up by Burns in reference to his natural daughter, Elizabeth Burns, daughter of Elizabeth Paton. It was drawn up at the time he was talking of going to the West Indies. It was kindly communicated to us by Dr. Grierson, of Thornhill. Elizabeth Burns was born in 1784. She received her portion of £400 with another natural daughter of the Poet, which was subscribed after the death of Burns. Elizabeth Burns became the wife of John Bishop, overseer at Polkemmet, and died in December, 1816.

"Know all men by these Presents that I Robert Burns in Mossgiel: Whereas I intend to leave Scotland and go abroad, and having acknowledged myself the father of a child named Elizabeth, begot upon Elizabeth Paton in Largieside: And whereas Gilbert Burns in Mossgiel, my brother, has become bound, and hereby binds and oblidges himself to aliment, clothe, and educate my said natural child in a suitable manner as if she was his own, in case her Mother chuse to part with her, and that until she arrive at the age of fifteen years. Therefore, and to enable the said Gilbert Burns to make good his said engagement, Wit ye me to have assigned, disponed, conveyed and made over to, and in favors of, the said Gilbert Burns his Heirs, Executors and Assignees, who are always to be bound in like manner with himself, all and Sundry Goods, Gear, Corns, Cattle, Horses, Nott, Sheep, Household furniture, and all other moveable effects of whatever kind that I shall leave behind me on my departure from the kingdom, after allowing for my part of the conjunct debts due by the said Gilbert Burns and me as joint Tacksmen of the farm of Mossgiel, and particularly, without prejudice of the foresaid generality, the profits that may arise from the publication of my Poems presently in the press—And also, I hereby dispone and convey to him trust foor behoof of my said natural daughter, the Copyright of said Poems in so far as I can dispose of the same by law, after she arrives at the above age of fifteen years complete—Surrogating and substituting the said Gilbert Burns my brother and his foresaids in my full right, title, room and place of the whole Premises, with power to him to intromit with, and dispose upon the same at pleasure, and in general to do every other thing in the Premises that I could have done myself before granting hereof, but always with and under the conditions before expressed—And I oblige myself to warrand this disposition and assignation from my own proper fact and deed allenarly—Consenting to the Registration hereof in the Books of Council and Session, or any other Judges' Books competent, therein to remain for preservation and Constitute . . . . . . whereof, I have w . . . . . Procutars &c.—In witness whereof I have wrote and signed these Presents, consisting of this and the preceding page, on stamped paper, with my own hand, at Mossgiel the twenty second day of July, One thousand seven hundred and eighty six years.

ROBERT BURNS."

No. IV.—WILLIAM BURNESS' MANUAL OF RELIGIOUS BELIEF.

THROUGH the kindness of our clever friend and fellow-townsman, Charles Maxwell, Esq. (one of the most enthusiastic and well-informed *Burnsians* in Great Britain), we are favoured with the sight of a copy of this document. It was first mentioned by Dr. Currie in his Life of the Poet in the following terms:—" There is in Gilbert's hands a little Manual of religious belief, in the form of a Dialogue between a Father and a Son, composed by him for the use of his children, in which the benevolence of his heart seems to have led him to soften the rigid Calvinism of the Scottish Church into something approaching to Arminianism." This MS., which was in the handwriting of John Murdoch, Burns' early teacher, was, and remained in, the possession of Gilbert Burns, the Poet's brother, and it now belongs to his youngest son, Gilbert Burns, resident at Knockmaroon Lodge, Chapel-Izod, County Dublin; and with his permission a limited edition of 600 copies was printed in Kilmarnock, 1875, one of which now lies before us.

. This Manual can by no means be ranked very high as a theological treatise. It contains, however, the bones of a very fair *Moderate* sermon of the period, and is written in a clear, correct, and unimpassioned style. The author proves that there is a God by the common argument that nothing can make itse´f, and (writing before Hume's Essays) that Nature demonstrates its Creator to be possessed of all possible perfections; and that we ought to serve Him out of love. He accounts for the fact that all men do not serve or love God from the Fall and the power of the Devil, brings in the promise of the Woman's Seed as counteracting that power, and lays great stress on men aiming at salvation through the exercise of their own faculties, along with the seeking of grace. Proceeds to prove the Christian Revelation true by four marks—1st, It must be worthy of God; 2nd, Answer all the necessities of human nature; 3rd, Must be sufficiently attested by miracles, and known by prophecies and their fulfilment. He then distinguishes very acutely and clearly between the three Jewish laws, the Ceremonial, the Judicial, and the Moral. He then, and here his Arminianism peeps out, maintains, that if we be but upright in our endeavours to obey the Moral Law, and sincere in our repentance upon our failing or shortcoming, we shall be accepted according to what we have. He then ably defines faith, impresses the necessity of repentance, describes almost graphically the intestine conflict between the animal and the spiritual natures in man, and closes by a very ingenious attempt to reconcile the injunction of Christ to His disciple to take up His Cross, and His promise that godliness has the promise of this life and all its innocent enjoyments, as well as that to come.

Such is the sum and substance of this brief Manual. Nothing is said in it of the Trinity, of (properly speaking) the Atonement, of the Divinity of Christ, or of Eternal Punishment. Alike in what it has and what it wants, it is very much the Creed of the Poet, and in this age, while many will hold it to be bare as a birch tree in December, others will think it is covered over with very dubious propositions, as with the rich but loose and faded foliage of Autumn. As this is not a controversial work, we simply leave this outline of it with our readers. It was then, and would be thought still, a remarkable production from the pen of an uneducated man.

No. V.—THE GLENRIDDELL MS.

To Mr. Maxwell's kindness we are also indebted for a sight of a little book published in Liverpool in 1874, entitled, " Some Account of the Glenriddell MS. of Burns' Poems, with several Poems never before Published; Edited

APPENDIX.

by Henry Bright; Published for Private Circulation." In the preface to this *brochure* the editor mentions that the widow of Mr. Wallace Currie (son of Dr. Currie) presented to the Athenæum Library, Liverpool, two volumes, one of " Poems written by Burns, and selected by him from the imprinted collection for Robert Riddell of Glenriddell, Esq."—a quarto volume of 162 pages, exclusive of portrait, title, and an introductory letter; the letter and seventy-eight pages of the poems being entirely in the Poet's handwriting, the rest of the MS. being in the handwriting of amanuenses, with occasional corrections and remarks by Burns himself. The second is a volume of " Letters by Burns, selected for R. Riddell, Esq."—a quarto volume containing 103 pages, exclusive of title and portrait; the first six pages blank, the rest of the volume in Burns' autograph. These are now placed in a glass case in the library, and may be readily inspected. The unpublished matter of the Letters has appeared in the *Athenæum*, August 1, 1874. On the fly-leaf of the volume of poems are the arms of Mr. Riddell and a portrait of Burns; on the title-page is the inscription, " Poems written by Mr. Robert Burns," &c., and ten lines of verse about Burns, very poor, by some unknown hand. Then comes Burns' Preface, which we may transcribe, as it is characteristic:—

" As this Collection almost wholly consists of pieces local or unfinished, fragments the effusion of a poetical moment, and bagatelles strung in rhyme simply *pour passer le temps* —the Author trusts that nobody into whose hands it may come will, without his permission, give, or allow to be taken, copies of anything here contained, much less to give to the world at large what he never meant to see the light. At the gentleman's request, whose from this time it shall be, the Collection was made; and to him, and, I will add, to his amiable lady, it is presented, as a sincere though small tribute of gratitude for the many, many happy hours the Author has spent under their roof. *There*—what Poverty, even though accompanied with Genius, must seldom expect to meet with at the tables and in the circles of fashionable life—his welcome has ever been the cordiality of Kindness and the warmth of Friendship. As, from the situation in which it is now placed, this MS. may be preserved and this preface read when the hand that now writes and the heart that now dictates it may be mouldering in the dust, let these be regarded as the genuine sentiments of a man who seldom flattered any, and never those he loved.

"*27th April*, 1791."   ROBERT BURNS.

Mr. H. Bright proceeds to give a complete catalogue of the poems thus preserved, and full transcriptions of those not previously published, along with notes added to them in Burns' own hand, or others; and a number of alterations and various readings, few of much importance. They are altogether fifty-seven in number. Some of Burns' notes are curious. Thus to

" In Mauchline there dwells six proper young belles,"

he adds, " Miss Armour is now known under the designation of Mrs. Burns." To the song, " I murder hate by flood or field," he adds an additional stanza—

" I would not die like Socrates
For all the fuss of Plato;
Nor would I with Leonidas,
Nor yet would I with Cato."

To " Holy Willie's Prayer" he annexes a rather long and not very refined note, in which he speaks of his possessing that polemical chattering which ends in tippling orthodoxy, and that spiritualized bawdry which refines to liquorish devotion. In the copy of his letter to Dr. Moore Burns appends some queer and characteristic remarks on the work of the amanuensis who transcribed it. He says he is not answerable for the bad spelling and punctuation— " I have something generous in my temper that cannot bear to see or hear the absent wronged, and I am very much hurt to observe that in several instances the transcriber has injured and mangled the proper name and principal title of a Personage of the very first distinction in all that is valuable among men—antiquity, abilities, and power (virtue everybody knows is an obsolete business); I mean the Devil. Considering that the transcriber was one of the clergy, an order that owe the very bread they eat to the said Personage's exertions, the affair was absolutely unpardonable." Under the heading of the poem on the death of Sir James Hunter Blair he says, " He once pressed my hand and asked me, with the most friendly warmth, if it was in his power to serve me. I had nothing to ask him; but if ever a child of his should be so unfortunate as to be under the necessity of asking anything of so poor a man as I am, it may not be in my power to grant it, but, by ——, I shall try!"

In reference to the lines on the Water-fowl at Loch Turit, after saying, as already quoted, that it was the production of a solitary forenoon's walk from Ochtertyre, he says, " I lived there Sir William's guest for two or three weeks, and was much flattered by my hospitable reception. What a pity that the mere emotions of gratitude are so impotent in this world! 'Tis lucky that, as we are told, they will be of some avail in the world to come." The poems are " Epistle to John Goudie in Kilmarnock," author of the " Gospel Recovered," August, 1785; " Ode to the Departed Regency Bill," 1789; " Birthday Ode," 3rd December, 1787; " Jeremiah xv. 10;" From Clarinda, on Mr. B—— saying that " he had nothing else to do;" " Answer to the foregoing, extempore;" " A Fragment on Glenriddell's Fox Breaking his Chain."

No. VI.

THE indefatigable Dr. Grierson has presented us with the photograph of the inscription on a copy of Young's

"Night Thoughts," given by Burns to Clarinda. It has never been published before, and the original is in the possession of L. Gilchrist Clarkson, who kindly permitted Dr. Grierson to send it us.

Dr. Grierson says, "Years ago I saw three poems in Burns' own hand; one of them is the poem, "The Thames flows proudly to the Sea;" the other two were very gross, altogether unsuitable for publication. Dr.

> To Mrs. McIlhose this Poem, the sentiments of the heirs of immortality, told in the numbers of Paradise, is respectfully presented by
>
> Robt Burns
>
> Mrs McIlhose presents this book to Mr Balfour Ship as a small return for all his kindness

Grierson quotes part of one verse, which quite proves his proposition.

No. VII.—Burns' Connection with the Excise.

In the number of *Chambers' Journal* for 27th March, 1875, there is an interesting paper, written evidently by a well-known London litterateur, a Scotchman, and a warm admirer of our Poet, in which some new facts anent the above-named subject are brought to light. Mr. MacFadzean, of the Inland Revenue Office, found in Somerset House some documents of the old Excise Office in Edinburgh bearing favourably on the treatment of the Poet by that office. He was entered on the list of promotion for the office of Supervisor on the 27th July, 1791, and he remained on it till his death. Had he lived he would have been promoted on the 12th January, 1797.

His name is not mentioned for censure amid all the censures passed by the Board of Excise; and at that time the duties imposed on Excise officers were exceedingly numerous, the Amended Instructions issued in 1804 forming a volume, as large as a Family Bible, of 939 pages. None but a tolerably steady as well as active man could have adequately fulfilled the multifarious duties. An alphabetical list of the names of officers was drawn up with marginal notes, reflecting severely, many of them, on the character of the officers, calling one a "bad moral character," another "a good officer, but now tipples;" a third, a "blundering officer," and so forth. Burns is characterized, first as "Never tryed—a Poet," with a subsequent interlineation, "turns out well;" and the worst said of him is three years afterwards, "The Poet does pretty well." This can by no means be regarded as a severe censure; it is rather complimentary. Of course a supervisorship was valued by him, chiefly as a stepping-

APPENDIX.

stone to a collectorship, which would have insured him "leisure and a little fortune." Burns never could have become a "Collector Snail" (see "Guy Mannering"); he would have continued active and unwearied; but what a blessing might competence have been to himself and his family! It might have proved, what his enemies even yet deny, that, in reference to his errors, it was his poverty and not his will which consented, and that "what seemed guilt might be but woe."

We have at present lying before us an interesting document connected with this subject. It is a copy of a Round Diary, kept by Burns' great friend, Mr. A. Findlater, of his Excise Collections for the Dumfries district. It had been shown to Robert Chambers, who thus speaks of it in a letter with which we were favoured by Mr. C. Maxwell:—"It is curious," says Mr. Chambers, "as showing Burns the only one out of a dozen officers under censure. I possess a copy of a letter of his to a Mr. Edgar of the Excise Office, April, 1795, extenuating some blame with which he was to be visited, on account of another slight failure in duty; which shows that, as might have been expected, he was not quite the most perfect gauger in the world, as well as the most brilliant Poet." In Findlater's Round Diary we find the words, "Admonished Mr. Burns," and opposite are the following words, by Findlater:—"Examined books. Hides, p. 36. A notice to draw leather, May 25th, but no account taken thereof till my survey on the 26th. Journal not entered on the 6th and 8th June by Burns. Brewery gage 157, June 4th, a cleansing of ale not regularly taken account of, but entered on the margin by Adam Stobie, supernumerary." This was the head and front of Burns' offending, for which Findlater "admonished Mr. Burns." Poor fellow! what with Daddy Auld and Supervisor Findlater, the Poet was a favourite subject of "admonition." It was Mr. Stobie, as we saw in the LIFE, who generously performed Burns' Excise work for him when he was ill, without fee or reward.

Mr. Findlater, another document we have informs us, "ranked high as a man of refined taste, of manly and generous sentiments, of glowing and enlightened patriotism, and as a public officer of excellent business habits and strict integrity." Mr. Findlater rose to the highest rank in the out-door department of the Excise, and after a meritorious service of fifty-two years, retired upon the highest superannuation allowance ever granted to a collector.

Another correspondent says, in accounting for some omission of Findlater's, not giving him one of his letters to Burns, that "he became aged and devout." He went to reside in Glasgow, and we have on our table a letter by him to a gentleman in Dundee, dated 26th October, 1839.

No. VIII.

WE gladly insert the following letter from Manchester:—

"SIR,—As the biographer of Burns, I beg to acquaint you that I am possessed of a number of relics connected with Scotia's Bard. They are the furniture from the cottage in which Burns was born, near Alloway Kirk, purchased at the sale of them in 1845, after the death of Miller Goudie, who kept the cottage open for visitors. The furniture is of the humblest description, as depicted in the *Illustrated London News* at the time of the Eglinton tournament, and covered with the names and initials of visitors. The following is a list of it:—An arm chair, two chairs, two tables, a smaller table, chest of drawers, old clock and case, corner cupboard, handbell, drinking horn, and toddy ladle. Also a tea-caddie and curious cup, made from 'the thorn on which Mungo's mither hanged hersel';' an autograph memorandum of Burns', five books of signatures of visitors to the cottage, and twelve chairs, put into the cottage latterly by the Miller Goudie. I have the notes of sale and other documents of identification. My father purchased the articles in 1845, and made the collection, which, I think, ought to find a place in Scotland in some depositary, public or private, devoted to the memory of the poet, whose 'Cotter's Saturday Night' was very descriptive of the homely belongings of the 'auld clay biggin'.' If you consider these unique things really interesting to you, I should be glad to know if you, or a circle of admiring Scots, could secure them from dispersion either in England or America."

No. IX.

EVERY one remembers the poetic competition in 1859, and the successful poem of Isa Craig. Besides her chaste and tasteful effusion, a number of others were published of various merit. One by Mr. James Bogue, then a teacher in Omoa Academy, near Airdrie, was too late for the prescribed time. The author sent it to us, and we had much pleasure in getting it printed in an Edinburgh newspaper, the *News*, conducted by our ingenious friend Mr. Daniel Gorrie, now of London. Although a little too allegorical in its form, it was full of real enthusiasm, and its composition showed the scholar as well as the poet. A gifted Northumberland lady, whose *nom de plume* is "Eta Mawr," has sent us recently a fine strain, recited at the Anniversary Dinner of the Burns Club, Newcastle-on-Tyne, 25th January, 1869. Ere appending it as a *Grand Finale* to our book, we may say in reference to Burns Clubs that we by no means intend to derogate from the claims of other clubs when we say, that the Edinburgh one has always been specially distinguished. Its chairmen have included, if we mistake not, such names as Professors Wilson, Blackie, and Masson, Dr. Robert Wallace, Campbell Smith, Esq., and many more, including, we think, the late lamented James Ballantine, who was at all events the soul of the institution. And we look (we must be pardoned for saying) on it as one of the highest honours of our life that we were three times solicited to preside at this Annual Entertainment, although we were, owing to unavoidable circumstances, as often obliged most reluctantly to decline.

POETA NASCITUR.
ON THE ANNIVERSARY OF ROBERT BURNS.

The following original Ode, from the pen of Eta Mawr, the author of "Far and Near; or, Translations and Originals," was recited with loud applause at the Anniversary Dinner of the Burns Club, Newcastle-upon-Tyne, on the birthday of the Scottish Bard, the 25th of January:—

Nature would frame a poet all her own!
   Her tyrant sister, Art,
   In him should claim no part—
The glory should be hers, and hers *alone!*
   She cast her eyes around
   On all the hallowed ground
Which genius loves to haunt —
   Genius, whose favours fall
   Alike on cottage or on hall:
And he who hears the glorious call
Nor fortune can beguile, nor poverty can daunt!
Where shall the land be, where the clime,
Where she shall make her search sublime?
   Not beneath southern skies,
   Not where the Alps arise;
Though *these* her grandest scenes can show —
Though *there* her brightest aspects glow:
   She turns from them
   To her sea-bright gem—
Nature and freedom love to smile
Alike upon their British Isle!

And here in humble guise she sought
   A child of toil and care;
   A spell around his cradle wrought,
   And brightened all the air.
     From the bleak North
     She called him forth—
   It softened at her smile;
     In native plaid
     His limbs arrayed,
   And strung his nerves to toil;
   But toil that left him leisure still
With Nature's lore his heart to fill.
His very *name* had charms for *her* —
   The "wimpling *burns*," his native streams,
With their wild music fancy stir,
   And weave melodious dreams!
     She led him by the hand
     O'er all th' enchanted land,
     And bade his infant lyre
     To sound her praise aspire;
Dear were to her his "woodnotes wild,"
And dear the mother to the child!

She steeped his soul in tenderness—the flower,
The wayside flower, his delving share upturned; *
   The thistle's self, in which he scanned
   The emblem of his native land,
By others trampled on or spurned,
A train of patriot thoughts awoke—a tender pity earned. †
   The tiny tenant of the field, ‡
     With palpitating heart,
   Did he from injury shield,
     And bid in peace depart.
All Nature's children had a charm
   His kindred soul to melt;
All that had life his heart could warm —
   For all that *feel* he felt.

Nor only did the *sadder* Muse
   Bestow her touching strain!
Full oft the *comic* he would choose
   To woo—nor woo in vain.
And humour grave and mirthful wit,
Along the sportive chords would flit —
Wit that, like Falstaff's, could inspire
   A kindred vein—contagious fire—
   And wit in others wake; §
Teach Sculpture, hitherto confined
To grand embodiments of mind,
   A humbler phase to take;
In "Tam o' Shanter," "Souter John"—
Plebeian garb for once put on,
   Descending, for his sake,
Yet find, amazed, that humble life
With equal fame for her was rife.
She gave the shapes the bard had shown
   An immortality in stone,
And shared for aye the undying praise
Which hovers o'er that poet's lays.

Ah! that he lived not—as he might—
To see such genuine meed requite; *
Beyond all fame to him, I ween,
Had such congenial tribute been.
Yes! mourn, with me, the cruel fate
That ever on the bard doth wait,
Whose fatal motto is—Too Late!
Too Late! Too Late!—Those words of woe
From each true poet's pen may flow;
   For never does he see below
     The fame he shall attain;

---

* "Wee, modest, crimson-tipped flower," &c.
† Burns says in one of his letters, that he never could see a thistle in bloom but he turned aside his plough, and spared his country's emblem. What exquisite delicacy of feeling in an untaught son of the soil!
‡ The field-mouse.
§ Falstaff says he was not only witty himself, but inspired wit in others.—See Henry IV. Shakspeare.
* Had Burns lived to the common age of man, he would long have survived the production of the celebrated figures of "Tam o' Shanter" and "Souter John," and rejoiced, doubtless, in so admirable an embodiment of his ideas.

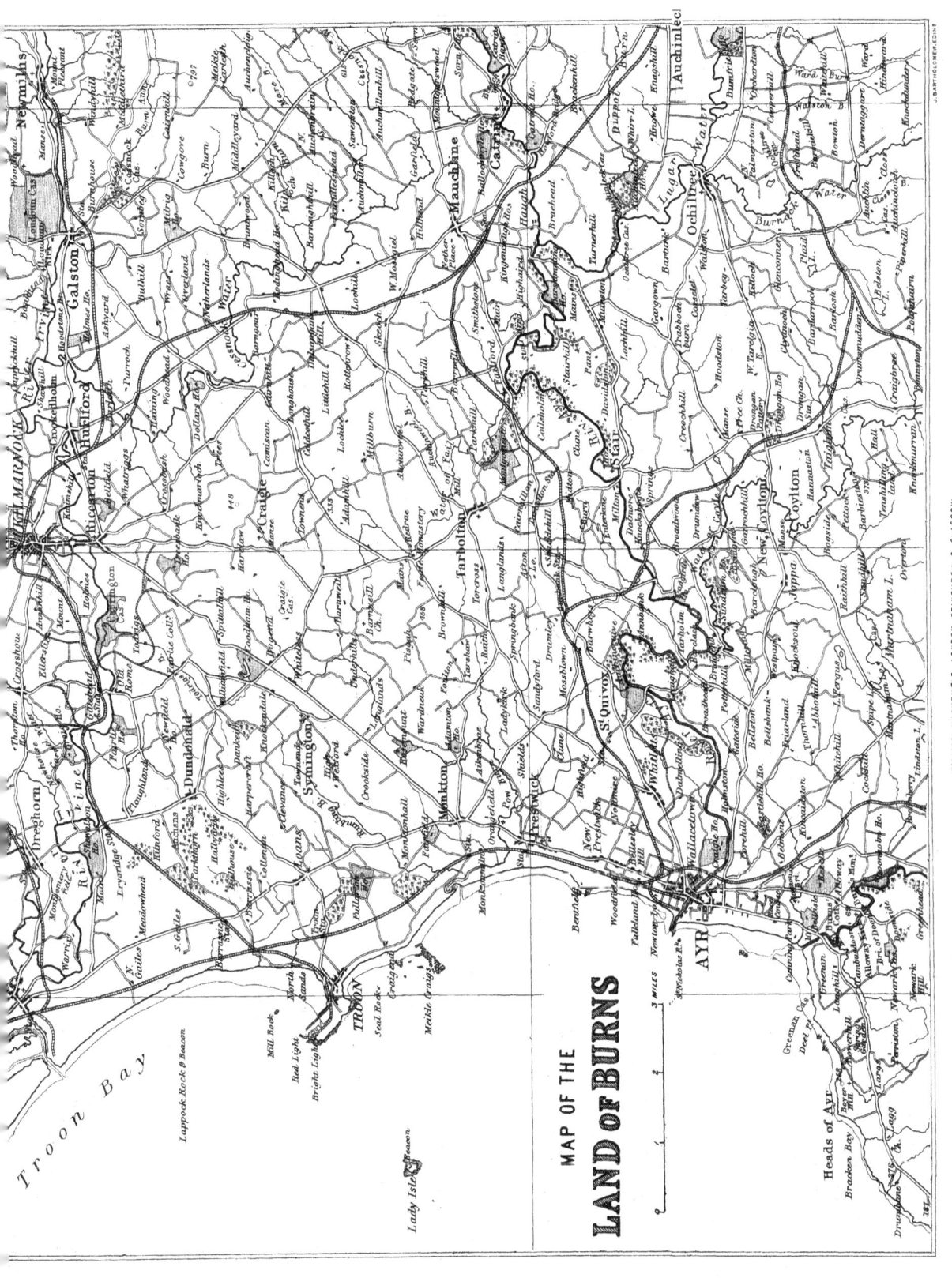

APPENDIX.

And doubt and fear distract his breast,
By cold Oblivion's dread opprest,
Till, sinking to his final rest,
    It comes, for *him*, in vain!

Too sad the theme! Ah, turn away,
And wake for him a loftier lay;
For Nature still has balm to heal
The pangs her gifted children feel,
    And soothe fate's keenest sting.
She fired his soul with patriot flame,
A glory o'er his country's name,
    In ages past, to fling.
For they who for their country bleed
Have ne'er received their crowning meed
Till their country's poets sing.
See! rising from their gory bed,
The Scots who once with Wallace bled,
The Scots whom Bruce so often led,
    Salute their gifted son;
Lo! in his strain
They live again,
A second race of glory run.
And bright the halo round them shed;
    For every line
    A wreath doth twine,
A deathless wreath of fame, for each devoted head.

Yet pause to bless the God of peace,
Who bade those cruel contests cease
    That tore the sister lands;
    And blending even in war their hands,
    Rends not from one pale bleeding brow
    The garland for the other now—
    The garland which they jointly claim,
    In union of immortal fame,
    Knit fast in concord's bands.
The Scots that once for Wallace bled
For England now their blood would shed,
    England would bleed for *them*!
In BRITAIN'S blending name they close
Those dire divisions, countless woes;
The Northern Thistle, Southern Rose,
    Now blooming on one stem.
Still may their serried ranks oppose
One dauntless front to their country's foes,
    Her thunders hurling from afar;
Still may they labour, hand in hand,
At home t' exalt each happy land,
And join, as now, in feasts of peace, not less than feats of war!

Hush the loud clarion's note!
List the low tones that float
    To sorrow's ear!
Breathe soft in solemn dirge
Sounds that from heaven's high verge
    Angels may stoop to hear!
So free from earthly taint
The undying love they paint,
    So pure the poet's tear!

But let the woe be brief,
    Sublimed from earthly leaven.
Ah! why for thee feel grief —
    "Mary—in Heaven!"

Nor only passion's purest form
The soul of Nature's bard could warm;
Domestic love! thou, too, hast claims
On kindred hearts and kindred names.
How sweetly thrill the poet's strings,
A pious father when he sings;
And where has Nature fitter place
Than bending at the throne of grace?
Draw near with reverence! on the earth
    No holier sight is seen:
The worship of the heart and hearth,
    Where angel steps have been;
The steps of virtue's hallowed train,
That o'er a humble household reign.
The patriarch of the cottage dome
Unfolds the Bible's ample tome—
    The Bible of his sires!
He calls to prayer! responsive hearts
In silence take their several parts,
And each impressive word to heaven's high court aspires.

And earthly friendship, warm and true,
A glory o'er the minstrel threw,
    Reflected from his line;
As hands and hearts, locked firm and fast,
Around the cup of kindness passed
    "For auld lang syne!"
Ah! from the Arctic to the zone,*
That song to Northern hearts is known;
A spell that shall for ever last,
To bind the present to the past
    In friendship's cordial growth;
Nor less the Southern Briton feels
The sighs it draws, the tear it steals—
    The smile that chases both!
That links, from youth's to age's span,
The heart of brother man to man.
Had he but breathed that strain alone,
The bard had made all hearts his own!
Then Nature on her minstrel smiled,
And owned him for her favourite child.
She clasped her chosen to her heart—
My son, my son, we ne'er will part!
Or grave or gay, thy heart my throne,
Still beats responsive to my own.
Whoe'er the race of glory run,
Still Burns shall be my favourite son;

---

* The Rev. J. Jeffrey, in his speech at the Anniversary Dinner, Newcastle, relates, that "being present, a few years ago, at a banquet given to some high dignitaries of the State, in the capital of an ancient Northern Kingdom, when the name of Burns happened at random to be mentioned, it was received by those distinguished foreigners with a burst of heartfelt appreciation and applause. They all knew his name, and they all had read and admired his writings—so true are the often-quoted words, "One touch of nature makes the whole world kin." And of none do these words hold good more thoroughly than of the peasant poet, Burns."

My rival sister well may claim
A share in every glorious name—
  In all save thine alone.
Fair are the works of Art,
But here she hath no part—
  Yes, thou art all my own.
  Kneel then before my throne,
  Receive the garland won!
From her own brow the bays she drew,
All bright with vernal dew;
Round *his* the garland wreathed,
And on the fadeless leaves immortal verdure breathed!

A hundred years have rolled away,
  And many another wreath been won;
But he whom Nature crowned that day
  Is still *her* favourite son.
Behold another century rise,
And still he claims and keeps the prize,
  By *her* sole hand assigned.
Far distant is that century's goal—
Fresh minstrels rise as ages roll—
  Fresh phases of the mind;
But when its goal is reached, e'en then shall Burns, as now,
Be Nature's Laureate Bard—her POET OF THE PLOUGH!

Poems & Songs by Robert Burns

HANDSOME NELL.*

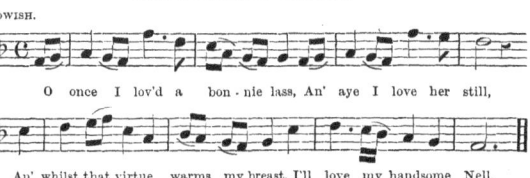

SLOWISH.

O once I lov'd a bonnie lass, An' aye I love her still,
An' whilst that virtue warms my breast, I'll love my handsome Nell.

As bonnie lasses I ha'e seen,
 And mony full as braw,
But for a modest gracefu' mien,
 The like I never saw.

A bonnie lass, I will confess,
 Is pleasant to the e'e,
But without some better qualities
 She's no a lass for me.

But Nelly's looks are blithe and sweet,
 And, what is best of a',
Her reputation is complete,
 And fair without a flaw.

She dresses aye sae clean and neat,
 Both decent and genteel;
And then there's something in her gait
 Gars ony dress look weel.

A gaudy dress and gentle air
 May slightly touch the heart,
But it's innocence and modesty
 That polishes the dart.

* "Handsome Nell:" Burns' first composition. She was Nelly Kilpatrick, daughter of a blacksmith near Mount Oliphant. She inspired the song in Autumn, 1773, when the Poet was only fifteen.

'Tis this in Nelly pleases me,
 'Tis this enchants my soul;
For absolutely in my breast
 She reigns without control.

HAIRST—A SONG COMPOSED IN AUGUST.

SLOW, WITH EXPRESSION.   TUNE—"When the King Came o'er the Water."

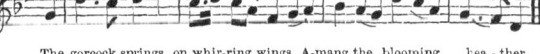

Now westlin winds and slaughterin' guns Bring Autumn's pleasant weather;
The gorcock springs, on whirring wings, A-mang the blooming heather.
Now waving grain, wide o'er the plain, Delights the weary farmer,

The moon shines bright, as I rove by night, To muse upon my charmer.

The partridge loves the fruitful fells;
 The plover loves the mountains;
The woodcock haunts the lonely dells;
 The soaring hern the fountains:
Through lofty groves the cushat roves,
 The path of man to shun it;
The hazel bush o'erhangs the thrush,
 The spreading thorn the linnet.

Thus every kind their pleasure find,
  The savage and the tender;
Some social join, and leagues combine;
  Some solitary wander;
Avaunt, away! the cruel sway,
  Tyrannic man's dominion;
The sportsman's joy, the murdering cry,
  The fluttering, gory pinion!

But Peggy, dear, the evening's clear,
  Thick flies the skimming swallow;
The sky is blue, the fields in view,
  All fading-green and yellow:

Come let us stray our gladsome way,
  And view the charms of nature;
The rustling corn, the fruited thorn,
  And every happy creature.

We'll gently walk, and sweetly talk,
  Till the silent moon shine clearly;
I'll grasp thy waist, and, fondly press'd,
  Swear how I love thee dearly;
Not vernal showers to budding flowers,
  Not autumn to the farmer,
So dear can be as thou to me,
  My fair, my lovely charmer!

TIBBIE, I HAE SEEN THE DAY.*

SLOWISH.   TUNE—"Invercauld's Reel."

CHORUS—O Tibbie I hae seen the day, Ye wad na been sae shy;
For lack o' gear ye lightly me, But, trowth, I care na by.

VERSE 1.—Yestreen I met you on the moor, Ye spak na, but gaed by like stour;
Ye geck at me because I'm poor, But fient a hair care I.

I doubt na, lass, but ye may think,
Because ye hae the name o' clink,
That ye can please me at a wink,
   Whene'er ye like to try.

   O Tibbie, I hae seen the day, &c.

* Tibby Stein, a Tarbolton lass. So says Mrs. Begg.

But sorrow tak him that's sae mean,
Although his pouch o' coin were clean,
Wha follows ony saucy quean
   That looks sae proud and high.

   O Tibbie, I hae seen the day, &

Although a lad were e'er sae smart,
If that he want the yellow dirt,
Ye'll cast your head anither airt,
   And answer him fu' dry.

   O Tibbie, I hae seen the day, &c.

But if he hae the name o' gear,
Ye'll fasten to him like a brier,
Though hardly he, for sense or lear,
   Be better than the kye.

   O Tibbie, I hae seen the day, &c.

But, Tibbie, lass, tak my advice:
Your daddie's gear maks you sae nice;
The deil a ane wad spier your price,
   Were ye as poor as I.

   O Tibbie, I hae seen the day, &c.

There lives a lass in yonder park,
I would na gie her in her sark,
For thee, wi' a' thy thousan' mark;
Ye need na look sae high.
    O Tibbie, I hae seen the day, &c.

I DREAM'D I LAY.*

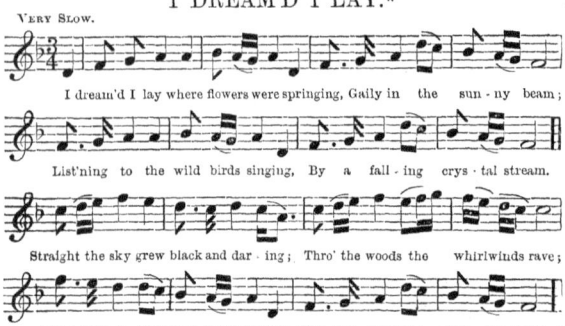

Such was my life's deceitful morning,
  Such the pleasures I enjoy'd;
But lang ere noon, loud tempests storming
  A' my flow'ry bliss destroy'd.
Though fickle fortune has deceived me,
  (She promised fair, and perform'd but ill;)
Of mony a joy and hope bereaved me,
  I bear a heart shall support me still.

TRAGIC FRAGMENT.

"In my early years nothing less would serve me than courting the Tragic Muse. I was, I think, about eighteen or nineteen when I sketched the outlines of a tragedy forsooth; but the bursting of a cloud of family misfortunes, which had for some time threatened us, prevented my farther progress. In those days I never wrote down any thing; so, except a speech or two, the whole has escaped my memory. The following, which I most distinctly remember, was an exclamation from a great character—great in occasional instances of generosity, and daring at times in villanies. He is supposed to meet with a child of misery, and exclaims to himself:—(B.)

"ALL devil as I am, a damnèd wretch,
A harden'd, stubborn, unrepenting villain,
Still my heart melts at human wretchedness;
And with sincere though unavailing sighs
I view the helpless children of distress.†
With tears indignant I behold th' oppressor
Rejoicing in the honest man's destruction,
Whose unsubmitting heart was all his crime.

* Composed when Burns was only seventeen. Probably suggested by Mrs. Cockburn's "Flowers of the Forest."
† He alludes to his family misfortunes at Mount Oliphant.—See LIFE.

Even you, ye helpless crew, I pity you;
Ye, whom the seeming good think sin to pity:
Ye poor, despised, abandon'd vagabonds,
Whom vice, as usual, has turn'd o'er to ruin.
Oh, but for kind, though ill-requited friends,
I had been driven forth like you forlorn,
The most detested, worthless wretch among you!"

THE TARBOLTON LASSES.

IF ye gae up to yon hill-tap,
  Ye'll there see bonnie Peggy;
She kens her father is a laird,
  And she forsooth's a leddy.

There Sophy tight, a lassie bright,
  Besides a handsome fortune:
Wha canna win her in a night,
  Has little art in courtin.

Gae down by Faile, and taste the ale,
  And tak a look o' Mysie;
She's dour and din, a deil within,
  But aiblins she may please ye.

If she be shy, her sister try,
  Ye'll may be fancy Jenny;
If ye'll dispense wi' want o' sense—
  She kens hersel she's bonnie.

As ye gae up by yon hillside,
  Spier in for bonnie Bessie;
She'll gie ye a beck, and bid ye light,
  And handsomely address ye.

There's few sae bonnie, nane sae guid,
  In a' King George' dominion;
If ye should doubt the truth o' this—
  It's Bessy's ain opinion!

AH, WOE IS ME, MY MOTHER DEAR.

Paraphrase of Jeremiah, 15th Chap., 10th verse.

AH, woe is me, my Mother dear!
  A man of strife ye've born me:
For sair contention I maun bear;
  They hate, revile, and scorn me.

I ne'er could lend on bill or band,
   That five per cent. might blest me;
And borrowing, on the tither hand,
   The de'il a ane wad trust me.

Yet I, a coin-denièd wight,
   By Fortune quite discarded;
Ye see how I am, day and night,
   By lad and lass blackguarded!

MONTGOMERY'S PEGGY.*

VERY SLOW.   TUNE—"Galla Water."

Although my bed were in yon muir, A-mang the heather in my plaidie,
Yet happy, happy would I be, Had I my dear Mont-gom-ery's Peggy.

When o'er the hill beat surly storms,
   And winter nights were dark and rainy;
I 'd seek some dell, and in my arms
   I 'd shelter dear Montgomery's Peggy.

* She became Mrs. Derbishire, and lived in London. Housekeeper at Coilsfield House; engaged ere Burns knew her.

Were I a baron proud and high,
   And horse and servants waiting ready,
Then a' 'twad gie o' joy to me,
   The sharin't with Montgomery's Peggy.

THE PLOUGHMAN'S LIFE.

As I was a-wandering ae morning in spring,
I heard a young ploughman sae sweetly to sing;
And as he was singin' thir words he did say,
"There 's nae life like the ploughman's in the month o' sweet May.

"The laverock in the morning she'll rise frae her nest,
And mount to the air wi' the dew on her breast;
And wi' the merry ploughman she'll whistle and sing,
And at night she'll return to her nest back again."

THE RONALDS OF THE BENNALS.*

In Tarbolton, ye ken, there are proper young men,
 And proper young lasses and a', man;
But ken ye the Ronalds that live in the Bennals,
 They carry the gree frae them a', man.

Their father's a laird, and weel he can spare't,
 Braid money to tocher them a', man;
To proper young men, he'll clink in the hand
 Gowd guineas a hunder or twa, man.

There's ane they ca' Jean, I'll warrant ye've seen
 As bonnie a lass or as braw, man;
But for sense and guid taste she'll vie wi' the best,
 And a conduct that beautifies a', man.

The charms o' the min', the langer they shine,
 The mair admiration they draw, man;
While peaches and cherries, and roses and lilies,
 They fade and they wither awa, man.

If ye be for Miss Jean, tak this frae a frien',
 A hint o' a rival or twa, man;
The Laird o' Blackbyre wad gang through the fire,
 If that wad entice her awa, man.

The Laird o' Braehead has been on his speed,
 For mair than a towmond or twa, man;
The Laird o' the Ford will straught on a board,
 If he canna get her at a', man.

Then Anna comes in, the pride o' her kin,
 The boast of our bachelors a', man:
Sae sonsy and sweet, sae fully complete,
 She steals our affections awa, man.

If I should detail the pick and the wale
 O' lasses that live here awa, man.
The fau't wad be mine if they didna shine
 The sweetest and best o' them a', man.

I lo'e her mysel, but darena weel tell,
 My poverty keeps me in awe, man;
For making o' rhymes, and working at times,
 Does little or naething at a', man.

* The Bennals, a farm in the west end of Tarbolton. Gilbert Burns courted one of these ladies in vain.

Yet I wadna choose to let her refuse,
 Nor hae 't in her power to say na, man:
For though I be poor, unnoticed, obscure,
 My stomach 's as proud as them a', man.

Though I canna ride in weel-booted pride,
 And flee o'er the hills like a craw, man,
I can haud up my head wi' the best o' the breed,
 Though fluttering ever so braw, man.

My coat and my vest, they are Scotch o' the best,
 O' pairs o' guid breeks I hae twa, man;
And stockings and pumps to put on my stumps,
 And ne'er a wrang steek in them a', man.

My sarks they are few, but five o' them new,
 Twal' hundred, as white as the snaw, man,
A ten-shillings hat, a Holland cravat;
 There are no mony poets sae braw, man.

I never had freens weel stockit in means,
 To leave me a hundred or twa, man;
Nae weel-tocher'd aunts, to wait on their drants,†
 And wish them in hell for it a', man.

I never was cannie for hoarding o' money,
 Or claughtin 't together at a', man;
I've little to spend, and naething to lend,
 But deevil a shilling I awe, man.

HERE'S TO THY HEALTH.

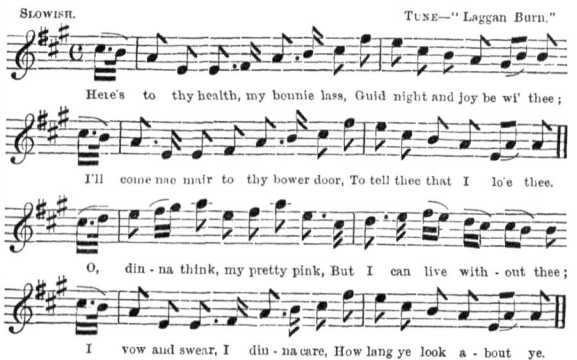

Slowish.   Tune—"Laggan Burn."

Here's to thy health, my bonnie lass, Guid night and joy be wi' thee;
I'll come nae mair to thy bower door, To tell thee that I lo'e thee.
O, dinna think, my pretty pink, But I can live without thee;
I vow and swear, I dinna care, How lang ye look about ye.

Thou 'rt aye sae free informing me
 Thou hast nae mind to marry;
I'll be as free informing thee
 Nae time hae I to tarry.
I ken thy friens try ilka means
 Frae wedlock to delay thee,
Depending on some higher chance;
 But fortune may betray thee.

† "Drants," long prayers.

I ken they scorn my low estate,
  But that does never grieve me;
But I 'm as free as any he,
  Sma' siller will relieve me.
I 'll count my health my greatest wealth,
  Sae lang as I 'll enjoy it:
I 'll fear nae scant, I 'll bode nae want,
  As lang 's I get employment.

But far-off fowls hae feathers fair,
  And aye until ye try them:
Though they seem fair, still have a care,
  They may prove waur than I am.
But at twal at night, when the moon shines bright,
  My dear, I 'll come and see thee;
For the man that lo'es his mistress weel,
  Nae travel makes him weary.

THE LASS OF CESSNOCK BANKS.*

On Cessnock banks there lives a lass,
  Could I describe her shape and mien;
The graces of her weel-fared face,
  And the glancin' of her sparkling e'en.

She 's fresher than the morning dawn,
  When rising Phœbus first is seen,
When dew-drops twinkle o'er the lawn;
  And she 's twa glancin', sparklin' e'en.

She 's stately like yon youthful ash,
  That grows the cowslip braes between,
And shoots its head above each bush;
  And she 's twa glancin', sparklin' e'en.

She 's spotless as the flowering thorn
  With flowers so white and leaves so green,
When purest in the dewy morn;
  And she 's twa glancin', sparklin' e'en.

Her looks are like the sportive lamb,
  When flowery May adorns the scene,
That wantons round its bleating dam;
  And she 's twa glancin', sparklin' e'en.

Her hair is like the curling mist
  That shades the mountain-side at e'en,
When flower-reviving rains are past;
  And she s twa glancin', sparklin' e'en.

Her forehead 's like the show'ry bow,
  When shining sunbeams intervene,
And gild the distant mountain's brow;
  And she 's twa glancin', sparklin' e'en.

Her voice is like the evening thrush
  That sings on Cessnock banks unseen,
While his mate sits nestling in the bush;
  And she 's twa glancin', sparklin' e'en.

Her lips are like the cherries ripe,
  That sunny walls from Boreas screen,
They tempt the taste and charm the sight;
  And she 's twa glancin', sparklin' e'en.

Her teeth are like a flock of sheep,
  With fleeces newly washen clean,
That slowly mount the rising steep;
  And she 's twa glancin', sparklin' e'en.

Her breath is like the fragrant breeze
  That gently stirs the blossom'd bean,
When Phœbus sinks behind the seas;
  And she 's twa glancin', sparklin' e'en.

But it's not her air, her form, her face,
  Though matching beauty's fabled queen;
But the mind that shines in every grace,
  And chiefly in her sparklin' e'en!

BONNIE PEGGY ALISON.†

* Ellison Begbie, daughter of a small farmer, who served with a family on Cessnock water, near Lochlea. She rejected Burns' suit.

† Supposed to be the same with Ellison Begbie.

When in my arms, wi' a' thy charms,
    I clasp my countless treasure, O!
I seek nae mair o' Heaven to share,
    Than sic a moment's pleasure, O!

And by thy e'en, sae bonnie blue,
    I swear I'm thine for ever, O!
And on thy lips I seal my vow,
    And break it shall I never, O!

MARY MORISON.*

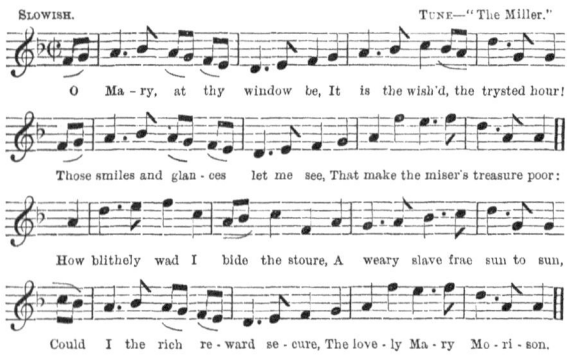

SLOWISH.   TUNE—"The Miller."

O Ma-ry, at thy window be, It is the wish'd, the trysted hour!
Those smiles and glan-ces let me see, That make the miser's treasure poor:
How blithely wad I bide the stoure, A weary slave frae sun to sun,
Could I the rich re-ward se-cure, The love-ly Ma-ry Mo-ri-son.

Yestreen, when, to the trembling string,
    The dance gaed through the lighted ha',
To thee my fancy took its wing,
    I sat, but neither heard nor saw:

* Heroine uncertain. Song repeated in the "Thomson Correspondence." In our opinion the most exquisite of all Burns' love songs. See also "Hazlitt's English Poets."

Though this was fair, and that was braw,
    And yon the toast of a' the town,
I sigh'd, and said amang them a',
    "Ye are na Mary Morison."

Oh, Mary, canst thou wreck his peace,
    Wha for thy sake wad gladly die?
Or canst thou break that heart of his,
    Whase only faut is loving thee?
If love for love thou wilt na gie,
    At least be pity to me shown;
A thought ungentle canna be
    The thought o' Mary Morison.

WINTER, A DIRGE.†

THE wintry west extends his blast,
    And hail and rain does blaw;
Or, the stormy north sends driving forth
    The blinding sleet and snaw:
While, tumbling brown, the burn comes down,
    And roars frae bank to brae;
And bird and beast in covert rest,
    And pass the heartless day.

"The sweeping blast, the sky o'ercast,"‡
    The joyless winter-day,
Let others fear, to me more dear
    Than all the pride of May:

† Written probably at Irvine in 1781, when in a very dark mood.
‡ "O'ercast:" Dr. Young.—(B.)

The tempest's howl, it soothes my soul,
  My griefs it seems to join;
The leafless trees my fancy please,
  Their fate resembles mine!

Thou Power Supreme, whose mighty scheme
  These woes of mine fulfil,
Here, firm, I rest, they must be best,
  Because they are Thy will!
Then all I want (oh, do Thou grant
  This one request of mine!)
Since to enjoy Thou dost deny,
  Assist me to resign.

PRAYER UNDER VIOLENT ANGUISH.*

O Thou Great Being! what Thou art,
  Surpasses me to know:
Yet sure I am that known to Thee
  Are all Thy works below.
Thy creature here before Thee stands,
  All wretched and distress'd,
Yet sure those ills that wring my soul
  Obey Thy high behest.
Sure Thou, Almighty, canst not act
  From cruelty or wrath!
Oh free my weary eyes from tears,
  Or close them fast in death!
But if I must afflicted be,
  To suit some wise design;
Then man my soul with firm resolves,
  To bear and not repine!

* Written at Irvine about the same time with "Winter, a Dirge."

PARAPHRASE OF THE FIRST PSALM.

The man, in life wherever placed,
   Hath happiness in store,
Who walks not in the wicked's way,
   Nor learns their guilty lore!

Nor from the seat of scornful pride
   Casts forth his eyes abroad,
But with humility and awe
   Still walks before his God.

That man shall flourish like the trees
   Which by the streamlets grow;
The fruitful top is spread on high,
   And firm the root below.

But he whose blossom buds in guilt
   Shall to the ground be cast,
And, like the rootless stubble, tost
   Before the sweeping blast.

For why? that God the good adore
   Hath given them peace and rest,
But hath decreed that wicked men
   Shall ne'er be truly blest.

FIRST SIX VERSES OF THE NINTIETH PSALM.

O Thou, the first, the greatest Friend
   Of all the human race!
Whose strong right hand has ever been
   Their stay and dwelling-place!

Before the mountains heaved their heads
   Beneath Thy forming hand,
Before this ponderous globe itself
   Arose at Thy command;

That Power which raised and still upholds
   This universal frame,
From countless, unbeginning time
   Was ever still the same.

Those mighty periods of years
   Which seem to us so vast,
Appear no more before Thy sight
   Than yesterday that's past.

Thou giv'st the word: Thy creature, man,
   Is to existence brought:

Again Thou say'st, "Ye sons of men,
   Return ye into nought!"

Thou layest them, with all their cares,
   In everlasting sleep;
As with a flood Thou tak'st them off
   With overwhelming sweep.

They flourish like the morning flower,
   In beauty's pride array'd;
But long ere night, cut down, it lies
   All wither'd and decay'd.

PRAYER IN THE PROSPECT OF DEATH.*

O Thou unknown, Almighty Cause
   Of all my hope and fear!
In whose dread presence, ere an hour,
   Perhaps I must appear!

---

* Dated August, 1784, when the poet was attacked by fainting fits, &c.: see his Common-place Book.

If I have wander'd in those paths
  Of life I ought to shun—
As something, loudly, in my breast,
  Remonstrates I have done—

Thou know'st that Thou hast formèd me
  With passions wild and strong;
And listening to their witching voice
  Has often led me wrong.

Where human weakness has come short,
  Or frailty stept aside,
Do thou, All-good! for such thou art,
  In shades of darkness hide.

Where with intention I have err'd,
  No other plea I have,
But, Thou art good; and goodness still
  Delighteth to forgive.

ON THE SAME OCCASION.

Why am I loth to leave this earthly scene?
  Have I so found it full of pleasing charms?
Some drops of joy with draughts of ill between:
  Some gleams of sunshine 'mid renewing storms:
Is it departing pangs my soul alarms?
Or death's unlovely, dreary, dark abode?
For guilt, for guilt, my terrors are in arms;
  I tremble to approach an angry God,
And justly smart beneath his sin-avenging rod.

Fain would I say, "Forgive my foul offence!"
  Fain promise never more to disobey;
But, should my Author health again dispense,
  Again I might desert fair virtue's way;
  Again in folly's path might go astray;
  Again exalt the brute, and sink the man:
Then how should I for heavenly mercy pray,
  Who act so counter heavenly mercy's plan?
Who sin so oft have mourn'd, yet to temptation ran?

O Thou, great Governor of all below!
  If I may dare a lifted eye to Thee,
Thy nod can make the tempest cease to blow,
  Or still the tumult of the raging sea:
With that controlling power assist even me,
  Those headlong furious passions to confine;
For all unfit I feel my powers to be,
  To rule their torrent in the allowèd line;
Oh, aid me with Thy help, Omnipotence Divine!

FICKLE FORTUNE.—"A FRAGMENT."

Though fickle Fortune has deceived me,
  She promis'd fair and perform'd but ill;
Of mistress, friends, and wealth bereav'd me,
  Yet I bear a heart shall support me still.

I'll act with prudence as far as I'm able,
  But if success I must never find,
Then come misfortune, I bid thee welcome,
  I'll meet thee with an undaunted mind.

RAGING FORTUNE.

O raging Fortune's withering blast
  Has laid my leaf full low!
O raging Fortune's withering blast
  Has laid my leaf full low!

My stem was fair, my bud was green,
  My blossom sweet did blow;
The dew fell fresh, the sun rose mild,
  And made my branches grow;

But luckless Fortune's northern storms
  Laid a' my blossoms low,—
But luckless Fortune's northern storms
  Laid a' my blossoms low!

NO CHURCHMAN AM I.*

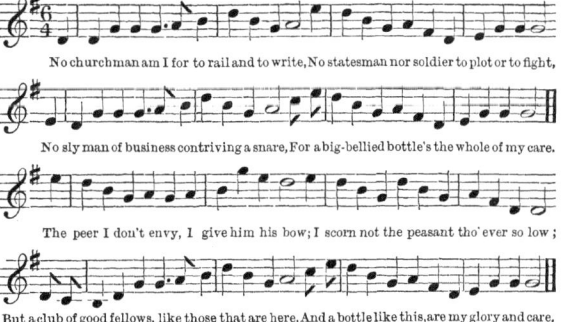

No churchman am I for to rail and to write, No statesman nor soldier to plot or to fight,
No sly man of business contriving a snare, For a big-bellied bottle's the whole of my care.
The peer I don't envy, I give him his bow; I scorn not the peasant tho' ever so low;
But a club of good fellows, like those that are here, And a bottle like this, are my glory and care.

Here passes the squire on his brother—his horse;
There centum per centum, the cit with his purse;
But see you The Crown, how it waves in the air!
There a big-bellied bottle still eases my care.

The wife of my bosom, alas! she did die;
For sweet consolation to church I did fly;

* Written after Burns had joined the Free Masons in 1781.

I found that old Solomon provèd it fair,
That a big-bellied bottle 's a cure for all care.

I once was persuaded a venture to make;
A letter inform'd me that all was to wreck;
But the pursy old landlord just waddled up stairs,
With a glorious bottle that ended my cares.

"Life's cares they are comforts"*—a maxim laid down
By the bard, what d' ye call him, that wore the black gown;
And, faith! I agree with the old prig to a hair;
For a big-bellied bottle 's a heaven of care.

ADDED IN A MASON LODGE.

Then fill up a bumper, and make it o'erflow,
And honours masonic prepare for to throw;
May every true brother of the compass and square
Have a big-bellied bottle when harass'd with care!

MY FATHER WAS A FARMER.

Then out into the world
  My course I did determine, O!
Though to be rich was not my wish,
  Yet to be great was charming, O!
My talents they were not the worst,
  Nor yet my education, O!
Resolved was I, at least to try
  To mend my situation, O!

In many a way, and vain essay,
  I courted fortune's favour, O!

* "Comforts:" Young's "Night Thoughts."—(P.)

Some cause unseen still stept between,
  To frustrate each endeavour, O!
Sometimes by foes I was o'erpower'd;
  Sometimes by friends forsaken, O!
And when my hope was at the top
  I still was worst mistaken, O!

Then sore harass'd, and tired at last,
  With fortune's vain delusion, O!
I dropt my schemes, like idle dreams,
  And came to this conclusion, O!
The past was bad, the future hid;
  Its good or ill untrièd, O!
But the present hour was in my power,
  And so I would enjoy it, O!

No help, nor hope, nor view had I,
  Nor person to befriend me, O!
So I must toil, and sweat, and broil,
  And labour to sustain me, O!
To plough and sow, and reap and mow,
  My father bred me early, O!
For one, he said, to labour bred,
  Was a match for fortune fairly, O!

Thus all obscure, unknown, and poor,
  Through life I 'm doom'd to wander, O!
Till down my weary bones I lay
  In everlasting slumber, O!
No view nor care, but shun whate'er
  Might breed me pain or sorrow, O!
I live to-day as well 's I may,
  Regardless of to-morrow, O!

But cheerful still, I am as well
  As a monarch in a palace, O!
Though fortune's frown still hunts me down,
  With all her wanton malice, O!
I make indeed my daily bread,
  But ne'er can make it farther, O!
But as daily bread is all I need,
  I do not much regard her, O!

When sometimes by my labour
  I earn a little money, O!
Some unforeseen misfortune
  Comes generally upon me, O!
Mischance, mistake, or by neglect,
  Or my good-natured folly, O!
But come what will, I 've sworn it still,
  I 'll ne'er be melancholy, O!

All you who follow wealth and power
  With unremitting ardour, O!
The more in this you look for bliss,
  You leave your view the farther, O!
Had you the wealth Potosi boasts,
  Or nations to adore you, O!
A cheerful, honest-hearted clown
  I will prefer before you, O!

IMPROMPTU—"I'LL GO AND BE A SODGER."*

Oh, why the deuce should I repine,
    And be an ill foreboder?
I'm twenty-three, and five feet nine—
    I'll go, and be a sodger!

I gat some gear wi' meikle care,
    I held it weel thegither;
But now it's gane, and something mair—
    I'll go and be a sodger!

JOHN BARLEYCORN.†

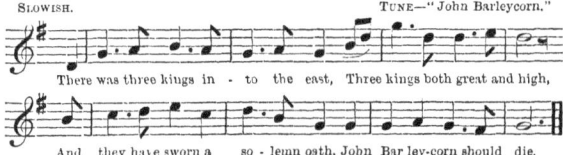

They took a plough and plough'd him down,
    Put clods upon his head;
And they hae sworn a solemn oath
    John Barleycorn was dead.

But the cheerful spring came kindly on,
    And showers began to fall;
John Barleycorn got up again,
    And sore surprised them all.

The sultry suns of summer came,
    And he grew thick and strong,
His head weel arm'd wi' pointed spears,
    That no one should him wrong.

The sober autumn enter'd mild,
    When he grew wan and pale;
His bending joints and drooping head
    Show'd he began to fail.

His colour sicken'd more and more,
    He faded into age;
And then his enemies began
    To show their deadly rage.

They've taen a weapon, long and sharp,
    And cut him by the knee;
Then tied him fast upon a cart,
    Like a rogue for forgerie.

They laid him down upon his back,
    And cudgell'd him full sore;
They hung him up before the storm,
    And turn'd him o'er and o'er.

They fill'd up a darksome pit
    With water to the brim;
They heaved in John Barleycorn,
    There let him sink or swim.

They laid him out upon the floor,
    To work him further woe;
And still, as signs of life appear'd,
    They toss'd him to and fro.

They wasted, o'er a scorching flame,
    The marrow of his bones;
But a miller used him worst of all,
    For he crush'd him between two stones.

And they hae ta'en his very heart's blood,
    And drank it round and round;
And still the more and more they drank,
    Their joy did more abound.

John Barleycorn was a hero bold,
    Of noble enterprise;
For if you do but taste his blood,
    'Twill make your courage rise.

'Twill make a man forget his woe;
    'Twill heighten all his joy;
'Twill make the widow's heart to sing,
    Though the tear were in her eye.

Then let us toast John Barleycorn,
    Each man a glass in hand;
And may his great posterity
    Ne'er fail in old Scotland!

POOR MAILIE,‡ AND ELEGY ON HER.

THE AUTHOR'S ONLY PET YOWE:
AN UNCO MOURNFU' TALE.

As Mailie and her lambs thegither
Were ae day nibbling on the tether,
Upon her cloot she coost a hitch,
And owre she warsled in the ditch:
There, groaning, dying, she did lie,
When Hughoc § he cam doytin' by.
Wi' glowrin' e'en, and lifted han's,
Poor Hughoc like a statue stan's;
He saw her days were near-hand ended,
But, waes my heart! he couldna mend it!
He gaped wide, but naething spak;
At length poor Mailie silence brak:
"O thou, whase lamentable face
Appears to mourn my woefu' case,

---

* Written at Lochlea, after being at Irvine in deep depression.
† "John Barleycorn:" this is partly composed on the plan of an old song known by the same name.—*B.* It will be found in Jamieson's Ballads, copied from black-letter in the Pepy's Library, Cambridge.

‡ Mailie, a pet yowe that got entangled in its tether.
§ "Hughoc:" a neighbour herd-callan, an odd, gapin, glowrin callant, about three-fourths wise.—(B). This took place at Lochlea.

My dying words attentive hear,
An' bear them to my master dear.

"Tell him, if e'er again he keep
As muckle gear as buy a sheep,
Oh, bid him never tie them mair
Wi' wicked strings o' hemp or hair!
But ca' them out to park or hill,
And let them wander at their will;
So may his flock increase, and grow
To scores o' lambs, an' packs o' woo'!

"Tell him, he was a master kin',
And aye was guid to me and mine;
And now my dying charge I gie him—
My helpless lambs I trust them wi' him.

"Oh, bid him save their harmless lives,
Frae dogs, an' tods, an' butcher's knives!
But gie them guid cow-milk their fill,
Till they be fit to fend themsel';
And tent them duly, e'en an' morn,
Wi' teats o' hay, an' ripps o' corn.

"And may they never learn the gaets
Of other vile, wanrestfu' pets!
To slink through slaps, and reave an' steal,
At stacks o' pease, or stocks o' kail.
So may they, like their great forbears,
For mony a year come through the sheers:
So wives will gie them bits o' bread,
An' bairns greet for them when they're dead.

"My poor toop-lamb, my son an' heir,
Oh, bid him breed him up wi' care!
And if he live to be a beast,
To pit some havins in his breast!
And warn him, what I winna name,
To stay content wi' yowes at hame;
And no to rin an' wear his cloots,
Like ither menseless, graceless brutes.

"And neist my yowie, silly thing,
Gude keep thee frae a tether string!
O! may thou ne'er forgather up
Wi' ony blastit moorland toop;
But aye keep mind to moop an' mell
Wi' sheep o' credit like thysel'!

"And now, my bairns, wi' my last breath,
I lea'e my blessin' wi' you baith:
And when you think upo' your mither,
Mind to be kin' to ane anither.

"Now, honest Hughoc, dinna fail
To tell my maister a' my tale;
And bid him burn this cursed tether,
And, for thy pains, thou'se get my blether."

This said, poor Mailie turn'd her head,
And closed her e'en amang the dead.

POOR MAILIE'S ELEGY.

Lament in rhyme, lament in prose,
Wi' saut tears trickling down your nose;
Our Bardie's fate is at a close,
  Past a' remead;
The last sad cap-stane o' his woes—
  Poor Mailie's dead!

It's no the loss o' warl's gear,
That could sae bitter draw the tear,
Or make our Bardie, dowie, wear
  The mourning weed:
He's lost a friend and neebour dear,
  In Mailie dead.

Through a' the toun she trotted by him;
A lang half-mile she could descry him;
Wi' kindly bleat, when she did spy him,
  She ran wi' speed:
A friend mair faithfu' ne'er cam nigh him
  Than Mailie dead.

I wat she was a sheep o' sense
And could behave hersel' wi' mense:
I'll say't, she never brak a fence,
  Through thievish greed.
Our Bardie, lanely, keeps the spence
  Sin' Mailie's dead.

Or, if he wanders up the howe,
Her living image in her yowe
Comes bleating to him, owre the knowe,
  For bits o' bread;
An' down the briny pearls rowe
  For Mailie dead.

She was nae get o' moorland tips,
Wi' tawted ket, an' hairy hips:
For her forbears were brought in ships
  Frae yont the Tweed:
A bonnier fleesh ne'er cross'd the clips
  Than Mailie dead.

Wae worth the man wha first did shape
That vile, wanchancie thing—a rape!
It maks guid fellows girn an' gape,
  Wi' chokin' dread;
And Robin's bonnet wave wi' crape,
  For Mailie dead.

O a' ye bards on bonny Doon!
An' wha on Ayr your chanters tune!
Come join the melancholious croon
  O' Robin's reed!
His heart will never get aboon
  His Mailie dead.

The following verse was deleted by the Poet:—

She was nae get o' runted rams,
Wi' woo like goats, and legs like trams:
She was the flower o' Fairlie* lambs—
  A famous breed;
Now Robin, greetin', chews the hams,
  O' Mailie dead.

* Fairlie, the first place where Burns' father got employment.

IT WAS UPON A LAMMAS NIGHT.

The sky was blue, the wind was still,
The moon was shining clearly;

* "Annie:" Anne Mary, youngest daughter of John Rankine, of Adamhill, near Lochlea; she became the keeper of a hostelry at Cumnock. Mrs. Mirry by name.

I set her down, wi' right good will,
  Amang the rigs o' barley;
I ken't her heart was a' my ain;
  I loved her most sincerely;
I kiss'd her owre and owre again,
  Amang the rigs o' barley.

I lock'd her in my fond embrace;
  Her heart was beating rarely:
My blessings on that happy place,
  Amang the rigs o' barley!
But by the moon and stars so bright,
  That shone that hour so clearly,
She aye shall bless that happy night,
  Amang the rigs o' barley!

I hae been blithe wi' comrades dear;
  I hae been merry drinkin';
I hae been joyfu' gath'rin' gear;
  I hae been happy thinkin':
But a' the pleasures e'er I saw,
  Though three times doubled fairly,
That happy night was worth them a',
  Amang the rigs o' barley.

MY NANNIE O!

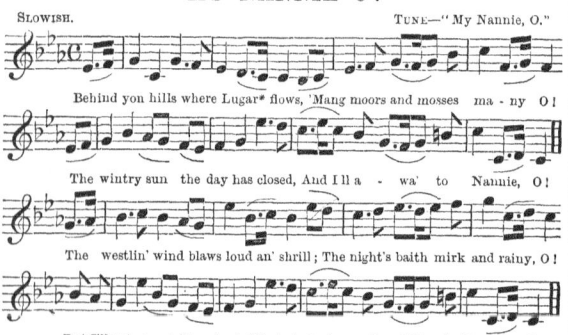

* "Lugar:" originally Stinchar. Stinchar has local verity in its favour. Lugar rises in Cumnock and reaches the Ayr at Barskimming. Nannie, according to Gilbert Burns, was Nannie Fleming, a farmer's daughter in Tarbolton.

My Nannie's charming, sweet, an' young;
  Nae artfu' wiles to win ye, O!
May ill befa' the flattering tongue
  That wad beguile my Nannie, O!
Her face is fair, her heart is true,
  As spotless as she's bonnie, O!
The opening gowan, wat wi' dew,
  Nae purer is than Nannie, O!

A country lad is my degree,
  And few there be that ken me, O!
But what care I how few they be?
  I'm welcome aye to Nannie, O!
My riches a's my penny-fee,
  And I maun guide it cannie, O!
But warl's gear ne'er troubles me,
  My thoughts are a'—my Nannie, O!

Our auld guidman delights to view
  His sheep an' kye thrive bonnie, O!
But I 'm as blithe that hauds his pleugh,
  And has nae care but Nannie, O!

Come weel, come woe, I care na by,
  I 'll tak what Heaven will sen' me, O!
Nae ither care in life have I,
  But live, an' love my Nannie, O!

GREEN GROW THE RASHES.*

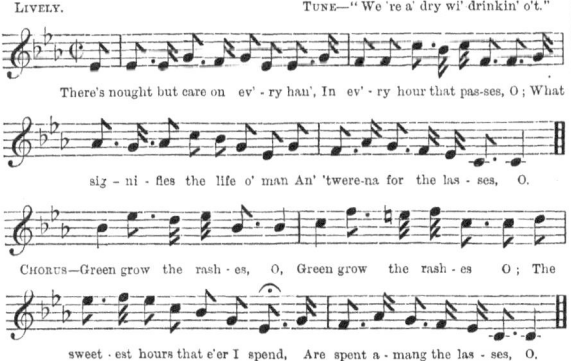

The warly race may riches chase,
  And riches still may fly them, O!

* This is an improvement on an old song.—(B.)

And though at last they catch them fast,
  Their hearts can ne'er enjoy them, O!
    Green grow, &c.

But gie me a canny hour at e'en,
  My arms about my dearie, O!
And warly cares, an' warly men,
  May a' gae tapsalteerie, O!
    Green grow, &c.

For you sae douse, ye sneer at this;
  Ye 're nought but senseless asses, O!
The wisest man the warl' e'er saw,
  He dearly loved the lasses, O!
    Green grow, &c.

Auld Nature swears, the lovely dears
  Her noblest work she classes, O!
Her 'prentice han' she tried on man,
  And then she made the lasses, O!
    Green grow, &c.

INDEED WILL I, QUO' FINDLAY.*

LIVELY.   TUNE—"Lass, an I come near thee."

Wha is that at my bower door? O wha is it but Findlay;
Then gae your gate, ye'se no be here! Indeed maun I, quo' Findlay.
What mak ye, sae like a thief? O come and see, quo' Findlay;
Before the morn ye'll work mischief; Indeed will I, quo' Findlay.

* Perhaps James Findlay, an officer of excise in Tarbolton, who trained Burns in that profession.

Gif I rise and let ye in
  (Let me in, quo' Findlay)
Ye 'll keep me waukin' wi' your din';
  (Indeed will I, quo' Findlay.)
In my bower if you should stay
  (Let me stay, quo' Findlay)
I fear ye 'll bide till break o' day;
  (Indeed will I, quo' Findlay.)

Here this night if ye remain
  (I 'll remain, quo' Findlay)
I dread ye 'll learn the gate again;
  (Indeed will I, quo' Findlay.)
What may pass within this bower
  (Let it pass, quo' Findlay)
Ye maun conceal till your last hour;
  (Indeed will I, quo' Findlay!)

REMORSE,* A FRAGMENT.

Of all the numerous ills that hurt our peace,
That press the soul, or wring the mind with anguish,
Beyond comparison the worst are those
That to our folly or our guilt we owe.
In every other circumstance, the mind
Has this to say—"It was no deed of mine!"
But when to all the evil of misfortune
This sting is added—"Blame thy foolish self!"
Or worser far, the pangs of keen remorse,
The torturing, gnawing consciousness of guilt—
Of guilt, perhaps, where we've involvèd others;
The young, the innocent, who fondly loved us,
Nay, more, that very love their cause of ruin!
O burning hell! in all thy store of torments
There's not a keener lash!
Lives there a man so firm, who, while his heart
Feels all the bitter horrors of his crime,
Can reason down its agonizing throbs;
And, after proper purpose of amendment,
Can firmly force his jarring thoughts to peace?
O happy, happy, enviable man!
O glorious magnanimity of soul!

EPITAPH ON JAMES GRIEVE, LAIRD OF BOGHEAD,† TARBOLTON.

Here lies Boghead amang the dead,
  In hopes to get salvation;
But if such as he in Heaven may be,
  Then welcome—hail! damnation.

EPITAPH ON WILLIAM HOOD.

Here souter Hood‡ in death does sleep:
  To hell if he's gane thither,
Satan, gie him thy gear to keep,
  He'll haud it weel thegither.

EPITAPH ON A FRIEND.§

An honest man here lies at rest,
As e'er God with his image blest;

The friend of man, the friend of truth,
The friend of age, and guide of youth:
Few hearts like his, with virtue warm'd,
Few heads with knowledge so inform'd.
If there's another world, he lives in bliss;
If there is none, he made the best of this.

EPITAPH FOR THE AUTHOR'S FATHER.

O ye whose cheek the tear of pity stains,
  Draw near with pious reverence and attend!
Here lie the loving husband's dear remains,
  The tender father, and the generous friend;

The pitying heart that felt for human woe;
  The dauntless heart that fear'd no human pride;
The friend of man, to vice alone a foe;
  "For even his failings lean'd to virtue's side." ‖

ON THE AMERICAN WAR. ¶

TUNE—"The Black Watch."

When Guildford good our pilot stood, An' did our helm thraw, man, Ae night, at tea, began a plea, Within America, man; Then up they gat the maskin' pat, And in the sea did jaw, man; An' did nae less, in full Congress, Than quite refuse our law, man.

Then through the lakes Montgomery takes,
  I wat he was na slaw, man:
Down Lowrie's burn he took a turn,
  And Carleton did ca', man:
But yet, what reck, he at Quebec,
  Montgomery-like, did fa', man,
Wi' sword in hand, before his band,
  Amang his enemies a', man.

---

* From the Poet's Commonplace Book.
† Boghead lies a mile due west from Lochlea, near Adamhill.
‡ A Tarbolton elder, very penurious.
§ William Muir of Tarbolton Mill (of "Willie's Mill").

‖ "Virtue's side:" Goldsmith.
¶ Burns' politics always smell of the smithy, said Dr. Blair. True enough, but in the smithy there is often found the news of the country in a fiery essence.

Poor Tammy Gage within a cage
  Was kept at Boston Ha', man;
Till Willie Howe took o'er the knowe
  For Philadelphia, man:
Wi' sword an' gun he thought a sin
  Guid Christian blood to draw, man;
But at New York, wi' knife an' fork,
  Sir-loin he hackèd sma', man.

Burgoyne gaed up, like spur an' whip
  Till Fraser brave did fa', man;
Then lost his way, ae misty day,
  In Saratoga shaw, man.
Cornwallis fought as lang 's he dought,
  And did the buckskins claw, man;
But Clinton's glaive frae rust to save,
  He hung it to the wa', man.

Then Montague, an' Guildford too,
  Began to fear a fa', man;
And Sackville dour, wha stood the stoure,
  The German Chief to thraw, man:
For Paddy Burke, like ony Turk,
  Nae mercy had at a', man;
And Charlie Fox threw by the box,
  And lowsed his tinkler jaw, man.

Then Rockingham took up the game;
  Till death did on him ca', man;
When Shelburne meek held up his cheek,
  Conform to gospel law, man.
Saint Stephen's boys, wi' jarring noise,
  They did his measures thraw, man,
For North an' Fox united stocks,
  And bore him to the wa', man.

Then clubs and hearts were Charlie's cartes,
    He swept the stakes awa', man,
Till the diamond's ace, of Indian race,
    Led him a sair *faux pas*, man:
The Saxon lads, wi' loud placads,
    On Chatham's boy did ca', man;
An' Scotland drew her pipe, an' blew
    "Up, Willie, waur them a', man!"

Behind the throne then Grenville's gone,
    A secret word or twa, man;
While slee Dundas aroused the class
    Be-north the Roman wa', man:
And Chatham's wraith, in heavenly graith,
    (Inspirèd bardies saw, man)
Wi' kindling eyes cried, "Willie, rise!
    Would I hae fear'd them a', man?"

But, word an' blow, North, Fox, and Co.,
    Gowff'd Willie like a ba', man,
Till Southron raise, and coost their claise
    Behind him in a raw, man;
And Caledon threw by the drone,
    And did her whittle draw, man;
And swore fu' rude, through dirt an' blood,
    To mak it guid in law, man.

EPISTLE TO J. RANKINE, ENCLOSING SOME POEMS.*

O ROUGH, rude, ready-witted Rankine,
The wale o' cocks for fun and drinkin'!
There's mony godly folks are thinkin',
    Your dreams † an' tricks
Will send you, Korah-like, a-sinkin',
    Straught to Auld Nick's.

Ye hae sae mony cracks and cants,
And in your wicked, drucken rants,
Ye mak a devil o' the saunts,
    And fill them fu':
And then their failings, flaws, an' wants,
    Are a' seen through.

Hypocrisy, in mercy spare it!
That holy robe, O dinna tear it!
Spare 't for their sakes wha aften wear it,
    The lads in black!
But your curst wit, when it comes near it,
    Rives 't aff their back.

Think, wicked sinner, wha ye're skaithing:
It's just the blue-gown ‡ badge and claithing
O' saunts; tak that, ye lea'e them naething
    To ken them by,
Frae ony unregenerate heathen
    Like you or I.

I've sent you here some rhyming ware,
A' that I bargain'd for, and mair;
Sae, when ye hae an hour to spare,
    I will expect
Yon sang,§ ye'll sen't wi' cannie care,
    And no neglect.

Though, faith, sma' heart hae I to sing!
My Muse dow scarcely spread her wing;
I've play'd mysel' a bonnie spring,
    And danced my fill!
I'd better gaen an' sair'd the king
    At Bunker's Hill.

'Twas ae night lately, in my fun,
I gaed a roving wi' the gun,
And brought a paitrick to the grun',
    A bonnie hen;
And, as the twilight was begun,
    Thought nane wad ken.

The poor wee thing was little hurt;
I straikit it a wee for sport,
Ne'er thinkin' they wad fash me for 't;
    But, deil-ma-care!
Somebody tells the poacher-court
    The hale affair.

Some auld-used hands had ta'en a note,
That sic a hen had got a shot;
I was suspected for the plot;
    I scorn'd to lie;
So gat the whissle o' my groat,
    An' pay't the fee.

But, by my gun, o' guns the wale,
And by my pouther an' my hail,
And by my hen, and by her tail,
    I vow an' swear!
The game shall pay o'er moor an' dale,
    For this, neist year.

As soon 's the clockin'-time is by,
And the wee pouts begun to cry,
L—d, I 'se hae sportin' by an' by
    For my gowd guinea:
Though I should herd the buckskin kye
    For 't, in Virginia.

---

* See LIFE.

† "Dreams:" a certain humorous *dream* of his was then making a noise in the countryside.—(B.) Rankine was a farmer in Adamhill, near Lochlea, a boon companion of Burns. He once, by filling a kettle with spirits instead of hot water, made a great professor of religion very drunk.

‡ "Blue-gown:" see "The Antiquary."

§ "Yon sang:" a song he had promised to the author.—(B.)

Trowth, they had muckle for to blame!
'Twas neither broken wing nor limb,
But twa-three draps about the wame
    Scarce through the feathers;
And baith a yellow George to claim,
    And thole their blethers!

It pits me aye as mad 's a hare;
So I can rhyme nor write nae mair;
But pennyworths again is fair,
    When time 's expedient;
Meanwhile I am, respected Sir,
    Your most obedient.

REPLY TO JOHN RANKINE,*

ON HIS WRITING TO THE POET THAT A GIRL IN THAT PART OF THE COUNTRY WAS WITH CHILD BY HIM.

I AM a keeper of the law
In some sma' points, although not a';
Some people tell me gin I fa',
    Ae way or ither,
The breaking of ae point, though sma',
    Breaks a' thegither.

I hae been in for't ance or twice,
And winna say o'er far for thrice,
Yet never met with that surprise
    That broke my rest;
But now a rumour 's like to rise—
    A whaup 's i' the nest.

A POET'S WELCOME TO HIS ILLEGITIMATE CHILD.†

THOU 's welcome, wean! mishanter fa' me,
If ought of thee, or of thy mammy,
Shall ever danton me, or awe me,
    My sweet wee lady,
Or if I blush when thou shalt ca' me
    Tit-ta, or daddy.

* See LIFE.
† The subject of these verses was the poet's illegitimate daughter, whom in "The Inventory" he styles his

    "Sonsy, smirking, dear-bought Bess."

She was married to Mr. John Bishop, overseer at Polkemmet, near Whitburn, and is long dead.—See LIFE.

Wee image of my bonnie Betty,
As fatherly I kiss and daut thee,
As dear and near my heart I set thee
    Wi' as gude will,
As a' the priests had seen me get thee
    That 's out o' hell.

What though they ca' me fornicator,
And tease my name in kintra clatter:
The mair they talk I'm kent the better,
    E'en let them clash;
An auld wife's tongue 's a feckless matter
    To gie ane fash.

Sweet fruit o' mony a merry dint,
My funny toil is now a' tint,
Sin' thou cam to the warl' asklent,
    Which fools may scoff at;
In my last plack thy part 's be in 't—
    The better half o 't.

And if thou be what I would hae thee,
And tak the counsel I shall gie thee,
A lovin' father I 'll be to thee,
    If thou be spared:
Through a' thy childish years I 'll e'e thee,
    And think 't weel wared.

Gude grant that thou may aye inherit
Thy mither's person, grace, and merit,
And thy poor worthless daddy's spirit,
    Without his failins;
'Twill please me mair to hear and see it,
    Than stockit mailins.

O, LEAVE NOVELS, YE MAUCHLINE BELLES.

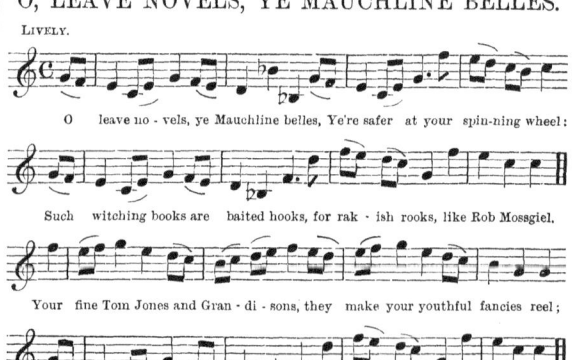

O leave no-vels, ye Mauchline belles, Ye're safer at your spin-ning wheel:
Such witching books are baited hooks, for rak-ish rooks, like Rob Mossgiel.
Your fine Tom Jones and Gran-di-sons, they make your youthful fancies reel;
They heat your brains and fire your veins, And then you're prey for Rob Mossgiel.

Beware a tongue that 's smoothly hung,
  A heart that warmly seems to feel;
That feeling heart but acts a part—
  'Tis rakish art in Rob Mossgiel.
The frank address, the soft caress,
  Are worse than poison'd darts of steel;
The frank address and politesse
  Are all finesse in Rob Mossgiel.

WHEN FIRST I CAME TO STEWART KYLE.*

VERY SLOW.   TUNE—"I had a Horse, and I had nae mair."

When first I came to Stewart Kyle, My mind it was nae steady;
Where'er I gaed, where'er I rade, A mistress still I had aye;
But when I came roun' by Mauchline town, Not dreading a-ny bo-dy,
My heart was caught be-fore I thought, And by a Mauchline la-dy.†

MY GIRL SHE'S AIRY, SHE'S BUXOM AND GAY.

My girl she's airy, she's buxom and gay;
  Her breath is as sweet as the blossoms in May;
  A touch of her lips it ravishes quite:
She's always good natur'd, good humor'd, and free;
  She dances, she glances, she smiles upon me;
  I never am happy when out of her sight.

Her slender neck, her handsome waist,
  Her hair well curled, her stays well lac'd,
  Her taper white leg with . . . .
  For her . . . .
  And O for the joys of a long winter night.

---

* Stewart Kyle—the district between the rivers Irvine and Ayr. Burns originally belonged to King's Kyle, between the Ayr and the Doon.

† Mauchline "lady"—Jean Armour.

IN MAUCHLINE THERE DWELLS.

SLOW.   TUNE—"Adieu Dundee."

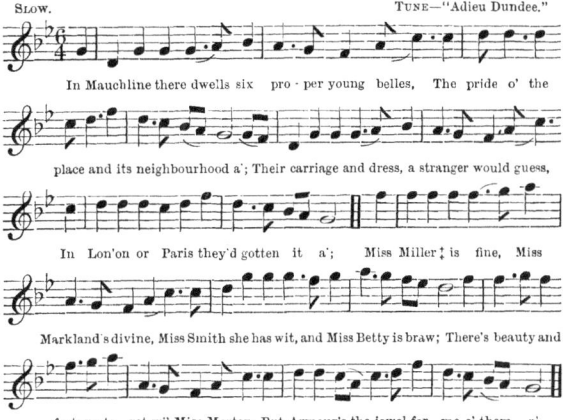

In Mauchline there dwells six pro-per young belles, The pride o' the place and its neighbourhood a'; Their carriage and dress, a stranger would guess, In Lon'on or Paris they'd gotten it a'; Miss Miller‡ is fine, Miss Markland's divine, Miss Smith she has wit, and Miss Betty is braw; There's beauty and fortune to get wi' Miss Morton, But Armour's the jewel for me o' them a'.

EPITAPH ON A NOISY POLEMIC.

BELOW thir stanes lie Jamie's§ banes:
  O Death, it 's my opinion,
Thou ne'er took such a bleth'rin bitch
  Into thy dark dominion!

ON A HENPECKED COUNTRY SQUIRE.‖

As father Adam first was fool'd
  (A case that 's still too common),
Here lies a man a woman ruled—
  The devil ruled the woman.

ON THE SAME.

O DEATH, hadst thou but spared his life,
  Whom we this day lament!
We freely wad exchanged the wife,
  And a' been weel content.

---

‡ "Miss Miller:" married Dr. Mackenzie, a friend of Burns; Miss Markland, Mr. Findlay, a gauger in Greenock; Miss Betty (Miller), sister of the former Miss Miller, became Mrs. Templeton; Miss Morton, Mrs. Paterson of Mauchline; Miss Smith married Mr. Candlish, and became the mother of the celebrated Dr. Candlish, and died in 1874.

§ "Jamie:" Humphrey, a west country mason, fond of controversy. He died in 1844, at the age of 86, an inmate of Faile poor-house.

‖ Campbell of Netherplace, between Mauchline and Mossgiel.

Even as he is, cauld in his graff,
  The swap we yet will do 't;
Tak thou the carlin's carcase aff,
  Thou 'se get the saul o' boot.

ONE QUEEN ARTEMISA.

One Queen Artemisa, as old stories tell,
When deprived of her husband she lovèd so well,
In respect for the love and affection he 'd show'd her,
She reduced him to dust, and she drank off the powder.

But Queen Netherplace, of a different complexion,
When call'd on to order the funeral direction,
Would have eat her dead lord, on a slender pretence,
Not to show her respect, but—to save the expense.

ON TAM THE CHAPMAN.*

As Tam the Chapman, on a day,
Wi' Death forgather'd by the way,
Weel pleased, he greets a wight sae famous,
And Death was nae less pleased wi' Thomas,
Wha cheerfully lays down the pack,
And there blaws up a hearty crack:
His social, friendly, honest heart
Sae tickled Death, they could na part:
Sae, after viewing knives and garters,
Death takes him hame to gi'e him quarters.

VERSES TO J. RANKINE.†

Ae day, as Death, that gruesome carle,
Was driving to the tither warl'
A mixtie-maxtie motley squad,
And mony a guilt bespotted lad;
Black gowns of each denomination,
And thieves of every rank and station,
From him that wears the star and garter,
To him that wintles in a halter:
Ashamed himsel' to see the wretches,
He mutters, glow'rin' at the bitches,
" By G—d, I'll not be seen behint them,
Nor 'mang the sp'ritual core present them,
Without at least ae honest man
To grace this damned infernal clan."
By Adamhill a glance he threw,
" L—d G—d!" quoth he, "I have it now:
There's just the man I want, i' faith,"
And quickly stoppit Rankine's breath.

LINES WRITTEN BY BURNS ON HIS OWN SUPPOSED DEATH, AND ADDRESSED TO RANKINE.

He who of Rankine sang lies stiff and dead,
And a green grassy hillock hides his head;
Alas! alas! an awful change indeed!

MAN WAS MADE TO MOURN: ‡

A DIRGE.

" Young stranger, whither wanderest thou?"
  Began the reverend sage;
" Does thirst of wealth thy step constrain,
  Or youthful pleasure's rage?
Or haply, press'd with cares and woes,
  Too soon thou hast began
To wander forth, with me, to mourn
  The miseries of man!

---

* "Tam the Chapman:" one Kennedy of Ayr, who had recovered from an illness, and met the poet. Communicated by William Cobbett, who met Tam in London, and published the lines in his Register. Tam became a commercial traveller, and died in London.

† 'J. Rankine:" the person to whom a former epistle was addressed, while Rankine occupied the farm of Adamhill, in Ayrshire.

‡ Partly imitated from an old ballad, "The Life and Age of Man." This was the song Burns' old grand-uncle used to like to listen to and weep at, from his mother's lips. This poem of Burns' was a special favourite of De Quincey. It was written in November, 1784, to the fine old tune of "Peggy Bawn."

"The sun that overhangs yon moors,
  Out-spreading far and wide,
Where hundreds labour to support
  A haughty lordling's pride—
I 've seen yon weary winter-sun
  Twice forty times return;
And every time has added proofs
  That man was made to mourn.

"O man! while in thy early years,
  How prodigal of time!
Mis-spending all thy precious hours,
  Thy glorious, youthful prime!
Alternate follies take the sway;
  Licentious passions burn;
Which tenfold force gives Nature's law,
  That man was made to mourn.

"Look not alone on youthful prime,
  Or manhood's active might;
Man then is useful to his kind,
  Supported is his right:

"But see him on the edge of life,
  With cares and sorrows worn,
Then Age and Want—oh! ill-match'd pair!—
  Show man was made to mourn.

"A few seem favourites of fate,
  In pleasure's lap caress'd;
Yet, think not all the rich and great
  Are likewise truly blest.
But, oh! what crowds in every land,
  All wretched and forlorn,
Through weary life this lesson learn—
  That man was made to mourn.

"Many and sharp the numerous ills
  Inwoven with our frame!
More pointed still we make ourselves,
  Regret, remorse, and shame!
And man, whose heaven-erected face
  The smiles of love adorn—
Man's inhumanity to man
  Makes countless thousands mourn!

"See yonder poor, o'erlabour'd wight,
   So abject, mean, and vile,
Who begs a brother of the earth
   To give him leave to toil;
And see his lordly fellow-worm
   The poor petition spurn,
Unmindful, though a weeping wife
   And helpless offspring mourn.

"If I 'm design'd yon lordling's slave—
   By Nature's law design'd—
Why was an independent wish
   E'er planted in my mind?
If not, why am I subject to
   His cruelty or scorn?
Or why has man the will and power
   To make his fellow mourn?

"Yet, let not this too much, my son,
   Disturb thy youthful breast:
This partial view of human-kind
   Is surely not the last!
The poor, oppressèd, honest man,
   Had never, sure, been born,
Had there not been some recompense
   To comfort those that mourn!

"O Death! the poor man's dearest friend—
   The kindest and the best!
Welcome the hour my aged limbs
   Are laid with thee at rest!
The great, the wealthy, fear thy blow,
   From pomp and pleasure torn;
But, oh! a blest relief to those
   That weary-laden mourn!"

THE HOLY TULZIE, OR TWA HERDS.*

O a' ye pious godly flocks,
Weel fed on pastures orthodox,
Wha now will keep you frae the fox,
   Or worrying tykes?
Or wha will tent the waifs and crocks,
   About the dykes?

The twa best herds in a' the wast,
That e'er gae gospel horn a blast,
These five-and-twenty simmers past,
   Oh! dool to tell,
Hae had a bitter black outcast
   Atween themsel'.

O, Moody, man, and wordy Russell,
How could you raise so vile a bustle?
Ye'll see how New-Light herds will whistle,
   And think it fine!
The Lord's cause ne'er gat sic a twistle,
   Sin' I hae min'.

O, sirs! wha e'er wad hae expeckit,
Your duty ye wad sae negleckit,
Ye wha were ne'er by lairds respeckit
   To wear the plaid,
But by the brutes themselves eleckit,
   To be their guide.

What flock wi' Moody's flock could rank,
Sae hale and hearty every shank!
Nae poison'd sour Arminian stank
   He let them taste;
Frae Calvin's well aye clear they drank—
   O sic a feast!

The thummart, wil'-cat, brock, and tod,
Weel kenn'd his voice through a' the wood,
He smelt their ilka hole and road,
   Baith out and in;
And weel he lik'd to shed their bluid,
   And sell their skin.

What herd like Russell tell'd his tale?
His voice was heard through muir and dale,
He kenn'd the L—d's sheep, ilka tail,
   O'er a' the height,
And saw gin they were sick or hale,
   At the first sight.

He fine a mangy sheep could scrub,
Or nobly fling the gospel club,
And New-Light herds could nicely drub,
   Or pay their skin;
Could shake them o'er the burning dub,
   Or heave them in.

Sic twa—oh! do I live to see 't!—
Sic famous twa should disagree 't,
And names like "villain," "hypocrite,"
   Ilk ither gi'en,
While New-Light herds, wi' laughin' spite,
   Say neither's lien'!

A' ye wha tent the gospel fauld,
There 's Duncan † deep, and Peebles ‡ shaul,
But chiefly thou, apostle Auld, §
   We trust in thee,
That thou wilt work them, hot and cauld,
   Till they agree.

---

* "Twa Herds:" the two herds or pastors were Mr. Moody, minister of Riccartoun, and that favourite victim of Burns, John Russell, then minister at Kilmarnock, and afterwards of Stirling — See HOLY FAIR. This was the first of Burns' productions that saw the light; it was founded on a dispute—subject uncertain—between the two divines.—See LIFE.

† Minister of Dundonald.   § Minister of Newton-on-Ayr.
‡ Minister of Mauchline.

Consider, sirs, how we 're beset;
There 's scarce a new herd that we get,
But comes frae 'mang that cursed set
    I winna name;
I hope frae heaven to see them yet
        In fiery flame!

Dalrymple* has been lang our fae,
M'Gill † has wrought us meikle wae,
And that curs'd rascal ca'd M'Quhae,‡
    And baith the Shaws,§
That aft hae made us black and blae,
    Wi' vengefu' paws.

Auld Wodrow ‖ lang has hatch'd mischief;
We thought aye death would bring relief,
But he has gotten, to our grief,
    Ane to succeed him,
A chiel wha 'll soundly buff our beef;
    I meikle dread him. ¶

And mony a ane that I could tell,
Wha fain would openly rebel,
Forby turn-coats amang oursel';
    There 's Smith ** for ane,
I doubt he 's but a gray-nick quill,
    And that ye 'll fin'.

O! a' ye flocks o'er a' the hills,
By mosses, meadows, moors, and fells,
Come, join your counsel and your skills
    To cowe the lairds,
And get the brutes the power themsel's
    To choose their herds.

Then Orthodoxy yet may prance,
And Learning in a woodie dance,
And that fell cur ca'd Common Sense,
    That bites sae sair,
Be banish'd o'er the sea to France:
    Let him bark there.

Then Shaw's and D'rymple's eloquence,
M'Gill's close nervous excellence,
M'Quhae's pathetic manly sense,
    And guid M'Math,
Wi' Smith, wha through the heart can glance,
    May a' pack aff.

---

* Minister of Ayr, who baptized Burns.
† Minister of Ayr.   ‡ Minister of St. Quivox.
§ Ministers of Craigie and Coylton.   ‖ Minister of Tarbolton.
¶ "Dread him:" alluding to the Rev. Mr. M'Math, mentioned above.
** One of the preachers at the Holy Fair.

EPISTLE TO DAVIE, A BROTHER POET.††

While winds frae aff Ben-Lomond blaw,
And bar the doors wi' driving snaw,
    And hing us owre the ingle,
I set me down to pass the time,
And spin a verse or twa o' rhyme,
    In hamely westlin' jingle.
While frosty winds blaw in the drift,
    Ben to the chimla lug,
I grudge a wee the great folks' gift,
    That live sae bien an' snug:
      I tent less, and want less,
        Their roomy fireside;
      But hanker and canker
        To see their cursed pride.

It 's hardly in a body's power
To keep, at times, frae being sour,
    To see how things are shared;
How best o' chiels are whiles in want,
While coofs on countless thousands rant,
    And ken na how to ware 't:
But, Davie, lad, ne'er fash your head,
    Though we hae little gear;
We 're fit to win our daily bread,
    As lang 's we 're hale and fier.
      "Mair spier na, nor fear na," ‡‡
        Auld age ne'er mind a feg,
      The last o 't, the warst o 't,
        Is only for to beg.

To lie in kilns and barns at e'en,
When banes are crazed and bluid is thin,
    Is, doubtless, great distress!
Yet then content could make us blest;
Even then, sometimes, we 'd snatch a taste
    Of truest happiness.
The honest heart that 's free frae a'
    Intended fraud or guile,
However Fortune kick the ba',
    Has aye some cause to smile:
      And mind still, you 'll find still,
        A comfort this nae sma';
      Nae mair then, we 'll care then,
        Nae farther we can fa'.

What though, like commoners of air,
We wander out, we know not where,
    But either house or hall?

---

†† "Brother poet:" David Sillar, one of the club at Tarbolton, and author of a volume of poems in the Scottish dialect. The original address was to "Davy, a brither-poet, lover, ploughman, and fiddler." He was the son of a small farmer at Tarbolton; became poet, grocer, schoolmaster, and magistrate at Irvine.
‡‡ "Fear na:" Ramsay.—(B.)

Yet nature's charms, the hills and woods,
The sweeping vales, and foaming floods,
  Are free alike to all.
In days when daisies deck the ground,
  And blackbirds whistle clear,
With honest joy our hearts will bound,
  To see the coming year:
    On braes when we please, then
      We 'll sit an' sowth a tune;
    Syne rhyme till 't, we 'll time till 't,
      And sing 't when we hae dune.

It 's no in titles nor in rank,
It 's no in wealth like Lon'on bank,
  To purchase peace and rest;
It 's no in making muckle mair,
It 's no in books, it 's no in lear,
  To make us truly blest:
If happiness hae not her seat
  And centre in the breast,
We may be wise, or rich, or great,
  But never can be blest:
    Nae treasures, nor pleasures,
      Could make us happy lang;
    The heart aye 's the part aye
      That makes us right or wrang.

Think ye, that sic as you and I,
Wha drudge and drive through wet an' dry,
  Wi' never-ceasing toil;
Think ye, are we less blest than they,
Wha scarcely tent us in their way,
  As hardly worth their while?
Alas! how aft in haughty mood,
  God's creatures they oppress!
Or else, neglecting a' that 's guid,
  They riot in excess!
    Baith careless and fearless
      Of either heaven or hell;
    Esteeming and deeming
      It 's a' an idle tale!

Then let us cheerfu' acquiesce,
Nor make our scanty pleasures less
  By pining at our state;
And, even should misfortunes come,
I, here wha sit, hae met wi' some,
  An 's thankfu' for them yet:
They gie the wit of age to youth;
  They let us ken oursel';
They make us see the naked truth,
  The real guid and ill.
    Though losses and crosses
      Be lessons right severe,
    There 's wit there, ye 'll get there,
      Ye 'll find nae other where.

But tent me, Davie, ace o' hearts!
(To say aught less wad wrang the cartes,
  And flattery I detest)
This life has joys for you and I;
And joys that riches ne'er could buy,
  And joys the very best.
There 's a' the pleasures o' the heart,
  The lover an' the frien';
Ye hae your Meg,* your dearest part
  And I my darling Jean!
    It warms me, it charms me,
      To mention but her name:
    It heats me, it beets me,
      And sets me a' on flame?

O all ye Powers who rule above!
O Thou, whose very self art Love!
  Thou know'st my words sincere!
The life-blood streaming through my heart,
Or my more dear immortal part,
  Is not more fondly dear!
When heart-corroding care and grief
  Deprive my soul of rest,
Her dear idea brings relief
  And solace to my breast.
    Thou Being, All-seeing,
      O hear my fervent prayer;
    Still take her, and make her
      Thy most peculiar care!

All hail, ye tender feelings dear!
The smile of love, the friendly tear,
  The sympathetic glow!
Long since, this world's thorny ways
Had number'd out my weary days,
  Had it not been for you!
Fate still has blest me with a friend,
  In every care and ill;
And oft a more endearing band,
  A tie more tender still.
    It lightens, it brightens,
      The tenebrific scene,
    To meet with, and greet with,
      My Davie or my Jean!

Oh, how that name inspires my style!
The words come skelpin', rank and file,
  Amaist before I ken!
The ready measure rins as fine,
As Phœbus and the famous Nine
  Were glowrin' owre my pen.
My spaviet Pegasus will limp,
  Till ance he 's fairly het;
And then he 'll hilch, and stilt, and jump,
  An' rin an unco fit:

---

* "Meg:" Margaret Orr, a servant of Mrs. Stewart of Stair. She did *not* marry Davie.

But lest then the beast then
Should rue this hasty ride,
I 'll light now, and dight now
His sweaty wizen'd hide.

HOLY WILLIE'S PRAYER.*

O THOU, wha in the heavens dost dwell,
Wha, as it pleases best thysel',
Sends ane to heaven, and ten to hell,
    A' for thy glory,
And no for ony guid or ill
    They've done afore thee!

I bless and praise thy matchless might,
Whan thousands thou hast left in night,
That I am here afore thy sight,
    For gifts and grace,
A burnin' and a shinin' light
    To a' this place.

What was I, or my generation,
That I should get sic exaltation,
I wha deserve sic just damnation
    For broken laws,
Five thousand years 'fore my creation,
    Through Adam's cause!

When frae my mither's womb I fell,
Thou might hae plungèd me in hell,
To gnash my gums, to weep and wail,
    In burnin' lake,
Whare damnèd devils roar and yell,
    Chain'd to a stake.

Yet I am here, a chosen sample,
To show thy grace is great and ample;
I'm here a pillar in thy temple,
    Strong as a rock,
A guide, a buckler, and example,
    To a' thy flock.

O L—d! thou kens what zeal I bear,
When drinkers drink, and swearers swear,
And singin' there, and dancin' here,
    Wi' great an' sma';
For I am keepit by thy fear
    Free frae them a'.

* "Holy Willie:" William Fisher, a hypocritical elder in Mauchline.—See LIFE.

But yet, O L—d! confess I must,
At times I'm fash'd wi' fleshly lust;
And sometimes, too, wi' warldly trust
    Vile self gets in:
But thou remembers we are dust,
    Defiled in sin.

O L—d! yestreen, thou kens, wi' Meg—
Thy pardon I sincerely beg,
Oh! may 't ne'er be a livin' plague,
    To my dishonour,
And I 'll ne'er lift a lawless leg
    Again upon her.

Besides, I farther maun avow,
Wi' Leezie's lass, three times I trow;
But, L—d! that Friday I was fou,
    When I cam near her,
Or else, thou kens, thy servant true
    Wad ne'er hae steer'd her.

Maybe thou lets this fleshly thorn
Beset thy servant e'en and morn,
Lest he owre high and proud should turn,
    'Cause he's sae gifted;
If sae, thy han' maun e'en be borne,
    Until thou lift it.

L—d, bless thy chosen in this place,
For here thou hast a chosen race;
But G—d confound their stubborn face,
    And blast their name,
Wha bring thy elders to disgrace
    And public shame.

L—d! mind Gaw'n Hamilton's deserts;
He drinks, and swears, and plays at cartes,
Yet has sae mony takin' arts,
    Wi' grit and sma',
Frae G—d's ain priests the people's hearts
    He steals awa'.

And when we chasten'd him therefor,
Thou kens how he bred sic a splore,
As set the warld in a roar
    O' laughin' at us:
Curse thou his basket and his store,
    Kail and potatoes.

L—d, hear my earnest cry and prayer,
Against that Presbyt'ry of Ayr;
Thy strong right hand, L—d, make it bare,
    Upo' their heads,
L—d, weigh it down, and dinna spare,
    For their misdeeds.

O L—d my G—d! that glib-tongued Aiken,
My very heart and saul are quakin',
To think how I sat sweatin', shakin',
    And p—d wi' dread,
While he, wi' hingin' lip an' snakin',
    Held up his head.

L—d, in the day of vengeance try him,
L—d, visit them wha did employ him,
And pass not in thy mercy by 'em,
    Nor hear their prayer;
But for thy people's sake destroy 'em,
    And dinna spare.

But, L—d, remember me and mine
Wi' mercies temporal and divine,
That I for gear and grace may shine,
    Excell'd by nane,
And a' the glory shall be thine,
    Amen! Amen!

EPITAPH ON HOLY WILLIE.

Here Holy Willie's sair-worn clay
    Taks up its last abode;
His saul has ta'en some other way,
    I fear, the left-hand road.

Stop! there he is, as sure 's a gun,
    Poor silly body, see him;
Nae wonder he's as black's the grun'
    Observe wha's standing wi' him.

Your brunstane devilship, I see,
    Has got him there before ye;
But haud your nine-tail cat a wee,
    Till ance ye've heard my story.

Your pity I will not implore,
    For pity ye hae nane!
Justice, alas! has gi'en him o'er,
    And Mercy's day is gane.

But hear me, sir, deil as ye are,
    Look something to your credit;
A coof like him would stain your name,
    If it were kent ye did it.

DEATH AND DOCTOR HORNBOOK:

A TRUE STORY.

Some books are lies frae end to end,
And some great lies were never penn'd:
Ev'n ministers, they hae been kenn'd,
    In holy rapture,
A rousing whid * at times to vend,
    And nail't wi' Scripture.

But this that I am gaun to tell,
Which lately on a night befell,
Is just as true 's the deil 's in hell,
    Or Dublin city:
That e'er he nearer comes oursel'
    'S a muckle pity.

The clachan yill had made me canty:
I was na fou, but just had plenty;
I stacher'd whyles, but yet took tent aye
    To free the ditches;
An' hillocks, stanes, and bushes kenn'd aye
    Frae ghaists an' witches.

The rising moon began to glowre
The distant Cumnock hills outowre:
To count her horns, wi' a' my power,
    I set mysel';
But whether she had three or four,
    I could na tell.

I was come round about the hill,
And todlin' down on Willie's mill,†
Setting my staff wi' a' my skill,
    To keep me sicker;
Though leeward whyles, against my will,
    I took a bicker.

I there wi' Something did forgather,
That pat me in an eerie swither;
An awfu' scythe, outowre ae shouther,
    Clear-dangling, hang;
A three-taed leister on the ither
    Lay, large an' lang.

Its stature seem'd lang Scotch ells twa,
The queerest shape that e'er I saw,
For fient a wame it had ava;
    And then its shanks,
They were as thin, an' sharp, an' sma',
    As cheeks o' branks.

---

* "A rousin whid:" in Second Edition—
    "Great lies and nonsense baith to vend."

† "Willie's mill:" a mill near Mauchline, on the river Faile, occupied by William Muir, a crony of Burns, and whose name appears as a subscriber to the Edinburgh edition of Burns' works.

DEATH AND DOCTOR HORNBOOK

"Guid-e'en'," quo' I; "Friend, hae ye been mawin',
When ither folk are busy sawin'?"*
It seem'd to mak a kind o' stan',
　　　But naething spak;
At length, says I, "Friend, whare ye gaun?—
　　　Will ye go back?"

It spak right howe—"My name is Death,
But be na fley'd." Quoth I, "Guid faith,
Ye 're maybe come to stap my breath;
　　　But tent me, billie—
I red ye weel, tak care o' skaith,
　　　See, there 's a gullie!"

"Guidman," quo' he, "put up your whittle,
I 'm no design'd to try its mettle;
But if I did, I wad be kittle
　　　To be mislear'd,

I wad na mind it, no that spittle
　　　Outowre my beard."

"Weel, weel," says I, "a bargain be 't;
Come, gie 's your hand, an' sae we 're gree 't;
We 'll ease our shanks an' tak a seat—
　　　Come, gie 's your news;
This while † ye hae been mony a gate,
　　　At mony a house."

"Ay, ay!" quo' he, an' shook his head,
"It 's e'en a lang, lang time indeed
Sin' I began to nick the thread,
　　　An' choke the breath:
Folk maun do something for their bread,
　　　An' sae maun Death.

* "Busy sawin':" this rencounter happened in seed-time, 1785.—(B.)

† "This while:" an epidemical fever was then raging in that country.—(B.)

"Sax thousand years are near-hand fled,
Sin' I was to the butching bred,
An' mony a scheme in vain 's been laid,
  To stap or scaur me;
Till ane Hornbook * 's ta'en up the trade,
  An' faith! he 'll waur me.

"Ye ken Jock Hornbook † i' the clachan,
Deil mak his king's-hood in a spleuchan!
He 's grown sae weel acquant wi' Buchan ‡
  An' ither chaps,
The weans haud out their fingers laughin'
  And pouk my hips.

"See, here 's a scythe, and there 's a dart,
They hae pierced mony a gallant heart;
But Doctor Hornbook, wi' his art
  And cursed skill,
Has made them baith no worth a f—t;
  Damn'd haet they 'll kill.

"'Twas but yestreen, nae farther gaen,
I threw a noble throw at ane;
Wi' less, I 'm sure, I 've hundreds slain;
  But deil-ma-care,
It just play'd dirl on the bane,
  But did nae mair.

"Hornbook was by, wi' ready art,
And had sae fortified the part,
That when I lookèd to my dart,
  It was sae blunt,
Fient haet o 't wad hae pierced the heart
  O' a kail-runt.

"I drew my scythe in sic a fury,
I near-hand cowpit wi' my hurry,
But yet the bauld apothecary
  Withstood the shock;
I might as weel hae tried a quarry
  O' hard whin rock.

"Ev'n them he canna get attended,
Although their face he ne'er had kenn'd it,
Just s—— in a kail-blade, and send it,
  As soon 's he smells 't,
Baith their disease, and what will mend it,
  At once he tells 't.

"And then a' doctor's saws and whittles,
Of a' dimensions, shapes, an' mettles,
A' kinds o' boxes, mugs, an' bottles,
  He 's sure to hae;
Their Latin names as fast he rattles
  As A, B, C.

"Calces o' fossils, earths, and trees;
True sal-marinum o' the seas;
The farina of beans an pease,
  He has 't in plenty;
Aqua-fontis, what you please,
  He can content ye.

"Forbye some new, uncommon weapons,
Urinus spiritus of capons;
Or mite-horn shavings, filings, scrapings,
  Distill'd *per se;*
Sal-alkali o' midge-tail clippings,
  And mony mae."

"Waes me for Johnny Ged's hole § now,"
Quo' I; "if that the news be true,
His braw calf-ward, whare gowans grew
  Sae white and bonnie,
Nae doubt they 'll rive it wi' the plew;
  They 'll ruin Johnny!"

The creature grain'd an eldritch laugh,
And says, "Ye needna yoke the pleugh,
Kirkyards will soon be till'd eneugh,
  Tak ye nae fear:
They 'll a' be trench'd wi' mony a sheugh
  In twa-three year.

"Whare I kill'd ane a fair strae death,
By loss o' blood or want o' breath,
This night I 'm free to tak my aith,
  That Hornbook's skill
Has clad a score i' their last claith,
  By drap an' pill.

"An honest wabster to his trade,
Whase wife's twa nieves were scarce weel-bred,
Gat tippence-worth to mend her head,
  When it was sair;
The wife slade cannie to her bed,
  But ne'er spak mair.

"A countra laird had ta'en the batts,
Or some curmurring in his guts;
His only son for Hornbook sets,
  An' pays him well:
The lad, for twa guid gimmer pets,
  Was laird himsel'.

---

* "Hornbook:" this gentleman, Dr. Hornbook, is professionally a brother of the Sovereign Order of the Ferula; but, by intuition and inspiration, is at once an apothecary, surgeon, and physician.—(B.)

† "Jock Hornbook:" John Wilson, a grocer, schoolmaster, and would-be apothecary in Tarbolton.—(B.) He and Burns had a quarrel. He became teacher and session-clerk in the Gorbals, Glasgow, and died in 1839.

‡ "Buchan:" Buchan's "Domestic Medicine"—once a most popular book. We have seen its 20th edition.

§ 'Johnny Ged's hole:" the grave-digger.

"A bonnie lass, ye kend her name,
Some ill-brewn drink had hoved her wame;
She trusts hersel', to hide the shame,
   In Hornbook's care;
Horn sent her aff to her lang hame,
   To hide it there.

"That 's just a swatch o' Hornbook's way;
Thus goes he on from day to day,
Thus does he poison, kill, an' slay,
   An 's weel paid for 't;
Yet stops me o' my lawfu' prey,
   Wi' his damn'd dirt.

"But, hark! I 'll tell you of a plot,
Though dinna ye be speaking o 't;
I 'll nail the self-conceited sot
   As dead 's a herrin':
Neist time we meet, I 'll wad a groat,
   He gets his fairin'!"

But just as he began to tell,
The auld kirk-hammer strak the bell
Some wee short hour ayont the twal,
   Which raised us baith:
I took the way that pleased mysel',
   And sae did Death.

FIRST EPISTLE TO JOHN LAPRAIK,* AN OLD SCOTTISH BARD.

APRIL 1, 1785.

WHILE briars an' woodbines budding green,
An' paitricks scraichin' loud at e'en,
An' morning poussie whiddin' seen,
   Inspire my muse,
This freedom in an unknown frien'
   I pray excuse.

On Fasten-e'en † we had a rockin',
To ca' the crack and weave our stockin';
And there was muckle fun an' jokin'
   Ye need na doubt:
At length we had a hearty yokin'
   At sang about.

There was ae sang, amang the rest,
Aboon them a' it pleased me best,
That some kind husband had address'd
   To some sweet wife:
It thirled the heart-strings through the breast,
   A' to the life.

---

* "Lapraik:" an old rhymster, residing in Muirkirk. The song that pleased Burns was borrowed from an old ditty.
† "Fasten-e'en:" Shrovetide, a festival that used to be religiously held in Scotland.

I 've scarce heard ought described sae weel,
What generous, manly bosoms feel;
Thought I, "Can this be Pope, or Steele,
   Or Beattie's wark?"
They tauld me 'twas an odd kind chiel
   About Muirkirk.

It pat me fidgin-fain to hear 't,
And sae about him there I spier't;
Then a' that kent him round declared
   He had ingine,
That nane excell'd it, few cam near 't,
   It was sae fine;

That, set him to a pint of ale,
An' either douce or merry tale,
Or rhymes an' sangs he 'd made himsel',
   Or witty catches,
'Tween Inverness an' Teviotdale,
   He had few matches.

Then up I gat, and swoor an aith,
Though I should pawn my pleugh and graith,
Or die a cadger pownie's death
   At some dyke back,
A pint and gill I 'd gie them baith
   To hear your crack.

But, first and foremost, I should tell,
Amaist as soon as I could spell,
I to the crambo-jingle fell;
   Though rude and rough.
Yet crooning to a body's sel'
   Does weel eneugh.

I am nae poet, in a sense,
But just a rhymer, like, by chance,
And hae to learning nae pretence;
   Yet, what the matter?
Whene'er my muse does on me glance,
   I jingle at her.

Your critic-folk may cock their nose,
And say, "How can you e'er propose,
You, wha ken hardly verse frae prose,
   To mak a sang?"
But, by your leave, my learned foes,
   Ye 're maybe wrang.

What 's a' your jargon o' your schools,
Your Latin names for horns an' stools?
If honest Nature made you fools,
   What sairs your grammars?
Ye 'd better ta'en up spades and shools,
   Or knappin'-hammers.

A set o' dull, conceited hashes,
Confuse their brains in college classes!
They gang in stirks, and come out asses,
   Plain truth to speak;
And syne they think to climb Parnassus
   By dint o' Greek!

Gie me ae spark o' Nature's fire,
That's a' the learning I desire;
Then though I trudge through dub an' mire
   At pleugh or cart,
My muse, though hamely in attire,
   May touch the heart.

O for a spunk o' Allan's glee,
Or Fergusson's, the bauld and slee,
Or bright Lapraik's, my friend to be,
   If I can hit it!
That would be lear eneugh for me,
   If I could get it.

Now, sir, if ye hae friends enow,
Though, real friends, I b'lieve, are few,
Yet, if your catalogue be fu',
   I 'se no insist;
But, gif ye want ae friend that's true,
   I 'm on your list.

I winna blaw about mysel',
As ill I like my fauts to tell;
But friends, and folk that wish me well,
   They sometimes roose me;
Though, I maun own, as mony still
   As far abuse me.

There's ae wee faut they whyles lay to me,
I like the lasses—Gude forgie me!
For mony a plack they wheedle frae me
   At dance or fair;
Maybe some ither thing they gie me,
   They weel can spare.

But Mauchline race, or Mauchline fair,
I should be proud to meet you there;
We 'se gie ae night's discharge to care,
   If we forgather,
And hae a swap o' rhymin'-ware
   Wi' ane anither.

The four gill chap, we 'se gar him clatter,
And kirsen him wi' reekin' water;
Syne we 'll sit down and tak our whitter,
   To cheer our heart;
And faith, we 'se be acquainted better
   Before we part.

Awa', ye selfish, warly race,
Wha think that havins, sense, an' grace,
Even love an' friendship, should give place
   To catch-the-plack!
I dinna like to see your face,
   Nor hear your crack.

But ye whom social pleasure charms,
Whose heart the tide of kindness warms,
Who hold your being on the terms,
   "Each aid the others,"
Come to my bowl, come to my arms,
   My friends, my brothers!

But, to conclude my lang epistle,
As my auld pen's worn to the grissle,
Twa lines frae you wad gar me fissle,
   Who am most fervent,
While I can either sing or whistle,
   Your friend and servant.

SECOND EPISTLE TO JOHN LAPRAIK.*

APRIL 21, 1785.

WHILE new-ca'd kye rowte at the stake,
An' pownies reek in pleugh or braik,
This hour on e'enin's edge I take,
   To own I 'm debtor
To honest-hearted, auld Lapraik,
   For his kind letter.

Forjesket sair, wi' weary legs,
Rattlin' the corn outowre the rigs,
Or dealing through amang the naigs
   Their ten-hours' bite,
My awkward muse sair pleads and begs,
   I would na write.

The tapetless, ramfeezled hizzie,
She's saft at best and something lazy;
Quo' she, "Ye ken we 've been sae busy
   This month an' mair,
That, trowth! my head is grown right dizzie,
   An' something sair."

Her dowff excuses pat me mad:
"Conscience," says I, "ye thowless jad!
I 'll write, and that a hearty blaud,
   This vera night;
So dinna ye affront your trade,
   But rhyme it right.

---

* Burns, when he received Lapraik's reply, was sowing. As he eagerly perused the letter, which was in rhyme, he dropt the sheet and spilt the corn.

"Shall bauld Lapraik, the king o' hearts,
Though mankind were a pack o' cartes,
Roose you sae weel for your deserts,
  In terms sae friendly,
Yet ye 'll neglect to shaw your parts,
  And thank him kindly?"

Sae I gat paper in a blink,
An' down gaed stumpie in the ink :
Quoth I, "Before I sleep a wink,
  I vow I 'll close it ;
And if ye winna mak it clink,
  By Jove, I 'll prose it !"

Sae I 've begun to scrawl, but whether
In rhyme, or prose, or baith thegither,
Or some hotch-potch that 's rightly neither,
  Let time mak proof ;
But I shall scribble down some blether
  Just clean aff-loof.

My worthy friend, ne'er grudge an' carp,
Though fortune use you hard an' sharp ;
Come, kittle up your moorland harp
  Wi' gleesome touch !
Ne'er mind how Fortune waft an' warp—
  She 's but a bitch.

She 's gien me mony a jirt an' fleg,
Sin' I could striddle owre a rig ;
But, by the L—d, though I should beg
  Wi' lyart pow,
I 'll laugh, an' sing, an' shake my leg,
  As lang 's I dow !

Now comes the sax-and-twentieth simmer
I 've seen the bud upo' the timmer,
Still persecuted by the limmer
  Frae year to year ;
But yet, despite the kittle kimmer,
  I, Rob, am here.

Do ye envy the city gent,
Behint a kist to lie and sklent,
Or purse-proud, big wi' cent. per cent.
  An' muckle wame,
In some bit brugh to represent
  A bailie's name ?

Or is 't the paughty feudal Thane,
Wi' ruffled sark and glancing cane,
Wha thinks himsel' nae sheep-shank bane,
  But lordly stalks,
While caps and bonnets aff are taen,
  As by he walks ?

O Thou, wha gies us each guid gift !
Gie me o' wit an' sense a lift,
Then turn me, if Thou please, adrift
  Through Scotland wide ;
Wi' cits nor lairds I wadna shift,
  In a' their pride !

Were this the charter of our state,
"On pain o' hell be rich an' great,"
Damnation then would be our fate,
  Beyond remead ;
But, thanks to Heaven ! that's no the gate
  We learn our creed.

For thus the royal mandate ran,
When first the human race began—
"The social, friendly, honest man,
  Whate'er he be,
'Tis he fulfils great Nature's plan,
  An' none but he !"

O mandate glorious and divine !
The ragged followers of the Nine—
Poor, thoughtless devils—yet may shine
  In glorious light,
While sordid sons of Mammon's line
  Are dark as night.

Though here they scrape, an' squeeze, an' growl,
Their worthless nievefu' of a soul
May in some future carcase howl,
  The forest's fright ;
Or in some day-detesting owl
  May shun the light.

Then may Lapraik * and Burns arise,
To reach their native, kindred skies,
And sing their pleasures, hopes, and joys,
  In some mild sphere,
Still closer knit in friendship's ties,
  Each passing year !

EPISTLE TO WILLIAM SIMSON.†

OCHILTREE.—MAY, 1785.

I GAT your letter, winsome Willie ;
Wi' gratefu' heart I thank you brawlie ;
Tho' I maun say 't, I wad be silly,
  And unco vain,
Should I believe, my coaxin billie,
  Your flatterin' strain.

---

* Lapraik published his poems in 1788, but they had no success. Burns was his only admirer.
† "Simson :" parish teacher in Cumnock ; a rhymer, and a man of considerable talent. He had got a copy of the "Twa Herds."

But I 'se believe ye kindly meant it:
I sud be laith to think ye hinted
Ironic satire, sidelins sklented
    On my poor musie;
Tho' in sic phraisin terms ye 've penn'd it,
    I scarce excuse ye.

My senses wad be in a creel,
Should I but dare a hope to speel,
Wi' Allan, or wi' Gilbertfield,*
    The braes o' fame;
Or Fergusson, the writer-chiel,
    A deathless name.

(O Fergusson! thy glorious parts
Ill suited law's dry, musty arts!
My curse upon your whunstane hearts,
    Ye E'nbrugh gentry!
The tythe o' what ye waste at cartes
    Wad stow'd his pantry!)

Yet when a tale comes i' my head,
Or lasses gie my heart a screed,
As whiles they're like to be my dead,
    (O sad disease!)
I kittle up my rustic reed;
    It gies me ease.

Auld Coila, now, may fidge fu' fain,
She's gotten poets o' her ain;
Chiels wha their chanters winna hain,
    But tune their lays,
Till echoes a' resound again
    Her weel-sung praise.

Nae poet thought her worth his while,
To set her name in measur'd style;
She lay like some unkenn'd-of isle
    Beside New Holland,
Or whare wild-meeting oceans boil
    Besouth Magellan.

Ramsay an' famous Fergusson
Gied Forth an' Tay a lift aboon;
Yarrow an' Tweed, to monie a tune,
    Owre Scotland rings;
While Irwin, Lugar, Ayr, an' Doon
    Naebody sings.

* "Gilbertfield:" Wm. Hamilton, a poet contemporary with Allan Ramsay.

Th' Illissus, Tiber, Thames, an' Seine,
Glide sweet in monie a tunefu' line:
But, Willie, set your fit to mine,
    An' cock your crest;
We'll gar our streams an' burnies shine
    Up wi' the best!

We'll sing auld Coila's plains an' fells,
Her moors red-brown wi' heather bells,
Her banks an' braes, her dens an' dells,
    Whare glorious Wallace
Aft bure the gree, as story tells,
    Frae Suthron billies.

At Wallace' name what Scottish blood
But boils up in a spring-tide flood!
Oft have our fearless fathers strode
    By Wallace' side,
Still pressing onward, red-wat-shod,
    Or glorious dy'd!

O sweet are Coila's haughs an' woods,
When lintwhites chant amang the buds,
And jinkin hares, in amorous whids,
   Their loves enjoy;
While thro' the braes the cushat croods
   With wailfu' cry!

Ev'n winter bleak has charms to me,
When winds rave thro' the naked tree;
Or frosts on hills of Ochiltree
   Are hoary gray;
Or blinding drifts wild-furious flee,
   Dark'ning the day!

O Nature! a' thy shews an' forms
To feeling, pensive hearts hae charms!
Whether the summer kindly warms,
   Wi' life an' light;
Or winter howls, in gusty storms,
   The lang, dark night!

The muse, nae poet ever fand her,
Till by himsel' he learn'd to wander,
Adown some trottin burn's meander,
   An' no think lang:
O sweet to stray, an' pensive ponder
   A heart-felt sang!

The warly race may drudge an' drive,
Hog-shouther, jundie, stretch, an' strive;
Let me fair Nature's face descrive,
   And I, wi' pleasure,
Shall let the busy, grumbling hive
   Bum owre their treasure.

Fareweel, "my rhyme-composing" brither!
We 've been owre lang unkenn'd to ither:
Now let us lay our heads thegither,
   In love fraternal:
May envy wallop in a tether,
   Black fiend, infernal!

While Highlandmen hate tolls an' taxes;
While moorlan' herds like guid, fat braxies;
While terra firma, on her axis,
   Diurnal turns;
Count on a friend, in faith an' practice,
   In Robert Burns.

POSTSCRIPT.

My memory 's no worth a preen;
I had amaist forgotten clean,
Ye bade me write you what they mean
   By this New-Light,*
'Bout which our herds sae aft hae been
   Maist like to fight.

* *New-Light* is a cant phrase in the West of Scotland for those religious opinions which Dr. Taylor of Norwich has defended so strenuously.—(B.)

In days when mankind were but callans
At grammar, logic, an' sic talents,
They took nae pains their speech to balance,
   Or rules to gie;
But spak their thoughts in plain, braid Lallans,
   Like you or me.

In thae auld times, they thought the moon,
Just like a sark or pair o' shoon,
Wore by degrees, till her last roon
   Gaed past their viewin';
And shortly after she was done
   They gat a new ane.

This past for certain, undisputed;
It ne'er cam i' their heads to doubt it,
Till chiels gat up an' wad confute it,
   And ca'd it wrang;
And muckle din there was about it,
   Baith loud and lang.

Some herds, well learn'd upo' the beuk,
Wad threap auld folk the thing misteuk;
For 'twas the auld moon turn'd a neuk,
   An' out o' sight,
An' backlins-comin' to the leuk,
   She grew mair bright.

This was denied—it was affirm'd;
The herds an' hirsels were alarm'd:
The reverend gray-beards rav'd an' storm'd
   That beardless laddies
Should think they better were inform'd
   Than their auld daddies.

Frae less to mair it gaed to sticks;
Frae words an' aiths to clours an' nicks;
And monie a fallow gat his licks,
   Wi' hearty crunt;
And some, to learn them for their tricks,
   Were hang'd an' brunt.

This game was play'd in mony lands,
And Auld-Light caddies bure sic hands,
That, faith! the youngsters took the sands
   Wi' nimble shanks,
Till lairds forbade, by strict commands,
   Sic bluidy pranks.

But New-Light herds gat sic a cowe,
Folk thought them ruin'd stick-an'-stowe,
Till now amaist on every knowe
   Ye 'll find ane placed;
An' some their New-Light fair avow,
   Just quite barefaced.

Nae doubt the Auld-Light flocks are bleatin';
Their zealous herds are vex'd an' sweatin';
Mysel' I 've even seen them greetin'
　　Wi' girnin' spite,
To hear the moon sae sadly lied on
　　By word an' write.

But shortly they will cowe the louns!
Some Auld-Light herds in neibour touns
Are mind't, in things they ca' balloons,
　　To tak a flight,
And stay a month amang the moons,
　　An' see them right.

Guid observation they will gie them;
And when the auld moon 's gaun to lea'e them,
The hindmost shaird, they 'll fetch it wi' them,
　　Just i' their pouch,
An' when the New-Light billies see them,
　　I think they 'll crouch!

Sae, ye observe that a' this clatter
Is naething but a "moonshine matter;"
But though dull prose-folk Latin splatter
　　In logic tulzie,
I hope, we bardies ken some better
　　Than mind sic brulzie.

ONE NIGHT AS I DID WANDER.

FRAGMENT OF SONG.

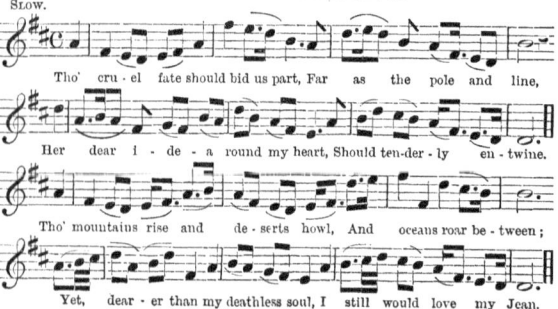

RANTIN', ROVIN' ROBIN.*

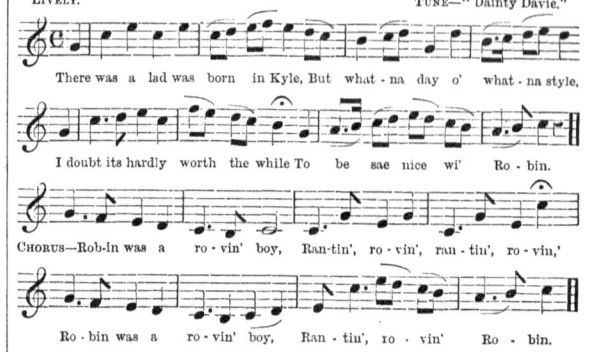

Our monarch's hindmost year but ane
Was five-and-twenty days begun,
'Twas then a blast o' Janwar' win'
　　Blew hansel in on Robin.
　　　　Robin was, &c.

The gossip keekit in his loof,
Quo' scho, "Wha lives will see the proof,
This waly boy will be nae coof;
　　I think we 'll ca' him Robin."
　　　　Robin was, &c.

"He 'll hae misfortunes great and sma',
But aye a heart aboon them a';
He 'll be a credit till us a'—
　　We 'll a' be proud o' Robin."
　　　　Robin was, &c.

"But sure as three times three mak nine,
I see by ilka score and line,
This chap will dearly like our kin',
　　So leeze me on thee, Robin!"
　　　　Robin was, &c.

"Guid faith, quo' scho, I doubt you 'll gar
The bonnie lasses lie aspar;
But twenty fauts ye may hae waur—
　　So blessin's on thee, Robin!"
　　　　Robin was, &c.

* The following tune, "O' Gin ye were Dead, Gudeman," is the modern adaptation to the words of "Rantin', Rovin' Robin;" but as it necessitates general alterations in the words, the original tune, "Dainty Davie," is given above:—

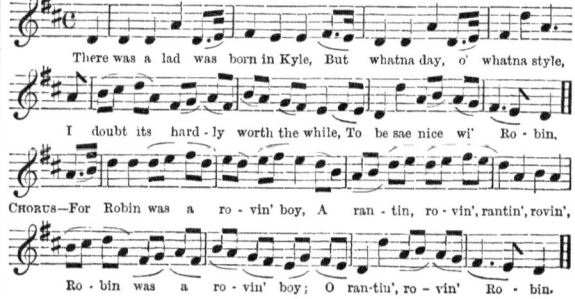

ELEGY

ON THE DEATH OF ROBERT RUISSEAUX.*

Now Robin lies in his last lair,
He'll gabble rhyme, nor sing nae mair;
Cauld poverty, wi' hungry stare,
    Nae mair shall fear him;
Nor anxious fear, nor cankert care,
    E'er mair come near him.

To tell the truth, they seldom fash'd him,
Except the moment that they crush'd him;
For soon as chance or fate had hush'd 'em,
    Though e'er sae short,
Then wi' a rhyme or sang he lash'd 'em,
    And thought it sport.

Though he was bred to kintra wark,
And counted was baith wight and stark,
Yet that was never Robin's mark
    To mak a man;
But tell him he was learn'd and clark,
    Ye roosed him then!

LETTER TO JOHN GOUDIE, KILMARNOCK,†

ON THE PUBLICATION OF HIS ESSAYS.

O GOUDIE! terror o' the Whigs,
Dread o' black coats and reverend wigs,
Sour Bigotry, on her last legs,
    Girnin', looks back,
Wishin' the ten Egyptian plagues
    Wad seize you quick.

Poor gapin', glowrin' Superstition,
Waes me, she's in a sad condition;
Fie! bring Black Jock,‡ her state physician,
    To see her water;
Alas! there 's ground o' great suspicion
    She 'll ne'er get better.

Auld Orthodoxy lang did grapple,
But now she's got an unco ripple;
Haste, gie her name up i' the chapel,
    Nigh unto death;
See how she fetches at the thrapple,
    And gasps for breath!

Enthusiasm 's past redemption,
Gane in a gallopin' consumption,
Not a' the quacks, wi' a' their gumption,
    Can ever mend her,
Her feeble pulse gie's strong presumption
    Death soon will end her.

'Tis you and Taylor § are the chief
Wha are to blame for this mischief;
But gin the L—d's ain folks gat leave,
    A toom tar barrel
And twa red peats wad send relief,
    And end the quarrel.

For me, my skill 's but very sma',
An' skill in prose I 've nane ava';
But quietlenswise, between us twa,
    Weel may ye speed!
And tho' they sud you sair misca',
    Ne'er fash your head.

E'en swinge the dogs, and thresh them sicker!
The mair they squeel aye chap the thicker;
And still 'mang hands a hearty bicker
    O' something stout;
It gars an owthor's pulse beat quicker,
    And helps his wit.

There 's naething like the honest nappy;
Whare 'll ye e'er see men sae happy,
Or women sonsie, saft and sappy,
    'Tween morn and morn,
As them wha like to taste the drappie,
    In glass or horn?

I 've seen me daez't upon a time,
I scarce could wink or see a styme;
Just ae hauf-mutchkin' does me prime,
    (Ought less is little,)
Then back I rattle on the rhyme,
    As gleg 's a whittle.

THIRD EPISTLE TO J. LAPRAIK.

SEPTEMBER 13, 1785.

GUID speed and furder to you, Johnnie,
Guid health, hale han's, and weather bonnie;
Now when ye're nickin down fu' canny
    The staff o' bread,
May ye ne'er want a stoup o' bran'y
    To clear your head!

---

* "Ruisseaux:" a play upon his own name, meaning, in French, *burns*.
† See LIFE.   ‡ "Black Jock:" see LIFE.
§ "Taylor:" Dr. Taylor of Norwich.

May Boreas never thrash your rigs,
Nor kick your rickles aff their legs,
Sendin' the stuff o'er muirs and haggs,
    Like drivin' wrack ;
But may the tapmost grain that wags
    Come to the sack !

I'm bizzie, too, and skelpin' at it,
But bitter, daudin' showers hae wat it;
Sae my auld stumpie pen I gat it,
    Wi' muckle wark,
And took my jocteleg* and whatt it,
    Like ony clark.

It 's now twa month that I 'm your debtor
For your braw, nameless, dateless letter,
Abusin' me for harsh ill-nature
    On holy men,
While deil a hair yoursel' ye 're better,
    But mair profane.

But let the kirk-folk ring their bells,
Let 's sing about our noble sel's :
We 'll cry nae jauds frae heathen hills
    To help, or roose us ;
But browster wives and whisky stills,
    They are the Muses.

Your friendship, sir, I winna quat it,
And, if ye mak objections at it,
Then han' in nieve some day we 'll knot it,
    And witness take,
And when wi' usquebae we 've wat it,
    It winna break.

But if the beast and branks be spared
Till kye be gaun without the herd,
And a' the vittel in the yard,
    An' theekit right,
I mean your ingle-side to guard
    Ae winter night.

Then muse-inspirin' aqua-vitæ
Shall make us baith sae blythe and witty,
Till ye forget ye 're auld and gatty,
    And be as canty
As ye were nine year less than thretty,
    Sweet ane an' twenty !

But stooks are coupit wi' the blast,
And now the sin keeks in the west,
Then I maun rin amang the rest,
    And quat my chanter ;
Sae I subscribe mysel' in haste,
    Yours, RAB THE RANTER.

---

* "Jocteleg:" from *Jacque de Liege*, the name of a French cutler.

TO THE REVEREND JOHN M'MATH,†

INCLOSING A COPY OF "HOLY WILLIE'S PRAYER," WHICH HE HAD REQUESTED, SEPT. 17, 1785.

WHILE at the stook the shearers cower
To shun the bitter blaudin' shower ;
Or in gulravage rinnin' scowr,
    To pass the time,
To you I dedicate the hour
    In idle rhyme.

My Musie, tired wi' mony a sonnet,
On gown, and ban', and douse black bonnet,
Is grown right eerie now she 's done it,
    Lest they should blame her,
And rouse their holy thunder on it,
    And anathem her.

I own 'twas rash, and rather hardy,
That I, a simple, kintra bardie,
Should meddle wi' a pack sae sturdy,
    Wha, if they ken me,
Can easy, wi' a single wordie,
    Louse hell upon me.

But I gae mad at their grimaces,
Their sighin', cantin', grace-proud faces,
Their three-mile prayers, and hauf-mile graces,
    Their raxin' conscience,
Whase greed, revenge, and pride disgraces
    Waur nor their nonsense.

There 's Gawn,‡ misca't waur than a beast,
Wha has mair honour in his breast
Than mony scores as guid 's the priest
    Wha sae abused him ;
And may a bard no crack his jest
    What way they 've used him ?

See him, the poor man's friend in need,
The gentleman in word and deed ;
And shall his fame and honour bleed
    By worthless skellums,
And not a muse erect her head
    To cowe the blellums ?

O Pope ! had I thy satire's darts,
To gie the rascals their deserts,
I 'd rip their rotten, hollow hearts,
    And tell aloud
Their jugglin', hocus-pocus arts,
    To cheat the crowd.

---

† "Rev. John M'Math·" assistant to the Rev. Peter Woodrow of Tarbolton. He fell into dissipated habits, and died at Rossal in the Isle of Mull. The harvest of 1785 was a bad one, to which there is allusion above.

‡ "Gawn:" Gavin Hamilton, Esq.

"THEN MUSE-INSPIRIN' AQUA-VITÆ
SHALL MAKE US BAITH SAE BLYTHE AND WITTY"

God knows, I 'm no the thing I should be,
Nor am I even the thing I could be;
But twenty times I rather would be
   An atheist clean,
Than under gospel colours hid be,
   Just for a screen.

An honest man may like a glass,
An honest man may like a lass,
But mean revenge and malice fause
   He 'll still disdain,
And then cry zeal for gospel laws,
   Like some we ken.

They take religion in their mouth;
They talk o' mercy, grace, an' truth;
For what?—to gie their malice skouth
   On some puir wight,
And hunt him down, o'er right and ruth,
   To ruin straight.

All hail, Religion! maid divine!
Pardon a muse sae mean as mine,
Who in her rough imperfect line
   Thus daurs to name thee;
To stigmatise false friends of thine,
   Can ne'er defame thee.

Though blotch't and foul wi' mony a stain,
And far unworthy of thy train,
With trembling voice I tune my strain
   To join with those
Who boldly dare thy cause maintain
   In spite of foes:

In spite o' crowds, in spite o' mobs,
In spite of undermining jobs,
In spite of dark banditti stabs
   At worth and merit,
By scoundrels, even wi' holy robes,
   But hellish spirit.

O Ayr! my dear, my native ground!
Within thy presbyterial bound
A candid, liberal band is found
   Of public teachers,
As men, as Christians too, renown'd,
   And manly preachers.

Sir, in that circle you are named;
Sir, in that circle you are famed;
And some, by whom your doctrine 's blamed,
   (Which gies you honour)
Even, sir, by them your heart 's esteemed,
   And winning manner.

Pardon this freedom I have ta'en,
And if impertinent I 've been,
Impute it not, good sir, in ane
   Whase heart ne'er wrang'd ye,
But to his utmost would befriend
   Ought that belang'd ye.

SECOND EPISTLE TO DAVIE, A BROTHER POET.*

AULD NEIBOUR,
 I 'M three times doubly owre your debtor
For your auld-farrant, frien'ly letter;
Though I maun say 't, I doubt ye flatter,
   Ye speak sae fair;
For my puir, silly, rhymin' clatter
   Some less maun sair.

Hale be your heart, hale be your fiddle;
Lang may your elbuck jink and diddle,
To cheer you through the weary widdle
   O' war'ly cares,
Till bairns' bairns kindly cuddle
   Your auld gray hairs.

But, Davie lad, I 'm rede ye 're glaikit;
I 'm tauld the Muse ye hae negleckit;
And gif it 's sae, ye sud be licket
   Until ye fyke;
Sic hauns as you sud ne'er be faiket,*
   Be hain't wha like.

For me, I 'm on Parnassus' brink,
Rivin' the words to gar them clink;
Whyles daez't wi' love, whyles daez't wi' drink,
   Wi' jauds or masons;
And whyles, but aye owre late, I think
   Braw sober lessons.

Of a' the thoughtless sons o' man,
Commen' me to the bardie clan;
Except it be some idle plan
   O' rhymin' clink,
The devil-hae't, that I sud ban,
   They ever think.

Nae thought, nae view, nae scheme o' livin',
Nae cares to gie us joy or grievin':
But just the pouchie put the nieve in,
   And while ought 's there,
Then, hiltie skiltie, we gae scrievin',
   And fash nae mair.

---

* "Brother poet:" this was prefixed to the poems of David Sillar, published at Kilmarnock, 1789.
† "Faiket:" folded.

Leeze me on rhyme! it 's aye a treasure,
My chief, amaist my only pleasure;
At hame, a-fiel', at wark, or leisure,
   The muse, poor hizzie!
Though rough an' raploch be her measure
  She 's seldom lazy.

Haud to the muse, my dainty Davie:
The warl' may play you mony a shavie;
But for the muse, she 'll never leave ye,
   Though e'er sae puir,
Na, even though limpin' wi' the spavie
  Frae door to door.

THE CATRINE WOODS WERE YELLOW SEEN.

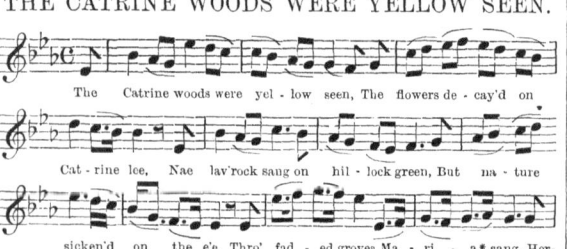

* "Maria:" eldest daughter of Sir John Whitefoord of Ballochmyle, who, owing to misfortunes connected with the Ayr Bank, had to sell his estate of Ballochmyle.

Low in your wintry beds, ye flowers,
 Again ye 'll flourish fresh and fair;
Ye birdies dumb, in with'ring bowers,
 Again ye 'll charm the vocal air.

But here, alas! for me nae mair
    Shall birdie charm, or floweret smile;
Fareweel the bonnie banks of Ayr,
    Fareweel, fareweel, sweet Ballochmyle!

YOUNG PEGGY BLOOMS.*

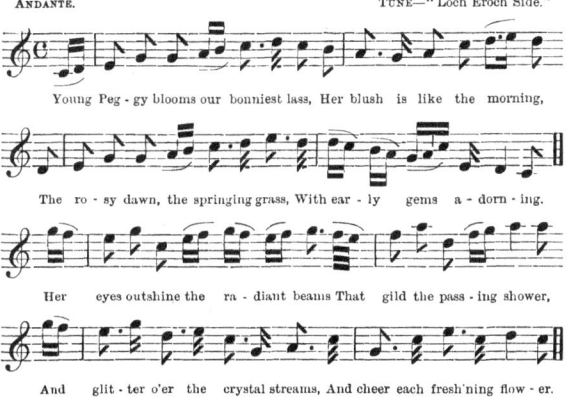

Young Peggy blooms our bonniest lass, Her blush is like the morning, The rosy dawn, the springing grass, With early gems adorning. Her eyes outshine the radiant beams That gild the passing shower, And glitter o'er the crystal streams, And cheer each fresh'ning flow-er.

Her lips, more than the cherries bright,
    A richer dye has graced them;
They charm th' admiring gazer's sight,
    And sweetly tempt to taste them;
Her smile is as the evening mild,
    When feather'd pairs are courting,
And little lambkins wanton wild,
    In playful bands disporting.

Were Fortune lovely Peggy's foe,
    Such sweetness would relent her;
As blooming spring unbends the brow
    Of surly, savage winter.
Detraction's eye no aim can gain,
    Her winning powers to lessen;
And fretful envy grins in vain
    The poison'd tooth to fasten.

Ye Powers of honour, love, and truth,
    From every ill defend her:
Inspire the highly-favour'd youth
    The Destinies intend her:

* Daughter of a Carrick laird, and relative of Mrs. Gavin Hamilton. Was unfortunate in her after life. See "Banks and Braes o' Bonny Doon."

Still fan the sweet connubial flame
    Responsive in each bosom;
And bless the dear parental name
    With many a filial blossom.

POWERS CELESTIAL! WHOSE PROTECTION.

Powers celestial, whose protection, ever guards the virtuous fair, While in distant climes I wander, Let my Mary† be your care: Let her form, sae fair and faultless, Fair and faultless as your own; Let my Mary's kindred spirit, Draw your choicest influence down.

Make the gales you waft around her,
    Soft and peaceful as her breast;
Breathing in the breeze that fans her,
    Soothe her bosom into rest:
Guardian angels! O protect her
    When in distant lands I roam;
To realms unknown while Fate exiles me,
    Make her bosom still my home.

HER FLOWING LOCKS.‡

HER flowing locks, the raven's wing,
    Adown her neck and bosom hing;
How sweet unto that breast to cling,
    And round that neck entwine her!
Her lips are roses wat wi' dew,
    O, what a feast her bonnie mou'!
Her cheeks a mair celestial hue,
    A crimson still diviner.

† "Mary:" written on Mary Campbell, at the time Burns was preparing to go abroad.
‡ "Her flowing locks:" an impromptu composed at Mauchline on seeing a beautiful young lady on horseback— probably Miss Whitefoord.

HALLOWE'EN.*

"Yes! let the rich deride, the proud disdain,
The simple pleasures of the lowly train;
To me more dear, congenial to my heart,
One native charm, than all the gloss of art."
                                    GOLDSMITH.

The following poem will, by many readers, be well enough understood; but for the sake of those who are unacquainted with the manners and traditions of the country where the scene is cast, notes are added, to give some account of the principal charms and spells of that night, so big with prophecy to the peasantry in the west of Scotland. The passion of prying into futurity makes a striking part of the history of human nature in its rude state, in all ages and nations; and it may be some entertainment to a philosophical mind, if any such should honour the author with the perusal, to see the remains of it among the more enlightened in our own.—(B.)

UPON that night, when fairies light
   On Cassilis Downans † dance,
Or owre the lays, in splendid blaze,
   On sprightly coursers prance;
Or for Colean the route is ta'en,
   Beneath the moon's pale beams;
There, up the Cove,‡ to stray an' rove,
   Amang the rocks and streams
        To sport that night:

Amang the bonnie winding banks,
   Where Doon rins, wimplin, clear;
Where Bruce § ance ruled the martial ranks,
   An' shook his Carrick spear:
Some merry, friendly, country-folks
   Together did convene,
To burn their nits, an' pu' their stocks,
   An' haud their Halloween
        Fu' blythe that night.

The lasses feat, an' cleanly neat,
   Mair braw than when they're fine;
Their faces blythe fu' sweetly kythe
   Hearts leal, an' warm, an' kin':
The lads sae trig, wi' wooer-babs
   Weel-knotted on their garten;
Some unco blate, an' some wi' gabs
   Gar lasses' hearts gang startin'
        Whyles fast at night.

Then, first an' foremost, thro' the kail,
   Their "stocks"‖ maun a' be sought ance;
They steek their een, an' grape an' wale
   For muckle anes, an' straught anes.
Poor hav'rel Will fell aff the drift,
   An' wandered thro' the "bow-kail,"
An' pu't, for want o' better shift,
   A runt, was like a sow-tail
        Sae bow't that night.

Then, straught or crooked, yird or nane,
   They roar an' cry a' throw'ther;
The vera wee-things, toddlin, rin,
   Wi' stocks out owre their shouther:
An' gif the custoc 's sweet or sour,
   Wi' joctelegs they taste them;
Syne coziely, aboon the door,
   Wi' cannie care they've plac'd them,
        To lie that night.

The lasses staw frae 'mang them a',
   To pu' their stalks o' corn;¶
But Rab slips out, an' jinks about,
   Behint the muckle thorn;
He grippet Nelly hard an' fast;
   Loud skirl'd a' the lasses;
But her tap-pickle maist was lost,
   Whan kiutlin in the "fause-house"**
        Wi' him that night.

The auld guid-wife's weel-hoordet nits ††
   Are round an' round divided,
An' mony lads an' lasses' fates
   Are there that night decided:
Some kindle couthie, side by side,
   An' burn thegither trimly;
Some start awa wi' saucy pride,
   An' jump out owre the chimlie
        Fu' high that night.

---

* "Hallowe'en:" is thought to be a night when witches, devils, and other mischief-making beings, are all abroad on their baneful midnight errands; particularly those aerial people, the Fairies, are said on that night to hold a grand anniversary.—(B.)

† "Cassilis Downans:" certain little, romantic, rocky, green hills, in the neighbourhood of the ancient seat of the Earls of Cassilis.

‡ "Cove:" a noted cavern near Colzean-house, called the Cove of Colzean; which, as well as Cassilis Downans, is famed in country story for being a favourite haunt of fairies.—(B.)

§ "Bruce:" the famous family of that name, the ancestors of Robert, the great deliverer of his country, were Earls of Carrick.—(B.)

‖ "Stocks:" the first ceremony of Hallowe'en is pulling each a *stock*, or plant of kail. They must go out, hand in hand, with eyes shut, and pull the first they meet with: its being big or little, straight or crooked, is prophetic of the size and shape of the grand object of all their spells—the husband or wife. If any *yird*, or earth, stick to the root, that is *tocher*, or fortune; and the state of the *custoc*, that is, the heart of the stem, is indicative of the natural temper and disposition. Lastly, the stems, or to give them their ordinary appellation, the *runts*, are placed somewhere above the head of the door; and the Christian names of the people whom chance brings into the house are, according to the priority of placing the *runts*, the names in question.—(B.)

¶ "Stalks o' corn:" they go to the barnyard and pull each, at three several times, a stalk of oats. If the third stalk wants the *top-pickle*, that is, the grain at the top of the stalk, the party in question will come to the marriage-bed anything but a maid.—(B.)

** "Fause-house:" when the corn is in a doubtful state, by being too green or wet, the stack-builder, by means of old timber, &c., makes a large apartment in his stack, with an opening in the side which is fairest exposed to the wind: this he calls a *fause-house*.—(B.)

†† "Nits:" burning the nuts is a favourite charm. They name the lad and lass to each particular nut, as they lay them in the fire, and accordingly as they burn quietly together, or start from beside one another, the course and issue of the courtship will be.—(B.)

Jean slips in twa, wi' tentie e'e;
  Wha 'twas she wadna tell;
But this is Jock, an' this is me,
  She says in to hersel:
He bleez'd owre her, an' she owre him,
  As they wad never mair part;
Till fuff! he started up the lum,
  And Jean had e'en a sair heart
      To see't that night.

Poor Willie, wi' his bow-kail runt,
  Was brunt wi' primsie Mallie;
An' Mary, nae doubt, took the drunt,
  To be compar'd to Willie:
Mall's nit lap out wi' pridefu' fling,
  An' her ain fit it brunt it;
While Willie lap, an' swoor by "jing,"
  'Twas just the way he wanted
      To be that night.

Nell had the "fause-house" in her min',
  She pits hersel' an' Rob in;
In loving bleeze they sweetly join,
  Till white in ase they're sobbin':
Nell's heart was dancin' at the view;
  She whisper'd Rob to leuk for't:
Rob, stowlins, prie'd her bonnie mou,
  Fu' cozie in the neuk for't,
      Unseen that night.

But Merran sat behint their backs,
  Her thoughts on Andrew Bell;

She lea'es them gashin at their cracks,
  An' slips out-by hersel':
She thro' the yard the nearest taks,
  An' for the kiln she goes then,
An' darklins grapit for the "bauks,"
  And in the "blue-clue"* throws then,
      Right fear't that night.

* "Blue-clue:" whoever would, with success, try this spell, must strictly observe these directions:—Steal out, all alone, to the kiln, and, darkling, throw into the pot a clue of blue yarn; wind it in a new clue off the old one; and, towards the latter end, something will hold the thread; demand, Wha hauds? *i.e.*, who holds? An answer will be returned from the kiln-pot, by naming the Christian and surname of your future spouse.—(B.)

An' aye she win't, an' aye she swat—
  I wat she made nae jaukin';
Till something held within the pat,
  Guid L—d! but she was quaukin'!
But whether 'twas the deil himsel',
  Or whether 'twas a bauk-en',
Or whether it was Andrew Bell,
  She did na wait on talkin'
      To spier that night.

Wee Jenny to her grannie says,
  "Will ye go wi' me, grannie?
I'll eat the apple* at the glass,
  I gat frae uncle Johnnie:"
She fuff't her pipe wi' sic a lunt,
  In wrath she was sae vap'rin',
She notic't na an aizle brunt
  Her braw, new, worset apron
      Out thro' that night.

"Ye little skelpie-limmer's-face!
  I daur you try sic sportin'
As seek the foul thief ony place,
  For him to spae your fortune:
Nae doubt but ye may get a sight!
  Great cause ye hae to fear it;
For mony a ane has gotten a fright,
  An' liv'd an' died deleerit,
      On sic a night.

"Ae hairst afore the Sherra-moor,
  I mind 't as weel's yestreen—
I was a gilpey then, I'm sure
  I was na past fyfteen:
The simmer had been cauld an' wat,
  An' stuff was unco green;
An' ay a rantin' kirn we gat,
  An' just on Hallowe'en
      It fell that night.

"Our 'stibble-rig'† was Rab M'Graen,
  A clever, sturdy fallow;
His sin gat Eppie Sim wi' wean,
  That liv'd in Achmacalla:
He gat hemp-seed,‡ I mind it weel,
  An' he made unco light o't;
But mony a day was by himsel',
  He was sae sairly frighted
      That vera night."

Then up gat fechtin' Jamie Fleck,
  An' he swoor by his conscience,
That he could saw hemp-seed a peck;
  For it was a' but nonsense:
The auld guidman raught down the pock,
  An' out a handfu' gied him;
Syne bad him slip frae 'mang the folk,
  Sometime when nae ane see'd him,
      An' try't that night.

He marches thro' amang the stacks,
  Tho' he was something sturtin';
The graip he for a harrow taks,
  An' haurls at his curpin:
And ev'ry now an' then he says,
  "Hemp-seed I saw thee,
An' her that is to be my lass
  Come after me, an' draw thee
      As fast this night."

He whistl'd up "Lord Lennox' March,"
  To keep his courage cheery;
Altho' his hair began to arch,
  He was sae fley'd an' eerie:
Till presently he hears a squeak,
  An' then a grane an' gruntle;
He by his shouther gae a keek,
  An' tumbled wi' a wintle
      Out-owre that night.

He roar'd a horrid murder-shout,
  In dreadfu' desperation!
An' young an' auld come rinnin out,
  An' hear the said narration:
He swoor 'twas hilchin Jean M'Craw,
  Or crouchie Merran Humphie—
Till stop! she trotted thro' them a';
  An' wha was it but grumphie
      Asteer that night?

Meg fain wad to the barn gaen,
  To winn three wechts o' naething;§
But for to meet the deil her lane,
  She pat but little faith in:

---

* "Eat the apple:" take a candle, and go alone to a looking-glass; eat an apple before it, and some traditions say, you should comb your hair all the time; the face of your conjugal companion, to be, will be seen in the glass, as if peeping over your shoulder.—(B.)

† "Stibble-rig:" leader of the reapers.

‡ "Hemp-seed:" steal out, unperceived, and sow a handful of hemp-seed, harrowing it with anything you can conveniently draw after you. Repeat now and then, "Hemp-seed, I saw thee; hemp-seed, I saw thee; and him (or her) that is to be my true-love, come after me and pu' thee." Look over your left shoulder, and you will see the appearance of the person invoked, in the attitude of pulling hemp. Some traditions say, "Come after me and shaw thee," that is, show thyself: in which case it simply appears. Others omit the harrowing, and say, "Come after me, and harrow thee."

§ "Win three wechts o' naething:" this charm must likewise be performed unperceived, and alone. You go to the barn, and open both doors, taking them off the hinges, if possible; for there is danger that the being about to appear may shut the doors, and do you some mischief. Then take that instrument used in winnowing the corn, which, in our country dialect, we call a *wecht*; and go through all the attitudes of letting down corn against the wind. Repeat it three times; and the third time an apparition will pass through the barn, in at the windy door, and out at the other, having both the figure in question, and the appearance or retinue marking the employment or station in life.—(B.)

She gies the herd a pickle nits,
 An' twa red cheekit apples,
To watch, while for the barn she sets,
 In hopes to see Tam Kipples
  That vera night.

She turns the key wi' cannie thraw,
 An' owre the threshold ventures;
But first on Sawnie gies a ca',
 Syne bauldly in she enters:
A ratton rattl'd up the wa',
 An' she cried, L—d preserve her!
An' ran thro' midden-hole an' a',
 An' pray'd wi' zeal and fervour,
  Fu' fast that night.

They hoy't out Will, wi' sair advice;
 They hecht him some fine braw ane;

It chanc'd the stack he faddom'd thrice,*
 Was timmer-propt for thrawin':
He taks a swirlie auld moss-oak
 For some black, grousome carlin;
An' loot a winze, an' drew a stroke,
 Till skin in blypes cam haurlin'
  Aff 's nieves that night.

A wanton widow Leezie was,
 As cantie as a kittlen;
But och! that night, amang the shaws,
 She gat a fearfu' settlin'!
She thro' the whins, an' by the cairn,
 An' owre the hill gaed scrievin',

* "Faddom'd thrice:" take an opportunity of going unnoticed to a bear-stack, and fathom it three times round. The last fathom of the last time, you will catch in your arms the appearance of your future conjugal yoke-fellow.—(B.)

Whare three lairds' lan's met at a burn,*
   To dip her left sark-sleeve in,
         Was bent that night.

Whyles owre a linn the burnie plays,
   As thro' the glen it wimpl't;
Whyles round a rocky scaur it strays,
   Whyles in a wiel it dimpl't;
Whyles glitter'd to the nightly rays,
   Wi' bickerin', dancin' dazzle;
Whyles cookit underneath the braes,
   Below the spreading hazle,
         Unseen that night.

Amang the brachens, on the brae,
   Between her an' the moon,
The deil, or else an outler quey,
   Gat up an' ga'e a croon:
Poor Leezie's heart maist lap the hool;
   Near lav'rock-height she jumpit,
But mist a fit, an' in the pool
   Out-owre the lugs she plumpit
         Wi' a plunge that night.

In order, on the clean hearth-stane,
   The "luggies"† three are ranged;
An' ev'ry time great care is ta'en
   To see them duly changed:
Auld uncle John, wha wedlock's joys
   Sin' "Mar's year"‡ did desire,
Because he gat the toom dish thrice
   He heav'd them on the fire,
         In wrath that night.

Wi' merry sangs, an' friendly cracks,
   I wat they did na weary;
An' unco tales, an' funnie jokes—
   Their sports were cheap an' cheery:
Till butter'd sow'ns,§ wi' fragrant lunt,
   Set a' their gabs a steerin';
Syne, wi' a social glass o' strunt,
   They parted aff careerin'
         Fu' blythe that night.

---

* "Met at a burn:" you go out, one or more, for this is a social spell, to a south running spring or rivulet, where "three lairds' lands meet," and dip your left shirt sleeve. Go to bed in sight of a fire, and hang your wet sleeve before it to dry. Lie awake; and some time near midnight an apparition, having the exact figure of the grand object in question, will come and turn the sleeve, as if to dry the other side of it.—(B.)

† "Luggies three:" take three dishes; put clean water in one, foul water in another, leave the third empty; blindfold a person, and lead him to the hearth where the dishes are ranged; he (or she) dips the left hand, if by chance in the clean water, the future husband or wife will come to the bar of matrimony a maid; if in the foul, a widow; if in the empty dish, it foretells, with equal certainty, no marriage at all. It is repeated three times, and every time the arrangement of the dishes is altered.—(B.)

‡ "Mar's Year:" 1715, when the Earl of Mar's rebellion took place.
§ "Butter'd sow'ns:" sowens, with butter instead of milk to them, is always the *Hallowe'en supper.*—(B.)

TO A MOUSE, ‖

ON TURNING HER UP IN HER NEST WITH THE PLOUGH, NOVEMBER, 1785.

WEE, sleekit, cow'rin', tim'rous beastie,
O, what a panic 's in thy breastie!
Thou need na start awa sae hasty,
         Wi' bickerin' brattle!
I wad be laith to rin an' chase thee,
         Wi' murderin' pattle!

I 'm truly sorry man's dominion
Has broken Nature's social union,
And justifies that ill opinion,
         Which makes thee startle
At me, thy poor earth-born companion,
         An' fellow-mortal!

I doubt na, whiles, but thou may thieve;
What then? poor beastie, thou maun live!
A daimen icker in a thrave
         'S a sma' request;
I 'll get a blessin' wi' the lave,
         And never miss 't!

Thy wee bit housie, too, in ruin!
Its silly wa's the win's are strewin'!
And naething, now, to big a new ane
         O' foggage green!
And bleak December's winds ensuin',
         Baith snell and keen!

Thou saw the fields laid bare and waste,
And weary winter comin' fast,
And cozie here, beneath the blast,
         Thou thought to dwell,
Till crash! the cruel coulter pass'd
         Out through thy cell.

That wee bit heap o' leaves and stibble
Has cost thee mony a weary nibble!
Now thou 's turn'd out, for a' thy trouble,
         But house or hald,
To thole the winter's sleety dribble,
         And cranreuch cauld!

But, Mousie, thou art no thy lane,
In proving foresight may be vain;
The best laid schemes o' mice an' men,
         Gang aft a-gley,
And lea'e us nought but grief and pain,
         For promised joy.

‖ Burns composed this while holding the plough in a field near Mossgiel. He had first saved its life from the gadsman, who wanted to kill it.—See LIFE.

Still thou art blest, compared wi' me !
The present only toucheth thee :
But, och ! I backward cast my e'e
    On prospects drear !
And forward, though I canna see,
    I guess an' fear.

HERE LIES JOHNNIE PIGEON.*

Here lies Johnnie Pigeon;
What was his religion
    Whae'er desires to ken,
To some other warl'
Maun follow the carl,
    For here Johnnie Pigeon had nane !

Strong ale was ablution,
Small beer persecution,
    A dram was *memento mori;*
But a full flowing bowl
Was the saving his soul,
    And port was celestial glory.

EPITAPH ON JAMES SMITH.†

Lament him, Mauchline husbands a',
    He aften did assist ye;
For had ye staid whole weeks awa',
    Your wives they ne'er had miss'd ye.

Ye Mauchline bairns, as on ye pass,
    To school in bands thegither,
O, tread ye lightly on his grass;
    Perhaps he was your faither !

THE JOLLY BEGGARS.‡

RECITATIVO.

When lyart leaves bestrew the yird,
Or wavering like the bauckie-bird, §
    Bedim cauld Boreas' blast;
When hailstanes drive wi' bitter skyte,
And infant frosts begin to bite,
    In hoary cranreuch dress'd;
Ae night at e'en a merry core
O' randie, gangrel bodies,
In Poosie Nansie's held the splore,
    To drink their orra duddies :
      Wi' quaffing and laughing,
        They ranted and they sang;
      Wi' jumping and thumping,
        The vera girdle rang.

First, neist the fire, in auld red rags,
Ane sat, weel braced wi' mealy bags,
    And knapsack a' in order;
His doxy lay within his arm,
Wi' usquebae and blankets warm—
    She blinket on her sodger;
And aye he gies the touzie drab
    The tither skelpin' kiss,
While she held up her greedy gab,
    Just like an aumous dish.
      Ilk smack still did crack still,
        Just like a cadger's whip;
      Then staggering and swaggering
        He roar'd this ditty up—

AIR.

I am a son of Mars, who have been in many wars, And show my cuts and scars wher-ev-er I come; This here was for a wench, and that other in a trench, When wel-com-ing the French at the sound of the drum. My 'prenticeship I past where my leader breathed his last, When the bloody die was cast on the heights of Abram; ‖ I serv'd out my trade when the gallant game was play'd, And the Moro ¶ low was laid at the sound of the drum. I served out my trade when the gallant game was played, I served out my trade when the gallant game was play'd, And the Moro low was laid at the sound of the drum.

---

* Host of Whitefoord Arms, Mauchline, where met an odd bachelor's club, of which Burns was a member.
† James Smith, to whom Burns wrote an epistle.—See Life.
‡ This Cantata was written in 1785; but not published till after the death of the poet.—See Life.
§ Bat.

‖ "The heights of Abram :" the battle-field near Quebec, where General Wolfe fell in the arms of victory, 1759.
¶ "The Moro low was laid :" the capture of Havanah, the capital of the island of Cuba, by the British, in 1762, is here alluded to. Moro was a castle defending its entrance.

I lastly was with Curtis, among the floating batteries,*
   And there I left for witness an arm and a limb;
Yet let my country need me, with Elliot † to lead me,
   I'd clatter on my stumps at the sound of a drum.

And now though I must beg with a wooden arm and leg, ‡
   And many a tatter'd rag hanging over my bum,
I'm as happy with my wallet, my bottle and my callet,
   As when I used in scarlet to follow a drum.

What though with hoary locks I must stand the winter shocks,
   Beneath the woods and rocks oftentimes for a home,
When the 'tother bag I sell, and the 'tother bottle tell,
   I could meet a troop of hell at the sound of the drum.

RECITATIVO.

He ended; and the kebars sheuk
   Aboon the chorus roar;
While frighted rattons backward leuk,
   And seek the benmost bore;
A fairy fiddler frae the neuk,
   He skirl'd out "Encore!"
But up arose the martial chuck,
   And laid the loud uproar.

AIR.
LIVELY.   TUNE—"The Sodger Laddie."

I once was a maid, though I cannot tell when, And still my delight is in proper young men; Some one of a troop of dragoons was my daddie, No wonder I'm fond of a sod-ger lad-die. Sing lal de lal, &c.

The first of my loves was a swaggering blade,
   To rattle the thundering drum was his trade;
His leg was so tight, and his cheek was so ruddy,
   Transported I was with my sodger laddie,
         Sing, lal de lal, &c.

But the godly old chaplain left him in the lurch,
   So the Sword I forsook for the sake of the Church;
He ventured the soul, and I risk'd the body—
   'Twas then I proved false to my sodger laddie.
         Sing, lal de lal, &c.

---

* "I lastly was with Curtis, among the floating batteries:" referring to the destruction of the Spanish floating batteries by Captain Curtis, during the famous siege of Gibraltar, 1782.

† "Elliot:" George Augustus Elliot, Lord Heathfield.

‡ This verse is generally omitted when the song is sung.

Full soon I grew sick of the sanctified sot,
   The regiment at large for a husband I got;
From the gilded spontoon to the fife I was ready,
   I askèd no more but a sodger laddie.
         Sing, lal de lal, &c.

But the peace it reduced me to beg in despair,
   Till I met my old boy at a Cunningham fair;
His rags regimental they flutter'd so gaudy,
   My heart it rejoiced at my sodger laddie.
         Sing, lal de lal, &c.

And now I have lived—I know not how long,
   And still I can join in a cup and a song;
But whilst with both hands I can hold the glass steady,
   Here's to thee, my hero, my sodger laddie!
         Sing, lal de lal, &c.

RECITATIVO.

Poor Merry Andrew, in the neuk,
   Sat guzzling wi' a tinkler hizzie;
They mind't na wha the chorus teuk,
   Between themselves they were sae busy
At length, wi' drink an' courting dizzy,
   He stoiter'd up an' made a face;
Then turn'd, an' laid a smack on Grizzy,
   Syne tun'd his pipes wi' grave grimace.

AIR.
LIVELY.   TUNE—"Auld Sir Symon the King."

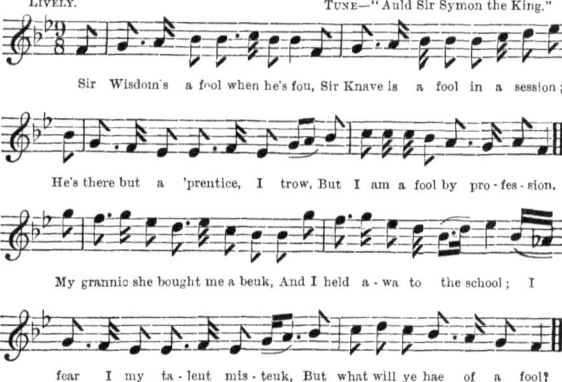

Sir Wisdom's a fool when he's fou, Sir Knave is a fool in a session; He's there but a 'prentice, I trow, But I am a fool by pro-fes-sion. My grannie she bought me a beuk, And I held a-wa to the school; I fear I my ta-lent mis-teuk, But what will ye hae of a fool?

For drink I would venture my neck;
   A hizzie's the half o' my craft;
But what could ye other expect
   Of ane that's avowedly daft?

I ance was tied up like a stirk,
   For civilly swearing and quaffing;
I ance was abused i' the kirk,
   For towzling a lass i' my daffin'.

Poor Andrew that tumbles for sport
  Let naebody name wi' a jeer;
There's even, I'm tauld, i' the court,
  A tumbler ca'd the Premier.

Observed ye yon reverend lad
  Mak faces to tickle the mob?
He rails at our mountebank squad—
  It's rivalship just i' the job.

And now my conclusion I'll tell,
  For faith I'm confoundedly dry;
The chiel that's a fool for himsel',
  Gude L—d! he's far dafter than I.

RECITATIVO.

Then neist outspak a raucle carlin,
Wha kent fu' weel to cleek the sterlin',
For mony a pursie she had hookit,
An' had in mony a well been doukit;
Her love had been a Highland laddie,
But weary fa' the waefu' woodie!
Wi' sighs and sobs she thus began
To wail her braw John Highlandman.

AIR.

With his philibeg an' tartan plaid,
An' guid claymore down by his side,
The ladies' hearts he did trepan,
My gallant, braw John Highlandman.
  Sing hey, &c.

We rangèd a' from Tweed to Spey,
An' liv'd like lords an' ladies gay;
For a Lalland face he fearèd none—
My gallant, braw John Highlandman.
  Sing hey, &c.

They banish'd him beyond the sea;
But ere the bud was on the tree,
Adown my cheeks the pearls ran,
Embracing my John Highlandman.
  Sing hey, &c.

But, och! they catch'd him at the last,
And bound him in a dungeon fast:
My curse upon them every one,
They've hang'd my braw John Highlandman!
  Sing hey, &c.

And now a widow, I must mourn
The pleasures that will ne'er return;
No comfort but a hearty can,
When I think on John Highlandman.
  Sing hey, &c.

RECITATIVO.

A pigmy scraper wi' his fiddle,
Wha us'd at trystes an' fairs to driddle,
Her strappin' limb and gausy middle
            (He reach'd nae higher)
Had hol'd his heartie like a riddle,
            An' blawn't on fire.

Wi' hand on hainch, and upward e'e,
He croon'd his gamut, one, two, three,
Then in an arioso key,
            The wee Apollo
Set off wi' allegretto glee
            His giga solo.

AIR.

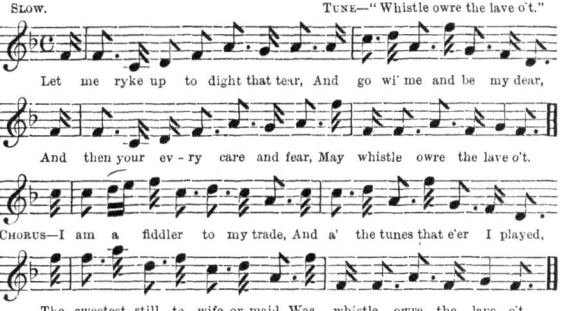

At kirns an' weddin's we'se be there,
An' O sae nicely's we will fare!
We'll bowse about till Daddie Care
  Sing whistle owre the lave o't.
    I am, &c.

Sae merrily's the banes we'll pyke,
An' sun oursells about the dyke;
An' at our leisure, when ye like,
  We'll whistle owre the lave o't.
    I am, &c.

But bless me wi' your heaven o' charms,
An' while I kittle hair on thairms,
Hunger, cauld, an' a' sic harms,
  May whistle owre the lave o't.
    I am, &c.

RECITATIVO.

Her charms had struck a sturdy caird,
  As weel as poor gut-scraper;
He taks the fiddler by the beard,
  An' draws a roosty rapier:
He swoor by a' was swearing worth,
  To speet him like a pliver,
Unless he would from that time forth
  Relinquish her for ever.

Wi' ghastly e'e poor tweedle-dee
  Upon his hunkers bended,
An' pray'd for grace wi' ruefu' face,
  An' so the quarrel ended.
But tho' his little heart did grieve
  When round the tinkler prest her,
He feign'd to snirtle in his sleeve,
  When thus the caird address'd her:

AIR.

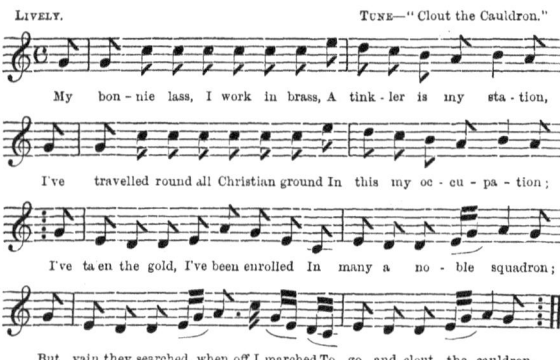

Tune—"Clout the Cauldron."

My bonnie lass, I work in brass, A tinkler is my station,
I've travelled round all Christian ground In this my occupation;
I've ta'en the gold, I've been enrolled In many a noble squadron;
But vain they searched, when off I marched To go and clout the cauldron.

Despise that shrimp, that wither'd imp,
  Wi' a' his noise and cap'rin',
And tak a share wi' those that bear
  The budget and the apron.
And by that stoup, my faith and houp,
  And by that dear Kilbaigie,*
If e'er ye want, or meet wi' scant,
  May I ne'er weet my craigie.
          And by that stoup, &c.

RECITATIVO.

The caird prevail'd—the unblushing fair
  In his embraces sunk,
Partly wi' love o'ercome sae sair,
  And partly she was drunk.

Sir Violino, with an air
  That show'd a man of spunk,
Wish'd unison between the pair,
  And made the bottle clunk
          To their health that night.

But hurchin Cupid shot a shaft,
  That play'd a dame a shavie;
The fiddler raked her fore and aft,
  Behint the chicken cavie.
Her lord, a wight o' Homer's craft,†
  Though limping with the spavie,
He hirpled up, and lap like daft,
  And shored them Daintie Davie
          O' boot that night.

He was a care-defying blade,
  As ever Bacchus listed!
Though Fortune sair upon him laid,
  His heart she ever miss'd it.
He had no wish but to be glad,
  Nor want but when he thirsted;
He hated nought but to be sad,
  And thus the Muse suggested
          His sang that night.

AIR.

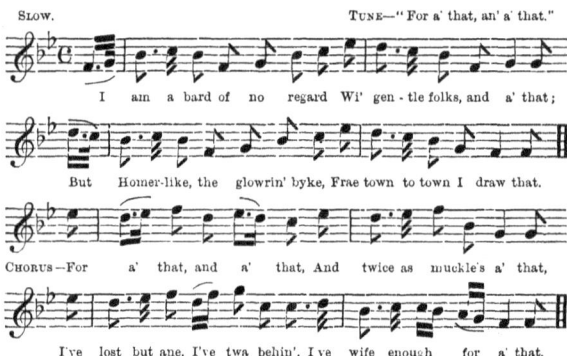

Tune—"For a' that, an' a' that."

I am a bard of no regard Wi' gentle folks, and a' that;
But Homer-like, the glowrin' byke, Frae town to town I draw that.

Chorus—For a' that, and a' that, And twice as muckle's a' that,
I've lost but ane, I've twa behin', I've wife enough for a' that.

I never drank the Muses' stank,
  Castalia's burn, and a' that;
But there it streams, and richly reams,
  My Helicon I ca' that.

Great love I bear to a' the fair,
  Their humble slave, and a' that;
But lordly will, I hold it still
  A mortal sin to thraw that.

In raptures sweet, this hour we meet,
  Wi' mutual love and a' that;
But for how lang the flee may stang,
  Let inclination law that.

---

* "Kilbaigie:" a peculiar sort of whisky, so called from Kilbaigie distillery in Clackmannanshire, and a great favourite with Poosie Nansie's clubs.—(B).

† "Homer's craft:" Homer is allowed to be the oldest ballad-singer on record.—(B).

Their tricks and craft hae put me daft,
    They've ta'en me in, and a' that:
But clear your decks, and here 's the Sex!
    I like the jauds for a' that.
        For a' that, an' a' that,
            And twice as muckle 's a' that;
        My dearest bluid, to do them guid,
            They 're welcome till 't for a' that.

RECITATIVO.

So sung the bard—and Nansie's wa's
    Shook wi' a thunder o' applause,
        Re-echoed from each mouth;
They toom'd their pocks, and pawn'd their duds,
They scarcely left to co'er their fuds,
    To quench their lowin' drouth.
Then owre again the jovial thrang
    The poet did request
To lowse his pack, an' wale a sang,
    A ballad o' the best:
        He rising, rejoicing,
            Between his twa Deborahs,
        Looks round him, and found them
            Impatient for the chorus.

AIR.

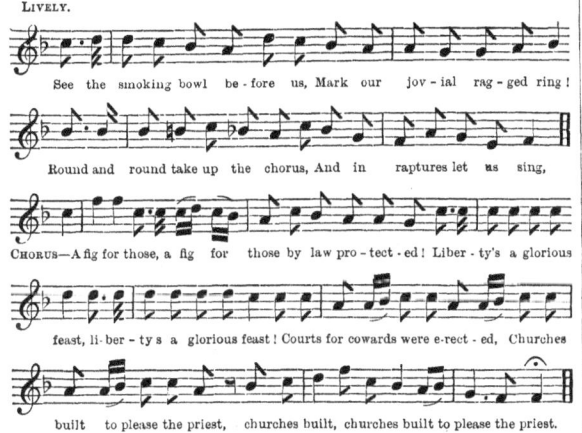

What is title? what is treasure?
    What is reputation's care?
If we lead a life of pleasure,
    'Tis no matter how or where!
        A fig for, &c.

With the ready trick and fable,
    Round we wander all the day;
And at night, in barn or stable,
    Hug our doxies on the hay.
        A fig for, &c.

Does the train-attended carriage
    Through the country lighter rove?
Does the sober bed of marriage
    Witness brighter scenes of love?
        A fig for, &c.

Life is all a variorum,
    We regard not how it goes:
Let them cant about decorum
    Who have character to lose.
        A fig for, &c.

Here 's to budgets, bags, and wallets!
    Here 's to all the wandering train!
Here 's our ragged brats and callets!
    One and all cry out—Amen!
        A fig for, &c.

KISSIN' MY KATIE.*

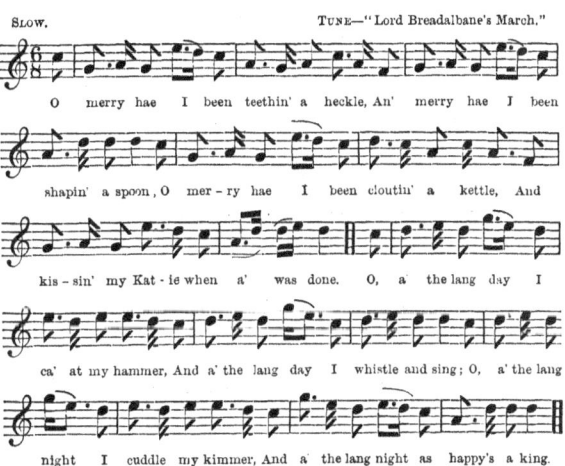

Bitter in dool I lickit my winnins
    O' marrying Bess, to gie her a slave:
Blest be the hour she cool'd in her linnen,
    And blythe be the bird that sings on her grave!
Come to my arms, my Katie, my Katie;
    O come to my arms and kiss me again!
Drucken or sober, here's to thee, Katie!
    An' blest be the day I did it again.

---

* Supposed to have been once intended for insertion in "The Jolly Beggars."

THE COTTAR'S SATURDAY NIGHT.

INSCRIBED TO R. AIKEN,* ESQ.

"Let not Ambition mock their useful toil,
   Their homely joys, and destiny obscure;
Nor Grandeur hear with a disdainful smile
   The short and simple annals of the poor."
                                           GRAY.

My loved, my honour'd, much respected friend!
   No mercenary bard his homage pays;
With honest pride, I scorn each selfish end;
   My dearest meed, a friend's esteem and praise.
To you I sing, in simple Scottish lays,
   The lowly train in life's sequester'd scene;
The native feelings strong, the guileless ways;
   What Aiken in a cottage would have been;
Ah! though his worth unknown, far happier there I ween!

November chill blaws loud wi' angry sough;
   The shortening winter-day is near a close:
The miry beasts retreating frae the pleugh;
   The blackening trains o' craws to their repose:

* "Aiken:" a writer in Ayr and great friend of Burns. Burns at Mossgiel always made family worship.—See LIFE.

The toil-worn Cottar frae his labour goes,
   This night his weekly moil is at an end,
Collects his spades, his mattocks, and his hoes,
   Hoping the morn in ease and rest to spend,
And weary, o'er the moor, his course does hameward bend.

At length his lonely cot appears in view,
   Beneath the shelter of an aged tree:
The expectant wee things, toddlin', stacher through
   To meet their dad, wi' flichterin' noise an' glee.
His wee bit ingle, blinkin' bonnilie,
   His clean hearth-stane, his thriftie wifie's smile,
The lisping infant, prattling on his knee,
   Does a' his weary kiaugh and care beguile,
And makes him quite forget his labour an' his toil.

Belyve, the elder bairns come drapping in,
   At service out amang the farmers roun';
Some ca' the pleugh, some herd, some tentie rin
   A cannie errand to a neibour town:
Their eldest hope, their Jenny, woman-grown,
   In youthfu' bloom, love sparkling in her e'e,
Comes hame, perhaps, to show a braw new gown
   Or deposite her sair-won penny-fee,
To help her parents dear, if they in hardship be.

Wi' joy unfeign'd brothers and sisters meet,
    And each for other's weelfare kindly speirs:
The social hours, swift-wing'd, unnoticed fleet;
    Each tells the uncos that he sees or hears;
The parents, partial, eye their hopeful years;
    Anticipation forward points the view.
The mother, wi' her needle an' her shears,
    Gars auld claes look amaist as weel's the new:
The father mixes a' wi' admonition due.

Their master's and their mistress's command
    The younkers a' are warned to obey;
And mind their labours wi' an eydent hand,
    And ne'er, though out o' sight, to jauk or play:
" And O! be sure to fear the Lord alway,
    And mind your *duty*, duly, morn an' night!
Lest in temptation's path ye gang astray,
    Implore His counsel and assisting might;
They never sought in vain that sought the Lord aright!"

But hark! a rap comes gently to the door;
    Jenny, wha kens the meaning o' the same,
Tells how a neibour lad cam o'er the moor,
    To do some errands, and convoy her hame.
The wily mother sees the conscious flame
    Sparkle in Jenny's e'e, and flush her cheek;
With heart-struck anxious care, inquires his name,
    While Jenny hafflins is afraid to speak;
Weel pleased, the mother hears its nae wild, worthless rake.

Wi' kindly welcome Jenny brings him ben;
    A strappin' youth, he taks the mother's eye;
Blythe Jenny sees the visit 's no ill ta'en;
    The father cracks of horses, pleughs, and kye.
The youngster's artless heart o'erflows wi' joy,
    But blate an' laithfu', scarce can weel behave;
The mother, wi' a woman's wiles, can spy
    What makes the youth sae bashfu' and sae grave;
Weel pleased to think her bairn 's respected like the lave.

O happy love! where love like this is found;
    O heart-felt raptures! bliss beyond compare!
I 've pacèd much this weary, mortal round,
    And sage experience bids me this declare—
" If Heaven a draught of heavenly pleasure spare,
    One cordial in this melancholy vale,
'Tis when a youthful, loving, modest pair,
    In other's arms breathe out the tender tale,
Beneath the milk-white thorn that scents the evening gale."

Is there, in human form, that bears a heart—
  A wretch! a villain! lost to love and truth!
That can, with studied, sly, ensnaring art,
  Betray sweet Jenny's unsuspecting youth?
Curse on his perjured arts! dissembling smooth!
  Are honour, virtue, conscience, all exiled?
Is there no pity, no relenting ruth,
  Points to the parents fondling o'er their child;
Then paints the ruin'd maid, and their distraction wild?

But now the supper crowns their simple board,
  The halesome parritch, chief o' Scotia's food:
The soupe their only hawkie does afford,
  That 'yont the hallan snugly chows her cood:
The dame brings forth, in complimental mood,
  To grace the lad, her weel-hain'd kebbuck, fell;
And aft he 's press'd, and aft he ca's it guid;
  The frugal wifie, garrulous, will tell
How 'twas a towmond auld, sin' lint was i' the bell.

The cheerfu' supper done, wi' serious face,
  They round the ingle form a circle wide;
The sire turns o'er, wi' patriarchal grace,
  The big ha'-bible, ance his father's pride:
His bonnet reverently is laid aside,
  His lyart haffets wearing thin an' bare;
Those strains that once did sweet in Zion glide,
  He wales a portion with judicious care;
And "Let us worship God!" he says with solemn air.

They chant their artless notes in simple guise;
  They tune their hearts, by far the noblest aim:
Perhaps "Dundee's" wild warbling measures rise,
  Or plaintive "Martyrs," worthy of the name;
Or noble "Elgin" beets the heavenward flame,
  The sweetest far of Scotia's holy lays:
Compared with these, Italian trills are tame;
  The tickled ears no heartfelt raptures raise;
Nae unison hae they with our Creator's praise.

The priest-like father reads the sacred page—
  How Abram was the friend of God on high!
Or Moses bade eternal warfare wage
  With Amalek's ungracious progeny;
Or how the royal bard did groaning lie
  Beneath the stroke of Heaven's avenging ire;
Or Job's pathetic plaint and wailing cry;
  Or rapt Isaiah's wild, seraphic fire;
Or other holy seers that tune the sacred lyre.

Perhaps the Christian volume is the theme—
  How guiltless blood for guilty man was shed;
How He, who bore in heaven the second name,
  Had not on earth whereon to lay His head:
How His first followers and servants sped;
  The precepts sage they wrote to many a land;
How he, who lone in Patmos banishèd,
  Saw in the sun a mighty angel stand;
And heard great Babylon's doom pronounced by Heaven's command.

Then kneeling down, to HEAVEN'S ETERNAL KING
  The saint, the father, and the husband prays:
Hope "springs exulting on triumphant wing,"*
  That thus they all shall meet in future days:
There ever bask in uncreated rays,
  No more to sigh, or shed the bitter tear,
Together hymning their Creator's praise
  In such society, yet still more dear;
While circling time moves round in an eternal sphere.

Compared with this, how poor Religion's pride,
  In all the pomp of method and of art,
When men display to congregations wide
  Devotion's every grace, except the heart!
The Power, incensed, the pageant will desert,
  The pompous strain, the sacerdotal stole;
But haply, in some cottage far apart,
  May hear, well-pleased, the language of the soul,
And in His Book of Life the inmates poor enrol.

Then homeward all take off their several way:
  The youngling cottagers retire to rest:
The parent-pair their secret homage pay,
  And proffer up to Heaven the warm request
That He who stills the raven's clamorous nest,
  And decks the lily fair in flowery pride,
Would, in the way His wisdom sees the best,
  For them and for their little ones provide;
But, chiefly, in their hearts with grace divine preside.

From scenes like these old Scotia's grandeur springs.
  That makes her loved at home, revered abroad:
Princes and lords are but the breath of kings,
  "An honest man 's the noblest work of God:"
And certes, in fair virtue's heavenly road,
  The cottage leaves the palace far behind;
What is a lordling's pomp? a cumbrous load,
  Disguising oft the wretch of human kind,
Studied in arts of hell, in wickedness refined!

O Scotia, my dear, my native soil!
  For whom my warmest wish to Heaven is sent!
Long may thy hardy sons of rustic toil
  Be blest with health, and peace, and sweet content!
And O! may Heaven their simple lives prevent
  From luxury's contagion, weak and vile!
Then, howe'er crowns and coronets be rent,
  A virtuous populace may rise the while,
And stand a wall of fire around their much-loved isle.

* Pope's "Windsor Forest."—(B.)

O Thou! who pour'd the patriotic tide
  That stream'd through Wallace's undaunted *
    heart;
Who dared to nobly stem tyrannic pride,
  Or nobly die, the second glorious part:
(The patriot's God peculiarly thou art,
  His friend, inspirer, guardian, and reward!)
O never, never Scotia's realm desert;
  But still the patriot, and the patriot bard,
In bright succession raise, her ornament and guard!

ADDRESS TO THE DEIL.

"O Prince! O chief of many thronèd pow'rs!
That led th' embattled seraphim to war.'—
                                    MILTON.

O THOU! whatever title suit thee,
Auld Hornie, Satan, Nick, or Clootie,
Wha in yon cavern grim an' sootie,
        Closed under hatches,
Spairges about the brunstane cootie, †
        To scaud poor wretches!

Hear me, auld Hangie, for a wee,
An' let poor damnèd bodies be;
I 'm sure sma' pleasure it can gie,
        E'en to a deil,
To skelp an' scaud poor dogs like me,
        An' hear us squeel!

Great is thy power, an' great thy fame;
Far kenn'd an' noted is thy name;
An' though yon lowin' heugh 's thy hame,
        Thou travels far;
An' faith! thou 's neither lag nor lame,
        Nor blate nor scaur.

* "Undaunted:" it was originally "great unhappy."
VOL. I.

† "Cootie:" a foot-pail, supposed to be filled with brimstone.
8

Whyles, rangin' like a roarin' lion,
For prey a' holes an' corners tryin';
Whyles on the strong-winged tempest flyin',
    Tirlin' the kirks;
Whyles in the human bosom pryin',
    Unseen thou lurks.

I've heard my reverend grannie say,
In lanely glens ye like to stray;
Or where auld ruin'd castles, gray,
    Nod to the moon,
Ye fright the nightly wanderer's way,
    Wi' eldritch croon.

When twilight did my grannie summon,
To say her prayers, douce, honest woman!
Aft yont the dyke she's heard you bummin',
    Wi' eerie drone;
Or, rustlin', through the boortrees comin',
    Wi' heavy groan.

Ae dreary, windy, winter night,
The stars shot down wi' sklentin' light,
Wi' you, mysel', I gat a fright,
    Ayont the lough;
Ye, like a rash-bush, stood in sight,
    Wi' wavin' sough.

The cudgel in my nieve did shake,
Each bristled hair stood like a stake,
When wi' an eldritch, stour, "quaick, quaick,"
    Amang the springs,
Awa' ye squatter'd, like a drake,
    On whistling wings.

Let warlocks grim an' wither'd hags
Tell how wi' you, on ragweed nags,
They skim the muirs and dizzy crags,
    Wi' wicked speed;
And in kirkyards renew their leagues,
    Owre howkit dead.

Thence countra wives, wi' toil an' pain,
May plunge an' plunge the kirn in vain;
For, oh! the yellow treasure 's taen
    By witching skill;
And dawtit, twal-pint hawkie 's gaen
    As yeld 's the bill.

Thence mystic knots mak great abuse
On young guidmen, fond, keen, an' crouse;
When the best wark-lume i' the house,
    By cantrip wit,
Is instant made no worth a louse,
    Just at the bit.

When thowes dissolve the snawy hoord,
And float the jinglin' icy-boord,
Then water-kelpies haunt the foord
    By your direction,
And 'nighted travellers are allured
    To their destruction.

An' aft your moss-traversin' spunkies
Decoy the wight that late an' drunk is:
The bleezin', curst, mischievous monkeys
    Delude his eyes,
Till in some miry slough he sunk is,
    Ne'er mair to rise.

When masons' mystic word an' grip
In storms an' tempests raise you up,
Some cock or cat your rage maun stop,
    Or, strange to tell!
The youngest brother ye wad whip
    Aff straught to hell.

Lang syne, in Eden's bonnie yard,
When youthfu' lovers first were paired,
And all the soul of love they shared,
    The raptured hour,
Sweet on the fragrant, flowery swaird,
    In shady bower:

Then you, ye auld, snick-drawing dog!
Ye cam to Paradise *incog.*,
An' play'd on man a cursed brogue,
    (Black be your fa'!)
And gied the infant warld a shog,
    'Maist ruin'd a'.

D'ye mind that day when in a bizz,
Wi' reekit duds an' reestit gizz,
Ye did present your smootie phiz
    'Mang better folk,
An' sklented on the man of Uz
    Your spitefu' joke?

An' how ye gat him i' your thrall,
An' brak him out o' house an' hall,
While scabs an' blotches did him gall,
    Wi' bitter claw,
An' lowsed his ill-tongued, wicked scawl,
    Was warst ava?

But a' your doings to rehearse,
Your wily snares an' fechtin' fierce,
Sin' that day Michael* did you pierce,
    Down to this time,
Wad ding a Lallan tongue, or Erse,
    In prose or rhyme.

* "Michael:" *Vide* Milton, Book vi.—(B.)

ADDRESS TO THE DEIL

And now, auld Cloots, I ken ye 're thinkin'
A certain Bardie 's rantin', drinkin',
Some luckless hour will send him, linkin',
    To your black pit;
But, faith! he 'll turn a corner jinkin',
    An' cheat you yet.

But fare you weel, auld Nickie-ben!
O wad ye tak a thought and men'!
Ye aiblins might—I dinna ken—
    Still hae a stake:
I 'm wae to think upo' yon den,
    E'en for your sake!

SCOTCH DRINK.

"Gie him strong drink, until he wink,
    That 's sinking in despair;
An' liquor guid to fire his bluid,
    That 's prest wi' grief an' care;
There let him bouse, an' deep carouse,
    Wi' bumpers flowing o'er,
Till he forgets his loves or debts,
    An' minds his griefs no more."
        Solomon's Proverbs, xxxi. 6, 7.

Let other Poets raise a fracas
'Bout vines, an' wines, an' drucken Bacchus,
An' crabbit names an' stories wrack us,
    An' grate our lug;
I sing the juice Scotch beare can mak us,
    In glass or jug.

O thou, my Muse! guid auld Scotch drink;
Whether through wimplin' worms thou jink,
Or, richly brown, ream o'er the brink,
    In glorious faem,
Inspire me till I lisp and wink,
    To sing thy name!

Let husky wheat the haughs adorn,
An' aits set up their awnie horn,
An' pease an' beans, at e'en or morn,
    Perfume the plain;
Leeze me on thee, John Barleycorn,
    Thou king o' grain!

On thee aft Scotland chows her cood,
In souple scones, the wale o' food!
Or tumblin' in the boilin' flood
    Wi' kail an' beef;
But when thou pours thy strong heart's blood,
    There thou shines chief.

Food fills the wame, an' keeps us leevin';
Though life 's a gift no worth receivin'
When heavy dragg'd wi' pine an' grievin';
    But oil'd by thee,
The wheels o' life gae downhill, scrievin',
    Wi' rattlin' glee.

Thou clears the head o' doited Lear;
Thou cheers the heart o' drooping Care;
Thou strings the nerves o' Labour sair,
    At 's weary toil;
Thou even brightens dark Despair
    Wi' gloomy smile.

Aft, clad in massy siller weed,
Wi' gentles thou erects thy head;
Yet humbly kind in time o' need,
    The poor man's wine,
His wee drap parritch, or his bread,
    Thou kitchens fine.

Thou art the life o' public haunts;
But thee, what were our fairs and rants?
Even godly meetings o' the saunts,
    By thee inspired,
When gaping they besiege the tents,
    Are doubly fired.

That merry night we get the corn in,
O sweetly then thou reams the horn in!
Or reekin' on a New-year mornin'
    In cog or bicker,
An' just a wee drap sp'ritual burn in,
    An' gusty sucker!

When Vulcan gies his bellows breath,
An' ploughmen gather wi' their graith,
Oh rare! to see thee fizz an' freath
    I' th' lugget cup!
Then Burnewin comes on like death
    At every chap.

Nae mercy then for airn or steel;
The brawnie, bainie, ploughman chiel
Brings hard owrehip, wi' sturdy wheel,
    The strong forehammer,
Till block and studdie ring and reel
    Wi' dinsome clamour.

When skirlin' weanies see the light,
Thou maks the gossips clatter bright,
How fumblin' cuifs their dearies slight;
    Wae worth the name!
Nae howdie gets a social night,
    Or plack frae them.

When neibours anger at a plea,
An' just as wud as wud can be,
How easy can the barley bree
  Cement the quarrel!
It 's aye the cheapest lawyer's fee
  To taste the barrel.

Alake! that e'er my Muse has reason
To wyte her countrymen wi' treason!
But mony daily weet their weason
  Wi' liquors nice,
An' hardly, in a winter's season,
  E'er speir her price.

Wae worth that brandy, burnin' trash!
Fell source o' mony a pain an' brash!
Twins mony a poor, doylt, drucken hash,
  O' half his days!
An' sends, beside, auld Scotland's cash
  To her warst faes.

Ye Scots, wha wish auld Scotland well!
Ye chief, to you my tale I tell;
Poor plackless devils like mysel',
  It sets you ill,
Wi' bitter, dearthfu' wines to mell,
  Or foreign gill.

May gravels round his blather wrench,
An' gouts torment him inch by inch,
Wha twists his gruntle wi' a glunch
  O' sour disdain,
Out owre a glass o' whisky punch
  Wi' honest men.

O Whisky, soul o' plays an' pranks!
Accept a Bardie's gratefu' thanks;
When wantin' thee, what tuneless cranks
  Are my poor verses!
Thou comes—they rattle i' their ranks
  At ither's a—s!

Thee, Ferintosh! O sadly lost!
Scotland lament frae coast to coast!
Now colic grips an' barkin' hoast
  May kill us a';
For loyal Forbes'* charter'd boast
  Is ta'en awa!

Thae curst horse-leeches o' th' Excise,
Wha mak the whisky stells their prize!
Haud up thy han', Deil! ance, twice, thrice!
  There, seize the blinkers!
An' bake them up in brunstane pies
  For poor d——d drinkers.

* "Forbes" of Culloden, who first by an Act of Parliament was empowered to distil whisky at his barony of Ferintosh, free of duty. In 1785 this privilege was abolished, but a handsome compensation was made to the Forbes family.

Fortune! if thou 'll but gie me still
Hale breeks, a scone, an' whisky gill,
An' rowth o' rhyme to rave at will,
  Tak' a' the rest,
An' deal 't about as thy blind skill
  Directs thee best.

THE AULD FARMER'S NEW-YEAR MORNING SALUTATION TO HIS AULD MARE MAGGIE,

ON GIVING HER THE ACCUSTOMED RIPP OF CORN TO HANSEL IN THE NEW-YEAR.

A GUID new-year I wish thee, Maggie!
Hae, there 's a ripp to thy auld baggie:
Though thou 's howe-backit now, and knaggie,
  I 've seen the day
Thou could hae gaen like ony staggie
  Out-owre the lay.

Though now thou 's dowie, stiff, an' crazy,
And thy auld hide 's as white 's a daisy,
I 've seen thee dapplet, sleek, an' glaizie,
  A bonnie gray:
He should been tight that daur't to raise thee,
  Ance in a day.

Thou ance was i' the foremost rank,
A filly buirdly, steeve, an' swank,
An' set weel down a shapely shank,
  As e'er tread yird;
An' could hae flown out-owre a stank,
  Like ony bird.

It 's now some nine-an'-twenty year,
Sin' thou was my guid-father's meare;
He gied me thee, o' tocher clear,
  An' fifty mark;
Though it was sma', 'twas weel-won gear,
  An' thou was stark.

When first I gaed to woo my Jenny,
Ye then was trottin' wi' your minnie:
Though ye was trickie, slee, an' funnie,
  Ye ne'er was donsie;
But hamely, tawie, quiet, an' cannie,
  And unco sonsie.

That day ye pranced wi' muckle pride,
When ye bure hame my bonnie bride:
An' sweet an' gracefu' she did ride,
  Wi' maiden air!
Kyle Stewart I could bragget wide
  For sic a pair.

Though now ye dow but hoyte and hobble,
And wintle like a saumont-coble,
That day ye was a jinker noble,
   For heels an' win'!
And ran them till they a' did wauble,
   Far, far behin'.

When thou an' I were young and skeigh,
And stable-meals at fairs were driegh,
How thou wad prance, an' snore, an' skreigh,
   An' tak the road!
Town's bodies ran, an' stood abeigh,
   An' ca't thee mad.

When thou was corn't, an' I was mellow,
We took the road aye like a swallow:
At brooses* thou had ne'er a fellow
   For pith and speed;
But every tail thou pay't them hollow,
   Where'er thou gaed.

* "Broose:" a race at a wedding, see "Hogg's Tales," or "The Noctes," *passim*.

The sma', droop-rumpl't hunter cattle,
Might aiblins waur't thee for a brattle;
But sax Scotch miles thou try't their mettle
   And gar't them whaizle:
Nae whip nor spur, but just a wattle
   O' saugh or hazel.

Thou was a noble fittie-lan'
As e'er in tug or tow was drawn!

Aft thee an' I, in aught hours' gaun,
    In guid March weather,
Hae turn'd sax rood beside our han',
    For days thegither.

Thou never braindg't, an' fetch't, an' fliskit,
But thy auld tail thou wad hae whiskit,
An' spread abreed thy weel-fill'd brisket,
    Wi' pith an' power,
Till spritty knowes wad rair't an' riskit,
    An' slypet owre.

When frosts lay lang, and snaws were deep,
And threaten'd labour back to keep,
I gied thy cog a wee-bit heap
    Aboon the timmer;
I kenn'd my Maggie wad na sleep
    For that, or simmer.

In cart or car thou never reestit;
The steyest brae thou wad hae faced it;
Thou never lap, and sten't, and breastit,
    Then stood to blaw;
But just thy step a wee thing hastit,
    Thou snoov't awa'.

My pleugh is now thy bairn-time a',
Four gallant brutes as e'er did draw;
Forbye sax mae I 've selt awa',
    That thou hast nurst:
They drew me thretten pund an' twa,
    The vera warst.

Mony a sair daurg we twa hae wrought
An' wi' the weary warl' fought!
An' mony an anxious day I thought
    We wad be beat!
Yet here to crazy age we 're brought,
    Wi' something yet.

An' think na, my auld trusty servan',
That now perhaps thou 's less deservin',
An' thy auld days may end in starvin',
    For my last fou;
A heapit stimpart I 'll reserve ane,
    Laid by for you.

We 've worn to crazy years thegither;
We 'll toyte about wi' ane anither;
Wi' tentie care I 'll flit thy tether
    To some hain'd rig,
Whare ye may nobly rax your leather,
    Wi' sma' fatigue.

THE TWA DOGS.

A TALE.

'Twas in that place o' Scotland's isle,
That bears the name o' Auld King Coil,*
Upon a bonnie day in June,
When wearin' through the afternoon,
Twa dogs, that were na thrang at hame,
Forgather'd ance upon a time.
  The first I 'll name, they ca'd him Cæsar,
Was keepit for his honour's pleasure;
His hair, his size, his mouth, his lugs,
Show'd he was nane o' Scotland's dogs,
But whalpit some place far abroad,
Whare sailors gang to fish for cod.
  His lockèd, letter'd, braw brass collar
Shew'd him the gentleman an' scholar;
But though he was o' high degree,
The fient a pride, nae pride had he;
But wad hae spent an hour caressin',
Ev'n wi' a tinkler-gipsey's messan:
At kirk or market, mill or smiddie,
Nae tawted tyke, though e'er sae duddie,
But he wad stand, as glad to see him,
An' stroan'd on stanes an' hillocks wi' him.
  The tither was a ploughman's collie—
A rhyming, ranting, raving billie,
Wha for his friend an' comrade had him,
And in his freaks had Luath ca'd him,
After some dog† in Highland sang,
Was made lang syne—Lord knows how lang.
  He was a gash an' faithfu' tyke,
As ever lap a sheugh or dyke.
His honest, sonsie, baws'nt face
Aye gat him friends in ilka place;
His breast was white, his tousie back
Weel clad wi' coat o' glossy black;
His gawsie tail, wi' upward curl,
Hung owre his hurdies wi' a swirl.
  Nae doubt but they were fain o' ither,
An' unco pack an' thick thegither;
Wi' social nose whyles snuff'd an' snowket;
Whyles mice an' moudieworts they howket;
Whyles scour'd awa' in lang excursion,
An' worry'd ither in diversion;
Till tir'd at last wi' mony a farce,‡
They set them down upon their a—e,
An' there began a lang digression
About the lords o' the creation.

---

* "Auld King Coil:" the ancient King of the Picts.
 † "Dog:" Cuchullin's dog in Ossian's "Fingal."—(B.). Luath, a dog of Burns', killed the night before his father's death; Burns said he would immortalize him. Cæsar is imaginary.

   ‡ "Until wi' daffin weary grown,
     Upon a knowe they sat them down."

CÆSAR.

I've aften wonder'd, honest Luath,
What sort o' life poor dogs like you have;
An' when the gentry's life I saw,
What way poor bodies liv'd ava.

Our laird gets in his rackèd rents,
His coals, his kane, an' a' his stents:
He rises when he likes himsel';
His flunkies answer at the bell;
He ca's his coach; he ca's his horse;
He draws a bonnie silken purse

As lang's my tail, whare, through the steeks,
The yellow letter'd Geordie keeks.
  Frae morn to e'en it's nought but toiling
At baking, roasting, frying, boiling;
An' though the gentry first are stechin,
Yet ev'n the ha' folk fill their pechan
Wi' sauce, ragouts, an' sic like trashtrie,
That's little short o' downright wastrie.
Our whipper-in, wee, blastet wonner,
Poor, worthless elf, it eats a dinner
Better than ony tenant-man
His honour has in a' the lan':

An' what poor cot-folk pit their painch in,
I own it's past my comprehension.

LUATH.

  Trowth, Cæsar, whyles they're fash't eneugh:
A cottar howkin in a sheugh,
Wi' dirty stanes biggin a dyke,
Baring a quarry, an' sic like;
Himself, a wife, he thus sustains,
A smytrie o' wee duddie weans,
An' nought but his han'-daurg to keep
Them right an' tight in thack an' rape.

An' when they meet wi' sair disasters,
Like loss o' health or want o' masters,
Ye maist wad think, a wee touch langer,
An' they maun starve o' cauld and hunger:
But how it comes I never kent yet,
They 're maistly wonderfu' contented;
An' buirdly chiels, an' clever hizzies,
Are bred in sic a way as this is.

CÆSAR.

But then to see how ye 're negleckit,
How huff'd, and cuff'd, and disrespeckit!
L—d, man, our gentry care as little
For delvers, ditchers, an' sic cattle;
They gang as saucy by puir folk
As I wad by a stinkin' brock.

I 've noticed, on our laird's court-day,
An' mony a time my heart 's been wae,
Puir tenant bodies, scant o' cash,
How they maun thole a factor's snash;
He 'll stamp an' threaten, curse an' swear,
He 'll apprehend them, poind their gear;
While they maun stan', wi' aspect humble,
An' hear it a', an' fear and tremble!

I see how folk live that hae riches;
But surely poor folk maun be wretches!

LUATH.

They 're nae sae wretched 's ane wad think,
Though constantly on poortith's brink:
They 're sae accustom'd wi' the sight,
The view o 't gies them little fright.
Then chance and fortune are sae guided,
They 're aye in less or mair provided;
An' though fatigued wi' close employment,
A blink o' rest 's a sweet enjoyment.
The dearest comfort o' their lives,
Their grushie weans and faithfu' wives;
The prattling things are just their pride,
That sweetens a' their fireside.
An' whyles twalpenny worth o' nappy
Can mak the bodies unco happy;
They lay aside their private cares,
To mind the Kirk and State affairs:
They 'll talk o' patronage and priests,
Wi' kindling fury i' their breasts,
Or tell what new taxation 's comin',
An' ferlie at the folk in Lon'on.

As bleak-faced Hallowmas returns,
They get the jovial, rantin' kirns,
When rural life, o' every station,
Unite in common recreation;
Love blinks, Wit slaps, an' social Mirth
Forgets there 's Care upo' the earth.

That merry day the year begins,
They bar the door on frosty win's;
The nappy reeks wi' mantling ream,
An' sheds a heart-inspiring steam;
The luntin' pipe, an' sneeshin mill,
Are handed round wi' right guid will;
The canty auld folks crackin' crouse,
The young anes rantin' through the house—
My heart has been sae fain to see them,
That I for joy hae barkit wi' them.

Still it 's owre true that ye hae said,
Sic game is now owre aften play'd.
There 's mony a creditable stock
O' decent, honest, fawsont folk,
Are riven out baith root and branch,
Some rascal's pridefu' greed to quench,
Wha thinks to knit himsel' the faster
In favour wi' some gentle master,
Wha, aiblins, thrang a parliamentin',
For Britain's guid his saul indentin'—

CÆSAR.

Haith, lad, ye little ken about it:
For Britain's guid!—guid faith, I doubt it!
Say rather, gaun as Premiers lead him,
An' saying Aye or No 's they bid him:
At operas an' plays parading,
Mortgaging, gambling, masquerading;
Or may be, in a frolic daft,
To Hague or Calais takes a waft,
To make a tour, an' tak a whirl,
To learn *bon ton*, an' see the worl'.

There, at Vienna or Versailles,
He rives his father's auld entails;
Or by Madrid he takes the route,
To thrum guitars, and fecht wi' nowte;
Or down Italian vista startles,
Whore-hunting amang groves o' myrtles;
Then bowses drumly German water,
To mak himsel' look fair and fatter,
An' clear the consequential sorrows,
Love-gifts of Carnival signoras.
For Britain's guid!—for her destruction!
Wi' dissipation, feud, an' faction.

LUATH.

Hech man! dear sirs! is that the gate
They waste sae mony a braw estate?
Are we sae foughten and harass'd
For gear to gang that gate at last?

O would they stay aback frae courts,
An' please themsel's wi' countra sports,
It wad for every ane be better,
The laird, the tenant, an' the cottar!
For thae frank, rantin', ramblin' billies,
Fient haet o' them 's ill-hearted fellows;
Except for breakin' o' their timmer,
Or speakin' lightly o' their limmer,

THE DEVIL'S PICTURD BEUKS.

Or shootin' of a hare or moor-cock,
The ne'er-a-bit they're ill to poor folk.

But will ye tell me, Master Cæsar,
Sure great folk's life 's a life o' pleasure?
Nae cauld nor hunger e'er can steer them,
The vera thought o't need na fear them.

CÆSAR.

Lord, man, were ye but whyles whare I am,
The gentles ye wad ne'er envy them!
It 's true, they need na starve nor sweat
Thro' winter's cauld or simmer's heat;
They've nae sair-work to craze their banes,
An' fill auld-age wi' grips an' granes:
But human bodies are sic fools,
For a' their colleges and schools,
That when nae real ills perplex them,
They mak enow themsel's to vex them;
An' aye the less they hae to sturt them,
In like proportion less will hurt them.
A country fellow at the pleugh,
His acres till'd, he 's right eneugh;
A country girl at her wheel,
Her dizzens done, she 's unco weel;
But gentlemen, an' ladies warst,
Wi' ev'ndown want o' wark are curst.
They loiter, lounging, lank an' lazy;
Though deil-haet ails them, yet uneasy:
Their days insipid, dull, an' tasteless;
Their nights unquiet, lang, an' restless.
An' ev'n their sports, their balls an' races,
Their galloping through public places,
There 's sic parade, sic pomp an' art,
The joy can scarcely reach the heart.
The men cast out in party-matches,
Then sowther a' in deep debauches.
Ae night they're mad wi' drink an' wh-ring,
Niest day their life is past enduring.
The ladies arm-in-arm in clusters,
As great an' gracious a' as sisters;
But hear their absent thoughts o' ither,
They're a' run deils an' jads thegither.
Whyles, owre the wee bit cup and platie,
They sip the scandal-potion pretty;
Or lee-lang nights, wi' crabbit leuks
Pore owre the devil's pictur'd beuks;
Stake on a chance a farmer's stackyard,
And cheat like ony unhang'd blackguard.
There 's some exceptions, man an' woman;
But this is gentry's life in common.

By this, the sun was out o' sight,
An' darker gloamin' brought the night;
The bum-clock humm'd wi' lazy drone;
The kye stood rowtin' i' the loan;

When up they gat, and shook their lugs,
Rejoic'd they were na men, but dogs;
And each took aff his several way,
Resolv'd to meet some ither day.

THE AUTHOR'S EARNEST CRY AND PRAYER *
TO THE SCOTCH REPRESENTATIVES IN THE HOUSE OF COMMONS.

> "Dearest of distillation! last and best,
> How art thou lost!"
> PARODY ON MILTON.

YE Irish lords, ye knights an' squires,
Wha represent our brughs an' shires,
An' doucely manage our affairs
    In Parliament,
To you a simple Bardie's prayers
    Are humbly sent.

Alas! my roopit muse is hearse!
Your honours' hearts wi' grief 'twad pierce,
To see her sittin' on her a—e
    Low i' the dust,
An' screechin' out prosaic verse,
    An' like to brust!

Tell them wha hae the chief direction,
Scotland an' me 's in great affliction,
E'er sin' they laid that curst restriction
    On aqua vitæ;
An' rouse them up to strong conviction,
    An' move their pity.

Stand forth, an' tell yon premier youth †
The honest, open, naked truth;
Tell him o' mine an' Scotland's drouth,
    His servants humble:
The muckle devil blaw ye south,
    If ye dissemble!

Does ony great man glunch an' gloom?
Speak out, an' never fash your thoom!
Let posts an' pensions sink or soom
    Wi' them wha grant them:
If honestly they canna come,
    Far better want them.

---

* "Prayer:" this was written before the Act anent the Scotch Distilleries, of session 1786; for which Scotland and the author return their most grateful thanks.—(B.) Previous to that the excise laws were enforced with the utmost rigour. The Act abolished the duties on drink and put a tax on stills.

† "Premier youth:" Pitt.

In gath'rin' votes you were na slack;
Now stand as tightly by your tack;
Ne'er claw your lug, an' fidge your back,
  An' hum an' haw;
But raise your arm, an' tell your crack
  Before them a'.

Paint Scotland greetin' owre her thrissle;
Her mutchkin stoup as toom 's a whistle;
An' d——d excisemen in a bussle,
  Seizin' a stell,
Triumphant, crushin' 't like a mussel,
  Or lampit shell.

Then on the tither hand present her,
A blackguard smuggler right behint her,
An' cheek-for-chow, a chuffie vintner,
  Colleaguing join,
Picking her pouch as bare as winter
  Of a' kind coin.

Is there that bears the name o' Scot,
But feels his heart's bluid rising hot,
To see his poor auld mither's pot
  Thus dung in staves,
An' plunder'd o' her hindmost groat
  By gallows knaves?

Alas! I 'm but a nameless wight,
Trod i' the mire out o' sight!
But could I like Montgomeries* fight,
  Or gab like Boswell,†
There 's some sark-necks I wad draw tight,
  An' tie some hose well.

God bless your Honours! can ye see 't,
The kind, auld, cantie carlin greet,
An' no get warmly to your feet,
  An' gar them hear it,
An' tell them wi' a patriot heat
  Ye winna bear it?

Some o' you nicely ken the laws,
To round the period and pause,
An' wi' rhetoric clause on clause
  To mak harangues;
Then echo through Saint Stephen's wa's
  Auld Scotland's wrangs.

Dempster,‡ a true-blue Scot I 'se warran';
Thee, aith-detesting, chaste Kilkerran;§

An' that glib-gabbet Highland baron,
  The Laird o' Graham: ‖
An' ane, a chap that 's d——d auldfarran,
  Dundas ¶ his name.

Erskine,** a spunkie Norland billie;
True Campbells, Frederick an' Ilay; ††
An' Livingstone, the bauld Sir Willie:
  An' mony ithers,
Whom auld Demosthenes or Tully
  Might own for brithers.

See, sodger Hugh, my watchman stented,
If poets e'er are represented;
I ken if that your sword were wanted,
  Ye 'd lend a hand;
But when there 's ought to say anent it,
  Ye 're at a stand.

Arouse, my boys! exert your mettle
To get auld Scotland back her kettle;
Or faith! I 'll wad my new pleugh-pettle,
  Ye 'll see 't or lang,
She 'll teach you, wi' a reekin' whittle,
  Anither sang.

This while she 's been in crankous mood,
Her lost militia ‡‡ fired her bluid;
(Deil nor they never mair do guid,
  Play'd her that pliskie!)
An' now she 's like to rin red-wud
  About her whisky.

An' L——d, if ance they pit her till 't,
Her tartan petticoat she 'll kilt,
An' durk an' pistol at her belt,
  She 'll tak the streets,
An' rin her whittle to the hilt,
  I' th' first she meets!

For God-sake, sirs! then speak her fair,
An' straik her cannie wi' the hair,
An' to the muckle house repair
  Wi' instant speed,
An' strive wi' a' your wit and lear
  To get remead.

Yon ill-tongued tinkler Charlie Fox,
May taunt you wi' his jeers an' mocks;

---

* "Montgomeries:" Hugh Montgomery of Coilsfield, afterwards the twelfth Lord Eglinton.
† "Boswell:" Johnson's Bozzy.
‡ "Dempster:" of Dunnichen, Angusshire.
§ "Kilkerran:" Sir Adam Ferguson.

‖ "The Laird o' Graham:" Duke of Montrose.
¶ "Dundas:" afterwards Lord Melville.
** "Erskine:" probably Thomas, afterwards Lord Erskine.
†† "Frederick and Ilay:" one Lord Register, and the other Lord Advocate, for Scotland, brothers of the Duke of Argyle.
‡‡ "Militia:" a Militia Bill in 1782, when the country was threatened with invasion, was mangled by Rockingham, and lost.

But gie him 't het, my hearty cocks!
   E'en cowe the cadie!
An' send him to his dicing box
   An' sportin' lady.

Tell yon guid bluid o' auld Boconnock's*
I 'll be his debt twa mashlum bannocks,
An' drink his health in auld Nanse Tinnock's †
   Nine times a week,
If he some scheme, like tea an' winnocks, ‡
   Wad kindly seek.

Could he some commutation broach,
I 'll pledge my aith in guid braid Scotch,
He need na fear their foul reproach,
   Nor erudition,
Yon mixtie-maxtie, queer hotch-potch,
   The "Coalition." §

Auld Scotland has a raucle tongue;
She 's just a devil wi' a rung;
An' if she promise auld or young
   To tak their part,
Tho' by the neck she should be strung,
   She 'll no desert.

And now, ye chosen Five-and-Forty,
May still your mither's heart support ye;
Then, tho' a minister grow dorty,
   An' kick your place,
Ye 'll snap your fingers, poor an' hearty,
   Before his face.

God bless your Honours, a' your days,
Wi' sowps o' kail and brats o' claise,
In spite o' a' the thievish kaes,
   That haunt St. Jamie's!
Your humble poet sings an' prays,
   While Rab his name is.

POSTSCRIPT.

LET half-starv'd slaves in warmer skies
See future wines, rich-clust'ring, rise;
Their lot auld Scotland ne'er envies,
   But, blythe and frisky,
She sees her freeborn, martial boys
   Tak aff their whisky.

What tho' their Phœbus kinder warms,
While fragrance blooms and beauty charms,
When wretches range, in famish'd swarms,
   The scented groves;
Or, hounded forth, dishonour arms
   In hungry droves!

Their gun 's a burden on their shouther;
They downa bide the stink o' powther;
Their bauldest thought 's a hank'ring swither
   To stand or rin,
Till skelp—a shot—they 're aff, a throw'ther,
   To save their skin.

But bring a Scotchman frae his hill,
Clap in his cheek a Highland gill,
Say, such is royal George's will,
   An' there 's the foe!
He has nae thought but how to kill
   Twa at a blow.

Nae cauld, faint-hearted doubtings tease him;
Death comes, wi' fearless eye he sees him;
Wi' bluidy hand a welcome gies him;
   An' when he fa's,
His latest draught o' breathin' lea'es him
   In faint huzzas.

Sages their solemn een may steek,
An' raise a philosophic reek,
An' physically causes seek,
   In clime an' season;
But tell me whisky's name in Greek,
   I 'll tell the reason.

Scotland, my auld, respected mither!
Tho' whiles ye moistify your leather
Till, whare ye sit on craps o' heather,
   Ye tine your dam;
Freedom and whisky gang thegither!
   Tak aff your dram!

THE ORDINATION. ||

"For sense, they little owe to frugal Heaven—
To please the mob they hide the little given."

KILMARNOCK wabsters, fidge an' claw,
   An' pour your creeshie nations;
An' ye wha leather rax an' draw,
   Of a' denominations;

---

* "Boconnock:" the Earl of Chatham was the son of Robert Pitt of Boconnock, in Cornwall.
† "Nanse Tinnock:" a worthy old hostess of the author's in Mauchline, where he sometimes studies politics over a glass of guid auld Scotch drink.—(B.)
‡ "Tea an' winnocks:" Pitt reduced the tax on tea, and laid one on windows, in 1784.
§ "Coalition:" between Fox, North, and Burke.

|| "The Ordination:" of Rev. James Mackinlay, in Kilmarnock, whose call and ordination, in place of a moderate, gave the highfliers a great triumph. His life in Kilmarnock was not a bed of roses, owing to a clamour at his marriage.

Swith! to the Laigh Kirk, ane an' a',
　　An' there tak up your stations;
Then aff to Begbie's* in a raw,
　　An' pour divine libations
　　　　　　For joy this day.

Curst Common-sense, that imp o' h—l,
　　Cam in wi' Maggie Lauder:†
But Oliphant‡ aft made her yell,
　　An' Russell§ sair misca'd her:
This day Mackinlay taks the flail,
　　An' he's the boy will blaud her!
He'll clap a shangan on her tail,
　　An' set the bairns to daud her
　　　　　　Wi' dirt this day.

Mak haste an' turn King David owre,
　　An' lilt wi' holy clangor;
O' double verse come gie us four,
　　An' skirl up "the Bangor:"
This day the kirk kicks up a stoure,
　　Nae mair the knaves shall wrang her;
For Heresy is in her pow'r,
　　And gloriously she'll whang her,
　　　　　　Wi' pith this day.

Come, let a proper text be read,
　　An' touch it aff wi' vigour,
How graceless Ham‖ leugh at his dad,
　　Which made Canaan a nigger;
Or Phineas¶ drove the murdering blade,
　　Wi' whore-abhorring rigour;
Or Zipporah,** the scauldin' jad,
　　Was like a bluidy teeger,
　　　　　　I' th' inn that day.

There, try his mettle on the creed,
　　And bind him down wi' caution—
That stipend is a carnal weed
　　He taks but for the fashion;
And gie him o'er the flock to feed,
　　And punish each transgression;
Especial, rams that cross the breed,
　　Gie them sufficient threshin';
　　　　　　Spare them nae day.

Now, auld Kilmarnock, cock thy tail,
　　An' toss thy horns fu' canty;
Nae mair thou'lt rowte out-owre the dale,
　　Because thy pasture's scanty;
For lapfu's large o' gospel kail
　　Shall fill thy crib in plenty,
An' runts o' grace the pick an' wale,
　　No gi'en by way o' dainty,
　　　　　　But ilka day.

Nae mair by "Babel's streams" we'll weep,
　　To think upon our "Zion;"
An' hing our fiddles up to sleep,
　　Like baby-clouts a-dryin'!
Come, screw the pegs wi' tunefu' cheep,
　　And o'er the thairms be tryin';
O, rare! to see our elbucks wheep,
　　And a' like lamb-tails flyin',
　　　　　　Fu' fast this day!

Lang, Patronage, wi' rod o' airn,
　　Has shor'd the Kirk's undoin;
As lately Fenwick,†† sair forfairn,
　　Has proven to its ruin:
Our patron, honest man! Glencairn,
　　He saw mischief was brewin';
An' like a godly, elect bairn,
　　He's waled us out a true ane,
　　　　　　And sound this day.

Now, Robertson,‡‡ harangue nae mair,
　　But steek your gab for ever;
Or try the wicked town of Ayr,
　　For there they'll think you clever;
Or, nae reflection on your lear,
　　Ye may commence a shaver;
Or to the Netherton§§ repair,
　　An' turn a carpet-weaver,
　　　　　　Aff-hand this day.

Mu'trie‖‖ and you were just a match,
　　We never had sic twa drones;
Auld Hornie did the Laigh Kirk watch,
　　Just like a winkin baudrons,
And aye he catch'd the tither wretch,
　　To fry them in his caudrons;
But now his Honour maun detach,
　　Wi' a' his brimstone squadrons,
　　　　　　Fast, fast this day.

See, see auld Orthodoxy's faes
　　She's swingein' through the city!
Hark, how the nine-tail'd cat she plays!
　　I vow it's unco pretty:

---

* "Begbie's:" a tavern near the church.
† "Maggie Lauder:" alluding to a scoffing ballad which was made on the admission of the late reverend and worthy Mr. Lindsay to the Laigh Kirk.—(B.). His wife, Margaret Lauder, had been housekeeper to Lord Glencairn; and he owed, it was said, his promotion to this.
‡ "Oliphant" an Evangelical minister in Kilmarnock.
§ "Russell:"—see note on "The Holy Fair," and LIFE.
‖ "Ham:" Genesis ix. 22.
¶ "Phinehas:" Numbers xxv. 8.　** "Zipporah:" Exodus iv. 25.

†† "Fenwick:" one Boyd was forced upon the parish of Fenwick in 1782.
‡‡ "Robertson:" the colleague of Mackinlay, a moderate.
§§ "Netherton:" a part of Kilmarnock full of weavers.
‖‖ "Mu'trie:" Mackinlay's predecessor.

There, Learning, with his Greekish face,
   Grunts out some Latin ditty;
And Common-sense is gaun, she says,
   To mak to Jamie Beattie*
           Her plaint this day.

But there's Morality himsel',
   Embracing all opinions;
Hear, how he gies the tither yell,
   Between his twa companions!
See, how she peels the skin an' fell,
   As ane were peelin' onions!
Now there, they 're packèd aff to hell,
   An' banish'd our dominions,
           Henceforth this day.

O happy day! rejoice, rejoice!
   Come bouse about the porter!
Morality's demure decoys
   Shall here nae mair find quarter:
Mackinlay, Russell, are the boys
   That Heresy can torture;
They 'll gie her on a rape a hoyse,
   And cowe her measure shorter
           By th' head some day.

Come, bring the tither mutchkin in,
   And here's—for a conclusion—
To ev'ry New-light† mother's son,
   From this time forth, confusion!
If mair they deave us wi' their din,
   Or Patronage intrusion,
We 'll light a spunk, and ev'ry skin,
   We 'll rin them aff in fusion,
           Like oil, some day.

YE SONS OF OLD KILLIE.

Ye powers who preside o'er the wind and the tide,
   Who markèd each element's border;
Who formed this frame with beneficent aim,
   Whose sovereign statute is order;
Within this dear mansion may wayward contention
   Or witherèd envy ne'er enter;
May secrecy round be the mystical bound,
   And brotherly love be the centre!

TO JAMES SMITH.‡

"Friendship! mysterious cement of the soul,
Sweetener of life, and solder of society,
I owe thee much!"
           BLAIR.

DEAR SMITH, the slee'st, pawkie thief
That e'er attempted stealth or rief,
Ye surely hae some warlock-breef
           Owre human hearts;
For ne'er a bosom yet was prief
           Against your arts.

For me, I swear by sun and moon,
And every star that blinks aboon,
Ye 've cost me twenty pair o' shoon,
           Just gaun to see you;
And every ither pair that 's done,
           Mair ta'en I 'm wi' you.

That auld, capricious carlin, Nature,
To mak amends for scrimpit stature,
She 's turn'd you aff, a human creature
           On her first plan,
And, in her freaks, on every feature
           She 's wrote the Man.

Just now I 've ta'en the fit o' rhyme,
My barmie noddle 's working prime,
My fancy yerkit up sublime
           Wi' hasty summon:
Hae ye a leisure moment's time
           To hear what 's comin'?

Some rhyme a neibour's name to lash;
Some rhyme (vain thought!) for needfu' cash;
Some rhyme to court the countra clash,
           And raise a din;
For me, an aim I never fash—
           I rhyme for fun.

---

* "James Beattie:" the author of the "Essay on Truth," and the "Minstrel."

† "New-light:" is a cant phrase in the West of Scotland for those religious opinions which Dr. Taylor of Norwich has defended so strenuously.—(B.).

‡ "James Smith:" a calico-printer near Linlithgow, who died in the West Indies. Burns wrote on him as a "Wag in Mauchline." He was a little vivacious man.

The star that rules my luckless lot
Has fated me the russet coat,
And damn'd my fortune to the groat;
    But in requit,
Has blest me wi' a random shot
    O' countra wit.

This while my notion 's ta'en a sklent,
To try my fate in guid black prent;
But still the mair I 'm that way bent,
    Something cries, "Hoolie!
I red you, honest man, tak tent!
    Ye 'll shaw your folly.

"There 's ither poets, much your betters,
Far seen in Greek, deep men o' letters,
Hae thought they had insured their debtors
    A' future ages;
Now moths deform, in shapeless tatters,
    Their unknown pages."

Then fareweel hopes o' laurel-boughs,
To garland my poetic brows!
Henceforth I 'll rove where busy ploughs
    Are whistling thrang,
And teach the lanely heights an' howes
    My rustic sang.

I 'll wander on, wi' tentless heed
How never-halting moments speed,
Till Fate shall snap the brittle thread;
    Then, all unknown,
I 'll lay me with the inglorious dead,
    Forgot and gone!

But why o' death begin a tale?
Just now we 're living sound an' hale,
Then top and maintop crowd the sail,
    Heave Care o'er side!
And large, before enjoyment's gale,
    Let 's tak the tide.

This life, sae far 's I understand,
Is a' enchanted fairy-land.
Where Pleasure is the magic wand,
    That, wielded right,
Maks hours like minutes, hand in hand,
    Dance by fu' light.

The magic wand then let us wield;
For, ance that five-an'-forty 's speel'd,
See crazy, weary, joyless eild,
    Wi' wrinkled face,
Comes hoastin', hirplin' owre the field,
    Wi' creepin' pace.

When ance life's day draws near the gloamin',
Then fareweel vacant, careless roamin';
And fareweel cheerfu' tankards foamin',
    An' social noise;
An' fareweel dear, deluding woman,
    The joy of joys!

O Life! how pleasant in thy morning,
Young Fancy's rays the hills adorning!
Cold-pausing Caution's lesson scorning,
    We frisk away
Like schoolboys, at the expected warning,
    To joy and play.

We wander there, we wander here,
We eye the rose upon the brier,
Unmindful that the thorn is near,
    Among the leaves;
And though the puny wound appear,
    Short while it grieves.

Some, lucky, find a flowery spot,
For which they never toil'd nor swat,
They drink the sweet and eat the fat,
    But care or pain;
And, haply, eye the barren hut
    With high disdain.

With steady aim some Fortune chase;
Keen hope does every sinew brace;
Through fair, through foul, they urge the race,
    And seize the prey:
Then cannie, in some cozie place,
    They close the day.

And others, like your humble servan',
Poor wights! nae rules nor roads observin'
To right or left eternal swervin',
    They zig-zag on;
Till curst with age, obscure and starvin',
    They aften groan.

Alas! what bitter toil an' straining—
But truce with peevish, poor complaining!
Is Fortune's fickle Luna waning?
    E'en let her gang!
Beneath what light she has remaining,
    Let 's sing our sang.

My pen I here fling to the door,
And kneel, Ye Powers! and warm implore,
"Though I should wander Terra o'er,
    In all her climes,
Grant me but this, I ask no more,
    Aye rowth o' rhymes.

"Gie dreeping roasts to countra lairds,
 Till icicles hing frae their beards;
Gie fine braw claes to fine life-guards,
    And maids of honour!
And yill and whisky gie to cairds,
    Until they sconner.

"A title—Dempster* merits it;
A garter gie to Willie Pitt;
Gie wealth to some be-ledger'd cit,
    In cent. per cent.;
But give me real, sterling wit,
    And I'm content.

"While ye are pleased to keep me hale,
I'll sit down o'er my scanty meal,
Be 't water-brose or muslin-kail,
    Wi' cheerfu' face,
As lang 's the Muses dinna fail
    To say the grace."

An anxious e'e I never throws
Behint my lug, or by my nose;
I jouk beneath Misfortune's blows
    As weel 's I may;
Sworn foe to sorrow, care, and prose,
    I rhyme away.

O ye douce folk that live by rule,
Grave, tideless-blooded, calm and cool,
Compared wi' you—O fool! fool! fool!
    How much unlike!
Your hearts are just a standing pool,
    Your lives, a dyke!
Nae hair-brain'd sentimental traces
In your unletter'd, nameless faces!
In *arioso* trills and graces
    Ye never stray,
But *gravissimo*, solemn basses
    Ye hum away.

Ye are sae grave, nae doubt ye're wise;
Nae ferly though ye do despise
The hairum-scairum, ram-stam boys,
    The rattlin' squad:
I see ye upward cast your eyes—
    Ye ken the road.

Whilst I—but I shall haud me there—
Wi' you I'll scarce gang ony where—
Then, Jamie, I shall say nae mair,
    But quat my sang,
Content wi' you to mak a pair,
    Whare'er I gang.

* "Dempster:" see note in "Earnest Cry and Prayer"—an eminent parliamentary patriot.

THE VISION.

DUAN FIRST.*

The sun had closed the winter day,
The curlers quat their roaring play,
And hunger'd maukin ta'en her way
    To kail-yards green,
While faithless snaws ilk step betray
    Whare she has been.

The thrasher's weary flingin'-tree,
The lee-lang day, had tirëd me;
And whan the day had closed his e'e,
    Far i' the west,
Ben i' the spence, right pensivelie,
    I gaed to rest.

There, lanely, by the ingle-cheek
I sat and eyed the spewing reek,
That fill'd wi' hoast-provoking smeek
    The auld clay biggin';
And heard the restless rattons squeak
    About the riggin'.

All in this mottie, misty clime,
I backward mused on wasted time,
How I had spent my youthfu' prime,
    An' done nae thing,
But stringin' blethers up in rhyme,
    For fools to sing.

Had I to guid advice but harkit,
I might, by this, hae led a market,
Or strutted in a bank, and clarkit
    My cash-account:
While here, half-mad, half-fed, half-sarkit,
    Is a' the amount.

I started, muttering blockhead! coof!
And heaved on high my waukit loof,
To swear by a' yon starry roof,
    Or some rash aith,
That I, henceforth, would be rhyme-proof
    Till my last breath—

When, click! the string the sneck did draw;
An' jee! the door gaed to the wa';
An' by my ingle-lowe I saw,
    Now bleezin' bright,
A tight, outlandish hizzie, braw,
    Come full in sight,

Ye need na doubt, I held my whisht;
The infant aith, half-form'd, was crusht;
I glowr'd as eerie 's I 'd been dusht
    In some wild glen;
When sweet, like modest Worth, she blusht,
    And steppit ben.

Green, slender, leaf-clad holly-boughs
Were twisted, gracefu', round her brows;
I took her for some Scottish Muse,
    By that same token,
And come to stop those reckless vows
    Wad soon been broken.

A "hair-brain'd, sentimental trace"
Was strongly markèd in her face;
A wildly-witty, rustic grace
    Shone full upon her;
Her eye, even turn'd on empty space,
    Beam'd keen with honour.

Down flow'd her robe, a tartan sheen,
Till half a leg was scrimply seen;
And such a leg! my bonnie Jean
    Could only peer it;
Sae straught, sae taper, tight, and clean,
    Nane else cam near it.

Her mantle large, of greenish hue,
My gazing wonder chiefly drew;
Deep lights and shades, bold-mingling, threw
    A lustre grand;
And seem'd, to my astonish'd view,
    A well known land.

Here rivers in the sea were lost;
There mountains to the skies were tost;
Here tumbling billows mark'd the coast
    With surging foam;
There distant shone Art's lofty boast,
    The lordly dome.

Here Doon pour'd down his far-fetch'd floods;
There well-fed Irwine stately thuds:
Auld hermit Ayr staw through his woods,
    On to the shore;
And many a lesser torrent scuds,
    With seeming roar.

Low, in a sandy valley spread,
An ancient burgh rear'd her head;
Still, as in Scottish story read,
    She boasts a race
To every nobler virtue bred,
    And polish'd grace.

---

* "Duan:" a term of Ossian's for the different divisions of a digressive poem. See his *Cath-Loda*, vol. ii. of M'Pherson's translation.—(B.).

THE VISION

By stately tower, or palace fair,
Or ruins pendent in the air,
Bold stems of heroes, here and there,
    I could discern;
Some seem'd to muse, some seem'd to dare,
    With feature stern.

My heart did glowing transport feel,
To see a race* heroic wheel,
And brandish round the deep-dyed steel
    In sturdy blows;
While, back-recoiling, seem'd to reel
    Their Southron foes.

His Country's Saviour,† mark him well!
Bold Richardton's‡ heroic swell;
The chief on Sark§ who glorious fell
    In high command;
And he whom ruthless fates expel
    His native land.

There, where a sceptred Pictish shade ||
Stalk'd round his ashes lowly laid,
I mark'd a martial race, portray'd
    In colours strong;
Bold, soldier-featured, undismay'd,
    They strode along.

Through many a wild romantic grove,¶
Near many a hermit-fancied cove,
(Fit haunts for friendship or for love)
    In musing mood,
An aged Judge, I saw him rove,
    Dispensing good.

With deep-struck, reverential awe,
The learned sire and son** I saw:
To Nature's God and Nature's law
    They gave their lore
This, all its source and end to draw;
    That, to adore.

---

* "A race:" the Wallaces.—(B.).

† "Country's saviour:" William Wallace.—(B.)

‡ "Richardton:" Adam Wallace, of Richardton, cousin to the immortal preserver of Scottish independence.—(B.)

§ "Sark:" Wallace, Laird of Craigie, who was second in command, under Douglas, Earl of Ormond, at the famous battle on the banks of Sark, fought *anno* 1448. That glorious victory was principally owing to the judicious conduct and intrepid valour of the gallant Laird of Craigie, who died of his wounds after the action.—(B.) Wallace of Craigie was in later days a very zealous reformer.

|| "Pictish shade:" Coilus, king of the Picts, from whom the district of Kyle is said to take its name, lies buried, as tradition says, near the family-seat of the Montgomeries of Coilsfield, where his burial place is still shown.—(B.).

¶ "Romantic grove:" Barskimming, the seat of the late Lord Justice Clerk.—(B.). Sir T. Miller, afterwards President of the Court of Session.

** "Learned sire and son:" Catrine, the seat of the late Doctor and present Professor Stewart.—(B.).

Vol. I.

Brydone's brave ward†† I well could spy
Beneath old Scotia's smiling eye;
Who call'd on Fame, low-standing by,
    To hand him on,
Where many a patriot name on high,
    And hero shone.

DUAN SECOND.

With musing-deep, astonish'd stare,
I view'd the heavenly-seeming Fair;
A whispering throb did witness bear
    Of kindred sweet,
When with an elder sister's air
    She did me greet.

"All hail! my own inspirèd bard!
In me thy native Muse regard;
Nor longer mourn thy fate is hard,
    Thus poorly low.
I come to give thee such reward
    As we bestow.

"Know, the great Genius of this land
Has many a light aërial band,
Who, all beneath his high command,
    Harmoniously,
As arts or arms they understand,
    Their labours ply.

"They Scotia's race among them share:
Some fire the soldier on to dare;
Some rouse the patriot up to bare
    Corruption's heart;
Some teach the bard, a darling care,
    The tuneful art.

"'Mong swelling floods of reeking gore,
They, ardent, kindling spirits pour;
Or 'mid the venal senate's roar
    They, sightless, stand,
To mend the honest patriot-lore,
    And grace the hand.

"And when the bard or hoary sage
Charm or instruct the future age,
They bind the wild poetic rage
    In energy,
Or point the inconclusive page
    Full on the eye.

"Hence Fullerton, the brave and young;
Hence Dempster's‡‡ zeal-inspired tongue;

---

†† "Brydone's brave ward:" Colonel Fullerton.—(B). Fullerton had travelled with Patrick Brydone, the once celebrated traveller, as his ward.

‡‡ See Epistle to James Smith.

Hence sweet harmonious Beattie sung
        His " Minstrel " lays,
Or tore, with noble ardour stung,
        The sceptic's bays.

" To lower orders are assign'd
The humbler ranks of human-kind,
The rustic bard, the labouring hind,
        The artisan;
All choose, as various they 're inclined,
        The various man.

" When yellow waves the heavy grain,
The threatening storm some strongly rein;
Some teach to meliorate the plain
        With tillage-skill;
And some instruct the shepherd-train,
        Blythe o'er the hill.

" Some hint the lover's harmless wile;
Some grace the maiden's artless smile;
Some soothe the labourer's weary toil
        For humble gains,
And make his cottage-scenes beguile
        His cares and pains.

" Some, bounded to a district-space,
Explore at large man's infant race,
To mark the embryotic trace
        Of rustic bard;
And careful note each opening grace,
        A guide and guard.

" Of these am I—Coila my name;
And this district as mine I claim,
Where once the Campbells,* chiefs of fame,
        Held ruling power:
I mark'd thy embryo tuneful flame,
        Thy natal hour.

" With future hope I oft would gaze,
Fond, on thy little early ways,
Thy rudely caroll'd, chiming phrase,
        In uncouth rhymes;
Fired at the simple, artless lays
        Of other times.

" I saw thee seek the sounding shore,
Delighted with the dashing roar;
Or when the North his fleecy store
        Drove through the sky,
I saw grim Nature's visage hoar
        Struck thy young eye.

" Or when the deep green-mantled earth
Warm cherish'd every floweret's birth,
And joy and music pouring forth
        In every grove,
I saw thee eye the general mirth
        With boundless love.

" When ripen'd fields and azure skies
Call'd forth the reaper's rustling noise,
I saw thee leave their evening joys,
        And lonely stalk,
To vent thy bosom's swelling rise
        In pensive walk.

" When youthful love, warm-blushing, strong,
Keen-shivering shot thy nerves along,
Those accents, grateful to thy tongue,
        The adored Name,
I taught thee how to pour in song,
        To soothe thy flame.

" I saw thy pulse's maddening play,
Wild send thee Pleasure's devious way
Misled by Fancy's meteor ray,
        By passion driven;
But yet the light that led astray
        Was light from Heaven.

" I taught thy manners-painting strains,
The loves, the ways of simple swains,
Till now o'er all my wide domains
        Thy fame extends;
And some, the pride of Coila's plains,
        Become thy friends.

" Thou canst not learn, nor can I show,
To paint with Thomson's landscape glow;
Or wake the bosom-melting throe,
        With Shenstone's art;
Or pour, with Gray, the moving flow
        Warm on the heart.

" Yet, all beneath the unrivall'd rose,
The lowly daisy sweetly blows;
Though large the forest's monarch throws
        His army shade,
Yet green the juicy hawthorn grows
        Adown the glade.

" Then never murmur nor repine;
Strive in thy humble sphere to shine;
And, trust me, not Potosi's mine,
        Nor kings' regard,
Can give a bliss o'ermatching thine,
        A rustic Bard.

---

* " Campbells:" the Loudoun branch of that family; Mossgiel was the Earl of Loudoun's property.

"To give my counsels all in one—
Thy tuneful flame still careful fan;
Preserve the dignity of man,
    With soul erect;
And trust the Universal Plan
    Will all protect.

"And wear thou *this*"—she solemn said,
And bound the holly round my head:
The polish'd leaves and berries red
    Did rustling play;
And, like a passing thought, she fled
    In light away.

SUPPRESSED STANZAS OF "THE VISION."*

After 18th stanza:—

With secret throes I marked that earth,
That cottage, witness of my birth;
And near I saw, bold issuing forth
    In youthful pride,
A Lindsay race of noble worth,
    Famed far and wide.

Where, hid behind a spreading wood,
An ancient Pict-built mansion stood,
I spied, among an angel brood,
    A female pair;
Sweet shone their high maternal blood,
    And father's air. †

An ancient tower‡ to memory brought
How Dettingen's bold hero fought;
Still, far from sinking into nought,
    It owns a lord
Who far in western climates fought,
    With trusty sword.

Among the rest I well could spy
One gallant, graceful, martial boy,
The *soldier* sparkled in his eye,
    A diamond water;
I blest that noble badge with joy
    That owned me *frater*. §

After 20th stanza:—

Near by arose a mansion fine, ||
The seat of many a muse divine;
Not rustic muses such as mine,
    With holly crown'd,
But th' ancient, tuneful, laurell'd Nine,
    From classic ground.

I mourn'd the card that Fortune dealt,
To see where bonnie Whitefoords dwelt;*
But other prospects made me melt,
    That village near;†
There Nature, Friendship, Love, I felt,
    Fond-mingling dear!

Hail! Nature's pang, more strong than death!
Warm Friendship's glow, like kindling wrath!
Love, dearer than the parting breath
    Of dying friend!
Not ev'n with life's wild devious path,
    Your force shall end!

The Pow'r that gave the soft alarms
In blooming Whitefoord's rosy charms,
Still threats the tiny, feather'd arms,
    The barbèd dart,
While lovely Wilhelminia warms
    The coldest heart. ‡

After 21st stanza:—

Where Lugar leaves his moorland plaid,§
Where lately Want was idly laid,
I markèd busy, bustling trade,
    In fervid flame,
Beneath a Patroness's aid,
    Of noble name.

Wild, countless hills I could survey,
And countless flocks as wild as they;
But other scenes did charms display,
    That better please,
Where polish'd manners dwell with Gray,
    In rural ease. ||

Where Cessnock pours with gurgling sound; ¶
And Irwine, marking out the bound,
Enamour'd of the scenes around,
    Slow runs his race,
A name I doubly honour'd found,**
    With knightly grace.

Brydon's brave ward,†† I saw him stand,
Fame humbly offering her hand,
And near, his kinsman's rustic band,‡‡
    With one accord,
Lamenting their late blessed land
    Must change its lord.

The owner of a pleasant spot,
Near sandy wilds, I last did note;§§
A heart too warm, a pulse too hot
    At times, o'erran;
But large in ev'ry feature wrote,
    Appear'd, the Man.

---

* These stanzas, along with the rest, were presented to Mrs. Stewart of Stair, in a manuscript book of ten leaves, called the "Stair Manuscript."

† Sundrum.—(B.) Hamilton of Sundrum was married to a sister of Colonel Montgomerie of Coilsfield

‡ Stair.—(B.) That old mansion was then possessed by General Stewart and his lady, to whom the MS. was presented.

§ Captain James Montgomerie, Master of St. James' Lodge, Tarbolton, to which the author has the honour to belong.—(B.)

|| Auchinleck.—(B.)

* Ballochmyle.   † Mauchline.

‡ A compliment to Miss Wilhelmina Alexander as successor, in that locality, to Miss Maria Whitefoord.

§ Cumnock.--(B.) || Mr. Farquhar Gray.-(B.)   ¶ Auchinskieth.-(B.)
** Caprington.—(B.)   †† Colonel Fullerton (see note, p. 73).—(B.)
‡‡ Dr. Fullerton.—(B.)   §§ Orangefield.—(B.)

WINTER NIGHT.

" Poor naked wretches, wheresoe'er you are,
That bide the pelting of this pitiless storm!
How shall your houseless heads and unfed sides,
Your loop'd and window'd raggedness, defend you
From seasons such as these?"
SHAKSPEARE.

When biting Boreas, fell and doure,
Sharp shivers through the leafless bower;
When Phœbus gies a short-lived glower
    Far south the lift,
Dim-darkening through the flaky shower,
    Or whirling drift:

Ae night the storm the steeples rock'd,
Poor Labour sweet in sleep was lock'd,
While burns, wi' snawy wreaths up-chok'd,
    Wild-eddying swirl,
Or through the mining outlet bock'd,
    Down headlong hurl.

Listening the doors and winnocks rattle,
I thought me on the ourie cattle,
Or silly sheep, wha bide this brattle
    O' winter war,
And through the drift, deep-lairing, sprattle
    Beneath a scaur.

Ilk happing bird, wee, helpless thing,
That, in the merry months o' spring,
Delighted me to hear thee sing,
    What comes o' thee?
Whare wilt thou cower thy chittering wing,
    And close thy e'e?

Even you, on murdering errands toil'd,
Lone from your savage homes exiled,
The blood-stain'd roost, and sheep-cote spoil'd,
    My heart forgets,
While pitiless the tempest wild
    Sore on you beats.

Now Phœbe, in her midnight reign,
Dark muffled, view'd the dreary plain;
Still crowding thoughts, a pensive train,
    Rose in my soul,
When on my ear this plaintive strain
    Slow, solemn, stole :—

" Blow, blow, ye winds, with heavier gust!
And freeze, thou bitter-biting frost!
Descend, ye chilly, smothering snows!
Not all your rage, as now united, shows
  More hard unkindness, unrelenting,
  Vengeful malice unrepenting,
Than Heaven-illumined man on brother man bestows!

"See stern Oppression's iron grip,
  Or mad Ambition's gory hand,
Sending, like blood-hounds from the slip,
  Woe, want, and murder o'er a land!
Even in the peaceful rural vale,
Truth, weeping, tells the mournful tale,
How pamper'd Luxury, Flattery by her side,
  The parasite empoisoning her ear,
  With all the servile wretches in the rear,
Looks o'er proud Property, extended wide;
  And eyes the simple rustic hind,
  Whose toil upholds the glittering show,
A creature of another kind,
  Some coarser substance, unrefined,
Placed for her lordly use thus far, thus vile, below.

"Where, where is Love's fond, tender throe,
  With lordly Honour's lofty brow,
    The powers you proudly own?
Is there, beneath Love's noble name,
Can harbour, dark, the selfish aim,
    To bless himself alone?
Mark maiden-innocence a prey
    To love-pretending snares,
This boasted Honour turns away,
Shunning soft Pity's rising sway,
Regardless of the tears, and unavailing prayers!
Perhaps, this hour, in Misery's squalid nest,
She strains your infant to her joyless breast,
And with a mother's fears shrinks at the rocking blast!

"O ye who, sunk in beds of down,
Feel not a want but what yourselves create,
  Think, for a moment, on his wretched fate,
  Whom friends and fortune quite disown!
Ill-satisfied keen Nature's clamorous call,
Stretch'd on his straw he lays himself to sleep,
While through the ragged roof and chinky wall,
Chill o'er his slumbers piles the drifty heap!
    Think on the dungeon's grim confine,
    Where Guilt and poor Misfortune pine!
  Guilt, erring man, relenting view!
  But shall thy legal rage pursue
  The wretch already crushèd low
By cruel Fortune's undeservèd blow?
Affliction's sons are brothers in distress,
A brother to relieve, how exquisite the bliss!"

  I heard nae mair, for chanticleer
    Shook off the pouthery snaw,
  And hail'd the morning with a cheer,
    A cottage-rousing craw.

  But deep this truth impress'd my mind—
    Through all His works abroad,
  The heart benevolent and kind
    The most resembles God.

THE RANTIN' DOG, THE DADDIE O'T.

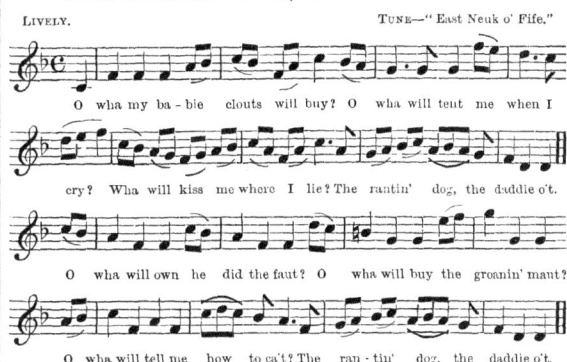

When I mount the creepie chair,
Wha will sit beside me there?
Gie me Rob, I'll seek nae mair—
  The rantin' dog, the daddie o't.

Wha will crack to me my lane?
Wha will mak me fidgin' fain?
Wha will kiss me o'er again?
  The rantin' dog, the daddie o't.

ADDRESS TO THE UNCO GUID, OR THE RIGIDLY RIGHTEOUS.

  " My son, these maxims make a rule,
    And lump them aye thegither;
  The Rigid Righteous is a fool,
    The Rigid Wise anither:
  The cleanest corn that e'er was dight
    May hae some pyles o' caff in;
  So ne'er a fellow-creature slight
    For random fits o' daffin."
          SOLOMON.—*Eccles.* vii. 16.

O YE wha are sae guid yoursel'
  Sae pious and sae holy,
Ye 've nought to do but mark and tell
  Your neibours' fauts and folly!
Whase life is like a weel-gaun mill,
  Supplied wi' store o' water,
The heapit happer's ebbing still,
  And still the clap plays clatter.

Hear me, ye venerable core,
  As counsel for poor mortals,
That frequent pass douce Wisdom's door
  For glaiket Folly's portals;

I, for their thoughtless, careless sakes,
    Would here propone defences,
Their donsie tricks, their black mistakes,
    Their failings and mischances.

Ye see your state wi' theirs compared,
    And shudder at the niffer;
But cast a moment's fair regard
    What maks the mighty differ?
Discount what scant occasion gave,
    That purity ye pride in,
And (what 's aft mair than a' the lave)
    Your better art o' hidin'.

Think, when your castigated pulse
    Gies now and then a wallop,
What ragings must his veins convulse,
    That still eternal gallop!
Wi' wind and tide fair i' your tail,
    Right on ye scud your sea-way;
But in the teeth o' baith to sail,
    It maks an unco lee-way.

See Social Life and Glee sit down,
    All joyous and unthinking,
Till, quite transmugrified, they 're grown
    Debauchery and Drinking:
O, would they stay to calculate
    The eternal consequences;
Or, your more dreaded hell to state,
    Damnation of expenses!

Ye high, exalted, virtuous dames,
    Tied up in godly laces,
Before ye gie poor frailty names,
    Suppose a change o' cases;
A dear-loved lad, convenience snug,
    A treacherous inclination;
But, let me whisper i' your lug,
    Ye 're aiblins nae temptation.

Then gently scan your brother man,
    Still gentler, sister woman;
Though they may gang a kennin' wrang,
    To step aside is human:
One point must still be greatly dark,
    The moving *why* they do it:
And just as lamely can ye mark,
    How far perhaps they rue it.

Who made the heart, 'tis He alone
    Decidedly can try us;
He knows each chord, its various tone,
    Each spring, its various bias:

Then at the balance let 's be mute,
    We never can adjust it;
What 's done we partly may compute,
    But know not what 's resisted.

HERE'S HIS HEALTH IN WATER.

THE INVENTORY.

IN ANSWER TO A MANDATE SENT BY THE SURVEYOR OF TAXES.

Sir, as your mandate did request,
I send you here a faithfu' list,
O' gudes an' gear, an' a' my graith,
To which I 'm free to tak my aith.
    Imprimis, then, for carriage cattle,
I hae four brutes o' gallant mettle,
As ever drew before a pettle;
My han'-afore 's* a guid auld has-been,
And wight and wilfu' a' his days been;
My han'-ahin'† 's a weel gaun filly,
That aft has borne me safe frae Killie,‡
And your auld borough mony a time,
In days when riding was nae crime.
But ance, when in my wooing pride,
I, like a blockhead, boost to ride,
The wilfu' creature sae I pat to,
(L⸺d, pardon a' my sins, and that too!)
I play'd my filly sic a shavie,
She 's a' bedevill'd wi' the spavie.

---

* " Han'-afore:" the fore-horse on the left-hand in the plough.
† " Han'-ahin:" the hindmost on the left-hand in the plough.
‡ " Killie:" Kilmarnock.

My fur-ahin'* 's a wordy beast
As e'er in tug or tow was traced :
The fourth 's a Highland Donald hastie,
A d——d red-wud Kilburnie blastie !
Forby a cowte, o' cowtes the wale,
As ever ran afore a tail.
An' he be spared to be a beast,
He 'll draw me fifteen pund at least.

  Wheel carriages I hae but few—
Three carts, and twa are feckly new;
An auld wheel-barrow, mair for token,
Ae leg and baith the trams are broken :
I made a poker o' the spin'le
And my auld mither brunt the trin'le.
For men, I 've three mischievous boys,
Run-deils for rantin' and for noise;
A gadsman ane, a thrasher t' other,
Wee Davoc hauds the nowt in fother.
I rule them, as I ought, discreetly,
And often labour them completely;
And aye on Sundays, duly, nightly,
I on the questions targe them tightly;
Till, faith, wee Davoc's grown sae gleg,
Though scarcely langer than my leg,
He 'll screed you aff Effectual Calling,
As fast as ony in the dwalling.

  I 've nane in female servant station,
(Lord, keep me aye frae a' temptation !)
I hae nae wife, and that my bliss is,
And ye hae laid nae tax on misses;
Wi' weans I 'm mair than weel contented,
Heaven sent me ane mair than I wanted ;
My sonsie, smirking, dear-bought Bess,
She stares the daddie in her face,
Enough of ought ye like but grace.
But her, my bonnie, sweet, wee lady,
I 've said enough for her already ;
And if ye tax her or her mither,
By the L—d ! ye'se get them a' thegither.

  And now, remember, Mr. Aiken,
Nae kind of licence out I 'm takin';
Frae this time forth, I do declare
I 'se ne'er ride horse nor hizzie mair ;
Through dirt and dub for life I 'll paidle,
Ere I sae dear pay for a saddle;
I 've sturdy bearers, Gude be thankit !
My travel a' on foot I 'll shank it.
The kirk an' you may tak you that,
It puts but little in your pat;
Sae dinna put me in your book,
Nor for my ten white shillings look.

  This list wi' my ain hand I 've wrote it,
The day and date as under notit;
Then know, all ye whom it concerns,
  Subscripsi huic,   ROBERT BURNS.

* " Fur-ahin' : " the same on the right-hand in the plough.

TO MR. JOHN KENNEDY.†

Now, Kennedy, if foot or horse
E'er bring you in by Mauchline Corse,
L—d, man, there 's lasses there wad force
    A hermit's fancy ;
And down the gate, in faith, they 're worse,
    And mair unchancy.

But, as I 'm sayin', please step to Dow's,
And taste sic gear as Johnnie brews,
Till some bit callant bring me news
    That you are there;
And if we dinna haud a bouse
    I 'se ne'er drink mair.

It 's no I like to sit and swallow,
Then like a swine to puke and wallow ;
But gie me just a true good fallow,
    Wi' right ingine,
And spunkie ance to make us mellow,
    And then we 'll shine.

Now, if ye 're ane o' warl's folk,
Wha rate the wearer by the cloak,
And sklent on poverty their joke,
    Wi' bitter sneer,
Wi' you no friendship will I troke,
    Nor cheap nor dear.

But if, as I 'm informèd weel,
Ye hate, as ill 's the vera deil,
The flinty heart that canna feel,
    Come, sir, here 's to you !
Hae, there 's my haun', I wiss you weel,
    And gude be wi' you !

TO MR. M'ADAM, OF CRAIGEN-GILLAN,‡

IN ANSWER TO AN OBLIGING LETTER HE SENT IN THE COMMENCEMENT OF MY POETIC CAREER.

  SIR, o'er a gill I gat your card,
    I trow it made me proud ;
  " See wha taks notice o' the bard ! "
    I lap and cried fu' loud.

  Now deil-ma-care about their jaw,
    The senseless, gawky million ;
  I 'll cock my nose aboon them a',
    I 'm roosed by Craigen-Gillan !

  'Twas noble, sir; 'twas like yoursel',
    To grant your high protection :
  A great man's smile, ye ken fu' well,
    Is aye a blest infection—

† A humble clerk near Mauchline, afterwards factor to Lord Breadalbane.
‡ " Craigen-Gillan : " an estate in Carrick.

Though, by his banes* wha in a tub
  Match'd Macedonian Sandy!
On my ain legs through dirt and dub,
  I independent stand aye.

And when those legs to gude warm kail
  Wi' welcome canna bear me;
A lee dyke-side, a syboe-tail,
  And barley-scone, shall cheer me.

Heaven spare you lang to kiss the breath
  O' mony flowery simmers;
And bless your bonnie lasses baith:
  I 'm tauld they 're lo'esome kimmers!

And God bless young Dunaskin's laird,
  The blossom of our gentry!
And may he wear an auld man's beard,
  A credit to his country!

TO A LOUSE,

ON SEEING ONE ON A LADY'S BONNET AT CHURCH.

HA! whare ye gaun, ye crowlin' ferlie?
Your impudence protects you sairly:
I canna say but ye strunt rarely,
      Owre gauze and lace;
Though, faith! I fear ye dine but sparely
      On sic a place.

Ye ugly, creepin', blastit wonner,
Detested, shunn'd by saunt an' sinner,
How daur ye set your fit upon her,
      Sae fine a lady?
Gae somewhere else, and seek your dinner
      On some poor body.

Swith, in some beggar's haffet squattle,
There ye may creep, and sprawl, and sprattle
Wi' ither kindred, jumpin' cattle,
      In shoals and nations;
Whare horn or bane ne'er daur unsettle
      Your thick plantations.

Now haud ye there, ye 're out o' sight,
Below the fatt'rels, snug an' tight;
Na, faith ye yet! ye 'll no be right
      Till ye 've got on it,
The vera tapmost, tow'rin' height
      O' Miss's bonnet.

* "His banes:" Diogenes.

My sooth! right bauld ye set your nose out,
As plump and gray as ony grozet;
O for some rank mercurial rozet,
      Or fell, red smeddum,
I 'd gie you sic a hearty doze o 't,
      Wad dress your droddum!

I wad na been surprised to spy
You on an auld wife's flannen toy;
Or aiblins some bit duddie boy,
      On 's wyliecoat;
But Miss's fine Lunardi!† fie!
      How daur ye do 't?

O Jenny, dinna toss your head,
An' set your beauties a' abroad!
Ye little ken what cursed speed
      The blastie's makin'!
Thae winks and finger-ends, I dread,
      Are notice takin'!

O wad some Power the giftie gie us
To see oursel's as ithers see us!
It wad frae mony a blunder free us,
      And foolish notion:
What airs in dress an' gait wad lea'e us,
      And even devotion!

TO MRS. CUNNINGHAM,‡

ON RECEIVING A WORK OF HANNAH MORE'S.

THOU flattering mark of friendship kind,
Still may thy pages call to mind
  The dear, the beauteous donor:
Though sweetly female every part,
Yet such a head, and more the heart,
  Does both the sexes honour.
She show'd her taste refined and just
  When she selected thee,
Yet deviating, own I must,
  For so approving me;
    But kind still, I mind still,
      The giver in the gift,
    I 'll bless her, and wiss her
      A Friend aboon the lift.

† "Lunardi:" the famous aeronaut—bonnets were called after him in 1785.
‡ Mrs. Cunningham of Enterkin, daughter of Mrs. Stewart of Stair, and a distant relative of Robert Aiken. It was inclosed in a letter to Aiken by Burns, April, 1786.

"O WAD SOME POWER THE GIFTIE GIE US,
TO SEE OURSEL'S AS ITHERS SEE US!"

THE HOLY FAIR.*

"A robe of seeming truth and trust
 Hid crafty observation;
And secret hung, with poison'd crust,
 The dirk of defamation:
A mask that like the gorget show'd
 Dye-varying on the pigeon;
And for a mantle, large and broad,
 He wrapt him in Religion."
                     HYPOCRISY A-LA-MODE.

Upon a simmer Sunday morn,
 When Nature's face is fair,
I walkèd forth to view the corn,
 An' snuff the caller air.
The risin' sun owre Galston muirs
 Wi' glorious light was glintin';
The hares were hirplin' down the furs,
 The lav'rocks they were chantin'
                     Fu' sweet that day.

As lightsomely I glowr'd abroad,
 To see a scene sae gay,
Three hizzies, early at the road,
 Cam skelpin' up the way;
Twa had manteeles o' dolefu' black,
 But ane wi' lyart lining;
The third, that gaed a wee a-back,
 Was in the fashion shining,
                     Fu' gay that day.

The twa appear'd like sisters twin,
 In feature, form, an' claes;
Their visage, wither'd, lang, an' thin,
 An' sour as ony slaes:
The third cam up, hap-stap-an'-lowp,
 As light as ony lambie,
An' wi' a curchie low did stoop,
 As soon as e'er she saw me,
                     Fu' kind that day.

Wi' bonnet aff, quoth I, "Sweet lass,
 I think ye seem to ken me;
I 'm sure I 've seen that bonnie face,
 But yet I canna name ye."
Quo' she, an' laughin' as she spak,
 An' taks me by the hands,
"Ye, for my sake, hae gi'en the feck
 Of a' the ten commands
                     A screed some day.

"My name is Fun—your cronie dear,
 The nearest friend ye hae;
An' this is Superstition here,
 An' that 's Hypocrisy.

I 'm gaun to Mauchline Holy Fair,
 To spend an hour in daffin':
Gin ye 'll go there, yon runkled pair,
 We will get famous laughin'
                     At them this day."

Quoth I, "Wi' a' my heart I 'll do 't;
 I 'll get my Sunday's sark on,
An' meet you on the holy spot—
 Faith, we 'se hae fine remarkin'!"
Then I gaed hame at crowdie-time,
 An' soon I made me ready;
For roads were clad frae side to side
 Wi' mony a wearie body,
                     In droves that day.

Here farmers gash, in ridin' graith,
 Gaed hoddin by their cottars;
There swankies young, in braw braid-claith,
 Are springin' o'er the gutters;
The lasses, skelpin' barefit, thrang,
 In silks an' scarlets glitter;
Wi' sweet-milk cheese, in mony a whang,
 An' farls baked wi' butter,
                     Fu' crump that day.

When by the plate we set our nose,
 Weel heapèd up wi' ha'pence,
A greedy glowr Black-bonnet † throws,
 An' we maun draw our tippence.
Then in we go to see the show,
 On every side they 're gatherin',
Some carrying deals, some chairs an' stools,
 An' some are busy blethrin'
                     Right loud that day.

Here stands a shed to fend the showers
 An' screen our countra gentry,
There racer Jess,‡ an' twa-three wh-res,
 Are blinkin' at the entry.
Here sits a raw of tittlin' jades,
 Wi' heavin' breasts an' bare neck,
An' there a batch of wabster lads,
 Blackguardin' frae Kilmarnock,
                     For fun this day.

Here some are thinkin' on their sins,
 An' some upo' their claes;
Ane curses feet that fyl'd his shins,
 Anither sighs an' prays;
On this hand sits a chosen swatch,
 Wi' screw'd-up grace-proud faces;
On that a set o' chaps at watch,
 Thrang winkin' on the lasses
                     To chairs that day.

---

* "Holy Fair" is a common phrase in the west of Scotland for a sacramental occasion.—(B.)

† "Black-bonnet:" the elder at the *plate*.
‡ "Racer Jess:" a half-witted girl named Gibson, of remarkable pedestrian powers, daughter of Poosie Nancy.

O happy is that man an' blest!
  (Nae wonder that it pride him!)
Whase ain dear lass, that he likes best,
  Comes clinkin' down beside him!
Wi' arm repos'd on the chair back,
  He sweetly does compose him;
Which, by degrees, slips round her neck,
  An' 's loof upon her bosom,
        Unkenn'd that day.

Now a' the congregation o'er
  Is silent expectation;
For Moodie* speels the holy door
  Wi' tidings o' damnation.
Should Hornie, as in ancient days,
  'Mang sons o' God present him,
The vera sight o' Moodie's face
  To 's ain het hame had sent him
        Wi' fright that day.

Hear how he clears the points o' Faith
  Wi' rattlin' an' wi' thumpin'!
Now meekly calm, now wild in wrath,
  He 's stampin' an' he 's jumpin'!
His lengthen'd chin, his turn'd-up snout,
  His eldritch squeel and gestures,
O how they fire the heart devout,
  Like cantharidian plaisters,
        On sic a day!

But hark! the tent has changed its voice;
  There 's peace an' rest nae langer:
For a' the real judges rise,
  They canna sit for anger.
Smith † opens out his cauld harangues
  On practice and on morals;
An' aff the godly pour in thrangs,
  To gie the jars an' barrels
        A lift that day.

What signifies his barren shine
  Of moral powers an' reason?
His English style, an' gesture fine,
  Are a' clean out o' season.
Like Socrates or Antonine,
  Or some auld pagan heathen,
The moral man he does define,
  But ne'er a word o' faith in
        That 's right that day.

In guid time comes an antidote
  Against sic poison'd nostrum;
For Peebles,‡ frae the Water-fit,
  Ascends the holy rostrum;
See, up he 's got the word o' God,
  An' meek an' mim has view'd it,
While Common-Sense § has ta'en the road,
  An' aff an' up the Cowgate, ‖
        Fast, fast, that day.

Wee Miller ¶ niest the guard relieves,
  An' Orthodoxy raibles,
Though in his heart he weel believes,
  An' thinks it auld wives' fables:
But, faith, the birkie wants a manse,
  So, cannily he hums them;
Although his carnal wit an' sense
  Like hafflins-ways o'ercomes him
        At times that day.

Now butt an' ben, the change-house fills,
  Wi' yill-caup commentators:
Here 's crying out for bakes and gills,
  An' there the pint-stoup clatters;
While thick an' thrang, an' loud an' lang,
  Wi' logic an' wi' scripture,
They raise a din, that in the end
  Is like to breed a rupture
        O' wrath that day.

Leeze me on drink! it gies us mair
  Than either school or college:
It kindles wit, it waukens lear,
  It pangs us fou o' knowledge.
Be 't whisky gill, or penny wheep,
  Or ony stronger potion,
It never fails, on drinking deep,
  To kittle up our notion
        By night or day.

The lads an' lasses, blythely bent
  To mind baith saul an' body,
Sit round the table, weel content,
  An' steer about the toddy.
On this ane's dress, an' that ane's leuk,
  They 're makin' observations:
While some are cozy i' the neuk,
  An' formin' assignations
        To meet some day.

But now the Lord's ain trumpet touts,
  Till a' the hills are rairin',
An' echoes back return the shouts;
  Black Russell ** is na sparin':

---

* "Moodie:" minister of Riccarton, a great preacher of terror, one of the heroes of the "Twa Herds."
† "Smith:" minister of Galston, see "Kirk's Alarm."
‡ "Peebles," Dr. William, minister of Newton-on-Ayr, called the "Water-foot;" an Evangelical preacher.
§ "Common-Sense:" one Mackenzie, doctor in the village, who had written on some controversial topic under that sobriquet.
‖ "Cowgate:" a street so called, which faces the tent in Mauchline.—(B.)
¶ "Miller:" afterwards minister of Kilmaurs, a man of low stature, but great girth. The above obstructed his promotion.
** "Black Russell:" afterwards of Stirling.—See LIFE.

His piercin' words, like Highland swords,
    Divide the joints an' marrow;
His talk o' hell, whare devils dwell,
    Our vera sauls does harrow *
          Wi' fright that day!

A vast, unbottom'd, boundless pit,
    Fill'd fou o' lowin' brunstane,
Whase ragin' flame an' scorchin' heat
    Wad melt the hardest whun-stane!
The half-asleep start up wi' fear,
    An' think they hear it roarin',
When presently it does appear
    'Twas but some neibour snorin'
          Asleep that day.

'T wad be owre lang a tale to tell
    How mony stories past,
An' how they crowded to the yill,
    When they were a' dismist:
How drink gaed round, in cogs an' caups,
    Amang the furms and benches:
An' cheese an' bread, frae women's laps,
    Was dealt about in lunches
          An' dauds that day.

In comes a gawsie, gash guidwife,
    An' sits down by the fire,
Syne draws her kebbuck an' her knife;
    The lasses they are shyer.
The auld guidmen, about the grace,
    Frae side to side they bother,
Till some ane by his bonnet lays,
    An' gi'es them 't like a tether,
          Fu' lang that day.

Waesucks! for him that gets nae lass,
    Or lasses that hae naething!
Sma' need has he to say a grace,
    Or melvie his braw claithing!
O wives, be mindfu' ance yoursel
    How bonnie lads ye wanted,
An' dinna, for a kebbuck-heel,
    Let lasses be affronted
          On sic a day!

Now Clinkumbell, wi' rattlin' tow,
    Begins to jow an' croon;
Some swagger hame the best they dow,
    Some wait the afternoon.
At slaps the billies halt a blink,
    Till lasses strip their shoon:
Wi' faith an' hope, an' love an' drink,
    They 're a' in famous tune
          For crack that day.

* "Sauls does harrow:" Shakspeare's "Hamlet."—(B.)

How mony hearts this day converts
    O' sinners and o' lasses!
Their hearts o' stane, gin night, are gane
    As saft as ony flesh is.
There 's some are fou o' love divine;
    There 's some are fou o' brandy;
An' mony jobs that day begin,
    May end in houghmagandie †
          Some ither day.

SONG IN SPRING.

TUNE—"Johnnie's Grey Breeks."

A-gain rejoicing Nature sees Her robe assume its vernal hues,
Her leafy locks wave in the breeze, All freshly steep'd in morning dews.

CHORUS—And maun I still on † Menie doat, And bear the scorn that's in her e'e?
For it's jet, jet black, an' it's like a hawk, An' it winna let a body be!
And maun I still on Menie doat, And bear the scorn that's in her e'e?
For its jet, jet black, an' it's like a hawk, An' it winna let a body be! ‡

In vain to me the cowslips blaw,
    In vain to me the violets spring;
In vain to me, in glen or shaw,
    The mavis and the lintwhite sing.
          And maun I still, &c.

The merry ploughboy cheers his team,
    Wi' joy the tentie seedsman stalks;
But life to me 's a weary dream,
    A dream of ane that never wauks.
          And maun I still, &c.

The wanton coot the water skims,
    Amang the reeds the ducklings cry,
The stately swan majestic swims,
    And everything is blest but I.
          And maun I still, &c.

† See LIFE.
‡ "Menie:" is the common abbreviation of Marianne.
§ This chorus is part of a song composed by a gentleman in Edinburgh, a particular friend of the author's.—(B.)

The shepherd steeks his faulding slap,
  And owre the moorlands whistles shrill;
Wi' wild, unequal, wandering step,
  I meet him on the dewy hill.
            And maun I still, &c.

And when the lark, 'tween light and dark,
  Blythe waukens by the daisy's side,
And mounts and sings on flittering wings,
  A woe-worn ghaist I hameward glide.
            And maun I still, &c.

Come, Winter, with thine angry howl,
  And raging, bend the naked tree;
Thy gloom will soothe my cheerless soul,
  When Nature all is sad like me!
            And maun I still, &c.

TO A MOUNTAIN DAISY,*

ON TURNING ONE DOWN WITH THE PLOUGH
IN APRIL, 1786.

WEE, modest, crimson-tippèd flower,
Thou 's met me in an evil hour;
For I maun crush amang the stoure
        Thy slender stem;
To spare thee now is past my power,
        Thou bonnie gem.

Alas! it 's no thy neibour sweet,
The bonnie lark, companion meet!
Bending thee 'mang the dewy weet,
        Wi' spreckled breast,
When upward-springing, blythe, to greet
        The purpling east.

* Called originally "To a Gowan."

Cauld blew the bitter-biting north
Upon thy early, humble birth;
Yet cheerfully thou glinted forth
    Amid the storm,
Scarce rear'd above the parent-earth
    Thy tender form.

The flaunting flowers our gardens yield,
High sheltering woods and wa's maun shield;
But thou, beneath the random bield
    O' clod or stane,
Adorns the histie stibble-field,
    Unseen, alane.

There, in thy scanty mantle clad,
Thy snawie bosom sunward spread,
Thou lifts thy unassuming head
    In humble guise;
But now the share uptears thy bed,
    And low thou lies!

Such is the fate of artless maid,
Sweet floweret of the rural shade!
By love's simplicity betray'd,
    And guileless trust;
Till she, like thee, all soil'd, is laid
    Low i' the dust.

Such is the fate of simple bard,
On life's rough ocean luckless starr'd!
Unskilful he to note the card
    Of prudent lore,
Till billows rage, and gales blow hard,
    And whelm him o'er!

Such fate to suffering worth is given,
Who long with wants and woes has striven,
By human pride or cunning driven
    To misery's brink,
Till wrench'd of every stay but Heaven,
    He, ruin'd, sink!

Even thou who mourn'st the daisy's fate,
That fate is thine—no distant date;
Stern Ruin's plough-share drives, elate,
    Full on thy bloom,
Till crush'd beneath the furrow's weight,
    Shall be thy doom.

TO RUIN.

All hail, inexorable lord!
At whose destruction-breathing word,
  The mightiest empires fall!
Thy cruel, woe-delighted train,
The ministers of grief and pain,
  A sullen welcome, all!
With stern-resolv'd, despairing eye,
  I see each aimèd dart;
For one has cut my dearest tie,
  And quivers in my heart.
    Then low'ring and pouring,
      The storm no more I dread;
    Though thick'ning, and black'ning,
      Round my devoted head.

And thou grim Pow'r by life abhorr'd,
While life a pleasure can afford,
  Oh! hear a wretch's pray'r!
No more I shrink appall'd, afraid;
I court, I beg thy friendly aid,
  To close this scene of care!
When shall my soul, in silent peace,
  Resign life's joyless day—
My weary heart its throbbings cease,
  Cold mouldering in the clay?
    No fear more, no tear more,
      To stain my lifeless face,
    Enclaspèd, and graspèd,
      Within thy cold embrace!

THE LAMENT,

OCCASIONED BY THE UNFORTUNATE ISSUE OF A FRIEND'S AMOUR.

"Alas! how oft does goodness wound itself,
And sweet affection prove the spring of woe!"

O thou pale orb that silent shines
  While care-untroubled mortals sleep!
Thou seest a wretch who inly pines,
  And wanders here to wail and weep!
With woe I nightly vigils keep,
  Beneath thy wan, unwarming beam;
And mourn, in lamentation deep,
  How life and love are all a dream!

I joyless view thy rays adorn
  The faintly-markèd, distant hill;
I joyless view thy trembling horn
  Reflected in the gurgling rill:
My fondly-fluttering heart, be still!
  Thou busy pow'r, remembrance, cease!
Ah! must the agonizing thrill
  For ever bar returning peace?

No idly-feign'd, poetic pains,
  My sad, love-lorn lamentings claim:
No shepherd's pipe—Arcadian strains;
  No fabled tortures, quaint and tame.
The plighted faith, the mutual flame,
  The oft-attested Pow'rs above,
The promis'd father's tender name;
  These were the pledges of my love!

Encircled in her clasping arms,
  How have the raptur'd moments flown!
How have I wish'd for fortune's charms,
  For her dear sake, and her's alone!
And, must I think it! is she gone,
  My secret heart's exulting boast?
And does she heedless hear my groan?
  And is she ever, ever lost?

Oh! can she bear so base a heart,
  So lost to honour, lost to truth,
As from the fondest lover part,
  The plighted husband of her youth?
Alas! life's path may be unsmooth!
  Her way may lie through rough distress!
Then, who her pangs and pains will soothe,
  Her sorrows share, and make them less?

Ye wingèd hours that o'er us pass'd,
  Enraptur'd more, the more enjoy'd,
Your dear remembrance in my breast
  My fondly-treasur'd thoughts employ'd:
That breast, how dreary now, and void,
  For her too scanty once of room!
Ev'n ev'ry ray of hope destroy'd,
  And not a wish to gild the gloom!

The morn, that warns th' approaching day,
  Awakes me up to toil and woe;
I see the hours in long array,
  That I must suffer, lingering slow:
Full many a pang, and many a throe,
  Keen recollection's direful train,
Must wring my soul, ere Phœbus, low,
  Shall kiss the distant western main.

And when my nightly couch I try,
  Sore harass'd out with care and grief,
My toil-beat nerves, and tear-worn eye,
  Keep watchings with the nightly thief:
Or if I slumber, fancy, chief,
  Reigns, haggard-wild, in sore affright:
Ev'n day, all-bitter, brings relief
  From such a horror-breathing night.

O thou bright queen, who, o'er th' expanse
  Now highest reign'st with boundless sway!
Oft has thy silent-marking glance
  Observ'd us, fondly-wand'ring, stray!
The time, unheeded, sped away,
  While love's luxurious pulse beat high,
Beneath thy silver-gleaming ray,
  To mark the mutual-kindling eye.

Oh! scenes in strong remembrance set!
  Scenes, never, never to return!
Scenes, if in stupor I forget,
  Again I feel, again I burn!
From every joy and pleasure torn,
  Life's weary vale I'll wander through;
And hopeless, comfortless, I'll mourn
  A faithless woman's broken vow!

DESPONDENCY—AN ODE.*

Oppress'd with grief, oppress'd with care,
A burden more than I can bear,
  I set me down and sigh;
O life! thou art a galling load,
Along a rough, a weary road,
  To wretches such as I!
Dim-backward as I cast my view,
  What sick'ning scenes appear!
What sorrows yet may pierce me through,
  Too justly I may fear!
    Still caring, despairing,
      Must be my bitter doom;
    My woes here shall close ne'er
      But with the closing tomb!

Happy! ye sons of busy life,
Who, equal to the bustling strife,
  No other view regard!
Ev'n when the wishèd end's denied,
Yet while the busy means are plied,
  They bring their own reward:

---

* The three preceding poems all allude to the unfortunate affair with Jean Armour.—See Life.

Whilst I, a hope-abandon'd wight,
  Unfitted with an aim,
Meet ev'ry sad returning night,
  And joyless morn, the same!
    You, bustling and justling,
      Forget each grief and pain;
    I, listless, yet restless,
      Find ev'ry prospect vain.

How blest the solitary's lot,
Who, all-forgetting, all-forgot,
  Within his humble cell—
The cavern, wild with tangling roots—
Sits o'er his newly-gather'd fruits,
  Beside his crystal well!
Or haply, to his ev'ning thought,
  By unfrequented stream,
The ways of men are distant brought,
  A faint, collected dream;
    While praising, and raising
      His thoughts to heav'n on high,
    As wand'ring, meand'ring,
      He views the solemn sky.

Than I, no lonely hermit plac'd
Where never human footstep trac'd,
  Less fit to play the part;
The lucky moment to improve,
And just to stop, and just to move,
  With self-respecting art:
But ah! those pleasures, loves, and joys,
  Which I too keenly taste,
The solitary can despise—
  Can want, and yet be blest!
    He needs not, he heeds not,
      Or human love or hate;
    Whilst I here must cry here
      At perfidy ingrate!

O enviable early days,
When dancing thoughtless pleasure's maze,
  To care, to guilt unknown!
How ill exchang'd for riper times,
To feel the follies, or the crimes,
  Of others, or my own!
Ye tiny elves that guiltless sport,
  Like linnets in the bush,
Ye little know the ills ye court,
  When manhood is your wish!
    The losses, the crosses,
      That active man engage;
    The fears all, the tears all,
      Of dim declining Age!

TO GAVIN HAMILTON, ESQ., MAUCHLINE,

(RECOMMENDING A BOY).

I HOLD it, sir, my bounden duty
To warn you how that Master Tootie,*
  Alias, Laird M'Gaun,
Was here to hire yon lad away
'Bout whom ye spak the tither day,
  And wad hae done 't aff han':
But lest he learn the callan tricks—
  An' faith I muckle doubt him—
Like scrapin' out auld Crummie's nicks
  An' tellin' lies about them;
    As lieve, then, I 'd have, then,
      Your clerkship he should sair,
    If sae be ye may be
      Not fitted otherwise.

Although I say 't, he 's gleg enough,
An' 'bout a house that 's rude and rough,
  The boy might learn to swear;
But then wi' you he 'll be sae taught,
An' get sic fair example straught,
  I hae na ony fear.
Ye 'll catechise him every quirk,
  And shore him weel wi' hell;
An' gar him follow to the kirk—
  Aye when ye gang yoursel'.
    If ye, then, maun be, then,
      Frae hame this comin' Friday;
    Then please, sir, to lea'e, sir,
      The orders wi' your lady.

My word of honour I hae gi'en,
In Paisley John's, that night at e'en,
  To meet the warld's worm;
To try to get the twa to gree,
And name the airles an' the fee,
  In legal mode an' form:
I ken he weel a snick can draw,
  When simple bodies let him;
An' if a Devil be at a',
  In faith he 's sure to get him.
    To phrase you an' praise you,
      Ye ken your Laureate scorns;
    The prayer still, you share still,
      Of grateful MINSTREL BURNS.

---

* "Master Tootie" then lived in Mauchline; a dealer in cows. It was his practice often to cut the nicks or markings from the horns of cattle, to disguise their age.

![Illustration]

THE HIGHLAND LASSIE.*

Nae gentle dames, tho' e'er sae fair, Shall ever be my muse's care;
Their titles a' are empty show; Gi'e me my Highland lassie, O.

CHORUS—Within the glen sae bushy, O, Aboon the plain sae rashy, O,
I set me down wi' right guid will, To sing my Highland lassie, O.

* Highland Mary.—See LIFE.

O were yon hills and valleys mine,
Yon palace and yon gardens fine!
The world then the love should know
I bear my Highland lassie, O!
    Within the glen, &c.

But fickle fortune frowns on me,
And I maun cross the raging sea;
But while my crimson currents flow,
I'll love my Highland lassie, O!
    Within the glen, &c.

Although through foreign climes I range,
I know her heart will never change,

For her bosom burns with honour's glow,
My faithful Highland lassie, O!
    Within the glen, &c.

For her I'll dare the billows' roar,
For her I'll trace a distant shore,
That Indian wealth may lustre throw
Around my Highland lassie, O!
    Within the glen, &c.

She has my heart, she has my hand,
By sacred truth and honour's band!
Till the mortal stroke shall lay me low,
I'm thine, my Highland lassie, O!

    Farewell, the glen sae bushy, O!
    Farewell, the plain sae rushy, O!
    To other lands I now must go,
    To sing my Highland lassie, O!

EPISTLE TO A YOUNG FRIEND.*

I LANG hae thought, my youthfu' friend,
  A something to have sent you,
Though it should serve nae ither end
  Than just a kind memento:
But how the subject-theme may gang,
  Let time and chance determine;
Perhaps it may turn out a sang;
  Perhaps turn out a sermon.

Ye'll try the world fu' soon, my lad,
  And, Andrew dear, believe me,
Ye'll find mankind an unco squad,
  And muckle they may grieve ye:
For care and trouble set your thought,
  E'en when your end's attained!
And a' your views may come to nought,
  Where every nerve is strained.

I'll no say, men are villains a';
  The real, harden'd wicked,
Wha hae nae check but human law,
  Are to a few restricket;
But och! mankind are unco weak,
  An' little to be trusted;
If self the wavering balance shake,
  It's rarely right adjusted!

---

* "Young friend:" usually thought to be Andrew Aiken, son of Robert Aiken, Burns' friend. Andrew was English consul at Riga. Willy Niven of Kilbride always pretended to be the "young friend," and Hamilton Paul thought him so.

Yet they wha fa' in fortune's strife,
  Their fate we shouldna censure,
For still th' important end of life
  They equally may answer:
A man may hae an honest heart,
  Though poortith hourly stare him;
A man may tak a neibour's part,
  Yet hae nae cash to spare him.

Aye free, aff han', your story tell,
  When wi' a bosom crony:
But still keep something to yoursel'
  Ye scarcely tell to ony.
Conceal yoursel' as weel 's ye can
  Frae critical dissection;
But keek through every other man,
  Wi' sharpen'd, sly inspection.

The sacred lowe o' weel-placed love,
  Luxuriantly indulge it;
But never tempt th' illicit rove,
  Though naething should divulge it:
I waive the quantum o' the sin,
  The hazard of concealing;
But, och! it hardens a' within,
  And petrifies the feeling!

To catch dame Fortune's golden smile,
  Assiduous wait upon her;
And gather gear by every wile
  That's justified by honour;
Not for to hide it in a hedge,
  Nor for a train-attendant;
But for the glorious privilege
  Of being independent.

The fear o' hell's a hangman's whip
  To haud the wretch in order;
But where ye feel your honour grip,
  Let that aye be your border;
Its slightest touches, instant pause—
  Debar a' side pretences;
And resolutely keep its laws,
  Uncaring consequences.

The great Creator to revere
  Must sure become the creature;
But still the preaching cant forbear,
  And e'en the rigid feature;
Yet ne'er with wits profane to range,
  Be complaisance extended;
An atheist-laugh's a poor exchange
  For Deity offended.

When ranting round in pleasure's ring,
  Religion may be blinded;
Or if she gie a random sting,
  It may be little minded;

But when on life we 're tempest-driven,
  A conscience but a canker,
A correspondence fix'd wi' Heaven,
  Is sure a noble anchor!

Adieu, dear, amiable youth!
  Your heart can ne'er be wanting;
May prudence, fortitude, and truth,
  Erect your brow undaunting!
In ploughman phrase, "God send you speed,'
  Still daily to grow wiser!
And may ye better reck the rede
  Than ever did th' adviser!*

FROM BEELZEBUB,

To the Right Honourable the Earl of Breadalbane, president of the Right Honourable and Honourable the Highland Society, which met on the 23rd of May last, at the Shakspeare, Covent Garden, to concert ways and means to frustrate the designs of five hundred Highlanders who, as the Society were informed by Mr. M'Kenzie of Applecross, were so audacious as to attempt an escape from their lawful lords and masters, whose property they are, by emigrating from the lands of Mr. Macdonald of Glengary to the wilds of Canada, in search of that fantastic thing—Liberty!—(B.) This is thought a very unjustifiable and undue attack on Breadalbane and on M'Kenzie.

Long life, my lord, and health be yours,
Unskaith'd by hunger'd Highland boors!
Lord grant nae duddie, desperate beggar,
Wi' durk, claymore, or rusty trigger,
May twin auld Scotland o' a life
She likes—as lambkins like a knife!

Faith, you and Applecross were right
To keep the Highland hounds in sight:
I doubtna, they would bid nae better
Than, let them ance out owre the water,
Then up amang thae lakes and seas
They 'll mak what rules and laws they please!
Some daring Hancock, or a Franklin,
May set their Highland bluid a ranklin';
Some Washington again may head them,
Or some Montgomery, fearless, lead them;
Till (God knows what may be effected,
When by such heads and hearts directed)
Poor dunghill sons of dirt and mire,
May to patrician rights aspire!
Nae sage North now, nor sager Sackville,
To watch and premier owre the pack vile!

* Burns put out the following stanza:—

  "If ye hae made a step aside—
    Some hap mistake o'erta'en you,
  Yet still keep up a decent pride,
    And ne'er o'er far demean you;
  Time comes wi' kind oblivious shade,
    And daily darker sets it;
  And if nae mair mistakes are made,
    The warld soons forgets it."

An' whare will ye get Howes and Clintons
To bring them to a right repentance,
To cowe the rebel generation,
And save the honour o' the nation?
They, and be d——! what right hae they
To meat, or sleep, or light o' day?
Far less to riches, power, or freedom,
But what your lordship likes to gi'e them!
But hear, my lord! Glengary, hear!
Your hand 's owre light on them, I fear:
Your factors, grieves, trustees, and bailies,
I canna say but *they* do gaylies;
They lay aside a' tender mercies,
And tirl the hallions to the birses;
Yet, while they 're only poind't and herriet,
They 'll keep their stubborn Highland spirit:
But *smash* them! crash them a' to spails!
And rot the dyvours i' the jails!
The young dogs, swinge them to the labour;
Let wark and hunger mak them sober!
The hizzies, if they 're aughtlins fawsont,
Let them in Drury Lane be lesson'd!
And if the wives and dirty brats
Come thiggin' at your doors and yetts,
Flaffin wi' duds and gray wi' beas',
Frightin' awa' your deucks and geese,
Get out a horse-whip or a jowler,
The langest thong, the fiercest growler,
And gar the tatter'd gipsies pack
Wi' a' their bastards on their back!

  Go on, my lord! I lang to meet you,
And in my *house at hame* to greet you!
Wi' common lords ye shanna mingle;
The benmost neuk beside the ingle,
At my right hand assign'd your seat,
'Tween Herod's hip and Polycrate;
Or if ye on your station tarrow,
Between Almagro and Pizarro.
A seat I 'm sure ye 're weel deservin't;
And till ye come—Your humble servant,
                                    BEELZEBUB.

June 1st, Anno Mundi 5790 [A.D. 1786.]

A DREAM.

" Thoughts, words, and deeds, the Statute blames with reason;
  But surely dreams were ne'er indicted treason?'

On reading, in the public papers, the Laureate's Ode, with the other parade of June 4, 1786, the Author was no sooner dropped asleep, than he imagined himself transported to the birthday levee; and in his dreaming fancy made the following Address.—(B.) The "Ode" was by Thomas Warton.

Guid-mornin' to your Majesty!
  May Heaven augment your blisses

On every new birthday ye see,
   A humble poet wishes!
My bardship here, at your levee
   On sic a day as this is,
Is sure an uncouth sight to see,
   Amang thae birthday dresses
        Sae fine this day.

I see ye 're complimented thrang,
   By mony a lord and lady;
"God save the King!" 's a cuckoo sang
   That 's unco easy said aye;
The poets, too, a venal gang,
   Wi' rhymes weel-turn'd an' ready,
Wad gar you trow ye ne'er do wrang,
   But aye unerring steady,
        On sic a day.

For me! before a monarch's face,
   Ev'n there I winna flatter;
For neither pension, post, nor place,
   Am I your humble debtor:
So, nae reflection on your Grace,
   Your kingship to bespatter;
There 's mony waur been o' the race,
   And aiblins ane been better
        Than you this day.

'Tis very true, my sovereign King,
   My skill may weel be doubted;
But facts are chiels that winna ding,
   An' downa be disputed:
Your royal nest,* beneath your wing,
   Is e'en right reft an' clouted,
And now the third part o' the string,
   And less, will gang about it
        Than did ae day.

Far be 't frae me that I aspire
   To blame your legislation,
Or say ye wisdom want, or fire,
   To rule this mighty nation!
But, faith! I muckle doubt, my Sire,
   Ye 've trusted ministration
To chaps wha in a barn or byre
   Wad better fill'd their station,
        Than courts yon day.

And now ye 've gi'en auld Britain peace,
   Her broken shins to plaister,
Your sair taxation does her fleece,
   Till she has scarce a tester;
For me, thank God! my life 's a lease,
   Nae bargain wearin' faster,
Or, faith! I fear, that wi' the geese
   I shortly boost to pasture
        I' the craft some day.

* "Royal nest:" alluding to the loss of America.

I 'm no mistrusting Willie Pitt,
   When taxes he enlarges,
(An' Will 's a true guid fallow's get,
   A name not envy spairges)
That he intends to pay your debt,
   An' lessen a' your charges;
But, G—d sake let nae saving fit
   Abridge your bonnie barges †
        An' boats this day.

Adieu, my liege! may Freedom geck
   Beneath your high protection;
And may ye rax Corruption's neck,
   And gie her for dissection!
But since I 'm here, I 'll no neglect,
   In loyal, true affection,
To pay your Queen, wi' due respect,
   My fealty an' subjection
        This great birthday.

Hail, Majesty Most Excellent!
   While nobles strive to please ye,
Will ye accept a compliment
   A simple poet gies ye?
Thae bonnie bairntime Heaven has lent,
   Still higher may they heeze ye
In bliss, till fate some day is sent
   For ever to release ye
        Frae care that day.

For you, young potentate o' Wales,
   I tell your Highness fairly,
Down Pleasure's stream, wi' swelling sails,
   I 'm tauld ye 're driving rarely;
But some day ye may gnaw your nails,
   And curse your folly sairly,
That e'er ye brak Diana's pales,
   Or rattled dice wi' Charlie,
        By night or day.

Yet aft a ragged cowte 's been known
   To mak a noble aiver;
So, ye may doucely fill a throne,
   For a' their clish-ma-claver:
There, him ‡ at Agincourt wha shone,
   Few better were or braver;
And yet, wi' funny, queer Sir John, §
   He was an unco shaver
        For mony a day.

For you, right reverend Osnaburg, ‖
   Nane sets the lawn-sleeve sweeter,

† "Barges:" alluding to a proposition, in 1786, by Captain Macbride, to give up 64-gun ships, and make other reductions in the navy.
‡ "Him:" King Henry V.—(B.)
§ "Sir John:" Sir John Falstaff, *vide* Shakspeare.—(B.)
‖ "Osnaburg:" afterwards the Duke of York.

Although a ribbon at your lug
  Wad been a dress completer:
As ye disown yon paughty dog
  That bears the keys of Peter,
Then, swith! and get a wife to hug,
  Or, trowth! ye 'll stain the mitre
        Some luckless day.

Young royal Tarry Breeks,* I learn,
  Ye 've lately come athwart her—
A glorious galley, † stem and stern,
  Weel rigg'd for Venus' barter;
But first hang out that she 'll discern
  Your hymeneal charter,
Then heave aboard your grapple airn,
  And large upo' her quarter
        Come full that day.

Ye, lastly, bonnie blossoms a',
  Ye royal lasses dainty,
Heav'n mak you guid as weel as braw,
  An' gie you lads a-plenty:
But sneer na British boys awa';
  For kings are unco scant aye;
An' German gentles are but sma',
  They 're better just than want aye,
        On ony day.

God bless you a'! consider now,
  Ye 're unco muckle dautet;
But ere the course o' life be through,
  It may be bitter sautet;
An' I hae seen their coggie fou,
  That yet hae tarrow 't at it;
But or the day was done, I trow,
  The laggen they hae clautet
        Fu' clean that day.

TO GAVIN HAMILTON, ESQ.‡

EXPECT na, Sir, in this narration,
A fleechin', flethrin' dedication,
To roose you up, an' ca' you guid,
An' sprung o' great an' noble bluid,
Because ye 're surnamed like his Grace, §
Perhaps related to the race;
Then when I 'm tired, and sae are ye,
Wi' mony a fulsome, sinfu' lie,
Set up a face, how I stop short
For fear your modesty be hurt.

This may do—maun do, Sir, wi' them wha
Maun please the great folk for a wamefu';
For me, sae laigh I needna bow,
For, L—d be thankit, I can plough:
And when I downa yoke a naig,
Then, L—d be thankit, I can beg;
Sae I shall say, an' that 's nae flatt'rin',
It 's just sic poet an' sic patron.

The Poet, some guid angel help him,
Or else, I fear, some ill ane skelp him;
He may do weel for a' he 's done yet,
But only—he 's no just begun yet.

The Patron (Sir, ye maun forgie me,
I winna lie, come what will o' me),
On every hand it will allow'd be,
He 's just—nae better than he should be.

I readily and freely grant,
He downa see a poor man want;
What 's no his ain, he winna tak it,
What ance he says, he winna brak it;
Ought he can lend he 'll no refuse 't,
Till aft his guidness is abused;
And rascals whyles that do him wrang,
Even that, he does na mind it lang:
As master, landlord, husband, father,
He does na fail his part in either.

But then, nae thanks to him for a' that;
Nae godly symptom ye can ca' that;
It 's naething but a milder feature
Of our poor, sinfu', corrupt nature:
Ye 'll get the best o' moral works
'Mang black Gentoos and pagan Turks,
Or hunters wild on Ponotaxi,
Wha never heard of Orthodoxy.
That he 's the poor man's friend in need,
The gentleman in word and deed,
It 's no through terror of damnation;
It 's just a carnal inclination.

Morality, thou deadly bane,
Thy tens o' thousands thou hast slain!
Vain is his hope, whase stay an' trust is
In moral mercy, truth, and justice!

No—stretch a point to catch a plack;
Abuse a brother to his back;
Steal through the winnock frae a wh—re,
But point the rake that taks the door;
Be to the poor like onie whunstane,
And haud their noses to the grunstane;
Ply ev'ry art o' legal thieving;
No matter—stick to sound believing.

Learn three-mile pray'rs, an' half-mile graces,
Wi' weel-spread looves, an' lang, wry faces;
Grunt up a solemn, lengthen'd groan,
And damn a' parties but your own;
I 'll warrant then, ye 're nae deceiver,
A steady, sturdy, staunch believer.

---

* "Tarry Breeks:" afterwards William IV.
† "Galley:" alluding to the newspaper account of a certain royal sailor's amour.—(B.)
‡ Meant to preface the first edition of his Poems, but inserted elsewhere in them.
§ "His Grace:" the Duke of Hamilton.

O ye wha leave the springs o' Calvin,
For gumlie dubs of your ain delvin!
Ye sons of Heresy and Error,
Ye'll some day squeel in quaking terror,
When Vengeance draws the sword in wrath,
And in the fire throws the sheath;
When Ruin, with his sweeping besom,
Just frets till Heaven commission gies him;
While o'er the harp pale Misery moans,
And strikes the ever-deep'ning tones,
Still louder shrieks, and heavier groans!

Your pardon, Sir, for this digression:
I maist forgat my Dedication;
But when divinity comes 'cross me,
My readers still are sure to lose me.

So, Sir, you see 'twas nae daft vapour;
But I maturely thought it proper,
When a' my works I did review,
To dedicate them, Sir, to you:
Because (ye need na tak' it ill),
I thought them something like yoursel'.

Then patronize them wi' your favour,
And your petitioner shall ever ——
I had amaist said, ever pray,
But that's a word I need na say;
For prayin', I hae little skill o 't,
I'm baith dead-sweer, an' wretched ill o 't;
But I 'se repeat each poor man's pray'r,
That kens or hears about you, Sir ——

"May ne'er Misfortune's gowling bark,
Howl through the dwelling o' the Clerk!
May ne'er his generous, honest heart,
For that same generous spirit smart!
May Kennedy's far-honour'd name
Lang beet his hymeneal flame
Till Hamiltons, at least a dizzen,
Are frae their nuptial labours risen:
Five bonnie lasses round their table,
And sev'n braw fellows, stout an' able,
To serve their king an' country weel
By word, or pen, or pointed steel!
May health and peace, with mutual rays,
Shine on the ev'ning o' his days;
Till his wee, curlie John's ier-oe,
When ebbing life nae mair shall flow,
The last, sad, mournful rites bestow!"

I will not wind a lang conclusion,
With complimentary effusion;
But, whilst your wishes and endeavours
Are blest with Fortune's smiles and favours,
I am, dear Sir, with zeal most fervent,
Your much indebted, humble servant.

But if (which Pow'rs above prevent)
That iron-hearted carl, Want,
Attended, in his grim advances,
By sad mistakes and black mischances,
While hopes, and joys, and pleasures fly him,
Make you as poor a dog as I am,
Your "humble servant" then no more;
For who would humbly serve the poor?
But, by a poor man's hopes in Heaven
While recollection's power is given—
If, in the vale of humble life,
The victim sad of fortune's strife,
I, through the tender-gushing tear,
Should recognize my master dear;
If friendless, low, we meet together,
Then, Sir, your hand—my friend and brother!

NOTE TO DR. MACKENZIE,*
INVITING HIM TO ATTEND A MASONIC ANNIVERSARY MEETING.

FRIDAY first 's the day appointed,
By our Right Worshipful anointed,
  To hold our grand procession;
To get a blaud o' Johnnie's † morals,
And taste a swatch o' Manson's barrels,‡
  I' the way of our profession.
Our Master and the Brotherhood
  Wad a' be glad to see you;
For me I would be mair than proud
  To share the mercies wi' you.
    If death, then, wi' skaith, then,
      Some mortal heart is hechtin',
    Inform him, and storm § him,
      That Saturday ye'll fecht him.
                    ROBERT BURNS.

MOSSGIEL, *An. M.* 5790 [A.D. 1786.]

FAREWELL TO THE MASON LODGE, TARBOLTON. ‖

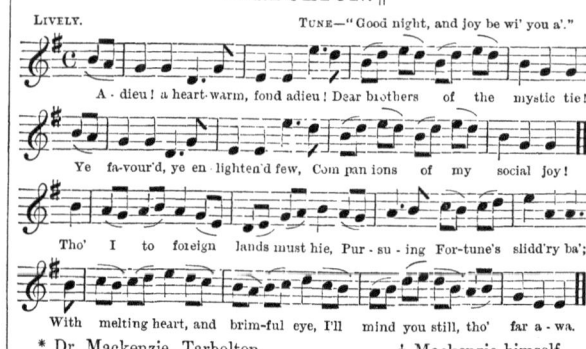

LIVELY.   TUNE—"Good night, and joy be wi' you a'."

A-dieu! a heart-warm, fond adieu! Dear brothers of the mystic tie!
Ye fa-vour'd, ye en-lighten'd few, Companions of my social joy!
Tho' I to foreign lands must hie, Pur-su-ing For-tune's slidd'ry ba';
With melting heart, and brim-ful eye, I'll mind you still, tho' far a-wa.

* Dr. Mackenzie, Tarbolton.   † Mackenzie himself.
‡ Manson, an inn-keeper.   § "Storm:" that is, threaten him.
‖ Written on the 23rd of June, 1786. Burns expected to sail for Jamaica in the August following.

Oft have I met your social band
   And spent the cheerful, festive night;
Oft, honour'd with supreme command,
   Presided o'er the Sons of Light;
And by that Hieroglyphic Bright,
   Which none but Craftsmen ever saw!
Strong Mem'ry on my heart shall write
   Those happy scenes, when far awa'.

May Freedom, Harmony, and Love,
   Unite you in the grand design,
Beneath the Omniscient Eye above—
   The glorious Architect Divine,
That you may keep the unerring line,
   Still rising by the plummet's law,
Till Order bright completely shine,
   Shall be my pray'r when far awa.

And you, farewell! whose merits claim
   Justly that highest badge to wear!
Heaven bless your honour'd, noble name,
   To Masonry and Scotia dear!
A last request permit me here,
   When yearly ye assemble a',
One round, I ask it with a tear,
   To him, the Bard that's far awa.

A SCOTCH BARD GOING TO THE WEST INDIES.

(WRITTEN IN 1786.)

A' YE wha live by sowps o' drink,
A' ye wha live by crambo-clink,
A' ye wha live and never think,
      Come, mourn wi' me!
Our billie 's gi'en us a' a jink,
      An' owre the sea.

Lament him, a' ye rantin' core,
Wha dearly like a random-splore;
Nae mair he 'll join the merry roar,
      In social key;
For now he 's ta'en anither shore,
      An' owre the sea.

The bonnie lasses weel may wiss him,
And in their dear petitions place him:
The widows, wives, an' a' may bless him
      Wi' tearfu' e'e;
For weel I wat they 'll sairly miss him
      That 's owre the sea.

O Fortune, they hae room to grumble!
Hadst thou ta'en aff some drowsy bummle,
Wha can do nought but fyke an' fumble,
      'Twad been nae plea;
But he was gleg as ony wumble,
      That 's owre the sea.

Auld, cantie Kyle may weepers wear,
And stain them wi' the saut, saut tear;
'Twill mak her poor auld heart, I fear,
      In flinders flee;
He was her laureate mony a year,
      That 's owre the sea.

He saw Misfortune's cauld nor'-wast
Lang mustering up a bitter blast;
A jillet brak his heart at last,
      Ill may she be!
So, took a berth afore the mast,
      An' owre the sea.

To tremble under Fortune's cummock,
On scarce a bellyfu' o' drummock,
Wi' his proud, independent stomach
      Could ill agree;
So, row't his hurdies in a hammock,
      An' owre the sea.

He ne'er was gi'en to great misguidin',
Yet coin his pouches wad na bide in,
Wi' him it ne'er was under hidin'—
      He dealt it free;
The Muse was a' that he took pride in,
      That 's owre the sea.

Jamaica bodies, use him weel,
And hap him in a cozie biel:
Ye 'll find him aye a dainty chiel,
      An' fou o' glee;
He wad na wrang'd the vera deil,
      That 's owre the sea.

Fareweel, my rhyme-composing billie!
Your native soil was right ill-willie;
But may ye flourish like a lily,
      Now bonnilie!
I 'll toast ye in my hinmost gillie,
      Though owre the sea.

FROM THEE, ELIZA, I MUST GO.

Slow.   Tune—"Gilderoy."

From thee, E-li-za,* I must go, And from my na-tive shore;
The cru-el fates be-tween us throw A boundless ocean's roar;
But boundless oceans, roar-ing wide, Between my love and me,
They ne-ver, ne-ver can divide My heart and soul from thee.

Farewell, farewell, Eliza dear,
  The maid that I adore !
A boding voice is in mine ear,
  We part to meet no more !
But the last throb that leaves my heart,
  While death stands victor by,
That throb, Eliza, is thy part,
  And thine that latest sigh !

      * Elizabeth Black.—See Life.

THE HEATHER WAS BLOOMING, THE MEADOWS WERE MAWN.

Tune—"The Tailor's March."

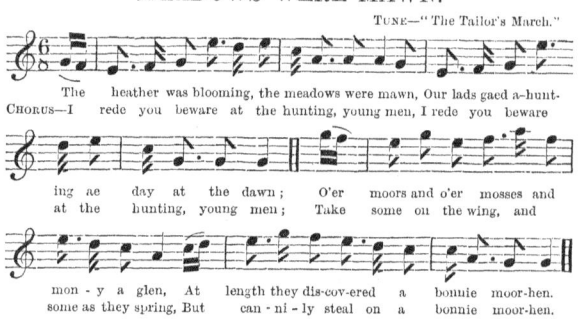

The heather was blooming, the meadows were mawn, Our lads gaed a-hunt-
Chorus—I rede you beware at the hunting, young men, I rede you beware
ing ae day at the dawn; O'er moors and o'er mosses and
at the hunting, young men; Take some on the wing, and
mon-y a glen, At length they dis-cov-ered a bonnie moor-hen.
some as they spring, But can-ni-ly steal on a bonnie moor-hen.

Sweet brushing the dew from the brown heather-bells,
Her colours betray'd her on yon mossy fells ;
Her plumage outlustred the pride o' the spring,
And O ! as she wantonèd gay on the wing.
          I rede you beware, &c.

Auld Phœbus himsel', as he peep'd o'er the hill,
In spite at her plumage he trièd his skill ;
He levell'd his rays where she bask'd on the brae—
His rays were outshone, and but mark'd where she lay.
          I rede you beware, &c.

"THE HEATHER WAS BLOOMING"

They hunted the valley, they hunted the hill;
The best of our lads wi' the best o' their skill;
But still as the fairest she sat in their sight,
Then, whirr! she was over a mile at a flight.
     I rede you beware, &c.

EPITAPHS.

A BARD'S EPITAPH.

Is there a whim-inspirèd fool,
Owre fast for thought, owre hot for rule,
Owre blate to seek, owre proud to snool,
    Let him draw near;
And owre this grassy heap sing dool,
    And drap a tear.

Is there a bard of rustic song,
Who, noteless, steals the crowds among,
That weekly this area throng,
    O, pass not by!
But, with a frater-feeling strong,
    Here heave a sigh.

Is there a man, whose judgment clear,
Can others teach the course to steer,
Yet runs, himself, life's mad career,
    Wild as the wave;
Here pause—and, through the starting tear,
    Survey this grave.

The poor inhabitant below
Was quick to learn, and wise to know,
And keenly felt the friendly glow,
    And softer flame;
But thoughtless follies laid him low,
    And stain'd his name!

Reader, attend! whether thy soul
Soars fancy's flights beyond the pole,
Or darkling grubs this earthly hole,
    In low pursuit;
Know, prudent, cautious, self-control,
    Is wisdom's root.

FOR ROBERT AIKEN, ESQ.

Know thou, O stranger to the fame
Of this much loved, much honour'd name!
(For none that knew him need be told)
A warmer heart death ne'er made cold.

FOR GAVIN HAMILTON, ESQ.

The poor man weeps—here Gavin sleeps,
 Whom canting wretches blamed;
But with such as he, where'er he be,
 May I be saved or damn'd!

ON WEE JOHNNY.*

"*Hic jacet* wee Johnnie."

Whoe'er thou art, O reader, know,
 That death has murder'd Johnnie!
An' here his body lies fu' low—
 For saul he ne'er had ony.

THE BONNIE LASS O' BALLOCHMYLE.†

'Twas even—the dewy fields were green, On every blade the pearls hang;
The zephyr wanton'd round the bean, And bore its fragrant sweets alang;
In ev'ry glen the mavis sang, All nature list'ning seem'd the while,
Except where greenwood echoes rang, Amang the braes o' Ballochmyle.

With careless step I onward stray'd,
 My heart rejoiced in Nature's joy,
When, musing in a lonely glade,
 A maiden fair I chanced to spy;
Her look was like the morning's eye,
 Her air like Nature's vernal smile:
Perfection whisper'd, passing by,
 Behold the lass o' Ballochmyle!

Fair is the morn in flowery May,
 And sweet is night in Autumn mild;
When roving through the garden gay,
 Or wand'ring in the lonely wild:
But woman, Nature's darling child!
 There all her charms she does compile;
Even there her other works are foil'd
 By the bonnie lass o' Ballochmyle.

---

* "Wee Johnny:" Wilson, the printer of Burns' Kilmarnock edition, who died in Ayr, 1821, a prosperous man.
† This took place in July, 1786.—See Life.

Oh, had she been a country maid,
   And I the happy country swain !
Though shelter'd in the lowest shed
   That ever rose on Scotland's plain,
Through weary winter's wind and rain,
   With joy, with rapture, I would toil;
And nightly to my bosom strain
   The bonnie lass o' Ballochmyle.

Then pride might climb the slippery steep,
   Where fame and honours lofty shine ;
And thirst of gold might tempt the deep,
   Or downward seek the Indian mine :
Give me the cot below the pine,
   To tend the flocks, or till the soil,
And every day have joys divine,
   With the bonnie lass o' Ballochmyle.

LINES TO AN OLD SWEETHEART.*

Once fondly loved, and still remember'd dear,
   Sweet early object of my youthful vows,
Accept this mark of friendship, warm, sincere ;
   Friendship ! 'tis all cold duty now allows.

* Peggy, mentioned in his letter to Dr. Moore.—See Life.

And when you read the simple, artless rhymes,
   One friendly sigh for him—he asks no more—
Who, distant, burns in flaming torrid climes,
   Or haply lies beneath th' Atlantic roar.

LINES WRITTEN ON A BANK NOTE.†

Wae worth thy power, thou cursed leaf,
   Fell source o' a' my woe and grief !
For lack o' thee I 've lost my lass,
   For lack o' thee I scrimp my glass :
I see the children of affliction
   Unaided, through thy cursed restriction :

† Written on a one pound bank note, dated 1st March, 1780.

I 've seen the oppressor's cruel smile
Amid his hapless victim's spoil,
And for thy potence vainly wish'd
To crush the villain in the dust.
For lack o' thee I leave this much-loved shore,
Never, perhaps, to greet old Scotland more.
                    R. B., Kyle.

STANZAS ON NAETHING.

EXTEMPORE EPISTLE TO GAVIN HAMILTON, ESQ.

To you, Sir, this summons I 've sent,
  Pray, whip till the pownie is fraething;
But if you demand what I want,
  I honestly answer you—naething.

Ne'er scorn a poor Poet like me,
  For idly just living and breathing,
While people of every degree
  Are busy employed about—naething.

Poor Centum-per-centum may fast,
  And grumble his hurdies their claithing;
He 'll find, when the balance is cast,
  He 's gane to the devil for—naething.

The courtier cringes and bows,
  Ambition has likewise its plaything;
A coronet beams on his brows;
  And what is a coronet?—naething.

Some quarrel the Presbyter gown,
  Some quarrel Episcopal graithing;
And every good fellow will own
  The quarrel is a' about—naething.

The lover may sparkle and glow,
  Approaching his bonnie bit gay thing;
But marriage will soon let him know
  He 's gotten—a buskit up naething.

The Poet may jingle and rhyme,
  In hopes of a laureate wreathing,
And when he has wasted his time,
  He 's kindly rewarded wi'—naething.

The thundering bully may rage,
  And swagger and swear like a heathen;
But collar him fast, I 'll engage,
  You will find that his courage is—naething.

Last night wi' a feminine whig—
  A poet she couldna put faith in;
But soon we grew lovingly big,
  I taught her, her terrors were—naething.

Her whigship was wonderful pleased,
  But charmingly tickled wi' ae thing;
Her fingers I lovingly squeezed,
  And kissed her, and promised her—naething.

The priest anathèmas may threat—
  Predicament, Sir, that we 're baith in;
But when honour's reveillé is beat,
  The holy artillery 's—naething.

And now I must mount on the wave—
  My voyage perhaps there is death in;
But what is a watery grave?
  The drowning a Poet is—naething.

And now, as grim death's in my thought,
  To you, sir, I make this bequeathing;
My service as long as ye 've ought,
  And my friendship, by G—d, when ye 've--
                                  naething.

FAREWELL, OLD SCOTIA.

" The valiant, in himself, what can he suffer?
Or what does he regard his single woes?
But when, alas! he multiplies himself,
To dearer selves, to the lov'd tender fair,
To those whose bliss, whose beings, hang upon him,
To helpless children!—then, Oh then, he feels
The point of misery fest'ring in his heart,
And weakly weeps his fortunes like a coward.
Such, such am I! undone!"—
        THOMSON'S " EDWARD AND ELEANORA."

FAREWELL, old Scotia's bleak domains,
Far dearer than the torrid plains
    Where rich ananas blow!
Farewell, a mother's blessing dear!
A brother's sigh! a sister's tear!
    My Jean's heart-rending throe!
Farewell, my Bess! though thou 'rt bereft
    Of my parental care;
A faithful brother I have left,
    My part in him thou 'lt share!
        Adieu too, to you too,
          My Smith, my bosom frien';
        When kindly you mind me,
          O then befriend my Jean!

What bursting anguish tears my heart!
From thee, my Jeany, must I part?
   Thou, weeping, answ'rest—"No!"
Alas! misfortune stares my face,
And points to ruin and disgrace;
   I for thy sake must go!
Thee Hamilton, and Aiken dear,
   A grateful, warm adieu!
I, with a much-indebted tear,
   Shall still remember you!
      All-hail, then, the gale, then,
         Wafts me from thee, dear shore!
      It rustles and whistles—
         I'll never see thee more!

THE CALF.

TO THE REV. MR. JAMES STEVEN,*

On his Text, Malachi iv. 2—"And ye shall go forth, and grow up, as calves of the stall."

RIGHT, Sir! your text I'll prove it true,
   Though heretics may laugh;
For instance, there's yoursel' just now,
   God knows, an unco calf!

And should some patron be so kind,
   As bless you wi' a kirk,
I doubt na, Sir, but then we'll find,
   Ye're still as great a stirk.

But, if the lover's raptured hour
   Shall ever be your lot,
Forbid it, every heavenly Power,
   You e'er should be a stot!

Though, when some kind, connubial dear,
   Your but-an'-ben adorns,
The like has been that you may wear
   A noble head of horns.

And in your lug, most reverend James,
   To hear you roar and rowte,
Few men o' sense will doubt your claims
   To rank amang the nowte.

And when ye're number'd wi' the dead,
   Below a grassy hillock,
Wi' justice they may mark your head—
   "Here lies a famous bullock!"

---

* "Rev. Mr. James Steven:" minister, afterwards, of Kilwinning, Ayrshire. These verses were written for a wager with Gavin Hamilton. He wrote them in Hamilton's house in a few minutes after returning from church.

TAM SAMSON'S ELEGY.†

"An honest man's the noblest work of God."—POPE.

HAS auld Kilmarnock seen the Deil?
Or great Mackinlay‡ thrawn his heel?
Or Robertson§ again grown weel,
      To preach an' read?
"Na, waur than a'!" cries ilka chiel—
      "Tam Samson's dead!"

Kilmarnock lang may grunt and grane,
And sigh, and sab, and greet her lane,
And cleed her bairns, man, wife, an' wean,
      In mourning weed;
To death, she's dearly paid the kane—
      Tam Samson's dead!

The brethren o' the mystic level
May hing their head in woefu' bevel,
While by their nose the tears will revel,
      Like ony bead;
Death's gien the lodge an unco devel—
      Tam Samson's dead!

When Winter muffles up his cloak,
And binds the mire up like a rock;
When to the lochs the curlers flock
      Wi' gleesome speed;
Wha will they station at the cock?—
      Tam Samson's dead!

He was the king o' a' the core,
To guard, or draw, or wick a bore,
Or up the rink like Jehu roar
      In time o' need;
But now he lags on death's hog-score—
      Tam Samson's dead!

Now safe the stately sawmont sail,
And trouts bedropp'd wi' crimson hail,
And eels weel kenn'd for souple tail,
      And geds for greed,
Since dark in death's fish-creel we wail
      Tam Samson dead!

---

† "Tam Samson's Elegy:" when this worthy old sportsman went out last muirfowl season, he supposed it was to be, in Ossian's phrase, "the last of his fields," and expressed an ardent wish to die and be buried in the muirs. On this hint the author composed his elegy and epitaph.—(B.) Samson was a nursery and seedsman, and a great sportsman.

‡ "Mackinlay:" a certain preacher, a great favourite with the million.—See "The Ordination," stanza ii.—(B.)

§ "Robertson:" another preacher, an equal favourite with the few, who was at that time ailing. For him, see also "The Ordination," stanza ix.—(B.)

Rejoice, ye birring paitricks a';
Ye cootie muircocks, crousely craw;
Ye maukins, cock your fud fu' braw,
    Withouten dread;
Your mortal fae is now awa'—
    Tam Samson 's dead!

That woefu' morn be ever mourn'd
Saw him in shootin' graith adorn'd,
While pointers round impatient burn'd,
    Frae couples freed;
But och! he gaed and ne'er return'd—
    Tam Samson 's dead!

In vain auld age his body batters;
In vain the gout his ancles fetters;
In vain the burns cam' down like waters,
    An acre braid!
Now every auld wife, greetin', clatters
    Tam Samson 's dead!

Owre mony a weary hag he limpit,
An' aye the tither shot he thumpit,
Till coward Death behint him jumpit
    Wi' deadly feide;
Now he proclaims, wi' tout o' trumpet,
    Tam Samson 's dead!

When at his heart he felt the dagger,
He reel'd his wonted bottle swagger,
But yet he drew the mortal trigger
    Wi' weel-aim'd heed;
"L—d, five!" he cried, an' owre did stagger—
    Tam Samson 's dead!

Ilk hoary hunter mourn'd a brither;
Ilk sportsman youth bemoan'd a father;
Yon auld gray stane, amang the heather,
    Marks out his head,
Whare Burns has wrote, in rhyming blether,
    Tam Samson 's dead!

There low he lies, in lasting rest;
Perhaps upon his mouldering breast
Some spitefu' muirfowl bigs her nest,
    To hatch an' breed;
Alas! nae mair he 'll them molest!—
    Tam Samson 's dead!

When August winds the heather wave,
And sportsmen wander by yon grave,
Three volleys let his memory crave
    O' pouther an' lead,
Till Echo answer frae her cave,
    Tam Samson 's dead!

Heaven rest his saul, whare'er he be!
Is the wish o' mony mae than me:
He had twa fauts, or maybe three,
    Yet what remead?
Ae social, honest man want we:
    Tam Samson 's dead!

THE EPITAPH.

Tam Samson's weel-worn clay here lies,
  Ye canting zealots, spare him!
If honest worth in Heaven rise,
  Ye 'll mend or ye win near him.

PER CONTRA.

Go, Fame, and canter like a filly,
Through a' the streets and neuks o' Killie,*
Tell every social, honest billie
    To cease his grievin',
For, yet unskaith'd by Death's gleg gullie,
    Tam Samson 's leevin'.

NATURE'S LAW—A POEM.

HUMBLY INSCRIBED TO GAVIN HAMILTON, ESQ.

"Great Nature spoke: observant man obey'd."—POPE.

Let other heroes boast their scars,
  The marks of sturt and strife;
And other poets sing of wars,
  The plagues of human life;
Shame fa' the fun; wi' sword and gun
  To slap mankind like lumber!
I sing his name, and nobler fame,
  Wha multiplies our number.

Great Nature spoke, with air benign,
  "Go on, ye human race;
This lower world I you resign;
  Be fruitful and increase.
The liquid fire of strong desire
  I 've pour'd it in each bosom;
Here, on this hand, does Mankind stand,
  And there, is Beauty's blossom."

The Hero of these artless strains,
  A lowly bard was he,
Who sung his rhymes in Coila's plains,
  With meikle mirth an' glee;
Kind Nature's care had given his share,
  Large, of the flaming current;
And, all devout, he never sought
  To stem the sacred torrent.

He felt the powerful, high behest
  Thrill, vital, through and through;
And sought a correspondent breast,
  To give obedience due:
Propitious Powers screen'd the young flow'rs,
  From mildews of abortion;
And lo! the bard—a great reward—
  Has got a double portion!

Auld cantie Coil may count the day,
  As annual it returns,
The third of Libra's equal sway,
  That gave another Burns,
With future rhymes, an' other times,
  To emulate his sire;
To sing auld Coil in nobler style,
  With more poetic fire.

Ye Powers of peace, and peaceful song,
  Look down with gracious eyes;
And bless auld Coila, large and long,
  With multiplying joys;
Long may she stand to prop the land,
  The flow'r of ancient nations;
And Burnses spring, her fame to sing,
  To endless generations!

---

* "Killie:" is a phrase the country-folks sometimes use for Kilmarnock.—(B.)

EPISTLE FROM A TAILOR,*

THOMAS WALKER, OCHILTREE, TO ROBERT BURNS.

WHAT waefu' news is this I hear?
Frae greeting I can scarce forbear,
Folk tells me ye 're gaun aff this year,
  Out owre the sea,
And lasses wham ye lo'e sae dear
  Will greet for thee.

Weel wad I like were ye to stay;
But, Robin, since ye will away,
I hae a word yet mair to say,
  And maybe twa;
May He protect us night and day,
  That made us a'!

Whare thou art gaun, keep mind frae me,
Seek Him to bear thee companie,
And, Robin, whan ye come to die,
  Ye 'll win aboon,
And live at peace and unity
  Ayont the moon.

Some tell me, Rab, ye dinna fear
To get a wean, and curse and swear;
I 'm unco wae, my lad, to hear
  O' sic a trade:
Could I persuade you to forbear,
  I wad be glad.

Fu' weel ye ken ye 'll gang to hell,
Gin ye persist in doin' ill:
Waes me! ye 're hurlin' down the hill
  Withouten dread;
And ye 'll get leave to swear your fill
  After ye 're dead.

There, walth o' women ye 'll get near,
But gettin' weans ye will forbear,
Ye 'll never say, My bonnie dear,
  Come, gie 's a kiss;
Nae kissing there—ye 'll girn and sneer,
  And ither hiss.

O Rab! lay by thy foolish tricks,
And steer nae mair the female sex,
Or some day ye 'll come through the pricks,
  And that ye 'll see;
Ye 'll fin' hard living wi' Auld Nicks—
  I 'm wae for thee!

But what 's this comes wi' sic a knell,
Amaist as loud as ony bell,
While it does mak my conscience tell
  Me what is true!
I 'm but a ragget cowt mysel',
  Owre sib to you!

We 're owre like those wha think it fit,
To stuff their noddles fu' o' wit,
And yet content in darkness sit,
  Wha shun the light,
Wad let them see to 'scape the pit
  That lang dark night.

But farewell, Rab, I maun awa';
May He that made us keep us a',
For that wad be a dreadfu' fa',
  And hurt us sair;
Lad, ye wad never mend ava,
  Sae, Rab, tak care.

ROBERT BURNS' ANSWER.

WHAT ails ye now, ye lousy bitch,
To thresh my back at sic a pitch?
Losh, man! hae mercy wi' your natch,
  Your bodkin 's bauld;
I didna suffer half sae much
  Frae Daddy Auld.

What though at times, when I grow crouse,
I gie their wames a random pouse,
Is that enough for you to souse
  Your servant sae?
Gae mind your seam, ye prick-the-louse,
  An' jag the flae!

King David, o' poetic brief,
Wrought 'mang the lasses sic mischief,
As fill'd his after-life wi' grief
  An' bluidy rants;
An' yet he 's ranked amang the chief
  O' langsyne saunts.

An' maybe, Tam, for a' my cants,
My wicked rhymes, an' drucken rants,
I 'll gie auld cloven Clootie's haunts
  An unco slip yet,
An' snugly sit amang the saunts,
  At Davie's hip yet.

---

* "Tailor:" Thomas Walker, who was probably assisted in it by Willie Simson.

But fegs! the Session says I maun
Gae fa' upo' anither plan
Than garrin' lasses coup the cran,
    Clean heels owre body,
An' sairly thole their mither's ban
    Afore the howdy.

This leads me on to tell for sport
How I did wi' the Session sort:
Auld Clinkum, at the Inner Port,
    Cried three times, "Robin!
Come hither, lad, and answer for 't,
    Ye 're blamed for jobbin'."

Wi' pinch I put a Sunday's face on,
And snooved awa' before the Session.
I made an open, fair confession,
    I scorn'd to lee;
An' syne Mess John, beyond expression,
    Fell foul o' me.

A fornicator loun he call'd me,
And said my faut frae bliss expell'd me;
I own'd the tale was true he tell'd me;
    "But what the matter?"
Quo' I, "I fear, unless ye geld me,
    I 'll ne'er be better."

"Geld you!" quo' he, "an' what for no?
If that your right hand, leg, or toe,
Should ever prove your spiritual foe,
    You should remember
To cut it aff, and what for no
    Your dearest member?"

"Na, na," quo' I, "I 'm no for that,
Gelding 's nae better than it 's ca't;
I 'd rather suffer for my faut,
    A hearty flewit,
As sair owre hip as ye can draw 't,
    Though I should rue it.

"Or gin ye like to end the bother,
To please us a', I 've just ae ither;
When next wi' yon lass I forgather,
    Whate'er betide it,
I 'll frankly gi'e her 't a' thegither,
    And let her guide it."

But, Sir, this pleased them warst of a',
An' therefore, Tam, when that I saw,
I said, "Gude-night," an' cam' awa',
    And left the Session;
I saw they were resolvèd a'
    On my oppression.

WILLIE CHALMERS.*

Wi' braw new branks in mickle pride,
    And eke a braw new brechan,
My Pegasus I 'm got astride,
    And up Parnassus pechin';
Whiles owre a bush, wi' downward crush,
    The doited beastie stammers;
Then up he gets, and off he sets,
    For sake o' Willie Chalmers.

I doubtna, lass, that weel-kenn'd name
    May cost a pair o' blushes;
I am nae stranger to your fame,
    Nor his warm-urgèd wishes.
Your bonnie face, sae mild and sweet,
    His honest heart enamours,
And, faith, ye 'll no be lost a whit,
    Though wair'd on Willie Chalmers.

Auld Truth hersel' might swear ye 're fair,
    And Honour safely back her,
And Modesty assume your air,
    And ne'er a ane mistak her:
And sic twa love-inspiring e'en
    Might fire even holy palmers;
Nae wonder, then, they 've fatal been
    To honest Willie Chalmers.

I doubtna fortune may you shore
    Some mim-mou'd pouther'd priestie,
Fu' lifted up wi' Hebrew lore,
    And band upon his breastie:
But oh! what signifies to you
    His lexicons and grammars?
The feeling heart 's the royal blue,
    And that 's wi' Willie Chalmers.

Some gapin', glowrin', countra laird,
    May warsle for your favour;
May claw his lug, and straik his beard,
    And hoast up some palaver.
My bonnie maid, before ye wed
    Sic clumsy-witted hammers,
Seek Heaven for help, and barefit skelp
    Awa' wi' Willie Chalmers.

Forgive the Bard! my fond regard
    For ane that shares my bosom,
Inspires my Muse to gie 'm his dues,
    For deil a hair I roose him.
May Powers aboon unite you soon,
    And fructify your amours,
And every year come in mair dear
    To you and Willie Chalmers!

---

* William Chalmers, writer in Ayr, being in love, got Burns to write the above verses for him to his *inamorata*.

SONG.*

Tune—"Roslin Castle."

The gloomy night is gath'ring fast, Loud roars the wild in-con-stant blast,
Yon murky cloud is foul with rain, I see it driv-ing o'er the plain;
The hunter now has left the moor, The scatt'red coveys meet se-cure;
While here I wan-der, prest with care, A-long the lone-ly banks of Ayr.

* Written on a dreary moor after leaving Mr. Laurie's house (Loudoun parish), and intended for Burns' last song on leaving Scotland.

The Autumn mourns her rip'ning corn
By early Winter's ravage torn;
Across her placid, azure sky,
She sees the scowling tempest fly;
Chill runs my blood to hear it rave;
I think upon the stormy wave,
Where many a danger I must dare,
Far from the bonnie banks of Ayr.

'Tis not the surging billow's roar,
'Tis not that fatal, deadly shore;
Though death in every shape appear,
The wretched have no more to fear!
But round my heart the ties are bound,
That heart transpierced with many a wound;
These bleed afresh, those ties I tear,
To leave the bonnie banks of Ayr.

Farewell, old Coila's hills and dales,
Her heathy moors and winding vales;
The scenes where wretched Fancy roves,
Pursuing past, unhappy loves!
Farewell, my friends! farewell, my foes!
My peace with these, my love with those—
The bursting tears my heart declare;
Farewell, the bonnie banks of Ayr!

A PRAYER.

LYING AT A REVEREND FRIEND'S* HOUSE ONE NIGHT, THE AUTHOR LEFT THE FOLLOWING VERSES IN THE ROOM WHERE HE SLEPT.

O Thou dread Power, who reign'st above!
  I know Thou wilt me hear,
When for this scene of peace and love
  I make my prayer sincere.

The hoary sire—the mortal stroke,
  Long, long, be pleased to spare!
To bless his little filial flock,
  And show what good men are.

She, who her lovely offspring eyes
  With tender hopes and fears,
O bless her with a mother's joys,
  But spare a mother's tears!

Their hope, their stay, their darling youth,
  In manhood's dawning blush—
Bless him, Thou God of love and truth.
  Up to a parent's wish!

The beauteous, seraph sister-band,
  With earnest tears I pray—
Thou know'st the snares on ev'ry hand—
  Guide Thou their steps alway!

When soon or late they reach that coast,
  O'er life's rough ocean driven,
May they rejoice, no wanderer lost,
  A family in heaven!

THE BRIGS OF AYR—A POEM.

INSCRIBED TO J. BALLANTYNE,† ESQ., AYR.

The simple Bard, rough at the rustic plough,
Learning his tuneful trade from every bough;
The chanting linnet, or the mellow thrush,
Hailing the setting sun, sweet, in the green thorn bush;
The soaring lark, the perching red-breast shrill,
Or deep-toned plovers, gray, wild-whistling o'er the hill.
Shall he—nurst in the peasant's lowly shed,
To hardy independence bravely bred,
By early poverty to hardship steel'd,
And train'd to arms in stern Misfortune's field—
Shall he be guilty of their hireling crimes,
The servile, mercenary Swiss of rhymes?
Or labour hard the panegyric close,
With all the venal soul of dedicating prose?
No! though his artless strains he rudely sings,
And throws his hand uncouthly o'er the strings,
He glows with all the spirit of the Bard,
Fame, honest fame, his great, his dear reward!
Still, if some patron's generous care he trace,
Skill'd in the secret to bestow with grace;
When Ballantyne befriends his humble name,
And hands the rustic stranger up to fame,
With heartfelt throes his grateful bosom swells;
The godlike bliss, to give, alone excels.

'Twas when the stacks get on their winter hap,
And thack and rape secure the toil-won crap;
Potatoe-bings are snuggèd up frae skaith
Of coming Winter's biting, frosty breath;
The bees, rejoicing o'er their summer toils,
Unnumber'd buds and flowers' delicious spoils,
Seal'd up with frugal care in massive waxen piles,
Are doom'd by Man, that tyrant o'er the weak,
The death o' devils, smoor'd wi' brimstone reek:
The thundering guns are heard on every side,
The wounded coveys, reeling, scatter wide;
The feather'd field-mates, bound by Nature's tie,
Sires, mothers, children, in one carnage lie:
(What warm, poetic heart but inly bleeds,
And execrates man's savage, ruthless deeds?)
Nae mair the flower in field or meadow springs:
Nae mair the grove with airy concert rings,
Except, perhaps, the robin's whistling glee,
Proud o' the height o' some bit half-lang tree:
The hoary morns precede the sunny days,
Mild, calm, serene, wide spreads the noontide blaze,
While thick the gossamer waves wanton in the rays.
'Twas in that season, when a simple Bard,
Unknown and poor, simplicity's reward,
Ae night, within the ancient brugh of Ayr,
By whim inspired, or haply press'd wi' care,
He left his bed, and took his wayward route,
And down by Simpson's‡ wheel'd the left about:
Whether impell'd by all-directing Fate,
To witness what I after shall narrate;
Or whether, wrapt in meditation high,
He wander'd out he knew not where, nor why.

---

* "Reverend Friend:" Mr. Laurie of Loudoun. See in LIFE an account of this gentleman, and Burns' visit to him.

† "Ballantyne:" an early friend and patron of Burns, who was superintending, as chief magistrate, the erection of a new bridge in Ayr in place of the old one.

‡ "Simpson's:" a noted tavern at the Auld Brig end.—(B.)

The drowsy Dungeon-clock * had number'd two,
And Wallace-tower * had sworn the fact was true:
The tide-swoln firth, with sullen-sounding roar,
Through the still night dash'd hoarse along the shore;
All else was hush'd as Nature's closèd e'e;
The silent moon shone high o'er tower and tree;
The chilly frost, beneath the silver beam,
Crept, gently-crusting, o'er the glittering stream.

When, lo! on either hand the listening Bard,
The clanging sugh of whistling wings is heard;
Two dusky forms dart through the midnight air,
Swift as the gos † drives on the wheeling hare;
Ane on th' Auld Brig his airy shape uprears,
The ither flutters o'er the rising piers:
Our warlock Rhymer instantly descried
The Sprites that owre the Brigs of Ayr preside.
(That Bards are second-sighted is nae joke,
And ken the lingo of the sp'ritual folk;
Fays, Spunkies, Kelpies, a', they can explain them,
And even the vera deils they brawly ken them).
Auld Brig appear'd of ancient Pictish race,
The very wrinkles Gothic in his face:
He seem'd as he wi' Time had warstled lang,
Yet, teughly doure, he bade an unco bang.
New Brig was buskit in a braw new coat,
That he at Lon'on, frae ane Adams, got;
In 's hand five taper staves as smooth 's a bead,
Wi' virls and whirlygigums at the head.
The Goth was stalking round with anxious search,
Spying the time-worn flaws in every arch;
It chanced his new-come neibour took his e'e,
And e'en a vex'd and angry heart had he!
Wi' thieveless sneer to see his modish mien,
He down the water gies him this guid-een :—

AULD BRIG.

I doubt na', frien', ye 'll think ye 're nae sheepshank,
Ance ye were streekit o'er frae bank to bank!
But gin ye be a brig as auld as me—
Though faith! that day I doubt ye 'll never see
There 'll be, if that date come, I 'll wad a bodle,
Some fewer whigmaleeries in your noddle.

NEW BRIG.

Auld Vandal, ye but show your little mense,
Just much about it wi' your scanty sense;
Will your poor, narrow footpath of a street—
Where twa wheelbarrows tremble when they meet—
Your ruin'd, formless bulk o' stane an' lime,
Compare wi' bonnie brigs o' modern time?
There 's men o' taste would tak the Ducat-stream, ‡
Though they should cast the very sark and swim,
Ere they would grate their feelings wi' the view
Of sic an ugly Gothic hulk as you.

* " Dungeon-clock and Wallace-tower:" the two steeples.—(B.)
† " Gos:" the gos-hawk, or falcon.—(B.)
‡ " Ducat-stream:" a noted ford, just above the Auld Brig.—(B.)

AULD BRIG.

Conceited gowk! puff'd up wi' windy pride!
This mony a year I 've stood the flood an' tide;
And though wi' crazy eild I 'm sair forfairn,
I 'll be a brig when ye 're a shapeless cairn! §
As yet ye little ken about the matter,
But twa-three winters will inform ye better.
When heavy, dark, continued, a'-day rains
Wi' deepening deluges o'erflow the plains;
When from the hills where springs the brawling Coil,
Or stately Lugar's mossy fountains boil,
Or where the Greenock winds his moorland course,
Or haunted Garpal ‖ draws his feeble source,
Aroused by blustering winds and spotting thowes,
In mony a torrent down his snaw-broo rowes;
While crashing ice, borne on the roaring spate,
Sweeps dams, an' mills, an' brigs a' to the gate;
And from Glenbuck, ¶ down to the Ratton-key, **
Auld Ayr is just one lengthen'd, tumbling sea—
Then down ye 'll hurl, (deil nor ye never rise!)
And dash the gumlie jaups up to the pouring skies;
A lesson sadly teaching, to your cost,
That Architecture's noble art is lost!

NEW BRIG.

Fine Architecture, troth, I needs must say 't o 't!
The Lord be thankit that we 've tint the gate o 't!
Gaunt, ghastly, ghaist-alluring edifices,
Hanging with threat'ning jut like precipices;
O'erarching, mouldy, gloom-inspiring coves,
Supporting roofs fantastic, stony groves:
Windows and doors in nameless sculptures dress'd,
With order, symmetry, or taste unbless'd;
Forms like some bedlam statuary's dream,
The crazed creations of misguided whim;
Forms might be worshipp'd on the bended knee,
And still the second dread command be free,
Their likeness is not found on earth, in air, or sea!
Mansions that would disgrace the building taste
Of any mason reptile, bird or beast:
Fit only for a doited monkish race,
Or frosty maids forsworn the dear embrace;
Or cuifs of later times, wha held the notion
That sullen gloom was sterling, true devotion:
Fancies that our guid Brugh denies protection,
And soon may they expire, unblest wi' resurrection!

AULD BRIG.

O ye, my dear remember'd, ancient yealings,
Were ye but here to share my wounded feelings!

§ This prediction was fulfilled in 1877.
‖ " Garpal:" the banks of Garpal Water is one of the few places in the West of Scotland where those fancy-scaring beings, known by the name of Ghaists, still continue pertinaciously to inhabit.—(B.)
¶ " Glenbuck:" the source of the river Ayr.—(B.)
** " Ratton-key:" a small landing-place above the large quay.—(B.)

Ye worthy Proveses, an' mony a Bailie,
Wha in the paths o' righteousness did toil aye;
Ye dainty Deacons, an' ye douce Conveeners,
To whom our moderns are but causey-cleaners;
Ye godly Councils, wha hae blest this town;
Ye godly Brethren o' the sacred gown,
Wha meekly gie your hurdies to the smiters;
And (what would now be strange) ye godly Writers:
A' ye douce folk I 've borne aboon the broo,
Were ye but here, what would ye say or do!
How would your spirits groan in deep vexation,
To see each melancholy alteration;
And, agonising, curse the time and place
When ye begat the base, degenerate race!
Nae langer reverend men, their country's glory,
In plain braid Scots hold forth a plain braid story;
Nae langer thrifty citizens, an' douce,
Meet owre a pint or in the council-house;
But staumrel, corky-headed, graceless gentry,
The herryment and ruin of the country;
Men, three-parts made by tailors and by barbers,
Wha waste your weel-hain'd gear on d——d new brigs and harbours!

NEW BRIG.

Now haud you there! for, faith, ye 've said enough,
And muckle mair than ye can mak to through;
As for your Priesthood, I shall say but little,
Corbies and Clergy are a shot right kittle:
But, under favour o' your langer beard,
Abuse o' Magistrates might weel be spared:
To liken them to your auld-warld squad,
I must needs say, comparisons are odd.
In Ayr, wag-wits nae mair can hae a handle
To mouth "a citizen," a term o' scandal;
Nae mair the Council waddles down the street,
In all the pomp of ignorant conceit;
Men wha grew wise priggin' owre hops an' raisins,
Or gather'd liberal views in bonds and seisins,
If haply Knowledge, on a random tramp,
Had shored them with a glimmer of his lamp,
And would to Common-sense for once betray'd them,
Plain, dull Stupidity stept kindly in to aid them.

What farther clishmaclaver might been said,
What bloody wars, if Sprites had blood to shed,
No man can tell: but all before their sight,
A fairy train appear'd in order bright.
Adown the glittering stream they featly danced;
Bright to the moon their various dresses glanced.
They footed o'er the watery glass so neat,
The infant ice scarce bent beneath their feet:
While arts of minstrelsy among them rung,
And soul-ennobling bards heroic ditties sung.

Oh had M'Lauchlan,* thairm-inspiring sage,
Been there to hear this heavenly band engage,
When through his dear strathspeys they bore with Highland rage;
Or when they struck old Scotia's melting airs,
The lover's raptured joys or bleeding cares;
How would his Highland lug been nobler fired,
And even his matchless hand with finer touch inspired!
No guess could tell what instrument appeared,
But all the soul of Music's self was heard;
Harmonious concert rung in every part,
While simple melody pour'd moving on the heart.

The Genius of the Stream in front appears,
A venerable chief advanced in years;
His hoary head with water-lilies crown'd,
His manly leg with garter-tangle bound.
Next came the loveliest pair in all the ring,
Sweet Female Beauty hand in hand with Spring;
Then, crown'd with flowery hay, came Rural Joy,
And Summer, with his fervid-beaming eye:
All-cheering Plenty, with her flowing horn,
Led yellow Autumn wreath'd with nodding corn;
Then Winter's time-bleach'd locks did hoary show,
By Hospitality with cloudless brow.
Next follow'd Courage, with his martial stride,
From where the Feal wild-woody coverts hide;
Benevolence, with mild benignant air,
A female form, came from the towers of Stair:†
Learning and Worth in equal measures trode
From simple Catrine,‡ their long-loved abode:
Last, white-robed Peace, crown'd with a hazel wreath,
To rustic Agriculture did bequeath
The broken, iron instruments of death;
At sight of whom our Sprites forgat their kindling wrath.

LINES ON MEETING WITH BASIL, LORD DAER.§

This wot ye all whom it concerns,
I, Rhymer Robin, alias Burns,
October twenty-third,
A ne'er-to-be-forgotten day,
Sae far I sprachled up the brae,
I dinner'd wi' a Lord.

---

* " M'Lauchlan:" a well-known performer of Scotch music on the violin.—(B.) He was from Argyleshire, and patronized by the Earl of Eglinton, himself a great musician, and alluded to in the last stanza as " Courage."

† " Towers of Stair:" the poet alludes here to Mrs. Stewart of Stair, his early patroness.

‡ " Catrine:" alluding to Dugald Stewart.

§ " Lord Daer:" son of the Earl of Selkirk.— See LIFE.

I 've been at drucken writers' feasts,
Nay, been bitch-fou 'mang godly priests,
    Wi' reverence be it spoken ;
I 've even join'd the honour'd jorum,
When mighty Squireships of the quorum
    Their hydra drouth did sloken.

But wi' a Lord—stand out my shin !
A Lord—a Peer—an Earl's son !
    Up higher yet, my bonnet !
An' sic a Lord !—lang Scotch ells twa,
Our Peerage he o'erlooks them a',
    As I look o'er my sonnet.

But oh for Hogarth's magic power !
To show Sir Bardie's willyart glower,
    An' how he stared an' stammer'd,
When, goavin, as if led wi' branks,
An' stumpin on his ploughman shanks,
    He in the parlour hammer'd.

I sidling shelter'd in a nook,
An' at his Lordship steal't a look,
    Like some portentous omen ;
Except good sense and social glee,
An' (what surprised me) modesty,
    I markèd nought uncommon.

I watch'd the symptoms o' the Great,
The gentle pride, the lordly state,
    The arrogant assuming ;
The feint a pride, nae pride had he,
Nor sauce, nor state, that I could see,
    Mair than an honest ploughman.

Then from his Lordship I shall learn,
Henceforth to meet with unconcern
    One rank as weel 's another ;
Nae honest, worthy man need care
To meet with noble, youthful Daer,
    For he but meets a brother.

EPISTLE TO MAJOR W. LOGAN.*

Hail, thairm-inspirin', rattlin' Willie !
Though Fortune's road be rough and hilly
To every fiddling, rhyming billie,
    We never heed,
But tak it like the unback'd filly,
    Proud o' her speed.

---

* Major Logan of Camlarg was one of the best fiddlers of his day. He was the brother of Miss Logan to whom Burns presented a copy of "Beattie's Minstrel." He was a retired military officer, residing at Park House, near Ayr, where Burns met him.

When, idly goavin, whiles we saunter,
Yirr ! Fancy barks, awa' we canter,
Up-hill, down-brae, till some mishanter,
    Some black bog-hole,
Arrests us ; then the scathe an' banter
    We 're forced to thole.

Hale be your heart ! hale be your fiddle !
Lang may your elbuck jink an diddle,
To cheer you through the weary widdle
    O' this wild warl' ;
Until you on a crummock driddle,
    A gray-hair'd carl.

Come wealth, come poortith, late or soon,
Heaven send your heart-strings aye in tune !
And screw your temper-pins aboon,
    A fifth or mair,
The melancholious, lazy croon
    O' cankrie care !

May still your life from day to day,
Nae "lente largo" in the play,
But "allegretto forte" gay,
    Harmonious flow,
A sweeping, kindling, bauld strathspey—
    Encore ! Bravo !

A blessing on the cheerie gang,
Wha dearly like a jig or sang,
An' never think o' right an' wrang
    By square an' rule,
But, as the clegs o' feeling stang,
    Are wise or fool !

My hand-waled curse keep hard in chase,
The harpy, hoodock, purse-proud race,
Wha count on poortith as disgrace :
    Their tuneless hearts,
May fireside discords jar a base
    To a' their parts !

But come—your hand, my careless brither;
I' th' ither warl', if there 's anither—
And that there is, I 've little swither
    About the matter—
We, cheek for chow, shall jog thegither ;
    I 'se ne'er bid better.

We 've faults and failings—granted clearly ;
We 're frail, backsliding mortals merely ;
Eve's bonnie squad, priests wyte them sheerly
    For our grand fa' ;
But still—but still—I like them dearly :
    God bless them a' !

Ochon for poor Castalian drinkers,
When they fa' foul o' earthly jinkers!
The witching, curst, delicious blinkers
    Hae put me hyte,
And gart me weet my waukrife winkers,
    Wi' girnin' spite.

But, by yon moon!—an' that's high swearin'—
An' every star within my hearin'!
An' by her e'en, wha was a dear ane
    I'll ne'er forget!
I hope to gie the jauds a clearin'
    In fair play yet.

My loss I mourn, but not repent it,
I'll seek my pursie whare I tint it;
Ance to the Indies I were wonted,
    Some cantrip hour,
By some sweet elf I'll yet be dinted,
    Then, *vive l'amour!*

Faites mes baissemains respectueuses
To sentimental sister Susie,
And honest Luckie; no to roose you,
    Ye may be proud
That sic a couple Fate allows ye,
    To grace your blood.

Nae mair at present can I measure,
An', troth, my rhymin' ware's nae treasure;
But when in Ayr, some half-hour's leisure,
    Be 't light, be 't dark,
Sir Bard will do himsel' the pleasure
    To call at Park.

                    ROBERT BURNS.
MOSSGIEL, *30th October,* 1786.

LINES TO MRS. LAWRIE.

RUSTICITY's ungainly form
    May cloud the highest mind;
But when the heart is nobly warm,
    The good excuse will find.

Propriety's cold, cautious rules
    Warm fervour may o'erlook;
But spare poor sensibility
    The ungentle, harsh rebuke.

THE COOPER O' CUDDIE.

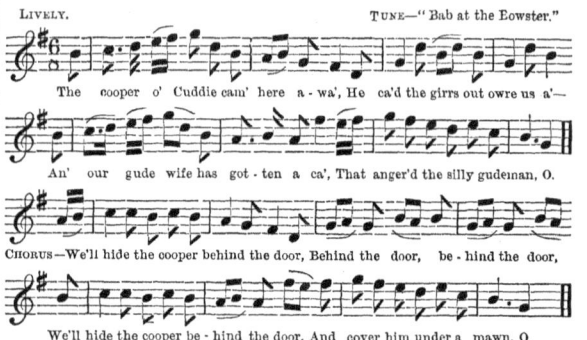

He sought them out, he sought them in,
Wi' deil hae her! and deil hae him!
But the body was sae doited and blin',
He wist na where he was gaun, O.
    We'll hide the cooper, &c.

They cooper'd at e'en, they cooper'd at morn,
Till our gudeman has gotten the scorn;
On ilka brow she's planted a horn,
And swears that they shall stan', O.
    We'll hide the cooper, &c.

ADDRESS TO EDINBURGH.

EDINA! Scotia's darling seat!
    All hail thy palaces and towers,
Where once, beneath a monarch's feet,
    Sat Legislation's sovereign powers!
From marking wildly-scatter'd flowers,
    As on the banks of Ayr I stray'd,
And singing, lone, the lingering hours,
    I shelter in thy honour'd shade.

Here wealth still swells the golden tide,
    As busy Trade his labours plies;
There Architecture's noble pride
    Bids elegance and splendour rise;
Here Justice, from her native skies,
    High wields her balance and her rod;
There Learning, with his eagle eyes,
    Seeks Science in her coy abode.

Thy sons, Edina! social, kind,
    With open arms the stranger hail;
Their views enlarged, their liberal mind,
    Above the narrow, rural vale;
Attentive still to Sorrow's wail,
    Or modest Merit's silent claim;
And never may their sources fail!
    And never Envy blot their name!

Thy daughters bright thy walks adorn,
  Gay as the gilded summer sky,
Sweet as the dewy milk-white thorn,
  Dear as the raptured thrill of joy!
Fair Burnet* strikes the adoring eye,
  Heaven's beauties on my fancy shine;
I see the Sire of Love on high,
  And own his work indeed divine!

There, watching high the least alarms
  Thy rough, rude fortress gleams afar;
Like some bold veteran, gray in arms,
  And mark'd with many a seamy scar;
The ponderous wall and massy bar,
  Grim-rising o'er the rugged rock,
Have oft withstood assailing war,
  And oft repell'd the invader's shock.

With awe-struck thought, and pitying tears,
  I view that noble, stately Dome,
Where Scotia's kings of other years,
  Famed heroes! had their royal home:
Alas! how changed the times to come!
  Their royal name low in the dust!
Their hapless race wild-wandering roam,
  Though rigid Law cries out, "'twas just!"

Wild beats my heart to trace your steps,
  Whose ancestors, in days of yore,
Through hostile ranks and ruin'd gaps
  Old Scotia's bloody Lion bore;
E'en I who sing in rustic lore,
  Haply, my sires have left their shed,
And faced grim Danger's loudest roar,
  Bold-following where your fathers led!

Edina! Scotia's darling seat!
  All hail thy palaces and towers,
Where once, beneath a monarch's feet,
  Sat Legislation's sovereign powers!
From marking wildly-scatter'd flowers,
  As on the banks of Ayr I stray'd,
And singing, lone, the lingering hours,
  I shelter in thy honour'd shade.

ODE ON CHARLES EDWARD'S BIRTHDAY.†

Afar the illustrious Exile roams,
  Whom kingdoms on this day should hail;
An inmate in the casual shed,
On transient pity's bounty fed,
  Haunted by busy memory's bitter tale!
Beasts of the forest have their savage homes,
  But He, who should imperial purple wear,
Owns not the lap of earth where rests his royal head!
  His wretched refuge, dark despair,
While ravening wrongs and woes pursue,
  And distant far the faithful few
    Who would his sorrows share.

False flatterer, Hope, away!
  Nor think to lure us as in days of yore:
We solemnize this sorrowing natal day,
  To prove our loyal truth—we can no more,
And owning Heaven's mysterious sway,
  Submissive, low adore.
Ye honoured, mighty Dead,
  Who nobly perished in the glorious cause,
  Your King, your Country, and her laws,
From great Dundee, who smiling Victory led,
And fell a martyr in her arms,
  (What breast of northern ice but warms!)
To bold Balmerino's undying name,
Whose soul of fire, lighted at Heaven's high flame,
Deserves the proudest wreath departed heroes claim:

Not unrevenged your fate shall lie,
  It only lags, the fatal hour;
Your blood shall with incessant cry
  Awake at last th' unsparing Power;
As from the cliff, with thundering course,
  The snowy ruin smokes along
With doubling speed and gathering force,
Till deep it, crushing, whelms the cottage in the vale;
  So Vengeance' arm, ensanguin'd, strong,
  Shall with resistless might assail,
  Usurping Brunswick's pride shall lay,
And Stuart's wrongs and yours, with tenfold weight,
    repay.

Perdition, baleful child of night!
  Rise and revenge the injured right
    Of Stuart's royal race:
Lead on the unmuzzled hounds of hell,
Till all the frighted echoes tell
    The blood-notes of the chase!
Full on the quarry point their view,
Full on the base usurping crew,
The tools of faction, and the nation's curse!
  Hark how the cry grows on the wind;
  They leave the lagging gale behind,
  Their savage fury, pityless, they pour;
With murdering eyes already they devour;
See Brunswick spent, a wretched prey,
  His life one poor despairing day,
Where each avenging hour still ushers in a worse!

---

* "Burnet:" Eliza, daughter of Lord Monboddo, who died of consumption, June, 1776.

† A small knot of enthusiasts met once a year to celebrate Prince Charles Edward's birthday. This ode was written for the meeting on the 31st December, 1787.

Such havoc, howling all abroad,
    Their utter ruin bring;
The base apostates to their God,
    Or rebels to their King.

TO MISS LOGAN,*

WITH BEATTIE'S POEMS FOR A NEW YEAR'S GIFT, JANUARY 1, 1787.

AGAIN the silent wheels of Time
    Their annual round have driven,
And you, though scarce in maiden prime,
    Are so much nearer heaven.

No gifts have I from Indian coasts
    The infant year to hail;
I send you more than India boasts,
    In Edwin's simple tale.

Our sex with guile and faithless love
    Is charged, perhaps too true;
But may, dear maid, each lover prove
    An Edwin still to you!

* "Miss Logan:" sister to Major Logan; see epistle to him.

THE BANKS O' DOON.

FIRST VERSION.

Thou'll break my heart, thou bonnie bird,
    That sings beside thy mate;
For sae I sat, and sae I sang,
    And wist na o' my fate.

Aft hae I rov'd by bonnie Doon,
  To see the woodbine twine;
And ilka bird sang o' its Luve,
  And sae did I o' mine:

Wi' lightsome heart I pu'd a rose,
  Upon its thorny tree;
But my fause Luver staw my rose,
  And left the thorn wi' me:

Wi' lightsome heart I pu'd a rose,
  Upon a morn in June;
And sae I flourished on the morn,
  And sae was pu'd or noon!

THE BANKS O' DOON.*

SECOND VERSION.

YE flowery banks o' bonnie Doon,
  How can ye blume sae fair?
How can ye chant, ye little birds,
  And I sae fu' o' care!

Thou 'll break my heart, thou bonnie bird,
  That sings upon the bough;
Thou minds me o' the happy days
  When my fause Luve was true.

Thou 'll break my heart, thou bonnie bird,
  That sings beside thy mate;
For sae I sat, and sae I sang,
  And wist na o' my fate.

Aft hae I roved by bonnie Doon,
  To see the woodbine twine,
And ilka bird sang o' its Luve,
  And sae did I o' mine.

Wi' lightsome heart I pu'd a rose,
  Frae aff its thorny tree,
But my fause luver staw the rose,
  And left the thorn wi' me.

EPIGRAM ON ROUGH ROADS.†

I 'M now arrived—thanks to the gods!—
  Through pathways rough and muddy,
A certain sign that makin' roads
  Is no this people's study:

Although I 'm not wi' Scripture cramm'd,
  I 'm sure the Bible says
That heedless sinners shall be damn'd,
  Unless they mend their *ways*.

THE GUIDWIFE OF WAUCHOPE-HOUSE‡
TO ROBERT BURNS.
February, 1787.

MY canty, witty, rhyming ploughman,
I hafflins doubt it is na true, man,
That ye between the stilts were bred,
Wi' ploughmen school'd, wi' ploughmen fed;
I doubt it sair, ye 've drawn your knowledge
Either frae grammar-school or college.
Guid troth, your saul and body baith
Were better fed, I 'd gie my aith,
Than theirs, wha sup sour-milk and parritch,
And bummil through the Single Carritch.
Wha ever heard the ploughman speak
Could tell gif Homer was a Greek?
He 'd flee as soon upon a cudgel,
As get a single line of Virgil.
And then sae slee ye crack your jokes
On Willie Pitt and Charlie Fox:
Our great men a' sae weel descrive,
And how to gar the nation thrive,
Ane maist wad swear ye dwalt amang them,
And as ye saw them, sae ye sang them.
But be ye ploughman, be ye peer,
Ye are a funny blade, I swear:
And though the cauld I ill can bide,
Yet twenty miles, and mair, I 'd ride,
O'er moss, and muir, and never grumble,
Though my auld yad should gie a stumble,
To crack a winter night wi' thee,
And hear thy sangs and sonnets slee.
A guid saut herring and a cake,
Wi' sic a chiel, a feast wad make;
I 'd rather scour your reaming yill,
Or eat o' cheese an' bread my fill,
Than wi' dull lairds on turtle dine,
And ferlie at their wit and wine.
Oh, gif I kenn'd but where ye baide,
I 'd send to you a marled plaid;
'Twad haud your shouthers warm and braw,
And douce at kirk or market shaw;
For south as weel as north, my lad,
A' honest Scotsmen lo'e the *maud*.
Right wae that we 're sae far frae ither,
Yet proud I am to ca' ye brither.
              Your most obedient, E. S.

---

* The young lady referred to in this song was Miss Kennedy (the blooming Peggy of a former song), an heiress in Carrick, who was seduced by a Captain M., in Wigtonshire, had a child to him, instituted an action against him in the Consistorial Court, but died, while it was going on, of a broken heart.

† The "Rough Roads" are those between Stewarton and Kilmarnock.

‡ "The guidwife of Wauchope-house:" was the late gifted Mrs. Scott of Wauchope, in Roxburghshire.

TO THE GUIDWIFE O' WAUCHOPE HOUSE.

GUIDWIFE, *March*, 1787.

I MIND it weel, in early date,
When I was beardless, young, an' blate,
  An' first could thresh the barn,
  Or haud a yokin' at the pleugh;
An' though forfoughten sair eneugh,
  Yet unco proud to learn:
When first amang the yellow corn
  A man I reckon'd was,
An' wi' the lave ilk merry morn
  Could rank my rig an' lass,
    Still shearing an' clearing
      The tither stookèd raw,
    Wi' claivers an' haivers
      Wearing the day awa'.

E'en then a wish (I mind its power),
A wish that to my latest hour
  Shall strongly heave my breast—
That I, for puir auld Scotland's sake,
Some usefu' plan or beuk could make,
  Or sing a sang at least.
The rough burr-thistle, spreading wide
  Amang the bearded bear,
I turn'd the weeder-clips aside,
  An' spared the symbol dear:
    No nation, no station,
      My envy e'er could raise;
    A Scot still, but blot still,
      I knew nae higher praise.

But still the elements o' sang
In formless jumble, right an' wrang,
  Wild floated in my brain:
Till on that hairst I said before
My partner in the merry core,
  She roused the forming strain;
I see her yet, the sonsie quean,
  That lighted up my jingle,
Her witching smile, her pauky een,
  That gart my heart-strings tingle;
    I firèd, inspirèd,
      At every kindling keek,
    But bashing, and dashing,
      I fearèd aye to speak.

Health to the sex! ilk guid chiel says,
Wi' merry dance in winter days,
  An' we to share in common:
The gust of joy, the balm of woe,
The soul o' life, the heaven below,
  Is rapture-giving woman.
Ye surly sumphs, who hate the name,
  Be mindfu' o' your mither;
She, honest woman, may think shame
  That ye 're connected with her.
    Ye 're wae men, ye 're nae men,
      That slight the lovely dears;
    To shame ye, disclaim ye,
      Ilk honest birkie swears.

For you, no bred to barn and byre,
Wha sweetly tune the Scottish lyre,
  Thanks to you for your line:
The marled plaid ye kindly spare,
By me should gratefully be ware;
  'Twad please me to the nine.
I 'd be mair vauntie o' my hap,
  Douce hingin' o'er my curple,
Than ony ermine ever lap,
  Or proud imperial purple.
    Farewell then, lang hale then,
      And plenty be your fa':
    May losses, and crosses,
      Ne'er at your hallan ca'!

THE POET'S PROGRESS.*

A POEM IN EMBRYO.

THOU, Nature, partial Nature, I arraign;
Of thy caprice maternal I complain.
  The peopled fold thy kindly care have found,
The horned bull, tremendous, spurns the ground;
The lordly lion has enough and more,
The forest trembles at his very roar;
Thou giv'st the ass his hide, the snail his shell,
The puny wasp, victorious, guards his cell.
Thy minions, kings defend, control, devour,
In all th' omnipotence of rule and power:
Foxes and statesmen subtile wiles ensure;
The cit and polecat stink, and are secure:
Toads with their poison, doctors with their drug,
The priest and hedgehog, in their robes, are snug:
E'en silly women have defensive arts,
Their eyes, their tongues—and nameless other parts.
  But O thou cruel stepmother and hard,
To thy poor fenceless, naked child, the Bard!
A thing unteachable in worldly skill,
And half an idiot too, more helpless still:
No heels to bear him from the op'ning dun,
No claws to dig, his hated sight to shun:
No horns, but those by luckless Hymen worn,
And those, alas! not Amalthea's horn:
No nerves olfact'ry, true to Mammon's foot,
Or grunting grub, sagacious, evil's root:
The silly sheep that wanders wild astray,
Is not more friendless, is not more a prey;

---
* Afterwards changed into an Epistle to Mr. Graham of Fintry.

Vampyre-booksellers drain him to the heart,
And viper-critics cureless venom dart.

Critics! appall'd I venture on the name,
Those cut-throat bandits in the paths of fame,
Bloody dissectors, worse than ten Monroes,
He hacks to teach, they mangle to expose:
By blockhead's daring into madness stung,
His heart by wanton, causeless malice wrung,
His well-won bays—than life itself more dear—
By miscreants torn who ne'er one sprig must wear;
Foil'd, bleeding, tortur'd in th' unequal strife,
The hapless Poet flounces on through life,
Till, fled each hope that once his bosom fired,
And fled each Muse that glorious once inspired,
Low-sunk in squalid, unprotected age,
Dead even resentment for his injur'd page,
He heeds no more the ruthless critics' rage.

So by some hedge the generous steed deceased,
For half-starved, snarling curs a dainty feast;
By toil and famine worn to skin and bone,
Lies, senseless of each tugging bitch's son.

. . . . . .

A little upright, pert, tart, tripping wight,
And still his precious self his dear delight;
Who loves his own smart shadow in the streets,
Better than e'er the fairest she he meets;
Much specious lore, but little understood,
(Veneering oft outshines the solid wood),
His solid sense by inches you must tell,
But mete his cunning by the Scottish ell!
A man of fashion too, he made his tour,
Learn'd "vive la bagatelle et vive l'amour;"
So travell'd monkeys their grimace improve,
Polish their grin—nay, sigh for ladies' love!
His meddling vanity, a busy fiend,
Still making work his selfish craft must mend.

. . . . . .

.   .   .   Crochallan came,
The old cock'd hat, the brown surtout—the same;
His grisly beard just bristling in its might—
'Twas four long nights and days from shaving-night!
His uncomb'd, hoary locks, wild-staring, thatch'd
A head, for thought profound and clear, unmatch'd;
Yet, though his caustic wit was biting-rude,
His heart was warm, benevolent, and good.

. . . . . .

O Dulness, portion of the truly blest!
Calm, shelter'd haven of eternal rest!
Thy sons ne'er madden in the fierce extremes
Of Fortune's polar frost, or torrid beams;
If mantling high she fills the golden cup,
With sober, selfish ease they sip it up;
Conscious the bounteous meed they well deserve,
They only wonder "some folks" do not starve!

The grave, sage hern thus easy picks his frog,
And thinks the mallard a sad worthless dog.
When disappointment snaps the thread of Hope,
When, thro' disastrous night, they darkling grope,
With deaf endurance sluggishly they bear,
And just conclude that "fools are Fortune's care;"
So, heavy, passive to the tempest's shocks,
Strong on the sign-post stands the stupid ox.

Not so the idle Muses' mad-cap train,
Not such the workings of their moon-struck brain;
In equanimity they never dwell,
By turns in soaring heaven, or vaulted hell!

RATTLIN', ROARIN' WILLIE.

As I cam by Crochallan, I cannilie kee-ket ben; Rat-tl-in', roar-in' Wil-lie Was sittin' at yon boord-en'; Sit-tin' at yon boord-en', And amang guid com-pan-ie, Rat-tl in', roarin' Willie, You're welcome hame to me.

VERSES

ADDRESSED TO THE LANDLADY OF THE INN AT ROSLIN.*

My blessings on ye, sonsy wife;
  I ne'er was here before;
You 've gi'en us walth for horn and knife,
  Nae heart could wish for more.

Heaven keep you clear o' sturt and strife,
  Till far ayont fourscore;
And while I toddle on through life,
  I 'll ne'er gang by your door.

INSCRIPTION FOR THE HEADSTONE OF FERGUSSON THE POET.

No sculptured marble here, nor pompous lay,
  "No storied urn nor animated bust;"
This simple stone directs pale Scotia's way,
  To pour her sorrows o'er the Poet's dust.

---

* She had supplied Burns with a good breakfast after a debauch and a sleepless night spent among the Pentland Hills.

She mourns, sweet tuneful youth, thy hapless fate;
  Though all the powers of song thy fancy fired,
Yet Luxury and Wealth lay by in state,
  And, thankless, starv'd what they so much admired.

This tribute, with a tear, now gives
  A brother Bard—he can no more bestow;
But dear to fame thy Song immortal lives,
  A nobler monument than Art can show.*

INSCRIBED UNDER FERGUSSON'S PORTRAIT.

CURSE on ungrateful man, that can be pleased,
And yet can starve the author of the pleasure.
O thou, my elder brother in misfortune,
By far my elder brother in the Muses,
With tears I pity thy unhappy fate!
Why is the bard unpitied by the world,
Yet has so keen a relish of its pleasures?

A BOTTLE AND A FRIEND.

"There 's nane that 's blest of human kind
  But the cheerful and the gay, man,
    Fal, la, la, &c.

HERE 's a bottle and an honest friend!
  What wad ye wish for mair, man?
Wha kens, before his life may end,
  What his share may be o' care, man?

Then catch the moments as they fly,
  And use them as ye ought, man:
Believe me, happiness is shy,
  And comes not aye when sought, man.

VERSES INTENDED TO BE WRITTEN BELOW A NOBLE EARL'S PICTURE.

WHOSE is that noble, dauntless brow?
  And whose that eye of fire?
And whose that generous princely mien,
  E'en rooted foes admire?

---

* The last two stanzas are from Alexander Smith's edition, 1865.

Stranger! to justly show that brow,
  And mark that eye of fire,
Would take *His* hand, whose vernal tints
  His other works inspire.

Bright as a cloudless summer sun,
  With stately port he moves;
His guardian seraph eyes with awe
  The noble ward he loves.

Among the illustrious Scottish sons,
  That Chief thou may'st discern;
Mark Scotia's fond-returning eye,
  It dwells upon Glencairn.

TO A HAGGIS.†

FAIR fa' your honest, sonsie face,
Great chieftain o' the puddin'-race!
Aboon them a' ye tak your place,
      Painch, tripe, or thairm:
Weel are ye wordy o' a grace
      As lang 's my arm.

The groaning trencher there ye fill,
Your hurdies like a distant hill,
Your pin wad help to mend a mill
      In time o' need,
While through your pores the dews distil
      Like amber bead.

His knife see rustic Labour dight,
An' cut you up wi' ready sleight,
Trenching your gushing entrails bright,
      Like ony ditch;
And then, O what a glorious sight,
      Warm-reekin', rich!

Then horn for horn they stretch an' strive,
Deil tak the hindmost! on they drive,
Till a' their weel-swall'd kytes belyve
      Are bent like drums;
Then auld Guidman, maist like to ryve,
      "Bethankit" hums.

Is there that owre his French ragout,
Or olio that wad staw a sow,
Or fricassee wad mak her spew
      Wi' perfect scunner,
Looks down wi' sneering, scornfu' view,
      On sic a dinner?

---

† Robert Chambers defines a haggis, Burns sings it, Wilson has painted it in flood (see "Noctes"); but the proof of this and all puddings is the preeing of it; and let the grace be the above poem.

Poor devil! see him owre his trash
As feckless as a wither'd rash,
His spindle-shank a guid whip-lash,
    His nieve a nit;
Through bloody flood or field to dash,
    O how unfit!

But mark the rustic, haggis-fed,
The trembling earth resounds his tread;
Clap in his walie nieve a blade,
    He 'll mak it whissle;
An' legs, an' arms, an' heads will sned,
    Like taps o' thrissle.

Ye Powers wha mak mankind your care,
And dish them out their bill o' fare,
Auld Scotland wants nae skinking ware
    That jaups in luggies;
But, if ye wish her gratefu' prayer,
    Gie her a haggis!

EXTEMPORE IN THE COURT OF SESSION.

LORD ADVOCATE.*

He clench'd his pamphlets in his fist,
  He quoted and he hinted,
Till in a declamation-mist,
  His argument he tint it:
He gapèd for 't, he graipèd for 't,
  He fand it was awa', man;
But what his common sense came short,
  He eked it out wi' law, man.

MR. ERSKINE.†

Collected, Harry stood a wee
  Then open'd out his arm, man:
His lordship sat wi' ruefu' e'e,
  And eyed the gathering storm, man;
Like wind-driven hail it did assail,
  Or torrents owre a linn, man;
The Bench sae wise lift up their eyes,
  Half-wauken'd wi' the din, man.

PROLOGUE,

SPOKEN BY MR. WOODS‡ ON HIS BENEFIT-NIGHT,
EDINBURGH, MONDAY, APRIL 16, 1787.

When, by a generous Public's kind acclaim,
That dearest meed is granted—honest fame;
When here your favour is the actor's lot,
Nor even the man in private life forgot;
What breast so dead to heavenly Virtue's glow,
But heaves impassion'd with the grateful throe!
  Poor is the task to please a barbarous throng,
It needs no Siddons' powers in Southern's song;
But here an ancient nation famed afar,
For genius, learning high, as great in war—
Hail, Caledonia, name for ever dear!
Before whose sons I 'm honour'd to appear!
Where every science, every nobler art,
That can inform the mind or mend the heart,
Is known; as grateful nations oft have found
Far as the rude barbarian marks the bound.
Philosophy, no idle pedant dream,
Here holds her search by heaven-taught Reason's beam;
Here History paints with elegance and force
The tide of Empire's fluctuating course;
Here Douglas forms wild Shakspeare into plan,
And Harley § rouses all the God in man.
When well-form'd taste and sparkling wit unite
With manly lore, or female beauty bright
(Beauty, where faultless symmetry and grace,
Can only charm us in the second place),
Witness my heart, how oft with panting fear
As on this night, I 've met these judges here!
But still the hope Experience taught to live,
Equal to judge, you 're candid to forgive.
No hundred-headed Riot here we meet,
With Decency and Law beneath his feet;
Nor insolence assumes fair Freedom's name:
Like Caledonians, you applaud or blame.
  O thou dread Power! whose empire-giving hand
Has oft been stretch'd to shield the honour'd land!
Strong may she glow with all her ancient fire!
May every son be worthy of his sire!
Firm may she rise, with generous disdain
At Tyranny's, or direr Pleasure's chain!
Still self dependent in her native shore,
Bold may she brave grim Danger's loudest roar,
Till Fate the curtain drop on worlds to be no more.

IMPROMPTU TO MISS AINSLIE.

Fair maid, you need not take the hint,
  Nor idle texts pursue:
'Twas guilty sinners that he meant—
  Not angels such as you!

---

* Mr. Islay Campbell, afterwards Lord President.
† The famous Henry Erskine, brother of Thomas, Lord Erskine and Lord Buchan.
‡ Joseph Woods, a player, and an old friend of Fergusson the poet.
§ "Harley:" "The Man of Feeling," wrote by Mr. Mackenzie.—(B.)

ON WILLIAM CREECH.

Auld chuckie Reekie's sair distrest,
Down droops her ance weel-burnish'd crest,
Nae joy her bonnie buskit nest
    Can yield ava,
Her darling bird that she lo'es best—
    Willie 's awa'!

O Willie was a witty wight,
And had o' things an unco sleight,
Auld Reekie aye he keepit tight,
    And trig an' braw:
But now they 'll busk her like a fright—
    Willie 's awa'!

The stiffest o' them a' he bow'd,
The bauldest o' them a' he cow'd;
They durst nae mair than he allow'd,
    That was a law:
We 've lost a birkie weel worth gowd—
    Willie 's awa'!

Now gawkies, tawpies, gowks, and fools,
Frae colleges and boarding schools,
May sprout like simmer puddock-stools
    In glen or shaw;
He wha could brush them down to mools—
    Willie 's awa'!

The brethren o' the commerce-chaumer
May mourn their loss wi' doolfu' clamour;
He was a dictionar and grammar
    Amang them a';
I fear they 'll now mak mony a stammer—
    Willie 's awa'!

Nae mair we see his levee door
Philosophers and Poets pour,
And toothy critics by the score,
    In bloody raw!
The adjutant o' a' the core—
    Willie 's awa'!

Now worthy Gregory's Latin face,
Tytler's and Greenfield's modest grace;
Mackenzie, Stewart, such a brace
    As Rome ne'er saw;
They a' maun meet some ither place—
    Willie 's awa'!

Poor Burns e'en Scotch drink canna quicken
He cheeps like some bewilder'd chicken
Scar'd frae its minnie and the cleckin'
    By hoodie-craw;
Grief 's gien his heart an unco kickin'—
    Willie 's awa'!

Now ev'ry sour-mou'd girnin' blellum,
And Calvin's folk, are fit to fell him;
Ilk self-conceited critic skellum
    His quill may draw;
He wha could brawlie ward their bellum—
    Willie 's awa'!

Up wimpling stately Tweed I 've sped,
And Eden scenes on crystal Jed,
And Ettrick banks, now roaring red,
    While tempests blaw;
But every joy and pleasure 's fled—
    Willie 's awa'!

May I be slander's common speech;
A text for infamy to preach;
And lastly, streekit out to bleach
    In winter snaw;
When I forget thee, Willie Creech,
    Tho' far awa'!

May never wicked fortune touzle him!
May never wicked men bamboozle him!
Until a pow as auld 's Methusalem
    He canty claw!
Then to the blessèd new Jerusalem
    Fleet wing awa'!

SYMON GRAY.

Dear Symon Gray, the other day,
  When you sent me some rhyme,
I could not then just ascertain
  Its worth, for want of time.
But now to-day, good Mr. Gray,
  I 've read it o'er and o'er,
Tried all my skill, but find I 'm still
  Just where I was before.
We auld wives' minions gi'e our opinions,
  Solicited or no;
Then of its faults my honest thoughts
  I 'll give—and here they go.*

NOTE TO MR. RENTON OF LAMERTON.

Your billet, Sir, I grant receipt;
Wi' you I 'll canter ony gate,
Though 'twere a trip to yon blue warl',
Whare birkies march on burning marl:
Then, Sir, God willing, I 'll attend ye,
And to his goodness I commend ye.
                      R. Burns.

---

* They were given in prose, and far from complimentary.

FAC-SIMILE OF THE HAND-WRITING
OF
ROBERT BURNS.

On reading in a Newspaper an account of the death of J— M— Esq.' brother to Miss Isabella M— a particular friend of the Author's ———

Sad thy tale, thou idle page,
   And rueful thy alarms;
Death tears the brother of her love
   From Isabella's arms. —

Sweetly deckt with pearly dew
   The morning rose may blow
But cold successive noontide blasts
   May lay its beauties low. —

Fair on Isabella's morn
   The sun propitious smil'd
But long ere noon succeeding clouds
   Succeeding hopes beguil'd.

EPIGRAM.

Whoe'er he be that sojourns here,
   I pity much his case,
Unless he come to wait upon
   The Lord their God, his Grace.

There's naething here but Highland pride,
   And Highland scab and hunger;
If Providence has sent me here,
   'Twas surely in his anger.*

A VERSE,

COMPOSED AND REPEATED BY BURNS, TO THE MASTER OF THE HOUSE, ON TAKING LEAVE OF A PLACE IN THE HIGHLANDS WHERE HE HAD BEEN HOSPITABLY ENTERTAINED.

When Death's dark stream I ferry o'er,
   (A time that surely shall come),
In heaven itself I'll ask no more,
   Than just a Highland welcome.

ON THE DEATH OF JOHN M'LEOD,† ESQ.,

BROTHER TO A YOUNG LADY, A PARTICULAR FRIEND OF THE AUTHOR.

Sad thy tale, thou idle page,
   And rueful thy alarms—
Death tears the brother of her love
   From Isabella's arms.

Sweetly deck'd with pearly dew
   The morning rose may blow;
But cold successive noontide blasts
   May lay its beauties low.

Fair on Isabella's morn
   The sun propitious smiled;
But, long ere noon, succeeding clouds
   Succeeding hopes beguiled.

Fate oft tears the bosom chords
   That Nature finest strung:
So Isabella's heart was formed,
   And so that heart was wrung.

Were it in the poet's power,
   Strong as he shares the grief
That pierces Isabella's heart,
   To give that heart relief!

Dread Omnipotence, alone,
   Can heal the wound he gave;
Can point the brimful grief-worn eyes
   To scenes beyond the grave.

Virtue's blossoms there shall blow,
   And fear no withering blast;
There Isabella's spotless worth
   Shall happy be at last.

ON THE DEATH OF SIR JAMES HUNTER BLAIR.‡

The lamp of day, with ill-presaging glare,
   Dim, cloudy, sank beneath the western wave;
Th' inconstant blast howl'd through the darkening air,
   And hollow whistled in the rocky cave.

Lone as I wander'd by each cliff and dell,
   Once the loved haunts of Scotia's royal train;
Or mused where limpid streams, once hallow'd, well,
   Or mouldering ruins mark the sacred fane;

Th' increasing blast roar'd round the beetling rocks,
   The clouds, swift-wing'd, flew o'er the starry sky,
The groaning trees untimely shed their locks,
   And shooting meteors caught the startled eye.

The paly moon rose in the livid east,
   And 'mong the cliffs disclos'd a stately form
In weeds of woe, that frantic beat her breast,
   And mix'd her wailings with the raving storm.

Wild to my heart the filial pulses glow,
   'Twas Caledonia's trophied shield I view'd:
Her form majestic droop'd in pensive woe,
   The lightning of her eye in tears imbued.

Revers'd that spear, redoubtable in war;
   Reclined that banner, erst in fields unfurl'd,
That like a deathful meteor gleam'd afar,
   And braved the mighty monarchs of the world.

"My patriot son fills an untimely grave!"
   With accents wild and lifted arms she cried;
"Low lies the hand that oft was stretch'd to save,
   Low lies the heart that swell'd with honest pride!

---

* This was written at Inverary by the poet, indignant at some fancied slight.

† Burns knew the M'Leods through the Campbells of Loudoun. To Isabella M'Leod he wrote the song, "Raving winds around her blowing." John died 2nd July, 1787.

‡ An Ayrshire squire, member of the banking house of Sir. W. Forbes; an excellent man.

"A weeping country joins a widow's tear,
  The helpless poor mix with the orphan's cry;
The drooping arts surround their patron's bier,
  And grateful science heaves the heartfelt sigh!

"I saw my sons resume their ancient fire;
  I saw fair Freedom's blossoms richly blow;
But, ah! how hope is born but to expire!
  Relentless fate has laid their guardian low.

"My patriot falls, but shall he lie unsung,
  While empty greatness saves a worthless name?
No; every muse shall join her tuneful tongue,
  And future ages hear his growing fame.

"And I will join a mother's tender cares,
  Through future times to make his virtues last,
That distant years may boast of other Blairs!"
  She said, and vanish'd with the sweeping blast.

TO MISS FERRIER,

INCLOSING THE ELEGY ON SIR J. H. BLAIR.

Nae heathen name shall I prefix,
  Frae Pindus or Parnassus;
Auld Reekie dings them a' to sticks,
  For rhyme-inspiring lasses.

Jove's tunefu' dochters three times three
  Made Homer deep their debtor;
But, gi'en the body half an e'e,
  Nine Ferriers wad done better!

Last day my mind was in a bog,
  Down George's Street I stoited;
A creeping cauld prosaic fog
  My very senses doited.

Do what I dought to set her free,
  My saul lay in the mire;
Ye turned a neuk—I saw your e'e—
  She took the wing like fire!

The mournfu' sang I here inclose,
  In gratitude I send you;
And pray, in rhyme as weel as prose,
  A' guid things may attend you!

EPIGRAM ON CARRON WORKS.*

We cam' na here to view your warks,
  In hopes to be mair wise,
But only, lest we gang to hell,
  It may be nae surprise:
But when we tirl'd at your door,
  Your porter dought na hear us;
Sae may, should we to hell's yetts come,
  Your billie Satan sair us!

LINES ON A WINDOW AT CROSS KEYS, FALKIRK.

Sound be his sleep and blythe his morn,
  That never did a lassie wrang;
Who poverty ne'er held in scorn,
  For misery ever tholed a pang.

LINES ON STIRLING.

WRITTEN ON A WINDOW IN WINGATE'S INN THERE.

Here Stuarts once in glory reign'd,
And laws for Scotia's weal ordain'd;
But now unroof'd their palace stands,
Their sceptre's sway'd by foreign hands;
Fallen indeed, and to the earth,
Whence grovelling reptiles take their birth.
The Stuarts' native race is gone!
A race outlandish fills their throne—
An idiot race, to honour lost:
Who know them best despise them most.†

THE REPROOF.

Rash mortal, and slanderous poet, thy name
Shall no longer appear in the records of Fame;
Dost not know that old Mansfield, who writes like the Bible,
Says the more 'tis a truth, Sir, the more 'tis a libel?

VERSES WRITTEN WITH A PENCIL

OVER THE CHIMNEY-PIECE IN THE PARLOUR OF THE INN AT KENMORE, TAYMOUTH.

Admiring Nature in her wildest grace,
These northern scenes with weary feet I trace:

---

* Carron Iron Works, near Falkirk, famous even then.

† Burns, who was then a zealous Jacobite, being challenged by a friend for these lines, replied, "I shall reprove myself;" and instantly wrote "The Reproof" on the same pane.

O'er many a winding dale and painful steep,
The abodes of covey'd grouse and timid sheep,
My savage journey, curious, I pursue,
Till famed Breadalbane opens to my view.
The meeting cliffs each deep-sunk glen divides,
The woods, wild-scatter'd, clothe their ample sides;
Th' outstretching lake, embosom'd 'mong the hills,
The eye with wonder and amazement fills;
The Tay meand'ring sweet in infant pride,
The palace rising on his verdant side;
The lawns wood-fringed in Nature's native taste;
The hillocks dropt in Nature's careless haste;

The arches striding o'er the new-born stream;
The village glittering in the noontide beam—

. . . .

Poetic ardours in my bosom swell,
Lone wand'ring by the hermit's mossy cell:
The sweeping theatre of hanging woods;
The incessant roar of headlong tumbling floods—

. . . .

Here Poesy might wake her heaven-taught lyre,
And look through Nature with creative fire;
Here, to the wrongs of Fate half reconciled,
Misfortune's lighten'd steps might wander wild;
And Disappointment, in these lonely bounds,
Find balm to soothe her bitter rankling wounds;
Here heart-struck Grief might heavenward stretch her scan,
And injured Worth forget and pardon man.

THE BIRKS OF ABERFELDY.

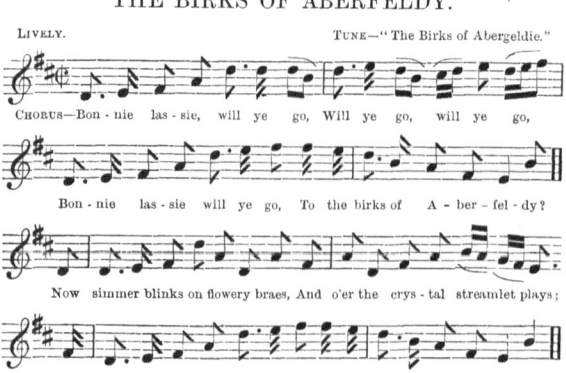

Chorus—Bonnie lassie, will ye go, Will ye go, will ye go, Bonnie lassie will ye go, To the birks of Aberfeldy?

Now simmer blinks on flowery braes, And o'er the crystal streamlet plays; Come let us spend the lightsome days In the birks of Aberfeldy.

The little birdies blythely sing,
While o'er their heads the hazels hing,
Or lightly flit on wanton wing
   In the birks of Aberfeldy.
        Bonnie lassie, &c.

The braes ascend like lofty wa's,
The foamy stream deep-roaring fa's,
O'erhung wi' fragrant spreading shaws—
   The birks of Aberfeldy.
        Bonnie lassie, &c.

The hoary cliffs are crown'd wi' flowers,
White o'er the linns the burnie pours,
And, rising, weets wi' misty showers
   The birks of Aberfeldy.
        Bonnie lassie, &c.

Let Fortune's gifts at random flee,
  They ne'er shall draw a wish frae me;
Supremely blest wi' love and thee,
  In the birks of Aberfeldy.
        Bonnie lassie, &c.

THE HUMBLE PETITION OF BRUAR WATER *

TO THE NOBLE DUKE OF ATHOLE.

My lord, I know, your noble ear
  Woe ne'er assails in vain;
Embolden'd thus, I beg you 'll hear
  Your humble slave complain,
How saucy Phœbus' scorching beams,
  In flaming summer-pride,
Dry-withering, waste my foamy streams,
  And drink my crystal tide.

---

* "Bruar Water:" Bruar Falls, in Athole, are exceedingly picturesque and beautiful; but their effect is much impaired by the want of trees and shrubs. — (B.) This charge no longer applies.

The lightly-jumpin', glowrin' trouts,
  That through my waters play,
If, in their random, wanton spouts,
  They near the margin stray;
If, hapless chance! they linger lang,
  I 'm scorching up so shallow,
They 're left the whitening stanes amang,
  In gasping death to wallow.

Last day I grat wi' spite and teen,
  As poet Burns came by,
That, to a bard, I should be seen
  Wi' half my channel dry;
A panegyric rhyme, I ween,
  Even as I was, he shor'd me;
But had I in my glory been,
  He, kneeling, wad ador'd me.

Here, foaming down the skelvy rocks,
  In twisting strength I rin;
There, high my boiling torrent smokes,
  Wild-roaring o'er a linn:

Enjoying large each spring and well
  As Nature gave them me,
I am, although I say 't mysel',
  Worth gaun a mile to see.

Would then my noble master please
  To grant my highest wishes,
He 'll shade my banks wi' tow'ring trees,
  And bonnie spreading bushes.
Delighted doubly then, my lord,
  You 'll wander on my banks,
And listen mony a grateful bird
  Return you tuneful thanks.

The sober lav'rock, warbling wild,
  Shall to the skies aspire;
The gowdspink, Music's gayest child,
  Shall sweetly join the choir;
The blackbird strong, the lintwhite clear,
  The mavis mild and mellow;
The robin pensive Autumn cheer,
  In all her locks of yellow.

This too, a covert shall ensure,
  To shield them from the storm;
And coward maukin sleep secure,
  Low in her grassy form.
Here shall the shepherd make his seat,
  To weave his crown of flowers;
Or find a shelt'ring, safe retreat,
  From prone-descending showers.

And here, by sweet, endearing stealth,
  Shall meet the loving pair,
Despising worlds, with all their wealth,
  As empty idle care;
The flowers shall vie in all their charms,
  The hour of heaven to grace;
And birks extend their fragrant arms
  To screen the dear embrace.

Here haply too, at vernal dawn,
  Some musing bard may stray,
And eye the smoking, dewy lawn,
  And misty mountain grey;
Or, by the reaper's nightly beam,
  Mild-chequering through the trees,
Rave to my darkly-dashing stream,
  Hoarse-swelling on the breeze.

Let lofty firs and ashes cool
  My lowly banks o'erspread,
And view, deep-bending in the pool,
  Their shadows' wat'ry bed:

Let fragrant birks, in woodbines drest,
  My craggy cliffs adorn;
And, for the little songster's nest,
  The close embow'ring thorn.

So may old Scotia's darling hope,
  Your little angel band,
Spring, like their fathers, up to prop
  Their honoured native land!
So may, through Albion's farthest ken,
  To social-flowing glasses,
The grace be—"Athole's honest men,
  And Athole's bonnie lasses!"

THE BONNIE LASS OF ALBANY.

In the rolling tide of spreading Clyde
  There sits an isle of high degree,
And a town of fame * whose princely name
  Should grace the Lass of Albany.

But there 's a youth, a witless youth,
  That fills the place where she should be;
We 'll send him o'er to his native shore,
  And bring our ain sweet Albany.

Alas the day, and woe the day,
  A false usurper wan the gree,
Who now commands the towers and lands—
  The royal right of Albany.

We 'll daily pray, we 'll nightly pray,
  On bended knees most fervently,
The time may come, with pipe and drum,
  We 'll welcome hame fair Albany.

* Rothesay: it gave the title Duke of Rothesay to the eldest sons of the Scottish kings.

ON THE FALL OF FYERS,* NEAR LOCH-NESS.

WRITTEN WITH A PENCIL ON THE SPOT.

Among the heathy hills and ragged woods
The roaring Fyers pours his mossy floods;
Till full he dashes on the rocky mounds,
Where, through a shapeless breach, his stream resounds.
As high in air the bursting torrents flow,
As deep recoiling surges foam below,
Prone down the rock the whitening sheet descends,
And viewless Echo's ear, astonished, rends.
Dim-seen, through rising mists and ceaseless showers,
The hoary cavern, wide-surrounding, lours.
Still through the gap the struggling river toils,
And still below, the horrid cauldron boils—
. . . .

* "Fyers:" called more frequently Foyers.

ON SCARING SOME WATER FOWL IN LOCH TURIT,

A WILD SCENE AMONG THE HILLS OF OCHTERTYRE.*

Why, ye tenants of the lake,
For me your wat'ry haunt forsake?
Tell me, fellow-creatures, why
At my presence thus you fly?
Why disturb your social joys,
Parent, filial, kindred ties?
Common friend to you and me,
Nature's gifts to all are free.
Peaceful keep your dimpling wave,
Busy feed, or wanton lave:

* "Ochtertyre:" near Crieff, Perthshire, famous for its beauty, as Loch Turit behind is for wild and lonely grandeur.

Or, beneath the sheltering rock,
Bide the surging billow's shock.
Conscious, blushing for our race,
Soon, too soon, your fears I trace.
Man, your proud usurping foe,
Would be lord of all below:
Plumes himself in Freedom's pride,
Tyrant stern to all beside.
The eagle, from the cliffy brow,
Marking you his prey below,
In his breast no pity dwells,
Strong necessity compels:
But Man, to whom alone is given
A ray direct from pitying Heaven,
Glories in his heart humane—
And creatures for his pleasure slain!
In these savage, liquid plains,

Only known to wand'ring swains,
Where the mossy riv'let strays,
Far from human haunts and ways,
All on Nature you depend,
And life's poor season peaceful spend.
  Or, if Man's superior might,
Dare invade your native right,
On the lofty ether borne,
Man with all his powers you scorn;
Swiftly seek, on clanging wings,
Other lakes and other springs;
And the foe you cannot brave,
Scorn at least to be his slave.

CASTLE GORDON.*

STREAMS that glide in orient plains
Never bound by winter's chains;
  Glowing here on golden sands,
There commix'd with foulest stains
  From Tyranny's empurpled hands:
These, their richly-gleaming waves,
I leave to tyrants and their slaves:
Give me the stream that sweetly laves
  The banks by Castle Gordon.

* See LIFE.

Spicy forests, ever gay,
Shading from the burning ray
　Hapless wretches sold to toil,
Or the ruthless native's way,
　Bent on slaughter, blood, and spoil:
Woods that ever verdant wave,
I leave the tyrant and the slave;
Give me the groves that lofty brave
　The storms, by Castle Gordon.

Wildly here, without control,
Nature reigns and rules the whole;
　In that sober, pensive mood,
Dearest to the feeling soul,
　She plants the forest, pours the flood.
Life's poor day I 'll musing rave,
And find at night a sheltering cave,
Where waters flow and wild woods wave,
　By bonnie Castle Gordon.

THERE 'S A YOUTH IN THIS CITY.*

For beauty and fortune the laddie 's been courtin';
　Weel-featur'd, weel-tocher'd, weel-mounted an' braw;
But chiefly the siller that gars him gang till her,
　The penny 's the jewel that beautifies a'.

There 's Meg wi' the mailen that fain wad a haen him,
　And Susie, wha's daddie was laird o' the Ha';
There 's lang-tocher'd Nancy maist fetters his fancy,
　But the laddie's dear sel' he lo'es dearest of a'.

HEE BALOU!

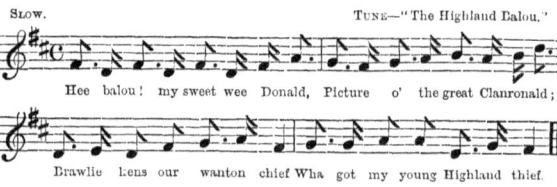

Leeze me on thy bonnie craigie,
An thou live thou 'lt steal a naigie,
Travel the country through and through,
And bring hame a Carlisle cow.

Through the Lawlands, o'er the border,
Weel, my baby, may thou furder;
Herry the louns o' the laigh countrie,
Syne to the Highlands hame to me.

TO MISS CRUICKSHANK,† A VERY YOUNG LADY.

WRITTEN ON THE BLANK LEAF OF A BOOK PRESENTED TO HER BY THE AUTHOR.

BEAUTEOUS rose-bud, young and gay,
Blooming on thy early May,
Never may'st thou, lovely flower,
Chilly shrink in sleety shower!
Never Boreas' hoary path,
Never Eurus' pois'nous breath,
Never baleful stellar lights,
Taint thee with untimely blights!
Never, never reptile thief
Riot on thy virgin leaf!
Nor even Sol too fiercely view
Thy bosom blushing still with dew!
　May'st thou long, sweet crimson gem,
Richly deck thy native stem;
Till some ev'ning, sober, calm,
Dropping dews, and breathing balm,
While all around the woodland rings,
And every bird thy requiem sings;
Thou, amid the dirgeful sound,
Shed thy dying honours round,
And resign to parent Earth
The loveliest form she e'er gave birth.

* Partly old.

† See LIFE.

BLYTHE WAS SHE.

Tune—"Andro and his Cutty Gun."

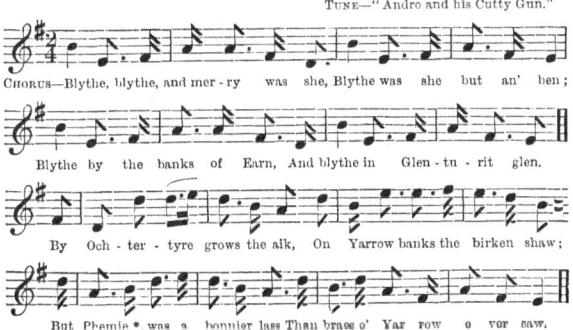

Chorus—Blythe, blythe, and merry was she, Blythe was she but an' ben;
Blythe by the banks of Earn, And blythe in Glenturit glen.

By Ochtertyre grows the aik, On Yarrow banks the birken shaw;
But Phemie* was a bonnier lass Than braes o' Yarrow ever saw.

* A cousin of Burns' host at Ochtertyre, a beautiful girl of eighteen, called the "Flower of Strathmore," afterwards married to Mr. Smythe of Methven, a judge of the Court of Session. See LIFE.

Her looks were like a flower in May,
  Her smile was like a simmer morn;
She trippèd by the banks of Earn,
  As light 's a bird upon a thorn.
        Blythe, blythe, &c.

Her bonnie face it was as meek
  As ony lamb upon a lea;
The evening sun was ne'er sae sweet
  As was the blink o' Phemie's e'e.
        Blythe, blythe, &c.

The Highland hills I 've wander'd wide,
  And o'er the Lowlands I hae been;
But Phemie was the blythest lass
  That ever trod the dewy green.
        Blythe, blythe, &c.

A ROSE-BUD BY MY EARLY WALK.

Canty.   "The Shepherd's Wife."

A rose-bud by my early walk,
A-down a corn-inclosed bawk,
Sae gently bent its thorny stalk,
    All on a dewy morning.
Ere twice the shades o' dawn are fled,
In a' its crimson glory spread,
And drooping rich the dewy head,
    It scents the early morning.

Within the bush her cover'd nest
A little linnet fondly prest,
The dew sat chilly on her breast,
    Sae early in the morning.

She soon shall see her tender brood,
The pride, the pleasure o' the wood,
Amang the fresh green leaves bedew'd,
    Awake the early morning.

So thou, dear bird, young Jeany fair,
On trembling string or vocal air,
Shalt sweetly pay the tender care
    That tents thy early morning.

So thou, sweet Rose-bud, young and gay,
Shalt beauteous blaze upon the day,
And bless the parent's evening ray
    That watch'd thy early morning.

BRAVING ANGRY WINTER'S STORMS.

Slowish.   Tune—"Neil Gow's Lamentation for Abercairny."

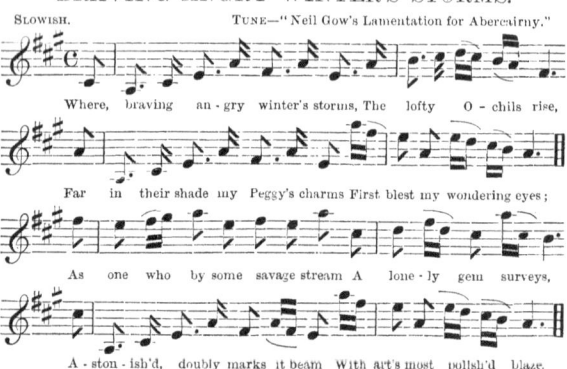

Where, braving angry winter's storms,
    The lofty Ochils rise,
Far in their shade my Peggy's charms
    First blest my wondering eyes;
As one who by some savage stream
    A lonely gem surveys,
Astonish'd, doubly marks it beam
    With art's most polish'd blaze.

Blest be the wild, sequester'd shade,
    And blest the day and hour,
Where Peggy's charms I first surveyed,
    When first I felt their power!

The tyrant Death, with grim control,
  May seize my fleeting breath;
But tearing Peggy* from my soul
  Must be a stronger death.

MY PEGGY'S FACE.†

The lily's hue, the rose's dye,
  The kindling lustre of an eye;
Who but owns their magic sway?
Who but knows they all decay?
The tender thrill, the pitying tear,
The generous purpose nobly dear,
The gentle look that age disarms—
These are all immortal charms.

WEARY FA' YOU, DUNCAN GRAY.

Bonnie was the Lammas moon—
  Ha, ha, the girdin' o't
Glowrin' a' the hills aboon—
  Ha, ha, the girdin' o't!

The girdin' brak, the beast cam down,
  I tint my curch and baith my shoon;
Ah! Duncan, ye 're an unco loon—
  Wae on the bad girdin' o't!

But, Duncan, gin ye 'll keep your aith—
  Ha, ha, the girdin' o't!
I'se bless you wi' my hindmost breath—
  Ha, ha, the girdin' o't!
Duncan, gin ye 'll keep your aith,
The beast again can bear us baith,
And auld Mess John will mend the skaith,
  And clout the bad girdin' o't.

ADDRESS TO MR. WILLIAM TYTLER, ‡

WITH THE PRESENT OF THE BARD'S PICTURE.

REVERED defender of beauteous Stuart,
  Of Stuart, a name once respected;
A name, which to love was the mark of a true heart,
  But now 'tis despised and neglected.

Though something like moisture conglobes in my eye,
  Let no one misdeem me disloyal;
A poor friendless wand'rer may well claim a sigh,
  Still more, if that wanderer were royal.

My fathers that name have revered on a throne:
  My fathers have fallen to right it;
Those fathers would spurn their degenerate son,
  That name should he scoffingly slight it.

Still in prayers for King George I most heartily join,
  The Queen, and the rest of the gentry:
Be they wise, be they foolish, is nothing of mine;
  Their title 's avow'd by my country.

But why of that epocha make such a fuss,
  That gave us th' Electoral stem?
If bringing them over was lucky for us,
  I 'm sure 'twas as lucky for them.

But loyalty, truce! we 're on dangerous ground;
  Who knows how the fashions may alter?
The doctrine, to-day, that is loyalty sound,
  To-morrow may bring us a halter!

I send you a trifle, a head of a bard,
  A trifle scarce worthy your care;
But accept it, good Sir, as a mark of regard,
  Sincere as a saint's dying prayer.

Now life's chilly evening dim shades on your eye,
  And ushers the long dreary night:
But you, like the star that athwart gilds the sky,
  Your course to the latest is bright.

---

* "Peggy:" Margaret Chalmers, afterwards Mrs. Lewis Hay, friend of Charlotte Hamilton.
† Margaret Chalmers.
‡ One of the soberest and ablest defenders of a bad cause—that of Mary Queen of Scots.

ON A YOUNG LADY,*

RESIDING ON THE BANKS OF THE SMALL RIVER DEVON, IN CLACKMANNANSHIRE, BUT WHOSE INFANT YEARS WERE SPENT IN AYRSHIRE.

Slow.   Tune—"The Brown Dairy-maid."

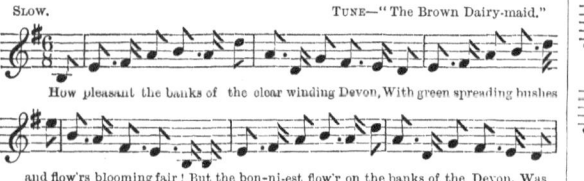

How pleasant the banks of the clear winding Devon, With green spreading bushes and flow'rs blooming fair! But the bon-ni-est flow'r on the banks of the Devon, Was

once a sweet bud on the braes of the Ayr. Mild be the sun on this sweet blushing flow-er, In the gay rosy morn as it bathes in the dew; And gentle the fall of the soft vernal shower, That steals on the evening each leaf to renew!

* "Young lady:" Charlotte Hamilton, whom Robert Burns very warmly loved, sister of Gavin Hamilton, born in Ayrshire.

O, spare the dear blossom, ye orient breezes,
  With chill hoary wing as ye usher the dawn!

And far be thou distant, thou reptile that seizes
　The verdure and pride of the garden or lawn!

Let Bourbon exult in his gay gilded lilies,
　And England triumphant display her proud rose;
A fairer than either adorns the green valleys
　Where Devon, sweet Devon, meandering flows.

ELEGY ON THE DEATH OF LORD PRESIDENT DUNDAS.*

Lone on the bleaky hills the straying flocks
Shun the fierce storms among the shelt'ring rocks;
Down foam the riv'lets, red with dashing rains;
The gathering floods burst o'er the distant plains;
Beneath the blast the leafless forests groan,
The hollow caves return a sullen moan.
Ye hills, ye plains, ye forests, and ye caves,
Ye howling winds, and wintry swelling waves!
Unheard, unseen, by human ear or eye,
Sad, to your sympathetic glooms I fly,
Where, to the whistling blast and water's roar,
Pale Scotia's recent wound I may deplore.

　O heavy loss, thy country ill could bear!
A loss these evil days can ne'er repair!
Justice, the high vicegerent of her God,
Her doubtful balance eyed and swayed her rod;
Hearing the tidings of the fatal blow,
She sunk, abandon'd to the wildest woe.

　Wrongs, injuries, from many a darksome den,
Now gay in hope explore the paths of men:
See, from his cavern grim Oppression rise,
And throw on Poverty his cruel eyes;
Keen on the helpless victim see him fly,
And stifle, dark, the feebly-bursting cry;
Mark ruffian Violence, distain'd with crimes,
Rousing elate in these degenerate times:
View unsuspecting Innocence a prey,
As guileful Fraud points out the erring way;
While subtile Litigation's pliant tongue
The life-blood equal sucks of Right and Wrong:
Hark, injured Want recounts the unlisten'd tale,
And much-wrong'd Misery pours the unpitied wail!

　Ye dark waste hills, and brown unsightly plains,
Inspire and soothe my melancholy strains!
Ye tempests, rage! ye turbid torrents, roll!
Ye suit the joyless tenor of my soul;
Life's social haunts and pleasures I resign;
Be nameless wilds and lonely wanderings mine,
To mourn the woes my country must endure,
That wound degenerate ages cannot cure.

* "Lord President:" Robert Dundas of Arniston, brother of Lord Melville, born 1713, died 1787. Charles Hay, advocate, urged Burns to write this venal and heartless ditty.

ON ELPHINSTONE'S TRANSLATION OF MARTIAL'S EPIGRAMS.

O thou whom Poesy abhors,
Whom Prose has turned out of doors!
Heard'st thou yon groan? proceed no further,
'Twas laurell'd Martial roaring "murther."

SYLVANDER TO CLARINDA.

EXTEMPORE REPLY TO VERSES ADDRESSED TO THE AUTHOR BY A LADY, UNDER THE SIGNATURE OF "CLARINDA."

When dear Clarinda, matchless fair,
　First struck Sylvander's raptur'd view,
He gaz'd, he listened to despair,
　Alas! 'twas all he dared to do.

Love, from Clarinda's heavenly eyes,
　Transfixed his bosom through and through;
But still in Friendship's guarded guise,
　For more the demon fear'd to do.

That heart, already more than lost,
　The imp beleaguer'd all *perdue;*
For frowning Honour kept his post—
　To meet that frown he shrunk to do.

His pangs the Bard refused to own,
　Though half he wish'd Clarinda knew:
But Anguish wrung the unweeting groan—
　Who blames what frantic pain must do?

That heart, where motley follies blend,
　Was sternly still to Honour true:
To prove Clarinda's fondest friend,
　Was what a lover sure might do.

The Muse his ready quill employed,
　No nearer bliss he could pursue;
That bliss Clarinda cold deny'd—
　"Send word by Charles how you do!"

The chill behest disarm'd his muse,
　Till passion all impatient grew:
He wrote, and hinted for excuse,
　'Twas 'cause "he'd nothing else to do."

But by those hopes I have above!
　And by those faults I dearly rue!
The deed, the boldest mark of love,
　For thee, that deed I dare to do!

O could the Fates but name the price
  Would bless me with your charms and you!
With frantic joy I 'd pay it thrice,
  If human art and power could do!

Then take, Clarinda, friendship's hand,
  (Friendship, at least, I may avow);
And lay no more your chill command—
  I 'll write, whatever I 've to do.
                                        SYLVANDER.

FAREWELL TO CLARINDA,
ON LEAVING EDINBURGH.

SLOW AND EXPRESSIVE.

Cla-rinda, mistress of my soul, The measur'd time is run!
The wretch beneath the drea-ry pole, So marks his lat-est sun.

To what dark cave of frozen night
  Shall poor Sylvander hie?

Deprived of thee, his life and light,
  The sun of all his joy!

We part—but, by these precious drops
  That fill thy lovely eyes,
No other light shall guide my steps
  Till thy bright beams arise.

She, the fair sun of all her sex,
  Has blest my glorious day;
And shall a glimmering planet fix
  My worship to its ray?

LOVE IN THE GUISE OF FRIENDSHIP.*

Very Slow.   Tune—"Banks of Spey."

Your friendship much can make me blest, O why that bliss destroy! Why urge the only one request you know I will deny! Your thought, if Love must harbour there, Conceal it in that thought; Nor cause me from my bosom tear, The very friend I sought.

WHEN I THINK ON THE HAPPY DAYS.

When I think on the happy days
I spent wi' you, my dearie;
And now what lands between us lie,
How can I be but eerie?

How slow ye move, ye heavy hours,
As ye were wae and weary!
It wasna sae ye glinted by
When I was wi' my dearie.

MACPHERSON'S FAREWELL.†

Slowish.   Tune—"M'Pherson's Rant."

Farewell, ye dungeons dark and strong, The wretch's destinie! MacPherson's time will not be long On yonder gallows tree.

Chorus—Sae rantingly, sae wantonly, Sae dauntingly gaed he; He play'd a spring, and danc'd it round, Below the gallows tree.

O what is death but parting breath?
On many a bloody plain

---

* Additional to a canzonette sent to Clarinda 3rd January, 1788.
† James Macpherson, a noted Norland freebooter, a man of vast strength, executed on Gallows Hill of Banff, 16th November, 1700. He played a tune on the gallows, offered the fiddle to any one who would accept it as a gift; and none accepting it, he indignantly broke the instrument and threw it away.

I've dared his face, and in this place
I scorn him yet again!
   Sae rantingly, &c.

Untie these bands from off my hands,
And bring to me my sword;
And there's no a man in all Scotland,
But I'll brave him at a word.
   Sae rantingly, &c.

I've lived a life of sturt and strife;
I die by treacherie:
It burns my heart I must depart,
And not avengèd be.
   Sae rantingly, &c.

Now farewell, light—thou sunshine bright,
And all beneath the sky!
May coward shame distain his name,
The wretch that dare not die!
   Sae rantingly, &c.

STAY, MY CHARMER, CAN YOU LEAVE ME!

Slow.   Tune—"The Black-haired Lad."

Stay, my charmer, can you leave me! Cruel, cruel to deceive me! Well you know how much you grieve me; Cruel charmer, can you go! Cruel charmer, can you go!

By my love so ill requited,
By the faith you fondly plighted,
By the pangs of lovers slighted,
  Do not, do not leave me so!
  Do not, do not leave me so!

THERE WAS A WIFE.

Slowish.   Tune—"Scroggam."

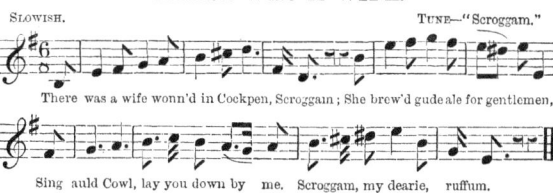

There was a wife wonn'd in Cockpen, Scroggam; She brew'd gude ale for gentlemen, Sing auld Cowl, lay you down by me. Scroggam, my dearie, ruffum.

The gudewife's dochter fell in a fever,
        Scroggam,
The priest o' the parish fell in anither;
Sing auld Cowl, lay you down by me,
Scroggam, my dearie, ruffum.

They laid the twa i' the bed thegither,
        Scroggam,
That the heat o' the tane might cool the tither;
Sing auld Cowl, lay you down by me,
Scroggam, my dearie, ruffum.

TO THEE, LOVED NITH.

To thee, loved Nith, thy gladsome plains,
  Where late wi' careless thought I ranged,
Though press'd wi' care and sunk in woe,
  To thee I bring a heart unchanged.

I love thee, Nith, thy banks and braes,
  Though memory there my bosom tear;
For therë he roved that brake my heart,
  Yet to that heart, ah, still how dear!

THE TAILOR.

Tune—"The Tailor's March."

The tailor fell through the bed, thimbles an' a', The tailor fell through the bed, thimbles an' a'; The blankets were thin and the sheets they were sma', The tailor fell through the bed, thimbles an' a'.

The sleepy bit lassie, she dreaded nae ill,
The sleepy bit lassie, she dreaded nae ill;
The weather was cauld, and the lassie lay still,
She thought that a tailor could do her nae ill.
Gie me the groat again, canny young man,
Gie me the groat again, canny young man;
The day it is short, and the night it is lang,
The dearest siller that ever I wan!
There 's somebody weary wi' lying her lane,
There 's somebody weary wi' lying her lane;
There 's some that are dowie, I trow wad be fain
To see the bit tailor come skippin' again.

VERSES TO MY BED.*

Thou bed, in which I first began
To be that various creature—*Man!*
And when again the Fates decree,
The place where I must cease to be;
When sickness comes, to whom I fly
To soothe my pain, or close mine eye;
When cares surround me where I weep,
Or lose them all in balmy sleep;
When sore with labour, whom I court,
And to thy downy breast resort;
Where, too, ecstatic joys I find,
When deigns my Delia to be kind,
And full of love, in all her charms,
Thou giv'st the fair one to my arms.
The centre thou, where grief and pain,
Disease and rest, alternate reign.
O, since within thy little space,
So many various scenes take place;
Lessons as useful shalt thou teach
As sages dictate—churchmen preach;
And man, convinc'd by thee alone,
This great important truth shall own:—
That thin partitions do divide
The bounds where good and ill reside;
That nought is perfect here below;
But bliss still bordering upon woe.

* A Glasgow Correspondent writes us that he found these verses, translated from the French, in the *London Magazine*, vol. xxviii., 1759 (the year of Burns' birth), and signed, R. B. The probability is that they were found in his possession, and supposed from the initials to be his.

STRATHALLAN'S LAMENT.*

Plaintive. Tune—"Strathallan's Lament."

Thickest night surround my dwelling! Howling tempests o'er me rave! Turbid torrents, wintry swelling, roaring by my lonely cave! Crystal streamlets, gently flowing, Busy haunts of base mankind, Western breezes, softly blowing, Suit not my distracted mind.

In the cause of Right engagèd,
  Wrongs injurious to redress,
Honour's war we strongly wagèd,
  But the Heavens denied success.
Ruin's wheel has driven o'er us,
  Not a hope that dare attend;
The wide world is all before us—
  But a world without a friend!

RAVING WINDS AROUND HER BLOWING.†

Very Slow. Tune—"M'Grigor of Roro's Lament."

Raving winds around her blowing, Yellow leaves the woodlands strowing, By a river hoarsely roaring, Isabella strayed, deploring, "Farewell hours that late did measure Sun-shine days of joy and pleasure; Hail, thou gloomy night of sorrow, Cheerless night that knows no morrow.

"O'er the past too fondly wandering,
  On the hopeless future pondering;
Chilly grief my life-blood freezes,
  Fell despair my fancy seizes.
Life, thou soul of every blessing,
  Load to misery most distressing,
Oh, how gladly I 'd resign thee,
  And to dark oblivion join thee!"

* "Strathallan:" fourth earl of that name, was one of the followers of the young Chevalier, and is supposed in the song to be lying concealed in some cave of the Highlands, after the battle of Culloden, but actually fell in the battle. The tune was by Allan Masterton, Burns' great friend.
† This was written in compliment to Isabella Macleod, afterwards Mrs. Ross, a very great friend of Burns. It alludes to the death of her sister and her sister's husband.

THE YOUNG HIGHLAND ROVER.*

Tune—"Morag."

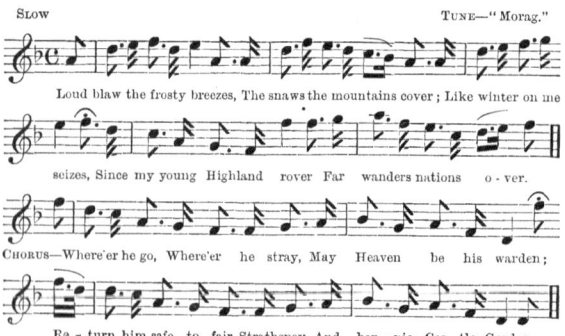

Loud blaw the frosty breezes,
    The snaws the mountains cover;
Like winter on me seizes,
    Since my young Highland rover
Far wanders nations over.
Where'er he go, where'er he stray,
    May Heaven be his warden;
Return him safe to fair Strathspey,
    And bonnie Castle Gordon!

The trees now naked groaning,
    Shall soon wi' leaves be hinging,
The birdies dowie moaning,
    Shall a' be blythely singing,
And every flower be springing.
Sae I 'll rejoice the lee-lang day,
    When by his mighty Warden
My youth 's returned to fair Strathspey,
    And bonnie Castle Gordon!

* "The Young Highland Rover:" is supposed to be the Chevalier, Prince Charles Edward.

GO ON, SWEET BIRD, AND SOOTHE MY CARE.

Go on, sweet bird, and soothe my care,
Thy cheerful notes will hush despair;
Thy tuneful warblings, void of art,
Thrill sweetly through my aching heart.

Now choose thy mate, and fondly love,
And all the charming transport prove;
Those sweet emotions all enjoy,
Let Love and Song thy hours employ;

Whilst I, a lovelorn exile, live,
And rapture nor receive nor give.
Go on, sweet bird, and soothe my care,
Thy cheerful notes will hush despair.

MUSING ON THE ROARING OCEAN.*

TUNE—"Druimion Dubh."

Musing on the roaring ocean, Which divides my love and me,
Wearying Heav'n in warm devotion, For his weal where'er he be:

Hope and fear's alternate billow
Yielding late to Nature's law,
Whisp'ring spirits round my pillow
Talk of him that's far awa'.

Ye whom sorrow never wounded,
Ye who never shed a tear,
Care-untroubled, joy-surrounded,
Gaudy day to you is dear.

Gentle night, do thou befriend me;
Downy sleep, the curtain draw;
Spirits kind, again attend me,
Talk of him that's far awa'!

* Burns says, "I composed these verses out of compliment to a Mrs. MacLachlane, whose husband is an officer in the East Indies."

THE GOWDEN LOCKS OF ANNA.

SLOWISH.   TUNE—"Banks of Banna."

Yestreen I had a pint o' wine, A place where body saw na;
Yestreen lay on this breast o' mine, The gowden locks o' Anna.
The hungry Jew in wilderness, Rejoicing o'er his manna,
Was nae-thing to the hin'-ny bliss, Upon the lips of Anna.

Ye monarchs, take the East and West,
Frae Indus to Savannah;
Gie me, within my straining grasp,
The melting form of Anna:
There I'll despise Imperial charms,
An Empress or Sultana,
While dying raptures, in her arms,
I give and take wi' Anna!

Awa, thou flaunting God of Day
Awa, thou pale Diana!

Ilk Star, gae hide thy twinkling ray,
    When I 'm to meet my Anna!
Come, in thy raven plumage, Night,
    (Sun, Moon, and Stars, withdrawn a';)
And bring an angel-pen to write
    My transports with my Anna!

POSTSCRIPT.

The Kirk an' State may join an' tell,
    To do sic things I maunna:
The Kirk an' State may gae to h—,
    And I 'll gae to my Anna.
She is the sunshine o' my e'e,
    To live but her I canna;
Had I on earth but wishes three,
    The first should be my Anna.

TO A LADY,*
WITH A PRESENT OF A PAIR OF DRINKING-GLASSES

FAIR Empress of the Poet's soul,
    And Queen of Poetesses;
Clarinda, take this little boon,
    This humble pair of glasses;

And fill them high with generous juice,
    As generous as your mind;
And pledge me in the generous toast—
    "The whole of human kind!"

"To those who love us!" second fill;
    But not to those whom we love,
Lest we love those who love not us;
    A third—"To thee and me, love!"

TO CLARINDA.

BEFORE I saw Clarinda's face
    My heart was blythe and gay,
Free as the wind, or feather'd race
    That hop from spray to spray.

But now dejected I appear,
    Clarinda proves unkind;
I, sighing, drop the silent tear,
    But no relief can find.

In plaintive notes my tale rehearses
    When I the fair have found;
On every tree appear my verses
    That to her praise resound.

But she, ungrateful, shuns my sight,
    My faithful love disdains,
My vows and tears her scorn excite,
    Another happy reigns.

* "Lady:" Mrs. M‘Lehose.

Ah, though my looks betray
    I envy your success,
Yet love to friendship shall give way—
    I cannot wish it less.

EPISTLE TO HUGH PARKER.†

IN this strange land, this uncouth clime,
A land unknown to prose or rhyme;
Where words ne'er cross'd the Muse's heckles,
Nor limpet in poetic shackles;
A land that Prose did never view it,
Except when drunk he stacher't through it;
Here, ambush'd by the chimla cheek,
Hid in an atmosphere of reek,
I hear a wheel thrum i' the neuk,
I hear it—for in vain I leuk.
The red peat gleams, a fiery kernel,
Enhuskèd by a fog infernal:
Here, for my wonted rhyming raptures,
I sit and count my sins by chapters;
For life and spunk like other Christians,
I 'm dwindled down to mere existence—
Wi' nae converse but Gallowa' bodies,
Wi' nae kent face but Jenny Geddes.
Jenny, my Pegasean pride!
Dowie she saunters down Nithside,
And aye a westlin' leuk she throws,
While tears hap o'er her auld brown nose!
Was it for this, wi' canny care,
Thou bure the Bard through mony a shire?
At howes or hillocks never stumbled,
And late or early never grumbled?
O had I power like inclination,
I 'd heeze thee up a constellation,
To canter with the Sagitarre,
Or loup the ecliptic like a bar;
Or turn the pole like any arrow;
Or, when auld Phœbus bids good-morrow,
Down the zodiac urge the race,
And cast dirt on his godship's face;
For I could lay my bread and kail
He 'd ne'er cast saut upo' thy tail.
Wi' a' this care and a' this grief,
And sma', sma' prospect of relief,
And nought but peat-reek i' my head,
How can I write what ye can read?
Tarbolton, twenty-fourth o' June,
Ye 'll find me in a better tune;
But till we meet and weet our whistle,
Tak this excuse for nae epistle.
                                ROBERT BURNS.

† This poetical letter, written at Ellisland, and dated June, 1788, is addressed to Hugh Parker, merchant Kilmarnock, an early friend of Burns.

THE CHEVALIER'S LAMENT.*

Tune—"Captain O Kean."

The small birds rejoice in the green leaves returning, The murmuring streamlet winds clear through the vale; The primroses blow in the dew of the morning, And wild scattered cowslips bedeck the green dale; But what can give pleasure, or what can seem fair, While the lingering moments are number'd by care? No flow'rs gaily springing, nor birds sweetly singing, Can soothe the sad bosom of joyless despair.

The deed that I dared, could it merit their malice,
    A king and a father to place on his throne?
His right are these hills, and his right are these valleys,
    Where the wild beasts find shelter, though I can find none.
But 'tis not my sufferings thus wretched, forlorn;
    My brave gallant friends, 'tis your ruin I mourn;
Your deeds proved so loyal in hot bloody trial—
    Alas! can I make you no sweeter return!

* Written in the moors between Galloway and Ayrshire, and sent to R. Cleghorn.

OF A' THE AIRTS.

Tune—"Miss Admiral Gordon's Strathspey."

Of a' the airts the wind can blaw, I dearly lo'e the west, For there the bonnie lassie lives, The lass that I lo'e best. Though wild woods grow, and rivers row, Wi' mony a hill between; Baith day and night my fancy's flight Is ever with my Jean.

I see her in the dewy flow'r, Sae lovely, sweet, and fair; I hear her voice in ilka bird, Wi' music charm the air! There's not a bonnie flow'r that springs By fountain, shaw, or green, Nor yet a bonnie bird that sings, But minds me o' my Jean.

WHEN JANUAR' WIND.

SLOW.   TUNE—"The Lass that Made the Bed to me."

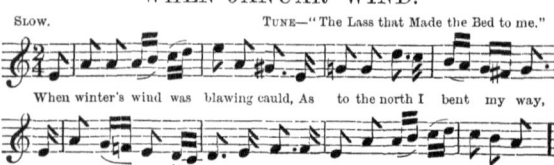

When winter's wind was blawing cauld, As to the north I bent my way,
The mirksome night did me enfauld, I knew na whare to lodge till day.

A charming girl I chanc'd to meet,
  Just in the middle o' my care;
And kindly she did me invite
  Her father's humble cot to share.

Her hair was like the gowd sae fine,
  Her teeth were like the ivorie;
Her cheeks like lilies dipt in wine,
  The lass that made the bed to me.

Her bosom was the drifted snaw,
  Her limbs like marble fair to see;
A finer form nane ever saw,
  Than her's that made the bed to me.

She made the bed baith lang and braid,
  Wi' twa white hands she spread it down;
She bade "gude night," and smiling, said
  "I hope ye 'll sleep baith saft and soun'."

Upon the morrow whan I raise,
  I thank'd her for her courtesie;
A blush cam o'er the comely face
  Of her that made the bed to me.

I clasp'd her waist, and kiss'd her syne;
  The tear stood twinkling in her e'e;
O dearest maid, gin ye 'll be mine,
  Ye aye sall mak the bed to me.

O WERE I ON PARNASSUS HILL.

SLOW.   TUNE—"My Love is Lost to me."

O were I on Parnassus hill, Or had o' Helicon my fill;
That I might catch poetic skill, To sing how dear I love thee.
But Nith maun be my Muse's well, My Muse maun be thy bonnie sel';
On Corsincon* I'll glow'r and spell, And write how dear I love thee.

Then come, sweet Muse, inspire my lay!
  For a' the lee-lang simmer's day
I couldna sing, I couldna say,
  How much, how dear, I love thee.

* "Corsincon:" a hill near Ellisland.

I see thee dancing o'er the green,
  Thy waist sae jimp, thy limbs sae clean,
Thy tempting lips, thy roguish een—
  By heaven and earth I love thee!

By night, by day, a-field, at hame,
  The thoughts o' thee my breast inflame;
And aye I muse and sing thy name—
  I only live to love thee.

Though I were doom'd to wander on,
  Beyond the sea, beyond the sun,
Till my last weary sand was run;
  Till then—and then—I love thee.

WRITTEN IN FRIARS CARSE HERMITAGE,† ON NITHSIDE.

FIRST VERSION.

THOU whom chance may hither lead,
Be thou clad in russet weed,
Be thou decked in silken stole,
Grave these maxims on thy soul:—
Life is but a day at most,
Sprung from night, in darkness lost;
Day, how rapid in its flight—
Day, how few may see the night;
Hope not sunshine every hour,
Fear not clouds will always lower;
Happiness is but a name,
Make content and ease thy aim.
Ambition is a meteor gleam;
Fame a restless, idle dream;
Pleasures, insects on the wing
Round Peace, the tenderest flower of Spring;
Those that sip the dew alone,
Make the butterflies thy own;
Those that would the bloom devour,
Crush the locusts—save the flower.
For the future be prepared,
Guard whatever thou canst guard;
But, thy utmost duly done,
Welcome what thou canst not shun.
Follies past give thou to air,
Make their consequence thy care:
Keep the name of Man in mind,
And dishonour not thy kind.
Reverence with lowly heart
Him whose wondrous work thou art;
Keep his goodness still in view,
Thy trust—and thy example too.

Stranger, go! Heaven be thy guide!
Quod the Bedesman on Nithside.

† "Friars Carse:" an estate near Ellisland, belonging to Mr. Riddell. See LIFE.

O WHA WILL TO ST. STEPHEN'S HOUSE?*

TUNE—"Killiecrankie."

O wha will to Saint Stephen's house, To do our er-rands there, man?
O wha will to Saint Stephen's house, O' th' mer-ry lads o' Ayr, man?
Or will ye send a man o' law? Or will ye send a sodger?
Or him wha led o'er Scot-land a' The mei-k'e Ur-sa Ma-jor?

Come, will ye court a noble lord,
  Or buy a score o' lairds, man?
For worth and honour pawn their word,
  Their vote shall be Glencaird's, man.
Ane gies them coin, ane gies them wine,
  Anither gies them clatter;
Annbank, wha guess'd the ladies' taste,
  He gies a *fête champêtre*.

When Love and Beauty heard the news,
  The gay green-woods amang, man;
Where, gathering flowers, and busking bowers,
  They heard the blackbird's sang, man;
A vow, they seal'd it with a kiss,
  Sir Politics to fetter,
As theirs alone, the patent bliss,
  To hold a *fête champêtre*.

Then mounted Mirth on gleesome wing,
  O'er hill and dale she flew, man;
Ilk wimpling burn, ilk crystal spring,
  Ilk glen and shaw she knew, man;
She summon'd every social sprite,
  That sports by wood or water,
On th' bonnie banks o' Ayr to meet,
  And keep this *fête champêtre*.

Cauld Boreas, wi' his boisterous crew,
  Were bound to stakes like kye, man;
And Cynthia's car, o' silver fu',
  Clamb up the starry sky, man:
Reflected beams dwell in the streams,
  Or down the current shatter;
The western breeze steals through the trees,
  To view this *fête champêtre*.

How many a robe sae gaily floats!
  What sparkling jewels glance, man,
To Harmony's enchanting notes,
  As moves the mazy dance, man!
The echoing wood, the winding flood,
  Like Paradise did glitter,
When angels met at Adam's yett
  To hold their *fête champêtre*.

When Politics came there, to mix,
  And make his ether-stane,† man,
He circled round the magic ground,
  But entrance found he nane, man;
He blush'd for shame, he quat his name,
  Forswore it every letter,
Wi' humble prayer to join and share
  This festive *fête champêtre*.

THE DAY RETURNS, MY BOSOM BURNS.‡

"Seventh of November."

The day returns, my bosom burns, The blissful day we twa did meet;
Though winter wild in tempest toil'd, Ne'er summer sun was half sae sweet.
Than a' the pride that loads the tide, And cros-ses o'er the sultry line;
Than kingly robes, than crowns and globes, Heaven gave me more— It made thee mine.

While day and night can bring delight,
  Or Nature aught of pleasure give;
While joys above my mind can move,
  For thee, and thee alone, I live!
When that grim foe of life below
  Comes in between to make us part;
The iron hand that breaks our band,
  It breaks my bliss—it breaks my heart!

---

* "Saint Stephen's House:" The occasion of this ballad was as follows:—When Mr. Cunninghame of Enterkin came to his estate, two mansion-houses on it—Enterkin and Annbank—were both in a ruinous state. Wishing to introduce himself with some *eclât* to the county, he got temporary erections made on the banks of Ayr, decorated with shrubs and flowers, and got up a supper and ball, to which most of the respectable families in the county were invited. It was a novelty in the county, and attracted great notice. A dissolution of Parliament was soon expected, and the festivity was thought to pave the way for a canvass for representing the county. Several other candidates were spoken of, particularly Sir John Whitefoord, then residing at Cloncaird, commonly pronounced Glencaird, and Mr. Boswell, the able biographer of Dr. Johnson. Mr. Cunninghame did not canvass the county, however, and the political views alluded to in the ballad were speedily laid aside.

† "Ether-stane:" alluding to the little annular stones, supposed to be formed from the sloughs of adders, but which in reality are Druidical.
‡ Composed for the anniversary of the marriage of Captain Riddell of Glenriddell.

THE WINTER IT IS PAST.

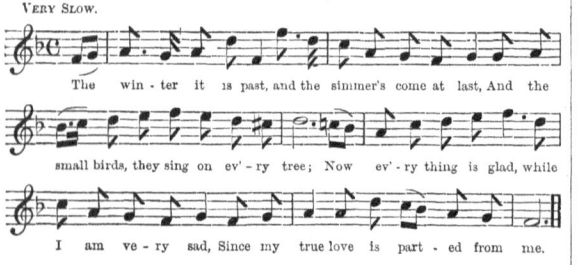

The winter it is past, and the simmer's come at last, And the small birds, they sing on ev'ry tree; Now ev'ry thing is glad, while I am very sad, Since my true love is parted from me.

The rose upon the breer, by the waters running clear,
  May have charms for the linnet or the bee;
Their little loves are blest, and their little hearts at rest,
  But my true love is parted from me.

BEHOLD, MY LOVE, HOW GREEN THE GROVES.

Behold, my love, how green the groves, The primrose banks how fair; The balmy gales awake the flowers, And wave thy flaxen hair. The lav'rock shuns the palace gay, And o'er the cottage sings; For nature smiles as sweet, I ween, To shepherds as to kings.

Let skilful minstrels sweep the string
  In lordly lighted ha',

The shepherd stops his simple reed
  Blythe in the birken shaw;
The princely revel may survey
  Our rustic dance wi' scorn,
But are their hearts as light as ours,
  Beneath the milk-white thorn?

The shepherd in the flowery glen
  In homely phrase will woo;
The courtier tells a finer tale,
  But is his heart as true?
These wild-wood flowers I 've pu'd to deck
  That spotless breast of thine;
The courtier's gems may witness love,
  But 'tis na love like mine.

SIMMER'S A PLEASANT TIME.

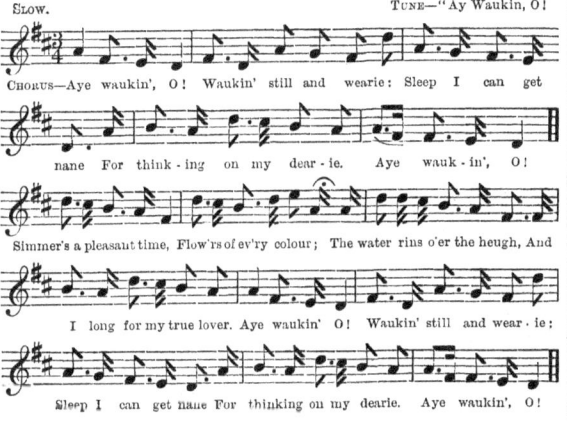

When I sleep I dream,
  When I wauk I 'm eerie:
Sleep I can get nane
  For thinking on my dearie.
      Aye waukin' O, &c.

Lanely night comes on,
  A' the lave are sleepin';
I think on my bonnie lad,
  And bleer my e'en wi' greetin'.
      Aye waukin' O, &c.

FIRST EPISTLE TO MR. GRAHAM OF FINTRY.*

WHEN Nature her great masterpiece design'd,
And framed her last, best work, the human mind,

* Written because Burns was told by some injudicious friends to try his hand at English instead of Scotch.

Her eye intent on all the mazy plan,
She form'd of various parts the various Man.
  Then first she calls the useful many forth;
Plain plodding industry, and sober worth:
Thence peasants, farmers, native sons of earth,
And merchandise' whole genus take their birth;
Each prudent cit a warm existence finds,
And all mechanics' many-apron'd kinds.
Some other rarer sorts are wanted yet,
The lead and buoy are needful to the net:
The *caput mortuum* of gross desires
Makes a material for mere knights and squires;
The martial phosphorus is taught to flow;
She kneads the lumpish philosophic dough,
Then marks the unyielding mass with grave designs,
Law, physic, politics, and deep divines;
Last, she sublimes the Aurora of the poles,
The flashing elements of female souls.
  The order'd system fair before her stood,
Nature, well-pleased, pronounced it very good;
But ere she gave creating labour o'er,
Half-jest, she tried one curious labour more.
Some spumy, fiery, *ignis fatuus* matter,
Such as the slightest breath of air might scatter;
With arch alacrity and conscious glee
(Nature may have her whim as well as we,
Her Hogarth-art perhaps she meant to show it),
She forms the thing, and christens it—a Poet:
Creature, though oft the prey of care and sorrow,
When blest to-day, unmindful of to-morrow.
A being form'd to amuse his graver friends,
Admired and praised—and there the homage ends:
A mortal quite unfit for Fortune's strife,
Yet oft the sport of all the ills of life;
Prone to enjoy each pleasure riches give,
Yet haply wanting wherewithal to live;
Longing to wipe each tear, to heal each groan,
Yet frequent all unheeded in his own.
But honest Nature is not quite a Turk;
She laugh'd at first, then felt for her poor work.
Pitying the propless climber of mankind,
She cast about a standard tree to find;
And, to support his helpless woodbine state,
Attach'd him to the generous, truly great;
A title, and the only one I claim,
To lay strong hold for help on bounteous Graham.
Pity the tuneful Muses' hapless train,
  Weak, timid landsmen on life's stormy main!
Their hearts no selfish, stern, absorbent stuff,
That never gives—though humbly takes enough;
The little fate allows they share as soon,
Unlike sage proverb'd wisdom's hard-wrung boon.
The world were blest did bliss on them depend,
Ah, that "the friendly e'er should want a friend!"
Let prudence number o'er each sturdy son,
Who life and wisdom at one race begun,

Who feel by reason and who give by rule
(Instinct 's a brute, and sentiment a fool!),
Who make poor "will do" wait upon "I should"—
We own they 're prudent, but who feels they 're good?
Ye wise ones, hence! ye hurt the social eye!
God's image rudely etch'd on base alloy!
But come, ye who the godlike pleasure know,
Heaven's attribute distinguish'd—to bestow!
Whose arms of love would grasp the human race:
Come *thou* who giv'st with all a courtier's grace;
Friend of my life, true patron of my rhymes,
Prop of my dearest hopes for future times!
Why shrinks my soul, half-blushing, half-afraid,
Backward, abash'd to ask thy friendly aid?
I know my need, I know thy giving hand,
I crave thy friendship at thy kind command.
But there are such who court the tuneful Nine—
Heavens! should the branded character be mine—
Whose verse in manhood's pride sublimely flows,
Yet vilest reptiles in their begging prose.
Mark, how their lofty independent spirit
Soars on the spurning wing of injured merit!
Seek you the proofs in private life to find?
Pity the best of words should be but wind!
So to heaven's gates the lark's shrill song ascends,
But grovelling on the earth the carol ends.

In all the clamorous cry of starving want,
They dun benevolence with shameless front;
Oblige them, patronize their tinsel lays,
They persecute you all your future days!
Ere my poor soul such deep damnation stain,
My horny fist assume the plough again;
The piebald jacket let me patch once more;
On eighteenpence a week I 've lived before.
Though, thanks to Heaven, I dare even that last shift,
I trust, meantime, my boon is in thy gift:
That, placed by thee upon the wished-for height,
Where, man and nature fairer in her sight,
My Muse may imp her wing for some sublimer flight.

A MOTHER'S LAMENT FOR THE DEATH OF HER SON.*

Fate gave the word, the ar - row sped, And pierc'd my dar - ling's heart; And with him all the joys are fled

* Burns here alludes to Mrs. Ferguson of Craigdarroch, who had lost her son—a youth of eighteen years of age, and of uncommon promise—at Glasgow College.

The mother linnet in the brake
Bewails her ravish'd young;
So I, for my lost darling's sake,
Lament the live-day long.
Death! oft I've fear'd thy fatal blow,
Now, fond, I bare my breast:
Oh, do thou kindly lay me low
With him I love, at rest!

THE JOYFUL WIDOWER.

We lived full one-and-twenty years
 A man and wife together;
At length from me her course she's steer'd,
 And gone I know not whither;
Would I could guess, I do profess,
 I speak and do not flatter,
Of all the women in the world,
 I never could come at her.

Her body is bestowèd well,
 A handsome grave does hide her;
But sure her soul is not in hell,
 The deil would ne'er abide her.
I rather think she is aloft,
 And imitating thunder;
For why—methinks I hear her voice
 Tearing the clouds asunder.

THE LAZY MIST.

How long I have lived—but how much lived in vain;
How little of life's scanty span may remain;
What aspects old Time, in his progress, has worn;
What ties cruel fate in my bosom has torn!
How foolish, or worse, till our summit is gain'd!
And downward, how weaken'd, how darken'd, how pain'd!
This life's not worth having with all it can give—
For something beyond it poor man, sure, must live.

NAEBODY.*

I am naebody's lord,
 I'll be slave to naebody;
I hae a guid braid sword,
 I'll tak dunts frae naebody.

I'll be merry and free,
 I'll be sad for naebody;
Naebody cares for me,
 I'll care for naebody.

* Written at Ellisland shortly after marriage.

LAMENT,

WRITTEN AT A TIME WHEN THE POET WAS ABOUT TO LEAVE SCOTLAND.

TUNE—"The Brown Dairy-maid."

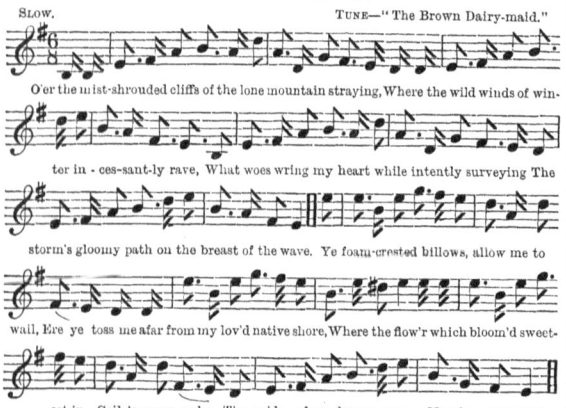

O'er the mist-shrouded cliffs of the lone mountain straying, Where the wild winds of winter in-ces-sant-ly rave, What woes wring my heart while intently surveying The storm's gloomy path on the breast of the wave. Ye foam-crested billows, allow me to wail, Ere ye toss me afar from my lov'd native shore, Where the flow'r which bloom'd sweetest in Coila's green vale, The pride of my bosom, my Mary's no more!

No more by the banks of the streamlet we'll wander,
   And smile at the moon's rimpled face in the wave;
No more shall my arms cling with fondness around her,
   For the dew-drops of morning fall cold on her grave.

No more shall the soft thrill of love warm my breast,
   I haste with the storm to a far distant shore;
Where unknown, unlamented, my ashes shall rest,
   And joy shall revisit my bosom no more.

WRITTEN IN FRIARS CARSE HERMITAGE, ON NITHSIDE.

SECOND VERSION.

THOU whom chance may hither lead,
Be thou clad in russet weed,

Be thou deckt in silken stole,
Grave these counsels on thy soul.
   Life is but a day at most,
Sprung from night, in darkness lost;
Hope not sunshine ev'ry hour,
Fear not clouds will always lower.
   As Youth and Love with sprightly dance
Beneath thy morning star advance,
Pleasure with her siren air
May delude the thoughtless pair;
Let Prudence bless Enjoyment's cup,
Then raptur'd sip, and sip it up.
   As thy day grows warm and high,
Life's meridian flaming nigh,
Dost thou spurn the humble vale?
Life's proud summits wouldst thou scale?
Check thy climbing step, elate,
Evils lurk in felon wait:

Dangers, eagle-pinion'd, bold,
Soar around each cliffy hold;
While cheerful Peace, with linnet song,
Chants the lowly dells among.
   As the shades of ev'ning close,
Beck'ning thee to long repose;
As life itself becomes disease,
Seek the chimney-nook of ease:
There ruminate with sober thought,
On all thou'st seen, and heard, and wrought;
And teach the sportive younkers round,
Saws of experience, sage and sound.
Say, man's true, genuine estimate,
The grand criterion of his fate,
Is not, Art thou high or low?
Did thy fortune ebb or flow?
Did many talents gild thy span?
Or frugal Nature grudge thee one?

Tell them, and press it on their mind,
As thou thyself must shortly find,
The smile or frown of awful Heaven,
To Virtue or to Vice is given;
Say, to be just, and kind, and wise—
There solid self-enjoyment lies;
That foolish, selfish, faithless ways
Lead to be wretched, vile, and base.

Thus resign'd and quiet, creep
To the bed of lasting sleep—
Sleep, whence thou shall ne'er awake,
Night, where dawn shalt never break,
Till future life, future no more,
To light and joy the good restore,
To light and joy unknown before.
Stranger, go! Heaven be thy guide!
Quod the Bedesman of Nithside.

MY BONNIE MARY.*

TUNE—"The Silver Tassie."

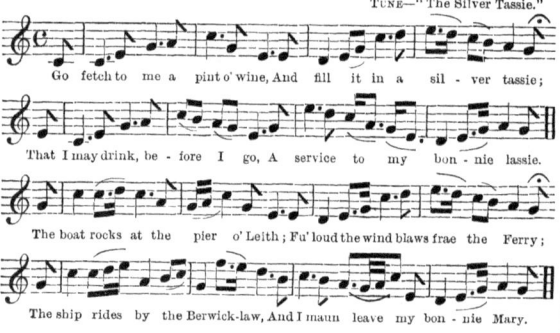

Go fetch to me a pint o' wine, And fill it in a sil-ver tassie;
That I may drink, be-fore I go, A service to my bon-nie lassie.
The boat rocks at the pier o' Leith; Fu' loud the wind blaws frae the Ferry;
The ship rides by the Berwick-law, And I maun leave my bon-nie Mary.

The trumpets sound, the banners fly,
  The glittering spears are rankèd ready;
The shouts o' war are heard afar,
  The battle closes deep and bloody;
It's not the roar o' sea or shore
  Wad make me langer wish to tarry;
Nor shouts o' war that's heard afar—
  It's leaving thee, my bonnie Mary.

TO ALEX. CUNNINGHAM, ESQ., WRITER, EDINBURGH.

ELLISLAND, NITHSDALE, *July 27th*, 1788.

My godlike friend—nay, do not stare,
  You think the phrase is odd-like;
But "God is Love," the saints declare,
  Then surely thou art god-like.

---

* The first four lines are from an old ballad by Alexander Lesslie of Edinburgh, Derwan-side, grandfather to Archbishop Sharpe.

And is thy ardour still the same?
  And kindled still at Anna? †
Others may boast a partial flame,
  But thou art a volcano!

Ev'n Wedlock asks not love beyond
  Death's tie-dissolving portal;
But thou, omnipotently fond,
  May'st promise love immortal!

Thy wounds such healing powers defy,
  Such symptoms dire attend them,
That last great anti hectic try:
  Marriage perhaps may mend them.

Sweet Anna has an air—a grace,
  Divine, magnetic, touching;
She talks, she charms—but who can trace
  The process of bewitching?

ELEGY ON THE YEAR 1788.

FOR Lords or Kings I dinna mourn,
E'en let them die—for that they're born!
But, oh! prodigious to reflec',
A towmont, sirs, is gane to wreck!
O Eighty-eight, in thy sma' space
What dire events hae taken place!
Of what enjoyments thou hast reft us!
In what a pickle thou hast left us!
  The Spanish empire's tint a head,
And my auld teethless Bawtie's dead;
The tulyie's teugh 'tween Pitt and Fox,
And our guidwife's wee birdie cocks;
The tane is game, a bluidy devil,
But to the hen-birds unco civil;
The tither's something dour o' treadin'
But better stuff ne'er claw'd a midden!
  Ye ministers, come mount the pu'pit,
And cry till ye be hearse and roopit;
For Eighty-eight, he wish'd you weel,
And gied you a' baith gear and meal;
E'en mony a plack, and mony a peck,
Ye ken yoursels, for little feck!
  Ye bonnie lasses, dight your e'en,
For some o' you hae tint a frien';
In Eighty-eight, ye ken, was ta'en
What ye'll ne'er hae to gie again.
  Observe the very nowte and sheep
How dowff and dowie now they creep;

---

† Anna was Anne Stewart, daughter of John Stewart of East Craigs. She did not marry Cunningham, but Mr. Forrest Dewar, surgeon, and afterwards bailie in Edinburgh.

Nay, even the yirth itsel' does cry,
For Embro' wells are grutten dry.
  O Eighty-nine, thou 's but a bairn,
And no owre auld, I hope, to learn!
Thou beardless boy, I pray tak care,
Thou now has got thy Daddy's chair,
Nae hand-cuff'd, muzzled, hap-shackled Regent,
But, like himsel', a full free agent.
Be sure ye follow out the plan
Nae waur than he did, honest man!
As meikle better as you can.

January 1, 1789.

SKETCH. [W. CREECH.*]

A LITTLE, upright, pert, tart, tripping wight,
And still his precious self his dear delight:
Who loves his own smart shadow in the streets,
Better than e'er the fairest she he meets.
A man of fashion, too, he made his tour,
Learn'd *vive la bagatelle, et vive l'amour;*
So travell'd monkeys their grimace improve,
Polish their grin, nay, sigh for ladies' love.
Much specious lore, but little understood;
Veneering oft outshines the solid wood:
His solid sense by inches you must tell,
But mete his cunning by the old Scots ell;
His meddling vanity, a busy fiend,
Still making work his selfish craft must mend.

TO CAPTAIN RIDDEL, GLENRIDDEL.†
EXTEMPORE LINES ON RETURNING A NEWSPAPER.
ELLISLAND, *Monday Evening.*

YOUR news and review, sir, I 've read through and
    through, sir,
  With little admiring or blaming:
The papers are barren of home-news or foreign,
  No murders or rapes worth the naming.

Our friends the reviewers, those chippers and hewers,
  Are judges of mortar and stone, sir;
But of meet or unmeet, in a fabric complete,
  I 'll boldly pronounce they are none, sir.

My goose-quill too rude is to tell all your goodness
  Bestow'd on your servant, the Poet;
Would to God I had one like a beam of the sun,
  And then all the world, sir, should know it!

ODE,‡ SACRED TO THE MEMORY OF MRS. OSWALD OF AUCHENCRUIVE.

DWELLER in yon dungeon dark,
Hangman of creation! mark
Who in widow-weeds appears,
Laden with unhonour'd years,
Noosing with care a bursting purse,
Baited with many a deadly curse!

STROPHE.

  View the wither'd Beldam's face;
Can thy keen inspection trace
Aught of Humanity's sweet, melting grace?
Note that eye, 'tis rheum o'erflows,
Pity's flood there never rose.
See those hands, ne'er stretch'd to save,
Hands that took, but never gave:
Keeper of Mammon's iron chest,
Lo, there she goes, unpitied and unblest,
She goes, but not to realms of everlasting rest!

ANTISTROPHE.

  Plunderer of Armies, lift thine eyes,
(A while forbear, ye torturing fiends;)
Seest thou whose step, unwilling, hither bends?
No fallen angel, hurl'd from upper skies;
'Tis thy trusty quondam mate,
Doom'd to share thy fiery fate;
She, tardy, hell-ward plies.

EPODE.

  And are they of no more avail,
Ten thousand glittering pounds a-year?
In other worlds can Mammon fail,
Omnipotent as he is here?
O, bitter mockery of the pompous bier,
While down the wretched vital part is driven!
The cave-lodg'd beggar, with a conscience clear,
Expires in rags, unknown, and goes to heaven.

---

* Creech Burns thought had used him ill. Their differences, however, are said to have been ultimately made up. See LIFE.

† Riddel had sent him a newspaper with some severe remarks on his poetry.

‡ His Correspondence describes the circumstances under which this savage ode was composed—driven out of comfortable quarters in an inn by Mrs. Oswald's funeral, and forced to ride on through tempests and over moors to the next inn.

EPISTLE TO JOHN TAYLOR.*

With Pegasus upon a day,
   Apollo weary flying,
Through frosty hills the journey lay,
   On foot the way was plying.

Poor slip-shod giddy Pegasus
   Was but a sorry walker;
To Vulcan then Apollo goes,
   To get a frosty caulker.

Obliging Vulcan fell to work,
   Threw by his coat and bonnet,
And did Sol's business in a crack;
   Sol paid him with a sonnet.

Ye Vulcan's sons of Wanlockhead,
   Pity my sad disaster;
My Pegasus is poorly shod—
   I'll pay you like my master.

ON AN EVENING VIEW OF THE RUINS OF LINCLUDEN ABBEY.

Ye holy walls, that, still sublime,
Resist the crumbling touch of time,
How strongly still your form displays
The piety of ancient days!
As through your ruins, hoar and gray—
Ruins yet beauteous in decay—
The silvery moonbeams trembling fly:
The forms of ages long gone by
Crowd thick on fancy's wand'ring eye,
And wake the soul to musings high.
E'en now, as lost in thought profound,
I view the solemn scene around,
And, pensive, gaze with wistful eyes,
The past returns, the present flies;
Again the dome, in pristine pride,
Lifts high its roof and arches wide,
That, knit with curious tracery,
Each Gothic ornament display.
The high arch'd windows, painted fair,
Show many a saint and martyr there.
As on their slender forms I'd gaze,
Methinks they brighten to a blaze!
With noiseless step and taper bright,
What are yon forms that meet my sight?
Slowly they move, while every eye
Is heavenward raised in ecstasy.
'Tis the fair, spotless, vestal train,
That seek in prayer the midnight fane.
And, hark! what more than mortal sound
Of music breathes the pile around?
'Tis the soft chanted choral song,
Whose tones the echoing aisles prolong;
Till, thence return'd, they softly stray
O'er Cluden's wave, with fond delay;
Now on the rising gale swell high,
And now in fainting murmurs die;
The boatmen on Nith's gentle stream,
That glistens in the pale moonbeam,
Suspend their dashing oars to hear
The holy anthem, loud and clear;
Each worldly thought awhile forbear,
And mutter forth a half-form'd prayer.
But, as I gaze, the vision fails,
Like frost-work touch'd by southern gales;
The altar sinks, the tapers fade,
And all the splendid scene's decay'd;
In window fair the painted pane
No longer glows with holy stain,
But through the broken glass the gale
Blows chilly from the misty vale:
The bird of eve flits sullen by,
Her home, these aisles and arches high;
The choral hymn, that erst so clear
Broke softly sweet on fancy's ear,
Is drown'd amid the mournful scream,
That breaks the magic of my dream!
Roused by the sound, I start and see
The ruin'd sad reality!

FRAGMENT.
INSCRIBED TO THE RIGHT HON. C. J. FOX.

How Wisdom and Folly meet, mix, and unite;
How Virtue and Vice blend their black and their white;
How Genius, th' illustrious father of fiction,
Confounds rule and law, reconciles contradiction—
I sing: If these mortals, the critics, should bustle,
I care not, not I—let the critics go whistle.

  But now for a Patron, whose name and whose glory
At once may illustrate and honour my story.
  Thou first of our orators, first of our wits;
Yet whose parts and acquirements seem mere lucky hits:
With knowledge so vast, and with judgment so strong,
No man with the half of 'em e'er could go wrong;
With passions so potent, and fancies so bright,
No man with the half of 'em e'er could go right:
A sorry, poor, misbegot son of the Muses,
For using thy name offers fifty excuses.

---

* Burns at Wanlockhead on a winter day wished Jenny Geddes frosted, but the smith, John Taylor, was busy, and refused till Burns handed him the above epistle. Taylor thought himself well paid for once with money, drink, and verse, "and all by a poet."

Good L—d, what is Man! for as simple he looks
Do but try to develop his hooks and his crooks;
With his depths and his shallows, his good and his evil,
And in all he's a problem must puzzle the devil.
On his one ruling passion Sir Pope hugely labours,
That, like th' old Hebrew walking-switch, eats up its
    neighbours:
Mankind are his show-box—a friend, would you know him?
Pull the string, ruling passion the picture will show him.
What pity, in rearing so beauteous a system,
One trifling particular—Truth—should have miss'd him;
For, spite of his fine theoretic positions,
Mankind is a science defies definitions.

Some sort all our qualities each to its tribe,
And think human nature they truly describe;
Have you found this, or t' other? there's more in the wind,
As by one drunken fellow his comrades you'll find;
But such is the flaw, or the depth of the plan,
In the make of that wonderful creature call'd Man,
No two virtues, whatever relation they claim,
Nor even two different shades of the same,
Though like as was ever twin-brother to brother,
Possessing the one shall imply you've the other.

But truce with abstraction, and truce with the Muse,
Whose rhymes you 'll perhaps, sir, ne'er deign to peruse;
Will you leave your joustings, your jars, and your quarrels,
Contending with Billy for proud-nodding laurels?
My much-honour'd Patron, believe your poor Poet,
Your courage much more than your prudence you show it;
In vain with Squire Billy for laurels you struggle,
He'll have them by fair trade, if not, he will smuggle.
Not cabinets even of kings would conceal 'em,
He'd up the back-stairs, and, by G—d, he would steal 'em!
Then feats like Squire Billy's you ne'er can achieve 'em;
It is not, outdo him—the task is, out-thieve him!

LETTER TO JAMES TENNANT,* GLENCONNER.

    AULD comrade dear, and brither sinner,
How's a' the folk about Glenconner?
How do you, this blae eastlin' win',
That's like to blaw a body blin'?
For me, my faculties are frozen,
My dearest member nearly dozen'.
I've sent you here by Johnnie Simpson
Twa sage philosophers to glimpse on;
Smith, wi' his sympathetic feeling,
An' Reid, to common sense appealing.
Philosophers have fought and wrangled,
An' meikle Greek an' Latin mangled,
Till, wi' their logic-jargon tired,
And in the depth of Science mired,
To Common Sense they now appeal,
What wives and wabsters see and feel.

But, hark ye, friend! I charge you strictly,
Peruse them, and return them quickly,
For now I'm grown sae cursèd douce,
I pray and ponder butt the house;
My shins, my lane, I there sit roastin',
Perusing Bunyan, Brown, and Boston,
Till by an' by, if I haud on,
I'll grunt a real gospel groan:
Already I begin to try it,
To cast my e'en up like a pyet,
When by the gun she tumbles o'er
Flutt'ring an' gasping in her gore:
Sae shortly you shall see me bright,
A burning an' a shining light.

My heart-warm love to guid auld Glen,
The ace an' wale of honest men:
When bending down wi' auld grey hairs
Beneath the load of years and cares,
May He who made him still support him,
An' views beyond the grave comfort him;
His worthy family far and near,
God bless them a' wi' grace and gear!

My auld school-fellow, Preacher Willie,
The manly tar, my mason billie,
And Auchenbay, I wish him joy;
If he's a parent, lass or boy,
May he be dad, and Meg the mither,
Just five-and-forty years thegither!
And no forgetting wabster Charlie,
I'm tauld he offers very fairly.
An', L—d, remember singing Sannock
Wi' hale breeks, saxpence, an' a bannock!
And next, my auld acquaintance, Nancy,
Since she is fitted to her fancy,
An' her kind stars hae airted till her
A guid chiel wi' a pickle siller.
My kindest, best respects I sen' it,
To cousin Kate and sister Janet;
Tell them, frae me, wi' chiels be cautious,
For, faith, they'll aiblins fin' them fashious:
To grant a heart is fairly civil,
But to grant a maidenhead's the devil.

An' lastly, Jamie, for yoursel',
May guardian angels tak a spell,
And steer you seven miles south o' hell:
But first, before you see heaven's glory,
May ye get mony a merry story,
Mony a laugh, and mony a drink,
An' aye eneugh o' needfu' clink!

    Now fare ye weel, an' joy be wi' you;
For my sake this I beg it o' you,
Assist poor Simpson a' ye can,
Ye'll fin' him just an honest man;
Sae I conclude, and quat my chanter,
Yours, saint or sinner,
                      ROB THE RANTER.

---

* An old friend of Burns', who assisted him in the choice of Ellisland.

ON SEEING A WOUNDED HARE LIMP BY ME,*

WHICH A FELLOW HAD JUST SHOT AT.

Inhuman man! curse on thy barbarous art,
  And blasted be thy murder-aiming eye:
  May never pity soothe thee with a sigh,
Nor ever pleasure glad thy cruel heart!

Go, live, poor wanderer of the wood and field!
  The bitter little that of life remains:
  No more the thickening brakes and verdant plains
To thee shall home, or food, or pastime yield.

Seek, mangled wretch, some place of wonted rest,
  No more of rest, but now thy dying bed!
  The sheltering rushes whistling o'er thy head,
The cold earth with thy bloody bosom press'd.

Oft as by winding Nith I, musing, wait
  The sober eve, or hail the cheerful dawn,
  I'll miss thee sporting o'er the dewy lawn,
And curse the ruffian's aim, and mourn thy hapless fate.

DELIA.†

Fair the face of orient day,
  Fair the tints of op'ning rose;
But fairer still my Delia dawns,
  More lovely far her beauty blows.

Sweet the lark's wild-warbled lay,
  Sweet the tinkling rill to hear;
But, Delia, more delightful still
  Steal thine accents on mine ear!

The flower-enamour'd, busy bee
  The rosy banquet loves to sip;
Sweet the streamlet's limpid laps
  To the sun-brown'd Arab's lip;

But, Delia, on thy balmy lips
  Let me, no vagrant insect, rove!
O let me steal one liquid kiss,
  For, oh! my soul is parch'd with love!

YE HAE LIEN A' WRANG, LASSIE.

Your rosy cheeks are turn'd sae wan,
  Ye're greener than the grass, lassie;
Your coatie's shorter by a span,
  Yet ne'er an inch the less, lassie.
      Ye hae lien a' wrang, lassie,
        Ye've lien a' wrang;
      Ye've lien in an unco bed,
        And wi' a fremit man.

O lassie, ye ha'e play'd the fool,
  And ye will feel the scorn, lassie;

---

* See Correspondence.
† "Delia:" doubtful if it be by Burns', said to have been sent by him to the *London Star*.

ADDRESS TO THE TOOTHACHE.

For aye the brose ye sup at e'en,
  Ye bock them e'er the morn, lassie.
    Ye hae lien a' wrang, &c.

Oh, ance ye danced upon the knowes,
  And through the wood ye sang, lassie,
But in the herrying o' a bee byke,
  I fear ye 've got a stang, lassie.
    Ye hae lien a' wrang, &c.

ADDRESS TO THE TOOTHACHE.

My curse upon your venom'd stang,
That shoots my tortur'd gums alang,
An' thro' my lug gies sic a twang,
    Wi' gnawing vengeance,
Tearing my nerves wi' bitter pang,
    Like racking engines!

When fevers burn, or agues freeze us,
Rheumatics gnaw, or colics squeeze us,
Our neibours' sympathy can ease us,
    Wi' pitying moan;
But thee—thou hell o' a' diseases—
    Aye mocks our groan!

Adown my beard the slavers trickle,
I throw the wee stools o'er the mickle,
While round the fire the giglets keckle,
    To see me loup;
An', raving mad, I wish a heckle
    Were in their doup!

In a' the numerous human dools—
Ill hairsts, daft bargains, cutty-stools,
Or worthy frien's rak'd i' the mools,
    Sad sight to see!
The tricks o' knaves, or fash o' fools—
    Thou bear'st the gree!

Where'er that place be priests ca' hell,
Where a' the tones o' misery yell,
An' ranket plagues their numbers tell,
    In dreadfu' raw,
Thou, Toothache, surely bear'st the bell,
    Amang them a'!

O thou, grim, mischief-making chiel,
That gars the notes o' discord squeel,
Till daft mankind aft dance a reel
    In gore, a shoe-thick,
Gie a' the faes o' Scotland's weal
    A towmond's toothache!

THE KIRK'S ALARM:*

A SATIRE.

Orthodox, orthodox, wha believe in John Knox,
  Let me sound an alarm to your conscience;
There 's a heretic blast has been blawn i' the Wast,
  That what is no sense must be nonsense.

Dr. Mac,† Dr. Mac, you should stretch on a rack,
  To strike evil-doers wi' terror;
To join faith and sense upon ony pretence,
  Is heretic, damnable error.

Town of Ayr, town of Ayr, it was mad, I declare,
  To meddle wi' mischief a-brewin';
Provost John is still deaf to the Church's relief,
  And orator Bob‡ is its ruin.

D'rymple mild, § D'rymple mild, though your heart 's like a child,
  And your life like the new-driven snaw,
Yet that winna save ye, auld Satan must have ye,
  For preaching that three 's ane an' twa.

Rumble John, ‖ Rumble John, mount the steps wi' a groan,
  Cry, the book is wi' heresy cramm'd;
Then lug out your ladle, deal brimstone like aidle,
  And roar every note of the damn'd.

Simper James,¶ Simper James, leave the fair Killie dames,
  There 's a holier chase in your view!
I 'll lay on your head that the pack ye 'll soon lead,
  For puppies like you there 's but few.

Singet Sawney,** Singet Sawney, are ye huirdin' the penny,
  Unconscious what evils await?
Wi' a jump, yell, and howl, alarm every soul,
  For the foul thief is just at your gate.

Daddy Auld, †† Daddy Auld, there 's a tod in the fauld,
  A tod meikle waur than the Clerk:‡‡
Though ye downa do skaith, ye 'll be in at the death,
  And gif ye canna bite, ye may bark.

Davie Bluster,§§ Davie Bluster, for a saint if ye muster,
  The corps is no nice of recruits;
Yet to worth let 's be just, royal blood ye might boast,
  If the ass was the king of the brutes.

---

* "The Kirk's Alarm:" written a short time after the publication of Dr. M'Gill's Essay, and referring to the polemical warfare which it excited.
† "Dr. Mac:" Dr. M'Gill.
‡ "Orator Bob:" Robert Aiken.
§ "D'rymple mild:" Dr. Dalrymple.—See Life.
‖ "Rumble John:" Mr. Russell.   ¶ "Simper James:" Mr. M'Kinlay.
** "Singet Sawney:" Mr. Moody.
†† "Daddy Auld:" Mr. Auld, Mauchline.
‡‡ "Clerk:" Mr. Gavin Hamilton.
§§ "Davie Bluster:" Mr. Grant, Ochiltree.

Jamie Goose,* Jamie Goose, ye ha'e made but toom roose,
  In hunting the wicked Lieutenant;
But the Doctor 's your mark, for the L—d's haly ark
  He has cooper'd an' ca 't a wrang pin in 't.

Poet Willie,† Poet Willie, gie the Doctor a volley,
  Wi' your "liberty's chain" and your wit;
O'er Pegasus' side ye ne'er laid a stride,
  Ye but smelt, man, the place where he sh— t.

Andro Gowk,‡ Andro Gowk, ye may slander the book,
  And the book nought the waur, let me tell ye;
Ye are rich and look big, but lay by hat and wig,
  And ye 'll hae a calf's head o' sma' value

Barr Steenie,§ Barr Steenie, what mean ye? what mean ye?
  If ye 'll meddle nae mair wi' the matter,
Ye may hae some pretence to havins and sense,
  Wi' people wha ken ye nae better

Irvine-side,‖ Irvine-side, wi' your turkey-cock pride,
  Of manhood but sma' is your share;
Ye 've the figure, 'tis true, even your faes will allow,
  And your friends they dare grant you nae mair.

Muirland Jock,¶ Muirland Jock, when the L-d makes a rock
  To crush Common Sense for her sins,
If ill-manners were wit, there 's no mortal so fit
  To confound the poor Doctor at ance.

Holy Will,** Holy Will, there was wit i' your skull,
  When ye pilfer'd the alms o' the poor;
The timmer is scant when ye 're ta'en for a saunt
  Wha should swing in a rape for an hour.

Calvin's sons, Calvin's sons, seize your spiritual guns,
  Ammunition you never can need;
Your hearts are the stuff will be powther enough,
  And your skulls are storehouses o' lead.

Poet Burns, Poet Burns, wi' your priest-skelping turns,
  Why desert ye your auld native shire?
Your Muse is a gipsy, e'en though she were tipsy,
  She could ca' us nae waur than we are.

THE WHISTLE,†† A BALLAD.

As the authentic prose history of the Whistle is curious, I shall here give it. In the train of Anne of Denmark, when she came to Scotland with our James VI., there came over also a Danish gentleman of gigantic stature and great prowess, and a matchless champion of Bacchus. He had a little ebony whistle, which at the commencement of the orgies he laid on the table, and whoever was last able to blow it, every body else being disabled by the potency of the bottle, was to carry off the Whistle as a trophy of victory. The Dane produced credentials of his victories, without a single defeat, at the courts of Copenhagen, Stockholm, Moscow, Warsaw, and several of the petty courts in Germany; and challenged the Scotch Bacchanalians to the alternative of trying his prowess, or else of acknowledging their inferiority. After many overthrows on the part of the Scots, the Dane was encountered by Sir Robert Lawrie of Maxwelton, ancestor of the present worthy baronet of that name: who, after three days and three nights' hard contest, left the Scandinavian under the table,

"And blew on the Whistle his requiem shrill."

Sir Walter, son to Sir Robert before-mentioned, afterwards lost the Whistle to Walter Riddel of Glenriddel, who had married a sister of Sir Walter's. On Friday, the 16th of October, 1760, at Friars Carse, the Whistle was once more contended for, as related in the ballad, by the present Sir Robert Lawrie of Maxwelton; Robert Riddel, Esq., of Glenriddel, lineal descendant and representative of Walter Riddel, who won the Whistle, and in whose family it had continued; and Alexander Ferguson, Esq., of Craigdarroch, likewise descended of the great Sir Robert; which last gentleman carried off the hard-won honours of the field.—(B.)

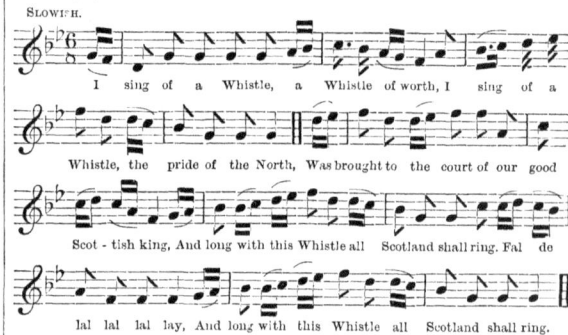

Old Loda,† still rueing the arm of Fingal,
  The god of the bottle sends down from his hall—
"This Whistle 's your challenge, to Scotland get o'er,
  And drink them to hell, Sir, or ne'er see me more!"
          Fal de lal, &c.

Old poets have sung, and old chronicles tell,
  What champions ventured, what champions fell;
The son of great Loda was conqueror still,
  And blew on the whistle their requiem shrill.
          Fal de lal, &c.

Till Robert, the lord of the Cairn and the Scaur,‡
  Unmatch'd at the bottle, unconquer'd in war,
He drank his poor godship as deep as the sea—
  No tide of the Baltic e'er drunker than he.
          Fal de lal, &c.

Thus Robert, victorious, the trophy has gain'd,
  Which now in his house has for ages remain'd;
Till three noble chieftains, and all of his blood,
  The jovial contest again have renew'd.
          Fal de lal, &c.

---

* "Jamie Goose:" Mr. Young. Cumnock.
† "Poet Willie:" Mr. Peebles, Ayr.
‡ "Andro Gowk:" Dr. A. Mitchell.
§ "Barr Steenie:" Mr. Stephen Young, Barr.
‖ "Irvine-side:" Mr. Smith, Galston.
¶ "Muirland Jock:" Mr. Shepherd.
** "Holy Will:" Holy Willie.
†† "Whistle:" Burns was present at this Bacchanalian encounter, and wrote the poem in the room. See CORRESPONDENCE and LIFE

* "Old Loda:" See Ossian's Caric-thura.—(B.)
† "Cairn and Skarr:" tributaries to the Nith.—(B.)

Three joyous good fellows, with hearts clear of flaw:
Craigdarroch, so famous for wit, worth, and law;
And trusty Glenriddel, so skill'd in old coins;
And gallant Sir Robert, deep read in old wines.
　　　　　Fal de lal, &c.

Craigdarroch began, with a tongue smooth as oil,
Desiring Glenriddel to yield up the spoil;
Or else he would muster the heads of the clan,
And once more, in claret, try which was the man.
　　　　　Fal de lal, &c.

"By the gods of the ancients," Glenriddel replies,
"Before I surrender so glorious a prize,
I'll conjure the ghost of the great Rorie More, §
And bumper his horn with him twenty times o'er."
　　　　　Fal de lal, &c.

Sir Robert, a soldier, no speech would pretend,
But he ne'er turn'd his back on his foe, or his friend,
Said, "Toss down the whistle, the prize of the field,"
And knee-deep in claret, he'd die or he'd yield.
　　　　　Fal de lal, &c.

To the board of Glenriddel our heroes repair,
So noted for drowning of sorrow and care;
But for wine and for welcome not more known to fame,
Than the sense, wit, and taste of a sweet lovely dame.
　　　　　Fal de lal, &c.

A Bard was selected to witness the fray,
And tell future ages the feats of the day;
A Bard who detested all sadness and spleen,
And wish'd that Parnassus a vineyard had been.
　　　　　Fal de lal, &c.

The dinner being over, the claret they ply,
And every new cork is a new spring of joy;
In the bands of old friendship and kindred so set,
And the bands grew the tighter the more they were wet.
　　　　　Fal de lal, &c.

Gay pleasure ran riot as bumpers ran o'er;
Bright Phœbus ne'er witness'd so joyous a core,
And vow'd that to leave them he was quite forlorn,
Till Cynthia hinted he'd see them next morn.
　　　　　Fal de lal, &c.

Six bottles a-piece had well wore out the night,
When gallant Sir Robert, to finish the fight,
Turn'd o'er in one bumper a bottle of red,
And swore 'twas the way that their ancestor did.
　　　　　Fal de lal, &c.

Then worthy Glenriddel, so cautious and sage,
No longer the warfare ungodly would wage;
A high Ruling Elder to wallow in wine!
He left the foul business to folks less divine.
　　　　　Fal de lal, &c.

The gallant Sir Robert fought hard to the end;
But who can with Fate and quart bumpers contend?
Though Fate said, a hero should perish in light;
So uprose bright Phœbus—and down fell the knight.
　　　　　Fal de lal, &c.

Next uprose our Bard, like a prophet in drink:—
"Craigdarroch, thou 'lt soar when creation shall sink!
But if thou would flourish immortal in rhyme,
Come—one bottle more—and have at the sublime!
　　　　　Fal de lal, &c.

"Thy line, that have struggled for freedom with Bruce,
Shall heroes and patriots ever produce;
So thine be the laurel, and mine be the bay;
The field thou hast won, by yon bright god of day!"
　　　　　Fal de lal, &c.

WILLIE † BREW'D A PECK O' MAUT.

Here are we met, three merry boys,
　Three merry boys I trow are we;
And mony a night we 've merry been,
　And mony mae we hope to be!
　　　We are na fou, &c.

It is the moon, I ken her horn,
　That 's blinkin' in the lift sae hie;
She shines sae bright to wyle us hame,
　But, by my sooth, she 'll wait a wee!
　　　We are na fou, &c.

Wha first shall rise to gang awa',
　A cuckold, coward loon is he!
Wha last beside his chair shall fa',
　He is the king among us three!
　　　We are na fou, &c.

* "Rorie More:" see Johnson's "Tour to the Hebrides."—(B.)

† The Willie who "brew'd a peck o' maut" was William Nicol; and Rob and Allan were the poet and Allan Masterton, a writing-master in Edinburgh. This meeting took place probably at Laggan, a farm purchased by Mr. Nicol, in Nithsdale, on the recommendation of our bard. See LIFE.

TO MARY IN HEAVEN.*

Tune—"The Death of Captain Cook."

Thou ling-'ring star, with less'-ning ray, That lov'st to greet the ear-ly morn, A-gain thou usher'st in the day My Mary from my soul was torn. O Ma-ry! dear de-parted shade! Where is thy place of bliss-ful rest? See'st thou thy lov-er lowly laid? Hear'st thou the groans that rend his breast?

That sacred hour can I forget,
  Can I forget the hallow'd grove,
Where by the winding Ayr we met,
  To live one day of parting love!
Eternity can not efface
  Those records dear of transports past;
Thy image at our last embrace;
  Ah! little thought we 'twas our last!

Ayr, gurgling, kiss'd his pebbled shore,
  O'erhung with wild woods, thickening green;
The fragrant birch and hawthorn hoar
  Twined amorous round the raptured scene;
The flowers sprang wanton to be press'd,
  The birds sang love on every spray—
Till too, too soon, the glowing west
  Proclaim'd the speed of wingèd day.

* See LIFE. These verses were transmitted to Johnston with a request that they should be set to the above air. They are, however, now generally sung to the tune "Mary's Dream," which will be found at page 124.

Still o'er these scenes my memory wakes,
  And fondly broods with miser care!
Time but the impression stronger makes,
  As streams their channels deeper wear.
My Mary! dear departed shade!
  Where is thy place of blissful rest?
Seest thou thy lover lowly laid?
  Hear'st thou the groans that rend his breast?

FROM DR. BLACKLOCK.
EDINBURGH, 24*th August*, 1789.

DEAR Burns, thou brother of my heart,
Both for thy virtues and thy art;
If art it may be call'd in thee,
Which Nature's bounty, large and free,
With pleasure in thy breast diffuses,
And warms thy soul with all the Muses.
Whether to laugh with easy grace,
Thy numbers move the sage's face,
Or bid the softer passions rise,
And ruthless souls with grief surprise,
'Tis Nature's voice distinctly felt,
Through thee, her organ, thus to melt.
  Most anxiously I wish to know
With thee of late how matters go;
How keeps thy much-loved Jean her health?
What promises thy farm of wealth?
Whether the Muse persists to smile,
And all thy anxious cares beguile?
Whether bright fancy keeps alive?
And how thy darling infants thrive?
  For me, with grief and sickness spent,
Since I my journey homeward bent,
Spirits depress'd no more I mourn,
But vigour, life, and health return.
No more to gloomy thoughts a prey,
I sleep all night, and live all day;
By turns my book and friend enjoy,
And thus my circling hours employ:
Happy while yet these hours remain,
If Burns could join the cheerful train,
With wonted zeal, sincere and fervent,
Salute once more his humble servant,
                THOS. BLACKLOCK.

TO DR. BLACKLOCK,
IN ANSWER TO THE PRECEDING EPISTLE.
ELLISLAND, 21*st October*, 1789.

Wow, but your letter made me vauntie!
And are ye hale, and weel, and cantie?
I ken'd it still, your wee bit jauntie
    Wad bring ye to:
Lord send you aye as weel 's I want ye,
    And then ye'll do.

The ill-thief blaw the Heron south!
And never drink be near his drouth!
He tauld mysel' by word o' mouth,
    He'd tak my letter;
I lippen'd to the chiel in truth,
    And bade nae better

But aiblins honest Master Heron[*]
Had, at the time, some dainty fair one
To ware his theologic care on,
    And holy study;
And tired o' sauls to waste his lear on,
    E'en tried the body.

But what d' ye think, my trusty fier,
I'm turn'd a gauger—Peace be here!
Parnassian queans, I fear, I fear,
    Ye'll now disdain me!
And then my fifty pounds a year
    Will little gain me.

Ye glaiket, gleesome, dainty damies,
Wha, by Castalia's wimplin' streamies,
Loup, sing, and lave your pretty limbies,
    Ye ken, ye ken,
That strang necessity supreme is
    'Mang sons o' men.

I hae a wife and twa wee laddies,
They maun hae brose and brats o' duddies;
Ye ken yoursel's my heart right proud is—
    I need na vaunt—
But I'll sned bosoms, thraw saugh woodies,
    Before they want.

Lord, help me through this warld o' care!
I'm weary sick o't late and air!
Not but I hae a richer share
    Than mony ithers;
But why should ae man better fare,
    And a' men brithers?

Come, firm Resolve! take thou the van,
Thou stalk o' carl-hemp in man!
And let us mind, faint heart ne'er wan
    A lady fair;
Wha does the utmost that he can,
    Will whyles do mair.

---

[*] "Heron:" author of a Life of Burns and other works. An unfortunate man.

But to conclude my silly rhyme,
(I 'm scant o' verse, and scant o' time),
To make a happy fireside clime
    To weans and wife,
That 's the true pathos and sublime
    Of human life.

My compliments to sister Beckie,
And eke the same to honest Lucky;
I wat she is a dainty chuckie,
    As e'er tread clay!
And gratefully, my guid auld cockie,
    I 'm yours for aye.
                  ROBERT BURNS.

ON THE LATE CAPTAIN GROSE'S*

PEREGRINATIONS THROUGH SCOTLAND, COLLECTING THE ANTIQUITIES OF THAT KINGDOM.

HEAR, Land o' Cakes, and brither Scots,
Frae Maidenkirk to Johnny Groat's;
If there 's a hole in a' your coats,
    I rede you tent it:
A chiel 's amang you takin' notes,
    And, faith! he 'll prent it.

If in your bounds ye chance to light
Upon a fine, fat, fodgel wight,
O' stature short, but genius bright,
    That 's he, mark weel;
And wow! he has an unco slight
    O' cauk and keel.

* Francis Grose, an Englishman who had seen better days, and betaken himself to authorship. He wrote works on Antiquities, was fat in person, small in stature, and, as Dominie Sampson says, "very facetious."

By some auld, houlet-haunted biggin',
Or kirk deserted by its riggin',
It's ten to ane ye'll find him snug in
    Some eldritch part,
Wi' deils, they say, L—d save 's! colleaguin'
    At some black art.

Ilk ghaist that haunts auld ha' or chaumer,
Ye gipsy-gang that deal in glamour,
And you, deep-read in hell's black grammar,
    Warlocks and witches;
Ye'll quake at his conjuring hammer,
    Ye midnight bitches.

It's tauld he was a sodger bred,
And ane wad rather fa'n than fled;
But now he's quat the spurtle blade,
    And dog-skin wallet,
And ta'en the—Antiquarian trade,
    I think they call it.

He has a fouth o' auld nick-nackets:
Rusty airn caps and jinglin' jackets,
Wad haud the Lothians three in tackets,
    A towmont guid;
And parritch-pats, and auld saut-backets,
    Before the Flood.

Of Eve's first fire he has a cinder;
Auld Tubal-Cain's fire-shool and fender;
That which distinguishèd the gender
    O' Balaam's ass;
A broom-stick o' the witch o' Endor,
    Weel shod wi' brass.

Forbye, he'll shape you aff, fu' gleg,
The cut of Adam's philibeg;
The knife that nicket Abel's craig,
    He'll prove you fully,
It was a faulding jocteleg
    Or lang-kail gullie.

But wad ye see him in his glee,
For meikle glee and fun has he,
Then set him down, and twa or three
    Guid fellows wi' him;
And port, O port! shine thou a wee,
    And then ye'll see him!

Now, by the powers o' verse and prose,
Thou art a dainty chiel, O Grose!
Whae'er o' thee shall ill suppose,
    They sair misca' thee;
I'd take the rascal by the nose,
    Wad say, Shame fa' thee!

ON CAPTAIN FRANCIS GROSE, THE CELEBRATED ANTIQUARIAN.

The Devil got notice that Grose was a-dying,
So whip! at the summons old Satan came flying;
But when he approach'd where poor Francis lay moaning,
And saw each bed-post with its burden a-groaning,
Astonish'd, confounded, cried Satan, "By ——,
I'll want 'im, ere I take such a damnable load!"

KEN YE OUGHT O' CAPTAIN GROSE,*

WRITTEN IN A WRAPPER INCLOSING A LETTER TO CAPTAIN GROSE, TO BE LEFT WITH MR. CARDONNEL, ANTIQUARIAN.

Slow.   Tune—"Sir John Malcolm."

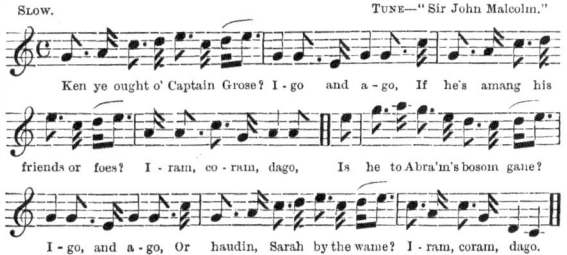

Is he south or is he north?
    Igo, and ago,
Or drownèd in the river Forth?
    Iram, coram, dago.

Is he slain by Highland bodies?
    Igo, and ago,
And eaten like a wether-haggis?
    Iram, coram, dago.

Where'er he be, the Lord be near him!
    Igo, and ago,
As for the Deil, he daur na steer him.
    Iram, coram, dago.

But please transmit th' inclosed letter,
    Igo, and ago,
Which will oblige your humble debtor.
    Iram, coram, dago.

So may you hae auld stanes in store,
    Igo, and ago,
The very stanes that Adam bore.
    Iram, coram, dago.

So may ye get in glad possession,
    Igo, and ago,
The coins o' Satan's corónation!
    Iram, coram, dago.

* See Life.

THE LADDIES BY THE BANKS O' NITH.
AN ELECTION BALLAD.

Slow.   Tune—"Up an' Warn a'."

The laddies by the banks o' Nith Wad trust his Grace* wi' a', Jamie;† But he'll sair them as he sair'd the King—Turn tail and rin awa', Jamie.

Chorus—*Up and waur them a', Jamie, Up and waur them a'; The Johnstones hae the guid-in' o't, Ye turn-coat Whigs, awa'!*

The day he stude his country's friend,
  Or gied her faes a claw, Jamie,
Or frae puir man a blessin' wan,
  That day the Duke ne'er saw, Jamie.
    Up and waur, &c.

But wha is he, his country's boast?
  Like him there is na twa, Jamie;
There's no a callant tents the kye,
  But kens o' Westerha', Jamie.
    Up and waur, &c.

To end the wark, here's Whistlebirk,‡
  Lang may his whistle blaw, Jamie;
And Maxwell true, o' sterling blue,
  And we'll be Johnstones a', Jamie.
    Up and waur, &c.

THE FIVE CARLINS.§
AN ELECTION BALLAD.

Very Slow.   Tune—"Chevy Chace."

There was five Carlins in the South, They fell upon a scheme To send a lad to Lon-'on town, To bring them tidings hame. Nor only bring them tidings hame, But do their errands there; And aib-lins gowd and honour baith Might be that laddie's share.

* The Duke of Queensberry had voted with the Whig Party against the king, and for the Prince of Wales, in the great struggle for the regency.
† "Jamie:" Sir James Johnstone of Westerhall, the sitting member. "The Johnstones hae the guidin' o't," an old Border proverb.
‡ "Whistlebirk:" Alexander Birkwhistle, a merchant and provost of Kirkcudbright.
§ See Life.

There was Maggy by the banks o' Nith,*
  A dame wi' pride eneugh;
And Marjory o' the mony Lochs,†
  A carlin auld and teugh.

And Blinkin' Bess o' Annandale, ‡
  That dwelt near Solway side,
And whisky Jean that took her gill,
  In Galloway § sae wide.

And black Joan, frae Crichton Peel, ||
  O' gipsy kith and kin:
Five wighter Carlins were na foun'
  The south countrie within.

To send a lad to Lon'on town,
  They met upon a day,
And mony a knight, and mony a laird,
  This errand fain wad gae.

O mony a knight and mony a laird
  This errand fain wad gae;
But nae ane could their fancy please,
  O ne'er a ane but twae.

The first ane was a belted knight,¶
  Bred o' a Border clan,
And he would gae to Lon'on town,
  Might nae man him withstan'.

And he wad do their errands weel,
  And meikle he wad say,
And ilka ane at Lon'on court,
  Would bid to him guid-day.

Then next came in a sodger youth,**
  And spak wi' modest grace,
And he wad gae to Lon'on town,
  If sae their pleasure was.

He wadna hecht them courtly gifts,
  Nor meikle speech pretend,
But he wad hecht an honest heart,
  Wad ne'er desert his friend.

Now, wham to choose, and wham refuse,
  At strife thir Carlins fell;
For some had gentle folks to please,
  And some wad please themsel'.

Then out spak mim-mou'd Meg o' Nith,
  And she spak up wi' pride,
And she wad send the sodger youth,
  Whatever might betide.

* "Nith:" Dumfries.   † "Mony Lochs:" Lochmaben
‡ "Annandale:" Annan.   § "Galloway:" Kirkcudbright
|| "Crichton Peel:' Sanquhar. ¶ "Belted knight:" Sir J. Johnstone
** "Sodger youth:" Major Miller.

For the auld Guidman o' Lon'on court*
  She didna care a pin;
But she wad send the sodger youth
  To greet his eldest son.†

Then up sprang Bess o' Annandale,
  And a deadly aith she 's ta'en,
That she wad vote the Border Knight,
  Though she should vote her lane.

For far-aff fowls hae feathers fair,
  And fools o' change are fain;
But I hae tried the Border Knight,
  And I 'll try him yet again.

Says black Joan frae Crichton Peel,
  A Carlin stoor and grim,
The auld Guidman, and the young Guidman,
  For me may sink or swim!

For fools will freit o' right or wrang,
  While knaves laugh them to scorn;
But the sodger's friends hae blawn the best,
  So he shall bear the horn.

Then whisky Jean spak owre her drink,
  Ye weel ken, kimmers a',
The auld Guidman o' Lon'on court,
  His back 's been at the wa';

And mony a friend that kiss'd his caup
  Is now a fremit wight:
But it 's ne'er be said o' whisky Jean—
  We 'll send the Border Knight.

Then slow raise Marjory o' the Lochs,
  And wrinkled was her brow;
Her ancient weed was russet gray,
  Her auld Scots bluid was true:

There 's some great folk set light by me—
  I set as light by them;
But I will sen' to Lon'on town
  Wham I like best at hame.

Sae how this weighty plea may end,
  Nae mortal wight can tell:
God grant the King and ilka man
  May look weel to himsel'.

  * "London court:" George III.
  † "Eldest son:" the Prince of Wales.

SKETCH—NEW YEAR'S DAY (1790).

TO MRS. DUNLOP.

This day Time winds th' exhausted chain,
To run the twelvemonth's length again:
I see the old, bald-pated fellow,
With ardent eyes, complexion sallow,
Adjust the unimpair'd machine,
To wheel the equal, dull routine.

The absent lover, minor heir,
In vain assail him with their prayer;
Deaf as my friend, he sees them press,
Nor makes the hour one moment less.
Will you (the Major‡ 's with the hounds,
The happy tenants share his rounds;
Coila's fair Rachel's§ care to-day,
And blooming Keith's engaged with Gray)
From housewife cares a minute borrow,
(That grandchild's cap will do to-morrow),
And join with me a-moralizing;
This day 's propitious to be wise in.

First, what did yesternight deliver?
"Another year has gone for ever."
And what is this day's strong suggestion?
"The passing moment 's all we rest on!"
Rest on—for what? what do we here?
Or why regard the passing year?
Will Time, amus'd with proverb'd lore,
Add to our date one minute more?
A few days may—a few years must—
Repose us in the silent dust.
Then, is it wise to damp our bliss?
Yes—all such reasonings are amiss!
The voice of Nature loudly cries,
And many a message from the skies,
That something in us never dies:
That on this frail, uncertain state,
Hang matters of eternal weight.
That future life in worlds unknown
Must take its hue from this alone;
Whether—as heavenly glory bright,
Or dark as Misery's woeful night.

Since then, my honour'd first of friends,
On this poor being all depends;
Let us th' important *now* employ,
And live as those who never die.
Though you, with days and honours crown'd
Witness that filial circle round,
(A sight life's sorrows to repulse,
A sight pale Envy to convulse),
Others now claim your chief regard;
Yourself, you wait your bright reward.

  ‡ "The Major:" afterwards General Dunlop of Dunlop.
  § "Rachel:" this young lady, daughter of Mrs. Dunlop, was drawing a picture of Coila from "The Vision."

I GAED A WAEFU' GATE YESTREEN.

SLOWISH. TUNE—"My only Joe and Dearie, O."

I gaed a wae-fu' gate yestreen, A gate, I fear, I'll dearly rue;
I gat my death frae twa sweet een, Twa lovely een o' bonnie blue.
'Twas not her golden ringlets bright; Her lips like roses wat wi' dew,
Her heaving bo-som, lily-white; It was her een sae bonnie blue.

She talk'd, she smil'd, my heart she wyl'd;
   She charm'd my soul I wist na how;
And aye the stound, the deadly wound,
   Cam frae her een sae bonnie blue.
But "spare to speak, and spare to speed;"
   She 'll aiblins listen to my vow:
Should she refuse, I 'll lay my dead
   To her twa een sae bonnie blue.*

---

* "Blue-eyed lass:" daughter of Rev. Mr. Jeffrey of Lochmaben married a Mr. Renwick of New York, and in 1822, when met by a son of George Thomson, Burns' friend, her eyes were as blue and bright as ever, and she talked of Burns with great respect and affection. Her memoirs, with a volume of her writings, were published after her death.

WHEN FIRST I SAW FAIR JEANIE'S FACE.

LIVELY. Tune—"Maggy Lauder."

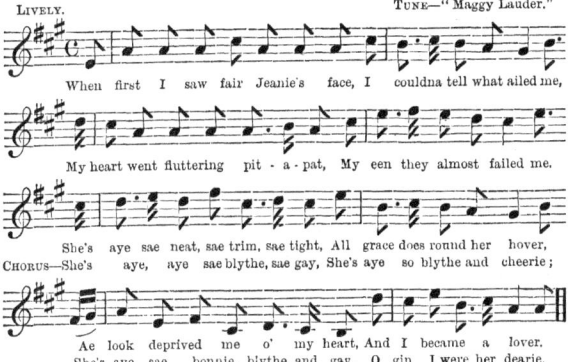

When first I saw fair Jeanie's face, I couldna tell what ailed me,
My heart went fluttering pit-a-pat, My een they almost failed me.
She's aye sae neat, sae trim, sae tight, All grace does round her hover,
Ae look deprived me o' my heart, And I became a lover.

CHORUS—She's aye, aye sae blythe, sae gay, She's aye so blythe and cheerie;
She's aye sae bonnie, blythe, and gay, O gin I were her dearie.

Had I Dundas's whole estate,
  Or Hopetoun's wealth to shine in;
Did warlike laurels crown my brow,
  Or humbler bays entwining—
I'd lay them a' at Jeanie's feet,
  Could I but hope to move her,
And prouder than a belted knight,
  I'd be my Jeanie's lover.
    She's aye, aye sae blythe, &c.

But sair I fear some happier swain
  Has gained sweet Jeanie's favour:
If so, may every bliss be hers,
  Though I maun never have her.
But gang she east, or gang she west,
  'Twixt Forth and Tweed all over,
While men have eyes, or ears, or taste,
  She'll always find a lover.
    She's aye, aye sae blythe, &c.

PROLOGUE SPOKEN AT THE THEATRE, DUMFRIES,

ON NEW YEAR'S EVENING, 1790.

No song nor dance I bring from yon great city
That queens it o'er our taste—the more's the pity:
Though, by the by, abroad why will ye roam?
Good sense and taste are natives here at home.
But not for panegyric I appear,
I come to wish you all a good New Year!
Old Father Time deputes me here before ye,
Not for to preach, but tell his simple story:
The sage grave Ancient cough'd, and bade me say—
"You're one year older this important day;"
If *wiser too*—he hinted some suggestion,
But 'twould be rude, you know, to ask the question;
And with a would-be roguish leer and wink,
He bade me on you press this one word—"*Think!*"
Ye sprightly youths, quite flush with hope and spirit,
Who think to storm the world by dint of merit!
To you the dotard has a deal to say,
In his sly, dry, sententious, proverb way.
He bids you mind, amid your thoughtless rattle,
That the first blow is ever half the battle;
That though some by the skirt may try to snatch him,
Yet by the forelock is the hold to catch him;
That whether doing, suffering, or forbearing,
You may do miracles by persevering.
  Last, though not least in love, ye youthful fair,
Angelic forms, high Heaven's peculiar care!
To you old Bald-pate smoothes his wrinkled brow,
And humbly begs you'll mind the important *Now!*
To crown your happiness he asks your leave,
And offers bliss to give and to receive.
  For our sincere, though haply weak endeavours,
With grateful pride we own your many favours;
And howsoe'er our tongues may ill reveal it,
Believe our glowing bosoms truly feel it.

PROLOGUE

FOR MR. SUTHERLAND'S BENEFIT-NIGHT, DUMFRIES.

WHAT needs this din about the town o' Lon'on,
How this new play and that new sang is comin'?
Why is outlandish stuff sae meikle courted?
Does nonsense mend, like whisky, when imported?
Is there nae poet, burning keen for fame,
Will try to gie us sangs and plays at hame?
For Comedy abroad he needna toil,
A fool and knave are plants of every soil;
Nor need he hunt as far as Rome and Greece
To gather matter for a serious piece;
There's themes enow in Caledonian story,
Would show the Tragic Muse in a' her glory.
  Is there no daring bard will rise, and tell
How glorious Wallace stood, how hapless fell?
Where are the Muses fled that could produce
A drama worthy o' the name o' Bruce?
How here, even here, he first unsheath'd the sword
'Gainst mighty England and her guilty lord;
And after mony a bloody, deathless doing,
Wrench'd his dear country from the jaws of ruin?
O, for a Shakspeare or an Otway scene,
To draw the lovely, hapless Scottish Queen!
Vain all th' omnipotence of female charms
'Gainst headlong, ruthless, mad Rebellion's arms.
She fell, but fell with spirit truly Roman,
To glut the vengeance of a rival woman;
A woman—though the phrase may seem uncivil—
As able and as cruel as the Devil!

One Douglas lives in Home's immortal page,
But Douglasses were heroes every age:
And though your fathers, prodigal of life,
A Douglas follow'd to the martial strife,
Perhaps, if bowls row right, and Right succeeds,
Ye yet may follow where a Douglas leads!

As ye hae generous done, if a' the land
Would take the Muses' servants by the hand;
Not only hear, but patronize, befriend them,
And where ye justly can commend, commend them:
And aiblins when they winna stand the test,
Wink hard, and say the folks hae done their best!
Would a' the land do this, then I'll be caution
Ye 'll soon hae poets o' the Scottish nation
Will gar Fame blaw until her trumpet crack,
And warsle Time, an' lay him on his back!

For us, and for our Stage, should ony spier
"Whase aught thae chiels maks a' this bustle here?"
My best leg foremost, I'll set up my brow,
We have the honour to belong to you!
We're your ain bairns, e'en guide us as ye like,
But, like good mithers, shore before ye strike.
And gratefu' still I hope ye 'll ever find us,
For a' the patronage and meikle kindness
We 've got frae a' professions, sets, and ranks;
God help us! we 're but poor—ye 'se get but thanks.

A NEW PSALM FOR THE CHAPEL OF KILMARNOCK,

ON THE THANKSGIVING-DAY FOR HIS MAJESTY'S * RECOVERY.

O SING a new song to the Lord,
   Make, all and every one,
A joyful noise, even for the king
   His restoration.

The sons of Belial in the land
   Did set their heads together;
Come, let us sweep them off, said they
   Like an o'erflowing river.

They set their heads together, I say,
   They set their heads together;
On right, on left, and every hand,
   We saw none to deliver.

Thou madest strong two chosen ones,
   To quell the Wicked's pride;
That Young Man, great in Issachar,
   The burden-bearing tribe:

And him, among the Princes, chief
   In our Jerusalem,
The judge that's mighty in thy law,
   The man that fears thy name.

Yet they, even they, with all their strength,
   Began to faint and fail;
Even as two howling, ravenous wolves
   To dogs do turn their tail.

Th' ungodly o'er the just prevail'd,
   For so thou hadst appointed;
That thou might'st greater glory give
   Unto thine own anointed.

And now thou hast restored our State,
   Pity our Kirk also;
For she by tribulations
   Is now brought very low.

Consume that high-place Patronage
   From off thy holy hill;
And in thy fury burn the book—
   Even of that man M'Gill.

Now hear our prayer, accept our song,
   And fight thy chosen's battle;
We seek but little, Lord, from thee;
   Thou kens we get as little.

TIBBIE DUNBAR.

TUNE—"Johnny M'Gill."

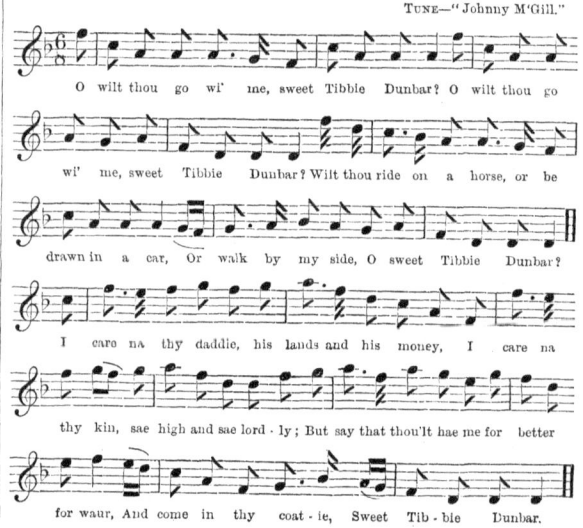

O wilt thou go wi' me, sweet Tibbie Dunbar? O wilt thou go wi' me, sweet Tibbie Dunbar? Wilt thou ride on a horse, or be drawn in a car, Or walk by my side, O sweet Tibbie Dunbar? I care na thy daddie, his lands and his money, I care na thy kin, sae high and sae lord-ly; But say that thou'lt hae me for better for waur, And come in thy coat-ie, Sweet Tib-bie Dunbar.

---

* "George III." went on 23rd April, 1789, to St. Paul's to return thanks for his recovery. These very pompous ceremonies were by no means pleasing to Burns.

WHEN ROSY MAY.*

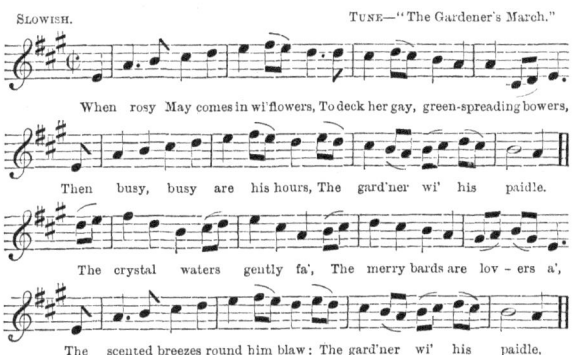

When purple morning starts the hare
To steal upon her early fare,
Then through the dews he maun repair—
  The gardener wi' his paidle.

When day, expiring in the west,
The curtain draws of Nature's rest,
He flies to her arms he lo'es best—
  The gardener wi' his paidle.

MY HARRY WAS A GALLANT GAY.†

When a' the lave gae to their bed,
  I wander dowie up the glen;
I set me down and greet my fill,
  And aye I wish him back again.
    O for him back again, &c.

* Burns produced a new version of this song with different corrections. See CORRESPONDENCE.

† Burns picked up the chorus from an old woman in Dunblane. He understood it in a Jacobite sense. It is said, however, to be founded on an old love story in Aberdeenshire. We remember the chorus happily applied by the *Spectator* to Lord Brougham when he had retired for a season from public life.

O, were some villains hangit high,
  And ilka body had their ain!
Then I might see the joyfu' sight,
  My Highland Harry back again.
    O for him back again, &c.

HER DADDIE FORBAD.

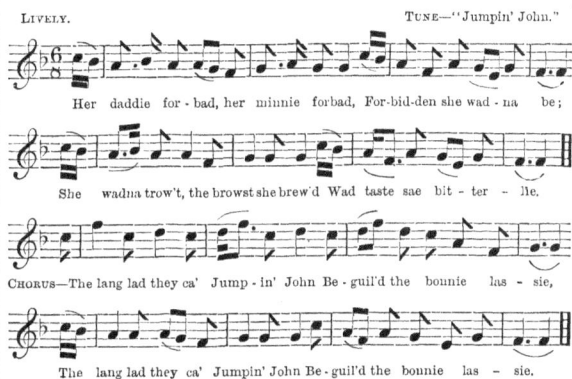

A cow and a cauf, a yowe and a hauf,
  And thretty gude shillin's and three;
A vera gude tocher, a cottar-man's dochter,
  The lass wi' the bonnie black e'e.
    The lang lad they ca', &c.

HAPPY FRIENDSHIP.

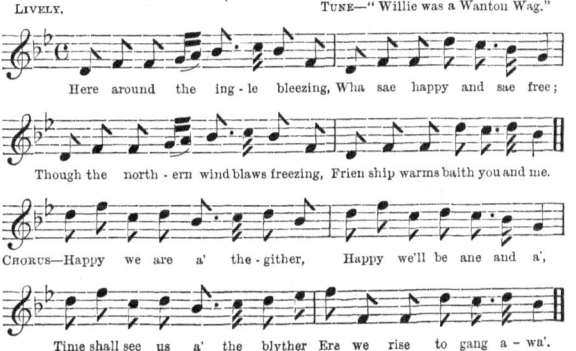

See the miser o'er his treasure
　Gloating wi' a greedy e'e !
Can he feel the glow o' pleasure
　That around us here we see ?
　　Happy we are a' thegither, &c.

Can the peer, in silk and ermine,
　Ca' his conscience half his own ;
His claes are spun an' edged wi' vermin,
　Though he stan' afore a throne !
　　Happy we are a' thegither, &c.

Thus, then, let us a' be tassing
　Aff our stoups o' generous flame ;
An' while roun' the board 'tis passing,
　Raise a sang in frien'ship's name.
　　Happy we are a' thegither, &c.

Frien'ship maks us a' mair happy,
　Frien'ship gies us a' delight ;
Frien'ship consecrates the drappie,
　Frien'ship brings us here to-night.
　　Happy we are a' thegither, &c

JOHN ANDERSON, MY JO.

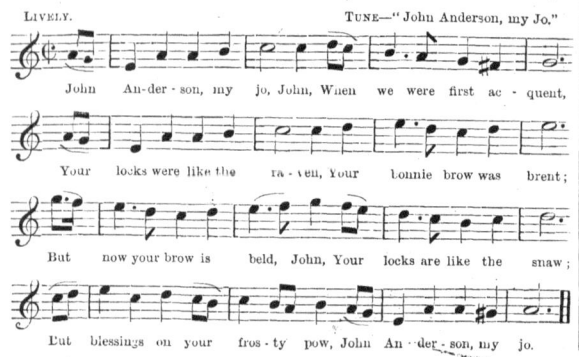

John Anderson, my jo, John,
　We clamb the hill thegither ;
And mony a canty day, John,
　We 've had wi' ane anither :

Now we maun totter down, John,
　But hand in hand we 'll go ;
And sleep thegither at the foot,
　John Anderson, my jo.*

* These are the only stanzas written by Burns. "John Anderson" was originally a loose song ; it was then adapted in derision to the tenets of the Roman Catholic church : it is now the most beautiful expression of true and time-tried tenderness in the world.

BEWARE O' BONNIE ANN.*

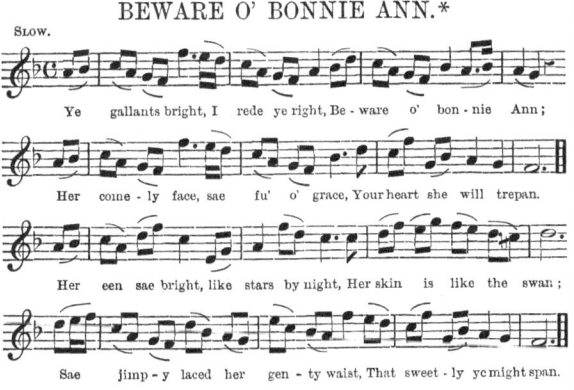

Ye gallants bright, I rede ye right, Beware o' bonnie Ann;
Her comely face, sae fu' o' grace, Your heart she will trepan.
Her een sae bright, like stars by night, Her skin is like the swan;
Sae jimpy laced her genty waist, That sweetly ye might span.
Youth, grace, and love, attendant move,
And pleasure leads the van;
In a' their charms and conquering arms,
They wait on bonnie Ann.
The captive bands may chain the hands,
But love enslaves the man.
Ye gallants braw, I rede ye a',
Beware o' bonnie Ann!

ODE ON THE DEPARTED REGENCY BILL.†

Daughter of Chaos' doting years,
Nurse of ten thousand hopes and fears,

---

* "Bonnie Ann," daughter of Allan Masterton, the third in the symposium when "Willie brew'd a peck o' maut." She became afterwards Mrs. Derbishire, and lived in London. The verses were probably composed during Burns' brief visit to Edinburgh in 1789.

† This poem alludes to Charles Fox and the Portland Party, and their debates with Pitt, and schemings during the illness and on to the "Convalescence" of George III.

Whether thy airy, unsubstantial shade
(The rights of sepulture now duly paid)
Spread abroad its hideous form
On the roaring civil storm,
Deafening din and warring rage
Factions wild with factions wage;
Or under-ground, deep-sunk, profound,
Among the demons of the earth,
With groans that make the mountains shake,
Thou mourn thy ill-starr'd, blighted birth;
Or in the uncreated Void,
Where seeds of future being fight,
With lessen'd step thou wander wide,
To greet thy Mother—Ancient Night,
And as each jarring, monster-mass is past,
Fond recollect what once thou wast:
In manner due, beneath this sacred oak,
Hear, Spirit, hear! thy presence I invoke!
  By a Monarch's heaven-struck fate,
  By a disunited State,
  By a generous Prince's wrongs,
  By a Senate's strife of tongues,
  By a Premier's sullen pride,
  Louring on the changing tide;
  By dread Thurlow's powers to awe—
  Rhetoric, blasphemy, and law;
  By the turbulent ocean,
  A Nation's commotion,
  By the harlot-caresses
  Of borough addresses,
  By days few and evil,
  (Thy portion, poor devil!)
By Power, Wealth, and Show,
  (The gods by men adored),
By nameless Poverty,
  (Their hell abhorred),
  By all they hope, by all they fear,
  Hear! and Appear!

Stare not on me, thou ghastly Power!
Nor, grim with chained defiance, lour:
No Babel-structure would *I* build
  Where, order exil'd from his native sway,
Confusion may the *Regent*-sceptre wield,
  While all would rule and none obey:
  Go, to the world of Man relate
  The story of thy sad, eventful fate;
  And call presumptuous Hope to hear,
  And bid him check his blind career;
  And tell the sore-prest sons of Care,
    Never, never to despair!

Paint Charles's speed on wings of fire,
The object of his fond desire,
Beyond his boldest hopes, at hand:
Paint all the triumph of the Portland Band;

Mark how they lift the joy-exulting voice,
And how their num'rous creditors rejoice;
But just as hopes to warm enjoyment rise,
Cry *Convalescence!* and the vision flies.

Then next pourtray a dark'ning twilight gloom,
  Eclipsing sad a gay, rejoicing morn,
While proud Ambition to th' untimely tomb
  By gnashing, grim, despairing fiends is borne:

Paint ruin, in the shape of high D[undas]
  Gaping with giddy terror o'er the brow;
In vain he struggles, the fates behind him press,
  And clam'rous hell yawns for her prey below:
How fallen *That*, whose pride late scaled the skies!
And *This*, like Lucifer, no more to rise!
Again pronounce the powerful word;
See Day, triumphant from the night, restored.

Then know this truth, ye Sons of Men!
  (Thus ends thy moral tale),
Your darkest terrors may be vain,
  Your brightest hopes may fail.

THE LASS OF ECCLEFECHAN.

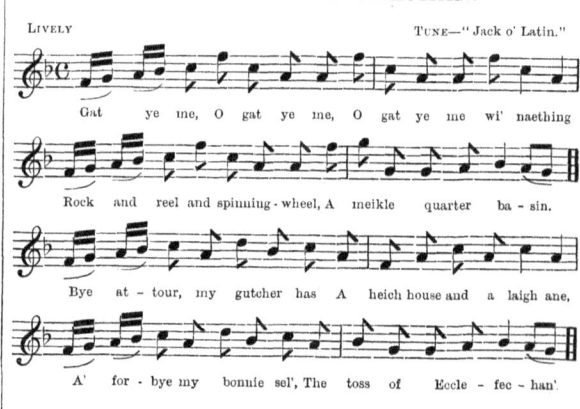

O haud your tongue now, Luckie Lang,
  O haud your tongue and jauner;
I held the gate till you I met,
  Syne I began to wander:
I tint my whistle and my sang,
  I tint my peace and pleasure;
But your green graff, now, Luckie Lang,
  Wad airt me to my treasure.

THE CAPTAIN'S LADY.

TUNE—"Mount your Baggage."

CHORUS—O mount and go, mount and make you ready, O mount and go, and be the Captain's Lady. When the drums do beat, and the cannons rattle, Thou shalt sit in state, and see thy love in battle: When the drums do beat, and the cannons rattle, Thou shalt sit in state, and see thy love in battle.

When the vanquish'd foe sues for peace and quiet,
To the shades we'll go, and in love enjoy it:
When the vanquish'd foe sues for peace and quiet,
To the shades we'll go, and in love enjoy it.
    O mount and go, &c.

ON THE BATTLE OF SHERIFF-MUIR,*

BETWEEN THE DUKE OF ARGYLE AND THE EARL OF MAR.

TUNE—"The Camerons' Rant."

"O can ye here the fight to shun, Or herd the sheep wi' me, man? Or were ye at the Sherra-muir, Or did the battle see, man?" "I saw the battle, sair and teugh, And reekin-red ran mony a sheugh; My heart, for fear, gaed sough for sough, To hear the thuds, and see the cluds O' clans frae woods, in tartan duds, Wha glaum'd at kingdoms three, man.

CHORUS—La, la, la, la, la, la, la, la, la, la, la, la, la, la, da.
La, la, la, la, la, la, la, la, la, la, la, la, la, da.

"The red-coat lads, wi' black cockauds,
  To meet them were na slaw, man;

---

* This is founded on an old song by Barclay the Berean, originally parish minister of Fettercairn, but who became a Berean, and preached to an immense congregation in Sauchieburn, in the neighbourhood—a very remarkable man.

They rush'd and push'd, and bluid outgush'd,
  And mony a bouk did fa, man:
The great Argyle led on his files,
I wat they glanc'd for twenty miles:
They houghed the clans like nine-pin kyles
They hack'd and hash'd, while broadswords clash'd,
And through they dash'd, and hew'd and smash'd,
  Till fey men died awa', man.
    La, la, la, la, &c.

"But had you seen the philabegs,
  And skyrin tartan trews, man,
When in the teeth they dared our Whigs,
  And Covenant true-blues, man;
In lines extended lang and large,
When bayonets opposed the targe,
And thousands hasten'd to the charge,
Wi' Highland wrath they frae the sheath
Drew blades o' death, till, out o' breath,
  They fled like frighted doos, man."
    La, la, la, la, &c.

"O how deil, Tam, can that be true?
  The chase gaed frae the north, man:
I saw, mysel', they did pursue
  The horsemen back to Forth, man;
And at Dunblane, in my ain sight,
They took the brig wi' a' their might,
And straught to Stirling wing'd their flight;
But cursèd lot! the gates were shut,
And mony a hunted, poor red-coat,
  For fear amaist did swarf, man."
    La, la, la, la, &c.

"My sister Kate cam up the gate
  Wi' crowdie unto me, man;
She swore she saw some rebels run
  To Perth and to Dundee, man:
Their left hand general had nae skill,
The Angus lads had nae good-will
That day their neibours' blood to spill;
For fear, by foes, that they should lose
Their cogs o' brose, they scar'd at blows,
  And hameward fast did flee, man."
    La, la, la, la, &c.

"They've lost some gallant gentlemen
  Amang the Highland clans, man;
I fear my Lord Panmure is slain,
  Or fallen in Whiggish hands, man.
Now wad ye sing this double flight,
Some fell for wrang and some for right;
But mony bade the world guid-night;
Say, pell and mell, wi' muskets' knell
How Tories fell, and Whigs to hell,
  Flew off in frighted bands, man!
    La, la, la, la, &c.

BLOOMING NELLY.

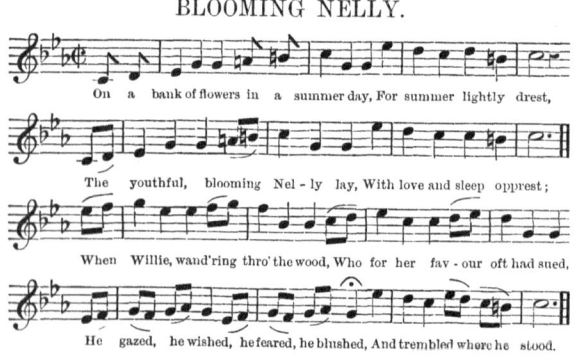

On a bank of flowers in a summer day, For summer lightly drest,
The youthful, blooming Nelly lay, With love and sleep opprest;
When Willie, wand'ring thro' the wood, Who for her favour oft had sued,
He gazed, he wished, he feared, he blushed, And trembled where he stood.

Her closèd eyes, like weapons sheathed,
  Were sealed in soft repose;
Her lip, still as she fragrant breathed,
  It richer dyed the rose.
The springing lilies, sweetly prest,
  Wild-wanton, kissed her rival breast;
He gazed, he wished, he feared, he blushed—
  His bosom ill at rest.

Her robes light waving in the breeze,
  Her tender limbs embrace;
Her lovely form, her native ease,
  All harmony and grace:
Tumultuous tides his pulses roll,
  A faltering, ardent kiss he stole;
He gazed, he wished, he feared, he blushed,
  And sighed his very soul.

As flies the partridge from the brake
  On fear-inspirèd wings,
So Nelly starting, half awake,
  Away affrighted springs:
But Willy followed, as he should;
  He overtook her in the wood;
He vowed, he prayed, he found the maid
  Forgiving all and good.

MY HEART'S IN THE HIGHLANDS.*

Farewell to the Highlands, farewell to the North,
The birth-place of valour, the country of worth;
Wherever I wander, wherever I rove,
The hills of the Highlands for ever I love.

Farewell to the mountains, high cover'd with snow;
Farewell to the straths and green valleys below:
Farewell to the forests and wild-hanging woods;
Farewell to the torrents and loud-pouring floods.

* An old song enlarged. Instead of the tune, "Failte na Miosg," originally set to this song, a much finer one, "Crochallan," is here substituted, to which it is now usually sung.

PEG NICHOLSON.†

Peg Nicholson was a good bay mare,
   As ever trod on airn;
But now she's floating down the Nith,
   And past the mouth o' Cairn.

Peg Nicholson was a good bay mare,
   And rode through thick and thin;
But now she's floating down the Nith,
   And wanting even the skin.

Peg Nicholson was a good bay mare,
   And ance she bore a priest;
But now she's floating down the Nith,
   For Solway fish a feast.

Peg Nicholson was a good bay mare,
   And the priest he rode her sair;
And much oppress'd and bruised she was,
   As priest-rid cattle are.

† "Peg Nicholson:" a name derived from the maniac, Margaret Nicholson, who attempted the life of George III.; she was the poet's mare, and the successor of Jenny Geddes, and was either sold or lent to him by William Nicol.

TAM GLEN.*

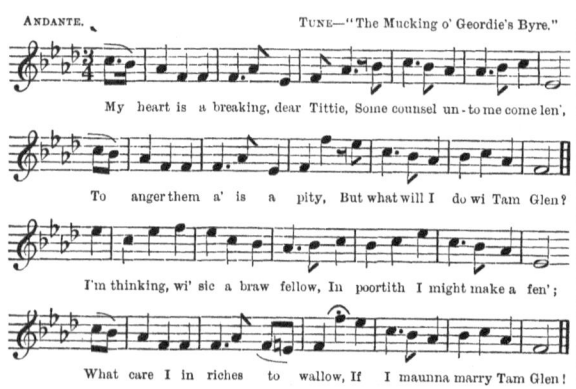

My heart is a breaking, dear Tittie, Some counsel un-to me come len',
To anger them a' is a pity, But what will I do wi Tam Glen?
I'm thinking, wi' sic a braw fellow, In poortith I might make a fen';
What care I in riches to wallow, If I maunna marry Tam Glen?

There 's Lowrie, the laird o' Drumeller,
  "Guid day to you, brute!" he comes ben;
He brags and he blaws o' his siller,
  But when will he dance like Tam Glen?

My minnie does constantly deave me,
  And bids me beware o' young men;
They flatter, she says, to deceive me,
  But wha can think sae o' Tam Glen?

My daddie says, gin I 'll forsake him,
  He 'll gie me guid hunder marks ten:
But, if it 's ordain'd I maun take him,
  O, wha will I get but Tam Glen?

Yestreen at the Valentines' dealing,
  My heart to my mou' gied a sten;
For thrice I drew ane without failing,
  And thrice it was written "Tam Glen!"

The last Hallowe'en I was waukin'
  My droukit sark-sleeve, as ye ken;
His likeness cam up the house staukin',
  And the very grey breeks o' Tam Glen!

Come, counsel, dear Tittie! don't tarry;
  I 'll gie ye my bonnie black hen,
Gif ye will advise me to marry
  The lad I lo'e dearly—Tam Glen!

---

* Stenhouse says that these verses were adapted to a very ancient air, of which the title "Tam Glen" is all that remains. The verses, however, are now sung to the air, "The Mucking o' Geordie's Byre."

DAMON AND SYLVIA.

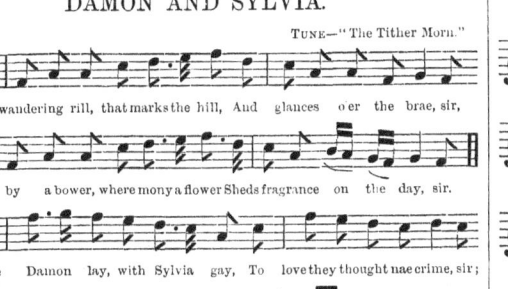

Tune—"The Tither Morn."

Yon wandering rill, that marks the hill, And glances o'er the brae, sir,
Slides by a bower, where mony a flower Sheds fragrance on the day, sir.
There Damon lay, with Sylvia gay, To love they thought nae crime, sir;
The wild birds sang, the echoes rang, While Damon's heart beat time, sir.

THE BANKS OF NITH.

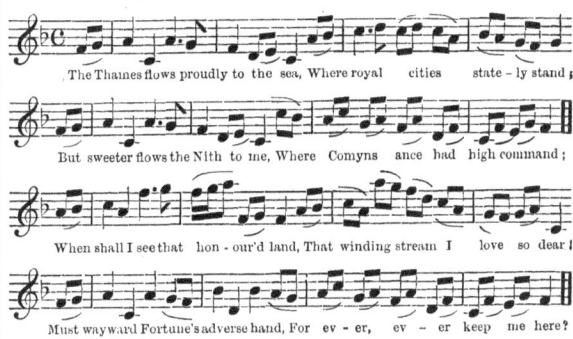

The Thames flows proudly to the sea, Where royal cities stately stand;
But sweeter flows the Nith to me, Where Comyns ance had high command;
When shall I see that honour'd land, That winding stream I love so dear!
Must wayward Fortune's adverse hand, For ever, ever keep me here?

How lovely, Nith, thy fruitful vales,
  Where spreading hawthorns gaily bloom;
How sweetly wind thy sloping dales,
  Where lambkins wanton through the broom!
Though wandering, now, must be my doom,
Far frae thy bonnie banks and braes,
May there my latest hours consume,
Amang the friends of early days!

POEM.

WRITTEN TO A GENTLEMAN WHO HAD SENT HIM A NEWSPAPER, AND OFFERED TO CONTINUE IT FREE OF EXPENSE.

KIND Sir, I've read your paper through,
  And, faith, to me 'twas really new!
How guessed ye, Sir, what maist I wanted?
This mony a day I've grain'd and gaunted,
To ken what French mischief was brewin';
Or what the drumlie Dutch were doin';
That vile doup-skelper, Emperor Joseph,
If Venus yet had got his nose off;
Or how the collieshangie works
Atween the Russians and the Turks;
Or if the Swede, before he halt,
Would play anither Charles the Twalt:
If Denmark, any body spak o't;
Or Poland, wha had now the tack o't;
How cut-throat Prussian blades were hingin';
How libbet Italy was singin';
If Spaniard, Portuguese, or Swiss,
Were sayin' or takin' aught amiss:

Or how our merry lads at hame,
In Britain's court, kept up the game;
How royal George—the Lord leuk o'er him!—
Was managing St. Stephen's quorum;
If sleekit Chatham Will was livin',
Or glaikit Charlie got his nieve in;
How daddie Burke the plea was cookin',
If Warren Hastings' neck was yeukin';
How cesses, stents, and fiars were rax'd
Or if bare a——s yet were tax'd;
The news o' princes, dukes, and earls,
Pimps, sharpers, bawds, and opera-girls;
If that daft buckie, Geordie Wales,
Was threshin' still at hizzies' tails,
Or if he was grown oughtlins douser,
And no a perfect kintra cooser.
A' this and mair I never heard of;
And, but for you, I might despair'd of.
So, gratefu', back your news I send you,
And pray a' guid things may attend you!

NOTE ON THE SAME,

COMPLAINING THAT THE PAPER ABOVE MENTIONED DID NOT COME REGULARLY.

DEAR Peter, dear Peter,*
  We poor sons of metre
Are often negleckit, ye ken;
  For instance, your sheet, man
  (Though glad I'm to see 't, man)
I get it no ae day in ten.

THE BAIRNS GAT OUT.

LIVELY.   TUNE—"The Deuks Dang o'er my Daddie."

The bairns gat out wi' an un-co shout, The deuks dang o'er my daddie, O!
The fient-ma-care, quo' the feirrie auld wife, He was but a paidlin' body, O!
He paidles out, and he paidles in, An' he paidles late and ear-ly, O:
This seven lang years I hae lien by his side, An' he is but a fu-sion-less car-lie, O.

* Mr. Peter Stewart of the *Star*, London, brother of David Stewart, of the *Courier*, Coleridge's friend.

O, haud your tongue, my feirrie auld wife,
  O, haud your tongue now, Nansie, O
I've seen the day, and sae hae ye,
  Ye wadna been sae donsie, O!
I've seen the day ye butter'd my brose,
  And cuddled me late and early, O!
But downa does come o'er me now,
  And, och! I feel it sairly, O!

SECOND EPISTLE TO MR. GRAHAM OF FINTRY.†

FINTRY, my stay in worldly strife,
Friend o' my Muse, friend o' my life!
  Are ye as idle 's I am?
Come, then, wi' uncouth kintra fleg,
O'er Pegasus I'll fling my leg,
  And ye shall see me try him.

But where shall I go rin a ride,
That I may splatter nane beside?
  I wad na be uncivil:
In manhood's various paths and ways
There's aye some doytin body strays,
  And I ride like the devil.

Thus I break aff wi' a' my birr,
An' down yon dark, deep alley spur,
  Where Theologics daunder
Alas! curst wi' eternal fogs,
And damn'd in everlasting bogs,
  As sure 's the Creed I'll blunder!

I'll stain a band, or jaup a gown,
Or rin my reckless, guilty crown
  Against the haly door:
Sair do I rue my luckless fate,
When, as the Muse an' Deil wad hae 't,
  I rade that road before.

Suppose I take a spurt, and mix
Amang the wilds o' Politics—
  Elector and elected,
Where dogs at Court (sad sons of bitches!)
Septennially a madness touches,
  Till all the land's infected.

All hail! Drumlanrig's haughty Grace,
Discarded remnant of a race
  Once godlike—great in story;
Thy forbears' virtues all contrasted,
The very name of Douglas blasted,
  Thine that inverted glory!

† Referring to a contested election between Sir J. Johnstone and Captain Miller for the Dumfries burghs.

Hate, envy, oft the Douglas bore,
But thou hast superadded more,
    And sunk them in contempt;
Follies and crimes have stain'd the name,
But, Queensberry, thine the virgin claim,
    From aught that 's good exempt.

I 'll sing the zeal Drumlanrig* bears,
Who left the all-important cares
    Of princes and their darlings;
And, bent on winning borough towns,
Came shaking hands wi' wabster loons,
    And kissing barefit carlins.

Combustion through our boroughs rode,
Whistling his roaring pack abroad,
    Of mad, unmuzzled lions;
As Queensberry blue and buff unfurl'd,
And Westerha' and Hopetoun † hurl'd
    To every Whig defiance.

But Queensberry, cautious, left the war,
The unmanner'd dust might soil his star,
    Besides, he hated *bleeding;*
But left behind him heroes bright,
Heroes in Cæsarean fight
    Or Ciceronian pleading.

O for a throat like huge Mons-Meg,‡
To muster o'er each ardent Whig
    Beneath Drumlanrig's banners;
Heroes and heroines commix
All in the field of politics,
    To win immortal honours.

M'Murdo ‡ and his lovely spouse
(Th' enamour'd laurels kiss her brows)
    Led on the Loves and Graces;
She won each gaping burgess' heart,
While he, all-conquering, play'd his part,
    Among their wives and lasses.

Craigdarroch ∥ led a light-arm'd corps;
Tropes, metaphors, and figures pour,
    Like Hecla streaming thunder;
Glenriddel,¶ skill'd in rusty coins,
Blew up each Tory's dark designs,
    And bared the treason under.

In either wing two champions fought,
Redoubted Staig, § who set at nought
    The wildest savage Tory,

And Welsh,* who ne'er yet flinch'd his ground,
High waved his magnum bonum round
    With Cyclopean fury.

Miller † brought up th' artillery ranks,
The many-pounders of the Banks,
    Resistless desolation!
While Maxwelton,‡ that baron bold,
'Mid Lawson's port entrench'd his hold,
    And threaten'd worse damnation.

To those what Tory hosts opposed,
With these what Tory warriors closed,
    Surpasses my descriving:
Squadrons, extended long and large,
With furious speed rush'd to the charge,
    Like raging devils driving.

What verse can sing, what prose narrate,
The butcher deeds of bloody Fate
    Amid this mighty tulyie?
Grim Horror girn'd, pale Terror roar'd,
As Murther at his thrapple shored,
    And Hell mix'd in the brulyie?

As Highland crags by thunder cleft,
When lightnings fire the stormy lift,
    Hurl down wi' crashing rattle;
As flames amang a hundred woods;
As headlong foam a hundred floods—
    Such is the rage of battle.

The stubborn Tories dare to die;
As soon the rooted oaks would fly
    Before th' approaching fellers;
The Whigs come on like Ocean's roar,
When all his wintry billows pour
    Against the Buchan Bullers.

Lo, from the shades of Death's deep night,
Departed Whigs enjoy the fight,
    And think on former daring!
The muffled murtherer of Charles
The Magna-Charter flag unfurls,
    All deadly gules its bearing.

Nor wanting ghosts of Tory fame:
Bold Scrimgeour § follows gallant Graham,
    Auld Covenanters shiver:
Forgive, forgive, much-wrong'd Montrose!
While death and hell engulf thy foes,
    Thou liv'st on high for ever!

---

* "Drumlanrig:" second title of the Duke of Queensberry.
† "Hopetoun:" Earl of.
‡ "Mons-Meg:" a piece of ordnance in Edinburgh Castle, founded in the reign of James IV., twenty inches in bore.
§ "M'Murdo:" the duke's chamberlain, friend of Burns.
∥ "Craigdarroch:" Fergusson of.
¶ "Glenriddel:" Captain Riddell.
** "Staig:" Provost of Dumfries.

* "Welsh:" sheriff of the county.
† Miller of Dalswinton, father of the candidate, once a banker
‡ "Maxwelton:" Sir Robert Lawrie, M.P. for the county.
§ "Scrimgeour:" the masked executioner of Charles I.

Still o'er the field the combat burns;
The Tories, Whigs, give way by turns;
    But Fate the word has spoken:
For woman's wit and strength of man
Alas! can do but what they can—
    The Tory ranks are broken.

O that my een were flowing burns!
My voice a lioness that mourns
    Her darling cubs' undoing!
That I might greet, that I might cry,
While Tories fall, while Tories fly,
    And furious Whigs pursuing!

What Whig but wails the good Sir James,
Dear to his country by the names,
    Friend, Patron, Benefactor?
Not Pulteney's wealth can Pulteney save!
And Hopetoun falls, the generous, brave!
    And Stewart,* bold as Hector!

Thou, Pitt, shalt rue this overthrow,
And Thurlow growl a curse of woe,
    And Melville melt in wailing!
Now Fox and Sheridan, rejoice!
And Burke shall sing: "O Prince, arise!
    Thy power is all-prevailing!"

For your poor friend, the Bard, afar
He only hears and sees the war,
    A cool spectator purely;
So when the storm the forest rends,
The robin in the hedge descends,
    And sober chirps securely.

Now, for my friends' and brethren's sakes,
And for my dear-lov'd Land o' Cakes,
    I pray with holy fire:
Lord, send a rough-shod troop o' Hell
O'er a' wad Scotland buy or sell,
    To grind them in the mire!

ELEGY ON CAPTAIN MATTHEW HENDERSON,†
A GENTLEMAN WHO HELD THE PATENT FOR HIS HONOURS IMMEDIATELY FROM ALMIGHTY GOD!

    "But now his radiant course is run,
      For Matthew's course was bright;
    His soul was like the glorious sun,
      A matchless, heavenly light!"

O Death! thou tyrant fell and bloody!
The meikle devil wi' a woodie

---

* Stewart of Hillside.—(B)
† "Captain M. Henderson:" a harmless, old, Edinburgh *bon vivant*, and a great boon companion of Burns', called "Captain" as a pet name. See LIFE.

Haurl thee hame to his black smiddie,
    O'er hurcheon hides,
And like stockfish come o'er his studdie
    Wi' thy auld sides!

He's gane! he's gane! he's frae us torn,
The ae best fellow e'er was born!
Thee, Matthew, Nature's sel' shall mourn
    By wood and wild,
Where, haply, Pity strays forlorn,
    Frae man exiled.

Ye hills, near neibours o' the starns,
That proudly cock your cresting cairns!
Ye cliffs, the haunts of sailing earns,
    Where Echo slumbers!
Come join, ye Nature's sturdiest bairns,
    My wailing numbers!

Mourn, ilka grove the cushat kens!
Ye hazelly shaws and briery dens!
Ye burnies, wimplin' down your glens
    Wi' toddlin' din,
Or foaming strang, wi' hasty stens,
    Frae lin to lin.

Mourn, little harebells o'er the lea;
Ye stately foxgloves, fair to see;
Ye woodbines hanging bonnilie
    In scented bowers;
Ye roses on your thorny tree,
    The first o' flowers.

At dawn, when every grassy blade
Droops with a diamond at its head,
At even, when beans their fragrance shed
    I' the rustling gale,
Ye maukins, whiddin' through the glade,
    Come join my wail!

Mourn, ye wee songsters o' the wood;
Ye grouse that crap the heather bud;
Ye curlews, calling through a clud;
    Ye whistling plover;
And mourn, ye whirring paitrick brood—
    He's gane for ever!

Mourn, sooty coots and speckled teals;
Ye fisher herons, watching eels;
Ye duck and drake, wi' airy wheels
    Circling the lake;
Ye bitterns, till the quagmire reels,
    Rair for his sake!

Mourn, clam'ring craiks at close o' day,
'Mang fields o' flow'ring clover gay;
And when ye wing your annual way
    Frae our cauld shore,
Tell thae far warlds wha lies in clay,
    Wham we deplore.

Ye houlets, frae your ivy bower
In some auld tree or eldritch tower,
What time the moon, wi' silent glower,
    Sets up her horn,
Wail through the dreary midnight hour
    Till waukrife morn!

O rivers, forests, hills, and plains!
Oft have ye heard my canty strains:
But now, what else for me remains
    But tales of woe?
And frae my een the drapping rains
    Maun ever flow.

Mourn, Spring, thou darling of the year!
Ilk cowslip cup shall kep a tear:
Thou, Simmer, while each corny spear,
    Shoots up its head,
Thy gay, green, flowery tresses shear
    For him that's dead!

Thou, Autumn, wi' thy yellow hair,
In grief thy sallow mantle tear!
Thou, Winter, hurling through the air
    The roaring blast,
Wide o'er the naked world declare
    The worth we've lost!

Mourn him, thou Sun, great source of light!
Mourn, Empress of the silent night!
And you, ye twinkling starnies bright,
    My Matthew mourn!
For through your orbs he's taen his flight,
    Ne'er to return.

O Henderson! the man! the brother!
And art thou gone, and gone for ever?
And hast thou cross'd that unknown river,
    Life's dreary bound?
Like thee where shall I find another,
    The world around?

Go to your sculptured tombs, ye great,
In a' the tinsel trash o' state!
But by thy honest turf I'll wait,
    Thou man of worth!
And weep the ae best fellow's fate
    E'er lay in earth.

THE EPITAPH.

Stop, passenger! my story's brief;
    And truth I shall relate, man:
I tell nae common tale o' grief—
    For Matthew was a great man.

If thou uncommon merit hast,
    Yet spurn'd at Fortune's door, man;
A look of pity hither cast—
    For Matthew was a poor man.

If thou a noble sodger * art,
    That passest by this grave, man;
There moulders here a gallant heart—
    For Matthew was a brave man.

If thou on men, their works and ways,
    Canst throw uncommon light, man;
Here lies wha weel had won thy praise—
    For Matthew was a bright man.

If thou at Friendship's sacred ca'
    Wad life itself resign, man;
Thy sympathetic tear maun fa'—
    For Matthew was a kind man.

If thou art staunch, without a stain,
    Like the unchanging blue, man;
This was a kinsman o' thy ain—
    For Matthew was a true man.

If thou hast wit, and fun, and fire,
    And ne'er guid wine did fear, man;
This was thy billie, dam, and sire—
    For Matthew was a queer man.

If ony whiggish, whingin' sot,
    To blame poor Matthew dare, man;
May dool and sorrow be his lot—
    For Matthew was a rare man.

LINES WRITTEN ON A COPY OF THOMSON'S SONGS,

PRESENTED TO MISS GRAHAM OF FINTRY.

Here, where the Scottish Muse immortal lives,
    In sacred strains and tuneful numbers join'd,
Accept the gift, though humble he who gives;
    Rich is the tribute of the grateful mind.

So may no ruffian feeling in thy breast,
    Discordant jar thy bosom-chords among;
But Peace attune thy gentle soul to rest,
    Or Love ecstatic wake his seraph song:

Or Pity's notes, in luxury of tears,
    As modest Want the tale of woe reveals,
While conscious Virtue all the strain endears,
    And heaven-born Piety her sanction seals.

---

* "Sodger:" this might induce us to suppose that Matthew had served in the army.

TAM O' SHANTER:

A TALE.

"Of Brownyis and of Bogillis full is this Buke."
Gawin Douglas.

WHEN chapman billies leave the street,
And drouthy neibours neibours meet;
As market days are wearing late,
An' folk begin to tak the gate;
While we sit bousing at the nappy,
An' getting fou and unco happy,
We think na on the lang Scots miles,
The mosses, waters, slaps, and styles,
That lie between us and our hame,
Where sits our sulky, sullen dame,
Gathering her brows like gathering storm,
Nursing her wrath to keep it warm.

This truth fand honest Tam o' Shanter,
As he frae Ayr ae night did canter:

(Auld Ayr, whom ne'er a town surpasses,
For honest men and bonnie lassies).

O Tam! had'st thou but been sae wise,
As taen thy ain wife Kate's advice!
She tauld thee weel thou was a skellum,
A bletherin', blusterin', drunken blellum;
That frae November till October,
Ae market-day thou was na sober;
That ilka melder wi' the miller,
Thou sat as lang as thou had siller;
That ev'ry naig was ca'd a shoe on
The smith and thee gat roaring fou on;
That at the L—d's * house, ev'n on Sunday,
Thou drank wi' Kirkton Jean till Monday.

* Leddie's: *Lord's* house is nonsense. How could he drink from Sunday to Monday in church? *Leddie's House* was the name of a tavern kept by the two sisters Kennedy, one of them called "Kirkton Jean." See LIFE.

She prophesied, that late or soon,
Thou wad be found deep drown'd in Doon,
Or catch'd wi' warlocks in the mirk,
By Alloway's auld, haunted kirk.

Ah, gentle dames! it gars me greet,
To think how mony counsels sweet,
How mony lengthen'd sage advices,
The husband frae the wife despises!

But to our tale:—Ae market night,
Tam had got planted unco right,
Fast by an ingle, bleezing finely,
Wi' reaming swats that drank divinely;
And at his elbow Souter Johnnie,
His ancient, trusty, drouthy crony:
Tam lo'ed him like a very brither;
They had been fou for weeks thegither.
The night drave on wi' sangs an' clatter;
And aye the ale was growing better:
The Landlady and Tam grew gracious,
Wi' secret favours, sweet and precious:
The Souter tauld his queerest stories;
The Landlord's laugh was ready chorus:
The storm without might rair and rustle,
Tam did na mind the storm a whistle.

Care, mad to see a man sae happy,
E'en drown'd himsel' amang the nappy.
As bees flee hame wi' lades o' treasure,
The minutes wing'd their way wi' pleasure:
Kings may be blest, but Tam was glorious,
O'er a the ills o' life victorious!

But pleasures are like poppies spread,
You seize the flow'r, its bloom is shed;
Or like the snow falls in the river,
A moment white—then melts for ever;
Or like the Borealis race,
That flit ere you can point their place;
Or like the rainbow's lovely form
Evanishing amid the storm.
Nae man can tether Time nor Tide,
The hour approaches Tam maun ride—
That hour, o' night's black arch the key-stane,
That dreary hour Tam mounts his beast in;
And sic a night he took the road in,
As ne'er poor sinner was abroad in.

The wind blew as 'twad blawn its last;
The rattling showers rose on the blast;
The speedy gleams the darkness swallow'd;
Loud, deep, and lang the thunder bellow'd:
That night, a child might understand,
The deil had business on his hand.

Weel mounted on his gray meare, Meg,
A better never lifted leg,
Tam skelpit on through dub and mire,
Despising wind, and rain, and fire;
Whiles holding fast his gude blue bonnet,
Whiles crooning o'er an auld Scots sonnet,
Whiles glow'ring round wi' prudent cares,
Lest bogles catch him unawares;
Kirk-Alloway was drawing nigh,
Where ghaists and houlets nightly cry.

By this time he was cross the ford,
Where in the snaw the chapman smoor'd;
And past the birks and meikle stane,
Where drunken Charlie brak 's neck-bane;
And through the whins, and by the cairn,
Where hunters fand the murder'd bairn;
And near the thorn, aboon the well,
Where Mungo's mither hang'd hersel'.
Before him Doon pours all his floods,
The doubling storm roars through the woods,
The lightnings flash frae pole to pole,
Near and more near the thunders roll;
When, glimmering through the groaning trees,
Kirk-Alloway seem'd in a bleeze.
Through ilka bore the beams were glancing,
And loud resounded mirth and dancing.

Inspiring bold John Barleycorn!
What dangers thou canst make us scorn!
Wi' tippenny we fear nae evil;
Wi' usquabae we'll face the devil!
The swats sae ream'd in Tammie's noddle,
Fair play, he cared na deils a boddle,
But Maggie stood, right sair astonish'd,
Till, by the heel and hand admonish'd,
She ventur'd forward on the light;
And, wow! Tam saw an unco sight!

Warlocks and witches in a dance:
Nae cotillon, brent new frae France,
But hornpipes, jigs, strathspeys, and reels,
Put life and mettle in their heels.
A winnock-bunker in the east,
There sat auld Nick, in shape o' beast;
A towzie tyke, black, grim, and large,
To gie them music was his charge:
He screw'd the pipes and gart them skirl,
Till roof and rafters a' did dirl.
Coffins stood round, like open presses,
That shaw'd the dead in their last dresses;
And (by some devilish cantraip sleight)
Each in his cauld hand held a light,
By which heroic Tam was able
To note upon the haly table—
A murderer's banes, in gibbet-airns;
Twa span-lang, wee, unchristen'd bairns;

A thief, new-cutted frae a rape,
Wi' his last gasp his gab did gape;
Five tomahawks wi' blude red-rusted:
Five scymitars wi' murder crusted;
A garter, which a babe had strangled:
A knife a father's throat had mangled,
Whom his ain son of life bereft,
The gray-hairs yet stack to the heft:
Wi' mair of horrible and awfu',
Which even to name wad be unlawfu'.

    As Tammie glowr'd, amaz'd and curious,
The mirth and fun grew fast and furious;
The piper loud and louder blew,
The dancers quick and quicker flew;

They reel'd, they set, they cross'd, they cleekit,
Till ilka carlin swat and reekit,
And coost her duddies to the wark,
And linket at it in her sark!

  Now Tam, O Tam! had thae been queans,
A' plump and strapping in their teens!
Their sarks, instead o' creeshie flainen,
Been snaw-white seventeen hunder linen!
Thir breeks o' mine, my only pair,
That ance were plush o' guid blue hair,
I wad hae gi'en them off my hurdies,
For ae blink o' the bonnie burdies!
But wither'd beldams, auld and droll,
Rigwoodie hags wad spean a foal,
Louping an' flinging on a crummock,
I wonder did na turn thy stomach.

  But Tam kent what was what fu' brawlie:
There was ae winsome wench and waulie,
That night enlisted in the core,
Lang after kenn'd on Carrick shore;

OLD AND NEW BRIGS OF DOON,
WITH BURNS MONUMENT.

(For mony a beast to dead she shot,
And perish'd mony a bonnie boat,
And shook baith meikle corn and bear,
And held the country-side in fear);
Her cutty sark, o' Paisley harn,
That while a lassie she had worn,
In longitude though sorely scanty,
It was her best, and she was vauntie.

Ah! little kent thy reverend grannie,
That sark she coft for her wee Nannie
Wi' twa pund Scots ('twas a' her riches),
Wad ever grac'd a dance of witches!

But here my Muse her wing maun cour,
Sic flights are far beyond her power;

To sing how Nannie lap an flang
(A souple jade she was and strang),
And how Tam stood, like ane bewitch'd,
And thought his very een enrich'd;
Even Satan glowr'd, and fidg'd fu' fain,
And hotch'd and blew wi' might and main:
Till first ae caper, syne anither,
Tam tint his reason a' thegither,
And roars out, "Weel done, Cutty-sark!"
And in an instant all was dark:
And scarcely had he Maggie rallied,
When out the hellish legion sallied.

As bees bizz out wi' angry fyke,
When plundering herds assail their byke;
As open pussie's mortal foes,
When, pop! she starts before their nose;
As eager runs the market-crowd,
When "Catch the thief!" resounds aloud;
So Maggie runs, the witches follow,
Wi' mony an eldritch skriech and hollow.

Ah, Tam! Ah, Tam! thou'll get thy fairin'!
In hell they'll roast thee like a herrin'!

In vain thy Kate awaits thy comin'!
Kate soon will be a woefu' woman!
Now, do thy speedy utmost, Meg,
And win the key-stane * o' the brig;
There at them thou thy tail may toss,
A running stream they dare na cross.
But ere the key-stane she could make,
The fient a tail she had to shake!
For Nannie, far before the rest,
Hard upon noble Maggie prest,
And flew at Tam wi' furious ettle;
But little wist she Maggie's mettle!
Ae spring brought off her master hale,
But left behind her ain grey tail:
The carlin claught her by the rump,
And left poor Maggie scarce a stump.

Now, wha this tale o' truth shall read,
Each man, and mother's son, take heed:
Whene'er to Drink you are inclin'd,
Or Cutty-sarks rin in your mind,
Think! ye may buy the joys o'er dear,
Remember Tam o' Shanter's meare.

ON THE BIRTH OF A POSTHUMOUS CHILD,†
BORN IN PECULIAR CIRCUMSTANCES OF FAMILY DISTRESS.

SWEET flow'ret, pledge o' meikle love,
  And ward o' mony a prayer,
What heart o' stane wad thou na move,
  Sae helpless, sweet, and fair!

November hirples o'er the lea,
  Chill, on thy lovely form;
And gane, alas! the sheltering tree,
  Should shield thee frae the storm.

May He who gives the rain to pour,
  And wings the blast to blaw,
Protect thee frae the driving shower,
  The bitter frost and snaw!

May He, the friend of woe and want,
  Who heals life's various stounds,

---

* "Keystane:" it is a well-known fact that witches, or any evil spirits, have no power to follow a poor wight any further than the middle of the next running stream. It may be proper likewise to mention to the benighted traveller, that when he falls in with bogles, whatever danger may be in his going forward, there is much more hazard in turning back.—(B.)

† "Posthumous child:" grand-child of Mrs. Dunlop, whose daughter had married M. Henri, a Frenchman. This son, after many vicissitudes, succeeded to his paternal estates. The father had died ere the birth.

Protect and guard the mother-plant,
  And heal her cruel wounds!

But late she flourish'd, rooted fast,
  Fair on the summer morn:
Now feebly bends she, in the blast,
  Unshelter'd and forlorn:

Blest be thy bloom, thou lovely gem,
  Unscathed by ruffian hand!
And from thee many a parent stem
  Arise to deck our land!

ELEGY
ON THE LATE MISS BURNET OF MONBODDO.

LIFE ne'er exulted in so rich a prize
As Burnet, lovely from her native skies;
Nor envious Death so triumph'd in a blow,
As that which laid th' accomplish'd Burnet low.

Thy form and mind, sweet maid, can I forget?
In richest ore the brightest jewel set!
In thee high Heaven above was truest shown,
As by his noblest work the Godhead best is known.

In vain ye flaunt in summer's pride, ye groves;
  Thou crystal streamlet with thy flowery shore,
Ye woodland choir that chant your idle loves,
  Ye cease to charm—Eliza is no more!

Ye heathy wastes immix'd with reedy fens;
  Ye mossy streams, with sedge and rushes stored;
Ye rugged cliffs, o'erhanging dreary glens,
  To you I fly, ye with my soul accord!

Princes, whose cumbrous pride was all their worth,
  Shall venal lays their pompous exit hail?
And thou, sweet Excellence! forsake our earth,
  And not a Muse with honest grief bewail?

We saw thee shine in youth and beauty's pride,
  And virtue's light, that beams beyond the spheres;
But like the sun eclipsed at morning tide,
  Thou left'st us darkling in a world of tears.

The parent's heart that nestled fond in thee,
  That heart how sunk, a prey to grief and care!
So deck'd the woodbine sweet yon aged tree;
  So, from it ravish'd, leaves it bleak and bare.

LAMENT OF MARY QUEEN OF SCOTS ON THE APPROACH OF SPRING.

Now Nature hangs her mantle green On ev'ry blooming tree, And spreads her sheets o' daisies white Out o'er the grassy lea.

Now Phœbus cheers the crystal streams,
   And glads the azure skies;
But nought can glad the weary wight
   That fast in durance lies.

Now lav'rocks wake the merry morn,
   Aloft on dewy wing;
The merle, in his noontide bower,
   Makes woodland echoes ring;

The mavis wild wi' mony a note,
   Sings drowsy day to rest:
In love and freedom they rejoice,
   Wi' care nor thrall opprest.

Now blooms the lily by the bank,
   The primrose down the brae;
The hawthorn 's budding in the glen,
   And milk-white is the slae:

The meanest hind in fair Scotland
   May rove thae sweets amang;
But I, the Queen of a' Scotland,
   Maun lie in prison strang.

I was the Queen o' bonnie France,
   Where happy I hae been;
Fu' lightly rase I in the morn,
   As blythe lay down at e'en:

And I 'm the sov'reign of Scotland,
  And mony a traitor there;
Yet here I lie in foreign bands,
  And never-ending care.

But as for thee, thou false woman!
  My sister and my fae,
Grim Vengeance yet shall whet a sword
  That through thy soul shall gae!

The weeping blood in woman's breast
  Was never known to thee:
Nor the balm that draps on wounds of woe
  Frae woman's pitying e'e.

My son! my son! may kinder stars
  Upon thy fortune shine!
And may those pleasures gild thy reign,
  That ne'er wad blink on mine!

God keep thee frae thy mother's faes,
  Or turn their hearts to thee:
And where thou meet'st thy mother's friend,
  Remember him for me!

O! soon, to me, may summer suns
  Nae mair light up the morn!
Nae mair, to me, the autumn winds
  Wave o'er the yellow corn!

And in the narrow house o' death
  Let winter round me rave;
And the next flowers that deck the spring,
  Bloom on my peaceful grave!

THERE 'LL NEVER BE PEACE.*

The Church is in ruins, the State is in jars,
  Delusions, oppressions, and murderous wars;
We dare na' weel say 't, but we ken wha 's to blame—
  There 'll never be peace till Jamie comes hame.

My seven braw sons for Jamie drew sword,
  And now I greet round their green beds in the yird:
It brak the sweet heart o' my faithfu' auld dame—
  There 'll never be peace till Jamie comes hame.

Now life is a burden that bows me down,
  Sin' I tint my bairns, and he tint his crown;
But till my last moment my words are the same—
  There 'll never be peace till Jamie comes hame.

LAMENT FOR JAMES, EARL OF GLENCAIRN.†

The wind blew hollow frae the hills,
  By fits the sun's departing beam
Look'd on the fading yellow woods
  That waved o'er Lugar's winding stream:
Beneath a craigy steep, a Bard,
  Laden with years and meikle pain,
In loud lament bewail'd his lord,
  Whom death had all untimely ta'en.

He lean'd him to an ancient aik,
  Whose trunk was mould'ring down with years;
His locks were bleachèd white with time,
  His hoary cheek was wet with tears;
And as he touch'd his trembling harp,
  And as he tuned his doleful sang,
The winds, lamenting through their caves,
  To Echo bore the notes alang:—

"Ye scatter'd birds, that faintly sing,
  The reliques o' the vernal queire!
Ye woods, that shed on a' the winds
  The honours o' the aged year!
A few short months, and glad and gay,
  Again ye 'll charm the ear and e'e;
But nocht in all revolving time
  Can gladness bring again to me.

"I am a bending, aged tree,
  That long has stood the wind and rain;
But now has come a cruel blast,
  And my last hald of earth is gane:
Nae leaf o' mine shall greet the spring,
  Nae simmer sun exalt my bloom;
But I maun lie before the storm,
  And ithers plant them in my room.

---

* The second strain of the music in *Johnson's Museum* being merely a repetition of the first an octave higher, and beyond the compass of any ordinary voice, the first is here only given.

† Lord Glencairn died in January, 1791, at Falmouth, on his way back from a voyage to Lisbon on a vain search for health, aged forty-two. Burns put on mourning for him, and called one of his sons James Glencairn.

"I 've seen sae mony changefu' years,
  On earth I am a stranger grown;
I wander in the ways of men,
  Alike unknowing and unknown:
Unheard, unpitied, unrelieved,
  I bear alane my lade o' care,
For silent, low, on beds of dust,
  Lie a' that would my sorrows share.

"And last (the sum of a' my griefs!)
  My noble master lies in clay;
The flower amang our barons bold,
  His country's pride, his country's stay:
In weary being now I pine,
  For a' the life of life is dead,
And hope has left my aged ken,
  On forward wing for ever fled.

"Awake thy last sad voice, my harp!
  The voice of woe and wild despair!
Awake! resound thy latest lay—
  Then sleep in silence evermair!
And thou, my last, best, only friend,
  That fillest an untimely tomb,
Accept this tribute from the Bard
  Thou brought from Fortune's mirkest gloom.

"In Poverty's low barren vale,
  Thick mists, obscure, involved me round;
Though oft I turn'd the wistful eye,
  Nae ray of fame was to be found.
Thou found'st me, like the morning sun
  That melts the fogs in limpid air;
The friendless Bard and rustic song
  Became alike thy fostering care.

"O! why has worth so short a date,
  While villains ripen gray with time?
Must thou, the noble, gen'rous, great,
  Fall in bold manhood's hardy prime?
Why did I live to see that day?
  A day to me so full of woe!
O! had I met the mortal shaft
  Which laid my benefactor low!

"The bridegroom may forget the bride
  Was made his wedded wife yestreen;
The monarch may forget the crown
  That on his head an hour has been;
The mother may forget the child
  That smiles sae sweetly on her knee;
But I'll remember thee, Glencairn,
  And a' that thou hast done for me!"

LINES SENT TO SIR JOHN WHITEFOORD, OF WHITEFOORD, BART.,*

WITH THE FOREGOING POEM.

THOU, who thy honour as thy God rever'st,
Who, save thy mind's reproach, nought earthly fear'st,
To thee this votive offering I impart,
The tearful tribute of a broken heart.
The Friend thou valued'st, I the Patron loved;
His worth, his honour, all the world approved.
We'll mourn till we, too, go as he has gone,
And tread the shadowy path to that dark world unknown.

THIRD EPISTLE TO MR. GRAHAM OF FINTRY.

LATE crippled of an arm, and now a leg,†
About to beg a pass for leave to beg;
Dull, listless, teased, dejected, and depress'd
(Nature is adverse to a cripple's rest);
Will generous Graham list to his Poet's wail?
(It soothes poor Misery, hearkening to her tale)

---

* Once laird of Ballochmyle, a great friend of Glencairn.
† After a fall from his horse. See CORRESPONDENCE.

And hear him curse the light he first survey'd,
And doubly curse the luckless rhyming trade?

Thou, Nature! partial Nature! I arraign;
Of thy caprice maternal I complain.
The lion and the bull thy care have found,
One shakes the forests, and one spurns the ground:
Thou giv'st the ass his hide, the snail his shell,
The envenom'd wasp, victorious, guards his cell;
Thy minions kings defend, control, devour,
In all th' omnipotence of rule and power;
Foxes and statesmen subtile wiles ensure,
The cit and polecat stink, and are secure;
Toads with their poison, doctors with their drug,
The priest and hedgehog in their robes, are snug;
Even silly woman has her warlike arts,
Her tongue and eyes, her dreaded spear and darts.

But, oh! thou bitter stepmother and hard,
To thy poor, fenceless, naked child, the Bard!
A thing unteachable in world's skill,
And half an idiot, too, more helpless still;
No heels to bear him from the op'ning dun;
No claws to dig, his hated sight to shun;
No horns, but those by luckless Hymen worn,
And those, alas! not Amalthea's horn:
No nerves olfactory, Mammon's trusty cur,
Clad in rich Dulness' comfortable fur;
In naked feeling, and in aching pride,
He bears the unbroken blast from ev'ry side:
Vampyre booksellers drain him to the heart,
And scorpion critics cureless venom dart.

Critics!—appall'd, I venture on the name—
Those cut-throat bandits in the paths of fame:
Bloody dissectors, worse than ten Monroes!‡
He hacks to teach, they mangle to expose.

His heart by causeless wanton malice wrung,
By blockheads' daring into madness stung;
His well-won bays, than life itself more dear,
By miscreants torn, who ne'er one sprig must wear:
Foil'd, bleeding, tortured in th' unequal strife,
The hapless poet flounders on through life;
Till, fled each hope that once his bosom fired,
And fled each Muse that glorious once inspired,
Low sunk in squalid, unprotected age,
Dead even resentment for his injured page,
He heeds or feels no more the ruthless critic's rage!
So, by some hedge, the gen'rous steed deceased,
For half-starved snarling curs a dainty feast;
By toil and famine wore to skin and bone,
Lies, senseless of each tugging bitch's son.

O Dulness! portion of the truly blest!
Calm shelter'd haven of eternal rest!

---

‡ "Monroe:" Alexander, Professor of Anatomy, Edinburgh.

Thy sons ne'er madden in the fierce extremes
Of Fortune's polar frost, or torrid beams.
If mantling high she fills the golden cup,
With sober selfish ease they sip it up:
Conscious the bounteous meed they well deserve,
They only wonder "some folks" do not starve.
The grave, sage hern thus easy picks his frog,
And thinks the mallard a sad worthless dog.
When Disappointment snaps the clue of hope,
And through disastrous night they darkling grope,
With deaf endurance sluggishly they bear,
And just conclude that "fools are fortune's care."
So, heavy, passive to the tempest's shocks,
Strong on the sign-post stands the stupid ox.
Not so the idle Muses' mad-cap train,
Not such the workings of their moon-struck brain;
In equanimity they never dwell,
By turns in soaring heaven, or vaulted hell.

I dread thee, Fate, relentless and severe,
With all a poet's, husband's, father's fear!
Already one stronghold of hope is lost.
Glencairn, the truly noble, lies in dust
(Fled, like the sun eclipsed as noon appears,
And left us darkling in a world of tears).
O! hear my ardent, grateful, selfish prayer!
Fintry, my other stay, long bless and spare!
Through a long life his hopes and wishes crown,
And bright in cloudless skies his sun go down!
May bliss domestic smooth his private path,
Give energy to life, and soothe his latest breath
With many a filial tear circling the bed of death!

ON GLENRIDDELL'S FOX BREAKING HIS CHAIN.*

A FRAGMENT, 1791.

Thou, Liberty, thou art my theme;
Not such as idle poets dream,
Who trick thee up a heathen goddess
That a fantastic cap and rod has;
Such stale conceits are poor and silly;
I paint thee out, a Highland fil'y,
A sturdy, stubborn, handsome dapple,
As sleek 's a mouse, as round 's an apple,
That when thou pleasest can do wonders;
But when thy luckless rider blunders,
Or if thy fancy should demur there,
Wilt break thy neck ere thou go further.

These things premised, I sing—a Fox
Was caught among his native rocks,

* From the Glenriddell MS. still preserved in Liverpool.

And to a dirty kennel chained,
How he his liberty regained.

Glenriddell! a Whig without a stain,
A Whig in principle and grain,
Could'st thou enslave a free-born creature,
A native denizen of Nature?
How could'st thou, with a heart so good
(A better ne'er was sluiced with blood),
Nail a poor devil to a tree,
That ne'er did harm to thine or thee?

The staunchest Whig Glenriddell was,
Quite frantic in his country's cause;
And oft was Reynard's prison passing,
And with his brother-Whigs canvassing
The Rights of Men, the Powers of Women,
With all the dignity of Freemen.

Sir Reynard daily heard debates
Of Princes', Kings', and Nations' fates,
With many rueful, bloody stories
Of Tyrants, Jacobites, and Tories:
From liberty how angels fell,
That now are galley-slaves in hell;
How Nimrod first the trade began
Of binding Slavery's chains on Man;
How fell Semiramis—G—d d—n her!
Did first, with sacrilegious hammer
(All ills till then were trivial matters)
For Man dethron'd forge hen-peck fetters;
How Xerxes, that abandoned Tory,
Thought cutting throats was reaping glory,
Until the stubborn Whigs of Sparta
Taught him great Nature's Magna Charta;
How mighty Rome her fiat hurl'd
Resistless o'er a bowing world,
And, kinder than they did desire,
Polish'd mankind with sword and fire;
With much, too tedious to relate,
Of ancient and of modern date,
But ending still, how Billy Pitt
(Unlucky boy!) with wicked wit,
Has gagg'd old Britain, drain'd her coffer,
As butchers bind and bleed a heifer.

Thus wily Reynard, by degrees,
In kennel listening at his ease,
Suck'd in a mighty stock of knowledge,
As much as some folks at a college;
Knew Britain's rights and constitution,
Her aggrandisement, diminution,
How fortune wrought us good from evil:
Let no man, then, despise the Devil,
As who should say, "I ne'er can need him,"
Since we to scoundrels owe our freedom.

. . . .

ADDRESS TO THE SHADE OF THOMSON,

ON CROWNING HIS BUST* AT EDNAM, ROXBURGHSHIRE,
WITH A WREATH OF BAYS.

WHILE virgin Spring, by Eden's flood,
   Unfolds her tender mantle green,
Or pranks the sod in frolic mood,
   Or tunes Æolian strains between;

While Summer, with a matron grace,
   Retreats to Dryburgh's cooling shade,
Yet oft, delighted, stops to trace
   The progress of the spiky blade;

While Autumn, benefactor kind,
   By Tweed erects his aged head,
And sees, with self-approving mind,
   Each creature on his bounty fed;

While maniac Winter rages o'er
   The hills whence classic Yarrow flows,
Rousing the turbid torrent's roar,
   Or sweeping, wild, a waste of snows:

So long, sweet Poet of the year,
   Shall bloom that wreath thou well hast won;
While Scotia, with exulting tear,
   Proclaims that Thomson was her son.

LOVELY DAVIES.†

Her smile's a gift frae 'boon the lift,
   That maks us mair than princes;
A sceptred hand, a king's command,
   Is in her darting glances.
The man in arms 'gainst female charms,
   Even he her willing slave is;
He hugs his chain, and owns the reign
   Of conquering, lovely Davies.

My Muse! to dream of such a theme,
   Thy feeble powers surrender:
The eagle's gaze alone surveys
   The sun's meridian splendour.
I wad in vain essay the strain,
   The deed too daring brave is;
I'll drap the lyre, and mute admire
   The charms o' lovely Davies.

BONNIE WEE THING.

Wit and Grace, and Love, and Beauty,
   In ae constellation shine;
To adore thee is my duty,
   Goddess o' this soul o' mine!
        Bonnie wee thing, &c.

---

* "Crowning his bust:" this was in September, 1790, under the eye of the Earl of Buchan. Burns was invited, but sent this instead of himself— a poor substitute.

† "Lovely Davies:" a young lady from Pembrokeshire, related to the Riddells—very pretty, witty, and *wee*. She was forsaken by her lover, a Captain Delany, and drooped and died in consequence. See LIFE.

TO TERRAUGHTY,* ON HIS BIRTHDAY.

HEALTH to the Maxwell's veteran chief!
Health, aye unsour'd by care or grief:
Inspired, I turn'd Fate's sibyl leaf
    This natal morn,
I see thy life is stuff o' prief,
    Scarce quite half-worn.

This day thou metes threescore eleven,
And I can tell that bounteous Heaven
(The second sight, ye ken, is given
    To ilka Poet)
On thee a tack o' seven times seven
    Will yet bestow it.

If envious buckies view wi' sorrow
Thy lengthen'd days on this blest morrow,
May Desolation's lang-teeth'd harrow,
    Nine miles an hour,
Rake them, like Sodom and Gomorrah,
    In brunstane stoure.

But for thy friends, and they are mony,
Baith honest men and lassies bonnie,
May couthie Fortune, kind and cannie,
    In social glee,
Wi' mornings blythe and e'enings funny,
    Bless them and thee!

Fareweel, auld birkie! Lord be near ye,
And then the deil he daurna steer ye;
Your friends aye love, your faes aye fear ye;
    For me, shame fa' me,
If neist my heart I dinna wear ye,
    While Burns they ca' me!

FOURTH EPISTLE TO MR. GRAHAM OF FINTRY.

I CALL no goddess to inspire my strains,
A fabled Muse may suit a bard that feigns;
Friend of my life! my ardent spirit burns,
And all the tribute of my heart returns,
For boons accorded, goodness ever new,
The gift still dearer, as the giver, you.
Thou orb of day! thou other paler light!
And all ye many sparkling stars of night!
If aught that giver from my mind efface,
If I that giver's bounty e'er disgrace;
Then roll to me, along your wandering spheres,
Only to number out a villain's years!
I lay my hand upon my swelling breast,
And grateful would, but cannot speak the rest.

* "To Terraughty:" Mr. Maxwell, of Terraughty, near Dumfries.

SONG OF DEATH.†

Scene.—A Field of Battle—Time of the day, evening—The wounded and dying of the victorious army are supposed to join in the following song.

Thou strik'st the dull peasant—he sinks in the dark,
    Nor saves e'en the wreck of a name;
Thou strik'st the young hero—a glorious mark;
    He falls in the blaze of his fame!
In the field of proud honour—our swords in our hands,
    Our king and our country to save;
While victory shines on Life's last ebbing sands—
    O who would not die with the brave?

O MAY, THY MORN.‡

And here's to them, that, like oursel',
    Can push about the jorum;
And here's to them that wish us weel,
    May a' that's guid watch o'er them!

† A powerful but gloomy song, which Burns once intended to have printed separately, and set to music.

‡ Alluding, it is thought, to one of his final meetings with Clarinda.

And here's to them, we daurna tell,
　The dearest o' the quorum:
And here's to them, we daurna tell,
　The dearest o' the quorum!

THE EXCISEMAN.*

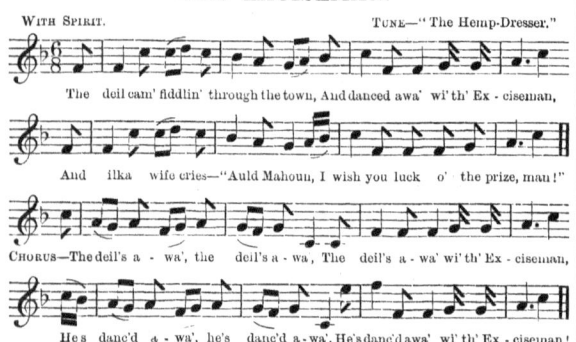

The deil cam' fiddlin' through the town, And danced awa' wi' th' Exciseman,
And ilka wife cries—"Auld Mahoun, I wish you luck o' the prize, man!"

CHORUS—The deil's a-wa', the deil's a-wa, The deil's a-wa' wi' th' Exciseman,
He's danc'd a-wa', he's danc'd a-wa', He's danc'd awa' wi' th' Exciseman!

We'll mak our maut, we'll brew our drink,
　We'll dance, and sing, and rejoice, man;
And mony braw thanks to the meikle black deil
　That danced awa' wi' th' Exciseman.
　　The deil's awa', &c.

There's threesome reels, there's foursome reels,
　There's hornpipes and strathspeys, man;
But the ae best dance e'er cam to the land
　Was—the deil's awa' wi' th' Exciseman.
　　The deil's awa', &c.

ON SENSIBILITY,

TO MY DEAR AND MUCH-HONOURED FRIEND, MRS. DUNLOP OF DUNLOP.

PLAINTIVE.　　TUNE—"Cornwallis' Lament for Colonel Muirhead."

Sensibility, how charming, Dearest Nancy, thou canst tell:
But distress, with horrors arming, Thou alas! hast known too well!
Fairest flower, behold the lily, Blooming in the sunny ray;
Let the blast sweep o'er the valley, See it prostrate in the clay.

* See LIFE.

Hear the wood-lark charm the forest,
　Telling o'er his little joys:
Hapless bird! a prey the surest
　To each pirate of the skies.
Dearly bought the hidden treasure
　Finer feelings can bestow;
Chords that vibrate sweetest pleasure,
　Thrill the deepest notes of woe.

AE FOND KISS.†

ANDANTE.

Ae fond kiss, and then we sever; Ae fareweel, and then for ever;
Deep in heart-wrung tears I'll pledge thee, Warring sighs and groans I'll wage thee.
Who shall say that Fortune grieves him, While the star of hope she leaves him!
Me, nae cheerfu' twinkle lights me, Dark despair around benights me.

I'll ne'er blame my partial fancy,
　Naething could resist my Nancy;
But to see her was to love her;
　Love but her, and love for ever.
Had we never loved sae kindly,
Had we never loved sae blindly,
Never met—or never parted—
We had ne'er been broken-hearted.‡

Fare-thee-weel, thou first and fairest!
Fare-thee-weel, thou best and dearest!
Thine be ilka joy and treasure,
Peace, enjoyment, love, and pleasure!
Ae fond kiss, and then we sever;
Ae fareweel, alas, for ever!
Deep in heart-wrung tears I'll pledge thee,
Warring sighs and groans I'll wage thee.

† Written on his parting from Clarinda. The verses are beautiful; but the idea of either party being "broken-hearted" is purely fanciful. See LIFE.
‡ These four lines, Sir Walter Scott said, "contain the essence of a thousand love tales."

GLOOMY DEGEMBER.*

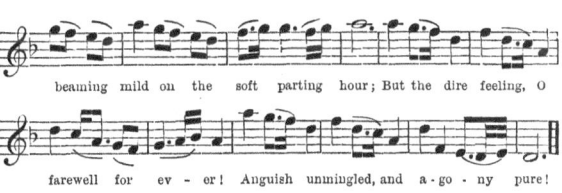

Wild as the winter now tearing the forest,
　Till the last leaf o' the summer is flown,
Such is the tempest has shaken my bosom,
　Till my last hope and last comfort is gone!
Still as I hail thee, thou gloomy December,
　Still shall I hail thee wi' sorrow and care;
For sad was the parting thou makes me remember,
　Parting wi' Nancy,† oh! ne'er to meet mair.

* The above air, along with the words, was communicated by Burns to *Johnson's Museum.* The song is also sung to the tune "Wandering Willie."

† "Nancy:" Clarinda.

FRAE THE FRIENDS AND LAND I LOVE.*

Frae the friends and land I love, Driv'n by Fortune's fel-ly spite;
Frae my best be-lov'd I rove, Nev-er mair to taste de-light:
Nev-er mair maun hope to find Ease frae toil, re-lief frae care;
When Re-mem-brance wracks the mind, Pleasures but un-veil de-spair.

Brightest climes shall mirk appear,
  Desert ilka blooming shore,
Till the Fates, nae mair severe,
  Friendship, love, and peace restore;
Till Revenge, wi' laurell'd head,
  Bring our banish'd hame again;
And ilk loyal, bonnie lad
  Cross the seas and win his ain.

MEIKLE THINKS MY LOVE.

O meikle thinks my luve o' my beauty, And meikle thinks my
luve o' my kin; But little thinks my luve I ken brawlie My tocher's
the jewel has charms for him. It's a' for the apple he'll nourish the tree, It's
a' for the hiney he'll cherish the bee, My laddie's sae meikle
in luve wi' the siller, He canna hae luve to spare for me.

Your proffer o' luve 's an airle-penny,
  My tocher 's the bargain ye wad buy;
But an ye be crafty, I am cunnin',
  Sae ye wi' anither your fortune maun try.
Ye 're like to the timmer o' yon rotten wood,
Ye 're like to the bark o' yon rotten tree,
Ye 'll slip frae me like a knotless thread,
  And ye 'll crack your credit wi' mae nor me.

* This song is only in part that of Burns.

LINES ON FERGUSSON, THE POET.

Ill-fated genius! Heaven-taught Fergusson,
  What heart that feels and will not yield a tear,
To think Life's sun did set e'er well begun
  To shed its influence on thy bright career.

O why should truest Worth and Genius pine
  Beneath the iron grasp of Want and Woe,
While titled knaves and idiot Greatness shine
  In all the splendour Fortune can bestow?

HOW CAN I BE BLYTHE AND GLAD?†

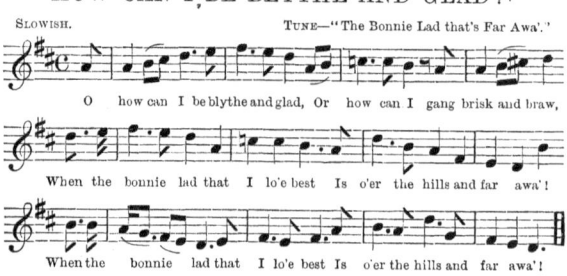

O how can I be blythe and glad, Or how can I gang brisk and braw
When the bonnie lad that I lo'e best Is o'er the hills and far awa'!
When the bonnie lad that I lo'e best Is o'er the hills and far awa'!

It's no the frosty winter wind,
  It's no the driving drift and snaw;
But aye the tear comes in my e'e,
  To think on him that's far awa';
But aye the tear comes in my e'e,
  To think on him that's far awa'.

My father pat me frae his door,
  My friends they hae disown'd me a';
But I hae ane will tak my part,
  The bonnie lad that's far awa';
But I hae ane will tak my part,
  The bonnie lad that's far awa'.

A pair o' gloves he bought to me,
  And silken snoods he gave me twa;
And I will wear them for his sake,
  The bonnie lad that's far awa';
And I will wear them for his sake,
  The bonnie lad that's far awa'.

The weary winter soon will pass,
  And spring will cleed the birken shaw;
And my sweet baby will be born,
  And he'll be hame that's far awa';
And my sweet baby will be born,
  And he'll be hame that's far awa'.

† Taken partly from an old song.

SWEET CLOSES THE EVENING.*

VERY SLOW WITH EXPRESSION.　　　　TUNE—"Craigieburn Wood."

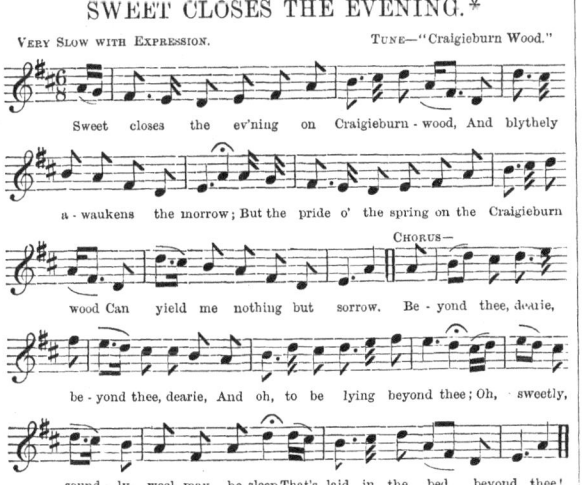

Sweet closes the ev'ning on Craigieburn-wood, And blythely a-waukens the morrow; But the pride o' the spring on the Craigieburn wood Can yield me nothing but sorrow. Be-yond thee, dearie, be-yond thee, dearie, And oh, to be lying beyond thee; Oh, sweetly, sound-ly, weel may he sleep That's laid in the bed beyond thee!

I see the spreading leaves and flowers,
　I hear the wild birds singing;
But pleasure they hae nane for me,
　While care my heart is wringing.
　　　Beyond thee, dearie, &c.

I canna tell, I maunna tell,
　I daurna for your anger;
But secret love will break my heart,
　If I conceal it langer.
　　　Beyond thee, dearie, &c.

I see thee gracefu', straight, and tall,
　I see thee sweet and bonnie;
But oh, what will my torments be,
　If thou refuse thy Johnnie!
　　　Beyond thee, dearie, &c.

* Written on Miss Lorimer, afterwards Mrs. Whelpdale, a flame of Burns, who lived at Craigieburn, near to Moffat. See LIFE.

To see thee in anither's arms,
   In love to lie and languish,
'Twad be my dead, that will be seen,
   My heart wad burst wi' anguish.
      Beyond thee, dearie, &c.

But Jeanie, say thou wilt be mine,
   Say thou lo'es nane before me;
And a' my days o' life to come
   I'll gratefully adore thee.
      Beyond thee, dearie, &c.

WHAT CAN A YOUNG LASSIE?

Tune—"What can a Young Lassie do wi' an Auld Man."

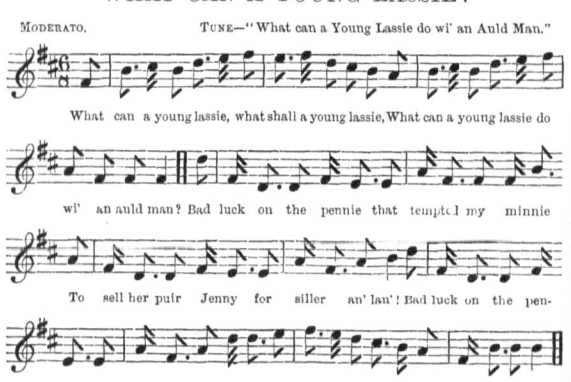

He's always compleenin' frae mornin' to e'enin',
   He hoasts and he hirples the weary day lang;
He's doyl't and he's dozin', his bluid it is frozen,
   dreary's the night wi' a crazy auld man!

He hums and he hankers, he frets and he cankers;
   I never can please him, do a' that I can;
He's peevish and jealous of a' the young fellows,
   O dool on the day I met wi' an auld man!

My auld Auntie Katie upon me takes pity,
   I'll do my endeavour to follow her plan;
I'll cross him and wrack him until I heart-break him,
   And then his auld brass will buy me a new pan.

YON WILD MOSSY MOUNTAINS.

Slow. Tune—"There's Few Guid Fellows when Jamie's Awa'."

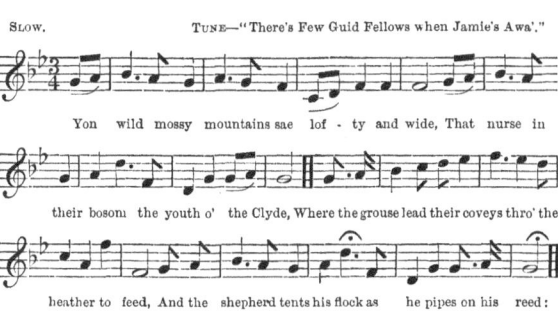

Yon wild mossy mountains sae lof-ty and wide, That nurse in their bosom the youth o' the Clyde, Where the grouse lead their coveys thro' the heather to feed, And the shepherd tents his flock as he pipes on his reed:

Not Gowrie's rich valley, nor Forth's sunny shores,
To me hae the charms o' yon wild, mossy moors;
For there, by a lanely, sequesterèd stream,
Resides a sweet lassie, my thought and my dream.

Amang thae wild mountains shall still be my path,
Ilk stream foaming down its ain green, narrow strath;
For there, wi' my lassie, the day lang I rove,
While o'er us unheeded flee the swift hours o' love.

She is not the fairest, although she is fair;
O' nice education but sma' is her share;
Her parentage humble as humble can be;
But I lo'e the dear lassie because she lo'es me.

To beauty what man but maun yield him a prize,
In her armour of glances, and blushes, and sighs?
And when wit and refinement hae polish'd her darts,
They dazzle our e'en, as they flee to our hearts.

But kindness, sweet kindness, in the fond sparkling e'e,
Has lustre outshining the diamond to me;
And the heart beating love, as I'm clasp'd in her arms,
O, these are my lassie's all-conquering charms!

I DO CONFESS THOU ART SAE FAIR.

SLOWISH. TUNE—"I do Confess thou'rt Smooth and Fair."

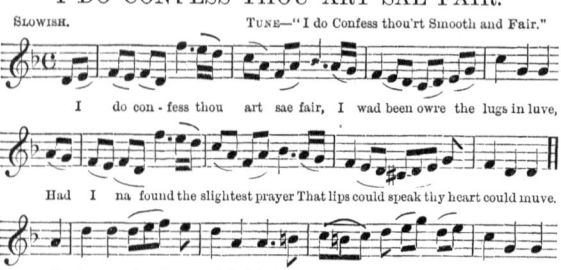

I do confess thou art sae fair, I wad been owre the lugs in luve,
Had I na found the slightest prayer That lips could speak thy heart could muve.
I do confess thee sweet, but find Thou art sae thriftless o' thy sweets,
Thy favours are the silly wind, That kisses ilka thing it meets.

    See yonder rose-bud, rich in dew,
      Amang its native briers sae coy;
    How sune it tines its scent and hue
      When pu'd and worn a common toy!
    Sic fate ere lang shall thee betide,
      Though thou may gaily bloom awhile;
    And sune thou shalt be thrown aside
      Like ony common weed and vile.

O SAW YE MY DEARIE?

SLOW. TUNE—"Eppie M'Nab."

O saw ye my dearie, my Eppie M'Nab? O saw ye my
dearie, my Eppie M'Nab? She's down in the yard, she's
kissin' the laird, She winna come hame to her ain Jock Rab.
O come thy ways to me, my Eppie M'Nab; O come thy ways
to me, my Eppie M'Nab; What-e'er thou hast dune, be it late, be
it sune, Thou's welcome again to thy ain Jock Rab.

What says she, my dearie, my Eppie M'Nab?
What says she, my dearie, my Eppie M'Nab?
    She lets thee to wot that she has thee forgot,
And for ever disowns thee, her ain Jock Rab.
Oh, had I ne'er seen thee, my Eppie M'Nab!
Oh, had I ne'er seen thee, my Eppie M'Nab!
    As light as the air, and as fause as thou's fair,
Thou's broken the heart o' thy ain Jock Rab.

O FOR ANE-AND-TWENTY, TAM!

CANTY. TUNE—"The Moudiewart."

CHORUS—An' O for ane an' twenty, Tam! An' hey, sweet ane an' twenty, Tam!
I'll learn my kin a rattlin sang, Gin I saw ane an' twenty, Tam.
SONG—They snool me sair, and haud me down, And gar me look like bluntie, Tam;
But three short years will soon run roun', And then comes ane an' twenty, Tam.

    A gleib o' lan', a claut o' gear,
      Was left me by my auntie, Tam;
    At kith or kin I need na spier,
      An I saw ane an' twenty, Tam!
      An' O for ane an' twenty, Tam, &c.

    They'll hae me wed a wealthy coof,
      Though I mysel' hae plenty, Tam;
    But hear'st thou, laddie—there's my loof—
      I'm thine at ane an' twenty, Tam!
      An' O for ane an' twenty, Tam, &c.

O WHARE GAT YE?

SLOW. TUNE—"Adieu Dundee."

Oh, whare gat ye that bonnie blue bonnet? Oh, what makes them
aye put the question to me? I gat it frae a bonnie Scots callan,
Atween Saint Johnston and bonnie Dundee. Oh, gin I saw the
laddie that gae me't! Aft has he doudled me upon his knee; May Heaven protect my bonnie Scots laddie, And send him safe hame to his baby and me!

    My heart has nae room when I think on my laddie,
      His dear rosy haffets bring tears to my e'e;
    But, O! he's awa, and I dinna ken whar he's—
      Gin we could ance meet, we'll ne'er part till we die.
    O light be the breezes around him saft blawin'!
    And o'er him sweet simmer still blink bonnilie,
    And the rich dews o' plenty, around him wide fa'in,
      Prevent a' his fears for my babie and me!

My blessings upon that sweet wee lippie!
  My blessings upon that bonnie e'e-bree!
Thy smiles are sae like my blythe sodger laddie,
  Thou's aye the dearer and dearer to me.

But I 'll big a bower on yon green bank sae bonnie,
  That 's lav'd by the waters o' Tay wimplin' clear,
And cleed thee in tartans, my wee smiling Johnnie,
  And make thee a man like thy daddie dear.

BESS AND HER SPINNING WHEEL.

Slow.   Tune—"Sweet's the Lass that Loves me."

O leeze me on my spinn-in wheel, And leeze me on my rock and reel; Frae tap to tae that cleeds me bien, And haps me biel and warm at e'en. I'll set me down and sing and spin, While laigh de-scends the simmer sun, Blest wi' con-tent, and milk and meal, O leeze me on my spinn-in' wheel.

On ilka hand the burnies trot,
  And meet below my theekit cot;
The scented birk and hawthorn white
  Across the pool their arms unite,
Alike to screen the birdie's nest,
  And little fishes' caller rest:
The sun blinks kindly in the biel',
  Where blythe I turn my spinnin' wheel.

On lofty aiks the cushats wail,
  And echo cons the doolfu' tale;
The lintwhites in the hazel braes,
  Delighted, rival ither's lays:
The craik amang the clover hay,
  The paitrick whirrin' o'er the ley,
The swallow jinkin' round my shiel,
  Amuse me at my spinnin' wheel.

Wi' sma' to sell, and less to buy,
  Aboon distress, below envy,
Oh, wha wad leave this humble state,
  For a' the pride of a' the great?
Amid their flaring, idle toys,
  Amid their cumbrous, dinsome joys,
Can they the peace and pleasure feel
  Of Bessy at her spinnin' wheel?

NITHSDALE'S WELCOME HAME.*

Though stars in skies may disappear,
   And angry tempests gather;
The happy hour may soon be near
   That brings us pleasant weather:
The weary night o' care and grief
   May hae a joyfu' morrow;
So dawning day has brought relief,
   Farweel our night o' sorrow.

THE COUNTRY LASSIE.

TUNE—"The Country Lass."

It 's ye hae wooers mony ane,
   And lassie, ye 're but young, ye ken;
Then wait a wee, and cannie wale
   A routhie butt, a routhie ben;
There 's Johnnie o' the Buskie-glen,
   Fu' is his barn, fu' is his byre;
Tak this frae me, my bonnie hen,
   It 's plenty beets the lover's fire.

* Composed when Lady Winifred Maxwell returned to Scotland and rebuilt Terreagles House, near Dumfries. She was descended from the forfeited Earl of Nithsdale.

For Johnnie o' the Buskie-glen,
   I dinna care a single flie;
He lo'es sae weel his craps and kye,
   He has nae love to spare for me;
But blythe 's the blink o' Robie's e'e,
   And weel I wat he lo'es me dear:
Ae blink o' him I wad na gie
   For Buskie-glen and a' his gear.

O thoughtless lassie, life 's a faught;
   The canniest gate, the strife is sair;
But aye fu'-han't is fechtin' best,
   A hungry care 's an unco care:
But some will spend and some will spare,
   An' wilfu' folk maun hae their will;
Syne as ye brew, my maiden fair,
   Keep mind that ye maun drink the yill.

O gear will buy me rigs o' land,
   And gear will buy me sheep and kye;
But the tender heart o' leesome love,
   The gowd and siller canna buy.
We may be poor—Robie and I;
   Light is the burden love lays on;
Content and love brings peace and joy—
   What mair hae queens upon a throne?

THE POSIE.

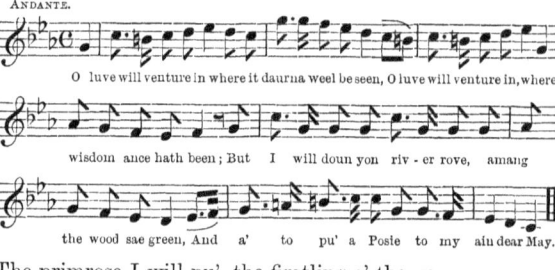

The primrose I will pu', the firstling o' the year,
And I will pu' the pink, the emblem o' my dear;
For she 's the pink o' womankind, and blooms without a peer,
   And a' to be a Posie to my ain dear May.

I 'll pu' the budding rose, when Phœbus peeps in view,
For its like a baumy kiss o' her sweet, bonnie mou;
The hyacinth's for constancy wi' its unchanging blue,
   And a' to be a Posie to my ain dear May.

The lily it is pure, and the lily it is fair,
And in her lovely bosom I 'll place the lily there;
The daisy 's for simplicity and unaffected air,
   And a' to be a Posie to my ain dear May.

The hawthorn I will pu', wi' its locks o' siller gray,
Where, like an aged man, it stands at break o' day;
But the songster's nest within the bush I winna tak away,
   And a' to be a Posie to my ain dear May.

The woodbine I will pu', when the e'ening star is near,
And the diamond draps o' dew shall be her een sae clear;
The violet 's for modesty, which weel she fa's to wear,
   And a' to be a Posie to my ain dear May.

I 'll tie the Posie round wi' the silken band o' luve,
And I 'll place it in her breast, and I 'll swear by a' above,
That to my latest draught o' life the band shall ne'er remove,
   And this will be a Posie to my ain dear May.

FAIR ELIZA.

Very Slow.   Tune—A Gaelic Air.

Turn again, thou fair Eliza! Ae kind blink before we part;
Rew on thy despairing lover, Can'st thou break his faithfu' heart?
Turn again, thou fair Eliza! If to love thy heart denies,
For pity hide the cruel sentence Under friendship's kind disguise!

Thee, sweet maid, hae I offended?
  My offence is loving thee;
Canst thou wreck his peace for ever,
  Wha for thine would gladly die?
While the life beats in my bosom,
  Thou shalt mix in ilka throe:
Turn again, thou lovely maiden,
  Ae sweet smile on me bestow.

Not the bee upon the blossom,
  In the pride o' sunny noon;
Not the little sporting fairy,
  All beneath the simmer moon;
Not the minstrel, in the moment
  Fancy lightens in his e'e,
Kens the pleasure, feels the rapture,
  That thy presence gies to me.

LANDLADY, COUNT THE LAWIN'.*

BOLDLY. TUNE—"Hey Tutti Taiti."

Landla-dy, count the law-in', The day is near the daw-in'; Ye're a' blind drunk, boys, And I'm but jol-ly fou. Hey tutti, tai-ti, How tutti, tai-ti, Hey tutti, tai-ti, Wha's fou now?

Cog, an ye were aye fu',
Cog, an ye were aye fu',
I wad sit and sing to you,
   If ye were aye fu'.
      Hey tutti, taiti, &c.

Weel may ye a'. be !
Ill may we never see !
God bless the king, boys,
   And the companie !
      Hey tutti, taiti, &c.

THE BANKS O' DOON.†

SLOW AND TENDER. TUNE—"The Caledonian Hunt's Delight."

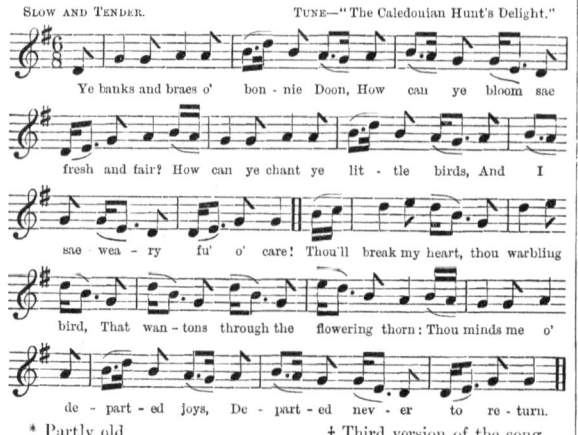

Ye banks and braes o' bon-nie Doon, How can ye bloom sae fresh and fair? How can ye chant ye lit-tle birds, And I sae wea-ry fu' o' care! Thou'll break my heart, thou warbling bird, That wan-tons through the flowering thorn: Thou minds me o' de-part-ed joys, De-part-ed nev-er to re-turn.

Aft hae I roved by bonnie Doon,
  To see the rose and woodbine twine ;
And ilka bird sang o' its luve,
  And fondly sae did I o' mine.
Wi' lightsome heart I pu'd a rose,
  Fu' sweet upon its thorny tree ;
And my fause luver staw my rose,
  But ah ! he left the thorn wi' me.

THE DISCREET HINT.

LASS, when your mither is frae hame,
  May I but be sae bauld
As come to your bower-window,
  And creep in frae the cauld ?

* Partly old.   † Third version of the song.

As come to your bower-window,
   And when it's cauld an' wat,
Warm me in thy fair bosom—
   Sweet lass, may I do that?

Young man, gin ye should be sae kind,
   When our guidwife's frae hame,
As come to my bower-window,
   Whare I am laid my lane,
To warm thee in my bosom—
   Tak tent, I'll tell thee what,
The way to me lies through the kirk:—
   Young man, do ye hear that?

SIC A WIFE AS WILLIE HAD.*

She has an e'e, she has but ane,
   The cat has twa the very colour;
Five rusty teeth forbye a stump,
   A clapper tongue wad deave a miller:
A whiskin' beard about her mou',
   Her nose and chin they threaten ither;
Sic a wife as Willie had,
   I wad na gie a button for her.

She's bow-hough'd, she's hen-shinn'd,
   Ae limpin' leg a hand-breed shorter;
She's twisted right, she's twisted left,
   To balance fair in ilka quarter:
She has a hump upon her breast,
   The twin o' that upon her shouther;
Sic a wife as Willie had,
   I wad na gie a button for her.

Auld baudrons by the ingle sits
   An' wi' her loof her face a washin';
But Willie's wife is nae sae trig,
   She dights her grunzie wi' a hushion:

* The music adapted to these words in the *Museum* is called "The Eight Men of Moidart," but it is now usually sung to the above tune.

Her walie nieves like midden-creels,
   Her face wad fyle the Logan Water;
Sic a wife as Willie had,
   I wad na gie a button for her.

THENIEL MENZIES' BONNIE MARY.

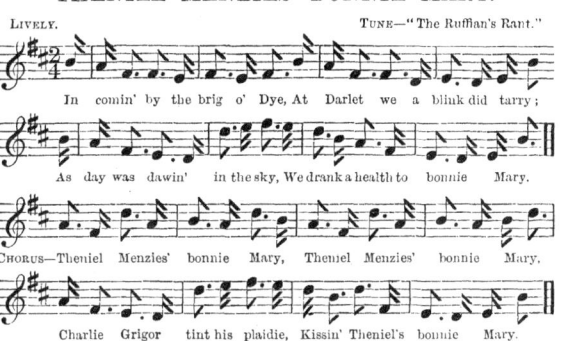

Her een sae bright, her brow sae white,
   Her haffet locks as brown 's a berry;
And aye they dimpl't wi' a smile,
   The rosy cheeks o' bonnie Mary.
      Theniel Menzies' bonnie Mary, &c.

We lap an' danc'd the lee-lang day,
   Till piper lads were wae and weary;
But Charlie gat the spring to pay,
   For kissin' Theniel's bonnie Mary.
      Theniel Menzies' bonnie Mary, &c.

THE SMILING SPRING.

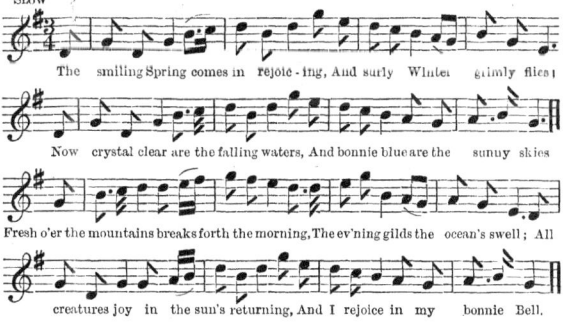

The flowery Spring leads sunny Summer,
   The yellow Autumn presses near;
Then in his turn comes gloomy Winter,
   Till smiling Spring again appear:
Thus seasons dancing, life advancing,
   Old Time and Nature their changes tell;
But never ranging, still unchanging,
   I adore my bonnie Bell.

AFTON WATER.*

Slow and Tender.

Flow gently, sweet Afton! among thy green braes, Flow gently, I'll sing thee a song in thy praise; My Mary's asleep by thy murmuring stream, Flow gently, sweet Afton, disturb not her dream.

* The above verses and tune were supplied by Burns to the *Museum*. They are, however, now generally sung to an air composed by Alexander Hume.

Thou stock dove whose echo resounds through the glen,
Ye wild whistling blackbirds, in yon thorny den,
Thou green crested lapwing thy screaming forbear,
I charge you, disturb not my slumbering Fair.

How lofty, sweet Afton, thy neighbouring hills,
Far mark'd with the courses of clear, winding rills;
There daily I wander as noon rises high,
My flocks and my Mary's sweet cot in my eye.

How pleasant thy banks and green valleys below,
Where, wild in the woodlands, the primroses blow;
There oft, as mild ev'ning weeps over the lea,
The sweet-scented birk shades my Mary and me.

Thy crystal stream, Afton, how lovely it glides,
And winds by the cot where my Mary resides;*
How wanton thy waters her snowy feet lave,
As, gathering sweet flowerets, she stems thy clear wave.

Flow gently, sweet Afton, amang thy green braes,
Flow gently, sweet river, the theme of my lays;
My Mary's asleep by thy murmuring stream,
Flow gently, sweet Afton, disturb not her dream.

THE GALLANT WEAVER.

My daddie sign'd my tocher-band,
To gie the lad that has the land,
But to my heart I'll add my hand,
  And give it to the weaver.
While birds rejoice in leafy bowers,
While bees delight in opening flowers,
While corn grows green in summer showers,
  I love my gallant weaver.

THE RIGHTS OF WOMAN.

AN OCCASIONAL ADDRESS SPOKEN BY MISS FONTENELLE ‡
ON HER BENEFIT NIGHT, NOVEMBER 26, 1792.

WHILE Europe's eye is fix'd on mighty things,
The fate of empires and the fall of kings;
While quacks of State must each produce his plan,
And even children lisp the Rights of Man;
Amid this mighty fuss just let me mention,
The Rights of Woman merit some attention.

* Dr. Currie says, "Afton Water is the stream on which stands Afton Lodge: to which Mrs. Stewart removed from Stair. Afton Lodge was Mrs. Stewart's property from her father. The song was presented to her in return for her notice, the first he ever received from any person in her rank of life." Gilbert Burns says it alludes to Highland Mary.
† "Cart:" a river near Paisley, sung by Campbell, and celebrated by Wilson, as well as by Burns.
‡ "Miss Fontenelle," a favourite actress in Dumfries.

First, in the sexes' intermix'd connection,
One sacred Right of Woman is *protection*.
The tender flower that lifts its head, elate,
Helpless, must fall before the blasts of fate,
Sunk on the earth, defac'd its lovely form,
Unless your shelter ward th' impending storm.

Our second Right—but needless here is caution,
To keep that right inviolate 's the fashion;
Each man of sense has it so full before him,
He'd die before he'd wrong it—'tis *decorum*.
There was, indeed, in far less polish'd days,
A time when rough, rude man had naughty ways;
Would swagger, swear, get drunk, kick up a riot,
Nay, even thus invade a lady's quiet.§
Now, thank our stars! these Gothic times are fled;
Now, well-bred men—and you are all well-bred—
Most justly think (and we are much the gainers)
Such conduct neither spirit, wit, nor manners.

For Right the third, our last, our best, our dearest,
That right to fluttering female hearts the nearest;
Which even the Rights of Kings, in low prostration
Most humbly own—'tis dear, dear *admiration!*
In that blest sphere alone we live and move;
There taste that life of life—immortal love.
Smiles, glances, sighs, tears, fits, flirtations, airs;
'Gainst such an host what flinty savage dares,
When awful Beauty joins with all her charms—
Who is so rash as rise in rebel arms?

But truce with kings, and truce with constitutions,
With bloody armaments and revolutions;
Let Majesty your first attention summon,
Ah! ça ira! THE MAJESTY OF WOMAN!

SHE'S FAIR AND FAUSE.

§ Ironical allusion to the Saturnalia of the Caledonian Hunt.

Whae'er ye be that woman love,
    To this be never blind;
Nae ferlie 'tis though fickle she prove,
    A woman has 't by kind.
O woman lovely, woman fair!
An angel form 's faun to thy share,
'Twad been owre meikle to gien thee mair—
    I mean an angel mind.

EPIGRAM ON SEEING MISS FONTENELLE IN A FAVOURITE CHARACTER.

Sweet naïveté of feature,
    Simple, wild, enchanting elf,
Not to thee, but thanks to Nature,
    Thou art acting but thyself.

Wert thou awkward, stiff, affected,
    Spurning Nature, torturing art;
Loves and graces all rejected,
    Then indeed thou 'd'st act a part.

EXTEMPORE ON SOME COMMEMORATIONS OF THOMSON.

Dost thou not rise, indignant shade,
    And smile wi' spurning scorn,
When they wha wad hae starved thy life,
    Thy senseless turf adorn?

Helpless, alane, thou clamb the brae,
    Wi' meikle honest toil,
And claught th' unfading garland there—
    Thy sair-won, rightful spoil.

And wear it there! and call aloud
    This axiom undoubted—
Would thou hae Nobles' patronage?
    First learn to live without it!

To whom hae much, more shall be given,
    Is every great man's faith;
But he, the helpless, needful wretch,
    Shall lose the mite he hath.

HERE 'S A HEALTH TO THEM THAT 'S AWA'.*

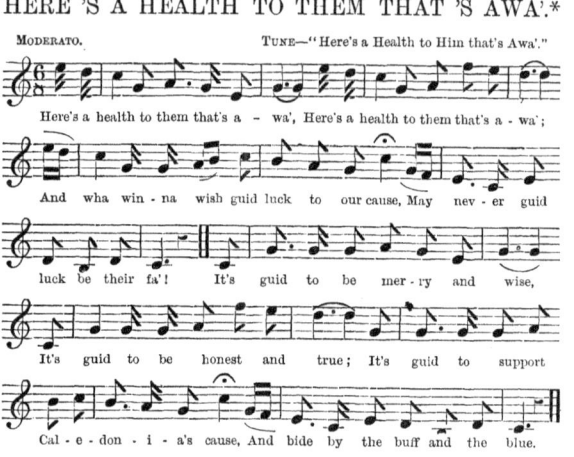

Here 's a health to them that 's awa',
    Here 's a health to them that 's awa',
Here 's a health to Charlie,† the chief o' the clan,
    Altho' that his band be sma'!
May Liberty meet wi' success!
    May Prudence protect her frae evil!
May tyrants and tyranny tine i' the mist,
    And wander their way to the devil!

Here 's a health to them that 's awa',
    Here 's a health to them that 's awa';
Here 's a health to Tammie,‡ the Norlan' laddie,
    That lives at the lug o' the law!
Here 's freedom to them that wad read,
    Here 's freedom to them that would write,
There 's nane ever fear'd that the truth should be heard,
    But they whom the truth would indite.

Here 's a health to them that 's awa',
    An' here 's to them that 's awa'!
Here 's to Maitland and Wycombe, let wha does na like 'em
    Be built in a hole in the wa'.
Here 's timmer that 's red at the heart,
    Here 's fruit that is sound at the core;
And may he that wad turn the buff and blue coat
    Be turn'd to the back o' the door.

Here 's a health to them that 's awa',
    Here 's a health to them that 's awa';
Here 's chieftain M'Leod,§ a chieftain worth gowd,
    Though bred amang mountains o' snaw.
Here 's friends on baith sides o' the firth,
    And friends on baith sides o' the Tweed;
And wha wad betray old Albion's right,
    May they never eat of her bread!

---

* Founded on an old favourite song.   † "Charlie:" Mr. Fox.
‡ "Tammie:" Lord Erskine.
§ M'Leod, M.P. for Inverness, a determined Reformer.

SONNET,

WRITTEN ON THE 25TH JANUARY, 1793, THE BIRTHDAY OF THE AUTHOR, ON HEARING A THRUSH SING IN A MORNING WALK.

Sing on, sweet thrush, upon the leafless bough,
   Sing on, sweet bird, I listen to thy strain,
   See aged Winter, 'mid his surly reign,
At thy blythe carol, clears his furrowed brow.

So in lone Poverty's dominion drear,
   Sits meek Content with light, unanxious heart;
   Welcomes the rapid moments, bids them part,
Nor asks if they bring ought to hope or fear.

I thank thee, Author of this opening day!
   Thou whose bright sun now gilds yon orient skies!
   Riches denied, thy boon was purer joys—
What wealth could never give nor take away!
Yet come, thou child of poverty and care,
The mite high Heav'n bestow'd, that mite with thee I'll share.

O CAN YE LABOUR LEA?

Chorus—O can ye labour lea, young man, O can ye labour lea?
It fee nor bountith shall us twine Gin ye can labour lea.

Song—I fee'd a man at Mic-hael-mas, Wi' airle pennies three;
But a' the faut I had to him, He could na labour lea.

   O clappin' 's gude in Febarwar,
     An' kissin' 's sweet in May;
   But my delight 's the ploughman lad,
     That weel can labour lea.
        O can ye labour lea, &c.

O kissin' is the key o' love,
    And clappin' is the lock;
An' makin' o' 's the best thing yet,
    That e'er a young thing gat.
        O can ye labour lea, &c.

ADDRESS TO GENERAL DUMOURIER.*

A PARODY ON "ROBIN ADAIR."

You 're welcome to despots, Dumourier;
You 're welcome to despots, Dumourier:
    How does Dampiere do?
    Ay, and Bournonville too?
Why did they not come along with you, Dumourier?

I will fight France with you, Dumourier;
I will fight France with you, Dumourier;
    I will fight France with you,
    I will take my chance with you;
By my soul, I 'll dance with you, Dumourier.

Then let us fight about, Dumourier;
Then let us fight about, Dumourier;
    Then let us fight about,
    Till Freedom's spark be out,
Then we 'll be d—d, no doubt, Dumourier.

IMPROMPTU,

ON MRS. RIDDELL'S BIRTHDAY, 4TH NOVEMBER, 1793.

Old Winter, with his frosty beard,
Thus once to Jove his prayer preferred:
"What have I done of all the year,
To bear this hated doom severe?
My cheerless suns no pleasure know;
Night's horrid car drags dreary slow;
My dismal months no joys are crowning,
But spleeny English hanging, drowning.

"Now Jove, for once be mighty civil,
To counterbalance all this evil;
Give me, and I 've no more to say,
Give me Maria's natal day!
That brilliant gift will so enrich me,
Spring, Summer, Autumn, cannot match me."
"'Tis done!" says Jove; so ends my story,
And Winter once rejoiced in glory.

---

* Chanted extempore when he heard of Dumourier deserting the Republican cause, April 5, 1793.

ON THE DEATH OF A LAP-DOG NAMED ECHO.†

In wood and wild, ye warbling throng,
    Your heavy loss deplore;
Now, half extinct your powers of song,
    Sweet "Echo" is no more.

Ye jarring, screeching things around,
    Scream your discordant joys;
Now, half your din of tuneless sound
    With "Echo" silent lies.

ON THE LAIRD OF LAGGAN.

When Morine, deceased, to the devil went down,
'Twas nothing would serve him but Satan's own crown;
"Thy fool's head," quoth Satan, "that crown shall wear never;
I grant thou 'rt as wicked, but not quite so clever."

EPIGRAM AT BROWNHILL INN.

At Brownhill we always get dainty good cheer,
And plenty of bacon each day in the year;
We 've a' thing that 's nice, and mostly in season,
But why always Bacon‡—come tell me the reason?

GRACE BEFORE AND AFTER MEAT

O Lord, when hunger pinches sore,
    Do thou stand us in stead,
And send us, from thy bounteous store,
    A tup or wether head! Amen.

O Lord, since we have feasted thus,
    Which we so little merit,
Let Meg § now take away the flesh,
    And Jock bring in the spirit! Amen.

---

† Belonging to Mrs. Gordon of Kenmure Castle.
‡ Bacon was the name of the landlord, who would seem to have been given to intruding on his guests.
§ Jock and Meg Hislop of the Globe Tavern.

TO THE OWL.

Sad bird of night! what sorrows call thee forth,
    To vent thy plaints thus in the midnight hour?
Is it some blast that gathers in the North,
    Threat'ning to nip the verdure of thy bower?

Is it, sad owl! that Autumn strips the shade,
    And leaves thee here, unshelter'd and forlorn?
Or fear that Winter will thy nest invade?
    Or friendless melancholy bids thee mourn?

Shut out, lone bird! from all the feather'd train,
    To tell thy sorrows to th' unheeding gloom;
No friends to pity when thou dost complain,
    Grief all thy thought, and solitude thy home.

Sing on, sad mourner! I will bless thy strain,
    And, pleased, in sorrow listen to thy song:
Sing on, sad mourner! to the night complain,
    While the lone echo wafts thy notes along.

Is beauty less, when down the glowing cheek
    Sad, piteous tears in native sorrows fall?
Less kind the heart when anguish bids it break?
    Less happy he who lists to pity's call?

Ah no, sad owl! nor is thy voice less sweet,
    That sadness tunes it, and that grief is there;
That spring's gay notes, unskill'd, thou can'st repeat;
    That sorrow bids thee to the gloom repair.

Nor that the treble songsters of the day
    Are quite estranged, sad bird of night! from thee;
Nor that the thrush deserts the evening spray,
    When darkness calls thee from thy reverie.

From some old tower, thy melancholy dome,
    While the gray walls, and desert solitudes,
Return each note, responsive to the gloom
    Of ivied coverts and surrounding woods;

There hooting, I will list more pleased to thee
    Than ever lover to the nightingale;
Or drooping wretch, oppress'd with misery,
    Lending his ear to some condoling tale.

LINES SENT TO A GENTLEMAN (MR. RIDDELL) WHOM HE HAD OFFENDED.

The friend whom, wild from wisdom's way,
  The fumes of wine infuriate send,
(Not moony madness more astray)
  Who but deplores that hapless friend?

Mine was th' insensate frenzied part,
  Ah! why should I such scenes outlive!
Scenes so abhorrent to my heart!
  'Tis thine to pity and forgive.

MONODY
ON A LADY FAMED FOR HER CAPRICE.*

How cold is that bosom which folly once fired,
  How pale is that cheek where the rouge lately glisten'd;
How silent that tongue which the echoes oft tired,
  How dull is that ear which to flatt'ry so listen'd!

If sorrow and anguish their exit await,
  From friendship and dearest affection remov'd;
How doubly severer, Maria, thy fate,
  Thou diedst unwept, as thou livedst unlov'd.

Loves, Graces, and Virtues, I call not on you;
  So shy, grave, and distant, ye shed not a tear:
But come, all ye offspring of Folly so true,
  And flowers let us cull for Maria's cold bier.

We'll search through the garden for each silly flower,
  We'll roam through the forest for each idle weed;
But chiefly the nettle, so typical, shower,
  For none e'er approach'd her but rued the rash deed.

We'll sculpture the marble, we'll measure the lay;
  Here Vanity strums on her idiot lyre; †
There keen Indignation shall dart on his prey,
  Which spurning Contempt shall redeem from his ire.

THE EPITAPH.

Here lies, now a prey to insulting neglect,
  What once was a butterfly, gay in life's beam:
Want only of wisdom denied her respect,
  Want only of goodness denied her esteem.

EPISTLE FROM ESOPUS TO MARIA.‡

From those drear solitudes and frowsy cells,
Where Infamy with sad Repentance dwells;
Where turnkeys make the jealous portal fast,
And deal from iron hands the spare repast;
Where truant 'prentices, yet young in sin,
Blush at the curious stranger peeping in;
Where strumpets, relics of the drunken roar,
Resolve to drink, nay half—to whore no more;
Where tiny thieves not destin'd yet to swing,
Beat hemp for others, riper for the string:
From these dire scenes my wretched lines I date,
To tell Maria her Esopus' fate.

"Alas! I feel I am no actor here!"
'Tis real hangmen real scourges bear!
Prepare, Maria, for a horrid tale
Will turn thy very rouge to deadly pale;
Will make thy hair, though erst from gipsy poll'd,
By barber woven, and by barber sold,
Though twisted smooth with Harry's nicest care,
Like hoary bristles to erect and stare.
The hero of the mimic scene, no more
I start in Hamlet, in Othello roar;
Or haughty chieftain, 'mid the din of arms,
In Highland bonnet, woo Malvina's charms;
While sans-culottes stoop up the mountain high,
And steal from me Maria's prying eye.
Blest Highland bonnet! once my proudest dress,
Now prouder still, Maria's temples press;
I see her wave thy towering plumes afar,
And call each coxcomb to the wordy war;
I see her face the first of Ireland's sons, §
And even out-Irish his Hibernian bronze;
The crafty colonel ‖ leaves the tartan'd lines
For other wars, where he a hero shines;
The hopeful youth, in Scottish senate bred,
Who owns a Bushby's heart without the head, ¶
Comes 'mid a string of coxcombs, to display
That *Veni, vidi, vici*, is his way;
The shrinking bard adown the alley skulks,
And dreads a meeting worse than Woolwich hulks;
Though there, his heresies in Church and State
Might well award him Muir and Palmer's fate:
Still she undaunted reels and rattles on,
And dares the public like a noontide sun.
What scandal call'd Maria's jaunty stagger
The ricket reeling of a crooked swagger?
Whose spleen (e'en worse than Burns' venom, when
He dips in gall unmix'd his eager pen,
And pours his vengeance in the burning line),
Who christen'd thus Maria's lyre divine
The idiot strum of vanity bemused,
And even the abuse of Poesy abused?

---

* Written on Mrs. Riddell.
† *N.B.*—The lady affects to be a poetess.—(B.)
‡ One Williamson, an actor, supposed to address Mrs. Riddell from a House of Correction.

§ "First of Ireland's sons:" Gillespie.
‖ "Crafty colonel:" Colonel M'Dowal of Logan, the Lothario of his day.
¶ Bushby Maitland, son of Mr. John Maitland of Tinwald-downs, a writer and banker with whom Burns had been on terms of intimacy.

Who call'd her verse a parish workhouse, made
For motley, foundling fancies, stolen or stray'd?

A workhouse! ah, that sound awakes my woes,
And pillows on the thorn my rack'd repose!
In durance vile here must I wake and weep,
And all my frowsy couch in sorrow steep!
That straw where many a rogue has lain of yore,
And vermin'd gipsies litter'd heretofore.

Why, Lonsdale, thus thy wrath on vagrants pour?
Must earth no rascal save thyself endure?
Must thou alone in guilt immortal swell,
And make a vast monopoly of hell?
Thou know'st the Virtues cannot hate thee worse;
The Vices also, must they club their curse?
Or must no tiny sin to others fall,
Because thy guilt's supreme enough for all?

Maria, send me too thy griefs and cares;
In all of thee sure thy Esopus shares.
As thou at all mankind the flag unfurls,
Who on my fair one Satire's vengeance hurls—
Who calls thee, pert, affected, vain coquette,
A wit in folly, and a fool in wit!
Who says that fool alone is not thy due,
And quotes thy treacheries to prove it true!

Our force united on thy foes we 'll turn,
And dare the war with all of woman born:
For who can write and speak as thou and I?
My periods that decyphering defy,
And thy still matchless tongue that conquers all reply!

MY EPPIE ADAIR.

A' pleasure exile me, dishonour defile me,
If e'er I beguile ye, my Eppie Adair!
A' pleasure exile me, dishonour defile me,
If e'er I beguile thee, my Eppie Adair!
And O my Eppie, &c.

A RED, RED ROSE.*

Till a' the seas gang dry, my dear,
And the rocks melt wi' the sun;
And I will luve thee still, my dear,
While the sands o' life shall run.
And fare-thee-well, my only luve!
And fare-thee-well, a while!
And I will come again, my luve,
Though 'twere ten thousand mile!

FRAGMENT—AMANG THE TREES.

Amang the trees, where humming bees,
At buds and flowers were hinging, O,
Auld Caledon drew out her drone,
And to her pipe was singing, O:
'Twas pibroch, sang, strathspeys and reels,
She dirl'd them aff fu' clearly, O;
When there cam' a yell o' foreign squeels,
That dang her tapsalteerie, O.

Their capon craws an' queer "ha, ha's,"
They made our lugs grow eerie, O;
The hungry bike did scrape and fyke,
Till we were wae and weary, O:
But a royal ghaist, wha ance was cas'd,
A prisoner, aughteen year awa',
He fir'd a fiddler in the North,
That dang them tapsalteerie, O.

* In the *Museum* the above words are set to two different airs—one called "Major Graham," which does not suit the words; the other, "Queen Mary's Lament" (see page 185). The song, however, is now usually sung to the tune given above.

THE LOVELY LASS O' INVERNESS.*

TUNE—"The Lovely Lass of Inverness."

The love-ly lass o' In-ver-ness, Nae joy nor pleasure can she see; For e'en to morn she cries a-las! And aye the saut tear blin's her e'e. Drum-os-sie moor, Drum-os-sie day; A waefu' day it was to me! For there I lost my fa-ther dear, My fa-ther dear, and breth-ren three.

Their winding-sheet the bluidy clay,
Their graves are growin' green to see;

* The first half stanza is old.

And by them lies the dearest lad
That ever blest a woman's e'e!
Now wae to thee, thou cruel lord,
A bluidy man I trow thou be;
For mony a heart thou has made sair,
That ne'er did wrang to thine or thee!

LOUIS, WHAT RECK I BY THEE?

TUNE—"Louis, what Reck I by thee?"

Louis, what reck I by thee, Or Geordie on his ocean? Dy-vour, beggar louns to me, I reign in Jean-ie's bosom!

Let her crown my love her law,
And in her breast enthrone me,
Kings and nations—swith awa'!
Reif randies, I disown ye!

THE MINSTREL AT LINCLUDEN.

FIRST VERSION.

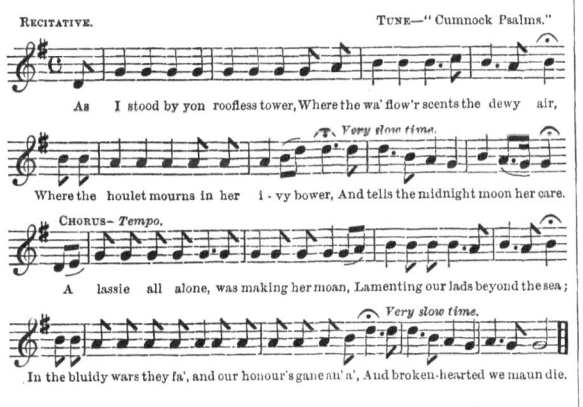

The winds were laid, the air was still,
    The stars they shot along the sky;
The tod was howling on the hill,
    And the distant-echoing glens reply.
        A lassie all alone, &c.

The burn, adown its hazelly path,
    Was rushing by the ruin'd wa',
Hasting to join the sweeping Nith,
    Whase roarings seem'd to rise and fa'.
        A lassie all alone, &c.

The cauld blae North was streaming forth
    Her lights, wi' hissing, eerie din,
Athort the lift they start and shift,
    Like Fortune's favours, tint as win.
        A lassie all alone, &c.

Now, looking over frith and fauld,
    Her horn the pale-faced Cynthia rear'd,
When lo! in form of minstrel auld,
    A stern and stalwart ghaist appear'd.
        A lassie all alone, &c.

And frae his harp sic strains did flow,
    Might rous'd the slumbering dead to hear;
But oh, it was a tale of woe,
    As ever met a Briton's ear!
        A lassie all alone, &c.

He sang wi' joy his former day,
    He, weeping, wail'd his latter times;
But what he said—it was nae play,
    I winna ventur 't in my rhymes.
        A lassie all alone, &c.

A VISION.

SECOND VERSION.

As I stood by yon roofless tower,*
  Where the wa'-flower scents the dewy air,
Where the howlet mourns in her ivy bower,
  And tells the midnight moon her care.

The winds were laid, the air was still,
  The stars they shot alang the sky;
The fox was howling on the hill,
  And the distant-echoing glens reply.

The stream, adown its hazelly path,
  Was rushing by the ruin'd wa's,
To join yon river on the Strath,
  Whase distant roaring swells and fa's.

The cauld blae North was streaming forth
  Her lights, wi' hissing, eerie din;
Athwart the lift they start and shift,
  Like Fortune's favours, tint as win.

By heedless chance I turn'd my eyes,
  And, by the moonbeam, shook to see
A stern and stalwart ghaist arise,
  Attir'd as minstrels wont to be.

Had I a statue been o' stane,
  His daring look had daunted me;
And on his bonnet grav'd was plain,
  The sacred posy—"LIBERTIE!"

And frae his harp sic strains did flow,
  Might rous'd the slumb'ring dead to hear;
But oh, it was a tale of woe,
  As ever met a Briton's ear!

He sang wi' joy his former day,
  He, weeping, wailed his latter times;
But what he said—it was nae play,
  I winna ventur't in my rhymes.

HAD I THE WYTE?

HAD I the wyte, had I the wyte,
  Had I the wyte? she bade me,
She watch'd me by the hie-gate side,
  And up the loan she shaw'd me.
And when I wadna venture in,
  A coward loon she ca'd me:
Had Kirk an' State been in the gate,
  I'd lighted when she bade me.

---

* "Roofless tower:" Lincluden Abbey. The "Song of Liberty" was probably written, but suppressed. See LIFE.

Sae craftilie she took me ben,
  And bade me mak nae clatter;
"For our ramgunshoch, glum guidman
  Is o'er ayont the water."
Whae'er shall say I wanted grace,
  When I did kiss and dawte her,
Let him be planted in my place,
  Syne say, I was the fautor.

Could I for shame, could I for shame,
  Could I for shame refus'd her?
And wadna manhood been to blame,
  Had I unkindly used her!
He claw'd her wi' the ripplin'-kame,
  And blae and bluidy bruis'd her;
When sic a husband was frae hame,
  What wife but wad excus'd her!

I dighted aye her e'en sae blue,
  An' bann'd the cruel randy,
And weel I wat, her willin' mou
  Was sweet as sugar-candie.
At gloamin'-shot, it was I wot,
  I lighted—on the Monday;
But I cam through the Tyseday's dew,
  To wanton Willie's brandy.†

OUT OVER THE FORTH.

---

† These verses certainly verge upon indecency; but they are much less objectionable than the old song on which they are founded.

FOR THE SAKE O' SOMEBODY.*

Ye Powers that smile on virtuous love,
O, sweetly smile on Somebody!
Frae ilka danger keep him free,
And send me safe my Somebody!
O-hon! for Somebody!
O-hey! for Somebody!
I wad do—what wad I not?
For the sake o' Somebody.

LOVELY POLLY STEWART.†

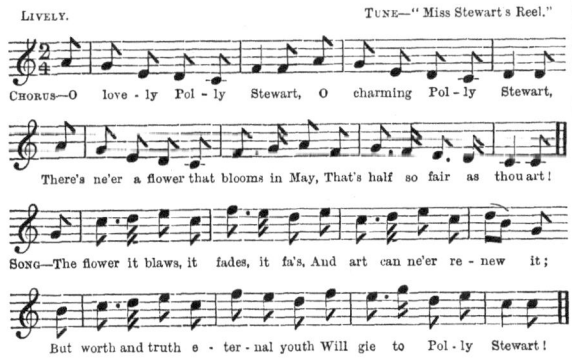

May he whase arms shall fauld thy charms
Possess a leal and true heart!
To him be given to ken the heaven
He grasps in Polly Stewart!
O lovely Polly Stewart, &c.

* The above tune, since it appeared in the *Museum*, has been vastly improved. The long-received and popular version is here given.
† Daughter of one Willy Stewart, near Ellisland, married to a large proprietor, fell into bad courses, and died in Florence.

JOHNNIE LAD, COCK UP YOUR BEAVER.‡

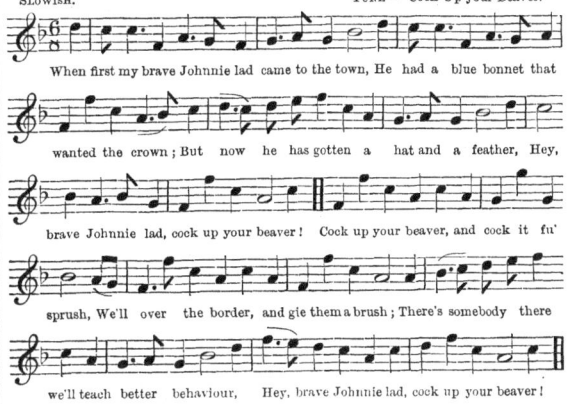

TO THE WEAVER'S GIN YE GO.

My mither sent me to the town,
To warp a plaiden wab;
But the weary, weary warpin' o't
Has gart me sigh and sab.
    To the weaver's, &c.

A bonnie, westlin' weaver lad
Sat working at his loom;
He took my heart as wi' a net,
In every knot and thrum.
    To the weaver's, &c.

I sat beside my warpin'-wheel,
And aye I ca'd it roun';
But every shot and every knock,
My heart it gae a stoun.
    To the weaver's, &c.

‡ Partly old.

The moon was sinking in the west,
  Wi' visage pale and wan,
As my bonnie, westlin' weaver lad
  Convoy'd me through the glen.
      To the weaver's, &c.

But what was said, or what was done,
  Shame fa' me gin I tell;
But Oh! I fear the kintra soon
  Will ken as weel 's mysel'!
      To the weaver's, &c.

WAE IS MY HEART.

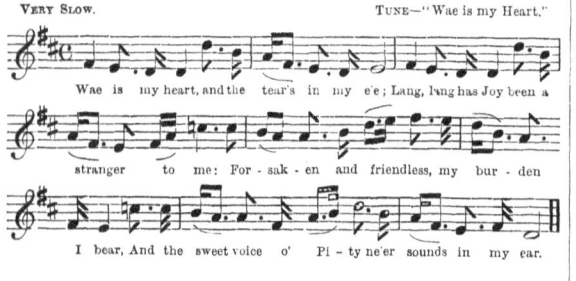

Love, thou hast pleasures, and deep hae I luv'd;
Love, thou hast sorrows, and sair hae I pruv'd;
But this bruisèd heart that now bleeds in my breast,
I can feel by its throbbings, will soon be at rest.

Oh, if I were—where happy I hae been—
Down by yon stream, and yon bonnie castle-green!
For there he is wand'ring and musing on me,
Wha wad soon dry the tear-drop that clings to my e'e.

MY LOVE, SHE'S BUT A LASSIE YET.*

Come draw a drap o' the best o't yet,
Come draw a drap o' the best o't yet;
Gae seek for pleasure whare ye will,
But here I never miss'd it yet.

    * An old song amended.

We 're a' dry wi' drinkin' o't,
We 're a' dry wi' drinkin' o't;
The minister kiss't the fiddler's wife;
He could na preach for thinkin' o't.

SONG—ANNA, THY CHARMS.

SLOW. TUNE—"Bonny Mary."

MY LADY'S GOWN, THERE 'S GAIRS UPON 'T.*

LIVELY. TUNE—"Gregg's Strathspey."

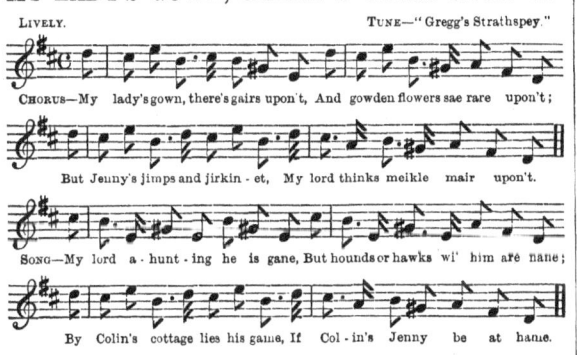

My lady 's white, my lady 's red,
And kith and kin o' Cassillis' blude;
But her ten-pund lands o' tocher gude
Were a' the charms his lordship lo'ed.
    My lady's gown, &c.

Out o'er yon muir, out o'er yon moss,
Whare gor-cocks through the heather pass,
There wons auld Colin's bonnie lass,
A lily in a wilderness.
    My lady's gown, &c.

Sae sweetly move her genty limbs,
Like music notes o' lovers' hymns:

    * An old song amended.

The diamond dew in her een sae blue,
Where laughing love sae wanton swims.
    My lady's gown, &c.

My lady's dink, my lady's drest,
The flower and fancy o' the west;
But the lassie that a man lo'es best,
O that 's the lass to mak him blest.
    My lady's gown, &c.

HEY, THE DUSTY MILLER.

LIVELY. TUNE—"Hey, the Dusty Miller."

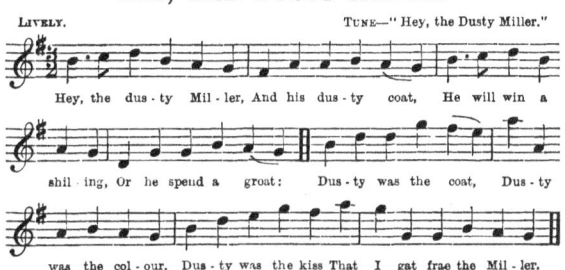

Hey, the dusty Miller,
  And his dusty sack;
Leeze me on the calling
  Fills the dusty peck:
Fills the dusty peck,
  Brings the dusty siller;
I wad gie my coatie
  For the dusty Miller.

O LAY THY LOOF IN MINE, LASS.

MODERATO. TUNE—"The Cordwainer's March."

There 's mony a lass has broke my rest,
That for a blink I hae lo'ed best;
But thou art queen within my breast,
For ever to remain.
    O lay thy loof, &c.

LINES WRITTEN EXTEMPORE IN A LADY'S POCKET-BOOK.

Grant me, indulgent Heaven, that I may live,
To see the miscreants feel the pains they give;
Deal Freedom's sacred treasures free as air,
Till slave and despot be but things that were.

INSCRIPTION ON A GOBLET
BELONGING TO MR. SYME.

There's Death in the cup, so beware!
  Nay, more—there is danger in touching;
But who can avoid the fell snare,
  The man and his wine's so bewitching!

JOCKEY'S TAEN THE PARTING KISS.

When the shades of evening creep
  O'er the day's fair, gladsome e'e,
Sound and safely may he sleep,
  Sweetly blythe his waukening be.
He will think on her he loves,
  Fondly he'll repeat her name;
For where'er he distant roves,
  Jockey's heart is still the same.

MALLY'S MEEK, MALLY'S SWEET.

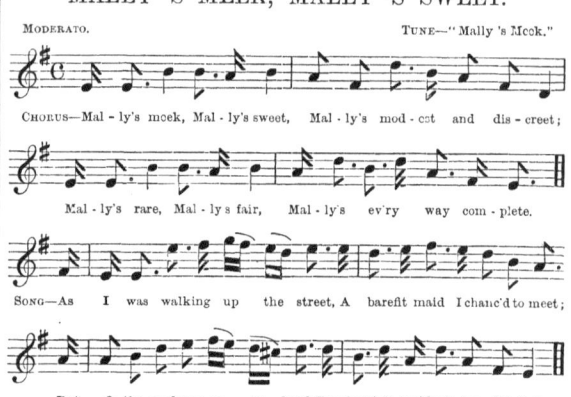

It were mair meet that those fine feet
  Were weel laced up in silken shoon,
And 'twere more fit that she should sit
  Within yon chariot gilt aboon.
    Mally's meek, &c.

Her yellow hair, beyond compare,
  Comes trinklin' down her swan-like neck;
And her two eyes, like stars in skies,
  Would keep a sinking ship frae wreck.
              Mally 's meek, &c.

SONNET ON THE DEATH OF ROBERT RIDDELL,

OF GLENRIDDELL AND FRIARS' CARSE.*

No more, ye warblers of the wood! no more;
  Nor pour your descant grating on my soul;
  Thou young-eyed Spring! gay in thy verdant stole,
More welcome were to me grim Winter's wildest roar.

How can ye charm, ye flowers, with all your dyes?
  Ye blow upon the sod that wraps my friend!
How can I to the tuneful strain attend?
That strain flows round the untimely tomb where Riddell
    lies.

Yes, pour, ye warblers! pour the notes of woe,
  And soothe the Virtues weeping o'er his bier:
The man of worth—and hath not left his peer!
Is in his "narrow house," for ever darkly low.

Thee, Spring! again with joy shall others greet;
Me, memory of my loss will only meet.

LIBERTY : A FRAGMENT.†

Thee, Caledonia, thy wild heaths among,
Thee, famed for martial deed and sacred song,
  To thee I turn with swimming eyes;
  Where is that soul of Freedom fled?
  Immingled with the mighty dead!
    Beneath the hallow'd turf where Wallace lies!
Hear it not, Wallace, in thy bed of death!
  Ye babbling winds, in silence sweep;
  Disturb not yet the hero's sleep,
Nor give the coward secret breath.
  Is this the power in freedom's war,
  That wont to bid the battle rage?
Behold that eye which shot immortal hate,
  Crushing the despot's proudest bearing,
That arm which, nerv'd me with thundering fate,
  Braved usurpation's boldest daring!
One quench'd in darkness like the sinking star,
And one the palsied arm of tottering, powerless age.

* Who died on 21st April, 1794.
† Designed as an irregular ode for Washington's birthday.

THE CREED OF POVERTY.

In Politics if thou would'st mix,
  And mean thy fortunes be;
Bear this in mind, be deaf and blind,
  Let great folk hear and see.

THERE 'S NEWS, LASSES, NEWS.

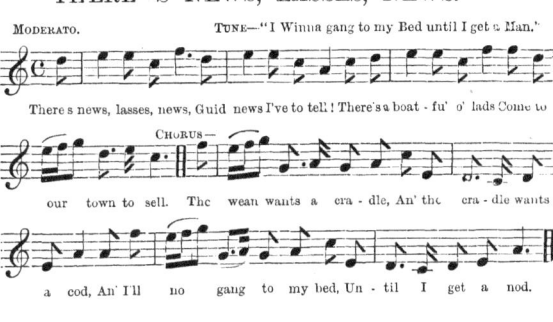

Father, quo' she, Mither, quo' she,
  Do what you can,
  I 'll no gang to my bed,
Until I get a man.
              The wean, &c.

I hae as guid a craft rig
  As made o' yird and stane;
And waly fa' the ley-crap,
  For I maun till'd again.
              The wean, &c.

THE TREE OF LIBERTY.‡

Heard ye o' the tree o' France,
  I watna what 's the name o't;
Around it a' the patriots dance,
  Weel Europe kens the fame o't:
It stands where ance the Bastile stood,
  A prison built by kings, man,
When Superstition's hellish brood
  Kept France in leading strings, man.

Upo' this tree there grows sic fruit,
  Its virtues a' can tell, man;
It raises man aboon the brute,
  It maks him ken himsel', man.

‡ Printed in the People's Edition of Burns, from a MS. belonging to James Duncan, Esq., Mosesfield, Glasgow.

Gif ance the peasant taste a bit,
　He 's greater than a lord, man,
An' wi' the beggar shares a mite
　O' a' he can afford, man.

This fruit is worth a' Afric's wealth,
　To comfort us 'twas sent, man :
To gie the sweetest blush o' health,
　And mak us a' content, man.
It clears the e'en, it cheers the heart,
　Maks high and low guid friends, man ;
And he wha acts the traitor's part
　It to perdition sends, man.

My blessings aye attend the chiel
　Wha pitied Gallia's slaves, man,
And staw a branch, spite o' the deil,
　Frae yont the western waves, man.
Fair Virtue water'd it wi' care,
　And now she sees wi' pride, man,
How weel it buds and blossoms there,
　Its branches spreading wide, man.

But vicious folks aye hate to see
　The works o' Virtue thrive, man ;
The courtly vermin 's bann'd the tree,
　And grat to see it thrive, man.
King Louis thought to cut it down,
　When it was unco sma', man ;
For this the watchman crack'd his crown,
　Cut aff his head and a', man.

A wicked crew syne, on a time,
　Did tak a solemn aith, man.
It ne'er should flourish to its prime,
　I wat they pledged their faith, man.
Awa' they gaed wi' mock parade,
　Like beagles hunting game, man.
But soon grew weary o' the trade,
　And wish'd they 'd been at hame, man.

For Freedom, standing by the tree,
　Her sons did loudly ca', man ;
She sang a sang o' liberty,
　Which pleased them ane and a', man.
By her inspired, the new-born race
　Soon drew the avenging steel, man ;
The hirelings ran—her foes gied chase,
　And bang'd the despot weel, man.

Let Britain boast her hardy oak,
　Her poplar and her pine, man,
Auld Britain ance could crack her joke,
　And o'er her neighbours shine, man.

But seek the forest round and round,
　And soon 'twill be agreed, man,
That sic a tree cannot be found,
　'Twixt London and the Tweed, man.

Without this tree, alake, this life
　Is but a vale o' woe, man ;
A scene o' sorrow mix'd wi' strife,
　Nae real joys we know, man.
We labour soon, we labour late,
　To feed the titled knave, man ;
And a the comfort we 're to get
　Is that ayont the grave, man.

Wi' plenty o' sic trees, I trow,
　The warld would live in peace, man ;
The sword would help to mak a plough,
　The din o' war would cease, man.
Like brethren in a common cause,
　We 'd on each other smile, man ;
And equal rights and equal laws
　Wad gladden every isle, man.

Wae worth the loon wha wadna eat
　Sic halesome, dainty cheer, man ;
I 'd gie my shoon frae aff my feet,
　To taste sic fruit, I swear, man.
Syne let us pray, auld England may
　Sure plant this far-famed tree, man ;
And blythe we 'll sing and hail the day
　That gave us liberty, man.

TO CHLORIS.*

'Tis Friendship's pledge, my young, fair Friend,
　Nor thou the gift refuse,
Nor with the unwilling ear attend
　The moralising Muse.

Since thou in all thy youth and charms,
　Must bid the world adieu,
(A world 'gainst Peace in constant arms)
　To join the Friendly Few ;

Since, thy gay morn of life o'ercast,
　Chill came the tempest's lour
(And ne'er Misfortune's eastern blast
　Did nip a fairer flower) ;

* Miss Lorimer, see LIFE.

Since life's gay scenes must charm no more;
　Still much is left behind;
Still nobler wealth hast thou in store—
　The comforts of the mind!

Thine is the self-approving glow,
　Of conscious Honour's part;
And (dearest gift of Heaven below)
　Thine Friendship's truest heart;

The joys refin'd of Sense and Taste,
　With every Muse to rove:
And doubly were the Poet blest,
　These joys could he improve.

LINES WRITTEN AND PRESENTED TO MRS. KEMBLE,

ON SEEING HER IN THE CHARACTER OF YARICO, DUMFRIES THEATRE, 1794.

KEMBLE, thou cur'st my unbelief
　Of Moses and his rod;
At Yarico's sweet note of grief
　The rock with tears had flow'd.

AH, CHLORIS!

AH, Chloris, since it may not be,
　That thou of love wilt hear;
If from the lover thou maun flee,
　Yet let the friend be dear.

Although I love my Chloris, mair
　Than ever tongue could tell;
My passion I will ne'er declare—
　I'll say, I wish thee well.

Though a' my daily care thou art,
　And a' my nightly dream,
I'll hide the struggle in my heart,
　And say it is esteem.

ON MR. WALTER RIDDELL.

SIC a reptile was Wat, sic a miscreant slave,
That the worms ev'n damned him when laid in his grave;
"In his flesh there's a famine!" a starved reptile cries;
"And his heart is rank poison!" another replies.

ELECTION BALLAD,*

WRITTEN IN 1795.

Wha sees Kerroughtree's open yett,
　(And wha is't never saw that?)
Wha ever wi' Kerroughtree met,
　And has a doubt of a' that?
　　For a' that, and a' that,
　　Here's Heron yet for a' that!
　The independent patriot,
　　The honest man, and a' that.

Though wit and worth, in either sex,
　St. Mary's Isle can shaw that,
Wi' dukes and lords let Selkirk mix,
　And weel does Selkirk fa' that.
　　For a' that, and a' that,
　　Here's Heron yet for a' that!
　The independent commoner
　　Shall be the man for a' that.

But why should we to nobles jouk,
　And is't against the law, that?
For why, a lord may be a gowk,
　Wi' ribband, star, and a' that,
　　For a' that, and a' that,
　　Here's Heron yet for a' that!
　A lord may be a lousy loun,
　　Wi' ribband, star, and a' that.

A beardless boy comes o'er the hills,
　Wi' uncle's purse and a' that;
But we'll hae ane frae 'mang oursels,
　A man we ken, and a' that.
　　For a' that, and a' that,
　　Here's Heron yet for a' that!
　For we're not to be bought and sold,
　　Like naigs, and nowte, and a' that.

Then let us drink—The Stewartry,
　Kerroughtree's laird, and a' that,

* See LIFE.

Our representative to be,
  For weel he's worthy a' that.
For a' that, and a' that,
  Here's Heron yet for a' that!
A House of Commons such as he,
  They wad be blest that saw that.

ELECTION BALLAD—ELECTION DAY.

With Spirit. Tune—"The Blythesome Bridal."

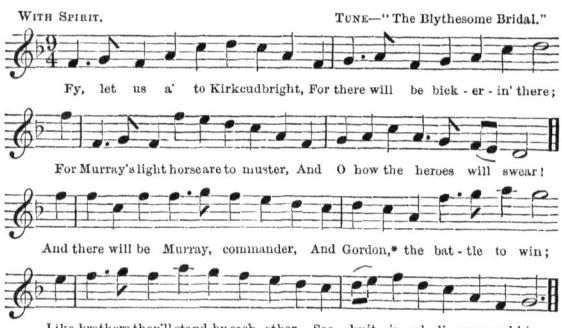

Fy, let us a' to Kirkcudbright, For there will be bick-er-in' there;
For Murray's light horse are to muster, And O how the heroes will swear!
And there will be Murray, commander, And Gordon,* the battle to win;
Like brothers they'll stand by each other, Sae knit in al-li-ance and kin.

And there will be black-nebbit Johnnie,†
  The tongue o' the trump to them a';
An he get na hell for his haddin',
  The Deil gets nae justice ava:
And there will be Kempleton's birkie, ‡
  A boy no sae black at the bane;
But as to his fine Nabob fortune,
  We'll e'en let the subject alane.

And there will be Wigton's new Sheriff; §
  Dame Justice fu' brawly has sped,
She's gotten the heart of a Bushby,
  But, Lord! what's become o' the head?
And there will be Cardoness, Esquire, ||
  Sae mighty in Cardoness' eyes;
A wight that will weather damnation,
  The Devil the prey will despise.

And there will be Douglasses doughty, ¶
  New christening towns far and near;
Abjuring their democrat doings,
  By kissin' the —— o' a peer:
And there will be folk frae St. Mary's,
  A house o' great merit and note;
The deil ane but honours them highly—
  The deil ane will gie them his vote!

And there will be Kenmure sae gen'rous, *
  Whose honour is proof to the storm,
To save them from stark reprobation,
  He lent them his name in the Firm.
And there will be lads o' the gospel,
  Muirhead † wha's as guid as he's true;
And there will be Buittle's Apostle, ‡
  Wha's mair o' the black than the blue.

And there will be Logan M'Dowall, §
  Sculdudd'ry an' he will be there,
And also the Wild Scot o' Galloway,
  Sogering, gunpowder Blair. ||
But we winna mention Redcastle, ¶
  The body, e'en let him escape!
He'd venture the gallows for siller,
  An 'twere na the cost o' the rape.

But where is the Doggerbank hero,
  That made "Hogan Mogan" to skulk?
Poor Keith's gane to hell to be fuel,
  The auld rotten wreck of a Hulk.
And where is our king's Lord Lieutenant,
  Sae fam'd for his gratefu' return?
The birkie is gettin' his questions
  To say in St. Stephen's the morn.

But mark ye! there's trusty Kerroughtree,**
  Whose honour was ever his law;
If the Virtues were pack'd in a parcel,
  His worth might be sample for a';
And strang an' respectfu' 's his backing,
  The maist o' the lairds wi' him stand;
Nae gipsy-like nominal barons,
  Wha's property 's paper—not land.

And there, frae the Niddisdale borders,
  The Maxwells will gather in droves,
Teugh Jockie,†† staunch Geordie,‡‡ an' Wellwood,§§
  That griens for the fishes and loaves;
And there will be Heron, the Major, ||||
  Wha'll ne'er be forgot in the Greys;
Our flatt'ry we'll keep for some other,
  Him, only it's justice to praise.

And there will be maiden Kilkerran, ¶¶
  And also Barskimming's guid Knight,***
And there will be roarin' Birtwhistle,†††
  Yet luckily roars i' the right.

---

* Murray of Broughton and Gordon of Balmaghie, great friends and brothers-in-law, although Murray had left his wife and eloped with a lady of rank.
† John Bushby.
‡ Bushby of Kempleton, who had made his fortune in India.
§ Bushby Maitland, son of John Bushby.
|| David Maxwell of Cardoness.
¶ Messrs. Douglas of Carlinwark, called by them "Castle Douglas."

* Gordon of Kenmure.　　† Muirhead of Urr—see Life.
‡ Rev. George Maxwell of Buittle.
§ Logan M'Dowall, the Lothario of "Ye Banks and Braes o' Bonnie Doon."
|| Mr. Blair of Dunskey.　　¶ William Sloan Lawrie.
** Patrick Heron of Kerroughtree.
†† John Maxwell, Esq., of Terraughty.
‡‡ George Maxwell of Carruchan.　§§ Mr. Wellwood Maxwell.
|||| Major Heron, brother of the Whig candidate.
¶¶ Sir Adam Fergusson of Kilkerran.
*** Sir William Miller of Barskimming, afterwards Lord Glenlee.
††† Mr. Alexander Birtwhistle of Kirkcudbright.

And there 'll be Stamp Office Johnnie,*
  (Tak tent how ye purchase a dram !)
And there will be gay Cassencarry,
  And there 'll be gleg Colonel Tam. †

And there 'll be wealthy young Richard,‡
  Dame Fortune should hing by the neck
For prodigal, thriftless bestowing—
  His merit had won him respect.
And there will be rich brother Nabobs,§
  (Though Nabobs, yet men not the worst,)
And there will be Collieston's whiskers, ∥
  And Quintin ¶—a lad o' the first.

Then hey ! the chaste Interest o' Broughton,
  And hey ! for the blessin's 'twill bring ;
It may send Balmaghie to the Commons,
  In Sodom 'twould make him a king ;
And hey ! for the sanctified Murray,
  Our land wha wi' chapels has stor'd ;
He founder'd his horse among harlots,
  And gied the auld naig to the Lord.

ELECTION BALLAD.

JOHN BUSHBY'S LAMENTATION.**

'Twas in the seventeen hunder year
  O' grace, and ninety-five,
That year I was the wae'est man
  Of ony man alive.

In March the three-an'-twentieth morn,
  The sun raise clear an' bright ;
But oh ! I was a waefu' man,
  Ere to-fa' o' the night.

Yerl Galloway lang did rule this land,
  Wi' equal right and fame,
And thereto was his kinsmen join'd,
  The Murray's noble name.

Yerl Galloway's man o' men was I,
  And chief o' Broughton's host ;
So twa blind beggars, on a string,
  The faithfu' tyke will trust.

But now Yerl Galloway's sceptre 's broke,
  And Broughton 's wi' the slain,
And I my ancient craft may try,
  Sin' honesty is gane.

* John Syme, Esq., distributor of stamps for Dumfries.
† Colonel Goldie, of Goldielea.
‡ Richard Oswald, Esq., of Auchincruive.
§ Messrs. Hannay.   ∥ Mr. Copeland of Collieston.
¶ Mr. Quintin M'Adam, of Cragingillan.
** "Bushby :" John Bushby of Tinwald-downs.

'Twas by the banks o' bonnie Dee,
  Beside Kirkcudbright's towers,
The Stewart and the Murray there,
  Did muster a' their powers.

Then Murray on the auld grey yaud,
  Wi' *winged spurs* * did ride,
That auld grey yaud a' Nidsdale rade,
  He staw upon Nidside.

An there had na been the Yerl himsel',
  O there had been nae play ;
But Garlies was to London gane,
  And sae the kye might stray.

And there was Balmaghie, I ween,
  In front rank he wad shine ;
But Balmaghie had better been
  Drinkin' Madeira wine.

And frae Glenkens cam to our aid
  A chief o' doughty deed ;
In case that worth should wanted be,
  O' Kenmure we had need.

And by our banners march'd Muirhead,
  And Buittle was na slack ;
Whase haly priesthood nane could stain,
  For wha could dye the black ?

And there was grave squire Cardoness,
  Look'd on till a' was done ;
Sae in the tower o' Cardoness
  A howlet sits at noon.

And there led I the Bushby clan,
  My gamesome billie, Will,
And my son Maitland, wise as brave,
  My footsteps follow'd still.

The Douglas and the Heron's name,
  We set nought to their score ;
The Douglas and the Heron's name,
  Had felt our weight before.

But Douglasses o' weight had we,
  The pair o' lusty lairds,
For building cot-houses sae fam'd,
  And christenin' kail-yards.

And then Redcastle drew his sword,
  That ne'er was stain'd wi' gore,
Save on a wand'rer lame and blind,
  To drive him frae his door.

And last cam creepin' Collieston,
  Was mair in fear than wrath ;
Ae knave was constant in his mind—
  To keep that knave frae scaith.

  .   .   .   .   .

* An allusion to the lady Murray had eloped with—Johnstone, whose crest was the *winged spurs*.

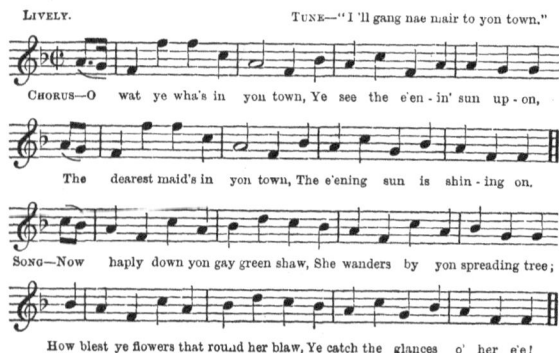

O WAT YE WHA'S IN YON TOWN.

LIVELY.   TUNE—"I'll gang nae mair to yon town."

CHORUS—O wat ye wha's in yon town, Ye see the e'en-in' sun up-on, The dearest maid's in yon town, The e'ening sun is shin-ing on.

SONG—Now haply down yon gay green shaw, She wanders by yon spreading tree; How blest ye flowers that round her blaw, Ye catch the glances o' her e'e!

How blest ye birds that round her sing,
   And welcome in the blooming year;
And doubly welcome be the Spring,
   The season to my Jeanie dear.
              O wat ye wha's, &c.

The sun blinks blythe in yon town,
   Amang the broomy braes sae green;
But my delight in yon town,
   And dearest pleasure, is my Jean.
              O wat ye wha's, &c.

Without my Fair, not a' the charms
   O' Paradise could yield me joy;

But give me Jeanie in my arms
  And welcome Lapland's dreary sky!
    O wat ye wha 's, &c.

My cave would be a lover's bower,
  Though raging Winter rent the air;
And she a lovely little flower,
  That I wad tent and shelter there.
    O wat ye wha 's, &c.

O sweet is she in yon town,
  The sinking Sun 's gane down upon;
A fairer than 's in yon town,
  His setting beam ne'er shone upon.
    O wat ye wha 's, &c.

If angry Fate is sworn my foe,
  And suff'ring I am doom'd to bear;
I careless quit aught else below,
  But spare, O spare me Jeanie dear.
    O wat ye wha 's, &c.

For while life's dearest blood is warm,
  Ae thought frae her shall ne'er depart,
And she, as fairest is her form,
  She has the truest, kindest heart.
    O wat ye wha 's, &c.

For never but by British hands
  Maun British wrangs be righted!
No! never but by British hands
  Shall British wrangs be righted!

The kettle o' the Kirk and State,
  Perhaps a clout may fail in 't;
But deil a foreign tinkler loun
  Shall ever ca' a nail in 't.
Our Fathers' blude the Kettle bought,
  And wha wad dare to spoil it,
By Heav'ns! the sacrilegious dog
  Shall fuel be to boil it!
By Heav'ns! the sacrilegious dog
  Shall fuel be to boil it!

The wretch that would a tyrant own,
  And the wretch, his true-born brother,
Who would set the mob aboon the throne,
  May they be damn'd together!
Who will not sing "God save the King,"
  Shall hang as high 's the steeple;
But while we sing "God save the King,"
  We 'll ne'er forget the People!
But while we sing "God save the King,"
  We 'll ne'er forget the People!

DOES HAUGHTY GAUL INVASION THREAT?

WITH SPIRIT.

O let us not, like snarling curs,
  In wrangling be divided,
Till, slap! come in an unco loun,
  And wi' a rung decide it!
Be Britain still to Britain true,
  Amang oursel's united;

Corsincon, a high hill at the source of the river Nith.

VOL. I.

COME BOAT ME O'ER TO CHARLIE.*

LIVELY.   TUNE—"O'er the Water to Charlie."

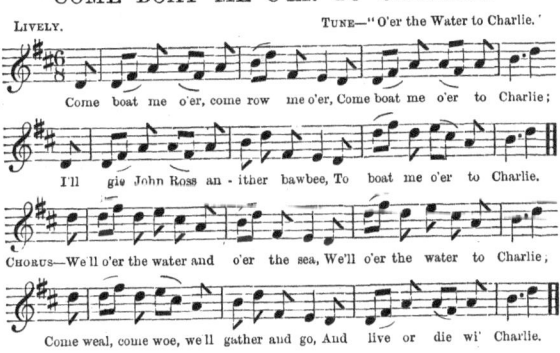

I lo'e weel my Charlie's name,
  Though some there be abhor him:
But oh, to see auld Nick gaun hame,
  And Charlie's faes before him!
    We 'll o'er the water, &c.

I swear and vow by moon and stars,
  And sun that shines so early,
If I had twenty thousand lives,
  I 'd die as aft for Charlie.
    We 'll o'er the water, &c.

† An old song amended.

29

A TOAST.*

Instead of a song, boys, I'll give you a toast;
Here's to the memory of those we have lost!—
That we lost, did I say?—nay, by Heav'n, that we found;
For their fame it will last while the world goes round.
The next in succession I'll give you's the King!
Whoe'er would betray him, on high may he swing!
And here's the grand fabric, the free Constitution,
As built on the base of our great Revolution!
And longer with Politics not to be cramm'd,
Be Anarchy curs'd, and be Tyranny damn'd!
And who would to Liberty e'er prove disloyal,
May his son be a hangman—and himself his first trial!

EXTEMPORE ON MR. SYME,

ON REFUSING TO DINE WITH HIM, AFTER HAVING BEEN PROMISED THE FIRST OF COMPANY AND THE FIRST OF COOKERY, 17TH DECEMBER, 1795.

No more of your guests, be they titled or not,
  And cookery the first in the nation;
Who is proof to thy personal converse and wit,
  Is proof to all other temptation.

THE LAST TIME I CAME O'ER THE MOOR.

The last time I came o'er the moor, And left Maria's dwelling,
What throes, what tortures passing cure, Were in my bosom swelling:
Condemn'd to drag a hopeless chain, And yet in secret languish;
To feel a fire in ev'ry vein, Yet dare not speak my anguish.

The wretch of love unseen, unknown,
  I fain my crime would cover:
The bursting sigh, th' unweeting groan,
  Betray the guilty lover.

I know my doom must be despair,
  Thou wilt nor canst relieve me;
But oh, Maria, hear my prayer,
  For Pity's sake, forgive me!

The music of thy tongue I heard,
  Nor wist while it enslav'd me:
I saw thine eyes, yet nothing fear'd,
  Till fear no more had sav'd me:
The unwary sailor thus, aghast,
  The wheeling torrent viewing,
'Mid circling horrors yields at last
  To overwhelming ruin.

TO MR. SYME,†

WITH A PRESENT OF A DOZEN OF PORTER.

O had the malt thy strength of mind,
  Or hops the flavour of thy wit,
'Twere drink for first of human kind,
  A gift that ev'n for Syme were fit.

POETICAL INSCRIPTION FOR AN ALTAR OF INDEPENDENCE,‡

AT KERROUGHTREE, THE SEAT OF MR. HERON.

Thou of an independent mind,
With soul resolv'd, with soul resign'd;
Prepar'd Power's proudest frown to brave,
Who wilt not be, nor have a slave;
Virtue alone who dost revere,
Thy own reproach alone dost fear—
Approach this shrine, and worship here.

STANZAS §

ON THE DUKE OF QUEENSBERRY.

How shall I sing Drumlanrig's grace—
Discarded remnant of a race
  Once great in martial story?
His forbears' virtues all contrasted—
The very name of Douglas blasted—
  His that inverted glory!

---

* "A toast:" A meeting of the Dumfriesshire Volunteers was held to commemorate the anniversary of Rodney's victory, April 12, 1782, and Burns was called on for a song, but instead he delivered the above lines extempore.

† See Life. ‡ Written in summer, 1795.

§ "Stanzas:" an impromptu on the tree-destroying Duke, made by the poet when once reproached for choosing nothing but low subjects. Perhaps part of an Election Ballad.

Hate, envy, oft the Douglas bore;
But he has superadded more,
    And sunk them in contempt;
Follies and crimes have stain'd the name:
But, Queensberry, thine the virgin claim,
    From aught that 's good exempt.

CHARLIE, HE 'S MY DARLING.

'Twas on a Monday morning, Right early in the year, That Charlie came to our town, The young Chevalier. An' Charlie, he's my darling, My darling, my darling, Charlie he's my darling, The young Chevalier.

As he was walking up the street
    The city for to view,
O there he spied a bonnie lass
    The window looking through.
        An' Charlie, &c.

Sae light 's he jumped up the stair,
    And tirl'd at the pin;
And wha sae ready as hersel'
    To let the laddie in!
        An' Charlie, &c.

He sat his Jenny on his knee,
    All in his Highland dress;
For brawly well he kenn'd the way
    To please a bonnie lass.
        An' Charlie, &c.

It 's up yon heathery mountain,
    An' down yon scroggie glen,
We daur na gang a milking,
    For Charlie and his men.
        An' Charlie, &c.

POEM ADDRESSED TO MR. MITCHELL,
COLLECTOR OF EXCISE, DUMFRIES, 1796.

FRIEND of the Poet, tried and leal,
Wha, wanting thee, might beg or steal;
Alake, alake, the meikle deil
    Wi' a' his witches
Are at it, skelpin jig and reel,
    In my poor pouches?

I modestly fu' fain wad hint it,
That One-pound-one, I sairly want it;
If wi' the hizzie down ye sent it,
    It would be kind;
And while my heart wi' life-blood dunted,
    I 'd bear 't in mind.

So may the Auld year gang out moanin'
To see the New come laden, groanin',
Wi' double plenty o'er the loanin',
    To thee and thine:
Domestic peace and comforts crownin'
    The hale design.

POSTSCRIPT.

Ye 've heard this while how I 've been licket,
And by fell Death was nearly nicket,
Grim loon! he got me by the fecket,
    And sair me sheuk;
But by guid luck I lap a wicket,
    And turn'd a neuk.

But by that health, I 've got a share o't,
And by that life, I 'm promis'd mair o't,
My hale and weel, I 'll tak a care o't,
    A tentier way;
Then farewell, folly, hide and hair o't,
    For ance and ay!

VERSES ON THE DESTRUCTION OF THE WOODS NEAR DRUMLANRIG.*

As on the banks of winding Nith,
    Ae smiling simmer morn I stray'd,
And traced its bonnie holms and haughs,
    Where linties sang and lammies play'd,
I sat me down upon a craig,
    And drank my fill o' fancy's dream,
When from the eddying deep below,
    Uprose the Genius of the stream.

Dark, like the frowning rock, his brow,
    And troubled, like his wintry wave,
And deep, as sughs the boding wind
    Amang his caves, the sigh he gave—
"And come ye here, my son," he cried,
    "To wander in my birken shade?
To muse some favourite Scottish theme,
    Or sing some favourite Scottish maid?

---

* Queensberry stript Drumlanrig of its woods to make a dowry for his supposed daughter, the Countess of Yarmouth. Burns wrote the following on the back of a window-shutter in a toll-house near the spot. See LIFE.

"There was a time, it 's nae lang syne,
  Ye might hae seen me in my pride,
When a' my banks sae bravely saw
  Their woody pictures in my tide;
When hanging beech and spreading elm
  Shaded my stream sae clear and cool;
And stately oaks their twisted arms
  Threw broad and dark across the pool;

"When, glinting through the trees, appear'd
  The wee white cot aboon the mill,
And peacefu' rose its ingle reek,
  That, slowly curling, clamb the hill.
But now the cot is bare and cauld,
  Its leafy bield for ever gane,
And scarce a stinted birk is left
  To shiver in the blast its lane."

"Alas!" quoth I, "what ruefu' chance
  Has twin'd ye o' your stately trees?
Has laid your rocky bosom bare—
  Has stripp'd the cleeding aff your braes!
Was it the bitter eastern blast,
  That scatters blight in early spring?
Or was 't the wil'fire scorched their boughs,
  Or canker-worm wi' secret sting?"

"Nae eastlin blast," the sprite replied;
  "It blaws na here sae fierce and fell,
And on my dry and halesome banks
  Nae canker-worms get leave to dwell:
Man! cruel man!" the Genius sighed—
  As through the cliffs he sank him down—
"The worm that gnaw'd my bonnie trees,
  That reptile wears a Ducal crown."

POEM ON LIFE.

ADDRESSED TO COLONEL DE PEYSTER,* DUMFRIES, 1796.

My honour'd Colonel, deep I feel
Your interest in the Poet's weal;
Ah! now sma' heart hae I to speel
    The steep Parnassus,
Surrounded thus by bolus pill,
    And potion glasses.

O what a canty warld were it,
Would pain and care and sickness spare it;
And Fortune favour worth and merit
    As they deserve;
And aye rowth o' roast-beef and claret,
    Syne wha wad starve?

Dame Life, though fiction out may trick her,
And in paste gems and frippery deck her;
Oh! flickering, feeble, and unsicker
    I've found her still,
Aye wavering like the willow-wicker,
    'Tween good and ill.

Then that curst carmagnole,† auld Satan,
Watches like baudrons by a ratton
Our sinfu' saul to get a claut on,
    Wi' felon ire;
Syne, whip! his tail ye 'll ne'er cast saut on,
    He 's aff like fire.

Ah Nick! ah Nick! it is na fair,
First showing us the tempting ware,
Bright wines, and bonnie lasses rare,
    To put us daft;
Syne weave, unseen, thy spider snare
    O' hell's damned waft.

Poor Man, the flie, aft bizzes by,
And aft, as chance he comes thee nigh,
Thy damn'd auld elbow yeuks wi' joy
    And hellish pleasure;
Already in thy fancy's eye,
    Thy sicker treasure.

Soon, heels o'er gowdie, in he gangs,
And, like a sheep-head on a tangs,
Thy girning laugh enjoys his pangs,
    And murdering wrestle,
As, dangling in the wind, he hangs
    A gibbet's tassle.

But lest you think I am uncivil
To plague you with this draunting drivel,

---

* "Peyster." a worthy military man, who had served in Canada, and lived till ninety-six years—dying in Dumfries in 1822. See LIFE.
† "Carmagnole;" a French Revolutionary nickname.

Abjuring a' intentions evil,
    I quat my pen.
The Lord preserve us frae the devil!
    Amen! Amen!

ADDRESS,

SPOKEN BY MISS FONTENELLE ON HER BENEFIT NIGHT, DECEMBER 4TH, 1793, AT THE THEATRE, DUMFRIES.

Still anxious to secure your partial favour,
And not less anxious, sure, this night than ever,
A Prologue, Epilogue, or some such matter,
'Twould vamp my bill, said I, if nothing better;
So sought a poet, roosted near the skies,
Told him I came to feast my curious eyes;
Said, nothing like his works was ever printed;
And last, my prologue-business slily hinted.
"Ma'am, let me tell you," quoth my man of rhymes,
"I know your bent—these are no laughing times:
Can you—but, Miss, I own I have my fears—
Dissolve in pause, and sentimental tears;
With laden sighs, and solemn-rounded sentence,
Rouse from his sluggish slumbers fell repentance;
Paint Vengeance as he takes his horrid stand,
Waving on high the desolating brand,
Calling the storms to bear him o'er a guilty land?"

I could no more—askance the creature eyeing,
D' ye think, said I, this face was made for crying?
I'll laugh, that 's poz—nay more, the world shall know it;
And so, your servant! gloomy Master Poet!

Firm as my creed, Sirs, 'tis my fix'd belief,
That Misery 's another word for Grief:
I also think—so may I be a bride!
That so much laughter, so much life enjoy'd.

Thou man of crazy care and ceaseless sigh,
Still under bleak Misfortune's blasting eye;
Doom'd to that sorest task of man alive—
To make three guineas do the work of five:
Laugh in Misfortune's face—the beldam witch!
Say, you 'll be merry, though you can't be rich.

Thou other man of care, the wretch in love,
Who long with jiltish arts and airs hast strove;
Who, as the boughs all temptingly project,
Measur'st in desperate thought—a rope—thy neck—
Or, where the beetling cliff o'erhangs the deep,
Peerest to meditate the healing leap:
Would'st thou be cur'd, thou silly, moping elf?
Laugh at her follies—laugh e'en at thyself:
Learn to despise those frowns now so terrific,
And love a kinder—that 's your grand specific.

To sum up all, be merry, I advise;
And as we 're merry, may we still be wise.

O WERT THOU IN THE CAULD BLAST.*

ANDANTE.   DUET BY MENDELSSOHN.

O wert thou in the cauld blast, On yon-der lea, on yon-der lea,

My plaidie to the angry airt, I'd shelter thee, I'd shelter thee

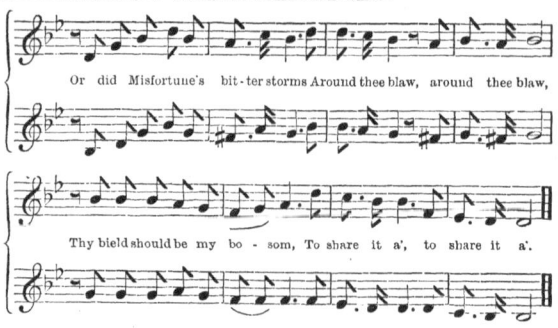

Or did Misfortune's bit-ter storms Around thee blaw, around thee blaw,

Thy bield should be my bo - som, To share it a', to share it a'.

* The Poet offered Jessie Lewars to write verses to any tune she would play. She played the air of an old song, "The Wren," and Burns wrote the above. This song is now, however, generally sung to the beautiful Duet by Mendelssohn given above.

Or were I in the wildest waste,
   Sae black and bare, sae black and bare,
The desert were a Paradise,
   If thou wert there, if thou wert there;
Or were I Monarch o' the globe,
   Wi' thee to reign, wi' thee to reign,
The brightest jewel in my crown
   Wad be my Queen, wad be my Queen.

THE DEAN OF FACULTY.*

A NEW BALLAD.

DIRE was the hate at old Harlaw,
   That Scot to Scot did carry;
And dire the discord Langside saw
   For beauteous, hapless Mary:
But Scot to Scot ne'er met so hot,
   Or were more in fury seen, Sir,
Then 'twixt Hal and Bob for the famous job,
   Who should be the Faculty's Dean, Sir.

This Hal for genius, wit, and lore,
   Amang the first was number'd;
But pious Bob, 'mid learning's store,
   Commandment the tenth remember'd:
Yet simple Bob the victory got,
   And wan his heart's desire,
Which shows that heaven can boil the pot,
   Though the devil piss in the fire.

Squire Hal, besides, had in this case
   Pretensions rather brassy;
For talents, to deserve a place,
   Are qualifications saucy.
So their worships of the Faculty,
   Quite sick of merit's rudeness,
Chose one who should owe it all, d' ye see,
   To their gratis grace and goodness.

As once on Pisgah purg'd was the sight
   Of a son of Circumcision,
So may be, on this Pisgah height,
   Bob's purblind mental vision—
Nay, Bobby's mouth—may be open'd yet,
   Till for eloquence you hail him,
And swear that he has the angel met
   That met the ass of Balaam.

In your heretic sins may you live and die,
   Ye heretic Eight-and-Thirty!

* These verses allude to the victory gained by the Tory Lord Advocate, Robert Blair, over the famous wit, Henry Erskine, brother of homas, Lord Erskine.

But accept, ye sublime Majority,
   My congratulations hearty.
With your honours, as with a certain king,
   In your servants this is striking,
The more incapacity they bring,
   The more they 're to your liking.

HERON ELECTION BALLAD.

THE TROGGER.

WHA will buy my troggin,* fine election ware,
Broken trade o' Broughton, a' in high repair?
   Buy braw troggin frae the banks o' Dee;
   Wha wants troggin let him come to me.

There 's a noble Earl's † fame and high renown,
For an auld sang—it 's thought the gudes were stown—
   Buy braw troggin, &c.

Here 's the worth o' Broughton ‡ in a needle's e'e;
Here 's a reputation tint by Balmaghie.§
   Buy braw troggin, &c.

Here 's its stuff and lining, Cardoness's head, ‖
Fine for a soger, a' the wale o' lead.
   Buy braw troggin, &c.

Here 's a little wadset, Buittle's ¶ scrap o' truth,
Pawn'd in a gin-shop, quenching holy drouth.
   Buy braw troggin, &c.

Here 's an honest conscience might a prince adorn;
Frae the downs o' Tinwald,** so was never worn.
   Buy braw troggin, &c.

Here 's armorial bearings frae the manse o' Urr;
The crest, a sour crab-apple, rotten at the core. ††
   Buy braw troggin, &c.

Here is Satan's picture, like a bizzard gled,
Pouncing poor Redcastle, ‡‡ sprawlin' like a taed.
   Buy braw troggin, &c.

Here 's the font where Douglas §§ stane and mortar names;
Lately used at Caily christening Murray's crimes.
   Buy braw troggin, &c.

Here 's the worth and wisdom Collieston ‖‖ can boast;
By a thievish midge they had been nearly lost.
   Buy braw troggin, &c.

* "Troggin:" a name for pedlers' wares.
  † The Earl of Galloway.   ‡ Mr. Murray of Broughton.
  § Gordon of Balmaghie.   ‖ Maxwell of Cardoness.
  ¶ Rev. George Maxwell of Buittle.   ** John Bushby of Tinwald.
  †† Muirhead of Urr.   ‡‡ Walter Sloan Lawrie.
  §§ Douglas of Carlinwark.   ‖‖ Copeland of Collieston.

Here is Murray's fragments o' the ten commands;
Gifted by black Jock* to get them aff his hands.
                Buy braw troggin, &c.

Saw ye e'er sic troggin? if to buy ye 're slack,
Hornie 's turnin' chapman—he 'll buy a' the pack.
                Buy braw troggin, &c.

JESSIE LEWARS.

TALK not to me of savages,
   From Afric's burning sun;
No savage e'er could rend my heart,
   As, Jessie, thou hast done:
But Jessie's lovely hand in mine,
   A mutual faith to plight,
Not even to view the heavenly choir,
   Would be so blest a sight.

THE TOAST.

FILL me with the rosy wine,
Call a toast, a toast divine;
Give the Poet's darling flame,
Lovely Jessie † be her name;
Then thou mayest freely boast,
Thou hast given a peerless toast.

ON JESSIE LEWARS' SICKNESS.

SAY, sages, what 's the charm on earth
   Can turn Death's dart aside?
It is not purity and worth,
   Else Jessie had not died.

* John Bushby.   † Jessie Lewars, see LIFE.

ON THE RECOVERY OF JESSIE LEWARS.

BUT rarely seen since Nature's birth,
   The natives of the sky;
Yet still one seraph 's left on earth,
   For Jessie did not die.

THE BLUDE-RED ROSE AT YULE MAY BLAW.

To daunton me, and me sae young,
Wi' his fause heart and flatt'ring tongue,
That is the thing you shall never see,
For an auld man shall never daunton me.
                To daunton me, &c.

For a' his meal and a' his maut,
For a' his fresh beef and his saut,
For a' his gold and white monie,
The auld man shall never daunton me.
                To daunton me, &c.

His gear may buy him kye and yowes,
His gear may buy him glens and knowes;
But me he shall not buy nor fee,
For an auld man shall never daunton me.
                To daunton me, &c.

He hirples twa-fauld as he dow,
Wi' his teethless gab and his auld beld pow,
And the rain rains down frae his red blear'd e'e;
That auld man shall never daunton me.
                To daunton me, &c.

www.ingramcontent.com/pod-product-compliance
Lightning Source LLC
Chambersburg PA
CBHW081944230426
43669CB00019B/2921